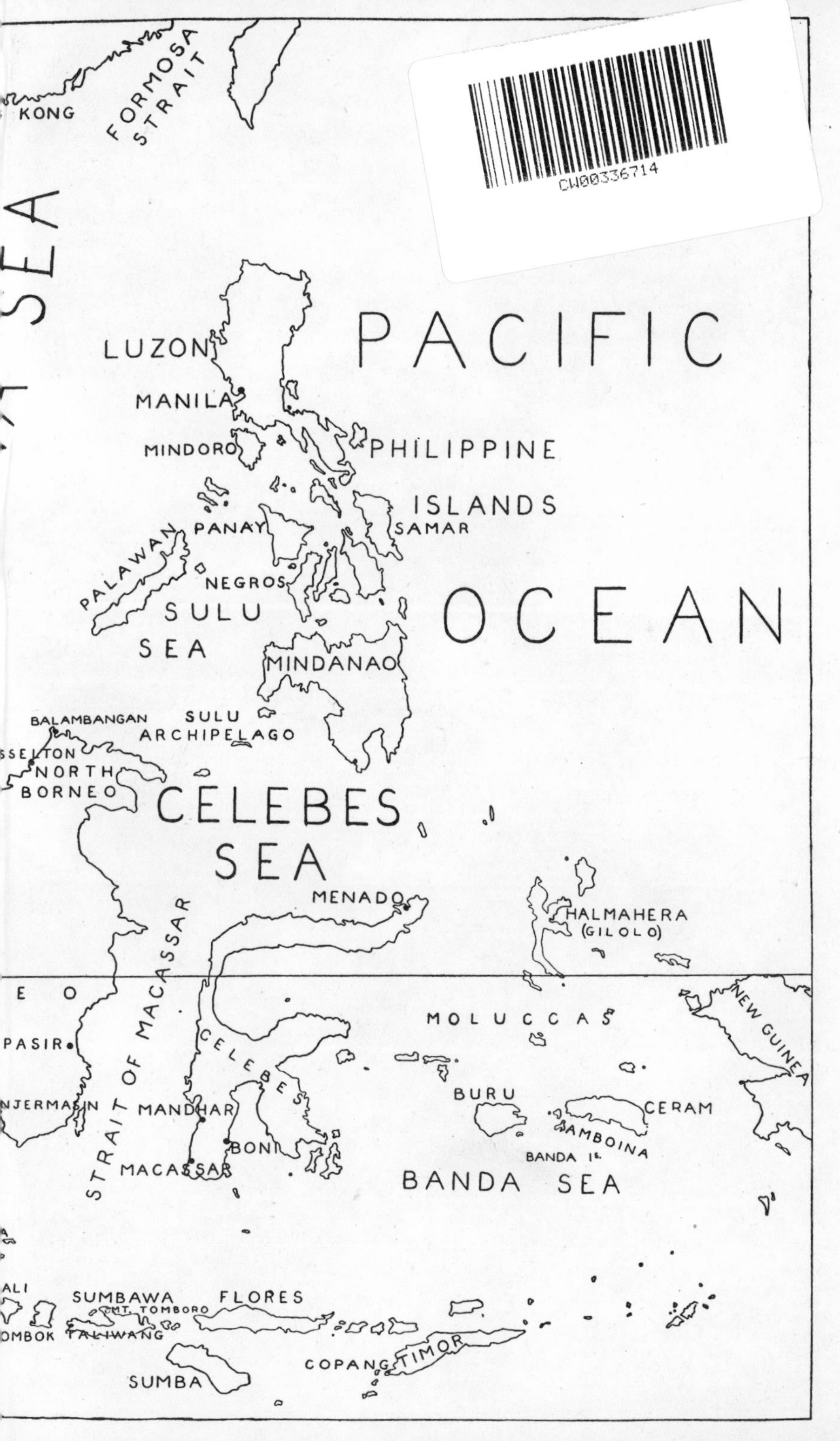

KONG
FORMOSA STRAIT
SEA
PACIFIC OCEAN
LUZON
MANILA
MINDORO
PHILIPPINE ISLANDS
PANAY
SAMAR
PALAWAN
NEGROS
SULU SEA
MINDANAO
BALAMBANGAN
SULU ARCHIPELAGO
SSELTON
NORTH BORNEO
CELEBES SEA
MENADO
HALMAHERA (GILOLO)
STRAIT OF MACASSAR
E O
PASIR
MOLUCCAS
NEW GUINEA
CELEBES
NJERMASIN
MANDHAR
BONI
MACASSAR
BURU
CERAM
AMBOINA
BANDA I[s]
BANDA SEA
ALI
SUMBAWA
FLORES
MT. TOMBORO
OMBOK
TALIWANG
COPANG
TIMOR
SUMBA
CW00336714

RAFFLES OF THE EASTERN ISLES

RAFFLES
OF THE
EASTERN ISLES

C. E. Wurtzburg

Edited for publication by Clifford Witting

"All I wish is to remain long enough to see my Settlement at Singapore firmly established. . . . My great object, the independence of the Eastern Isles, has been attained."

Extract from private letter from Sir Stamford Raffles to a friend in England (1820)

SINGAPORE
OXFORD UNIVERSITY PRESS
OXFORD NEW YORK

Oxford University Press

Oxford New York Toronto
Delhi Bombay Calcutta Madras Karachi
Petaling Jaya Singapore Hong Kong Tokyo
Nairobi Dar es Salaam Cape Town
Melbourne Auckland
and associated companies in
Berlin Ibadan

Oxford is a trade mark of Oxford University Press

First published by Hodder & Stoughton in 1954
First issued in Oxford in Asia Paperbacks *1984*
Reissued as an Oxford University Press paperback 1986
Second impression 1990

ISBN 0 19 582605 1

Printed in Malaysia by Peter Chong Printers Sdn. Bhd.
Published by Oxford University Press Pte. Ltd.,
Unit 221, Ubi Avenue 4, Singapore 1440

This book is published as a tribute to the memory of Charles Wurtzburg, and as a token of the affection and respect which his colleagues felt for him.

September 1954.

Glen Line Limited,
London.

FOREWORD

CHARLES EDWARD WURTZBURG was born on 5th June 1891. Educated at Aldenham School and Emmanuel College, Cambridge, where he obtained First Class Honours in Classics, he served during the First World War with the Liverpool Rifles (T.F.) and was awarded the Military Cross. In 1920 he went to Singapore, where he became chairman of Mansfield & Co. Ltd., chairman of the Straits Steamship Co. Ltd., and an unofficial member of the Legislative Council of the Colony.

On his appointment as managing director of the Glen Line Ltd., he returned in 1937 to London, where he became also chairman of McGregor Gow & Holland Ltd. During the Second World War he was chief representative of the Ministry of War Transport, South and East Africa. From 1946 to 1948 he was president of the Association of British Malaya, and in 1951 president of the Chamber of Shipping of the United Kingdom. He died on 30th April 1952 in his sixty-first year, leaving a widow, two sons and two daughters.

"In 1920," he wrote shortly before his death, "my business career took me to Singapore and a very brief residence there inevitably focused my attention on Sir Stamford Raffles, whose name is commemorated in so many ways. It has always been my hobby to read the history of any place where I have happened to live, and as Raffles was not unknown to one who had spent so many happy hours of boyhood at the London Zoo, I soon found myself busily collecting books dealing with his career.

"As my reading extended, the impression grew that the standard biographies were not entirely satisfactory. The mass of documents piously assembled by his widow, the rather stilted and very Victorian biography of Demetrius Boulger, for all his access to original sources, and even the more balanced Life by H. E. Egerton, still left me unsatisfied. I felt that the British point of view was perhaps too readily accepted. Presumably there was a Dutch point of view also.

"Having, as I supposed, settled down to complete my career in the Far East, with the prospect of retiring at about the age of fifty, as was the general expectation in those days, I deliberately set to work to collect from every possible source all the information I could about Raffles and his work, with the view to occupying the leisure of my retirement in writing a fully documented Life. I studied, for example, the local records; I obtained introductions to colonial historians in England and Holland; I pestered my friends in Java. An unexpected visit to India gave me the chance, in the appalling heat of midsummer, to examine the letter books of Dr Nathaniel Wallich in the Botanic Gardens, Calcutta, of which he was curator in Raffles' day.

"The more I studied Raffles at close range from contemporary documents, the more impressed I became with the greatness of the man and his achievements.

"My collection of material grew and grew, each new source suggesting another one. Then in 1936 I was offered an even more responsible and still more active position in London. Engulfed in fresh work and new responsibilities, I still went on collecting, but as the prospect of early retirement receded, the fear that the book would never be written at all began to haunt me.

"I found myself in a dilemma. If I waited until I retired, would I still have the energy or the powers of application to handle this mass of information—now almost embarrassing in quantity—and produce a satisfactory biography? Alternatively, was there any hope at all of achieving my purpose if the book had to be written in evenings at my London flat after long hours of work in the office, or at week-ends in Devon, when my instinct would rightly be to spend every possible minute out of doors? How should I manage when my library was in Devon and I was trying to write in London? Would not the books I wished to use always be at the wrong end?

"Although it would be hard to imagine anything less satisfactory than chapters written in bits and pieces at intervals over a long period of time, I yet felt that this was my only chance to write the book at all. Were I to succeed in making available in orderly shape at least the essential parts of the more important British and Dutch documents, without a study of which no biographer, however brilliant, can claim to produce a true portrait of Raffles, I should be content, leaving to a more accomplished pen than mine to paint in vivid portraiture the living features of the man."

Under these extremely difficult conditions Charles Wurtzburg laboured for four years, by the end of which time he had transcribed 450,000 words, covering the whole of Raffles' life and activities. This was the first step. Here assembled was the raw material for a book, certainly with some research still to be done, as the pencilled notes in the margins of the typescript show, but nevertheless with all the essential matter within a manageable compass.

Then Charles Wurtzburg died, and it became the task of others to complete the book that he did not live to put into final form. Among those who so readily co-operated in this undertaking, and to whom grateful acknowledgments are made, are the following:—

Baptist Missionary Society; Professor C. R. Boxer; John S. Gordon Clark, Esq.; Colonial Office Library; Directorate of Military Survey;

Major E. C. M. Flint, D.S.O.; Alfred Holt & Co.; India Office Library; Institute of Historical Research, University of London; Koninklijk Instituut voor Taal-, Land- en Volkenkunde; London Missionary Society; Stewart MacTier, Esq., C.B.E.; members of the staff of Glen Line Ltd.; Office of the Commissioner for Malaya in the U.K.; Captain H. F. Pearson; L. G. Pine, Esq., Managing Editor, *Burke's Peerage*; Major R. L. Stamford Raffles; Royal Asiatic Society; Royal United Service Institution; Rev. Charles E. Surman, M.A., Research Secretary, The Congregational Historical Society; War Office Library; Rev. Harold E. Wood, M.A., St Paul's Church, Mill Hill; Zoological Society of London.

To Sir Richard Winstedt we are under a deep obligation. At a considerable expenditure of time, he gave freely of his advice while the editorial work was in progress, and was then kind enough to read through the whole of the final text, which has greatly profited by his corrections and additions. It was he who prepared the family tree of the rulers of Rhio-Johore and Singapore; and his *English-Malay Dictionary*, augmented by his own patient guidance in a language of which the editor's knowledge was scant at the outset, is the authority for the Malay words and phrases included in these pages.

C. W.

CONTENTS

MAPS

Chapter One

EARLY YEARS, 1781-1805

ON Saturday, 30th June 1781, there was intense activity in the beautiful harbour of Port Morant, Jamaica. For months a huge convoy of merchantmen had been assembling, and now the imposing fleet of some two hundred vessels was to begin its hazardous course for England and North America. The first group was leaving that day; the remainder on the following Monday and Tuesday.

An escort worthy of the occasion had been assembled: the *Albion* (74 guns), under the command of George Bowyer, Esq., Commodore, the *Princess Royal* (90 guns), the *Ruby* (64 guns) and the *Janus* (44 guns). The *Ramillies* (74 guns) and a number of frigates were to go a certain distance and then return to Port Royal.

The Commodore's task was no light one. The American War of Independence was entering on its last and most critical stage. We were at war also with France, Spain and the Netherlands, and the Caribbean and the Atlantic were full of raiders and privateers. But if Commodore Bowyer had reason to be anxious, Captain Benjamin Raffles, master of the West Indiaman *Ann*, had his own personal worries, for, as was common in those days, his wife (*née* Anne Lyde) was sailing with him, and she was expecting her second baby. Two years before, a daughter had died in infancy. Now the second child was to arrive under conditions of discomfort and hazard. For four months or longer the vessel had been lying snugly in harbour, and it must have been provoking that the event could not have occurred even a few days earlier. However, on 6th July (5th July by sea reckoning[1]) a son was safely delivered.

Some kind of christening ceremony appears to have been performed on board; the baby was given the names of Thomas Stamford Bingley, Mr Stamford and Mr Bingley being mentioned as godfathers. Evidently this was not regarded as an official ceremony, for on 4th July 1784 he was christened, with his sister Harriet (born in 1783), at the parish church of Eaton Bishop in Herefordshire, where the Rev. John Lindeman, who had married the sister of Mrs Raffles, held the living. On this occasion the boy was given the single name of Thomas, after his grandfather, for thirty years a clerk in the Prerogative Office, Doctors' Commons. The name Stamford seems hardly to have been used until the Java period, and came into principal use only after Raffles had received his knighthood.

[1] A day at sea was reckoned, not from midnight to midnight, but from noon to noon.

The name Bingley was never used at all, and in later years Raffles denied that Mr Thomas Bingley was his godfather. This gentleman was at that time a man of wealth and, whether godfather or not, seems to have acted the part of a fairy one during young Raffles' early years. Who Mr Stamford was is not very clear; he was reputed to be concerned in the Jamaican trade, and there was in business in London at that period a Thomas Stamford who had some connexion with Jamaica.

Three months after Raffles was born—on the 19th October 1781—Cornwallis surrendered at York Town, and less than a year later, by his victory at the Battle of the Saints, Rodney re-established British command of the seas, thus making possible the building of a new empire in the East to balance the loss of the American colonies in the West. It was singularly appropriate that one who was to be described by the British admiral, Ballard, as "an English landsman with a range of maritime vision little inferior to that even of Albuquerque" should have been born at sea under the protection of the Royal Navy; and that one who was to rank among our empire-builders should have survived the perils of the West Indies to live and build in the East Indies.

Not very much is known of the Raffles family. Earlier biographers have traced them to Forfarshire. Later they appeared in Yorkshire, moving finally to London. The only one who made any public mark was a Sir Benjamin Raffles, a knight banneret of the seventeenth century.

Even of Raffles' parents our knowledge is not extensive. Of Mrs Raffles we have at least a portrait—she looks a masterful old lady, to whom her son bore a considerable facial likeness—but Captain Raffles remains a shadowy figure. Though one of the senior masters in the West India trade, he seems to have been financially a failure. Admittedly, thanks to the wars, the whole trade was in a depressed state, and shipowning could have been far from profitable. The *Ann*—260 tons, built in Scotland in 1765 and armed with eight four-pounders—was owned by Hibberts & Co. of Glasgow, and that Captain Raffles had a share in her is suggested by the fact that she bore the same name, if without an "e", as his wife. The ship was sold in 1782 to one Moran, who became master and owner, so it might well have been that Captain Raffles had already incurred losses.

Five more children followed Tom—all girls except Benjamin, who was born in 1788 and died the same year—and this growing family so strained resources that an ineffectual struggle against a mounting load of debt became the background of the Raffles' home.

How or where Raffles spent his early childhood is not known. Whether his mother continued to accompany her husband to sea and, if so, whether her baby boy went with her is equally obscure. At best, Captain Raffles could have meant little to his son, seeing him only at rare intervals, so that any physical or mental qualities Raffles may have derived from him—a tough Yorkshire strain, an instinct for the sea, a scientific bent—must have been inherited and not learned from example. Other virtues—extraordinary industry, powers of application in all circumstances, cheerfulness under all conditions—came surely from his mother, for the Raffles family would have gone under had she not possessed these qualities.

If she and her children lived in England, their place of residence cannot be established. All we do know is that, at the age of twelve—presumably in 1793, in which year the youngest of his four sisters, Ann, was born—Raffles entered as a boarder "a respectable academy at Hammersmith" kept by "a Dr Anderson". The school to which Lady Raffles, his second wife, thus refers in her *Memoir* was the Mansion House Boarding School, kept by a Dr Anderton, not Anderson. This was at the west end of King Street. Later the site was occupied, first by the Mansion House Inn and, in our day, by the Hammersmith Palace of Varieties. At this school according to Mr T. Faulkner, who published a history of the parish[1] in 1820, "many eminent persons have received their education, one of whom [was] Sir Stamford Raffles". In those days Hammersmith was a pleasant village and, thanks no doubt to its proximity to London, popular with schoolmasters.

After two years Raffles had to be removed because funds to continue his education were lacking. Who, one is prompted to ask, had been paying and why was financial support so suddenly withdrawn? Many years later in Java, when enemies levelled innumerable charges against Raffles, one complaint concerned Mr Bingley, to whom he had given employment in the government service. Raffles wrote: "He was not my godfather. He was a gentleman once possessed of large fortune, but times have changed with him—in my youth he had been my friend." Is it not possible that Mr Bingley paid for the boy's schooling until he could afford it no longer?

All his life Raffles lamented: "The deficiency of my early education has never been fully supplied." As late as 1824 he described himself as being "as ignorant as a Hottentot". Forster writes of Dickens: "Of the two kinds of education which Gibbon says that all men who rise above the common level receive; the first that of his teachers, and the second more personal and more important, *his own*, he had the advantage only of the last. It nevertheless suffices for him." No words could more happily describe the situation of young Raffles. Not only did he learn widely and deeply from being "forced to enter on the busy scenes of life, then a mere boy"; he also set himself to make good, by his own exertions, his lack of academic knowledge.

[1] *History and Antiquities of the Parish of Hammersmith*. I am indebted to Mr W. H. Warhurst, Town Clerk of Hammersmith, for this information.

With the shadow of a debtor's prison hanging over her, Mrs Raffles had to plot and plan to save every penny and beguile the last bit of credit. No wonder that her mind was concentrated on her only son, to find for him at the earliest possible moment some form of employment.

In 1795, at the age of fourteen, through the influence of his uncle, Mr Hamond, who was—if we can believe the story told to Crabb Robinson by his eccentric son, Elton Hamond[1]—a tea merchant, Raffles obtained employment with the East India Company in Leadenhall Street as a temporary clerk in the secretary's office. According to Mr C. Northcote Parkinson, the historian, this was the largest department, containing between fifty and sixty clerks.

The entry of Raffles into East India House coincided with the end of an epoch in Indian affairs. In that year the long agony of Warren Hastings had ended in acquittal. Whatever one's feelings may be towards his accuser, Burke, with his cruel and shameless oratory, whatever sympathy one may have for the great proconsul, it must be admitted that English opinion had been shocked by the revelations of Company rule. Already the wise and statesmanlike work of Lord Cornwallis had gone far to cleanse the Augean stables in India, and the humanitarian sentiments inspired by the French Revolution were taking root. Burke,[2] Adam Smith, Tom Paine and others spread new ideas in many minds, and the battle to end slavery, which was to outlast Raffles, was beginning. It was only the stress of war and the fear of France and French ideas that prevented a wider and more rapid spread of liberal principles. Even so, the sentimental cult of the Noble Savage was gaining some ground. It was already mentioned by Pope.

Holland, in that year, was drawn into the war with France, with the result that the Cape of Good Hope and Malacca fell into our hands. No one could guess then the part Malacca was to play in the rise to fame of the shabby and timid young temporary clerk in East India House.

Charles Lamb had entered this same office just three years before. He found the life hard and exacting. "I am cruelly engaged and likely to be; on Friday I was at office from 10 in the morning (two hours dinner excepting) to 11 at night. . . . I never leave till 4 and do not keep a Holy Day now once in ten times . . . confusion blast all mercantile transactions. . . . In this mournful weather I sit moping where I now write, jammed in between four walls and writing by candlelight, most melancholy. Never see the light of the sun six hours in the day, and am surprised to find how pretty it shines on Sunday."

Raffles worked fully as hard; only thus could he secure the few extra

[1] Diary of Crabb Robinson—entry for 1st January 1820.

[2] In Java, Raffles had a complete set of Burke's published works. He also revealed himself in his land policy in Java as a student of Adam Smith.

pounds that meant so much at home. His initial salary is not on record, but as he was receiving only £70 a year in 1802, two years after his appointment had been confirmed, it must have been small. By unremitting labour and staying late he managed to earn in most years gratuities of from £20 to £30, but it is doubtful if he ever averaged more than £100 a year. Allowing for the value of money a hundred and fifty years ago, it was still little enough, yet it meant much to a mother struggling to maintain a home for six young children, the more so after the death of her husband.

The year of this loss is not beyond all question. In a letter from Java to his uncle in 1812—the only known letter in which Raffles made any reference at all to his father—he mentioned his death. Boulger[1] assumed from this that Captain Raffles had died recently, but it is more probable that this occurred in June 1797, in which month it was recorded in *The Colombian Magazine: or Monthly Miscellany* that Captain Raffles, master of the *Sebastiana*, had died on a voyage to Falmouth, Jamaica. The absence in the record of any Christian name or initials leaves some doubt, yet it is unlikely that there were two shipmasters named Raffles in the West Indian trade at that time.

The only description of Raffles at East India House comes from one who was his junior—Robert Ibbetson, who, by remarkable powers of survival rather than by outstanding merit, reached in 1828 the respectable position of Governor of the Incorporated Settlements, later known as the Straits Settlements. In 1803, at the age of sixteen, Ibbetson was taken by his father to East India House to express thanks for a cadetship in the Penang Establishment. "On arrival at the Company's office, while his father was taken to interview the Directors, he was left in a room occupied by two clerks. One of these was standing before the fire, when the other came and, with a kick, sent him away. The one who was removed from the fire in so undignified a manner was Mr Raffles who became the celebrated Sir Stamford Raffles." Quite probably the story is true, and no doubt the egregious Mr Ibbetson enjoyed telling it.

"You always said", wrote Raffles in 1811 to one of his old associates, "I was a strange wild fellow, insatiable in ambition, though meek as a maiden, and perhaps there was more truth than otherwise in what you said; but with all, I will assure you this, that although from want of self-confidence and from natural shamefacedness (for I will not call it modesty or bashfulness) I am as unhappy at times as any poor wretch need be, I have times in which I am as happy as I think it possible for man to be."

This was to William Brown Ramsay, the son of William Ramsay, his chief. Mr Ramsay showed a benevolent interest in him, inviting him to

[1] *The Life of Sir Stamford Raffles* (London, 1897). Demetrius Charles Boulger founded and was for some time editor of the *Asiatic Quarterly Review*.

his house and encouraging a friendship with his son. By this kindness Raffles was enabled to acquire the ways of social life, the polish that gives poise. In a house peopled by intelligent folk, particularly those engaged in public affairs, the talk would have been on politics, the French Revolution, the future of India, the theatres of war, literature, art. . . . It was an age of change, and Raffles was the child of his age, developing his guiding principle that every man is entitled to justice, to live his own life and to work for his own benefit.

In spite of going early to East India House and staying late, he gave some time of each day to the improvement of his knowledge.

"My leisure hours, however," he wrote later, "still continued to be devoted to favourite studies; and with the little aid my allowance afforded, I contrived to make myself master of the French language, and to prosecute enquiries into some of the branches of literature and science; this was, however, in stolen moments, either before the office hours in the morning, or after them in the evening. . . . I shall never forget the mortification I felt when the penury of my family once induced my mother to complain of my extravagance in burning a candle in my room."

The strain on the growing lad of studious nights and long hours by day in a stuffy office began to impair his health. There was talk of tuberculosis. He was granted a fortnight's leave and, with that astonishing physical energy that later was to be the terror of his staff, he set off on foot for Wales, walking from thirty to forty miles a day.

No more is heard of tuberculosis, though his constitution was never robust.

The days of drudgery were drawing to a close. In 1805, when he was twenty-four and had been ten years in East India House, the opportunity came to apply for a post with the new Presidency that it had been decided to set up in Penang. Mr Ramsay forwarded the application to Sir Hugh Inglis, a director of the Company.

"Mr Ramsay, in performing this generous act," wrote Lady Raffles in the *Memoir*, "expressed his feeling in the strongest terms that, although in parting with so useful an assistant in his department, he should suffer the greatest inconvenience; that it was like the loss of a limb to him; yet he felt bound to further the views and promotion in life of one who possessed strong claims from such superior talents and amiable private character."

Raffles had done more than work hard in East India House. He had learned the lesson of unswerving attention to the task in hand; a mastery of detail that was to enable him to keep control of affairs various and complex; clarity of language; a lasting interest in scientific studies; a devotion to duty that was to burn up his body within the short span of thirty years.

On 8th March 1805 he was gazetted assistant secretary to the new Governor of Penang, the Hon. Philip Dundas. With the rank of junior merchant, he rose from the lowly grade of clerkship, and overnight £70 a year became £1,500.

Six days after the gazette notice, he was married at the parish church of St George, Bloomsbury, to Olivia Mariamne Fancourt (*née* Devenish). Born on 16th February 1771, she had married in 1793 Mr Jacob Cassivelaun Fancourt, an assistant surgeon in Madras. He had died in May 1800 at Raikot, in the Punjab, and in 1804 his widow had petitioned at East India House for a pension, being awarded twenty-five guineas and a pension of one shilling and eightpence a day. Whether Raffles handled her case, or how he met her, is not recorded.

No portrait of Olivia is known to exist. Lord Minto, who first met her in Malacca in 1811, wrote to his wife:

"Mrs Raffles is the great lady, with dark eyes, lively manner, accomplished and clever. She had a former husband in India; and I have heard that she was one of the beauties to whom Anacreontic Moore addressed many of his amatory elegies."

Authorities have dismissed this suggestion on the ground that Thomas Moore was only sixteen when Olivia left England, but he was, as we know, a very precocious youth.

In a not too scrupulous age, when the foulest calumnies were bandied about without a shred of supporting evidence, it was to be expected that Raffles' sudden promotion and his equally sudden marriage would give rise to ill-natured gossip. A slanderous story current at that time found its way into print in 1816, when, in a supplement to Colburn's *Biographical Dictionary of the Living Authors of Great Britain and Ireland*, it was implied that Olivia had been a mistress of Mr Ramsay and that Raffles had obtained his appointment as a reward for marrying her.

"Mr Raffles", ran the entry, "went out to India in an inferior capacity, through the interest of Mr Ramsay, Secretary to the Company, and in consequence of his marrying a lady connected with that gentleman."

Raffles' reply to this is contained in a letter to his cousin, Rev. Thomas Raffles,[1] on 13th October 1819.

"My first wife", he wrote, "was in no manner connected with Mr Ramsay; they never saw each other, neither could my advancement in life possibly be accelerated by that marriage. It gave me no connexions, no wealth but on the contrary a load of debt which I had to clear off. It increased my difficulties and thus increased my energies. It gave me domestic enjoyment and thus contributed to my happiness; but in no way can my advancement in life be accounted owing to that connexion. My resolution to proceed to India and my appointment to Prince of Wales's

[1] Their grandfather married twice. See genealogical tree, page 750.

Island [Penang] were made before the marriage took place, and when I was about to quit all other ties and affections it was natural that I should secure one bosom friend, one confidante on my journey who would soothe the adverse blasts of misfortune and gladden the sunshine of prosperity."

Not very romantic, but Raffles described both his marriages in most matter-of-fact terms. There seems, however, no reason to doubt the truth of what he wrote. Had Olivia been William Ramsay's mistress, it is hardly creditable that he would have allowed her to apply to his department for a widow's pension. Nor is it likely that Raffles would have remained the intimate friend of the Ramsays, father and son.[1]

The new Governor of Penang and the officials recruited at home left England in the *Ganges* in April 1805, Raffles and his wife being accompanied by his favourite sister, Mary Anne. Before they sailed, he discharged the family debts and arranged a secure financial position for his mother.

The amenities of modern travel by sea were then unknown. For a large sum a passenger was privileged to occupy a small and usually most inconvenient fraction of the ship, with practically no sanitary or other conveniences. No furniture was provided; the passenger had to bring his own and camp (that is really the right word) as best he could on the portion of deck to which he was allowed access. Their voyage, therefore, could not have been anything but horribly uncomfortable, with the added unpleasantness of continuous rain squalls, the damp heat and the heavy swell of the Indian Ocean in the south-west monsoon.

But the drudgery of East India House and the cramping grip of poverty lay astern; ahead a career where energy and talent could find their reward.

At Madras they changed from the *Ganges* to the *Warley*, in which they arrived at Penang on 19th September, a voyage—thanks to the south-west monsoon—of less than six months, which was speedy in those days. Before they reached there Raffles had achieved something that his colleagues never achieved at all—a working knowledge of Malay.

[1] For further details, and the results of enquiries into the parentage of Olivia, see Appendix I, page 744.

Chapter Two

THE FOURTH PRESIDENCY

IN 1599 the Dutch East India Company, which supplied the English market with pepper and spices, felt itself sufficiently strong against its only competitors, the Portuguese, to raise the price of pepper from three shillings to six shillings and eightpence a pound. Condiments were of special importance, for lack of winter fodder compelled farmers to slaughter heavily in the autumn, and the absence of such means as cold storage to preserve the meat made it unpalatable unless strongly seasoned. The English resented this arbitrary rise in price of a commodity so essential as pepper and decided to break the monopoly by going to fetch their own supplies. To this incident the English East India Company is said to owe its origin.

Despite some striking initial successes, the early history of the Company in the area east of India is one of failure rather than of permanent settlement. The Dutch resisted stoutly, and by the middle of the eighteenth century, British interest was so centred on India that the supremacy of the Dutch in the Malay Archipelago was in the main tacitly accepted. Our only permanent settlement was Bencoolen on the west coast of Sumatra, founded in 1685. It had been originally supposed that the best route to China was by the Strait of Sunda, and Bencoolen would be a convenient port of refreshment. It was also considered a suitable place to grow pepper and spices. But its commercial aspirations were not realized and its importance as a port of call faded when it was found that the best route to China was through the Straits of Malacca.

Towards the end of the eighteenth century, however, circumstances caused the English to look again with greater interest to the area east of India. During the war with France, considerable naval actions were fought in the Indian Ocean, and at times the very existence of our factories in India was imperilled by the activities of a French fleet in the Bay of Bengal. This was a new development. Formerly such operations had been confined to the Indian Ocean, and for these our forces were comfortably based on Bombay.

This change in naval strategy had, in a period before the invention of steam, serious implications. Sailing-vessels depend on the position of the wind, and in the eastern seas this dependence was intensified by the existence of two very strong seasonal winds. From May to October the south-west monsoon dominates the Indian Ocean; from November to March the north-east monsoon blows with equal force in the China Sea.

The two intervening periods are characterized by shifting winds and violent storms. Eastern traders from earliest times had regulated their operations according to these monsoons, so their effect on naval strategy can readily be seen. We had no base on the east coast of India where our ships could repair during the north-east monsoon; nor indeed was it possible for our fleet to remain at all on that coast during that period. A French squadron operating from Mergui or Achin,[1] Sumatra, could, and in fact did, raid the east coast of India with complete impunity, sinking our commerce or driving it out of the Bay of Bengal, and on one occasion blockading Calcutta. A further advantage to the French was the use of Trincomalee as a base for refitting. Moreover, when the change in the monsoon reopened activities in the Bay of Bengal, they had a convenient breathing space before the British could get round from their distant base at Bombay.

The search for a suitable base on the east coast of India seems to have begun about 1763, but as it was unsuccessful, the Admiralty was compelled to look eastward, where the attraction of a naval base would be enhanced by its value as a much-needed port of repair and refreshment for the China fleet, which was the key to the financial structure of the East India Company. As things stood, if any of these ships were damaged east of India, their only ports of refuge were Dutch—an appalling expense in time of peace, and in war an impossibility. It was thought also that a station to the east might attract local commerce and strike at least a small blow at Dutch monopoly. At any rate, such a trade might assist to defray the cost of the station, a matter of prime consequence to the directors of the East India Company.

The Madras government was instructed in 1771 to send a mission to Achin. The firm of Jourdan Sulivan and de Souza were consulted and they in turn sought the advice of one of their masters, Captain Francis Light, who was familiar with the west coast of Malaya and on terms of friendship with the Sultan of Kedah.

Francis Light was born in Suffolk in 1740. He entered the Navy in 1759 as a midshipman in H.M.S. *Captain*. After four years' service in various junior appointments, he found himself unemployed, and two years later went out to India. He became master of a country-ship[2] trading between India and the Malay Peninsula. With a good knowledge of colloquial Malay, he also possessed that happy personality that breaks down barriers between European and Asiatic races. He was able and energetic, zealous for the promotion of British interests and unrelenting in his opposition to Dutch monopoly.

On receiving the enquiry from the Madras government, Light, on

[1] Acheen, Atchin, Acheh, etc.

[2] A vessel owned in an Indian port.

22nd November 1771, recommended Penang as "a convenient magazine for trade". Missions were dispatched to both Achin and Kedah, but neither achieved anything, and a call by Light on Warren Hastings during a visit to Calcutta appears to have been equally unproductive. In 1780, on another visit to Calcutta, Light made a second attempt to influence Hastings against the growing danger of Dutch monopoly. This time he was received with more interest and cordiality, but unfortunately Hastings was then too preoccupied with Indian affairs to take immediate action. Four years later, however, perhaps as a result of Light's visit, two further missions were dispatched, this time to Rhio[1] (Capt. Forrest) and Achin (Kinlock). In both places results were negative; the Dutch had anticipated us in Rhio, and Achin, as always, was intractable.

Being again in Calcutta in 1786, Light had an interview with Sir John MacPherson, the Governor-General. He recommended two stations: Junk Ceylon,[2] where he had his own headquarters, and Penang, which he was able to offer on behalf of the young Sultan of Kedah, with whom he was even more friendly than he had been with the father. MacPherson thought two stations excessive, but authorized an agreement with the Sultan, and Light negotiated a settlement whereby the island of Penang was ceded to the Company for the annual payment of $6,000.[3] The British flag was hoisted on 12th August 1786, the birthday of the Prince of Wales, later George IV, to commemorate which Penang was renamed Prince of Wales (or Wales's) Island, and the capital became George Town (or Georgetown). Francis Light was the first superintendent, his reward for fifteen years' endeavour.

It was only the greater brilliance of his successor, Raffles, and the overshadowing of Penang by Singapore, that deprived Francis Light of the fame that should be his. Like Raffles, he had enthusiasm, and it was his pressure on the authorities that brought Penang into being. But for his vigorous efforts as its superintendent, the new colony might well have been abandoned almost as soon as it had been founded. Without Light, Raffles might never have had his chance.

Penang (Pulau Pinang—Areca Nut[4] Island—of the Malays) is some fifteen miles long and ten miles wide, with an area of about a hundred and ten square miles, and is separated from Kedah on the mainland by a narrow strait. The greater part of the island is occupied by a striking group of hills that rise to points over two thousand feet high. In 1786 it was almost uninhabited and covered with dense tropical vegetation. The

[1] Riau, Riouw, etc., an archipelago to the south of the Malay Peninsula.

[2] Now called Salang.

[3] £1,500. The Mexican (or Spanish) dollar, the trade dollar of the Far East, was at that time worth 5s.

[4] Erroneously known as betel nut. It is the nut with which betel leaves are chewed.

settlement was begun at the point of a flat triangle, which, with its base reaching to the foothills, faces with its apex the mainland. So marked is this triangle, which still contains the principal settlement on the island, that the Malays call the town of Penang (or Georgetown) Tanjong—the Spit.

The original purpose of the settlement is clear from a letter of Sir John MacPherson's dated 22nd January 1787: ". . . to secure a port of refreshment and repair for the King's, the Company's and the Country ships, and we must leave it to time and your good management to establish it as a port of commerce." To accelerate that development, the Governor-General, on the inspiration of his superintendent, laid down a novel commercial policy, of which Raffles was later to be such a keen exponent. "We desire you will refrain from levying any kind of duties or tax on goods landed or vessels importing, and it is our wish to make the port free to all nations."

Standing as Penang did on the fringe of Dutch monopoly, its early success was assured, and the Dutch had to take drastic steps to prevent wholesale migration from Malacca. But the East India Company was interested less in the achievements of local commerce than in the cost of the Penang establishment. Moreover, the colony was much affected by extravagant claims and by the reaction when these were disappointed. Steps to build up and consolidate its position were not taken, and within four years its fate hung in the balance. In 1790, during a period of Anglo-Dutch trade negotiations,[1] Henry Dundas (later Viscount Melville) discussed with his colleagues the possibility of getting Rhio from the Dutch in exchange for Penang. Dundas was then Treasurer of the Navy and a member of the Board of Control set up by the British Government under the India Act of 1784 to supervise the administration of the East India Company.

"The more I think on the subject," he wrote to the Home Secretary, W. W. Grenville, on 1st July 1790, "the more satisfied I am that a station for the purpose of Commerce is necessary in the Eastern seas; and all things considered there seems no reason to doubt that Rhio from its ideal situation ought to be that place, and reasons which render Rhio the most eligible go to prove that the Prince of Wales's Island is not so. . . . I think both Prince of Wales's Island and Nagapatam ought to be given up rather than the Rhio. . . ."

Nothing was done, except that in 1791 the agreement of 1786 was modified by a treaty whereby the Kedah government was to receive $6,000 every year from the East India Company "so long as the English continue in possession of Pulo Pinang".

Francis Light died on the island on 21st October 1794, and in place of a superintendent, Penang was controlled by a Lieutenant-Governor.

[1] *Dropmore Papers*, Vol. I.

In 1796 Arthur Wellesley was sent as a colonel to India. A younger brother of the Marquis Wellesley, then Earl of Mornington and Governor-General designate of India, he was engaged in the following year in the abortive Manila expedition and spent some time in Penang. No doubt at the request of his brother, he went carefully into the question as to whether the colony should be retained or not. As might be expected of the future Duke of Wellington, his report was lucid and practical. Remembering the purpose for which the colony had been founded, he pronounced: "It is a most desirable place to retain because scarcely a ship of the expedition has failed to sustain damage from the violence of the south-west monsoon." Then, as to refreshment: "Such was the diligence of the governing power, and the capabilities of the place, that not less than 10,000 people, in addition to the inhabitants, were daily fed: above 6,000 of these Europeans." Moreover, "The stillness of the water" enable the ships "to shift their cargo, and to perform numberless operations" without the slightest interference by wind or water. On the other hand, he found the defences contemptible, the colony liable to be "plundered or insulted by a single frigate".

"If it be a benefit", he wrote, "to live under the Company's Government, it cannot be expected that any man will spend his time and fortune upon a settlement which they intend to abandon; and as the settlement is, as I have above shown, of infinite advantage to the Company, and as it will undoubtedly be quitted by the settlers if the Company's Government does not declare its intention of keeping it, it is recommended that it should make that declaration in the most explicit terms, and adhere to it faithfully. . . ."

Notwithstanding this, the only real step taken to establish the new colony on a proper basis was the acquisition, for a further $4,000 per annum, of a strip of the mainland opposite the town.[1] This was named Province Wellesley, presumably in honour of the Governor-General and not of the Duke of Wellington to be.

In the following year the free-trade policy laid down by MacPherson was revoked. An attempt to maintain law and order was made by the appointment of John Dickens (often incorrectly taken to be an uncle of the novelist) as judge and magistrate. He had had considerable experience as a lawyer in India, but was greatly hampered in his new task by the absence, through the dilatoriness of the Company, of a proper charter, without which the magistracy and police had no legal standing. He was still further impeded by the conceit and self-importance of young Sir George Leith, then Lieutenant-Governor of the island. Between the stiff,

[1] The British Government, which took over the East India Company in 1858, concluded a treaty with Siam in 1869, one clause of which agreed to the annual payment of $10,000 for Penang and Province Wellesley. This amount is still being paid.

uncompromising legalism of the one and the inflated inexperience of the other, a state of deadlock arose that was as detrimental to the settlement as it was discreditable to the parties concerned.

Continuing to have doubts about the value of the colony, though quite clear as to the amount it was costing to keep it, the Company still hesitated to take any decisive step that might commit it to a definite forward policy.

Then once again something quite outside the Company's affairs put Penang in the limelight.

The Admiralty had been getting more and more apprehensive about the scarcity of seasoned oak to maintain the Navy. Philip Dundas, nephew of Henry Dundas, on his return in 1803 from Bombay, where he had been master attendant,[1] suggested to his uncle—by then Viscount Melville and First Lord of the Admiralty—that teak might be used in place of oak. This meant that ships would have to be built in the East, as facilities were lacking in those days for the transport to England of the quantities of timber required. Melville was much struck with this idea, and after various consultations as to the suitability of Bombay, Rangoon and Penang, it was finally decided that Penang would be the best place. The need for a naval arsenal and improved defences there, in view of the renewal of hostilities with France, was already apparent. The site for the shipyard was to be at Pulau Jerejak, and the cost was to be recovered from the Admiralty.

The East India Company now had to take a decisive step; and perhaps to make up for its previous dilatoriness and parsimony, it plunged straight into the astonishing decision to make Penang a fourth Presidency,[2] with Philip Dundas as its Governor.

At that time the colony was under the control of a Lieutenant-Governor, one Robert T. Farquhar, of exceptional merit. He had spent almost twelve years abroad in the Company's service—in Ceylon, the Moluccas and Borneo. He knew some Malay and was probably better acquainted than anyone else of the period with the islands of the Eastern Archipelago. He was thus well qualified to hold the additional office of Agent of the Governor-General with the Malay States. He had taken over at Penang as recently as 15th January 1804.

Bearing in mind the report of Colonel Wellesley, the Company relied on meeting the cost of the new Presidency by savings at Bencoolen and Malacca, which were to be reduced to very small establishments; it proposed to improve commerce by giving officials of the new government large salaries and prohibiting them from trading; and it hoped to obtain

[1] Executive assistant to superintendent of naval dockyard. He was reputed to have made a fortune of £70,000-£80,000. (*Diary of Joseph Farington*, IV, 254.)

[2] The other three were centred on Bombay, Madras and Calcutta.

direct revenue from duties, customs and land rent to cover the remaining deficit. As the cost of the new establishment was £43,500 a year, the Company was as optimistic as it was extravagant.

It must have been particularly galling to Robert Farquhar, not only that the Governor who was to supersede him was young and quite inexperienced, but also that, of the whole new government, only one was a civil servant, and he much junior to himself. Certainly the whole scheme was madness. As Farquhar wrote in his memorial to the Company:

"Every advantage that the Island was capable of affording was just beginning to bud—plans for the formation of docks and of a great Naval Arsenal had been commenced, defences equal to the protection of the inhabitants' property on the Island had been completed, cultivation had been facilitated, extended and improved by the formation of extensive and commodious roads and bridges . . . revenue had increased £17,000 in the course of 17 months and uncultivated land had risen in value from 8 to 50 dollars; land in the town and suburbs had gone up from 500 to 1,500 dollars."

But Farquhar got his reward later, becoming the first Governor of Mauritius and being duly knighted for his services there.

Chapter Three

PENANG, 1805-1806

CARRYING an imposing array of officials and their ladies, and escorted by H.M.S. *Blenheim*, the *Warley* arrived at Penang on 19th September 1805.

Another traveller of that period, recording his first sight of Penang, wrote:

"... It was about eight o'clock in the morning. The Island presented a most beautiful and irregular outline, involved in those delicate tints of grey which, as the sun rose, through a humid atmosphere, changed to a beautiful pink. In my younger days, I had frequently been puzzled how to understand the proper application of the expression 'rosy tinted Aurora', but now it was most completely illustrated, to my mind as well as to my eye, by the soft pink-grey which overspread the whole of this lovely mountain. We were about twenty miles distant and, as we approached, the deepening tints became more and more vivid, point after point opening gradually to our view, until the whole extent of the picturesque Isle formed one side of our splendid panorama; whilst, on the other side, not more than four miles off, the hilly and jungly coast of Queda [Kedah] displayed almost equal beauty, though of a bolder character. The narrowness of this passage between Penang and the coast of Malacca makes the sailing through this part of the Straits very interesting, the objects on both sides being always in view. ...

"The town spreads itself naturally over a little point of land jutting out into the sea, which seemed so expressly formed for its Establishment that one can scarcely believe that it was with such infinite labour and expense that the East India Company succeeded in making the space habitable by clearing away the thick jungle which formerly covered it. At present it is one of the prettiest places I ever saw; the red roofs of the houses glittered in the sun through the surrounding thick foliage of the trees. ..."

To-day the irregular ridge of mountain, which runs from north to south the whole length of the island, is sadly denuded of much of its forest, yet Penang remains one of the most beautiful, if least advertised, places in the world. Many of the flowering shrubs that make such a striking picture have been introduced since, but even in 1805 the yellow cassia, the scarlet flowers of hibiscus and ixora, the sweet-scented frangipane and the flaming cæsalpinia would have made a brilliant show.

If nature's reception was warm and exciting, the attitude of the

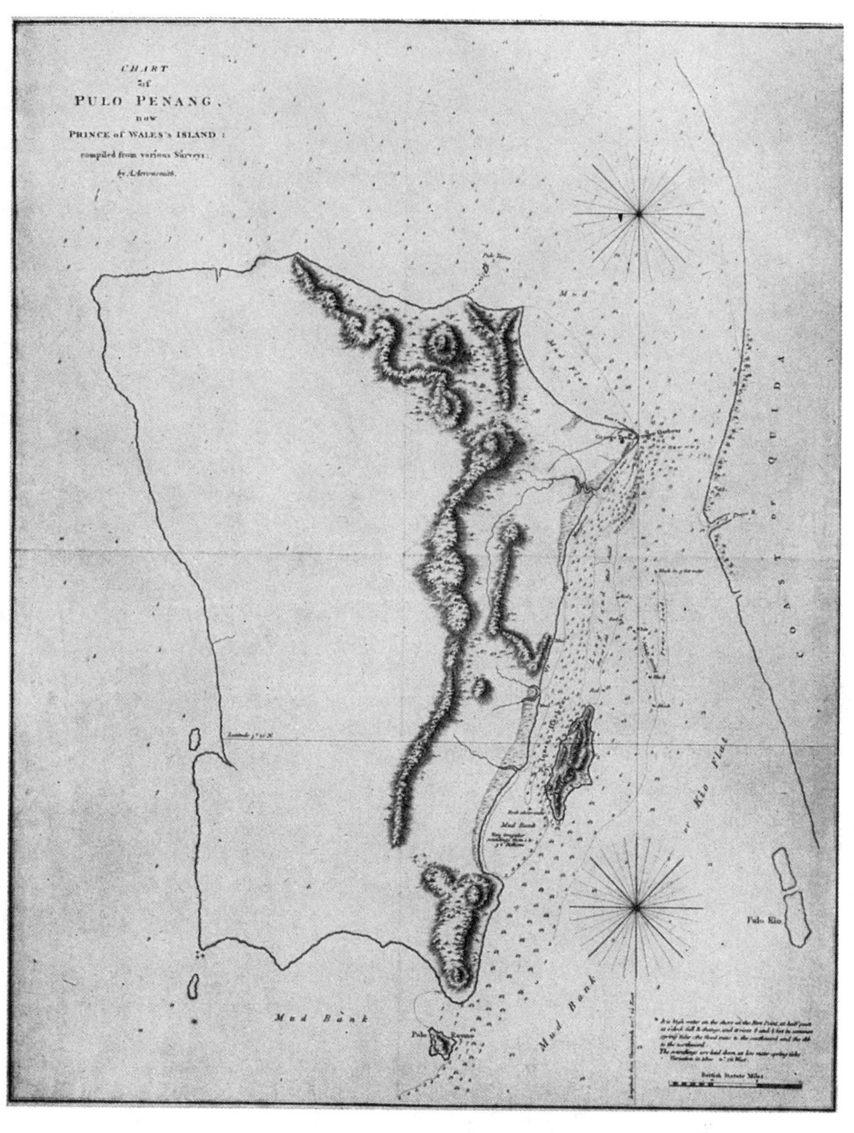

MAP OF PENANG

Prepared by J. Arrowsmith in 1805.
By courtesy of the British Museum.

inhabitants towards the newcomers was less exuberant. Robert Farquhar had bitterly opposed being supplanted by a Governor and Council of little standing and experience, and many of the displaced officials naturally shared his view. One of the most disgruntled was the secretary to the former government, William E. Phillips.

Born in 1769, Phillips had gone out to India in 1787. He had seen some active service with the 74th Regiment and had reached the rank of captain. Owing to ill health he had been sent to Penang as secretary to the government under Sir George Leith and had continued under Farquhar. With the departure of Farquhar, he was acting Governor when the new contingent arrived, and his reduction in position to collector of customs and land revenue was naturally displeasing to him. He seems to have taken an early dislike to Raffles, who perhaps failed to treat him with sufficient deference.

The new government was as follows:

	Council	*$ per annum*
Governor and Treasurer	Hon. Philip Dundas	32,000
Second in Council and Warehouse Keeper	John Hope Oliphant	18,000
Third in Council and Superintendent of Marine	Alexander Gray	18,000
Fourth in Council and Commandant	Capt. (later Col.) Norman Macalister	18,000
	Others	
Surgeon	Dr William Dick	10,720
Secretary	Henry Shepherd Pearson	8,000
Accountant and Auditor	James Philip Hobson	8,000
Chaplain	Rev. Atwill Lake	6,400
Assistant Secretary	Thomas Raffles	6,000
Assistant to Accountant and Auditor	William Robinson	6,000
Sub Warehouse Keeper and Paymaster	Quintin Dick Thompson	6,000
Collector of Customs and Land Revenue	William Edward Phillips	6,000
Assistant to Superintendent of Marine	John James Erskine	6,000

There were also various minor officials, including young Mr Ibbetson, then aged eighteen, making a total establishment of twenty-six. Two junior clerks—writers, as they were called—had died on the voyage out.

The advent of all these could only mean a general rise in living costs, which would benefit few and injure many. But the chief reaction of the inhabitants was, not unnaturally, one of astonishment that the home authorities should have decided to impose such a costly government machine on their small settlement. The new Governor, however, created a good impression as a mild and moderate man and one unlikely to embark on any sensational or dramatic schemes to obtain the required revenue. Meantime, there was money to be made supplying the new arrivals with their local needs, so they were inclined to regard the whole thing as a huge joke, though one rather impaired by the unpleasant thought that somehow they might be made to foot the bill—an impossible task, as the Company was to discover for itself only too soon.

On 20th September (just one month before the Battle of Trafalgar) the new government was installed, and a dispatch[1] embodying its instructions read to the Council. This consisted of no less than seventy-four paragraphs. Beginning with a brief explanation of the delay in setting up a permanent government and the reasons that had prompted action now, particularly the requirements of the Admiralty and the renewal of war, it reviewed the general situation in the area. There was an acid reference to Bencoolen being politically and commercially valueless. Malacca was not worth the expense, so its fortifications were to be destroyed and the European inhabitants evacuated. The enhanced trade, which a regular government should create at Penang, would, said the dispatch, enable commerce to support the cost of establishment. Woollens and other useful commodities from home to the value of £25,000 had been ordered to be sent to Penang, and expectations of good profits were held out from sales of opium, land regulations and the monopoly of marine stores. Other paragraphs dealt with coinage, the proposed naval arsenal, fortifications, military matters and the administration of justice. The last paragraph referred to the appointment of Mr Lake as chaplain, and the dispatch concluded with the pious exhortation: "We trust by Mr Lake's endeavours and your example, the interests of religion and morality will be promoted in the island."

The installation of a new government is not as simple as the official ceremony that empowers it to function. At Penang the confusion and dislocation, inherent in a wholesale change of office-holders and the inexperience of the new officials, were aggravated by the complete absence of Asiatic clerks. In the modern Colonial Service, these are the equivalent of the junior clerical service at home and form the essential background of any colonial administration. The lack of this vital part of the organization made the task of the Penang secretariat very difficult, and extremely onerous.

Raffles touched on this matter in a letter to London dated 10th November 1805, two months after his arrival. A draft of this has been

[1] *Journal of the Indian Archipelago*, Vol. VI, p. 18.

preserved, and though the addressee is not given, it can be assumed that it was to his old friend and patron, William Ramsay. In it is revealed his natural optimism, which never left him—and sometimes acted as a boomerang.

"I beg leave", wrote Raffles, "to state my opinion that the present Establishment is quite sufficient for the various duties of the different departments, provided five or six Writers are sent out annually. In the course of a year, those who are here will understand the business very well, and many of them, I hope, be capable of succeeding to the superior stations. I am, however, sorry to call your particular attention to a paragraph in our General Letter alluding to the employment of persons not regularly admitted into the Service and to observe that it cannot be expected the youths sent out will pay that attention necessary while they see strangers, with Government interests, put over their heads."

Another early problem was shortage of accommodation. Property owners saw their opportunity, and rents for houses and offices shot up. Raffles, for example, had to pay no less than £330 a year for a house. He was but the assistant secretary, so one can imagine the sums demanded of the Governor and members of the Council. The writers—or "young gentlemen of the Civil Service", as they were called—were boarded by a Mr Porter at Flower Pot Hall at a rate of one and a half dollars (seven and sixpence) a day, which included a bottle of wine among four. This house stood at the western corner of Love Lane and Farquhar Street and survived up to the Japanese invasion in December 1941, when it was demolished by a bomb.

In that first year of the Presidency, printing was introduced into Penang, and the *Government Gazette* appeared. This was brought out by private enterprise, though receiving official recognition. A Licenser of the Press (Raffles, unpaid) was appointed, and the *Gazette* contained copies of government notices and orders. After a few issues the title was changed to the *Prince of Wales's Island Gazette*, and the publisher did his best to collect and print all the news he could get together from visiting ships, letters and newspapers received by private individuals, and from gazettes and newspapers sent regularly from other countries. Local affairs received some degree of notice, but by far the greater part of each issue was taken up by long extracts from English, American, Continental and Indian papers, covering not merely political events and accounts of battles and other great stirs, but also dramatic trials, reviews of books and descriptions of strange lands. Scandals, duels and other social matter gave pungency to the paper. Caroline, Princess of Wales, occupied several closely printed sheets in issue after issue.

To our modern age a delay of six months or more in getting news would seem a terrible deprivation. The people of Penang did not expect it sooner. Tidings of victory at Trafalgar and the death of Nelson, of the struggle in the Peninsula, of the great defeats and victories of the Napoleonic wars were just as real and just as exciting to them half a year after the event as they would be to us if heard within a few hours.

Of Robert Farquhar's administration before the establishment of the Presidency, Raffles wrote in the letter of 10th November 1805:

"We found the Island in a much higher state of improvement than we expected. The Government of Mr Farquhar was very expensive and, although he may be condemned, as I have no doubt he will be, for extravagance and lavish expenditure of the public money, yet the new Government has no cause to complain as far as their individual and personal comforts are concerned. Our roads, houses and the comforts of life have improved to twice what they were when he took charge of this Government, and the state of Society and more general resort are both improved and encouraged. You will observe by our Consultations, correspondence that took place before his departure which may probably be the cause demanding a public enquiry into his conduct. We find him very much beloved by the inhabitants who have no doubt improved their fortunes under his administrations, but who have also improved the Island by following the instructions of a man of such superior abilities as the late Lieutenant-Governor. . . . A considerable difficulty has arisen to the servants acting under the new Government by the want of regularity in all the departments before their arrival, but we are now getting settled and into separate offices. . . ."

In referring to the favourable prospect of Penang "becoming a station of the highest political and commercial consequence", Raffles expressed regret that his want of experience and lack of opportunity for observation since his arrival prevented him from supplying full details, yet the letter is a foretaste of his prodigious energy and unflagging interest.

". . . I have been very particular in my enquiries respecting the construction of docks here, and the establishment of a Naval Arsenal, and I am happy that it is in my power to afford the most satisfactory information on this head:—There is no doubt whatever that the wishes of the Court and His Majesty's Ministers can be carried into effect to their fullest extent, and at much less expense than I believe to have been calculated upon before we left England. I forward by this conveyance [H.M.S. *Dédaigneuse*] two plans, of the harbour and that part of it, which offered itself as advantageous for this measure to the late Government. . . . With respect to timber, there is a considerable supply on the Island and on the adjacent shore that will be serviceable for ship-building, but the teak must come from Pegue[1] or thereabouts. . . . With the respect of the principal points of commercial advantage that may be expected from the new

[1] Pegu, Burma.

Government of this Island, I cannot state I think more satisfactory, except I add a few particulars on the subject of the Pepper produce. I find it here to be a fact well-known that the London markets have been supplied for several years with pepper, chiefly the produce of this Island, and the neighbourhood, although the same was shipped at Bencoolen for Europe —two ships were sent here last year from that Settlement and traded with pepper—and as late as June last a ship arrived here from thence for the same purpose, but the merchants, having received information respecting the new Government for the Island, raised their price and returned the ship without pepper. I am inclined to think nearly the whole of the pepper, the produce of the Island, is fit for the Europe market, being considerably heavier and better than what has frequently brought a high price there. There are several young plantains not yet bearing, and many pepper vineyards planting, and if the market in Europe was good, they might be very considerably increased. . . ."

This letter accompanied certain official reports—the "Consultations" mentioned above—of which he wrote:

". . . I have done everything that my situation enabled me to insert in the Proceedings of Government, whatever might be interesting to the Court of Directors, and I trust they will, in considering the very great times we have had to encounter, both in want of offices and proper assistance, approve of the exertions made by Mr Pearson and myself on whom the burthen has chiefly fallen, and look over the many official irregularities they may contain."

Shortly before this letter was written there had arrived in Penang a young man whose meeting with Raffles was to have far-reaching results, both for Raffles and the British Empire. This young man was an assistant surgeon from India, John Caspar Leyden.

Born of peasant stock on 8th September 1775 at Denholm on the Teviot—"in", wrote Lockhart,[1] "one of the wildest valleys of Roxburghshire"—he was educated at the village school. In 1790 he went to Edinburgh University and there studied Hebrew, Arabic, Theology and Medicine. Before he attained his nineteenth year he had, as Lockhart recorded, "confounded the doctors of Edinburgh by the portentous mass of his acquisitions in almost every department of learning. He had set the extremest penury at utter defiance, or rather he had never been conscious that it could operate as a bar; for bread and butter, and access to books and lectures, comprised all within the bounds of his wishes; and thus he toiled and battled at the gates of science after science, until his unconquerable perseverance carried everything before it; and yet with this monastic abstemiousness and iron hardness of will, perplexing those about him by manners and habits in which it was hard to say whether the

[1] J. G. Lockhart, *Life of Sir Walter Scott.*

moss-trooper or the schoolman of former days most prevailed, he was at heart a poet." In 1798 he obtained a licence to preach, but abandoned that pursuit in favour of literature and medicine, obtaining an M.D. at St Andrews. He produced various literary works and collaborated with Scott in his *Border Minstrelsy*.

In 1803 Leyden applied for an appointment on the medical establishment in India, and, on 7th April, sailed for Madras. He was ill on the voyage, and his health was further impaired by his work as assistant surgeon and naturalist attached to the Commission of Survey in Mysore. After a period in hospital he was sent to Penang to recuperate. The idea still persisted that Penang was a health resort and, compared, perhaps, with the mainland of India, it might well have been, though the sea voyage more probably deserved the credit.

He arrived in Penang on 22nd October 1805.

"Eight o'clock. With the utmost difficulty we have at last got into the harbour between five and six o'clock in the evening. The hills on both sides of the bay remained almost completely concealed by the haze, but the bay is wide and spacious, and extremely well sheltered on every side. The entrance is wide, open and safe. The fort and Government House are the first objects which present themselves to attract the attention. The town lies low, and is in a great measure concealed by wood. We found a considerable number of ships in the harbour, and among the rest two line-of-battle ships commanded by Sir Thomas Trowbridge,[1] namely, the 'Rattlesnake' and 'Dédaigneuse'. The town is full of strangers, and of persons who have been superseded by the erection of Puloo Penang into a Presidency, and who are consequently ready to take their departure, so that there is not only a great deal of confusion, but a sort of interregnum."

Leyden stayed at "a kind of naval tavern where all around me is ringing with the vociferation of tarpaulins, the hoarse bawling of sea oaths and the rattling of the dicebox". He was still far from recovered from his illness, so it was fortunate that Raffles rescued him from this primitive lodging and gave him hospitality in his home, where Olivia nursed the invalid back to health.

"Being confined entirely to the house, and having abundance of time on my hands", wrote Leyden, "to get rid of the *ennui* of a tedious convalescence, I applied vigorously to the acquisition of the Malay, the Hindustani of the East."

This accidental encounter with a versatile scholar was to mean much to Raffles. Probably for the first time it brought him into direct contact with a man who was his equal in enthusiasm and one, too, who had also acquired his knowledge in the face of extreme penury. All the amateur

[1] Troubridge.

enthusiasm that Raffles' natural bent had kindled was now directed by a trained mind filled with a varied stock of specialized knowledge. Here was a living model for him to follow, a guide to direct him on the path of learning. Such a teacher would have been an asset to any man anxious to learn; to Raffles—self-taught, his scholarship acquired haphazardly and as circumstances had permitted—the chance was of paramount importance. Among his colleagues in the new government there was no kindred spirit, and he might have wondered in his heart if study was really worth while. Yet, however indifferent Penang might have been to Eastern literature, to the habits and customs of the indigenous peoples, their history and lore, there were plenty of people in India who pursued these subjects with devotion. As long before as 1784 an Asiatic Society had been founded in Calcutta by Sir William Jones, judge of the Supreme Court, for the express purpose of studying Eastern languages and literature; and in 1786 Sir William had made what was in fact the first public reference to Sanskrit, which became the starting-point for the modern science of comparative philology. And now, in Raffles' own house, was another such scholar—a man who owed his career to that very devotion to the pursuit of knowledge so ridiculed by the pompous and ignorant dullards who composed the majority of the Penang administration.

J. T. Thomson, the writer on Singapore, tells us very seriously that in the early days Raffles and Olivia were ostracized by Penang society because of the story attaching to Olivia, but that good came out of evil because this forced them to cultivate the friendship of the Malays. This, in part at least, is nonsense. Evidence of ostracism is deficient, and Raffles' interest in the Malays requires no such curious explanation.

Captain Thomas Otho Travers, who got to know Raffles at an early date in Penang, wrote:

"Being of a cheerful lively disposition and very fond of Society it was surprising how he was able to entertain so hospitably as he did and yet labour so much as he was known to do at the time, not only in his official capacity but in acquiring a general knowledge of the history, Government and local interests of the neighbouring States; and this he was greatly aided in doing by conversing freely with the natives who were constantly visiting Penang at this period, many of whom were often found to be sensible, intelligent men and greatly pleased to find a person holding Mr Raffles's situation able and anxious to converse with them in their own language."

No, Thomson's story does not make sense. It is, one suspects, simply another attempt to find an explanation, however far-fetched, for a taste so unusual as to be almost incomprehensible. Officials in Penang did not make friends with the Malays: they could not even speak their language.

The three months Leyden spent in Penang were not unproductive. "Happy in the enjoyment of congenial society", he laid the foundation of his famous *Dissertation on the Indo-Persian, Indo-Chinese, and Dekkan Languages*, and a translation of the *Sĕjarah Mĕlayu* ("Malay Annals"), to which Raffles was to contribute a preface. But Leyden produced something much more important and much more lasting than either of those learned works; he produced a trained disciple, who, though he would never surpass his master in pure learning, would outstrip him immeasurably in the world of action and in fame.

Leyden was certainly correct in describing as congenial the society in which he found himself. Whatever truth there may have been in the story that Olivia was under a social cloud (it would have been from the women, certainly not the men), Leyden frankly fell in love with her. It was all perfectly seemly, giving Raffles cause to be nothing but pleased and flattered that Olivia found Leyden such a charming guest, as happy to flirt with her as to co-operate with himself over the mysteries of the Malay tongue.

Olivia was said to be the "Nona" to whom Tom Moore addressed his poems. She also inspired Leyden to a considerable outburst of lyric poetry. Sir Walter Scott rated him high as a poet. Modern opinion hardly supports that view, but the effusions do at least show what kindness Leyden received in the Raffles' home and how deeply attached he was to Olivia —and her husband.

Still may'st thou live in bliss secure
  Beneath that friend's protecting care,
And may his cherished life endure
  Long, long, thy holy love to share.[1]

Raffles and Leyden were kindred spirits, rapidly finding themselves on terms of that special intimacy kindled and sustained by an equally ardent passion for research and the pursuit of knowledge. Of much the same age, their enthusiastic and unselfish zeal established between them a bond of complete harmony. Unquestionably, John Leyden was closer to the heart of Raffles than was any other man.

Leyden left for Calcutta in the *St Antonio*, a Portuguese ship, early in January 1806. On the 7th of that month, a day or two out from Penang, he wrote to Olivia:

"My Dear Madam,—We have now lost sight of Pooloo Penang, more, I am sorry to say, from the darkness than from the distance, and while our Portuguese friends are recommending themselves with great

[1] *Dirge of the Departed Year. To Olivia.*

fervency of devotion to their patron saint, I have retired to pay the devoirs which I owe to her whom I have chosen my patroness for the voyage. I cannot help congratulating myself a good deal on the superiority of my choice of a living saint to a dead one, and am positive if you choose to exert yourself a little you have a great chance of rivalling his sublimest miracles, among which none of the least is his preaching on a certain day with great zeal and fervour to divers asses till their long ears betrayed powerful symptoms of devotion . . . if it be possible to overcome the irksomeness of light gales, a heaving cradle of a sea, and a barren, sweltering, tropical voyage, I flatter myself that I have adopted the best possible method by associating with all the pleasant recollections which I hoarded up at Penang in the society of you and your amiable husband. It is a terrible circumstance, after all, that there is little real difference between the recollections of past pleasures and past sorrows. Perhaps the most we can make of it is that the memory of past pleasures is pleasant and mournful, and the memory of past sorrows is mournful and pleasant. I remember to have read of some such distinction in a volume of sermons, but I will by no means vouch for the accuracy of the quotation, as on second thoughts the epithets, I imagine, might be reversed with equal propriety. However this may be, the recollection of the pleasure I enjoyed in your society is by no means so vivid as my distress at losing it, and the little prospect I have of soon recovering it. . . ."

When Leyden and Raffles next met, it was as actors in a great enterprise. Fate had many cruel strokes in hand for Raffles, more strokes than most men are called upon to withstand. That Leyden should be struck down at the very moment when their dreams came true was of all blows the most cruel, except only the death of Olivia herself, love for whom was the final and most perfect link that bound them together.

Another visitor to Penang in that period was one who was to be intimately associated with Raffles for the next twenty years. Thomas Otho Travers, born in Ireland in 1785, had gone out to India in 1804 and had been gazetted to 20th Native Infantry. He came to Penang as a member of the local garrison and, by a fortunate chance, kept a diary. Most of this has survived, but no volume before 1813, so that we are deprived of his jottings for some of the most important years. Quotations from his diary before that date as given in the *Memoir* by Raffles' second wife are, in fact, extracts from a memorandum prepared by Travers at her request. If he made any reference to Olivia, it was excised, for none appears in the memorandum as published. Lady Raffles permitted no mention of Olivia in the *Memoir*, except in one footnote!

Travers had this to say about Raffles:

"It was in the year 1806 I first became acquainted with Mr Raffles at the island of Penang. He was then Deputy Secretary to the new Government which had been recently sent out to that place. . . . The details of the Government proceedings, as far as related to local arrangements and regulations, together with the compilation of almost every public document, devolved on Mr Raffles, who possessed great quickness and facility in conducting and arranging the forms of a new Government as well as in drawing up and keeping records.

"The public dispatches were also entrusted to him and, in fact, he had the entire weight and trouble attendant on the formation of a new Government. This, however, did not prevent his attending closely to improve himself in the Eastern languages: and whilst his mornings were employed in his public office, where at first he had but little assistance, his evenings were devoted to Eastern literature. Few men, but those who were immediately on the spot at the time, can form any idea of the difficult task which he had to perform in conducting the public business of such a Government as existed on the first establishment of Penang as a Presidency. It would be irrelevant here to allude to, or to attempt any description of the different characters of whom this Government was formed, the more particularly so as they are all now dead, but it is due to Mr Raffles to state that he was respected and consulted by every member of it. In his official capacity, he gave most general satisfaction, whilst the settlers looked up to him for assistance and advice in every difficulty; and, when he afterwards became chief Secretary, the most general satisfaction was evinced throughout the Settlement."

At this time Raffles was indeed carrying, and for that matter continued to carry, the whole burden of the administrative machine. Yet he found time not only to continue his Malay studies, but also to take on any odd job for which no other suitable candidate was available. At all times he was the willing horse, ready to carry on his heavily burdened shoulders any additional work, either to gain practical experience or because he preferred this to seeing it shelved or bungled by his colleagues. But, as almost invariably happens, his energy and enthusiasm, in such striking contrast to that of his neighbours, later became a source of irritation and jealousy among his seniors. In the early days his position gave him, no doubt, a gratifying sense of power, and the rest of the Government were quite happy to sit back and let him do the work. He wrote home cheerfully that he was "on the best footing possible with the present Government. They leave everything to me that I wish, and are satisfied with my conduct."

In the first general letter to London, the Governor in Council had reported that unless the rent of houses and other expenses were reduced they would not be able to live on their salaries. These, in terms of sterling, had seemed princely, but they had soon discovered that, in the expression of the day, "a dollar here does not go as far as a rupee in the other

Provinces"—or, in the more modern and equally common parlance of Singapore, "a dollar here goes as far as a shilling".

In addition to having now to defray his normal living expenses, Raffles had had to repay substantial advances against his salary before he left England. Soon after his arrival he had sent home to his mother no less than £400 in one draft, and this sum he continued to allow her annually. Besides fitting out his wife and himself for life overseas, he had had to bear the cost of an outfit for his sister, Mary Anne, and to maintain her in Penang. It is true that, within six months of her arrival, she had secured a husband, Quintin Dick Thompson, but, knowing the character of Raffles, we can assume that she did not go entirely empty-handed. He was now arranging for two more of his sisters, Harriet and Leonora to join them in Penang.

Raffles had incurred other liabilities of a different kind, resulting from his researches into the Malay language and customs. He wrote to the Governor in Council on 20th February 1806:

"I have been at much expense in retaining in my service several natives whom I have selected as persons whose ability, and perhaps integrity, might be depended upon when they are being engaged in trade or other pursuits, wherein the occasional knowledge they might obtain of the affairs of Government might be improper. These men were engaged by me and, hitherto, have been maintained at my expense, but I have now to regret the narrow limits of my income will not longer admit of continuing so expensive an establishment on my own account, and more particularly so as I had reason to expect from them considerable assistance in explaining and commenting upon the customs and laws of the adjacent States, which I am endeavouring to collect, in the hope of laying a fair translation thereon before your Honourable Board.

"I cannot, however, omit adding that I was in a great measure induced to engage those men, from the circumstance of the *full* employment of Translator to Government not having been granted to any person at this Presidency. . . . And I trust that whenever the Honourable the Governor and Council shall take this appointment under consideration I shall be honoured by their favourable notice. . . ."

He said also that, "having paid considerable attention to the acquisition of the Malayee language", he felt himself competent, not only to detect any error or misrepresentation made in translating or transcribing letters, but also, when necessary, to translate or transcribe with is own hand letters of a confidential or secret nature, "and in many other respects to prevent, by my personal application, the affairs and interests of Government being intrusted in the hands of a native. . . ."

The regular interpreter at that time was a Thomas Hutton, a member of the former administration. It seems that he was not very satisfactory,

Dundas and the Council having little faith in him. Raffles' offer of his services as official translator was not immediately accepted. As for the other matter, on 6th March 1806 the Council passed the following resolution:

"Resolved that Mr Raffles be allowed the natives he requires, the Board relying on his not keeping them longer than is necessary for the completion of the work on which he is employed."

This work was probably the preliminary research that was later to form the material of his paper, *On the Malayu Nation*, which was published in the Proceedings of the Asiatic Society of Calcutta for the year 1816. Long before that date it was to form an essential link in the chain of circumstances that brought Raffles into public notice in a very much wider field.

His active prosecution of Malay studies brought another reward. Governor Dundas was approached by William Marsden for answers to various technical points affecting Malay language and history. William Marsden was at this time making a name for himself as one of the leading British orientalists. Later he was to be an original member of both the Royal Asiatic Society and the Royal Geographical Society. Born in 1754, the son of an Irish bank director, he had been intended for the Church, but, inspired by a wish to join his elder brother in Bencoolen, he had secured an appointment with the East India Company and had arrived there on 29th May 1771. Eight years later he had given up his appointment and returned to England, where in 1795 he had been appointed Second Secretary to the Navy, becoming First Secretary in 1803. He retired in 1807 and devoted his time to historical and linguistic studies.

Dundas naturally turned to Raffles for help, which was readily forthcoming. In a reply dated 6th July 1806, Raffles dealt with the queries at length. This letter initiated a long and fruitful correspondence between Raffles and Marsden, from which Marsden obtained, as he publicly acknowledged, a great deal of valuable information. Raffles, in his turn, derived great advantage also; it acted as a stimulant to his zeal for the studies he had begun from natural curiosity, and which Leyden had encouraged and probably in some degree directed in their earlier stages.

For some time past there had been friction between the Governor and the secretary, Pearson. So serious did this become that on 28th August 1806 Pearson departed on six months' leave. Though the excuse given was ill-health, the real reason was because he was "finding this office so ill to agree with him and furthermore not drawing well with the Hon. Governor". No one was more pleased at his departure than Raffles, who, on the following day, was appointed acting secretary and thus became in name what he had been all along in fact: the mainspring and pivot of the government. If the acting appointment was not a very lucrative one, it was "certainly a pleasanter one than that of Deputy under an ignoramus in his office".

One of his first steps was to write to the Governor (18th September), laying bare the state of the secretary's office and the arrears into which the work had already fallen. Here Raffles was on firm ground; there was no one who possessed his secretarial experience, certainly not Pearson, who lacked also ability and energy. It is true that internally there had been some extenuating circumstances. While the Company had been extravagant in higher appointments, it had been parsimonious in the lower grades. Only four writers had been appointed and two of these young men had died on the voyage out. There was no staff of Asiatic clerks, and for the first month there had been no supply of paper.

Having reported this letter to the Council, Dundas recorded the following minute:

"I must acknowledge I was a good deal surprised by the contents of the paper just read, being in substance neither more nor less than a communication from our Secretary's office (certainly of not very auspicious omen, as read on the anniversary day of our arrival in the Island) that now, when we have been twelve months in possession of the Government, there exists, not at this moment, any regular record of our proceedings . . . it ought long ago to have been communicated to the Board, and I think the Acting Secretary has done well in not allowing the real state of the Records in this respect to be longer concealed, with the view of remedying the evil, which must be immediately set about by the readiest means that can be devised."

At the meeting on 23rd September Raffles reported the rate at which the arrears could be made good, and expressed his opinion that the establishment should, in future, be able to cope with the work. The task was, in fact, no light one. The meetings of the Governor in Council provided the chief means whereby members could bring their supposed ability and sagacity to the notice of the Supreme Government and of the Court. The secretary's office, therefore, had not only to produce the weekly dispatches, which dealt with everything in flowery periods of immoderate length, but also to send with them reports on the weekly consultations, at which members seldom failed to deliver themselves of their views. These were not infrequently distinguished solely by their length, but they had to be recorded verbatim and four sets of each written up by hand. Their perusal to-day is a weary business. Their conceit and pomposity are astonishing. But notwithstanding these drawbacks, an examination of them is necessary to appreciate the strange mixture of subjects with which the Council had to deal; and these can have represented only a small fraction of the problems handled by Raffles on his own responsibility.

It must be remembered that, in such a small colony, the duties of government included also the functions normally executed by a municipal council. There had been very grave delay in the setting up of a proper judicial authority, and that in a settlement with a full quota of tough characters, a bewildering mixture of races, languages and customs, and a police force small and inexperienced.

To indicate the scope and variety of the work with which Raffles, in his capacity as secretary, had to deal, here are a few items picked out at random:

The great shipbuilding programme, the prime cause of the new Presidency, began with the placing of a contract with James Scott for the supply of timber for a 1,200-ton ship for the Company's service and a frigate for the Navy. These proved to be the only fruits of the project on which such high hopes, and such an expensive government, had been built.

The police magistrate was found to be involved in supporting the vices he was supposed to be suppressing. The man chosen to succeed him was Thomas McQuoid, whose name will appear again.

Control of prices in the market was the subject of a special committee, which recommended that the prices of local produce only should be regulated. Imported produce was to find its own price-level.

The chaplain complained of the indecorous behaviour of the church clerk. The Governor reported that he had himself often witnessed the unbecoming conduct of the church clerk and felt that he should be at once dismissed and returned to Europe. There was no likely opportunity of early repatriation, so the Governor recommended that the man be informed that, through the mercy and forbearance of the Governor, he was to be allowed to continue in his post for the time being, in the hope of "an amendment in the execution of his duty and his general conduct"—an ingenious solution of a practical difficulty.

There was the question of acquiring a piece of land "adjoining the hospital, and between it and the sea-breeze (which would be of great use to the hospital when cleared) and also afford sufficient space for a decent and properly enclosed burying ground".

At the same meeting, attention was called to an unoccupied plot "now nearly in the centre of the European habitation in Georgetown", which had "remained in the same state of nature as it then was, and has now become a noisome and pestilential swamp, the exhalations from which are highly deleterious to the health of the inhabitants, and highly disgraceful to the Police and Municipal regulations of the Island, being immediately contiguous to the principal entrance to the town from the country".

Such was the day-to-day business of the government, and such was the style in which their utterances were couched. No wonder Raffles was to remark: "I think five years as Secretary is as much as I can stand."

Chapter Four

PENANG AND MALACCA, 1806-1807

i

THE European community in Penang was not a large one. A petition signed in 1806, evidently by every European official and merchant of any importance, contains only seventy-eight names. In the absence of skilled Asiatics there was, it is true, a relatively larger number of small tradesmen and artisans than is to be found in Penang to-day—publicans, barbers, saddle-makers and others, besides men working at the building slips—but the total European population, including wives, would not have exceeded a hundred and twenty adults.

What sort of life did they lead? People at home thought it was one of ease and luxury, the same idea as persists in England to-day. Raffles gives a somewhat different description in a letter to his cousin, Thomas Raffles, then eighteen years of age and studying in London for the Congregational ministry.

"I suppose", he wrote, "you are calculating that by this time I am rolling in Rubies, a perfect Nabob, reviling religion and sloughing in immorality? In this however you would be mistaken. I am poorer than I was three months before I left England, and as to splendour and luxury, we have nothing of the kind on our little Island; some of the Nuisances with very few of the Comforts are alone afforded us. I must acknowledge that we cannot say much for our general appearance of Religion; we have a Clergyman but no Church, and tho' a very good man, like most others of the Church, too careless of the eternal interest of his flock."

Allowing for tropical conditions, the community probably differed very little in its outlook, habits and customs from one of similar size in a small town in the Great Britain of that period. To appreciate this comparison, one has to make some effort to realize to what a degree in contemporary England the small-town and village communities were isolated, by lack of communications, from the rest of the county, let alone the rest of the country. The majority, therefore, of those who came to live in a distant tropical island such as Penang would feel their isolation far less than would a modern Englishman if he were set down in a place six months' journey from home, with only such contact as that afforded by casual ships calling for cargo or refreshment, and the annual visitation of a convoy bringing mail and news from England.

Britons, we are told, take their habits with them; wherever they settle, they make it as much like the home they have left as the conditions and their resources permit. This was even more true then than now—and to that tradition must be added the not unimportant fact that the settler of those days went abroad to make his life in the new land. A six months' journey and all the cost of the voyage were not endured for a visit of two or three years. There was no prospect for him of six months' leave in England at regular intervals; no luxurious ships to take him home in three or four restful weeks, still less an aeroplane to do the trip in thirty hours. Even if at death's door, he could get a passage only once a year with the returning China fleet, during the period of the north-east monsoon. So he put thoughts of return out of his mind until he had amassed sufficient fortune to retire in style—that is, if he survived the requisite time.

Consequently, such European communities as that at Penang were self-contained entities, living their own lives independently, making their own interests and amusements, just as their families at home had to do. Had Jane Austen visited Penang at that date, as one of her sailor brothers did, she would have found just the sort of material of which she made such delightful use in her stories of middle-class homes in contemporary England.

The advertisements in the *Prince of Wales's Island Gazette* afford a number of clues to the interests and activities of the inhabitants. To take one example, there is the publicity given to the supply of books and periodicals. From this it is clear that the exiles were not so cut off from or so disinterested in literature as some writers have suggested. With the limitations of sailing-ships, consignments of reading matter could arrive only at rare intervals, but when they did come they included not only the various well-known periodicals, but also a remarkable range of books, from Blackstone's *Commentaries on the Laws of England*, volumes of sermons and books on history and geography, to the last new novel of Scott or the latest poems of Byron. These books seem to have been read and widely circulated, for notices of missing ones appeared regularly in the *Gazette* advertisements. Only a few years after Raffles left Penang, a library was established by public subscription.

Music of all kinds—instrumental and vocal, quartets, duets and solos—was also in considerable demand. Singing was not then one of the lost arts. There was no mechanical music, and doubtless, as in England, piano playing and singing were popular both for personal amusement and when company was being entertained. The songs ranged from the patriotic and martial to the romantic and comic, of which last "The Dream of Camphor Bug" was an example. "The Coy Blushing Sylvia" was described as a "favourite song", and "In My Youth I Was Careless and Gay" had obvious possibilities.

At banquets all important toasts were drunk with musical honours, and as banquets were numerous and toast-lists long, the supply of suitable tunes had to keep pace. Dance music must also have been in continuous request, because, apart from the grand balls on special occasions, there were subscription assemblies, just as there were in England. Dancing was very popular with both sexes and was carried on till the early hours of the morning. One can but hope that the costumes of the ladies were more suitable to the climate than those of their partners.

In the matter of dresses, the *Gazette* is full of advertisements. There was a wonderful assortment of stuffs in alluring colours. Much came from China and India, but there were annual importations from England of Welsh flannels, scarlet serge and broadcloth, which would not find a ready sale in Penang to-day. But doubtless velvet camlets, chintzes, ratteens, mock cashmere, and silks could be made into very entrancing costumes. Then there were all sorts of jewels and trinklets, suitable for ladies of fashion and a steady drain on their husbands' purses. Fashions—even though six or more months' old—were carefully studied. Here are two samples quoted in the *Gazette*:

> *Ball Dress*—a Light blue or grey chemise robe, of gossamer net, imperial crape, or Spanish gauze, worn over white pealing satin, ornamented up the front with French bows and knots of silver. A full melon sleeve, formed of the same material as the dress, and alternate stripes of white satin finished with bows and knots of silver. A double roll of white satin round the neck of the robe, by way of tucker. Hair falling in natural and irregular curls on the forehead, with a diamond comb, diamond bandeau, with necklace, armlets and drop-earrings of the same. Slippers of white satin with silver clasps. French kid gloves, just escaping the elbow. Fan of carved ivory.
>
> *Walking Dress*—a fine cambric or Indian muslin high gown, with long sleeves and falling collar, ornamented at the feet, and round the neck with appliquéd lace or needle-work. Deep amber broach, or gold filigree buckle, confining the dress at the throat and waist, with bracelets en suite. Gold chain and opera glass. The woodland hat of fine platted straw or chip, with ostrich feathers falling on one side. A French cloak of bright purple sarsnet or velvet, lined with amber, or rose colour, and trimmed entirely round with broad black lace and beading, purple parasol, with deep white or amber awning, Shoes, and Gloves of buff kid.

But the ladies of Penang had duties to perform as well as to consider their own adornment, or the rival wardrobes of their friends and neighbours. Apart from looking after their houses and planning their domestic meals or the entertainment of their guests, keeping an eye on the garden and arranging vases of the many tropical flowers, they mostly had to care for children who remained with them, not till they had reached the age of six or seven, but till the parents themselves went home, though the richer ones might send at least their sons to England to be educated. Various enterprising persons set up schools in Penang. One advertised by a Mr Peter Hart undertook to teach children "reading and writing, English language and Accounts". Later a school was established by public subscription.

Outdoor exercise in the modern sense was unknown. No one sailed or bathed; there was no tennis or cricket. A favourite pastime was riding or driving in the evening or early morning. The horses were mostly ponies from Achin, Sumatra, and there was much social rivalry in the saddlery and harness, as in the vehicles. "Neat light Bengal buggies" and "well built palanquins for one or two horses" were in demand. There were no horse-races in the modern sense for some years to come, but individual challenges over a specific distance for a wager of some sort were common. The men did a certain amount of shooting: snipe, green pigeon and perhaps other birds that would not be shot to-day. The occasional report of a "tyger" probably provoked as much enthusiasm among the local Nimrods as it would now, and with equally little result.

As for indoor amusements, amateur theatricals were much in vogue. Whist was played a great deal. There were subscription whist parties just as there were subscription dances. The former were probably reserved for men, as were the dinners of the Prince of Wales's Island Club. "Dinner will be on the table at 6 p.m. sharp, Camp Fashion, as usual." This can be taken to mean that these were alfresco affairs, for formal dinners were at 4.30 p.m. Undoubtedly, dinners, private or public, and balls were the high lights of social life.

Before the departure on 7th December 1806 of H.M.S. *Blenheim* on her last voyage, "a very elegant Entertainment was given by Tuan Syed Hussan,[1] at which the Honourable the Governor attended by his Suite, His Excellency Sir Thomas Troubridge, Bart., the Commander-in-Chief of the troops, and upwards of sixty Ladies and Gentlemen of the Settlement were present".

The report in the *Gazette* continues:

"The whole of the Syed's extensive Premises, as well as all the streets and avenues around, were illuminated; Peons were stationed and several Officers of the Police attended, for the purpose of preventing the access from being obstructed by the concourse of Native Spectators that had collected to view this, to them, novel entertainment.

"The Company began to assemble a little before 6 o'clock in the evening, and were conducted by the Managers of the Entertainment to a

[1] For a further description of Sayid Husain, see page 132.

Pavilion brilliantly illuminated, and elegantly fitted up for the occasion in the Eastern style, with various ornaments and rich carpets, where the Syed received and paid his compliments to the visitors.

"At half past 6, dinner was announced, when the Company repaired to a spacious hall, splendidly lighted up and tastefully decorated. The dinner consisted of every luxury and delicacy that the most extensive hospitality could procure; the Wines were excellent and abundant, and the utmost harmony and conviviality presided during the entertainment. . . .

"After dinner no less than nine Principal toasts were drunk with enthusiastic applause, each toast being accompanied by the appropriate tune from the Band which had been kindly supplied by His Majesty's Ship *Blenheim*.

"The company retired from the dinner table to the Pavilion at about half past 9 o'clock, to witness the display of a choice collection of fire-works, and the dances performed by young and beautiful Malayan Nautch Girls, which were strongly contrasted in their style, by others exhibited at the same time by the females from the Malabar coast.

"The Ladies having expressed a desire of enjoying the amusement of dancing themselves, the tables in the hall were immediately cleared, in which place the whole of the company having again assembled, the sprightly dance commenced, and was kept up with great spirit until nearly 2 in the morning, when the company retired by degrees, highly gratified at the entertainment, and at the hospitality and politeness of their host."

Although Penang, in its public avowals, prided itself on its moderation, there is no doubt that the vast meals and huge potations sanctioned in England of the period were prevalent here also. The advertisements of liquor are particularly frequent in the *Gazette*, and one or two examples of prices may be quoted. "Madeira, warranted 10 years in India" cost fourteen dollars (seventy shillings) a dozen. Port and brandy were ten dollars a case, and gin twenty-two dollars. Pale ale was seven dollars a dozen. "Most excellent Claret, warranted equal to any on the Island" was twenty-four dollars a dozen quart bottles.

To gauge the consumption of liquor, it is interesting to note that in 1797, during George Caunter's temporary charge of the settlement, when the European community was very much smaller, Government House managed to consume in twenty-one months:

Claret	85 dozen
Port	25 ,,
Brandy	10 ,,
Madeira	117 ,,
Beer	49 ,,
Cherry Brandy	2½ ,,

The total cost of this was 3,032 dollars—£758.

When one remembers the life, sedentary except for dancing, that both sexes largely lived, and the unsuitable clothing, heavy meals and heavier drinking, it is not surprising that the mortality was high; rather one is surprised that so many survived. Malaria and dysentery cannot be held alone responsible for the appallingly high death rate, though no doubt the "putrid fevers" that carried people off so suddenly were either typhoid or malignant malaria. Hygiene and medical science were in their infancy, and more than one hundred years had to pass before the mosquito was proved to be the instrument of malaria. Even then incredulity, not to say derision, was the background against which Ronald Ross carried out his great experiments.

Penang had at that time a remarkable reputation as a health resort. The climate was described by one enthusiast as "infallible", which has prompted modern writers to sarcastic agreement. Between 1807 and 1819 five Governors were to die, and the wife of one, Mrs Dundas; also Oliphant, the senior member of the Council, and many others in government and commercial circles. Yet compared with India, Penang had some justification for its good reputation. Taking the year round, the climate was incomparably better than anything that Calcutta, Madras or Bombay could offer. At no time did conditions in Penang approximate in the least to the appalling heat of India during the summer months.

"Here", wrote a correspondent to the *Gazette*, "are neither the great vicissitudes of Bombay, the marsh effluvia of Bengal, or the scorching heat of Madras. The climate is very salubrious. On the mountain, which occupies a great part of the island and is of considerable elevation, bungalows are erected, open to the sea and land breezes, where the thermometer ranges from 70 and 80 degrees, and where the heat is never reflected or oppressive. . . ."

Six years after the establishment of the Presidency there appeared another laudatory account from which can be quoted:

". . . The northern extremity is the most lofty; and here a Signal House has been erected, and several bungalows built. The whole of the ridge of mountains is covered with a forest of trees of immense size. The level ground from the base of the mountainous ridge to the Eastern coast opposite Queda extends about twelve miles in length, and is of different breadths from two to four miles. This slip of land is in a high state of cultivation, producing abundance of Pepper, Cocoanuts, Sugar-canes, Betel and Areka. The whole is interspersed with elegant garden-houses and bungalows surrounded by beautiful plantations. The roads are lined with a great variety of fragrant shrubs and trees which enjoy perpetual verdure. . . . Provisions of all kinds are in plenty and supplied at a very reasonable rate from the Queda shore. Fruits are so cheap that I purchased three dozen of Oranges for twopence and beautiful ripe Pineapples for twopence each. Culinary vegetables of all sorts were also to be had in abundance. A great variety of the most excellent fish is found in shoals in every direction round the Island which Mr Johnson says 'From the salubrity of the air is justly esteemed the Montpelier of India'. *Coups de Soleil* are seldom experienced in this Settlement, although the Europeans walk and ride about at all times of the day exposed to the vertical sun. From the dawn of day until the sun has emerged above the high mountains of Queda, and even for some time after this period, Penang rivals anything that has been fabled of the Elysian Fields. The dews which had fallen in the course of the night, and by remaining on the trees, shrubs and flowers have become impregnated with their odours early in the morning, begin to exhale, and fill the air with the most delightful perfumes, while the European inhabitants, taking advantage of this pleasant scene for air and exercise, crowd the road in carriages, on horseback and on foot till the sun, getting to some height above the mountains of Queda, becomes so powerful as to drive them into their bungalows to enjoy a good breakfast with a good appetite. The low lands of Penang, being liable to inundation in the rainy season, the houses of the Europeans are all elevated from the ground eight or ten feet on arches or pillars. They seldom consist of more than one floor, built of wood and thatched with leaves of trees."

Whether it was actually or relatively an Elysium is perhaps not relevant to our purpose. "Eat, drink and be merry" was certainly the motto of Penang. One of the party might die within the next forty-eight hours, but this possibility cast no shadow on the gaiety.

Sir Thomas Troubridge, Sir Edward Pellew and William O'Brien Drury had been brother captains under Nelson before they had been sent to tropical waters. At Penang, towards the end of 1806, Troubridge and Pellew quarrelled so violently that Troubridge decided to proceed home in H.M.S. *Blenheim*. Pellew knew, as did Troubridge, that the ship was in a rotten state, but Troubridge was in such a rage that he refused to listen to reason, and departed on 7th December. With him as guests went Alexander Gray, the member of the Council, and his wife, who were going on leave to Europe. The vessel was lost off Madagascar with all hands on 1st February 1807.

When, three weeks later, Pearson, the secretary, returned from leave, he was at once promoted to provisional membership of the Council in place of Gray. In March, Oliphant, senior member of the Council, died at the age of thirty-four and, subject to the confirmation of the Court, Pearson was appointed to the substantive vacancy thus created. On 22nd March, Raffles was appointed secretary to the Council, young William Clubley becoming assistant secretary.

Hutton, the translator, had gone on six months' leave in January, and

Raffles had taken over his duties. In recognition of this and other special services Pearson (apparently bearing no ill will for the revelations of Raffles' as to the state of the secretariat, and at this time very friendly) proposed that Raffles' salary, which had automatically risen to $8,000 on his promotion to secretary, should be further increased by $2,400, and that amount deducted from the assistant secretary's salary. The Governor in Council accepted this proposal and, seeking "approbation and confirmation", wrote to the Court in London:

". . . The salary which we have now taken upon ourselves to fix for the Secretary we deem to be no more than a full remuneration for the laborious duties and responsibility of the office, whilst that now annexed to the situation of Assistant is, we conceive, fully equal to any office which your Honourable Court would be desirous a young man of not more than two years' standing in your service should be appointed to. . . ."

In anticipation of the Court's approval of this arrangement, "by which no additional expense will attach to the Honourable Company, and which will prove equally beneficial to the Assistant in the event of his succession to the Secretaryship", Raffles' monthly salary became $866.66, and Clubley's $300.

1807 was a year of fatalities for the Penang government. Philip Dundas, whose wife had already died in Calcutta, where she had vainly gone for her health, was now himself seriously ill. On 1st April he left Penang in H.M.S. *Belliqueux*, in the hope that sea air would help, but he died on board a week later. He was forty-five.

During his absence, Pearson had been put in temporary charge of the government, and, on the death of Dundas, he claimed the position of acting Governor. Although he had been member of Council only for about six weeks, and a provincial member at that, he argued that it was impossible for Macalister, senior member since the death of Oliphant, to succeed, on the remarkable ground that the military member could not be both Governor and commander of the troops. An unseemly wrangle followed in the Council. Pearson behaved in an overbearing manner. Macalister was a milder character and acted with propriety, allowing Pearson to act as Governor on condition that the point was referred home. He was well advised. The Court replied that he should act as Governor, and he was sworn in on 16th October.

The incident is not in itself of particular importance except as a sidelight on the type of official appearing from time to time in positions of authority. There is little doubt that the dispute between Pearson and Macalister led to a division of the local authorities into two parties, with Raffles on the side of Macalister, and weaker men such as Phillips, secretary to the former administration and for a time acting Governor, on the side of Pearson. Certainly Macalister was on very cordial terms with Raffles, on whom Pearson later staged a sudden attack, explainable only as an act of spite or revenge.

July of that year, 1807, saw an event that was to have a decisive influence on Raffles' career: the appointment of Viscount Minto as Governor-General of India.

Gilbert Elliot, first Viscount Minto, was born in Teviotdale in 1751. He had grown up a kindly and sympathetic country gentleman whose Liberal instincts had prompted him to associate himself with Burke and Mirabeau. While his heart was still in his home and country pursuits, he became more and more entangled in London politics. Having entered Parliament in 1778, he moved the impeachment of Sir Elijah Impey in 1787. He was also one of the managers of the impeachment of Warren Hastings. During the temporary occupation of Corsica by the British he was appointed Viceroy and was evacuated with some difficulty in 1796 by Nelson, of whom he became a great friend and warm admirer. In 1798 he was raised to the peerage as a Viscount. On 3rd July 1807 he arrived at Calcutta to take up the appointment of Governor-General in succession to Sir George Barlow, who had acted after the departure of that magnificent figure, the Marquis Wellesley.

The contrast between the New Governor-General and Lord Wellesley was as marked as that between his descendant, the fourth Earl of Minto, and Lord Curzon, whom he succeeded as Viceroy in 1905. Wellesley was an imperious man, able and ambitious and, as far as the East India Company was concerned, uncontrollable, whether in annexation or expenditure. While not deliberately flouting the Court, he exploited to the full the distance between London and Calcutta and the slowness of the mail; and the Court watched with increasing anger the skilful way in which he managed to evade or misinterpret their most emphatic orders. While his policy may have contributed greatly to the position of England in India, he went near to wrecking the whole financial structure of the Company.

Minto was sent out because those at home were under the impression that he was a mild and relatively unambitious man, with liberal views on the treatment of Asiatics and no predilection for a career of costly magnificence or martial glory. He was a man of firm character, high principles and wide vision, but, like his descendant, lacking in the hauteur that both Wellesley and Curzon thought so requisite for a proconsul. No wonder Curzon described him as "one of the class of Governor-Generals who leave no particular mark on history and cease to be remembered for good or ill".

A less prejudiced historian, Vincent Smith, has recorded:

"The most brilliant chapter in Lord Minto's Indian Government is that of his foreign policy . . . every fresh gain of France in Europe was followed by a corresponding loss in Asia. It was the glory of Lord Minto's administration that whereas at its commencement dread of a French invasion of India haunted the imagination of statesmen, at its close France had lost all her acquisitions eastward of the Cape. The Isles of Bourbon and of France,[1] the Moluccas and Java had been added to the colonial possessions of Great Britain. The fleets of France were swept from the Indian Seas, and England was without a rival in the Eastern hemisphere.

"Many circumstances contributed to dim Lord Minto's fame. The six years of his administration coincided with the most critical period of the Napoleonic War, during which public attention was concentrated either on Wellington's glorious struggle in Spain and Portugal, or on Napoleon's Russian venture. Even the most brilliant success in the Eastern seas could not compete in interest with the events of the European drama."

Lord Minto was a friendly man. He disliked the splendid isolation that a Governor-General finds it difficult entirely to avoid. He had, also, too keen a sense of humour to regard the magnificence of his high office as seriously as had his lordly predecessor. His delightful letters to his wife are full of such amusing comments as:

"The first night I went to bed at Calcutta I was followed by fourteen persons in white muslin gowns into the dressing-room. One might have hoped that some of them were ladies; but on finding there were as many turbans and black beards as gowns, I was very desirious that these bearded handmaids should leave me. . . ."

Minto had another quality, one that was to prove of great importance to Raffles. Probably from his experience during the impeachment of Warren Hastings, Minto had come to realize how vitally the proper government of foreign races depends on the ability of the governors to understand and speak the language of the governed. This became a main plank in his policy. Addressing the College of Fort William, founded by Lord Wellesley, where young civil servants studied Asiatic languages, he referred to British ignorance of Indian languages having led to almost unlimited dependence on native and subordinate officers.

"How much prejudice to the interest of the Company," he said, "how much vexation, extortion and credulity towards our Native subjects, how much individual shame and ruin have resulted from this cause, a very short acquaintance with the affairs of India will quickly show."

To give backing to this point, he added that proficiency in Indian languages would be a key to promotion.

Holding as he did these views, Minto was naturally attracted at once to young John Leyden, who had achieved the position of Professor of Hindustani, particularly as Leyden could claim Teviotdale kinship. With such qualifications for patronage, Leyden's future was secure and there

[1] Later named Réunion and Mauritius respectively.

was no limit to the position he might have reached. And being the kind of man he was, he did not forget his friend and correspondent in Penang.

During the autumn of 1807 Raffles suffered his first serious illness. On 20th November his application to proceed to sea for the sake of his health was granted. Whether he took advantage of this—and, if he did, where he went—has long been in doubt. The *Prince of Wales's Island Gazette*, usually very informative on such matters, makes no reference to his departure. That he was either absent from the colony or completely incapacitated by illness is sufficiently obvious. His signature appears in no consultation from 20th November 1807 to 19th January 1808. Clubley was appointed acting secretary during that period, young John Curson Lawrence filling the post of assistant. Then there was the rather ludicrous affair of the Malay translator. Hutton who had more than once been regarded as unsatisfactory, overstepped the mark by refusing to obey an order—a thing the Council could not overlook. Nor was that all: he added to his insubordination by flatly declining to examine any of his possible successors. This put the Council in a quandary. None of them was able to conduct such an examination, so that on 27th November the following remarkable minute was recorded:

"The Board, not having the means of ascertaining how far any of the applicants are qualified, appoint the Assistant Secretary, Lawrence, to act as Malay Translator in addition to his other duties."

This decision would surely not have been taken had Raffles been available. In fact, he did leave Penang on this occasion and went to Malacca with Olivia, the first of his two health trips to that place, although no previous biographer, from Lady Raffles onward, appears to have been aware of this, recording the incidents of two visits as if they had belonged to one.

ii

The port of Malacca lies on the mainland of Malaya about two hundred and fifty miles south-east of Penang. It is thus about half-way down the Straits of Malacca and was ideally situated to act as the mistress of that ancient highway and as a central mart for the products of China, India and the Malay Archipelago. If to-day circumstances have dimmed its glory, the glamour of its name still persisted in 1807, though even then the growth of Penang had seriously affected its prosperity. The founding of Singapore twelve years later sealed its fate once and for all.

Here was the very heart of the Golden Chersonese of Greek and Roman tradition. Much legend surrounded, too, the founding of the city at the beginning of the fifteenth century by a Malay prince who came from Singapore after that *entrepôt* of Chinese trade with the Indies had been utterly destroyed about 1365. Under him and his descendants grew up an empire that included the Malay peninsula, the Rhio archipelago and the east coast of Sumatra. Malacca was captured by the Portuguese under d'Albuquerque in 1511 and later from the Portuguese by the Dutch after a protracted siege in 1641.

As Sir Richard Winstedt so happily puts it in his *Britain and Malaya*:

"Camoens served there as a soldier; St Francis Xavier preached and was originally buried in its Cathedral; Ralph Fitch, that amazing globe-trotter, stayed in the port in 1588 to study its commerce in nutmegs and mace from the Moluccas, in pepper and camphor and gold from Sumatra, in silk, porcelain and opium from China, tin and jungle produce from the Malay States, rice from Siam and Java, sugar from Manila and every kind of cloth from India."

Such was the *entrepôt* captured by the Portuguese, and a rich prize it had been. But in 1641 the Dutch had quite different ideas. The trade of the Indies was to be centred at Batavia, Java. Their only aim in capturing Malacca was to kill its *entrepôt* trade, which spoiled their monopoly; their main use for it was as a base from which the efforts of the native traders from the Spice Islands[1] to evade their cruisers and seek more profitable free markets elsewhere could be watched and frustrated.

Napoleon's seizure of Holland and the creation of the Batavian Republic had opened to our attack not only French colonial possessions, but also the former Dutch colonies. When Lord Howe's victory in 1794 restored to Britain the command of the seas, Pitt turned his attention abroad. The Cape of Good Hope, Ceylon and Malacca fell rapidly in turn in the following year, with the help, it is true, of the manifesto of the refugee Prince of Orange. In 1796 the Moluccas also were captured. Malacca was surrendered in August by the Dutch Governor, Abraham Couperus, to Captain Brown of H.M.S. *Orpheus* and Major Newcome of the East India Company. Shortly afterwards, an engineer officer, Captain William Farquhar, who is not to be confused with Robert T. Farquhar, was appointed Resident.

Under English rule, Malacca began rapidly to recover some of her old commercial importance. Traders from the Eastern Archipelago flocked to the port, and the Dutch were now impotent to prevent this inroad into their cherished monopoly. But as Penang grew in importance, mutual jealousy developed between the two ports. Malacca traders complained of the competition of their upstart neighbour, while Penang cast envious glances at the rich trade Malacca was rebuilding with the Spice Islands. Apart from sentimental and traditional connexions with Malacca, the Malay and Arab traders from the Eastern Archipelago were unwilling to incur the additional hazards of an extra two hundred and fifty miles to Penang. But the merchants of Penang could not forget the possibility that

[1] The Moluccas.

Malacca would be returned to the Dutch at the end of the war—for Great Britain was, by open profession, merely trustee on behalf of an occupied Holland—and that the revival of its prosperity might encourage the Dutch to maintain there the British free-trade policy, to the confusion of Penang.

The Court of Directors of the East India Company, being made aware of this situation, conceived a simple solution. Malacca was to be utterly destroyed; its fortifications and public buildings were to be razed to the ground, and the merchants and their business transferred *en bloc* to Penang. They felt that thus the prestige and power of Penang would be enhanced at the expense of Malacca. At the end of the French war, if Malacca had to be returned to the Dutch, the humble, undefended Malay settlement was unlikely, within measurable time, to be once more a thorn in the flesh of Penang.

These instructions had been incorporated in the dispatch read by Philip Dundas to the Council on the installation of the government of Penang on 20th September 1805. To the honour, or it may be to the common sense, of the Penang government, and no less to that of the Resident of Malacca, William Farquhar, the project of the Court was strongly opposed as being quite fantastic, but remonstrances were in vain. Orders had to be given for the destruction of the fortifications and other measures of obliteration. The Dutch inhabitants protested bitterly against the order "to proceed on paroles of honour to Batavia or to hold themselves in readiness to remove at the shortest notice to Prince of Wales Island or Calcutta". Farquhar forwarded a petition that he himself supported, but there the matter seems to have rested. The demolition of the defences began in 1807, but it is to the merit of Farquhar that, without any authority then or subsequently, he ordained on his own responsibility that the church, Government House and the principal public buildings should be preserved.

Three years later, Lord Minto wrote to his wife:

"Malacca stands on the banks of a small stream about the breadth of the Rule at Spittal but resembling it in no other respect. The town is built along the right bank of the river, one side of the houses projecting a few feet over the stream, supported on piles which elevate them seven or eight feet above the surface of the water. This gives the place in that quarter rather an amphibious appearance. The town runs down to the edge of the sea, and runs back in the direction of the beach, sometimes advancing into the tide upon piles, sometimes leaving a handsome terrace between the houses and the water. On the opposite bank of the river, close also to the sea, the Portuguese built a small fort on their acquisition of the place in the 16th Century. The Dutch dispossessed them in the following Century and maintained everything as it was. We came next about sixteen years ago and, by orders from home, have burnt down the fort. This work of destruction has been very recently accomplished at considerable expense—a most useless piece of gratuitous mischief as far as I can understand the subject. . . . The Government House, however, built by the Portuguese and a Church erected by the Dutch within the limits of the fort, are still on foot together with a few other buildings, public and private. I inhabit the Government House which is not magnificent, but answers my purposes perfectly in most respects. But it stands at the foot of a steep hill which covers the whole tenement from the sea. Now, as the sea breeze is, in these climates, a true vital air and as delicious as the gas of Paradise, suffocation is our portion at the Government House."

Although official correspondence must have been frequent between the secretary to the government of Penang and the Resident of Malacca, there is no record of Farquhar having visited Penang while Raffles was there. Presumably, therefore, the first time that the two men, who were later to be so actively associated, actually met was in 1807. We may also assume that on this, as certainly on their second visit to Malacca, Raffles and Olivia stayed with Farquhar in the stuffy house to which Minto referred.

This is not the place to consider at length the striking contrast in character that Raffles and Farquhar, later the two protagonists in the adventure of Singapore, inevitably reveal. But their obvious differences can be briefly indicated. Farquhar was older than Raffles by seven years (Raffles was twenty-six in 1807), but probably appeared considerably older than the difference in age might suggest. Like his house, there was something stuffy about him. He was a kindly and honourable man, by no means unintelligent, but such a cautious and such a strictly orthodox civil servant that his ideas, in more than one respect the same as and perhaps even anticipating those of Raffles, never really reached fruition. He lacked the will-power to drive them home in the face of official opposition. He suffered, it is to be suspected, from a complaint not so commonly recognized then as now—an inferiority complex. This made him rather stiff and formal, ready to see slights where they were not intended; essentially rather a weak and unambitious man, but with a good conceit of himself, and over-anxious to ensure that he got full or more than full credit for his part in affairs. Nor was he able to appreciate that others might, by their actions, be more entitled to the credit than one who merely had the conception, but not the power or will to put it into execution.

Raffles and Farquhar had one thing in common: they both had a genuine affection for and sympathy with the Malays, and were in return esteemed and respected. While that was instinctive in both, Farquhar's interest was not deep, consisting rather of a paternal interest such as became a humane and liberal Resident. Raffles, while equally humane and liberal—and certainly a far more consistent and politically advanced administrator—was also deeply interested in the Malays as a race; everything about them excited his eager study. It should be added in this connexion that Farquhar did make a collection of paintings of tropical flowers, their Malay names noted on them, but not their scientific names. These are now in the library of the Royal Asiatic Society, London. Farquhar had one great advantage over Raffles; he was an accomplished writer of Malay, which Raffles never managed to become, though he spoke it fluently.

How Raffles occupied his time at Malacca is nowhere on record, but all the circumstantial evidence suggests that, sick man though he was, he was not idle. After a second visit there, to which reference is made later, he submitted a long report as soon as he returned to Penang. Even a prodigy such as he could not have accumulated so much information and made so immediate and effective use of it after one short visit to Malacca. By far the greater part of that information could have been obtained only at Malacca, for few Malay traders from the islands went farther west than there. The strong assumption is, then, that it was during his first visit that he laid the foundation of the mass of accurate data of so many different kinds that was to enable him to produce his masterly criticism of official policy towards Malacca; and the foundation, too, of that almost encyclopaedic knowledge of the East Indian Archipelago that was to be a vital but by no means his only contribution to the success of the Java campaign.

Also, he may very well have completed and dispatched to Leyden the material from which his paper, *On the Malayu Nation*, was constructed; and instituted those enquiries into the little state of Rumbowe (Rembau) in the hinterland of Malacca that enabled him to confirm to Marsden its ancient connexion with the empire of Menangkabau, in Sumatra. This information was included by Marsden in his *History of Sumatra*, with acknowledgments to Raffles, "a gentleman whose intelligence and zeal in the pursuit of knowledge give the strongest hope of his becoming an ornament to oriental literature".

It is known that Raffles also wrote a series of letters to Governor Macalister. These clearly would not have dealt with obscure points of the Malay language or history, neither of which would have been of interest to this gunnery officer. More likely the letters dealt with the misgivings of Raffles as to the propriety, let alone the expediency, of the Company's policy towards Malacca.

The change of scene, the clean breezes of the Straits, coupled with his manifold interests and, above all, his relief from the petty irritations and incessant worries of official life in Penang, must soon have made a new man of Raffles. Then, with Olivia's anxiety on his behalf steadily fading, there came, all too soon, an urgent summons from his friend, the Governor.

"A thousand thanks", wrote Macalister, "for your kind letters which I had the pleasure to receive some days ago; and hearing then that there was a small vessel lying off for Malacca I wrote you a few hurried lines by her to inform you of the arrangement I had made for your coming back, in the event of your not meeting with a better conveyance. The 'Scourge' sailed five days ago and is to call at Salangore [Selangor] and Siak before she goes to Malacca. Captain Barratt has been desired to place himself under your orders whenever he arrives: and unless a more favourable conveyance offers I sincerely hope you will find yourself well enough to come back to us in the 'Scourge'. It is distressing to me, my dear Sir, to be under the necessity of stating in this pointed manner the unavoidable exigence of the case, but such is the case that we shall not be able to make up any dispatches for the Court without your assistance. It is truly hard upon you under the present circumstances in your delicate state of health, but I trust you will believe that nothing else would induce me to press so hard upon you at this time. With the exception of Mr Phillips the rest of the Board can give but little assistance in making out the General Letter, none, however, so little as myself."

The *Scourge* was a small craft, alleged to have been merely the converted longboat of an East Indiaman. She ran regularly between Penang and Malacca, but the conveniences offered to passengers were few indeed. Raffles, however, was never one to put personal comfort before duty, so he returned alone in her to Penang, though strongly urged to remain in Malacca until his health was fully restored. He arrived at Penang on 23rd January 1808. Olivia arrived a week later in the Portuguese ship *Theresa*, which was carrying the Governor of Macao and his lady to Goa.

Once more, after so short a respite, Raffles was back to the old daily grind, with the additional task of picking up the threads and preparing the dispatches that Clubley and Lawrence between them had been incapable of tackling—a task made more pressing and onerous by the fact that the vessel to bear these documents to England had been lying waiting in Penang harbour since the time Macalister had written his urgent letter of recall.

We can hardly blame Macalister; he was a decent soldier, but had no experience in the intricacies of the Company's methods of business. Pearson, the former secretary, was there, but as he was senior member of the Council, such affairs were beneath his dignity and possibly above his capacity. Moreover, he hated Macalister and was doubtless well pleased to see his rival in such an awkward dilemma. The sudden reappearance of Raffles must have been a great disappointment to him.

This incident, apart from demonstrating how completely the government of Penang depended on Raffles, also affords some explanation and justification for the contempt he felt for that government, a feeling that he was never at pains to disguise, affecting, as it did, many of his subsequent actions.

Chapter Five

PENANG AND MALACCA, 1808-1810

i

THE year 1808 had barely opened when news was received in Penang from Sir Edward Pellew that he had won a sweeping victory over the Dutch near the eastern extremity of Java. Such an event was not merely an occasion for public rejoicing. It brought home to people in Penang that the renewal of the great Napoleonic war, now raging in distant Europe, had repercussions in the East. France had engulfed Holland; Dutch colonial possessions had passed to France and become potential enemy bases. The resumption of hostilities reminded thinking people that one day the war might affect Penang.

The excitement over Pellew's victory was almost at once eclipsed by something nearer home. In March a disastrous fire devastated a large part of Georgetown. Most of the shops were built of wood, with *atap* (palm-leaf) roofs. Fire-fighting appliances were few and primitive, the organization quite inadequate to deal with such a conflagration, which spread with alarming rapidity and was suppressed only with very great difficulty, after damage to the extent of $300,000 had been done. £75,000 was a formidable figure for those days.

Such a catastrophe added greatly to Raffles' work, and the situation was made worse when, on 17th March, Clubley departed for Madras on four months' leave. Lawrence acted as assistant secretary in his place. He was quite willing, but still young and not experienced enough to undertake more than mere routine matters.

On 2nd April the first Recorder of Penang, Sir Edmond Stanley, reached the settlement, bringing with him the long-promised charter of justice. From the earliest days the lack of proper legal jurisdiction had been a serious problem and, as the Company had continually postponed a decision, the urgency had become greater and greater. It could hardly have been otherwise when the local magistracy and police lacked legal sanction for their acts, and that in a young settlement containing a fair proportion of pioneers. Unruly habits and defiance of authority are commonly associated with hardy adventurers, and in Penang they had certainly lived up to tradition. Many of the Asiatic immigrants, too, were unaccustomed to police control, and the *Gazette* contains frequent references to "horrid murders".

John Dickens had been appointed judge and magistrate in 1801. After the departure of Sir George Leith, conditions had improved under Robert Farquhar and Philip Dundas. Farquhar was an able administrator, Dundas of a reasonable and accommodating character; but in the absence of a charter the situation had remained most unsatisfactory. Dickens was waylaid in the street and abused by persons who had appeared before him in court. To give him his due, he displayed no lack of courage on such occasions, being ready to challenge his assailants to a duel to prove himself right. No litigant appears to have been willing to back his complaint as far as that.

Raffles had done his best to assist Dickens, and, as Licenser of the Press, had other official relations with him. The only record of this connexion is an official letter from the judge, somewhat ponderously calling attention to a failure to scratch out, as directed, an underlining—an inattention, he observed, that the Governor and Council could not have expected of Raffles when they made him Licenser of the Press.

When Dickens had gone back to Calcutta it looked at first as if the change was not for the better. "All was confusion here," wrote Raffles, "and that Court could not have been established had I not come forward and voluntarily acted as Regular Clerk of the Crown. . . . War was brewing between Sir Edmond Stanley and the Governor. . . . Stepping between them judiciously I am confident that I stopped a breach which might never have been healed up."

Sir Edmond acknowledged this help. "I must never forget to mention the cheerful disposition Mr Raffles has manifested to me and the Court in the operations, as far as was possible for him, consistent with his other occupations, to do."

Olivia did not like Dickens. She wrote to John Leyden on 3rd August 1808:

". . . His [Raffles'] old *enemy* Mr Dickens is going to Calcutta with his heart full of rancour and his mouth full of scurrility against him—for what Olivia? Because he has proved himself *almost* as learned in the law as himself, 'Great Judge and M.', because he has saved the Government, bad as it is, from his insolent and unmerited attacks—because he has proved himself above him in all things and has persevered in politeness to him—and last of all causes he would not allow an address from some of the Wapping Pedlers voting him a piece of plate and a reply from him to be published, as it reflected on the Government in a very severe manner—but I dare say you will see it, as a Copy is to be sent to the secretary at Calcutta—he says he will publish it there in spite of their teeth—he is really the most *impudent, ignorant, affected* envious ungrateful old *Jay* I ever heard of—he came to this island seven years ago in debt—he leaves it now worth £40,000—most part of which has been torn from the poor, Malays, Chinese, &c, &c, &c, under the title of *fees*! tho' he received a salary of

£3,000 a year with a House &c.—Yet *he* calls himself an *honest man*. He wished much to be appointed Registrar and told Sir Edmond Stanley that he would never be able to get through a cause without *him* or some such great and able personage—however Sir E. and the Governor and Council conjured Mr Raffles to act as Registrar and you will see that everything is going on perfectly correct—a cause of some consequence has been tried and gain'd for the plaintiff to the satisfaction of all—you know what a public spirit your friend has—he has taken the enormous task of Registrar and without a *fee* or present reward—secretary without an assistant, or anyone who can afford him the least possible assistance. The consequence begins to show itself very soon—he is ill and quite worn out and I dread another long lingeiing fit of illness such as he had last which was brought on by intense labour of mind and body—all here is dull stupidity. . . ."

This letter is now in the National Library of Scotland. It is the only letter of Olivia's that is known to have survived. It is a pity there are not more.

Of Olivia as she was then, at the age of thirty-seven, the following description is certainly not flattering. The author of it was at the time a young midshipman.

"This [Penang] was one of poor Sir Stamford Raffles' pet spots; and here I recollect right well his coming on board, with a rather elderly lady, dressed rather fantastically, a good and clever creature, and one already celebrated in song—'Rosa'[1]—of a certain little bard. Ye gods! Well, anything but Rosa! How well your poetic flights thus point to a discrepancy. Mr Raffles was at that time just coming into notice as a clever man and thorough Malay scholar. I forget what he did then besides giving good dinners to our local bigwigs, and being the life and soul of what little society (European) there was gathered up and down among the cocoa-nut trees."[2]

At this period Raffles and his wife were living in a bungalow on one of the foothills, which they called Mount Olivia, a name that has persisted to the present day. On an adjoining hill, Mount St Mary, lived Quintin Dick Thompson with his wife Mary Anne, who was Raffles' sister.

Olivia wrote in the letter referred to above:

"Mary Ann has a beautiful little girl two months old yesterday and has been living on the Hill for the last month. Mr R. is building a pretty brick house on the beach which I hope will be finished in eight or ten weeks. Did I tell you about *our* Hill? If not I will describe it in my next."

When the infant Charlotte was christened, Rear-Admiral Drury stood

[1] Presumably in error for the "Nona" of Thomas Moore.

[2] Anonymous contribution to *United Service Journal*, January 1836.

godfather, yet another indication that Raffles and his family were far from being ostracized by Penang society. It is worthy of mention that Charlotte married Charles Knox, fourth Earl Castle Stewart, in 1835, and died at a very advanced age in 1906.

There was a reference to the new bungalow in the *Gazette* of 4th January 1809:

"The north beach will, ere long, assume a very handsome appearance, when the several elegant villas, now building, are finished. The new buildings commence with Runnymede, the property of Mr Raffles, and adjoining are the grounds of Mr Hobson, Mr Robinson, Mr Erskine, Capt. Douglas, Mr Pearson and Mr Lawrence, on most of which houses are erecting."

The north beach would be about two miles from Fort Cornwallis, where the government offices were. It commands a view across the sea to the ever-changing and ever-beautiful Kedah Peak, which dominates the landscape on the mainland. Runnymede survived as a house in Northam Road up to September 1901, when the roof caught fire and the house was burned to the ground.

The letter from Olivia to Leyden was in answer to a communication from him to the effect that the article Raffles had sent to Leyden in Calcutta had received official recognition in the highest quarters. No less a person than the Governor-General had stated in a public address:

"The Malay language has been successfully cultivated by Mr Raffles . . . who, much to his honour, has long been employed in compiling a code of . . . Malay Laws from the best authorities in the Malay and Bugguese[1] languages."

It must have been very encouraging to Raffles to realize that his name at least was known to Lord Minto. True, it was only an academic connexion, but having succeeded so far, he might now obtain recognition in the political field also. There alone lay the hope of promotion from the narrow confines of Penang. The studies he had been pursuing at Malacca when his visit was cut short must be completed.

The grateful Olivia began her letter:

"My Very Dear Dr Leyden,—If you knew the real heartfelt joy I experienced on reading your dear kind letter you would be convinced how tenderly you are remembered by me. I feel an affection for you such as I feel for my only and beloved Brother. And when I heard you were dangerously ill I felt such a sudden pang as assured me of the sincerity of my regard. You cannot then blame me for having been unhappy when I imagined you had forgotten me when I knew you were well and yet thought not of me so far as to write and tell me so. For I have never received more than your first delightful letter and that which you sent by

[1] Bugis, natives of Celebes and born seamen.

Mr Bureau. I have written many many. But a truce with complainings, I am remembered and happy. . . . Who but you could, who but your dear self would have remembered my beloved and *every way worthy husband* in the elegant and honourable manner in which we saw his name. Ah my dear friend I shed many grateful tears on the paper, so did your friend. The little paltry wretches here were astonished and nearly maddened by envy, for after some battles your friends had succeeded in keeping them all at bay. They may bark as a dog does at the Moon and with as much effect. . . ."

She ended with this postscript:

> "Oh thou whom ne'er my constant heart
>   One moment hath forgot
> Tho Fate severe hath bid us part
>   Yet still forget me not—
>
> Yet let not distance from thy breast
>   My image ever blot
> Let our fond friendship bear this test,
>   Absent, forget me not—

"Now don't be like a Great Big larned Pundit finding a thousand and fifty faults in my poor unrefined & incorrect scrawl. I know about as much of fine writing as I do about Greek—but you will understand me—"

There is reason to remember the first verse of this little ode.

Raffles' hasty return from sick-leave at the request of Macalister was sooner than his health warranted. The additional duties of registrar, and the absence of Clubley, proved too much of a strain in the summer months, and a severe attack of jaundice developed. In July he was compelled to apply for leave "to proceed to the Eastward". He left with Olivia at the end of that month, a day or two before her letter to Leyden, on a second visit to Malacca—a visit that was to be the turning-point in his career.

They were the guests of William Farquhar. As far as his low state of health permitted, Raffles continued his enquiries on the subject of Malacca, making at the same time an intensive study of Java and the Eastern Archipelago. Malacca offered far better opportunities than Penang for meeting shipmasters and Asiatic traders from the Dutch East Indies. He was already formulating in his mind the possibility of England extending her activities against French maritime power by capturing Java instead of merely maintaining a blockade against it, as Rear-Admiral Drury was then doing.

No urgent summons came this time for Raffles to hurry back. He returned with Olivia by the *Wyndham*, arriving at Penang on 29th October

1808, after a bare three months' leave. Two days later he submitted the following report to the Governor and Council at Penang—the first example of Raffles, emancipated—if only for a moment—from the trammels of petty routine, speaking his mind out loud:

"Having lately had an opportunity of noticing the destruction of the works at Malacca as well as the general effect of the measures taken towards reducing and eventually abandoning that Settlement, I have been led to pay particular attention to the subject, and being impressed with a conviction that the future prosperity of Prince of Wales's Island is materially involved in the impending fate of Malacca, I feel it a duty incumbent on me respectfully to submit to your Honourable Board the result of my observations.

"The fortifications may be considered as completely demolished, the convicts being principally employed in removing the ruins, but the storehouses and some of the public buildings, such as the Government House, church, gaol, &c, still remain entire, in consequence, I believe, of a wish expressed on the part of His Excellency Sir Edward Pellew, and of the recommendation of the Honourable the Governor. As, however, the destruction of the latter must, under the Commandant's present instructions, be almost immediately proceeded on, and the last appearance of a respectable Government annihilated, I am induced to hope that a faithful report at this time of the actual state of Malacca and the dangers to be apprehended in eventually withdrawing the garrison, will be acceptable to your Honourable Board.

"On the political expedience of destroying the permanent fortifications it does not become me to remark. My observations are intended wholly to apply to the Settlement as it at present stand[s].

"The object of the measures taken with regard to Malacca appears to have been twofold—to discourage, by the destruction of the works, any European Power from setting a value on the place or turning it to account in the event of its falling into their hands; and to have improved the settlement at Prince of Wales's Island by the transfer of its population and trade. These objects were, undoubtedly, highly desirable and of great political importance. The former, perhaps, may, in some degree, have been effected by the destruction of the works and removal of the ordnance and stores to Penang; but with respect to the latter much remains to be done.

"Very incorrect information appears to have been received by the Honourable Court of Directors [in London] respecting the trade and advantages of the Settlement of Malacca. It has by them been considered as a place possessing no natural advantages in product or trade, and involving great expense without corresponding benefit, either in its revenues or commerce. Under such a representation it is not surprising that the destruction and abandonment of Malacca should have been determined on, the more particularly as it was stated, from personal knowledge, that the population and trade of the place might with ease be removed to Penang, a Settlement likely to unite every advantage desired by the British Government.

"The inaccuracy of the above statement will, I doubt not, fully appear in the course of this paper.

"The inhabitants resident within the territory of Malacca are estimated at 20,000 souls, of which the majority reside in the town and its neighbourhood. They consist chiefly of Europeans (few in number and mostly Dutch), the descendants of such (principally half-castes) born in the place, Chinese and their descendants by Malay women, Malays, Portuguese, Arabs, Javanese, and Chuliahs.[1]

"More than three-fourths of the above population were born in Malacca, where their families have been settled for centuries. The Chinese appear to have emigrated to this place at a very early period, as is evident from the remarks of Albuquerque, when it fell into the hands of the Portuguese in 1511, and the antiquity and extent of their tombs and burial-places, which occupy the base of the different hills in the neighbourhood.

"The Malays, a class of people not generally valued as subjects, are here industrious and useful members of society; attached to the place from their birth, they are accustomed to the local regulations; and in the bosom of their family feel that they are at home. Their peculiarities are attended to, their rank respected, and their necessities easily supplied.

"Independent of the fixed population above mentioned, there is a continual resort of native traders from the Eastward and the countries in the vicinity, Malacca being the centre of the native commerce within the Straits.

"From the antiquity and former celebrity of the place it follows that the country is well cultivated, and that valuable buildings, public and private, have been erected by the inhabitants; to which they must be attached, as well on account of their comforts as of their more absolute necessities. The prejudices of the natives are too well known to require comment here; and it is no common advantage that will induce them to quit the tombs of their ancestors, their temples sacred to the Deity, their independence, and estates on which they depend for their livelihood and respectability.

"The inhabitants of Malacca are very different from what they appear to have been considered. Three-fourths of the native population of Prince of Wales's Island might, with little encouragement, be induced to remove, having no fixed or permanent property; adventurers, ready to turn their hands to any employment. But the case is very different with the native

[1] Indians of the Coromandel Coast. See also footnote, page 671.

inhabitants of Malacca. Those answering the above description appear to have removed long ago, in consequence of the measures taken by the Government of Prince of Wales's Island. The inhabitants that remain are mostly proprietors of property or connected with those that are; and those possessing independence from their gardens, fishing, and the small traffic of the place. The more respectable, the majority, accustomed to independence and respect from their childhood, would ill brook the difficulties of establishing themselves at a new Settlement. They are not men that can easily be converted into artificers or artisans. The few of those now resident at Malacca obtain an easy livelihood in supplying the comforts of their superiors.

"The present population must therefore be considered as attached to the soil; and, from every appearance, it seems they have determined to remain by Malacca, let its fate be what it will. Into whatever hands it falls it cannot be much more reduced than at present, and they have a hope that any change must be for the better. The offer made by Government of paying the passage of such as would embark for Penang was not accepted by a single individual.

"Malacca, although it has ever been discouraged in raising its own supplies, produces sufficient rice for six months' consumption, and from the constant resort of prows from Java and its vicinity (commanded by Arabs and other neutrals), has never required any supply from Bengal till very lately, when, in consequence of the expected abandonment of the Settlement, and the conduct of some of our vessels to the Eastward, some trifling assistance has occasionally been required from Bengal.

"During a scarcity of rice, sago—always cheap, and received in the greatest quantities from the opposite coast of Siak [Sumatra]—may always be substituted. The country abounds in cattle, poultry, &c, which, notwithstanding the constant supplies to His Majesty's and other ships passing up and down the Straits, are always in plenty, and at the same price.

"The coast abounds with the finest fish—salted fish and fish roes, first imported from Siak, form an extensive export. Of the soil, and its produce in sugar, fruits, &c, &c, it is unnecessary to make any observations; its superiority being universally admitted.

"Thus situated, the population of Malacca is, in a great degree, independent; and when it is considered that no corresponding benefit can be offered to them at Penang, it cannot be expected that they will remove. Admitting even that they are indemnified for the loss of their fixed property, they would feel but little inclination to adventure at Penang, where they must either purchase land and houses from others, or undertake the clearing of an unhealthy jungle.

"The natives consider the British faith as pledged for their protection. When the Settlement fell into the hands of the English, they were invited to remain; protection and even encouragement were offered them. The latter has long ago ceased; and they are in daily expectation of losing the former. For our protection they are willing to make great sacrifices; and they pay the heavy duties imposed on them, with the cheerfulness of faithful and obedient subjects. The revenues of Malacca are never in arrear.

"With respect to the European inhabitants, it appears admitted that they should, in some measure, be indemnified for the loss of their property on the garrison being withdrawn. The estimate which has been formed of the fixed and immovable property of individuals, amounts to the sum of Dollars 300,000 (at 5s. a Dollar, £75,000), a principal part of which, it appears, must be paid before Penang can reap the expected advantage from the destruction of Malacca. No doubt many deductions might be made from the above estimate: and, by a liberal policy in the commencement, the few might follow the majority obtained by such means; but I am apprehensive that it would be neither fair nor honourable to indemnify one, and not the whole. Prince of Wales's Island would, of course, derive the benefit of an increase of population by these means, as the indemnifications would only be granted conditionally on their removal, and that condition strictly enforced; but whether so great an outlay of the public money can, for attaining such an object, at the present time be authorized, is, perhaps, very doubtful; and, admitting it were granted, and the population actually removed, what check could be placed over emigration? Malacca, the abode of their fathers and of the ancestors of their fathers, would alone be considered as their home.

"The trade of Malacca is now principally carried on with the Bugguese and Javanese (neutrals), with Rhio, Lingin [Lingga], and the ports in the immediate neighbourhood; the Indian and China trade having, with the exception of the resort of a few merchants from the coast and Surat, been annihilated by the superior advantages afforded at Penang in duties, &c.

"The Bugguese or Eastern trade, which now forms so important and valuable a branch of the commerce of Penang, appears originally to have entered at Malacca; but on an attentive observation of the share now enjoyed by it, it will be found that Penang cannot expect much further advantages, or that its remaining trade can be forced further up the Straits, whatever may be the fate of Malacca.

"The Bugguese prows are from Macassar, Passeir [Pasir, eastern Borneo], Banjarmassin, but mostly from Bally [Bali], Mandar [Mandhar, Celebes], Sambava [Sumbawa], &c, which ports they leave at the commencement of the South-West monsoon, and arrive in the Straits in the month of July, increasing in number during August, September, and October, and declining with the year. Having touched on the coasts of Borneo and Java on their way, their cargoes generally consist of Bugguese sarangs, mats and birds' nests; from their own country inferior spices, and diamonds clandestinely procured from the Dutch, gold dust, and dollars; and from the ports at which they touch occasionally, of rice, tobacco, oil, &c. In return they take away opium and cloths, mostly coarse Indian. Of these prows the whole touch at Malacca, but the rich and well-equipped proceed on to Penang for the advantage of obtaining opium at a better rate than the duties at Malacca will admit of. These endeavour to arrive early in the season to avoid the North-West winds that often set in in September, but are always uncertain; they are often driven back after leaving Malacca for Penang by the North-West winds setting in earlier than expected, and are in consequence forced to end their adventure at Malacca. The best equipped of their prows can only sail before the wind, and the voyages of the most must be made with the favourable monsoons. The smaller Bugguese prows and other[s] arriving late in the season, and those badly equipped, find it impossible to weather the North-West winds, and, of necessity, stop at Malacca. Of these there are many, but they are not so rich as those which proceed to Penang; they mostly bring sarangs, in constant demand by the Malays at Malacca and its neighbourhood, and of which only a certain quantity will obtain a favourable sale at Penang. The superior advantage in the sale of this article at Malacca and its neighbourhood, added to the quicker return they make to the Eastward, counterbalances, in some degree, the advantage of the lower duties at Penang, by enabling them to anticipate the return to the Eastward of their greater rivals who had extended their voyage; the prows first returning enjoying the readiest and most profitable sale. They time their voyages so well as generally to avoid adverse winds, except in the Straits; in which, from the uncertainty of the Seasons, they can never be depended on. The delay in proceeding on to Penang frequently lengthens their voyage for months, and always for many weeks, an object of the first importance to these traders, sailing but with the fair monsoon, and obliged to perform their voyages periodically.

"Besides those denominated Bugguese prows, there are also a few with birds' nests, camphor, pepper and sago from Borneo Proper, one with pepper from Tringano [Trengganu, Malaya], and one or two from Pahan [Pahang, Malaya] with gold dust for opium.

"From the nature of this trade it is apparent that, if the duties of Malacca were lowered to the standard of Penang, very few prows would proceed further up the Straits; and that the portion now stopping at Malacca is not of a description to be forced further on, but on being driven out of Malacca, if it is possible to do so by still heavier duties, would either cease altogether, or attain its object at a less advantage, at the native port of Rhio, or of the Dutch at Java.

"The average export of opium at Malacca by means of this trade may now be estimated at from one hundred to one hundred and fifty chests per annum. This is obtained, in the first instance, either by commission from Bengal, or by purchase from Bengal ships returning from an unsuccessful voyage to the Eastward. The Sultan of Rhio has lately been more settled in his Government, and may in like manner obtain opium from returning ships; while the Dutch Government at Batavia, notwithstanding every effort on our part, appear to obtain supplies by neutrals and others. It is stated that last year, from captures taken by these and other means, they obtained opium at the rate of from seven hundred to eight hundred dollars per chest; but, as they hold the monopoly of this article in their own hands, they, of course, sell it at a very different price.

"The great object in fixing the commerce of Prince of Wales's Island, is to establish it as an entrepôt between Eastern and Western India; and if the regulations and interests of the Bengal Government would have admitted of it, perhaps it might have been of the greatest advantage for the Company to have imported into Penang a quantity of opium on their own account, or, indeed, to have held the monopoly of it themselves, thereby forcing the Eastern prows to come up to Penang for the whole of their supplies of this article. Great delicacy is requisite in keeping the duties of Penang (and, perhaps, at Malacca, for the smaller prows) sufficiently low to prevent the merchants in Bengal from fitting out vessels direct from the Eastward. It should be more to their interest to be satisfied in leaving it at Penang; and the uncertainty and length of an Eastern voyage will always induce them to put up with less profit there. This trade from Bengal (which is now occasionally carried on) not only deprives Penang of its advantages as an entrepôt, but, in many instances, from overstocking the market to the Eastward at different seasons of the year, deprives the Bugguese prows on their return from Penang of that advantage they calculated upon; and finding themselves thus anticipated in the Eastern market, some are ruined, while others are discouraged in further voyages, trusting to future supplies being in the same way received from Bengal ships, which can always afford to undersell them.

"The Javanese trade is carried on by Java prows (commanded by Arabs, Malays, or Chinese, as neutrals), bringing rice, sugar, arrack, coffee, spices (cloves), and a little tin which they pick up on their way. They take in return Pulicat and Nagore cloths, gambier, salted fish and fish roes, putchuk [puchuk], tutenague (when it is to be procured), a few Surat piece goods, &c.

"This trade may be said properly to belong to Malacca, and were it driven out from thence, is not likely to find its way to Penang. The vessels are, in general, but badly equipped, and not calculated for a voyage up the Straits. The ancient connexion subsisting between Java and Malacca gave rise to it, and, with the decline of the latter, it has gradually decreased. The great supply of rice is obtained by means of this trade, and Malacca can always command through this channel the quantity it may require. The uncertain footing on which Malacca is at present held discourages the prows from coming until they ascertain what is to be done, now the works are demolished; but it will rapidly resume its former extent as soon as it may be settled and understood that the garrison is not to be withdrawn. Next to this trade may be ranked that from Rhio, Lingin [Lingga], Palembang [Sumatra], and the countries in the more immediate neighbourhood of Malacca.

"The Palembang and Lingin vessels import about 1,500 peculs[1] of tin annually, which, with what is brought from other quarters, may be estimated at from 2,000 to 3,000 peculs annually. Rumbo [Rembau], a Malay country in the interior of the Peninsula at the back of Malacca, formerly, under a contract with the Dutch Government, supplied of itself 2,000 peculs, but now only sends about 400 peculs annually, and this is obtained at some risk by advances. The remainder might, perhaps, be obtained the same way, but, at present, seems to take its course down the Pahan[g] River on the other side of the Peninsula, from whence it is transported in small prows to Rhio, &c, &c.

"The interior produce of the Malacca territory in pepper is but trifling, having been discouraged, but considerable quantities are constantly imported from Rhio, where it is produced in great abundance.

"A considerable trade was formerly carried on with Siak on the East Coast of Sumatra, nearly opposite Malacca. At this place the Dutch once had a factory and derived advantages; but for many years this trade has been on the decline owing to our Settlements on the West coast, and the subsequent usurpation of the government by the present Rajah; and it is now almost annihilated.

"The traders from the populous countries in the interior of Sumatra have turned their course to the other side; but, in the event of the English Settlements there being reduced, there seems no doubt but it might with ease be again brought into its original channel by an enterprising Government at Malacca. The trade from Malacca to Siak formerly consisted of raw silk, coarse and other cloths, and opium, in return for which was received gold, wax, sago, salted fish and fish roes, elephants' teeth, gambier, hogslard, camphor, rattans, &c. The Dutch Company were also in the habit of sending annually from Siak to Java several rafts of spars for masts; and we have lately had an opportunity of knowing its capability in the produce of frame timbers for shipbuilding.

"The Dutch had also a factory at Jamby [Jambi] on the same coast, and kept up a similar intercourse; but at present the trade with Malacca is very trifling. The returns are nearly the same as from Siak, with the

[1] *Pikul*, 'a man's load', 133·3 lb.

addition of coarse benjamin and dragon's blood. The smaller ports to the northward of Siak, as far as Assahan and Batta Bara, still send their small produce in rattans, wax, and rice, mostly to Malacca.

"The only Indian trade now carried on with Malacca is by a few Pulicat merchants freighting annually on the Indiaman from eighty to one hundred and fifty bales of cloth to the value of 80,000 to 140,000 dollars; by three or four Chuliah vessels, every monsoon bringing coarse cloths (blue), coir and seeds, &c, for the native bazaar; and by a few Surat merchants, passengers on the Bombay and China ships, and two annual native vessels from Surat, touching on their way to Siam and other ports, bringing silks and chintzes.

"Of the above trade almost the whole first goes to Penang, but the articles, being exclusively adapted for the Malacca market, or that of Penang being, perhaps, overstocked, cannot find a sale there. The finer, or Pulicat cloths, are taken away from Malacca in Javanese prows, as well as part of the coarse, and the silks and chintzes generally by the Eastern prows. Three or four Siamese junks arrive at Malacca in the course of the year, coming round the Peninsula, bringing rice, salt, salt fish, sticklack, sappan-wood, &c, and take cloths, opium, &c, and, until the last three years, a large annual junk came from China, bringing raw silk, coarse China ware, paper, tobacco, and supplies of various kinds required by the inhabitants of Malacca and the neighbouring States. On the arrival of the vessel the native prows from the adjacent States crowded to Malacca, and each bringing the produce of its country, were of some importance to the trade of the place. The junk, on its return, carried away tin, fish roes, bêche-de-mer, rattans, birds' nests, camphor, &c, to a great amount; the savings of the Chinese inhabitants of Malacca and the neighbouring countries invested in the above articles; and such of the Chinese as were desirious of returning to Macao. The savings of the Chinese inhabitants are also sent on in pepper and similar articles by the Macao Portuguese ships.

"The surplus arrack, sugar, &c, imported in the Javanese prows, is generally sent on to Penang, as opportunity offers; and, in addition to the trade carried on by the means of native vessels, as above mentioned, there are a few brigs and other small craft belonging to the inhabitants of Malacca, but mostly navigated by natives.

"I have deemed it necessary to be thus particular respecting the trade of Malacca, as it does not appear to be generally understood; and the nature of the population and trade being made known, I feel confident that I shall not stand alone in the opinion that Penang cannot expect much more of either than it already possesses; and, with regard to the latter, that it is now a trade almost exclusively belonging to Malacca from its natural advantages.

"Thus far it has been my object to explain the difficulties that will arise in transferring the present population and trade. It is now necessary to view the subject as to the dangerous consequences likely to ensue to Penang in the event of the garrison being withdrawn.

"Malacca, having been in the possession of a European Power for three centuries, and even previously to that period considered as the Capital of the Malay States, has obtained so great an importance in the eyes of the native Princes, that they are ever anxious to obtain the friendship of the nation in whose hands it may be. Its name carries more weight to a Malay ear than any new Settlement, whatever its importance. This pre-eminence ensures constant respect from the traders to and from the neighbouring ports: at least it has done so till very lately; and by this means affords a considerable check to piracy. Were Malacca in the hands of a native Prince, however respectable, or supported by us, this check would not only be lost, but fleets of piratical vessels and prows would be fitted out, even from its shores, whose depredations the enterprise of our cruisers would find it difficult to keep under.

"From the trade of Rhio—since it was given up to Sultaun Mahomed in 1795, to be attributed to the exactions being less there than at Malacca—and the advantages which Rhio seems likely to derive, now that its Government is more settled and the conduct of the Rajah more settled, it is but fair to infer that Malacca, in the hands of a native Prince, would, with its superior population and extent of resources, adopt a similar conduct, and obtain an equal, and in all probability a far superior advantage. It would still afford its usual facilities and accommodations to traders, and there is but too much reason to believe that Penang would be deprived of that great advantage she has hitherto derived in the Eastern trade.

"But to look at the subject in a more serious point of view still—for I am far from thinking it would ever remain in the hands of a native Power—although the permanent fortifications and public works of every description may be effectually destroyed, the possession of Malacca will ever be a most desirable object to a European Power and to our enemy. Prince of Wales's Island, though advantageously situated for commanding the bay and the Northern entrance of the Straits, has by no means the same advantage and command within the Straits that Malacca possesses. Every ship that passes up or down must be observed from the latter place, and should this station ever be held by an enterprising enemy, not only Penang, but our more important China trade, would be materially endangered. We have now the command. Why give it up, unless we are forced? and I trust we are not reduced to that extremity.

"Waiving the great advantages that might be derived from encouraging Malacca, or rather allowing it to have fair play, let the subject only be considered as it relates to the interests of Penang.

"It is well known that the Dutch Government had in contemplation to make Malacca a free port, with the view of destroying the English Settlement at Penang. Should the place ever fall into their hands again, or into that of their now superior authority, which it no doubt will if evacuated by the English, a similar, or more active policy must be expected. This alone, independent of every other consideration, should, I think, be a sufficient inducement for the British Government to retain it in support of their Settlement at Prince of Wales's Island. The Eastern trade, now so lucrative a source of commerce and revenue at Penang, would at once be destroyed, while passing vessels would never find it worth their while to submit to the delay of stopping at Penang. Trade must ever flourish most where the greatest advantages are afforded. Malacca has greater natural advantages than Penang, and these can only be counterbalanced by the policy of the Penang Government in exacting heavier duties there.

"The fortifications of Malacca were extensive but irregular and badly constructed, more formidable in appearance than in reality, and were of more use in inspiring awe in the natives than they ever would have been in resisting any regular force. Whoever is acquainted with the difficulty of clearing and settling a Malay country, knows well the value of the place upon cleared and cultivated [land]; [and] in what estimation it is held in respect to the extent of cleared lands, its orchards and plantations, the value of brick and other buildings, &c, &c. Malacca possesses an advantage in this respect beyond every other Malay Settlement. The houses, &c, &c, constructed after the style of the Dutch, are of brick and stone, and likely to resist the effects of ages. The public works may be demolished, the principal buildings levelled with the earth from which they sprang, but Malacca in its facilities for trade, its extent of cultivation, its permanent style of native buildings, must remain the same. Fortifications can in a short time be destroyed by the fiat of man, but who shall direct the forests to reassume their former extent, or the country of Malacca at once to become an impenetrable forest and unhealthy swamp? The industry of ages has been too effectually and too successful[ly] exerted to be effaced with common trouble. Time and the exterminating sword alone will ever be able to reduce it to its original state; and when it is so reduced, it will always be an object of importance to our European enemy, as well on account of superior advantages in trade and produce, as of its capability of annoying, and effectually destroying the English interests at Penang.

"It does not fall within my line to submit the actual advantages of Malacca as to its natural defences, or to set forth the various plan[s] that might be adopted for supporting them. They can be professionally and better pointed out by Captain Farquhar, the Engineer officer now in charge of the Government. For the present purpose it is sufficient to say that from that source and my own observation, I am enabled to assert with correctness that any European Power possessing Malacca would, in a very short time, be able to intrench themselves nearly as securely as they could have done within the old walls, and that we should find the greatest difficulty in again obtaining possession of the place.

"To evince more clearly the actual state of Malacca in regard to its revenues and disbursements, I take the liberty of referring to the official documents lately furnished by the Commandant, by which it will appear that the estimated revenues of the present year exceed the disbursements, the former being estimated at 83,000 and the latter at 79,000 Dollars, including military and all other charges.

"The foregoing statement will afford a more satisfactory proof than any I could offer of the Settlement being [maintained] at no expense to the Company; and if the actual annual cost of the Settlement were calculated on the same principle as that of Penang has been, by leaving out the military as chargeable to other Presidencies, a surplus revenue, after paying every charge, would arise to the amount of a lac of Rupees [100,000].

"It should, however, be stated that, while Malacca continues to be discouraged as it has been, the revenues cannot be expected materially to increase, although they have annually done so, in a trifling degree, for the last five years. Some relaxation in the very heavy duties now imposed may, perhaps, be deemed advisable, as they not only affect the inhabitants very seriously, but may be the means of forcing [a] considerable part of the trade to Rhio and other ports. Great care should be observed in fixing the extent of the duties, so as to ensure to Penang the whole of the trade that may be forced out of Malacca.

"The garrison and establishment at Malacca appear to have been reduced to the very lowest state consistent with the honour of the British Flag and the internal safety of the place; and no further reduction can, I think, with safety, be attempted. It may, however, be deemed sufficient; and if the Commandant is authorized to lay out a very small sum in repairing the works at Bookis China and on the hill of St John's, and in erecting some temporary works near the town, the Settlement may be considered as secure against any predatory force of the enemy, being defended by nature from any attack by shipping. It is at the same time fair to infer that, if the above temporary works are erected, and it is determined to continue the present garrison and Government, the superior advantages that may be derived from the revenues in consequence of the safety of the place, will fully reimburse any trifling expense incurred on that account.

"The policy of, at any rate, keeping Malacca in our possession until we are actually obliged to give it up, is, I must presume, made apparent in the remarks I have taken the liberty to submit, not only on account of the difficulty of doing justice to its inhabitants, but as such a measure can be of no real service to Penang, but in all probability [will be] most injurious. Notwithstanding our utmost efforts the Settlement will be an object of importance to our enemies, whenever they have the power to settle in it.

"It is unnecessary to dwell on the advantages of Malacca as a port of refreshment for His Majesty's and other ships. His Excellency, the Commander-in-Chief, I have reason to believe, is fully convinced of this, and has represented to the Supreme Government [of India] the advantage of holding the Settlement on this account alone; but I trust, and confidently hope, that enough has been said to prove the policy, not to say necessity, of continuing the present garrison till the conclusion of this war; and that, on a review of the actual importance of Malacca in its relation to Prince of Wales's Island, your Honourable Board will be induced to call the attention of the Supreme Government to the subject. Should the Right Honourable the Governor-General be inclined to interest His Majesty's Ministers in retaining it, on a peace, and eventually establishing it as a British Settlement, a more detailed statement can be drawn up, and from the memoranda I deemed it my duty to make while at Malacca, I may probably be able to furnish further information as to the real advantages that might be expected from Malacca as a permanent Settlement. Malacca ceded to the English, its rivalship with Penang would cease. No longer the oppressor and oppressed, they would mutually assist each other. The revenues of Malacca would immediately increase, while the Dutch law might be abolished by Proclamation from His Majesty, and the jurisdiction of the Court at Prince of Wales's Island with ease extended in its room.

"With the assistance of Malacca the whole of the Malay Rajahs in the Straits and to the Eastward might be rendered not only subservient, but, if necessary, tributary. But to dwell on the permanent advantages to Penang that, on a more extended and political point of view, might be derived from the possession of Malacca, under an enlightened and liberal policy, is not the object of this paper. Facts evincing the impracticability of destroying the Settlement, and the danger to be apprehended from any further attempts to effect such a measure, are simply stated. If I am wrong in the conclusions I have drawn, I trust to the Honourable Board's favourable construction of my intentions. Actuated from a sense of duty alone, I have presumed thus unasked to intrude on the time of your Honourable Board, and a consciousness of the correctness of my statement flatters me with the hope of your approbation."

This report, which has been printed before,[1] was dated 31st October, only two days after Raffles' return to Penang. It must have been almost,

[1] Demetrius C. Boulger, *The Life of Sir Stamford Raffles*.

if not entirely, in its final shape before he left Malacca. It is curious, therefore, to note that William Farquhar was completely unaware that Raffles, though a guest in his house, was drafting this long document. Nor, apparently did he subsequently see a copy. As late as 1830 he wrote to the *Asiatic Journal and Monthly Register* protesting against various statements made by Lady Raffles in her *Memoir*:

". . . With respect to Malacca Lady Raffles gives Sir Stamford credit for having laid the inhabitants under some particular obligation to him whilst there for the recovery of his health. Now I happened to be in command of Malacca at the period alluded to; and as Sir Stamford was at that time a guest of mine it would, one may conclude, in some way or other have been brought to my knowledge if such an obligation had actually existed. The truth is that the Dutch inhabitants forwarded through me a Petition to Government respecting the great hardship of their case in being ordered to quit Malacca, which Petition was recommended by me to the most favourable consideration of Government in my letters of the 6th and 7th February 1806. . . ."

That Raffles could have drafted such a report and not told Farquhar that he was doing so, let alone allow him to see the draft, confirms the supposition that the two men were not on terms of more than formal acquaintance; there could have been between them no close or cordial friendship. It might be said, of course, that Raffles adopted these tactics in order to keep all the credit—that he was, as Minto's son, Captain Hon. George Elliot, later described him, "full of trick".

The report reveals the mass of detailed and accurate information that, in three busy years, beset by endless official duties and interrupted by two serious illnesses, he had been able to collect and now assemble to support his argument. The logic, too, of that argument is as masterly as his control over language is striking. He was able to reveal himself as a statesman, for while his subject was really one of local interest, the treatment was that by a mind whose vision had no such restricted horizon. Most significant perhaps of all was the interest he was already displaying in what lay "to the Eastward".

The Governor-General in Council wasted no time in replying from Calcutta to the dispatch:

". . . As the circumstances in that report appear to us to render it highly inexpedient to withdraw the Garrison and inhabitants from the Settlement of Malacca, we do not hesitate in recommending to you that the measure be suspended until a further reference can be made on the subject to the Honourable the Court of Directors. The question appeared to us to be of so urgent a nature . . . that we have considered it expedient to give an immediate opinion on it without waiting the result of your further deliberations."

It appears that Raffles also sent a copy privately to Leyden, with the request that it be shown personally to Lord Minto. For a long time there was silence. He wrote a second letter. Meanwhile he found himself engulfed once more in the heavy duties of his exacting office, a strain on his body and a trial for his patience. Was this all life had to offer him? Might death not intervene before his chance came?

"I am convinced", he wrote to a friend at home during this period, "my health will never permit my holding this office many years. If therefore I am not to look for a seat in Council, or some quiet place in the Government, I must either fall a sacrifice or apply for the first vacancy in the Collectorship or other subordinate office. My constitution was always delicate; with care I have no doubt it could last as long here as in England. Without it, it will soon break up. I am afraid they will work the willing horse to death; all I ask is to see the end of it. . . ."

Again in November of that year, 1808:

"A Secretary is, in general the organ, but in some places the very soul. I am neither the one nor the other. We have not abilities to admit of my being the former, nor liberality to allow the other. You may, therefore, guess the situation. The arrogance that a temporary exaltation has given to some is scarce to be borne with, except by such a patient body as me."

And so, with the gloomy prospect of an eternal round of official duties, petty jealousies and parochial business, the year 1808 ended.

ii

A charming picture of domestic life in Penang is to be found in the *Narrative* of Edward Robarts. Not a great deal is known about Robarts beyond the *Narrative*, which is to be found in the Advocates' Library at Edinburgh, though there is no record as to how it came there. He was a sailor who visited the South Seas and married in Tahiti a girl of the country who was supposed to be a royal princess. On arrival in Penang with his wife and children, he became steward to Quintin Dick Thompson, Raffles' brother-in-law. He describes thus a small dinner party at the Thompsons' home on Mount St Mary:

"Dinner was sent to table at 7 o'clock. The Hon. Col. Maccallister Govnr., several Naval Captains Military Officers and gentlemen of the Civil Service, Mrs Raffles and Mrs Hobson graced the festive board. After dinner in rotation tea and coffee were served up and about ten o'clock the Merry Dance led off, afterwards several songs was sung. The Boyne water was sung by Mrs Raffles in high stile, the Banks of the Dee on the German Flute by Captain Phillips and sung to by Mrs Thompson, the sweetness of her voice would melt a heart of adamant, well might the poet say 'music hath charms to soothe the savage breast'. The evening was spent in the most agreeable and pleasant manner."

In March 1809, addressing his letter from "Runemede, Penang", Raffles wrote to Marsden:

". . . I have by me a sketch of a grammar which I have drawn up, and which I will send you as soon as I get time to correct and copy it; and I am gradually compiling a dictionary, which you shall be welcome to, if it can be of any service to you. . . ."

On 18th May he managed to assume yet another official duty, that of one of the three commissioners of the Court of Requests, with Caunter and Lawrence as colleagues, and one Julius Caesar as secretary. While this extra burden added materially to the strain upon him, he was to benefit greatly from the knowledge of the law and its methods of operation acquired in this active association with Sir Edmond Stanley.

Quintin Dick Thompson was acting as Naval agent at Penang and had in his charge certain moneys in connexion with Naval widows and orphans. On 1st July 1809 he died. As executor for his brother-in-law, and under strong pressure from Rear-Admiral Drury, who was godfather to Charlotte, daughter of Mary Anne, Raffles took over, as a temporary measure, the duties of Naval agent, this with the permission of Governor Macalister. There is no doubt that Raffles intended to retain the post beyond the time necessary to settle up Thompson's affairs; though the appointment carried no salary, the holder was allowed commission on all disbursements.

There came news of the arrival from Europe of eleven French frigates at Mauritius, then in the hands of the French, and of their intention to cruise those waters. The Governor in Council of Penang wrote on this matter to Admiral Drury on 4th August 1809:

"It appearing . . . to be the object of the enemy to establish at Acheen [Achin, Sumatra] a depot for small marine stores, and to obtain a ready supply of provisions and refreshments for such of their ships as may be there, the number of Frenchmen now in the service of the King of Acheen affording too much reason to believe that they have not been unsuccessful in obtaining the confidence of that Government, we have intimated to the King the information in our possession, and, at the same time, that we called upon him to support his good faith and alliance with the English, warned him of the dangers attending on unwary conduct. . . ."

The admonition to the king concluded:

". . . The English cannot allow any French ship shall receive refreshment or repairs at Acheen or at any ports under Your Majesty's authority. If such takes place, the English Admiral will, of course, deem it necessary to attend to such conduct. . . . As a mark of my friendship and esteem for

Your Majesty, I request Your Majesty's acceptance of the articles which will be delivered by the bearer of this letter."

The Admiralty had instructed Admiral Drury to institute a close blockade of Java and the Moluccas. The Supreme Government realized the repercussions this might have on the Malays, who already traded with Penang and would be likely to do so even more actively if the ports of Java were closed. This trade would be pure gain to us and a serious loss of revenue to the Franco-Dutch régime. Accordingly, on 15th August, Calcutta addressed to the Penang government a letter with which were enclosed copies of correspondence with Admiral Drury. While unable to go against his instructions from London, Drury appreciated their point of view and expressed his willingness to advise his officers to avoid interfering with our Malay friends. The Penang government was instructed to explain the position to the Malays, so that there should be no unfortunate incidents.

Experience has shown, however, how difficult it is to exercise an effective blockade without disturbing the legitimate trade of neutrals. And when these neutrals happened to be hardy Malay traders whose language no one could speak or understand and who were completely unaware of the international rules of blockade; when, too, the commanders of some of the blockading ships were enthusiastic young officers, ready and anxious to carry out their orders to the letter (with an eye to prize-money) without any discretion or appreciation of general policy, it was only too certain that such incidents would occur.

With pained regret, the Penang government reported to Calcutta that "the annual fleet of Boogies prows bound from the Eastward to Malacca and this place had about the 1st October fallen in with H.M.S. 'Piedmontaise'." This was about the worst thing that could have happened. The resulting action was due to a misunderstanding between the boarding officers and the Malays, so likely to arise from a mutual ignorance of each other's tongues, and it was a brisk one. The English had two killed and twenty wounded, including five officers. The Malays were thought to have had severe casualties also. The serious result was that "the whole of the fleet immediately put back and efforts to induce them to come on to Penang again had completely failed".

The strong representations already made to London did cause the blockade to be lifted the next year. But meanwhile other, though less serious, incidents kept occurring, and the strain imposed on Anglo-Malay relations was considerable.

In the midst of his efforts to recover Malay confidence, together with his other heavy duties, Raffles had to face a sudden attack by his erstwhile supporter, Pearson, who had just returned from leave in India. Whether the attack was really directed at Raffles or was intended to be a stick with which to beat Pearson's old enemy, Governor Macalister, one cannot tell.

The storm burst at a Council meeting on 19th October. It concerned the post of Naval agent.

"I think the Members of the Board", said Pearson, "are particularly called upon to second their entire disapprobation of Mr Raffles ever having been permitted to hold a situation so totally incompatible with that of a confidential Secretary of the Government, and in violation of the positive orders of the Honourable the Court of Directors. I have heard it casually mentioned shortly after the death of Mr Thompson that Mr Raffles was in possession of the office of Naval Agent, but I did not, for a moment, imagine that he could wish or expect to retain the situation, but that he was merely closing the accounts of his brother-in-law. . . ."

Pearson's minute, which was much longer than as quoted above, resulted in the following letter to Captain Christopher Cole, "Senior Officer of H.M. Ships now in Fort Cornwallis":

"Sir,—I am directed by the Honourable the Governor and Council to acknowledge receipt of your letter and to acquaint you in reply that your intimation of Mr Secretary Raffles being in possession of the office of Naval Agent at this Port is the first that has reached them on the subject, and the Board now cannot sufficiently express their regret that such an irregularity has tacitly been permitted to exist for a single day. . . . From the term on which Mr Raffles was permitted by the Governor to assume the temporary charge of the office of Naval Agent, he was aware that such indulgence in no way sanctioned arrangements unconnected with the accounts of his late brother-in-law; consequently the Governor and Council do not deem themselves responsible in any way for the possible inconvenience that may arise out of the present determination. . . .

(*Signed*) Thos. Raffles,
Secretary to Government, Fort Cornwallis."

Raffles' feelings as he transcribed the minute and signed the letter must be a matter for conjecture. It could not have affected his relations with the Naval officers, which were close and cordial. Nelson's captains knew a man when they met one. They had little respect for the Penang government, and letters from the Admiral to the Governor in Council were apt to be blunt and imperious. One fertile source of friction was the shore accommodation that the government had to find for the Admiral. This frequently produced an exchange of acid letters. Then there was the incident of the absent-minded gunner who rammed home a cannon ball during the firing of a salute. After all, the ship could hardly be blamed because an unfortunate coolie chose to be standing on the exact spot where the ball fell!

But the Navy only visited Penang occasionally; Raffles had to live and work there. After this stupid affair, the prospect of unremitting and unrewarded labour under such unpleasant conditions must have seemed well-nigh intolerable, though Pearson departed soon for England.

Fortunately for Raffles' peace of mind, the long-awaited answer from Leyden came to hand just about this time, It was dated from Calcutta, 9th October.

"MY DEAR RAFFLES,—I have received both your letters, and with great vexation have to inform you that Lord Minto is at present gone to the unfortunate Presidency of Madras, where I believe he has got his hands full.[1] I laid before him without delay the MS. concerning Malacca, with which he was greatly pleased, and desired me to say he should be gratified in receiving immediately from yourself any communications respecting the Eastern parts of a similar nature. I shall not fail to write to him as soon as I am a little recovered, for I have been for some time (days I mean) confined to bed by a smart attack of fever. . . ."

At Penang, every excuse was taken for official or public festivities. The Governor usually invited everyone who counted in the social world to a dinner and entertainment on the birthday of the King and the Prince of Wales—or Prince Regent, as he became—while private individuals or the regiment chose any public occasion that offered for a dinner and a ball. Sometimes the dinner was given by one and the ball by another. In the issue of the *Gazette* dated 11th November 1809 appeared the following:

"THE BEAU MONDE

"We have the pleasure to congratulate our numerous readers upon the happy return of gaieties to Pinang.

"On Thursday, being Lord Mayor's Day, Mr Robinson entertained a select party of friends to dinner at his Mansion on the North Beach. In the evening a most elegant fête was given by Messrs Clubley and Phipps. It is impossible for us to convey any idea of the styles and manner in which everything was conducted.

"The Honourable the Governor together with the beauty and fashion of the Island assembled at an early hour.

"The Ball commenced between 8 and 9. Mr Clubley had the honour to lead Mrs Raffles down the first Dance to the tune of 'Off She Goes'.

"The supper rooms were thrown open precisely at 12 o'clock. The tables were covered in every delicacy which India[2] could produce. The wines were of the most delicious quality; and that nothing might be

[1] Mutiny of army officers.
[2] See footnote, page 359.

wanting in rendering gratification perfect several ladies and gentlemen entertained the Company with Songs, displaying on the one part the most true delicacies of taste and on the other true original comicality.

"Dancing recommenced with increased life immediately after supper and continued until the early hours of the morning when the party separated with every appearance of regret. . . ."

Two months later, in the early weeks of 1810, Raffles suffered a severe blow. It related to the increase in salary agreed by the Council in 1807, subject to the approval of the Court of Directors in London. Although the mail took fully six months, there was little excuse for a delay of nearly two years in sending an unfavourable reply. Even then, though dated 28th April 1809, it was not received in Penang until 15th January 1810.

The dispatch, which was chilly and formal, was to the effect that the Court highly disapproved of the arrangement and could "never admit that because the salary of one office will bear reduction, another is therefore to be increased in a proportionate degree". Clubley's salary was to remain at $3,600 per annum; Raffles was to revert "to the sum originally fixed by us" and, further, he was to be "called upon to refund the amount which he may have received over and above the sum of dollars 8,000 per annum". This was $6,500—£1,625.

If there was little excuse for the delay, an explanation is to be found in the failure of the colony as far as the Company was concerned. Probably the proposal had raised at first little objection in London, but the ensuing disappointments and the huge expense of the colony (for which none but the Company was to blame) had brought the matter to a decision. Here at least was a chance to recover something; the amount must be written back. The logic of the decision was inescapable; by the hardship its delay would cause, it was unjust and arbitrary.

Raffles appealed to the Council in a letter dated 8th February 1810. ". . . most solemnly do I assure your Honourable Board of my total inability to comply with the heavy and unexpected demand now made—nearly three years subsequent to my appointment. The circumstances of the offices devolving upon me, as it did at the time, without the aid of an experienced Assistant, of which my predecessor had the advantage, added to the serious illnesses under which I have laboured, brought on chiefly from close attention to duty and a constant anxiety to perfect the public service . . . will, I hope meet with your favourable consideration; and when the increased demands on my earnings in consequence of the death of a near relative which has left a widow-sister and three infant children[1] entirely dependent on my support, are adverted to as connected with this

[1] Mary Anne had two sons and a daughter (Charlotte) by Quintin Dick Thompson. One of the sons, Acheson Quintin Dick Thompson (born 22nd October 1806), died in New Zealand on 14th January 1883, leaving three sons and a daughter.

statement, I hope that I may not be deemed improperly intrusive on your time. . . ."

This letter was supported by one from Pearson, who confirmed the truth of the statements contained in it. The Governor in Council resolved "that in consideration of the peculiar circumstances stated by Mr Raffles, and of the increased allowance in question having been given to him unconditionally as the spontaneous act of the Board, and not in consequence of any representation whatever on his part, the subject be again referred to the Honourable Court of Directors, and the representation now made by Mr Raffles recommended in the strongest manner to their favourable consideration. . . ."

Governor Macalister wrote accordingly to the Court, but no reply was given beyond a repeated demand for repayment. It was very unfortunate for Raffles that the East India Company should have been at that very time considering what retrenchment could be effected on the grounds that "the Ministers of the Crown had not fulfilled their intention of making the island an important Naval station. . . ." As a result in 1809 some reduction in the establishment had been ordered.

This was to hang over Raffles for years. It was not till 1817, when he was able to raise the matter personally in London, that the amount was at length written off. It is difficult to avoid the conclusion that this unlucky affair, resulting only from the well-intentioned efforts of the Council, later reacted very unfairly on Raffles—one more black mark against him.

Chapter Six

CALCUTTA, 1810

i

IT was Admiral Drury who, in 1810, unlocked the gates of Raffles' prison and pointed the road to escape.

The Moluccas, those islands of the East Indies lying between Celebes and New Guinea, fell into our hands in April of that year—a conquest, as Raffles wrote, "unexpectedly achieved by a small Naval force which had been merely sent to plunder them". The raiders found the garrison lacking in powder and shot, thereby unable to resist. Lord Minto, Governor-General of India, refused to accept the responsibility of administering the islands on behalf of the East India Company, while Admiral Drury did not consider himself empowered to set up a government on behalf of the King. Pending instructions from England, Drury suggested to Minto that Raffles should be put in charge of a provisional administration.

"Lord Minto immediately replied", wrote Raffles, "that I was not unknown to him; that he was perfectly satisfied of my fitness and claims, and that he would immediately appoint me if the Admiral would undertake that I would accept the office. . . . I might be unwilling to sacrifice a certainty for an uncertainty. . . . My advancement at Prince of Wales's Island was secure; but the Moluccas were only a war dependency. . . ."

A quick decision was necessary, for there might be other applicants, but Drury was reluctant to give the required undertaking without the assent of Raffles. He sent a ship to Penang.

"Some months", wrote Raffles, "had now elapsed . . . yet the chance of being in time, with the expectation of still further advance in my interest with Lord Minto, weighed with me in the resolution I took in proceeding in person to Bengal. . . ."

He applied for two months' leave of absence. There was no regular vessel available, but his impatience would brook no delay and on 7th June 1810 he left Penang for Calcutta in a frail local craft that nearly came to disaster on the dangerous sandbanks guarding the entrance to the Hooghly.

He arrived at Calcutta at the end of the month, a few days before his twenty-ninth birthday—a very different Raffles from the young clerk who had left England five years before. In spite of two serious illnesses, he had lost nothing of the energy, the sense of duty, the wide interest in his work that had distinguished him above his fellow-clerks at East

India House. The moist heat of Penang had, it is true, damaged his constitution, but it had not damped his enthusiasm. He had made the fullest use of his opportunities to collect political, ethnological and scientific information, besides getting to know and understand the Malays in a way that few men were then able to do. He was now a trained and experienced official, ready and willing to take over any appointment offering full scope for his talents. He had, too, the modest confidence in himself that inspires confidence in others.

The first thing he learned on reaching Calcutta was that the Moluccas appointment was not to be his. This did not greatly disappoint him; the Moluccas had served their purpose in giving him an excuse to visit Calcutta and make personal contact with Lord Minto. In fact, he gives as his main reason for the trip:

"My attention had long been directed to the state of the Dutch possessions to the Eastward, and, as rumours were afloat of a projected armament going against the Isle of France [Mauritius], it occurred to me that information I possessed respecting Java might be useful and possibly turn the attention of our Government to that direction."

Of his interview with the Governor-General, he writes:

". . . I met with the kindest reception from Lord Minto. I found that, though the appointment to the Moluccas had not actually taken place, it was promised to another. I, in consequence, relinquished all idea of it, and at once drew his Lordship's attention to Java, by observing that there were other islands worthy of his Lordship's consideration besides the Moluccas: Java, for instance. On the mention of Java, his Lordship cast a look of such scrutiny, anticipation, and kindness upon me, as I shall never forget. 'Yes,' said he, 'Java is an interesting Island; I shall be happy to receive any information you can give me concerning it.' This was enough to encourage me; and from this moment all my views, all my plans, and all my mind were devoted to create such an interest regarding Java as should lead to its annexation to our Eastern Empire. . . ."

ii

The island of Java is about six hundred miles long, and the mean of its width is about one hundred miles, with a total content of approximately fifty-one thousand square miles—a little larger than England. It is separated at its western from Sumatra by the Strait of Sunda, which, at its narrowest point, is only some fourteen miles wide. The island of Madura, which lies close along the northern coast opposite Surabaya, is about ninety-one miles long by about thirty-one miles wide. At its nearest point it is only one mile from the coast of Java. On the east, Java is separated from Bali by the Straits of Bali, which are about two miles wide at the nearest point. The population of Java, according to Dutch records, is reputed to have been at this date about three millions.

Java is almost wholly volcanic. From the coast at the Strait of Sunda the ground rises gradually, and from there to the other extremity of the island there is a more or less continuous chain of mountains, including some considerable peaks and active volcanoes. This chain divides the country into two main areas. Dutch control of the northern half of the island was more or less complete. Their control of the southern half was hardly nominal, large portions of it being still quite unexplored by Europeans. The island is immensely fertile and contains a wide variety of scenery of the greatest beauty.

To explain the obvious interest of Lord Minto in Java, it is necessary to sketch the circumstances that led up to it. That the capture of the island, third largest of the Sunda group, ranking only after Borneo and Sumatra, would be advantageous from certain points of view, no one so well informed as Raffles could fail to understand, but he could hardly have been aware how much British policy in regard to Java had wavered from year to year.

The connexion of the Dutch with Java dates from the founding of the Dutch East India Company in 1579. On the site of the old capital of Jakatra, whose ruling chief they put to death in 1619, they built a new capital, Batavia, which to-day, under the Indonesian Republic, is called Jakarta.

The Dutch came to Java and the other Spice Islands as traders, just as the English—after unfruitful efforts to follow in Dutch footsteps in the East Indies—did in India. They wanted trading posts and only enough territory in their vicinity to give them security, having no more desire to form large new colonies than had the servants of the British East India Company in India. But, like their British rivals, the Dutch were from time to time compelled, in self-protection, to interfere in local politics, so that, however unwillingly, they were gradually forced to extend their control farther and farther. The growth of British India is an exact parallel.

At no time was the whole island brought under direct administrative control. The original purpose of the Company, as a trading corporation, remained unchanged and the policy of exploitation by means of forced cultivation and fixed prices for spices and other special commodities was met by no serious challenge. This system is, in modern eyes, thoroughly vicious and immoral, and, apart from such ethical considerations, it proved not only disastrous for the native inhabitants of Java, but also financially ruinous to the Dutch East India Company. There was, too, the less obvious but very real effect on the Dutch officials. An oppressive system such as forced cultivation inevitably tends to debase the standard of morality of those called upon to carry it out, the extent of corruption being in proportion to the personal standards of those officials. As this was not high in the Dutch Colonial service in those days, frequent complaints were addressed to Holland concerning the poor quality of men sent out.

The wars in Europe and the virtual isolation of Java that resulted tended to encourage further deterioration. Such slight control as had previously been exercised from distant Europe now disappeared. To many of the Dutch in Java, the obvious course seemed to be to exploit the country and its inhabitants by any and every means to produce the maximum output of tropical crops, not now so much for the benefit of the mother country as for that, so far as each one dared, of the individual. Holland was far away. Salaries were grossly inadequate, and senior officials were too often lax and venal. The climate was enervating, the risk of death ever present. The standard of morals sank progressively lower. There were comparatively few European women. Slaves were plentiful and the half-caste population grew. Luxury and dissipation increased, the only purpose of life for many being to make as much hay as possible while the sun shone—and it shone most days of the year—in the hope, often frustrated by gross self-indulgence, that a fortune could be made quickly enough for them to escape the very real dangers of the climate and so return, as rich men, to Holland.

In contemporary British India also, much had been going on of which Englishmen must be ashamed. But it was the behaviour of individuals, not the official policy, that was to blame. No attempt was made by the British East India Company to introduce into India a system of compulsory cultivation or forced deliveries. It was not, one may suppose, because such a policy was regarded as immoral, for it was the one officially pursued in Bencoolen, but rather because it would have been impracticable; India was too vast, too far advanced in civilization and commercial experience for any such system to succeed.

As in the East Indies, the main source of trouble in India was the inadequate pay of the officials. It was tacitly recognized that they lived by private trading—indeed, many amassed fortunes in that way. While doubtless the natives were all too frequently grossly exploited, the chief sufferer was the Company itself, which was flagrantly defrauded by its own servants. Even the monopoly of overseas trade granted by its charter was undermined without scruple and eventually cancelled.

One important difference between India and Java was that India was much nearer to England than the East Indies were to Holland, and the movement of people between England and India was very much greater. While many adventurers and scoundrels went to seek ill-gotten fortunes in India, the average Englishman who went there was probably better educated and had a more developed sense of responsibility than the contemporary Dutchman who went to the Indies. The standard of education required by the British Company was considerably higher. English women accompanied their husbands to India to a degree beyond the general practice in the East Indies, and their influence was by no means negligible in maintaining reasonable standards of morality. The Army and Navy and the Company's servants contained a higher proportion of men of ability and personal integrity. In fact, when we read some of the grosser episodes of our Indian administration of the period, it is as well to remember that the good work of decent people has little news value; the black sheep were probably not so common as the lurid accounts of them suggest. In all fairness, this might well have applied to the Dutch East Indies also.

India, however, was, by comparison, more fortunate than the Eastern Archipelago in two other respects. In spite of the peculation of some of her servants, or perhaps thanks to the profitable China trade, the British East India Company, while in almost continuous financial straits, was never in acute danger of collapse, whereas when the Dutch East India Company collapsed in 1790, the crash was spectacular. The commissioners who went out to examine the financial system there had to report that the Company was not only insolvent, but also in debt to the sum of eighty-five million florins. Their opinion was given in extremely frank terms:

"When we take a view of our chief possession and establishment and when we attain to the real situation of the internal trade of India, which is still increasing, and the exorbitant rates of the expenses, the incessant want of cash, the mass of paper money in circulation, the unrestrained peculation and faithlessness of many of the Company's servants, the consequent clandestine trade of foreign nations, the perfidy of the native Princes, the weakness and connivance of the Indian Government, the excessive expenses in the Military department and for the public defences; in a word, when we take a view of all this collectively, we should almost despair of being able to fulfil our task, if some persons of great talents and ability among the Directors had not stepped forward to devise means by which, if not to eradicate, at least to stop the further progress of corruption and to prevent the total ruin of the Company."

There is this further point. The abuses in British India were given the widest publicity in England through the eloquence of one of her greatest orators, Edmund Burke, which so thoroughly aroused public opinion that there was an immediate and most salutary effect on British administration. In Holland, however, the revelations of the commissioners received no equivalent publicity and, possibly as a result, had no such early and happy effect. Certainly other circumstances proved adverse to reform, but it does seem as if committees and paper planning were thought to be a substitute for action, whereas agreement on a few simple principles, and the appointment of sufficient officials of experience and integrity to reorganize the details of the administration to accord with these, might well have been more speedily effective.

The story of the various plans adopted, and for one reason or another never implemented, has been told elsewhere—for example, in Mr J. S. Furnivall's book, *Netherlands India*. There is need to refer here only to such part of this halting urge to reform as directly concerns Java—and Raffles.

Mention must be made of Dirk van Hogendorp. He was born in 1761. On joining the Dutch army he was posted to Java. From there he transferred to India and in 1786 he was second in charge of the Dutch trading station at Patna, where he lived the extravagant life of a wealthy nabob so familiar to the readers of the memoirs of his friend William Hickey. He spent money recklessly and gambled without hesitation or skill, losing on one occasion 32,000 rupees at one sitting. But debts never troubled him; he simply handed over worthless IOUs or tendered drafts on Europe that were never honoured. When he returned to Java in 1789 he continued to live far beyond his means and equally without any thought as to how he would ultimately meet his creditors.

Yet, though in his style of living he resembled the silly young man of fashion so typical of the period, he had an entirely different side to his character. In *The Mandarin at Chinsurah*, Professor C. R. Boxer well describes him as "an interesting, active and intelligent, if vain and unstable character". Under the influence of the Abbé Raynal's famous book,[1] van Hogendorp interested himself in the land-settlement scheme, recently introduced in Bengal, under which the cultivator of land was taxed on the basis of its productivity. On his return to Java his interest in land administration remained unimpaired and he set to work to study the contrasting systems of Bengal and Java. In Java he found a very different system from that adopted in British India. Government monopoly was the rule, the cultivator paying for his land a rent arbitrarily fixed by the Regent and receiving prices for his crops arbitrarily fixed by the government. To a student of the Abbé Raynal, this seemed very wrong, but van Hogendorp prudently kept his ideas to himself till news reached Java of the revolution at home. Hearing that liberal principles were now being openly enunciated in Holland, he was encouraged to prepare a report, which it was his intention to dispatch to the authorities in Brussels. The local authorities, however, got to hear of it first and he was promptly put in prison.

He managed to escape and leave Java. As soon as he arrived home, he

[1] *A Philosophical and Political History of the Settlements and Trade of the Europeans in the East and West Indies*, originally published in Brussels in 1770.

completed his report,[1] which is usually known by the brief title, the *Bericht*. This was published at Delft in December 1799, and immediately reprinted in the following month. It is significant that a quotation from the Abbé Raynal appears on the title page.

The publication of the *Bericht* caused a great sensation and scandal in Holland, and not less so in Java when copies reached there. Inspired by the Abbé, who in turn, one may suppose, had been influenced by Adam Smith, van Hogendorp boldly asserts at the outset of the *Bericht* that there is, in economics, no difference between the East and the West. Self-interest "is the only motive which can spur men to industry", and in Java forced labour had deprived the Javanese of this incentive. Forced labour must, therefore, cease, and in its place the cultivator must be given a direct personal interest in his land. This could only be done by abolishing the control of the Regents and handing over the land to the cultivator, who should pay rent for it, not with cash, but with an assessed percentage of the crops produced.

This, for Java, was a very revolutionary doctrine, for it cut at the very roots of the whole system of Dutch commercial policy and practice. The *Bericht* touched on many other matters in which van Hogendorp considered reform was also necessary. Land policy, for example, was to be completely remodelled. While the rice lands were to be reserved for the Javanese, who were also to be encouraged to plant coffee and pepper on dry lands and receive fair prices for their crops, Europeans were to be allowed to purchase or lease waste lands and pay for them either in cash or produce. Chinese were to be allowed to lease lands, but no estates were to be farmed out to them for exploitation. All land was to be surveyed, classified and registered, and a service of forest officers introduced. No forced labour would be permitted. A capitation tax in cash or kind would be introduced, and labour paid a fair wage. Trade would be thrown open to all Dutchmen and, under certain restrictions, to other Europeans, with the exception of the spice trade and the trade with China. Regular postal services would be introduced, and a paid regular army substituted for native levies.

To a modern view there may be nothing very startling in all this, but to the Dutchmen of the day the proposals were revolutionary. Their adoption would have signalized a complete reorientation of colonial policy. The problems of the East Indies had so far been studied solely from a commercial angle, whether the best trading results were produced by exploitation of the government, the Company or by private individuals. For the first time the question was asked: What sort of *government* should be devised?

[1] *Bericht van den Tegenwoordigen Toestand der Bataafsche Bezittingen in Oost-Indië* ("Report on the Present State of the Batavian Possessions in the East Indies").

Meanwhile, the entry in 1795 of Holland into the war on the side of France had exposed Dutch colonies to British sea-power, and in that year Malacca, the Cape of Good Hope and a considerable part of Ceylon had been captured. William Pitt had also authorized the Supreme Government of India to capture Java. There is in existence in the India Office Library a series of reports by the Resident of Fort Marlborough, Bencoolen, as to the possibility of an attack on Java by forces based on Bencoolen and Penang.

Nothing came of this. The Indian government was far too preoccupied with its own wars to consider such a risky venture to a distant place of which so little was known. Napoleon's Eastern projects had also been halted, for the time being, by the Battle of the Nile in 1798.

When in 1801 yet another committee was set up in Holland, this time under Nederburgh, van Hogendorp was appointed a member. They were still deliberating on the question of the Dutch colonies when the short-lived Treaty of Amiens was signed in March 1802. By this, the Cape of Good Hope was restored to the Dutch, Ceylon remaining British. Malacca was also to have been restored, but the renewal of hostilities in the following year prevented this.

In August 1802 Nederburgh's committee presented its report. From the point of view of colonial policy, perhaps the most important conclusion was the reaffirmation that "the Colonies exist for the Mother Country and not the Mother Country for the Colonies", though this was not to be interpreted as allowing any actual injustice to the colony. Adam Smith had in England promulgated exactly opposite views. The report further recorded that the position of Holland and Java was not parallel with that of England and India; that Indian practice would not suit Java. The committee recommended that the transition to Free Trade must be slow and cautious. (Adam Smith would have agreed with this.) The habits of the Javanese were such as to make impossible a free use of the soil and what the soil could produce. Unpredictable results might follow from any such violent change. If the power of the Regents were undermined, the people would receive privileges that they would neither desire nor know how to use. The Javanese were by nature lazy, and the volume of production would drop sharply. Turning to European or Asiatic exploitation, private monopolies were dangerous and open to serious abuse (and with that both Adam Smith and the Abbé Raynal would have agreed). Capital investment and leases to Chinese were not favoured. The cost of administration would rise and a deficit would result. (This was one of the commonest arguments of that period.) While forced labour must continue, such improvement as could be introduced should be introduced (a sop to the liberal-minded). The function of the government was not to govern directly, but to supervise the Regents, who should continue to discharge that responsibility. The Dutch authority was to be of a paternal nature.

Van Hogendorp signed this report, and in doing so, for reasons which no doubt he considered adequate, surrendered some of his leading principles.

Some modern historians have regarded the report as the most important document on colonial policy, considering the times, that had so far been produced. This seems rather high praise. But whatever merits it had, its recommendations were not implemented. Fate intervened in the person of Napoleon.

During the short peace that followed the Treaty of Amiens, the First Consul did not lose interest in the Far East. He sent an efficient soldier, General Charles Decaen, to India with instructions to reinforce the garrisons of Pondicherry, Chandernagore, Mauritius (then Île de France) and Réunion (then Bourbon). The resumption of war with England in May 1803 did not lead to any hostilities outside Europe until the Cape of Good Hope was recaptured in January 1806, when the Dutch surrender was signed by the Governor, General Jan Willem Janssens. In the same year Napoleon placed his brother, Louis Bonaparte, on the throne of Holland.

Van Hogendorp lost no time in addressing a memorial to the new king, explaining the type of governor that Java so urgently needed. It required little imagination to grasp that the ideal man for this important post, an experienced colonial official, was no other than Dirk van Hogendorp. Unluckily Napoleon, with whom the choice rested, had no interest at all in liberal principles or the education and emancipation of native races anywhere, certainly not in the remote Far East. He had, however, a very keen and active interest in the military conquest of the East; the activities of the British Navy had exposed only too clearly the risk he ran of losing the valuable base for offensive operations that Java could offer. It was, therefore, a soldier he wanted, not a disciple of the Abbé Raynal.

The choice fell on Marshal Herman Willem Daendels. One of the leaders in the abortive rising against the House of Orange in 1787, he had fled from Holland and had returned there with the invading French army in 1795. Two years later he had been in command of 30,000 Dutchmen waiting in the Texel for the invasion of England, which had been frustrated by the naval battle off Camperdown. In 1799 he had narrowly escaped being taken prisoner in the Helder campaign.

Here was the active leader, with the necessary Dutch background, for whom Napoleon was looking, and so the "Thundering Marshal", as he was to be called in Java, was appointed to the governor-generalship of the island, where he arrived in January 1808.

His instructions were primarily military, but in the light of the endless committees and the general agreement that for financial if for not more lofty reasons some reforms at least were urgently necessary if the island was not to continue to be a grave liability instead of an asset, he was given some instructions in that direction also. He was to put a stop to the abuses that had grown up under the Company; the lot of the common man was to be ameliorated by protection against arbitrary treatment; the merit of the reforms advocated by Nederburgh's committee was to be reported upon, though no action was to be taken to implement them without reference home. But for his military objectives he had secret dictatorial powers.

He took with him as a member of his staff, Herman Warner Muntinghe. As Muntinghe was to occupy an important position during the British régime in Java, some account of his history is necessary. He was born in 1773 at Amsterdam and was educated partly in England. He first went out to Java in 1804 as Advocate Fiscal to the Asiatic Council. When he returned home, he came under considerable French influence. He was in sympathy with the ideas formulated by his friend, van Hogendorp.

Daendels could have had no illusions as to the reality of the British blockade of Java, for he narrowly missed capture on his way there. Yet when he came to formulate his economic policy he failed to appreciate that, except for neutral (American) ships, Java was effectually isolated from world trade. In his military policy also he seemed to forget the implications of the command of the sea.

The general situation revealed on his first arrival was even worse than he had been warned to expect. Siberg, who had been in control from 1801 to 1804, had been one of the worst governors who ever ruled Java. Lazy, incompetent and dishonest, he had made no attempt to control the abuses that were rampant, his sole preoccupation having been to fill his own pockets as rapidly and generously as possible. Lesser functionaries had followed his example to the fullest extent of their more restricted opportunities. Wiese, who had succeeded him, had effected little improvement.

The principal duty of the new Governor-General was to reorganize the defences of the island. He set to work accordingly. He replaced the native levies by a properly constituted army, recruited mainly—and forcibly—from outside Java. Though reorganization was a necessary step, it could not for some time be more than a paper reform. Conscripted native regiments and European troops of poor quality, the earlier ones thoroughly debauched and the later ones chiefly those whom it was undesirable to keep at home, could not be transformed by any stroke of the pen into an immediately effective fighting force. It was, however, a first step.

Daendels also embarked on two immense military projects: a grand trunk road through the island, from Bantam in the west to Pasuruan[1] in the east, and a series of forts in Bantam. Both these entailed heavy loss of life among the unfortunate natives requisitioned for the purpose; the road, which was some eight hundred miles in length when completed, was estimated to have cost over ten thousand lives.

Though the trunk road was later to prove very important for the economic development of Java, its immediate value for defence was questionable. Given a highly trained and mobile striking force, it might well have afforded a very desirable flexibility to Daendel's defences, but no such troops were at his disposal, nor had he in prospect either the necessary instructors, equipment or even the time to train his raw levies before the English invasion came, if it came at all.

The forts in Bantam had even less to commend them. The idea apparently was that these should act as defended bases for a powerful naval squadron. Apart from the fact that their construction involved Daendels in a local revolt of some magnitude, he must have known that the prospect of such a squadron being fitted out at home simply did not exist. Had, indeed, there been such a possibility, the chance of the squadron's escaping the British blockade in Europe or surviving in the East thereafter was equally slender.

Lastly, he built the fortified camp at Meester Cornelis, which was to prove a death-trap.

Whatever view expert opinion may take of his military plans, there can be little disagreement that in these, as in some of his political measures, he displayed a failure to grasp essentials, which suggests that violence and passion were allowed, at least at times, to dictate a policy that prudence and common sense would have rejected. For instance, the loss of life caused by his defence works, while it frightened the natives outwardly into abject servility, created such a degree of hatred and hostility, however veiled, as to jeopardize the security of his communications should his army at any time be involved in actual hostilities with the English. This was an unwarrantable risk. But not content with this, he went out of his way to alienate the Javanese princes.

Hitherto these had, as Regents, retained most of their princely prerogatives though little actual power. Daendels now converted them into civil servants, compelling them not only to accept the orders of their Dutch Residents "without the slightest variations", but also to give precedence to those Residents on all public occasions. Whether he realized what an insult this was to the pride of the Regents, and how greatly such a lowering of their prestige would anger both them and their subjects, is not clear. Even if he did realize it, he would not have cared. The Thundering Marshal was that type of man.

[1] From *Pesirehan*: "Place of the Betel Pepper".

Colonel Huibert Gerard Nahuijs (or Nahuys), Resident at the court of Surakarta and no lover of the new Governor-General, tells in his reminiscences of the treatment meted out to the brother of the Sultan of Mataram and his (the brother's) young son.

"Whereas these princes were placed in the stocks, like criminals of the lowest order, in a miserable dungeon of Fort Cheribon, as I can truly testify, having seen them in prison."

According to Colonel Nahuijs, Daendels wrote to the Dutch Resident at Cheribon:

"The Government cannot openly condemn them to death, but desires to hear of their being put out of the way."

Colonel Nahuijs tells us, too, about Colonel Filty, the commandant at Amboina when the Moluccas were surrendered to the British.

"Although aware of the dreadful fate that threatened him at Batavia, nothing could induce this honourable man to seek safety in flight. 'I have been weak,' said he, 'but my flight would prove me a cowardly traitor.'"

By the order of Daendels, Colonel Filty was court-martialled and shot.

Daendels administrative reforms were, in many instances, soundly conceived. The island was, for the first time, intelligently divided into prefectures, which in turn were subdivided into regencies. All officials were given military rank and suitable salaries. The office of director-general of trade was abolished. Instead, a head administrator of finance, with four assistants, was appointed, and a chamber of accounts established. Feudal levies were abolished and, though forced services were permissible, labour had (in theory) to receive a proper wage. Postal services were introduced and the residential quarter of the capital was moved back to the healthier district of Weltevreden.

In the judicial sphere, reform was certainly much overdue. Additional courts were set up in Surabaya and Samarang, a court of circuit instituted, and in each prefecture native courts were instituted by means of a bench of Regents with the Prefect as chairman. In principle, these were sound measures, but it seems doubtful whether reform was completed in any major degree.

On the economic side, the Forest Service was overhauled, the alienation of villages to Chinese stopped, and some attempt made to recover those alienated. Daendels went so far as to consider the introduction of a land tax on a basis of one-fifth of the gross produce, but eventually he decided that, until the people had advanced farther along the road of civilization, this substitute for forced labour was not practicable. Here he was supporting the views of the Nederburgh committee rather than those of van Hogendorp.

He intensified the production of coffee on the hills and cotton in the valleys, though he ordered that labour must be paid. What he expected to gain from this is not clear. The British blockade, in spite of its obvious effects on the life of the island, did not seem to cause him to see things in their true perspective. The chance of converting coffee into cash was at best not very good. American tonnage was the one and only hope, and he took such ill-judged steps as, for example, repudiating contracts properly made in Europe, requisitioning American ships for his own purposes and losing them to English frigates, that this sole means of export was soon denied him.

iii

Castlereagh, when Secretary of State for War and the Colonies in 1805, had given definite instructions to the Indian government that no expedition to Java was to be undertaken, and, though the Whig government of 1806 had taken a more favourable view, the return of Castlereagh to power in 1807 could only be interpreted to reaffirm his previous veto. Daendel's military prestige and his activities in Java, of which the Indian government must have been aware, put rather a different complexion on affairs.

Although Minto had been expressly selected as a moderate man, untainted with military or imperialistic ambitions, he was no fool. On his first arrival in India, the Company's finances had been too strained for any external operations to be thought of, yet he was by no means ignorant of the designs of Napoleon towards India, or of the havoc created among British shipping in the Indian Ocean by French naval forces based on Réunion and Mauritius. In his own mind he planned, as soon as finances would permit, the destruction of the French maritime power in the East by the capture of those two islands, followed by the final and even more ambitious attempt to seize Java.

By March 1810 Minto felt financially strong enough to put his plans into operation, and wrote to inform London of his intentions. Before his letter arrived in London, instructions were sent (13th June) for him to occupy Réunion and Mauritius. By the time these reached Calcutta, Réunion had surrendered on 8th July after a token resistance, and an expedition had been dispatched to Mauritius, where, at the expense of Réunion, Decaen had concentrated all his forces.

Calcutta, when Raffles came there from Penang, was thus in the throes of excitement about these two expeditions. So far there were no official instructions about Java, but Minto was fully determined to continue his policy of anticipating orders from home. But the capture of Java, however desirable, was not a task to be lightly undertaken. Except for John Leyden, whose knowledge was academic, and R. T. Farquhar,[1]

[1] Robert Farquhar had had unusual experience, as Civil Commissioner of the Spice Islands (Moluccas) in 1793, and later at Balambangan ("Place of Palm-planks") in Borneo. He spoke Dutch fluently.

then governor designate of Mauritius, few in India could give reliable information about Java. No wonder, then, that the arrival of Raffles was warmly welcomed. Nor had he come empty-handed. He had brought a memorandum proposing the annexation of Java, and purporting to show that the task was not so formidable as some might think.

". . . The power of the Dutch on the Island of Java, even in their most prosperous times, was much inferior to what it might have been considered in reference to the apparent authority exercised by that Nation in the Eastern Seas—a careful and jealous policy, successful for the time, having supplied the place of actual force. So far from possessing the entire Sovereignty of this extensive Island, they can only be said to this day to have unconditionally subdued the least considerable of the four principal Kingdoms into which they found it divided. The small Kingdom of Jakatra, extending from Cheribon to Bantam and in which the City of Batavia, so long the admiration and dread of the Eastern States, is situated, alone acknowledges the Sovereignty of the European Arms. . . .

"When Daendels arrived, the Native Powers had almost shaken off Dutch authority and there was fighting with the Rajahs of Cheribon, Mataram and Bantam. From the energy, however, of his measures and the wisdom of his policy, the Governor-General was enabled again to reduce them within the stated bounds, and once more to establish the Dutch authority on a footing which if not timely checked bids fair to be more permanent than ever.

"With regard to the Dutch themselves, they had so far degenerated from that enterprising Character necessary to keep such powerful neighbours in awe, that the Marshal found still greater difficulty in restoring them to some degree of activity and reforming the degrading abuses and Corruptions that had crept into every department of the State. He is supposed to have strengthened his military force by a corps of slaves from Bali and other Eastern States and, it is said, by Criminals from the public gaols. His greatest difficulty is the total want of European officers . . . and serious consequences would arise if no officers should arrive from Europe.

"That the attention of the French Government has been particularly directed to Java, and the Malay States from the time of their losing all hopes of establishing a solid footing on the Continent of Hindostan, may be inferred from a variety of circumstances, one of which is the cultivation of the Malay Language in Paris under the celebrated Professor Langlis.

"It is proposed to transfer the capital from the unhealthy Batavia to Samarang: the opposition of property owners of Batavia has delayed this step, but it is almost certain it has not been abandoned. Meanwhile a new military road is being built and communications with the chain of forts along the northern coast has been improved tenfold. But at the same time that so great an improvement has been lately made in their military resources, the Dutch can only be considered to hold possession on a very slight tenure. . . ."

After referring to the resentment of both Javanese and Dutch inhabitants at the measures taken by Marshal Daendels, and the tyrannous extension of the Dutch East India Company's monopoly of rice, "by which each Individual is literally rendered personally dependent on the Government for his immediate subsistence", he continued:

"It is a matter of surprise and certainly of regret, when the horrid Massacres that in so many instances have dyed those Seas with the blood of our Countrymen are recollected, that no measures have ever been adopted to convey to the minds of the different chieftains to the Eastward those mild principles of policy by which the British Government is so peculiarly distinguished from the other European Powers with whom they have had connexion, and that their knowledge of the English has been confined almost exclusively to the Reports of Noquedahs [*nakhoda*, master of a native vessel] frequenting our ports, and the notions received from the Commanders of trading Vessels, who however respectable their line cannot be considered the best qualified to represent the British Nation in its general Character.

"The necessity of establishing a proper understanding with the Malay Rajahs was seen by Mr [Robert] Farquhar, when Lieutenant-Governor of Prince of Wales's Island, who suggested the idea of Commercial Treaties being entered into with the most powerful . . . had this plan been carried into effect . . . we should not perhaps have now had to lament that unfortunate want of faith in our actions and general indifference which in a great measure paved the way for the open rupture that attended the enforcement of the Blockade.

"The immediate adoption of Mr Farquhar's plan would now have been peculiarly expedient with a view to the restoration of that confidence. The resources of Java are extensive. It is the rice granary of the East, supplying all the Dutch possessions without any prohibition of export elsewhere. If the Island was freed from restriction, it could more than cover its expenditure. Coffee, pepper, cotton, tobacco and indigo, &c can be cultivated with such success that every other Settlement in that quarter of the globe could be undersold. Its timber resources alone would render its possession an object of the greatest importance. For example, teak might be supplied from Samarang and the eastern shores for shipbuilding at a much lower rate than from Burma and so could crooked timbers, especially Caya Merbou[1] for the frames of the largest class of ships. . . ."

The surviving copy of this memorandum, which is in the India Office Library, is incomplete, and the extracts quoted above are not the whole

[1] *Kayu Mĕrbau*, of the Afzelia species.

content of the manuscript that remains to us. Yet Raffles' line of argument is clear.

On the evidence of the paragraphs quoted on page 89, some writers have condemned Raffles for claiming that it was he who put the capture of Java into Minto's mind. It is to be noted, however, that Raffles, who was not slipshod in his choice of words, referred to "annexation", not to "capture". As will emerge later in these pages, it was not until plans were well advanced that Minto decided on annexation and occupation for the good of the native inhabitants, rather than the precise carrying out of his instructions from London "to subdue the Dutch Government, to destroy the fortifications, to distribute the ordnance, arms and military stores amongst the native chiefs and inhabitants, and then to retire from the country".

Criticism has also been directed against Lady Raffles for stating in the *Memoir* (with the same alleged object in view) that her husband "communicated to Lord Minto information of so important a nature that his Lordship was induced to undertake without delay the reduction of Java". The significant words here are "without delay". The capture of such a large island as Java at such distance from India was a very formidable undertaking, and to have attempted it without adequate information would have been extremely hazardous. Clearly, Minto was determined on the operation before Raffles submitted his memorandum, yet it was the arrival of Raffles with authentic information and the means to supplement it to the maximum degree that alone enabled Minto to proceed with his project "without delay".

Naturally anxious not to return to the drab monotony of the Penang secretariat, Raffles could not afford to lose the initiative. On 11th July he wrote to Lord Minto:

"As it becomes necessary for me to make almost immediate preparations for returning to Penang, I am compelled to intrude on your Lordship more early than I should otherwise have desired by requesting permission to tender my services in the fullest extent for carrying into effect any arrangements which your Lordship may have in contemplation as regard to the Malay countries. . . ."

His suggestion was that he should act as *avant-courier*, with Malacca as his first objective.

". . . if therefore your Lordship should be pleased to authorize my proceeding thither with powers to communicate with the Malay States, I think I could venture to promise the most complete success in detaching at once the Sultan of Palembang from the Dutch and in obtaining possession of the person of the King of Bantam. At the same time that this point was carried into effect, a communication could with facility be opened with the great native powers of Java in order to ascertain fully how far they might be disposed to receive English Agents to co-operate in the common object, the reduction of the Dutch power in Java. This I am aware might be obtained without attracting the particular attention of the Dutch by my being directed ostensibly to proceed to Malacca with the purpose of explaining to the Maharaja of Linga and the other Eastern States the principles of Maritime Law on which the Blockading System which has excited such general dissatisfaction has been established . . . if at the same time my assistance can be of any utility in carrying into effect any further arrangement your Lordship may propose with regard to Acheen, that object may with facility and without immediate delay be obtained by touching at Acheen on the passage to Malacca or Penang as may be most advisable . . . the objects in view may be obtained without either incurring expense to the Company or producing inconvenience or mismanagement by my very temporary absence from my official Station."

Minto agreed. Here was the instrument to carry out his plans for Java, for no one else combined such energy and ability with such an extensive knowledge of the Eastern Archipelago. Robert Farquhar had, as Lieutenant-Governor of Penang, held the appointment of Agent to the Governor-General with the Malay States, and it was this title that Minto now proposed, subject to the consent of the Penang government, to bestow on Raffles. But whereas the appointment in the case of Farquhar merely gave the Lieutenant-Governor the necessary status to correspond with the Supreme Government on matters otherwise outside the scope of his government, it was to confer on Raffles extensive functions and wide responsibilities; on the volume and accuracy of the information he would collect and furnish, the success or failure of the expedition would largely depend. No greater compliment was ever paid to Raffles. Never did Minto make a better choice.

From then on the letters from Raffles to Minto disclose an ever-increasing range of advice. Raffles did not take his duties lightly. He wrote on 9th August:

"Enclosed I have the Honour to submit for your Lordship's consideration the result of my enquiries respecting the best season for operations against Java, accompanied by some general ideas relating to the mode of attack, on the principles suggested by your Lordship. As it is evident that no direct commencement of operations can be undertaken with advantage until the month of January, I am again induced to solicit your Lordship's particular attention to the propriety of treating in the meantime with the Native Powers, a policy rendered still more urgent from the official information contained in Mr Parry's [the Resident's] letter from Bencoolen, as your Lordship will at once see the connexion between Lampoon [Lampong, Sumatra], Bantam and Palembang. The advantages to be derived from an early communication with the latter, as suggested in the Paper I had the Honour to submit, becomes more particularly evident from the establishment which appears to have been formed by the people of the Western part of Java and the political importance which Marshal Daendels seems to have attached to their operations. Your Lordship is already aware of the ancient and intimate friendship subsisting between Bantam and Lampoon by the vicinity of the latter to Palembang, which, while it affords the most favourable opportunity, under present circumstances, for negotiations, may enable us successfully to annoy the Enemy in this quarter by throwing in Supplies of Stores to a formidable opponent and at the same time, taking advantage of existing hostilities, effectually to cut off all communication between the Dutch Government and the Island of Sumatra. I formerly stated that in treating with Bali we had the advantage of a friendly Power, the views of which have consistently been adverse to the Dutch interests. This circumstance would secure the cordial reception of an Agent on the Eastern side of Java and most probably the ready co-operation of the Bali Rajahs, which in the commencement of the attack on Java might be of the utmost importance in bringing over to our interests the Rajah of Sourabaya, whose union at this time with the Dutch is to be treated as it may occasion great loss of time. The terms on which the Rajahs of Bali stand with respect to the independent Rajahs of Java, especially the Susuhunan [Emperor], as well as the position of the Island, would in a great degree facilitate our negotiation. . . . I take the liberty of stating for your Lordship's consideration that in the event of my proceeding to Palembang it would be within my power, in carrying into effect your Lordship's views in that quarter, to establish an Agent at Bali, from whence a communication might be opened with the Susuhunan and the other Chiefs and after obtaining the latest and most accurate details of the enemy's force and positions, to return to Bengal in time to proceed from thence with the ultimate Expedition."

During the period of waiting, which was to keep him in Calcutta until the end of October, Raffles made his academic bow by reading before the Asiatic Society his paper *On the Malayu Nation.* When not working with Minto's staff, most of his time was spent with John Leyden, plotting and planning for the Java campaign and, more important still, what was to happen when the island had been captured.

Leyden introduced him into one of the intellectual circles of Calcutta —a circle that included Thomas Manning, the famous orientalist, and Dr Joshua Marshman, the great Baptist missionary. Frequently the four had supper together. Raffles took a great interest in comparative religion. In spite of a naturally religious nature, he was by no means an orthodox Christian, being unable to accept the view that Christianity was the only permissible doctrine. He took a keen interest in, for example, Mohammedanism, expressing the view that it was particularly well suited to Eastern races.

These conversations with three highly intelligent men were of special value to Raffles, who for only a short time had had the advantage of a brain of Leyden's calibre to match against his own. Nothing is more destructive to a clever man than to have no equals, or superiors, on whom to sharpen his wits.

Leyden wrote to Olivia on 22nd August of that year:

MY DEAR SISTER OLIVIA,—And so you had as nearly as possible been lady of Amboina [Moluccas] and then we should have had you writing a tragedy on the Dutch massacre. Never mind that accident, there are many Baratarias[1] between you and Amboina and you know I mean to be king of one of them myself some of these days.

"Well, next with respect to the Gudeman, as we Scotch folks have it, he is looking quite famously and the ladies one and all have done nothing but take him for a bachelor since his star first rose in our quarter of the world. In short he is at least a foot higher than he used to be in consequence of being puffed up by their flattery and it would not be possible for a homely fellow like me to endure it if I had not a conscious satisfaction of being able to rival him in a pair of jaws and grinders that do credit to an Ourang utang. In spite of his teeth I can match him there.

"However I have the pleasure of informing you that he has received the most cordial attentions from Ld. Minto and that it is my opinion everything will tend to the best possible issue—so said Solomon the Wise—now what will Dame Grundy say! As Lord Minto has chosen to detain him till his own time comes, you must not be impatient as he will certainly not budge in my opinion for these six weeks, but if nothing else will satisfy you send me notice by a Courier Dove or something of that sort and depend on it I will be with you in the twinkling of a handsaw to drink five and forty cups of tea and eat a wagonload of pineapples before you can say Jack Robinson, but you must not be frightened as I am not the same person as I was but have been changed like the Man in the Arabian Tales. Don't send my friend Raffles any more letters d'you see, for they make him quite allicholy and like to cry and then he goes dancing and fidgetting about, the dear fellow! (you will say) to my utter discomfiture and in especial to that of my ink horns and standishes.

"Moreover you must not think to escape with impunity the doing such an outlandish thing as send verses to your husband. I protest all Calcutta would be highly scandalized at such an incident; so take care next time to send the verses to me and don't suppose that I insist on their being quite so fine.

[1] Barataria, the island city of which Sancho Panza was made governor and gave up in disgust because it robbed him of his former liberty.—*Don Quixote*.

"Raffles is grievously alarmed about your health and I have great difficulty to keep up his spirits, so recollect if you happen to have sent us any more of that sort of intelligence to have it changed by the road, and don't you be the least alarmed about his health, as I will not suffer or permit him to be unwell here, but the truth is that if it were not for a few recollections relating to your Ladyship he would be a famously gay fellow and beat us all in spirits. There is one thing however which convinces me that he is quite impatient to be with you that I can seldom prevail upon him to talk on any other subject. On second thoughts, which it is said are always best, it appears to me now that Bourbon has fallen he may be with you within a fortnight after the receipt of this if not sooner. I therefore request you to behave pretty and get better as soon as possible. . . ."

Raffles' reunion with his wife was not to be so swift as predicted by Leyden. His appointment was not officially confirmed until 19th October. Following discussions, his instructions were drawn up.

"An application having been made to the Government of Prince of Wales's Island that you may be permitted to proceed to the Eastward for purposes connected with the operations which are in contemplation with regard to the Dutch Possessions on the Island of Java, I have the directions of the Rt. Hon. Governor-General in Council to communicate the following instructions for your direction and guidance. . . ."

H.C.C.[1] *Ariel*, commanded by Lieut. D. Macdonald of the Indian Navy, was placed at his disposal. He was to proceed in her to Penang, then to Malacca and then as far eastward as was necessary to obtain the information he sought. He was to discover the composition of the Franco-Dutch army, as to how far this was European and how far Asian; and if Asian, how far officered by Europeans. He was also to report on the facilities for landing, the nature of the country and the nature and strength of the defences.

"There being reason to believe from every information received, that in consequence of the oppressive conduct of the Dutch Government and the obnoxious restrictions which they have imposed on Industry and Commerce, nearly the whole of the native population of Java are obviously disaffected and would readily co-operate in any plan that may be concerted for the expulsion of the European Enemy, you are directed to avail yourself of every favourable opportunity that may offer for opening a communication with the different native powers on the Island of Java with the view of establishing a general good Understanding with them and ensuring their effectual support and aid in the measures that may hereafter be adopted by the British Government."

He was authorized, if satisfied as to their disaffection, to lead the

[1] Honourable Company's cruiser.

Javanese chiefs to expect English assistance, but he was to enjoin secrecy. It was desirable to ascertain the precise state of relations between the different Javanese states, but in the first instance he was not bound to any set plan. Particular attention was directed to Bali; if circumstances permitted, he was to make a personal visit.

As for Lampong, Sumatra, "should these people have still been able to keep their ground against the Dutch, or even continue in a condition at all capable of recommencing their attack, they may be encouraged in their exertions and so far as prudence may warrant, assisted with Stores".

Among other possibilities was to obtain the person of one of the former kings of Bantam, sent by the Dutch to Palembang in south-east Sumatra, "and to adopt with him such measures as may ensure not only the neutrality or co-operation of the State of Bantam, but facilitate the final establishment in that part of the Island, of a general pacific disposition after the Dutch may have been removed".

He was to make certain that interpreters and guides would be available, and ascertain to what extent provisions and labour could be expected in the different parts of the island at the time of the attack.

"As it will be advisable that the ostensible object of your proceeding Eastward should in some degree be foreign from the immediate point to which your attention is particularly required, his Lordship is pleased to appoint you Agent to the Governor-General in order that you may in that capacity explain to the Bugguese and other Eastern Traders the general and friendly intentions of the English, and satisfy them as well with regard to the obnoxious System of Blockade as to the misunderstanding which gave rise to the apparent hostility of the English in the late unfortunate affair in which several lives were lost."

If it proved possible, he was to proceed to Lingga and Rhio; and give the necessary assurances to the Malay rajas, especially those of Siak, Palembang and Achin.

When all relative information had been obtained, he was to return to Calcutta, leaving Captain William Farquhar or some other qualified person in charge of Malacca, but if circumstances seemed to make it advisable, he was to remain there.

There is little doubt that these instructions were drafted by Raffles himself.

The choice of Malacca for his headquarters was clearly the right one. Intercourse between the Malays of Malacca and those of the Eastern Archipelago was closer and more constant than that of the semi-urbanized Malays of Penang. A more personal reason was that he would have found it impossible to carry out this important and highly confidential mission in the atmosphere of jealousy and suspicion he would have encountered in Penang. He had escaped the life of a drudge there. He had no intention of entering the prison again, unless as Governor.

A glimpse of Raffles in Calcutta is to be found in the *Narrative* of Edward Robarts. On the death of Quintin Dick Thompson, "I hove up my situation and retired to the house of the Hon. T. S. Raffles, Esqre., brother to my lady. . . ." Under pressure from his Tahitian wife, he had moved from Penang to Calcutta at the beginning of 1810, in the hope of getting more lucrative employment there. In this he had been disappointed, being still out of a job when he met Raffles in October.

"One day," he writes, "as I was going thro' Tank Square Sir T. Raffles passed me in a palankeen. He looked at me but as it was raining very hard I did not stop as a great man is easy found when no one knows a poor one. Some few days afterwards I found out whence Sir T. R. lived. When I came to the house the first I saw was a malay boy that was formerly servant to Mr Thompson. On seeing me the Boy ran up stairs to inform Sir T. R. that I was below. He ran half way down stairs to meet me; he received me with that friendly manner as tho' I was his equal. He conducted me to the room where the Immortal Dr Leyden was sitting and introduced me to him; he had made every enquiry for me but could not find me out my being a stranger. . . .

"After some conversation Sir T. R. asked me how I employed my time. I answered looking for employment and writing my Narrative of what I had gone thro' since I had left London. What says he you have turned author, I replied anything to raise the wind for an honest morsel. He laughed. What says Dr L. raise the wind? Yes Sir replied I—I have been lying becalmed these ten months and if a breeze does not spring up my unfortunate Bark will founder on the rocks of Adversity. Well says Dr L. let me see your narrative and then I shall be a better judge of your abilities. Sir T. R. eagerly enquired about my family and wished to see them; a day was appointed. . . .

"The day arrived, we went to Dr Ls. house, some Persian writers being up stairs I waited untill they was gone, we was then sent for and went up stairs. On entering the room Sir T. R. met my wife, our past happy situation at Penang recalld to her mind she burst into tears and leand on his shoulder. He supported her kindly and conducted her to a chair. . . . My wife recovered she eagerly asked about Mrs T. and Mrs R. and in broken accents said I shall see them no more. Sir T. R. was touched at this last expression. Dr L. helpt my wife to a glass of wine, Sir T. R. then said to Dr L. you will do me a personal kindness in helping Robarts to some employment. He held a weighty charge at Penang, you may trust him with gold untold. Well replied Dr L. I will see what I can do for him. Dr L. then desired me to come every day to write my narrative. A room was appointed for me to write in. Sir T. R. being come on

Publick duty he was mostly at Government house. He desired me to see him before his departure but the pressure of his duty debarred me that happiness. . . ."

In a letter dated 22nd October 1810 Leyden wrote to Olivia:

"I take the opportunity of sending you a few lines by R. just as he is going off, therefore you are not to expect a letter. But it is impossible not to congratulate you upon his success here which I regard as in every respect compleat. If he succeeds in his present objects he will have a much finer game to play than he has hitherto had, and one to which Amboina is not in the least to be compared. What will Dame Grundy say to that! I think you will have a fine time of it if you listen either to speculation or speakulation. I have to conjure you now to take care to throw no obstacles in R.'s way as I see every moment of the next six or ten months must be precious to him. I am anxious that he should finish the Imdang-Imdang[1] or Malay Laws as fast as possible for the weight that this would give him in the settling of Java, but I am almost afraid to press it as his Public Reports are so very necessary in the first instance.

"I had some hopes and a great deal of desire to have joined in the expedition, and indeed when R. first arrived my health seemed absolutely to require the sea voyage, but I have now contrived to get closer tied by the leg than ever and verily there is very little hope of seeing me again in the eastern world unless something very curious occurs. . . .

"I am writing amid a perfect combustion of persons calling on R. and the jingling of knives, forks etcetera just as tiffing is going on the table you are not to expect any very lucid observations."

After a final request for copies of Burmese, Malay and Siamese vocabularies, and for the services of one John Scott, Raffles embarked in the *Ariel* in the fourth week of October. The brig arrived at Penang on 17th November.

[1] *Undang-undang.*

Chapter Seven

MALACCA, 1810–1811

THERE had been changes at Penang, and new arrivals. The Hon. Charles Andrew Bruce, a brother of Lord Elgin, had recently taken over as Governor. Two more of Raffles' sisters, Harriet and Leonora, had arrived from England, and Leonora had since married a widower, John Billington Loftie, a surgeon on the Madras establishment.

Olivia, Harriet, Leonora, Mary Anne and her three children were to go with Raffles to Malacca, so there was much packing and other preparations to be done in a short time, for they were due to leave at the beginning of December.

As an indication that this was really good-bye to Penang, this advertisement appeared:

> To be sold by auction by A. B. Bone on the premises on Saturday, 26th instant at 5 o'clock p.m. precisely (if not previously disposed of by private contract) that valuable and very eligible Estate on the North Beach, with a most excellent brick built dwelling house and offices erected thereon . . . and known by the name of "Runnymede".

Apart from the written instructions given to Raffles, the *Ariel* had brought a private and secret letter on the same matter to Governor Bruce. Raffles was thereby authorized to indent for supplies on the various departments and also to expend public money. As his mission was of a confidential nature, this authority could not be recorded in the consultations, but a limited explanation was given privately to the Council by the Governor. The Council took grave exception to this. That its late secretary should be given such obscure authority was hard to stomach.

Raffles wrote to Calcutta on 25th November:

"The mischievous effects of the attacks made this season on the Bugguese and other Prows by His Majesty's ships must far exceed that of the former unfortunate affair with the 'Piedmontaise'; independent of these occurrences two unsuccessful attacks have been meditated and in part proceeded on under the authority of the Admiral against Palembang—the consequence has been that the Sultan, whose people have materially suffered, has in conjunction with the Dutch made an attack on Lingen [Lingga] . . . the mode in which several Bali people have been plundered and disturbed by the British cruisers will also, I fear, materially prejudice our operations in that quarter. Fortunately, however, and certainly most opportunely I found on my arrival here that Orders had reached India from the Admiralty directing the blockade of Java and Moluccas to be taken off—this will enable me to assume a decided pacific character towards the Eastern states and effectually cover more political measures. . . . The Season does not admit of the Bugguese Prows taking advantage of the circumstances until June or July next, but it is of the utmost importance that they should carry back to their Country the most favourable impressions that it may be in my power to make on them. . . ."

Continuing, he stated that Mr Bruce had placed a small cutter at his disposal. He also requested that some arms be sent to Malacca.

Two days later he wrote that he had induced a local shipbuilder to take a new vessel to Calcutta. "I have little doubt that there will be a scarcity of tonnage in Bengal if transports are required." His practical mind was always busy with such details as this.

The party sailed from Penang in the *Ariel*, which brought them to Malacca on 4th December.

Raffles took up his quarters in the Bandar Hilir area and set about collecting a Malay staff to transcribe letters to chiefs, translate documents, and generally to act as his Malay Intelligence section. The chief translator was Lebai Isma'il, whose elder brother had acted in a similar capacity at Bencoolen for William Marsden. This brother had a young son named 'Abdullah, who was added to the staff. Many years later, when he was an old man resident in Singapore, 'Abdullah was persuaded to dictate his reminiscences. The greater part of these were translated by the Rev. R. G. Shellabear (*Autobiography of Munshi Abdullah*) and J. T. Thomson (*Translations from Hikayat Abdulla*). The old man's memory was not at all reliable on dates and facts, and as an accurate account of exact happenings his autobiography is quite untrustworthy—in many important respects demonstrably wrong. Notwithstanding this, his portraits are so vivid and his character-drawing so clear that they can be regarded without question as authentic. Here is a description of William Farquhar, the Resident; it comes from Thomson's *Hikayat Abdulla*:

"Now, Colonel Farquhar was a man of good parts, slow at fault-finding, having an equal bearing to poor as well as to rich, holding neither the one lower nor the other higher. If persons, however poor or mean, should come before him to lay a complaint, they had immediate access and the whole plaint was listened to, and he gave advice and counsel till he had appeased them. Thus they returned rejoicing. And if he went out walking, driving or riding, the poor people and others would salute him, on which occasions he would always return the same. He was an open hand to all God's slaves."

Here is Raffles:

"And when I first saw Mr Raffles, he struck me as being of middle stature, neither too short nor too tall. His brow was broad, the sign of large heartedness; his head betokened his good understanding; his hair being fair betokened courage; his ears being large betokened quick hearing: his eyebrows were thick, and his left eye squinted a little; his nose was high; his cheeks a little hollow; his lips narrow, the sign of oratory and persuasiveness; his mouth was wide; his neck was long, and the colour of his body was not purely white; his breast was well-formed; his waist slender; his legs to proportion and he walked with a stoop. . . .

"Now, I observed his habit was to be always in deep thought. He was most courteous in his intercourse with all men. He always had a sweet expression towards Europeans as well as native gentlemen. He was extremely affable and liberal, always commanding one's best attention. He spoke in smiles. He also was an earnest enquirer into past history and gave up nothing till he had probed it to the bottom. He loved most to sit in quietude, when he did nothing else but write or read; and it was his usage, when he was either studying or speaking, that he would see no one till he had finished. He had a time set apart for each duty, nor would he mingle one with another. Further, in the evenings, after tea, he would take ink, pen and paper, after the candles had been lighted, reclining with closed eyes in a manner that I often took to be sleep; but in an instant he would be up and write for awhile till he went to recline again. Thus he would pass the night, till twelve or one, before he retired to sleep. This was his daily practice. On the next morning he would go to what he had written and read it while walking backwards and forwards, when, out of ten sheets, probably he would only give three or four to his copying clerk to enter into the books, and the others he would tear up. Such was his daily habit. . . .

"He kept four persons on wages, each in their peculiar departments; one to go to the forests in search of various kinds of leaves, flowers, fungi, pulp and such like products. Another he sent to collect all kinds of flies, grasshoppers, bees in all their varieties, as well as scorpions, centipedes and such like, giving him needles as well as pins with a box to stick the creatures therein. Another he sent with a basket to seek for coral, shells, oysters, mussels, cockles and such like; also fishes of various species; and another to collect animals, such as birds, jungle fowl, deer, stags, mouse-deers and so forth. Then he had a large book with thick paper, whose use was for the keeping of the leaves and flowers. And when he could not put them there, he had a Chinese Macao painter, who was good at painting fruit and flowers to the life, these he set him to copy. Again, he kept a barrel full of arrack, or brandy, and when he had got snakes, scorpions, centipedes, or such like, he would put them into it till they were dead, before putting them in bottles. This occupation astonished the people of Malacca and many people profited from going to search for the living creatures that exist in the sky and the earth, sea or land, town or country; whether they flew or crawled, whether they sprouted or grew out of the earth, it was as above related. Further, people brought books of Malayan history to the number of many hundreds, so as to nearly finish the national literature. They brought them from all parts, owing to the good price given. Thus were sold two or three hundred books, also divers poems, pantuns and such like. At that time the histories stored up in Malacca were nearly exhausted, being sold by the people, and what were only to be borrowed, these he had copied.

"Thus daily people brought various kinds of animals and moths which are seldom seen by men, such as Javanese butterflies. Then came presents from the Rajah of Samba [Sambas, Borneo] in the shape of a *mawas*—which white men call orang outang[1]—a young tiger, birds and other kinds of brutes from various countries. So he put trowsers on the *mawas*, with coat and hat complete, which made it as like a little man as possible, and he let it go, when it soon became apparent that its habits were those of mankind; the only fault being that it could not speak. And when I was engaged writing, it would come so softly up to the table that you would not perceive its footsteps, just like apes and monkeys; then it would slowly take the pen up to its neck and when I told the animal to put the pen down, down it would put it. The belly of the *mawas* was large, but when the animal was sitting it puckered up like that of a sick person. So I asked of it, what ails you? when it held its stomach, as if it understood my language; but this by instinct only. There were a pair, male and female, but after they had been in Malacca for four or five months, the female died. After this the male had all the appearance of a man in sorrow; it left off its food and in a few days also died; and I was much touched at this, seeing that even brutes had such affection as between the sexes, and especially should we men take an example by this. Afterwards he had a great many beasts and birds, each with their cages. . . .

"Now, Mr Raffles took great interest in looking into the origin of nations, and their manners and customs of olden times, examining what would elucidate the same. He was especially quick in the uptake of Malay with its variations. He delighted to use the proper idioms as the natives do; he was active in studying words and their place in phrases and not until we had told him would he state that the English had another mode. It was his daily labour to order post letters to the various Malay countries to support their good understanding with his nation, and increase the bond of friendship—this with presents and agreeable words. This gained the goodwill of the various Rajahs, who returned the compliment with

[1] Man of the woods, used by the Malays in the sense of " wild man" or "savage". The ape is *mawas* to them, not *orang outang*.

respect and thanks, and moreover with presents. There also came a great many presents of books from various countries.

"Now, Mr Raffles' disposition was anything but covetous, for, in whatever undertakings or projects he had in view, he grudged no expense so that they were accomplished. Thus his intentions had rapid consummation. There were numbers of people always watching about his house, ready to seek for whatever he wanted, to sell to him or take orders; so that they might obtain profit. Thus loads of money came out of his chest daily, in buying various things, or in paying wages. I also perceived that he hated the habit of the Dutch who lived in Malacca of running down the Malays and they detested him in return; so much so that they would not sit down beside him. But Mr Raffles loved always to be on good terms with the Malays, the poorest could speak to him; and while all the great folk in Malacca came to wait on him daily, whether Malays or Europeans, yet they could not find out his object in coming there—his ulterior intentions. But it was plain to me that in all his sayings and doings there was the intelligence of a rising man, together with acuteness. And if my experience be not at fault, there was not his superior in this world in skill or largeness of heart."

And here is Olivia:

"Then as to his wife, she was not an ordinary woman, but was in every respect co-equal with her husband's position and responsibilities; bearing herself with propriety, politeness and good grace. She was very fond of studying the Malay language, saying 'What is this in Malay?' and 'what that?' Also, whatever she saw she wrote down, and, whatever her husband intended to undertake, or when buying anything, he always deferred to her. Thus if it pleased his wife it pleased him. Further, her alacrity in all work was apparent; indeed, she never rested for a moment, but she was always busy, day after day. In this diligence which I observed there is a very great distinction between the habits of the natives (of Malayan countries) and the white people. For it is the custom of the Malayan women, on their becoming the wives of great people, to increase their arrogance, laziness and habitual procrastination. Further, their talk is only of their bigness, and to their apprehension it is mean to do anything whatever, or to busy themselves in any way; thus all that they do is to sit, sleep or recline, or else order about their slaves; and as for the latter, all that they know is how to serve up meals on their knees. In the mornings they do not rise till ten or eleven, then they eat and drink and go again to sleep till evening. Thus it goes till they have got the name of being old;—thus marriage is entered into with great men. But to look at Mrs Raffles, her hands and feet were in continual motion, like chopping one bit after another. Then there was sewing, which was succeeded by writing; for it is a real truth that I never saw her sleep at mid-day, or even reclining for the sake of ease, but always at work with diligence, as day follows day. This the Almighty knows also. And if I am not wrong in the conclusion that I have arrived at, these are the signs of good sense and understanding, which qualify for the undertaking of great deeds. Thus her habits were active; so much so, that in fact she did the duty of her husband; indeed, it was she that taught him. Thus God had matched them as King and Counsellor, or as a ring with its jewels."

What were the fruits of those activities of Raffles' so graphically described by 'Abdullah? of all those questionings, those comings and goings of couriers, those burnings of the midnight candle? They were the material for a series of reports to India, covering not only every aspect of the forthcoming operation but also the wider issues of what was to be done with Java when it had been captured. As Raffles observed at a very early date, the seizure of the island was easy; it was its subsequent administration that would be difficult. There is a peculiarly modern ring about this comment.

Biographers in general have paid too little attention to this period of Raffles' life. Interest has been concentrated on his government of the island, with relatively little account of his activities prior to its capture, during those busy months from December 1810 to August 1811, when the first landing was made. It is no exaggeration to say that the success of the Java campaign as a combined operation, up to at least the first landing, including the route taken and the selected point of assault, together with a most accurate appreciation of such other vital military information as the strength and disposition of the enemy's forces, the attitude of the Dutch population and the reaction of the Javanese princes was, after due allowances for the specifically military details supplied by William Farquhar, the work of Raffles and no one else.

To do justice by quotation to the reports that Raffles passed in an unbroken stream to Penang for dispatch to India is not easy. Individual reports were of enormous length—a hundred pages or more. All the earlier ones covered a wide field: military, economic, geographical and political. Paragraphs ranged from small but practical points likely to affect the success of a military operation, to major political or economic questions affecting the future administration of the island. In his last dispatches he developed his ideas of a great new empire—"This other India". Everything he discovered, everything that occurred to him was immediately transmitted to Calcutta. That twenty different subjects were touched on in one dispatch mattered not at all. He was working against time. Information was only of value when it had reached Minto and his other correspondents. The important thing was to get it there quickly and leave them to sort it out. His comments on the lethargy of Penang in forwarding his letters were extremely scathing.

Such parts of these reports as are reproduced in the pages that follow will, it is hoped, give a good idea of Raffles' share in the preparations for the conquest of Java.

Having set up his headquarters in Malacca and assembled his staff of Malay clerks, his next step was to select suitable emissaries—*wakils*, as they were called—and dispatch them to the Javanese princes. In the India Office are preserved the English versions of some of the letters so sent. One, typical of them all, was addressed to "The Emperor of the Whole Country of Java" with a long list of titles. It begins after great compliments:

"Be it known to your illustrious Majesty by this Letter, which contains what I am desirous of stating by Speech, that the Great Governor General of Bengal and of all India has heard with Concern of the Conduct of the Dutch in the Island of Java and of their having broken through and destroyed long established Customs and the rights and dignity of your Majesty and that he is in consequence inclined to expel from the Island of Java and from the Eastern Countries all the Dutch and French Authority.

"It is therefore my desire to support your Majesty's dignity and Authority according to established Custom that I now write this letter with the authority of the Governor General of Bengal to inform your illustrious Majesty that the English will not act as the Dutch have done, and that they are in consequence in the first instance desirous of establishing a good understanding with your Majesty in order that hereafter when the English may arrive at the Country of Java no evil may befall your Majesty nor any of your Majesty's People—Let your Majesty be of one heart with the English, and after the receipt of this Letter enter into no further agreements with the Dutch, rather waiting in silence in anxious expectation for the arrival of the English in Java.

"I request your Majesty to send me an immediate answer to this by the Bearer thereof. . . ."

After warning him of the need for secrecy, he ends:

"I do not at this time send presents to your Majesty as this Letter is only to give Notice in Secret of great events likely to occur—but when I have the honour of meeting your Majesty hereafter, whatever your Majesty desires and whatever can be desired in this world, is to be procured from the great Country of Bengal—then will I make presents suitable to your Majesty's dignity. . . ."

He referred to this matter in a long dispatch to Minto on 15th December, eleven days after his arrival.

"As the season of the year does not admit of my approaching the Coast of Java myself . . . I have deemed it advisable . . . to delay my departure from hence until a reasonable time shall have been given to the political Agents . . . to establish their points so far in the Enemy's

Country as to render the subsequent possible discovery of the real object of my Mission of no serious importance to their personal safety, or the general success of my operations."

The report of a concerted attack on Lingga by the Dutch and the Sultan of Palembang had proved incorrect, so "at the same time that I send a Vakeel to Palembang I have deemed it advisable to send Mr Scott to Lingen [Lingga] to put the Sultan there on his guard against Palembang. . . ."

"As the Sultan of Palembang is one of the richest of the Malay Chieftains and is literally said to have Godowns stored with Dollars and Gold hoarded by his Ancestors, I considered it a point of some importance to prevent Daendels from availing himself of this extensive source of supply, and in consequence wrote to the Sultan immediately on my arrival here urging him to be on his guard against the Dutch operations and assuring him of the friendship of the English should he be desirous of getting rid of them. Having heard since that part of the Dutch vessels have been permitted to go up the River, and that they are likely to succeed in whatever object they have in view, I have this day dispatched a Second Letter entrusted to Toonkoo[1] Mahomed, a relation of the Sultan's. . . ."

The first letter to the sultan had been prompted by the receipt by Raffles of the news that a party of Dutch ships was approaching Palembang to enforce payment of a considerable sum of money alleged by the Dutch to be owed to them. Raffles was anxious to dissociate the sultan from his Dutch alliance. The correspondence was to have unexpected repercussions. Meanwhile:

"By the latest accounts from Java it appears that the Dutch are in possession of Bantam and that the party attached to the late King (headed by his brother, and termed Insurgents) has been obliged to retreat into the interior. As the measures best to be adopted in this part of the Island are of a very important and delicate nature, I have engaged my best assistant for the service, whom your Lordship may recollect by the name of Toonkoo Pangeran[2] of Siac. . . . I shall mention to the Sultan of Lingen that the Toonkoo is sent by me to examine the different harbours at Banca [Bangka] and the Lampoon [Lampong] Country for the purpose of ascertaining whether any of the Dutch vessels remain there—and at the same time request he will furnish him with a small war-like Prow for the purpose. As soon as the Toonkoo Pangeran quits Lingen for this service, he will direct his course to Cheribon and land the Cheribon Princes in the night in Creeks with which he is well acquainted—afterwards he will proceed to the Insurgents at Bantam, from whence communications will

[1] Tunku, prince.

[2] Pangeran, title, under Dutch rule, of a regent or headman.

be opened with the Susuhunan[1] at Solo. He hopes to receive information from him by way of Lampoon and Palembang. . . .

"I have also had the satisfaction of finding here . . . a Vakeel to the Commandant of Malacca from the Susuhunan himself . . . he was sent here a considerable time ago for the purpose of obtaining people skilful in working gold. . . . This man will leave Malacca either to-night or to-morrow a Passenger in a Bugguese Prow and will proceed from Lingen direct to Samarang. . . . I have also a skilful Agent to convey my communications to Madura and Sourabaya and from thence to the Susuhunan and the Sultan [of Mataram]. . . ."

Raffles proposed also to send a *wakil* to Bali if a suitable man could be found, but, as he observed, Bali would not be of much importance till operations were farther advanced.

As to the military side of the expedition, he advised Minto that, from information received, the Dutch forces in Java were between 12,000 and 14,000. In the view of Farquhar and himself, 3,000 Europeans, 6,000 natives, 500 cavalry and a train of horse artillery would be fully sufficient to ensure success against them.

"I am well satisfied in my mind that there will be very little serious opposition . . . were the English now to appear off the coast in any number, the whole of the native population, with the exception of those in the immediate pay of the Dutch, would declare in our favour. As regards the provisioning of the Expedition, Penang and Malacca would each, with notice, be able to look after half for a month or so. The plan of operations . . . cannot be acted upon with advantage if the attack is delayed beyond the early part of May. The Easterly winds set in so strong towards the end of April, increasing in May, that it will be tedious and difficult for our ships to beat to windward."

While the flow of reports from Malacca to India continued steadily, Minto's plans were taking shape. In India, formal dispatches had taken the place of private correspondence. On 17th January 1811, Fort William, Calcutta, addressed Fort St George, Madras, in an official communication:

". . . It is evident indeed that recent events in Europe, as they affect the United Provinces alone, increase in a high degree both the importance and urgency of extinguishing the Island of Java, a power which is now formally as well as substantially directed by French Counsels, and the seat of which is in fact a province of that new Empire. . . .

"The capture of the Moluccas and the expeditions against the French Islands [Réunion and Mauritius] must have awakened in the mind of Marshal Daendels an apprehension of an attack on the seat of his Government, which cannot have failed to lead him to apply to France for succour with additional earnestness. . . . Every information which we have

[1] Susuhunan (or Susunan): "Object of Adoration".

received to the condition of affairs in that quarter justifies a Confident expectation of the success of an Expedition. . . .

"We have the satisfaction to learn by a dispatch from the Honourable the Secret Committee [London] . . . that this projected Enterprise . . . has received the sanction of the Authorities in England. . . . The intention of prosecuting this Expedition was communicated confidentially to the Hon. Major-General Abercrombie[1] and the Governor of Bourbon [Réunion] . . . for the purpose of pointing out the Necessity of returning to India, at the earliest practicable period of time, the whole of the disposable force drawn from the three Presidencies [for the Mauritius operations]. . . ."

A similar communication was addressed to Rear-Admiral Drury, soliciting his co-operation in the transport of a force estimated to be one Company of the Royal Artillery, 200 Hon. Company's artillery with the regulated proportion of gun lascars, 4,000 European infantry, 4,000 native infantry and 300 pioneers.

"It is our expectation that the Bengal Division will be ready to sail from the River soon after the middle of March, and that it will reach Malacca where it is proposed that the troops should rendezvous, in the month of April. You will be pleased therefore to form your arrangements with a view to the dispatch of the Armament from Fort St George accordingly."

Lieutenant-General Sir Samuel Auchmuty had been nominated to the command of the troops. The curious situation whereby the naval commander could take his orders only from the Admiralty, whereas the military commander accepted orders from the Governor-General, who in turn was answerable to the India Board of Control, was not conducive to successful combined operations.

Drury asked that 1,000 men be embarked on a squadron and sent to the Strait of Sunda for the purpose of intercepting possible French reinforcements and protect the homeward-bound China fleet. Minto declined this request on the ground that the army and navy should act together "upon one joint and preconcerted plan" and not engage in "distinct partial and uncombined exertions". This wise policy has often been neglected to our cost.

Already the navy was becoming agitated about the route. Drury wrote to Auchmuty that a passage through the Durian and Bangka Straits would be unlikely to succeed unless performed in the month of March, and that no other route was convenient. The Governor-General in Council commented on this to Fort St George that, as they did not share these fears, preparations were to continue of the basis of the original instructions. This question of route was to arise again.

Minto wrote to London on 22nd January at great length, urging on

[1] Governor and Commander-in-Chief, Fort St George.

the Secret Committee the imperative need for at least a limited establishment to be retained in Java, in order to get the best results out of the expedition and to protect the European population. At the same time, he indicated his intention to go there in person. So slow were the mails that the reply was not sent from London until 10th July and did not reach Minto until long after he had returned from Java to India.

Minto let out the secret to his wife in his first letter to her in 1811.

"We are now in the agony of preparation for Java; and I will whisper in your ear that I am going there myself, not to command the Army but to see all the political work done to my mind. The 'Modeste' is to be my state coach."

This decision, that later excited Lord Curzon's contemptuous comment, was forced upon him by Raffles' inability to return to Calcutta before the expedition left. The magnitude of the issues in the event of the British remaining in Java was such that it could only be discussed in personal conference. If Raffles could not come to Calcutta, Minto must go to Malacca, an unprecedented but unavoidable step.

On 24th January Raffles emphasized again to Minto the importance of the time factor.

"To ensure the Passage, the force should at the latest be ready to leave this port [Malacca] by the 1st of April for its ultimate destination at which it should certainly arrive by the 1st of May. . . . Would it perhaps be advisable to dispatch to Malacca and Penang such troops as are coming from Bengal or Madras? Should the troops from Mauritius not be available it might be possible to seize and hold Madura and some of the Islands to the Eastward."

A small but not unimportant suggestion was the inclusion of the battalion of the 20th or Marine Regiment, "this Corps having been so frequently at Penang and Bencoolen where they have in some measure become acquainted with the manners, customs and language of the Eastern Nations. . . ."

He went on to recommend by name certain officers with Eastern experience.

On the following day, 25th January, India received the good news of the surrender of Mauritius, but nearly a month was to elapse before it became known to Raffles in Malacca.

A glimpse of the scene at Calcutta is to be had through the eyes of Captain Thomas Taylor, military secretary to the Governor-General. He wrote on 27th January 1811[1]:

"This day a long dispatch arrived from Mr Raffles at Malacca, of whom Lord M. thinks very highly and rightly so, though to my mind

[1] *Facing the Music*, by Colonel P. Carew (*Blackwood's Magazine*, October 1949), and additional unpublished material.

he is inclined to be a trifle self-opinionated, as I own I am myself. Raffles reports that Java is likely to prove a stiffish fence. . . . Captain Greigh of the 'Minto' has confounded the Navy's pessimism regarding the Caramata passage[1] and reports that it is perfectly feasible and that Borneo may be made through the Straits of Singapore. Mr Leyden, a friend of Raffles and a protégé of Lord M., has been a very useful channel of communication owing to his knowledge of Malay. Leyden is a curious mixture of apothecary, poet and scholar. He bled me for a fever when Assistant Surgeon at Madras, though goodness knows I was bloodless enough already. Having done so, he solaced me with porter and poetry. He is to accompany us on the expedition as interpreter and general adviser and will work well with Mr Raffles, whom we meet at Malacca. No-one save myself has an inkling that Lord M. is coming in person."

Early in February an important emissary from Palembang arrived at Malacca with information of such moment that Raffles decided to send Lieutenant Macdonald to Palembang in the *Ariel*. Since arrival at Malacca, Macdonald had been busy learning Malay.

"It being an object of importance", ran Raffles' instructions to Macdonald, "to ascertain the exact nature and strength of the Dutch force stated to be in the Lampoon [Lampong] country and in the vicinity of Palembang, you will be pleased to proceed without loss of time to the port of Muntok[2], where . . . you will adopt immediate measures for the delivery of the accompanying letters and presents to the Sultan of Palembang.

"In the neighbourhood of the Palembang river you will most probably find a small brig (the 'Friend's Adventure') engaged by me, and under the orders of Toonkoo Radin Mahomed, a native agent employed by me at the Court of Palembang, and for whom I also entrust you with a letter; from *this person* you will be able to obtain the latest information respecting the state of the country, and the disposition of the native Chieftains.

"It would be advisable that you should, if practicable, deliver the letters to the Sultan in person. . . . You will be *most minute* in your enquiries respecting the state of the enemy's force in the Lampoon and Bantam countries, and if the Sultan should require your advice and assistance in finally arranging with Dutch persons now residing at Palembang, you are authorized to attend thereto. You will of course make known to the Sultan the political change by which Holland is become a province of France. . . .

[1] Karimata Strait, between the island of Billiton (Belitong) and the west coast of Borneo, an alternative route to Java to that through Durian and Bangka Straits. For Durian, see glossary.

[2] On the north-east coast of the island of Bangka, off Sumatra.

"I cannot too strongly recommend to you the most conciliatory manners to the native inhabitants of whatever place you may touch at, whom you will endeavour to impress with the most favourable ideas of the English and of their views to the Eastward. . . . A small assortment of trifling presents to interior persons who may be useful, has been sent on board the 'Ariel'. . . ."

These written instructions were supplemented by certain verbal ones, which emerge in Macdonald's *Narrative of Early Life and Services*.

"I was instructed to go to Palembang and explain to his Highness the views of the British government, the attitude they were about to assume in the archipelago, and their wish that I should be allowed to convey the members of the Dutch residency to Malacca, until the result of our operations on Java should be known. Such were my *verbal instructions*: and taking with me Toonkoo Radin Mahomed, who was a near kinsman of the Sultan, and one of our most intelligent and active *employees*, whom I found, as I expected, at Mintow (now Minto),[1] we proceeded up the river, and very soon disposed of the mission I had in charge, but unfortunately found the Prince sternly resolved to permit none of the ill-fated Europeans to depart, basing his objections on the danger which his eldest son, the Pangeran Rattoo, then on a mission to Marshal Daendels, on this and other grievances, would be exposed to, should intelligence of his participation in such a measure as the surrender of the Factory into our custody reach that headstrong and irascible man. . . ."

Raffles' instructions were that, whatever the reply of the Sultan, Macdonald was, in no circumstances, to protract his stay beyond forty-eight hours. He continues:

". . . by this plausible excuse, we were constrained to return without fulfilling Sir S. Raffles' kind and benevolent intentions—I quote the expressions that fell from his Highness on that occasion, and am most accurate in rendering them, as in after times it was basely attempted to connect the name of Sir S. R. with the sanguinary catastrophe which ensued."

The tragic incident to which he refers has its place in a later chapter.

Immediately on his return to Malacca, Macdonald left (14th February) for Calcutta with secret dispatches from Raffles to Lord Minto and Neil Benjamin Edmonstone, chief secretary to the Supreme Government, and later a member of the Council. The need for this arose from, as already mentioned, the tardiness of the Penang authorities in forwarding mail.

"I am aware", wrote Raffles to Minto by the *Ariel*, "that nothing will be done (*except on paper*) without positive and decided Orders from the Supreme Government—for the presumed object of forcing the whole expedition into Penang in order to reduce the importance of Malacca,

[1] Muntok, renamed Minto in 1812.

the Penang Government would ruin the best and most extended political plan ever laid down."

The relations between Raffles and Penang were now less cordial than ever. Bruce having followed the example of former Penang Governors by dying (27th December 1810), Phillips was once more acting Governor. On learning this, Raffles had communicated to Phillips the information secretly given only to Bruce, and Phillips was very piqued not to have been taken earlier into his confidence.

The secret dispatch to Minto drew attention to the importance of having one or two Dutch translators. "The Dutch, I am sorry to say, have in all affairs of accounts and commercial arrangements, so much superiority to the generality of Englishmen, that it is necessary to guard against them over-reaching us." It referred also to the need for competent officials to accompany the expedition—for example, his intimate friend, William Robinson, senior civil servant at Penang, the only person on that island likely to be of use, "neither the attention of the Government or of its officers being turned to political objects or even conversant with the language and customs of the countries under their immediate control". It suggested further that Captain William Farquhar would be useful in some staff or civil appointment, and that John Leyden should be given a senior post in the new administration.

On the various points that would arise after Java had been captured he wrote:

"Precautions should be taken by proclamation on landing against emptying of public Treasury and Godowns and also as to the claims of capital in the form of Government notes. . . . Government in Java being the great and almost only Traders, monopolizing every produce of the Island and its dependencies, the Public Warehouses will be found to contain immense Treasures. . . .

"The system of bribery and corruption that prevails in the Dutch Settlements to the eastward is perhaps not to be equalled, and on this account as well as on every other connected with the eventual prosperity of our Measures to the eastward, I think it of importance that definite arrangements for the government should be put in force as soon as we effect a landing."

In his view, the civil authority must be supreme, and he recommended that all civil and judicial authorities and persons in office be continued for a time. Samarang seemed to be the place best adapted for residence of the chief authority, and it might be necessary to retain the splendour and pomp always observed by the Dutch.

He then touched on a vital point.

"By the acquisition of Java the whole of the Eastern Islands and ports are under our Control, which will thus be effectually united with Western

India, and form with our Conquests in other parts of the world such an Empire of Colonies, that must encourage the principles of commerce and in many cases dictate Monopoly."

He expressed his intention of drawing up some general memoranda for the government of the whole Eastern Archipelago.

". . . at present and in the first instance I would recommend that on the taking of Java we should keep in our hands as many of the advantages derived by the Dutch as possible. . . ."

The secret dispatch to Edmonstone also dealt with many matters, largely military.

"The Dutch possessing an extensive Sea Coast . . . which from the Straits of Sunda to those of Gressie,[1] does not appear to afford, by nature, one Commanding Station, adequate to resist with effect the attack of a well appointed Enemy from Sea, with a powerful and extensive native population in the interior of the country that they have never known how to manage, seem rather as the necessity of the occasion has dictated to have constructed their different fortifications more with the view of maintaining their ground against the Native States, than with any serious regard to the extent of defence that such fortifications might afford against an European Enemy. . . ."

Various small forts were scattered over the country and skirting the beach, but many of these were originally of native construction or, if built by the Dutch, primarily intended for the defence of their Residents and factories previous to the different provinces being regularly placed under their immediate government. Several of these forts, Raffles reported, were garrisoned only by "a small Malay Party and Sergeants Guard, and few have the advantage of an European Commandant".

"So insignificant were these defences previous to the arrival of Marshal Daendels and so feeble and worn out were the energies of the Dutch Government in Java, that had the smallest force been landed five years ago the whole of their possessions must have fallen an easy conquest.

"The measures, however, which have subsequently been adopted by Marshal Daendels must be considered as having in a Military point of view entirely changed the face of the country and deserve serious consideration".

Daendels had remodelled the Army by increasing pay, abolishing corruption and introducing Frenchmen into every Corps, and "by dis-

[1] This appears on various maps as Grissee, Grise, Gressik, Grisek, etc. "In Javanese correctly Gârsik, that is, 'dry land' or firm land, distinguished from muddy or marshy. . . . It lies along the shore of the narrow strait which divides Java from Mudura. . . . It was in Gressie that the Mahommedan strangers who eventually overthrew the ancient religion of Java, first established themselves in the 14th century. . . ." Crawfurd, *Descriptive Dictionary*.

charging the Javanese Troops and supplying in their place Amboynese Madurese Bugguese and Native Slaves from other foreign States".

The defences of Samarang had been improved and harbours fortified. A military road had been completed from one end of the island to the other—eight hundred miles in length, and "a superior mode of communication by Posts and Telegraph" established along it.

The army, Raffles explained, was divided into five divisions: a mobile division, a division each at Batavia, Surabaya, Samarang, and one division for the defence of distant dependencies. The nominal strength was 20,000, but "it seems well ascertained on good authority . . . that the actual force cannot at this time exceed 15,000 and these by no means well disciplined or appointed, the Dutch and country born officers in general dissatisfied, and the native troops who have generally speaking either been slaves or furnished by force levies, deserting daily in great numbers."

The Amboynese were reported to have declared after the capture of the Moluccas that they had no longer any right to serve the Dutch.

"The policy of Marshal Daendels in discharging the Javanese troops, tho' no doubt extremely politic and necessary in checking the Native States, is a measure that must in a great decree have alienated the regard and affection of the Javanese and at any rate has been the means of constituting the whole army into an army of foreigners of all ranks, castes and conditions, who it may be fairly presumed from former experience and the general information lately received would, officers and men, require but little invitation and promised assistance, to induce them to come over to the English. . . ."

The report goes on to deal with the fortifications and a long list of minor forts and other military information not covered by a separate report made by William Farquhar.

From then on, Raffles left more and more to Farquhar the collection and passing on of purely military intelligence, disclosing his intention to devote the whole of his time to "the political and commercial arrangements that it may be necessary to make on our first establishment to the Eastward". As he so rightly added: "I am aware of the jealousy with which such [military] information or advice is ever received from a Civilian."

His correspondence with India is particularly interesting for two reasons. In the first place it shows the extensive and detailed information he had been able to accumulate at Penang, in spite of the fact that he had been very seriously and continuously overworked. Then there had been the added difficulty that, latterly at any rate, Java had been enemy territory, with intercourse seriously restricted by the naval blockade. Secondly, some of the subjects touched on in these dispatches are very illuminating, giving as they do a foretaste of his subsequent actions as Lieutenant-Governor.

The lengthy memorandum, or rather, series of memoranda, to Edmonstone contained commercial as well as military intelligence. He explained, for example, the system of the Dutch in regard to the giving and receiving of presents in their dealings with Javanese princes, and pointed out that whatever the English view of such a practice might be, it was advisable, at any rate in the early days of occupation, that such a well-established custom should be maintained. On trade, produce and revenue he had a lot to say, as also on the open and clandestine traffic in opium.

"... while in the hands of the Company it would be the certain source of immense gain, at the same time that the cause of Humanity would be served by selling the least possible quantity of the poison for the greatest obtainable price. . . ."

This for many years was the policy of the government of the Straits Settlements.

"Cloths, Iron, China Goods and generally speaking every kind of merchandise except those produced in the Eastern Islands, were not permitted to enter for Trade anywhere but at Batavia, and consequently it was there that these Articles were to be procured—but latterly Marshal Daendels has allowed those of Java to be exported from Samarang and Sourabaya and even Spices from Amboyna. . . .

"The Revenues of the Dutch Government are so intimately connected with the profits they derive from their monopolies, that it would perhaps be difficult to separate them. It may therefore be sufficient to state that the Revenues are in every instance farmed, and arise principally from established profits on different articles the produce of Java, from annual sale of exclusive privileges, from a general export and import duty (of about 5 per cent) and from a Capitation Tax on the Chinese (about 6 Dollars a year). . . ."

In this connexion he made a shrewd comment on the Chinese:

"The Dutch seem long since to have been aware of the unprofitable result that must arise from a large Chinese population, a Class of people who though most useful in introducing Industry into a new country, must ever tend to impoverish it afterwards, from the immense remittances that they make to China, to which country they naturally return in great numbers as soon as they have acquired a fortune."

Lastly, he made an important and, in the light of later events, a very significant reference to Dirk van Hogendorp. He encloses "a Calculation (by Mr Hogendorp) of what the Island of Java, if well governed with freedom of calculation, commerce and navigation, is capable of producing".

It is interesting to find that at this early stage he was aware of the writings of van Hogendorp. Events were to show how much he was indebted to van Hogendorp and his friend Muntinghe for his land-revenue scheme. From Raffles' description of the document it is not absolutely certain that it was the *Bericht* itself. Van Hogendorp had circulated a manuscript document in the East Indies before he had been arrested, and it is possible that it was this that Raffles forwarded to India. In his *History of Java* Raffles states in a footnote that he had only just seen the *Bericht* when he was writing the chapter dealing with his own land-rental system. Whole sentences of this chapter are taken almost verbatim from the *Bericht*. If it was the *Bericht* that he sent to India from Malacca, he may well have forgotten the fact. Possibly one of the Dutch residents gave him a copy with a brief account of its thesis, and Raffles, not being able to read Dutch, sent it at once to Calcutta, where it could be translated. But undoubtedly Raffles' land policy was to be greatly influenced by the views of the Abbé Raynal, whether he imbibed them from van Hogendorp's *Bericht* direct or—which is more probable—through Muntinghe, a great friend of van Hogendorp's and a believer in the same liberal principles.

With these dispatches for Lord Minto and Edmonstone, Macdonald did the trip from Malacca to Calcutta in twenty-one days. On arrival he found letters being read that he had handed in to Penang to be forwarded, a fortnight before he himself had started. This supports the remark of Raffles to the effect that "the conduct of the Penang Government having been throughout so incomprehensible to me that I cannot rely upon them even for forwarding the present Dispatch".

For his services, Macdonald was promoted to Captain.

Four days after the *Ariel* had sailed from Malacca Raffles wrote to Lord Minto "by the first regular conveyance that offers" on the subject of the so-called mystery of the eastern trade.

"The Eastern Trade has hitherto been a mystery to the English, but it is certain that it was the foundation of the Dutch prosperity in Europe and that they derived greater resources from the Eastern part of India than the English have ever done from the Western. We have now the opportunity of uniting both, but political considerations must be allowed their due weight. If we wish to derive *every* advantage from the Eastward we must follow the Dutch. If we wish to destroy as much as possible the resources of Java, in the event of its ever being given up to a foreign European Power, we must forego immense advantages and annihilate for ever any regular Eastern Trade. But may we not pursue a middle course? May not the Company retain in their hands some of the few lucrative monopolies, such as Opium, Tin, &c, and yet effect their object? . . .

"The restrictions on trade and commerce have so long been established to the Eastward and have become so completely the *Law of Nations* among the Eastern Islands that caution would suggest enquiry and consideration previous to their being annulled. The Conquest of Java will open new relations and connexions and the British Interests to the Eastward will be completely changed. Hitherto we have been as Smugglers and Contraband Traders and the great Supporters of our Settlements the Bugguese who live by this Trade Alone, can exist only as a great Maritime Nation by the clandestine trade of Opium to Java. . . .

"Malacca, Penang and Bencoolen will naturally come under consideration, but whatever may be the nature of their respective Governments, they must in some measure co-operate or be directed to attend to the policy of Java, which must ever rule the Eastern Seas. . . ."

Minto wrote to Raffles at about this time, informing him that the expedition would sail from India at the beginning or middle of March, and that he himself would be coming "at least to Malacca and eventually, I may say, to Java".

"The expediency, not to say necessity of my approaching the scene, and bringing the authority of Government at least within reach of reference, is evident. The Resolution is therefore taken. I count upon meeting you at Malacca; and then in communication with yourself and Sir Samuel Auchmuty the final plans, military and political, will be settled. . . .

"I must tell you in confidence, that I have received the sanction of Government at Home for this Expedition, but that the views of the Directors do not go beyond the expulsion or reduction of the Dutch power, the destruction of their fortifications, the distribution of their arms and stores to the natives and the evacuation of the Island by our own troops. I conclude, therefore, that the disruptive and calamitous consequence of this plan to so ancient and populous a European Colony, the property and lives of which must fall as sacrifice to the vindictive sway of the Malay Chiefs . . . have not been fully contemplated; and I have already stated my reasons for considering the modification of all their orders. . . ."

In a further letter he wrote before leaving for Madras, where he was to call before proceeding eastward:

"I embark here on the 7th for Madras. . . . I bring Hope and Leyden with me in the Dutch and Malay departments. I also bring Mr Seton, the late Resident at Delhi, an Administrative man, and now Governor of Prince of Wales's Island. I shall probably install him at Penang; and then it is equally probable that he may accompany me to the eastward for counsel and general assistance. Not to alarm you, however, he will have no further relations with the Javanese affair than as *Amicus Curiae*. . . .

"It is proposed to style you Secretary to the Governor-General when we come together; for thus your character of Agent will naturally merge. Secretary is the highest office below the Council and was lately held by

Mr Edmonstone at Madras. I hope you do not doubt the prospective interest I have always taken, and do not cease to take, in your personal view and welfare. . . ."

Five months was quick promotion from secretary to the Governor of Penang to secretary to the Governor-General of India, and it was clear that, in so far as it lay in his power, Minto had a still higher post in mind.

John Leyden wrote to Raffles by the same mail:

". . . he was always talked of you to me, with a kindness very uncommon in a Governor-General and says that he is pleased when thinking he will be able to arrange matters very much to your satisfaction when he arrives. I am glad I have been able to keep him tied up in this point. He is still fluctuating between the two old plans of keeping the country or rendering it independent. The orders which he has received from Home are entirely and positively in favour of the last. . . . This his own good sense directly saw to be impossible, from the shoals of half castes at Batavia. Colebrook[e] and Lumsden have succeeded in making some impression on him by talking of accustoming the Malays to independence, and all that. But may I never be the second Draco, nor write my laws in blood, if they succeed. Succeed they shall not, that is flat, for the Malays must neither have independence, nor yet be very dependent, but we must have a general Malay league in which all the Rajahs must be united like the old Ban of Burgundy, or the late one of Germany, and these must be represented in a General Parliament of the Malay States, like the Amphictyonic Council of the Greeks, and this Council should meet in the Island of Madura or some celebrated ancient place and under the direction of the Governor of Java.

"We ought to retain in some shape or other all the Dutch possessions at first, while we are making ourselves known; and you should write to all the Rajahs and the Malays however far or where situated, to come in person to meet the Good Maharajah of Bengal, and state in your letters that the Malay States are expressly invited to send their most ancient and sagacious men to assist at a general meeting or Congress to take into consideration all their laws, institutions, Government, religion and policy. Publish far and wide the coming of the good Maharajah like another Secunder Zulkaram [Iskandar dzu'l-Karnain] to land in Malacca and conquer Java and drive out all the cruel Dutch and treacherous French and take away all embargoes and the restrictions on trade, abolish piracy and bring peace and happiness to all the Anak Malays. In short, make a great and mighty noise that will compel his Lordship to be a greater man than he would wish to be if left alone."

Minto wrote to his wife in a letter dated 25th February:

"I have here Mr Raffles . . . a very clever, able, active and judicious man, perfectly versed in the Malay language and manners and conversant in the interest and affairs of the Eastern States, in advance for some months past, to collect recent intelligence, to open communications with the Javanese Chiefs and to prepare the way for operations. I carry with me good assistants of every sort, though few in number. Among these are Mr Hope, the brother of Sir John Hope, a tolerable Dutchman, with excellent talents and habits of business; Dr Leyden, a perfect Malay; Mr Seton, now Resident at Delhi, who is to be Governor of Prince of Wales's Island (in the room of poor Mr Bruce, Lord Elgin's brother, lately dead) but who will go on with me to Java. . . I have John and Taylor [military secretary], Captain Robinson who married a Dutch beauty at the Cape and mastered his wife's tongue; and Lt. George, who is an excellent draughtsman . . . the object we have in view is of the greatest national importance and it is of infinite consequence that the first political arrangement is to be made on right principles."

Among the reasons he gave in this letter for his own participation in the expedition was: ". . . as Admiral Drury acts in a distinct authority and is best at acting for himself, I have no security for the execution of any plan I might adopt or any instructions which might be given by this Government. . . ."

The secret was kept as long as possible. Minto launched his bombshell at a Council meeting on 8th March.

"His Lordship", wrote Captain Taylor, "gave the big wigs at the seat of government a terrible shock. They threw up their hands in horror at the Governor-General demeaning himself over a paltry place like Java; would not believe that he really intended to go there and comforted themselves that he was merely going to quell an insurrection in Madras. When I told Lord M. he said 'Let them think what they please, it makes no odds to me'."

Leyden wrote to Raffles:

"All are utterly confounded by his Lordship's resolution, of which nobody had the slightest suspicion, and so completely were they all taken aback, that nobody volunteered for service, until the whole arrangements were settled. Indeed, more than the half are as yet thunderstruck, and are very far from believing that he has any real intention of visiting Java. . . ."

The party left Calcutta in the *Mornington* on 11th March. On arrival at Madras after a long, tedious passage, Minto decided that he had had enough of the ship, as, according to Taylor, the captain "preferred East India sherry in his interior to wind in his sails". The whole party transferred to the *Modeste*, a fast frigate commanded by Minto's son, the Hon. George Elliot. The voyage from Madras to Penang was quite a pleasant one, the time being happily spent in playing deck games and acting charades, in both of which Lord Minto revealed himself a very competent performer. Penang was reached on 9th May.

"A harmonious voyage of a week or so," recorded Taylor, "disturbed only by the incessant disputations between Leyden and Seton, of which no-one except themselves knows anything, and cares less. Even Lord M. became very bored and when we dropped Seton at Penang said 'Thank God for a calm before the storm'."

On the day of arrival, Archibald Seton was installed as Governor of Penang. Minto at the same time took his seat as Governor-General in Council, "converting this small Presidency into the Supreme Government of India, and acting myself the part of the great lady in the little parlour". This was in a letter to his wife, in which he continued: ". . . and so Penang will have upon its consultations some proceedings of the Governor-General, which is an odd accident in the history of both Governments". These consultations still exist with Minto's signature at the foot.

After some flattering references, which Raffles would not have endorsed, to the assistance afforded by the Penang government, Minto and his party, which included Seton, left for Malacca in the *Modeste* on 12th May.

Captain Taylor wrote on that day:

"Lord M. still sticks to his design of embarking. . . . After breakfast a rich Malay[1] who has large possessions in the peninsula and they say might have been King of Acheen in Sumatra but who prefers living under the protection of an English Government came to pay his respects to Lord M. That ceremony over we embarked from Government House. Sir C. [E.] Stanley near got a ducking in getting into the boat. About three o'clock two large prows came in and with yellow flags at mastheads and yellow ensign. A note from the shore informed us this was the King of Queda coming to pay his respects to Lord M. So we got under way and left His Majesty in the lurch."

This was most regrettable. In view of a threatened Siamese invasion of Kedah, Raffles had endeavoured to arrange this meeting. He had submitted to Minto a masterly summary of the position of Kedah in relation to Siam. Quoting long extracts from the reports of Captain Light, Robert Farquhar and others, he had pointed out not only the expediency but also the moral obligation of help being afforded to Kedah by the Company. It was a tragedy that Minto was always too much preoccupied with the forthcoming expedition to Java to give due attention to this report. Otherwise one of the less defensible acts of the Supreme Government, whereby Kedah was sacrificed to the Siamese invaders, would never have taken place and Kedah—perhaps even the whole of the Malay peninsula—would have come under British influence half a century sooner than it did.

[1] Sayid Husain, the giver of the "very elegant Entertainment" described on page 49.

Chapter Eight

MALACCA, 1811

i

MEANWHILE, in Malacca, Raffles had not been idle. On 14th March he had issued this proclamation for circulation in Java:

"Inhabitants of Java!

"The fortunate period is arrived when the English meditate an attack on Java. They will soon appear on your Coast, with a Naval and Military Force, which must render resistance vain. Already has the Mauritius and the whole of the French Naval and Military forces serving in this country, surrendered to the British Arms. It is now intended to establish the British Interests on the Island of Java.

"You cannot be ignorant of the much boasted strength of the Mauritius. You have heard with what facility it fell before English Prowess and Discipline. Be not, therefore, deceived in your own strength, nor calculate too highly on the means of resistance adopted by your Chief, who, to effect a temporary Military stand, may be heedless how far he involves you and the whole Island in Misery and Ruin. The English are fully aware of his resources and are prepared to meet them. For your own interests be cautious how you involve yourselves.

"Inhabitants who have long settled on Java with your families! It is to you that this Proclamation is more particularly addressed, altho' it deserves the consideration of all! What has been your situation for the last three years? How long, after the failure of every attempt at Clandestine Trade, have not the precious productions of your Island been blocked up within your Settlements and mouldering in your Stores? How long have you been deprived of every intercourse with neighbouring States, and of every advantage from Commerce? And for what? Are you not at this day subjected to the grossest Military oppression and Tyranny, to a system of forced loans and Levies, destroying alike every shadow of security, either for person or property?

"Alas! the politics that have latterly disturbed the Peace of Europe, have been fatally transplanted to your otherwise happy Island, but the period of their termination is fast approaching. The English are at hand; all they require is that you should individually consider the state of affairs, deliberate thereon and act for yourselves. Your future happiness or misery, as well as that of your families, is in your hands. The English character is not unknown to you—it is for you to decide.

"Inhabitants, remain neutral, reside on your Estates, maintain order and respect among your slaves, let not the Public Peace be disturbed! Each of you maintain and be ready to deliver a good and true account of the duty with which you are now respectively charged! Neither suffer sequestration nor the destruction of Property!

"Following this line of conduct, you may rely on the protection of the English. But if on the contrary, you abandon your property and admit of disorder in your department, or in any way make resistance to the British Troops, remember that you forfeit that Protection. The inhabitants of the Moluccas already enjoy the blessings of English Government. May your Conduct entitle you to its consideration.

"Given under my hand at Malacca, this 14th March

"1811

"Tho' Raffles

"Agent to the Governor General with the Malay States."

A copy of this had been sent to Minto while he was at Madras. He had found it "to be written with judgment and becoming moderation".

Rear-Admiral Drury died on 13th April, and the command of the naval forces with the expedition devolved on the very uninspiring Commodore Broughton.

In Java, Daendels' financial position was going from bad to worse. His defensive works, including the war with Bantam, which these involved, were proving very costly. It is true that much of the revenue that had filled the pockets of the officials was now—in theory, at any rate—diverted into the government's treasury, and officials were remunerated by a fixed monthy salary. But this was expected to be regularly paid, even though the irregularities it was supposed to replace had by no means ceased. In fact, the hatred Daendels inspired encouraged many officials to defraud him of every guilder they safely could. The native producers, too, completely alienated as they were, had no inducement to show any special enthusiasm to produce larger crops. Revenue from overseas Daendels had himself cut off by his treatment of American shipping.

Consequently he had found himself forced to reverse his own policy in material ways. Instead of recovering villages from the Chinese, he had to sell them additional lands on a larger scale. Instead of getting the finances on a sound basis, he had to issue larger and larger quantities of paper money, which naturally depreciated very rapidly. Instead of paying for the labour he required, as he himself had laid it down, he had no cash at all for it, while his requirements continued to grow.

The more difficult his position became, the greater became the opposition to his plans. The more he was opposed, the more violent he became, and the more hated. He tended to rely completely on his secret powers (limited in fact to purely military matters) to get his way. Having revised the judicial system, he had made it clear that he himself was above the law, and acted accordingly. Having set out to abolish graft and peculation, he had appropriated Buitenzorg for his headquarters and sold it to the government for 70,000 francs.

It has been said of Raffles that many of his reforms were paper reforms; this is certainly true of Daendels. Like Raffles, his good intentions were on occasions frustrated by force of circumstances. Unlike Raffles, his efforts were not infrequently negated by his own obstinacy, or the results of his own violence and impetuosity. In fact, by 1811 he had built round himself such a wall of hatred and passive resistance that his measures of reform, good and bad alike, were met with an almost equal degree of ill will. To crown this, he had raised the French flag and thus aroused the animosity of the Dutch, whose support was the more vital to him as he had already alienated Javanese opinion, both high and low.

Napoleon would have cared little for most of these things when news of them found its way to Europe, but there was one suggestion (perfectly unfounded, it is believed) that Daendels was intending to set himself up as supreme ruler of Java. This roused Napoleon to immediate action, and Daendels was recalled. Janssens, who had surrendered the Cape, was appointed in his place.

When he heard about this, Captain Taylor wrote in his diary: "Bonaparte apparently warned him that since he was now a French General, a second surrender would not be tolerated. We shall see. . . ."

Janssens arrived in Java on 27th April, accompanied by the French Major-General Jumel. As soon as Daendels embarked, he was arrested and travelled home a prisoner.

The new Governor-General of Java was a very different type of man from his predecessor. True, he had taken service under Napoleon, but in spite of this he remained at heart a Dutchman. He was quite a sound general, though not a brilliant one—a gentleman with a high sense of duty and of complete integrity.

If Daendels had found the situation bad when he arrived, Janssens found it desperate. The country was bankrupt. Most of the population, European and Javanese alike, were longing for the English invasion, not from any Anglomania, but as a deliverance from a brutal and savage tyranny. That the attack was imminent all were certain. Modern security measures were not then practised and, though the expedition was always described as "to the Eastward", no one was in any doubt as to its destination. Against this well-trained and experienced invasion force, Janssens would have a motley crowd of conscripted natives, ready to desert at the first suitable moment, a poor collection of French troops badly officered, and a general scarcity of equipment. In Jumel, he had a commander-in-chief as lazy as he was incompetent.

This change in the governor-generalship would not have been known to Raffles when, on 30th April, he passed on other important up-to-date information from Java.

"I learn that the Rajah of Bali Baliling[1] had received my communication and may be depended upon as far as we can desire and from Batavia we have certain accounts that Daendels is concentrated in the West. The ship 'Amboyna' arrived here this morning having sailed from Batavia on the 12th inst. She was engaged by Captain Court to land Prisoners. The French flag had been hoisted in Java. Very serious objections had been urged on the part of many of the Dutch inhabitants to take the Oath of Allegiance to France, and many respectable persons who had refused to receive it, are stated to have come off to our Ships of War in order to place themselves under the protection of the English. Everything was however understood to be peaceable in the interior.

"His Majesty's ships 'Leda', 'Bucephalus' and 'Baracouta' were in Batavia Roads and had taken one Dutch Cruiser and about 15 flat bottomed boats—the Marshal it appears considers the intended attack as inevitable. . . . The general report of the day was . . . that he would not resist our landing but attack us afterwards, and that he meant to retreat to the interior. He . . . has established an extensive System of Espionage as well over the natives as European population. He has, of course, forbid boats from affording supplies and coming off to English ships under pain of Death, but no difficulty whatever in this respect seems to be felt by our Squadron; the people who came off to the 'Amboyna' with provisions, came at night—said they did so at the risk of their lives—but that they were confident the English were coming and that they were desirous of assisting. . . ."

He reported also that the major part of the first division of transports had arrived at Malacca from Bengal and that the troops were encamped. On 6th May he sent further information, including the safe arrival of the second division of transports on the 5th.

"The return of most of my Agents", he wrote, "enables me to report to your Lordship that the intimations made by me to the several Javanese Chieftains appear to have had every effect that could have been desired."

He referred to the value of Captain Greigh's services.

"Considering it an object of the very first importance that the point should be well ascertained whether a safe Passage for the Fleet may be made between Caramatta and the Main, I have again dispatched Captain Greigh to the Eastward with Letters to the Sultan of Pontiana [Pontianak, Borneo] and every possible assistance to enable him to make an actual and regular Survey of this Passage and I am confident that he will effect

[1] More correctly Bleleng, a principality of Bali, covering most of its northern coast. A port some two miles from Singaraja, the capital, is now known as Buleleng.

his purpose and return to Malacca by the 25th inst. If we ascertain that a safe Passage may be made by this route I apprehend that there will be but one opinion on its advantage. . . .

"Daendels has demanded immense levies of people from all quarters, especially Madura. The Sultan however is stated to have positively refused granting him any further supply of Men—alleging that as the English were expected he thought it most prudent to keep them for the service of his own Dominions—this conduct—if correctly stated, must have been effected by means of the different communications I have sent in and of the Agents I have employed to the Eastward. . . . It is stated that the Susuhunang (or So'nang) as well as the Sultan [of Mataram] are very far from being in his interest and that he has not a single Chieftain of ancient power and consequence on whom he can depend; he seems to place his whole confidence in his Tumumggungs,[1] men whom he has selected and raised to consequence from low origin. . . .

"It seems to be fully expected that the Marshal will receive assistance from France almost immediately and the circumstance of his hoisting the French Flag, a measure certainly odious to a large proportion of the population, indicates that he places his reliance on some extraordinary assistance. . . .

"I am sorry to find that we are not yet to expect the Madras Division. Should there be any chance of the fleet being detained at Malacca beyond the 20th or 25th of the present month, I fear our supplies will fall very short. . . ."

He was not too much occupied with military and naval matters to lose sight of the difficult question of the paper money issued by the Dutch in Java. On 7th March he had written to Minto:

"I cannot but consider that the English Government, or rather the Company who in this instance represent it, in taking upon themselves as they most probably will be, to guarantee the Public Debt or Paper Currency, to stand by all existing Contracts to their loss and to become answerable for all further claims whether political or commercial, as well as for the maintenance of a principal part of the Dutch Establishment, are entitled to ensure themselves at least the Commercial or Trading Capital that may be in store."

Now he wrote (30th April):

"The value of Government Paper on Java was understood to be destroyed by the Proclamation hoisting the French Flag—which circumstances alone must have materially increased the disquiets of the Dutch and Chinese, the principal holders of that Capital, but must be considered as a very favourable circumstance for us."

[1] Temenggongs, title, under Dutch rule, of district officers appointed to collect revenue from the heads of villages.

ii

The *Modeste* arrived at Malacca from Penang in six days. Captain Taylor recorded in his diary:

"May 18th. 7 a.m. Now running into Malacca roads. The 'Amboyna' corvette met us with dispatches for Lord Minto, who was much put out by one from the Board of Control, putting all responsibility for the expedition on him and saying that as the Governor-General he should have remained at the seat of Government. Methinks the Marquess of Wellesley has a finger in the pie, sour grapes maybe. Directly we came to anchor, Sir Samuel Auchmuty and Mr Raffles came on board. Lord M. is highly impressed with Sir Samuel Auchmuty as a C.-in-C.; thinks he has all the qualities necessary."

'Abdullah has recorded his impressions of the expedition as it assembled at Malacca. The great variety of the troops struck him greatly, as did the diversity of their uniforms.

"There came to Malacca about three or four vessels daily, and afterwards, six or seven. All these carried Bengal lascars and sepoys, with a great many high people; these erected their tents from Lambongang as far as Tanjong Kling, this without break, each with their entrances. And amongst them were various races of Hondoos and Musselmen and I saw others who ate like dogs, to wit, they licked their food with their tongues; while there were others, who, on being seen eating, would throw the food away, and chase you, as if they would kill you, they were so angry . . . and there were others, who tied three strands of thread round their belly before they ate, nor did they stop eating until that thread had broken; there were others who took white and red earth and smeared it on their breasts, with three stripes on their arms and brow: then they bowed themselves in front, then to the right and to the left, then to the back, then off they ran into the sea . . . others there were who could not taste fish and flesh or things of blood, but only vegetables.

"How many forms of people did I thus not see and kinds of dresses that I had never in my life seen before! And it was to be perceived, that the English had provided their leaders with different dresses; some had tiger skins for coats, others had hats covered with fowls' feathers dyed red, white or black; while others had beasts' skins for trowsers; there were also others who had clothes spotted like leopards . . . again, after a few days came a very large ship carrying troops to the number of 300 men. These were all Musselmen, under three English Officers . . . many people went to see them, myself amongst the rest; and I saw them being exercised by their Officers, in the middle of the open ground, all on horseback and their horses were of the Arab breed; standing high and of the same colour of hair and beauty; and the men were alike of great height and build and all decorated, their coats, trowsers and hats being pearly, each having a musket slung from behind, with a cartridge box attached to the left side, also a forage bag hung to his shoulder and two pistols in the saddle locked . . . they raced their horses, as if they were flying . . . now, I was much more astonished at the intelligence of the horses than I was of that of the bullocks, which drew the cannon, for the former obeyed the sign of the trumpet, as if they had been spoken to, and this without a slip, however great the distance, neither did the rider guide with the bridle, but the horses manœuvred by their own intelligence."

Here is 'Abdullah's description of (presumably) Sir Samuel Auchmuty:

"The General disembarked when I had an opportunity of seeing his mightiness. His face was long and red, his body was stumpy, of half the usual height of men. He wore a long black coat, with a star on his heart. There were four or five gentlemen with him. Then Mr Raffles, Colonel Farquhar and other leading men of Malacca shook hands with him, with due respect, and then as his foot touched the shore, the guns were fired and the Guard of Honour presented arms as he proceeded to the Government House."

But the high light of his experience was the arrival of the Governor-General. His fancy had depicted that the Supreme Authority would be "great and his dress gorgeous". What he actually saw was "One who was middle aged, thin in body, of soft manners and sweet countenance; and I felt that he could not carry 20 catties [about thirty pounds], so slow were his motions. His coat was black cloth, trowsers the same, nor was there anything peculiar. And when the leading men desired to pay their respects, they remained at a distance, none daring to grasp his hand; but they took off their hats and bent their bodies . . . then after a short time having returned the salute of the people he walked on slowly bowing his head until he had arrived at the Government House, and ascended. Then all the leading men of Malacca followed him, to wait on him; but of those Mr Raffles, I saw, was the only one who dared approach close to him; as for the others, they stayed at some distance and having presented themselves, they retired."

For Raffles the occasion was momentous. The one-sided correspondence was ended. The finishing touches could now be made in personal discussion and then the expedition would start—an enterprise whose success depended so much on the accuracy of his information and the completeness of his preparations. His own future was at stake.

Lord Minto also described, in his own happy style, the scene at Malacca:

"There are about 15,000 souls in the town and adjoining district. About two-thirds of these are Malays—that is to say, natives; the remainder are principally Chinese, who have been long settled and have colonized here, contrary to their usual custom, which is to return to China, when they have made a little independence to live on at home. The Chinese emigrants never bring women with them, but foregather with Malay females—mostly slaves—and leave them behind when they go home. At Malacca they have married the daughters of these Malay mothers and these, inter-marrying, have, in a number of generations, converted the Malay coarse clay into fine China, so that the colony is now whole blood on both sides of the house, and may be accounted curious in that respect, as well as in that of the men not being emigrants from China, but descended from emigrant ancestors and born for several generations at Malacca. There are also some remains of the old Portuguese stock. These are very degenerate and little trace of European origin is left, except their professing the Catholic religion. There are people, both Mussulman and Hindoo, from different parts of India; but the most thriving class, though not the most numerous, is Dutch, pure and mixed with Malay blood. The better kind of Dutch are the more substantial part of the community. They continue, under our Government, to fill the principal offices, particularly the judicial, Dutch law being established by the capitulation. Some are merchants, several of them are well-informed, respectable people and one or two are polite, accomplished men. Of the ladies, the elder matrons preserve a smack of the primitive Dutch colonial fashion in dress and manners. The daughters dress, dance and flirt very much as well-educated young women do in Europe, with the advantage of being intensely and beautifully brown. You are lily-fair compared with the fairest of the Batavo-Malaya fair sex. My fidelity, you see, is put to the test. Of English there is but a Commandant, with one or two Officers and medical men attached to the small garrison, which consists of two companies of sepoys from Bengal. Malacca is a dependency of the Penang Government.

"This account of Malacca is for ordinary times. At present we have a great fleet and army officered by English gentlemen; we have also my establishment, including Mr Raffles, who has a pretty numerous family." Here follows the description quoted in Chapter One. "Mrs Raffles is the great lady, with dark eyes, lively manner, accomplished and clever. . . . The sisters are all fair, one a very pretty woman. You need not smile, Anna Maria, for George says so . . . the other two, to avoid sneering, I shall say are honest-like. I have exchanged dinners with them; have breakfasted and visited there."

The sister who had met with the Hon. George Elliot's approval was Mary Anne, who had married again (2nd May 1811) since coming to

Malacca, this time to Captain William Flint,[1] R.N., of H.M.S. *Teignmouth.* She was Raffles' favourite sister—his "dear Pussy".

Minto went on:

"I have mustered the whole female community of Malacca at a Ball, for I am now writing on June 7. I celebrated the King's birthday by a levee in the forenoon, a great dinner to all mankind, and a Ball in the evening to all womankind."

Apart from the social life of Malacca, stimulated into such exceptional activity by the presence of the Governor-General and the whole expedition, there was much work being done. The most vital point to be decided was the route to be taken. The Navy, in the person of Commodore Broughton, was so conservative—and, be it added, ignorant—that it could not conceive the possibility of the expedition proceeding by any route except the one actually known to itself, although all agreed that this route, through the Durian and Bangka Straits, could not be attempted till the end of the monsoon, some months later. Broughton, however, had not reckoned with the industry and resourcefulness of Raffles or the firm determination of the Governor-General.

Raffles had already instituted extensive enquiries, "but here I was surprised to find the utmost degree of obscurity and contradiction prevailed. The alternative of only two routes was presented, the first of which, or the direct course along the South West coast of Borneo, was very generally represented as remarkably difficult and uncertain if not altogether impracticable. The second course, round the North and East coast of Borneo and through the Straits of Macassar, though supposed to be practicable was admitted by all to be eminently dangerous as well as tedious. . . ."

Captain Greigh had, at his request, proved the ease with which the Karimata Strait could be navigated and had "likewise ascertained both the facility of working along the coast of Borneo by the sea and land breezes and likewise of making Borneo through the Straits of Singapore".

This information was given in the course of a long memorandum to Minto on 22nd May. Soon after Greigh's departure on his mission to the Sultan of Pontianak:

". . . I fortunately procured the opinion of Messrs R. Scott and Stewart, two of the best informed and most respectable of our Eastern traders in the Malay seas, both of whom were decidedly of opinion that the S.W. passage was not only practicable at this season of the year, but infinitely less dangerous and tedious than the N.W. passage. Both of them had passed through the Caramata Passage at different seasons of the

[1] William Lawrence Flint (1781-1828), a younger brother of Sir Charles Flint, private secretary to the Duke of Wellington (1808-1815). A sister, Anne Flint, married in 1824 Rear-Admiral Fane and, on his death, the Marquis of Thomond.

year. Both of them affirmed the practicability of effecting a passage between Caramata Passage and the mainland of Borneo. . . . On the whole, therefore, I am happy to say that no doubt can now be reasonably entertained that the S.W. passage may be effected by the Fleet sailing in divisions in the space of a month or six weeks at farthest, although it will certainly be desirable in case of accidents that the whole should be victualled and watered for two months."

While Minto and Raffles were discussing this momentous question, Leyden had seized the opportunity to go up country from Malacca to quench his insatiable thirst for knowledge. He wrote to Raffles on 31st May from Gappam:

"... I am very much pleased with the inhabitants of the Campong, or Vale of Gappam. They are [a] clean, healthy, stout looking race; and appear to me to be as excellend peasants as I have seen . . . as far as I can learn, the Pangula[1] of Nanning is as nearly as possible in a state of open rebellion and the people here say he has got a signet from Menangkabu, with which he flourishes away famously. If I were Mr Seton I would give him an opportunity of contemplating a company of Sepoys for a couple of days. The supineness of the former Government is only equalled by the wickedness of the maxims under which it acted. Tell Mr Seton, that I earnestly entreat him to give me a grant of a couple of hundred of ruined villages, for here there is nothing else to be met with. . . . I meant to have put Mrs Raffles in a postscript but have decided on considering that it is generally the most favourable part of a lady's letter and have reserved that honour for Miss Raffles; apropos all ladies, I have already become an immense favourite of that goodly old dame, the Pangulu of Gappam's wife, from having dined entirely on curries, &c, of her own dressing, the lady has not yet ventured to show herself; but I have been informed of the fact, which I hold for gospel."

The sister referred to was Harriet, the eldest. It has been said that they would have been married but for his untimely death. This seems improbable, for Leyden was engaged to a girl in Scotland, Janet Brown. Ultimately, in 1816, Harriet married a Somerset House official named Browne.

Captain Taylor, reporting to his wife (1st June) the arrival of a division, adds this note:

"This Division had passed the Commodore Broughton feeling his way down [the Straits of Malacca] with 'Phoenix' frigate ahead sounding."

Broughton certainly deserved his reputation.

With this division came Colonel Robert Rollo Gillespie, he who, in July 1806, had made the famous ride from Arcot to Vellore, where the fort was besieged by mutinous sepoys.

[1] Penghulu, territorial chief.

The days spent at Malacca must have been very busy, yet Raffles managed to organize a meeting of the Malacca Asiatic Society, which Minto attended. Minto also arranged for the instruments of torture found in the Malacca prison to be publicly destroyed.

Notwithstanding all the activity in which inevitably he was a central figure and alone able to answer the innumerable questions that kept cropping up, and in spite of endless conversations with the Governor-General and all his new functions as principal secretary, Raffles still found time to complete and present to Minto a series of immense dispatches in which were summarized all the facts he had collected on the Netherlands Indies, the state of Dutch administration and, above all, his own personal views on the future policy to be adopted. First of all he warned Minto (this memorandum is undated) of unwelcome activities that the enemy might contrive while surrender was taking place:

"As emptying the public Treasury and Godowns is so frequent a trick while surrender is negotiating and the great depression in value of paper currency afford such easy aggrandizement to those in the secret of public affairs, it might well be to notify by Proclamation, on landing, that 'The persons and property of the Governors or Residents and Council, with all those in public situations connected with the charge, when rumour may create sufficient suspicion, will be held accountable, unless it can be proved that the said Depositories have not been opened, or otherwise, equally to satisfaction, that no property has been moved from the time of receiving this notification' and 'that should any provision be hereafter deemed admissible for the claims of capital invested in Government notes, they will only be acknowledged at the lowest rate they can be ascertained to have passed, and if continued in circulation thereby, not allowed to represent more.' In such a moment of alarm the simple will, notwithstanding this precaution, sell, and the knowing, buy. . . . As these notes are like those of our own Bank, in payment of a debt, legal tender . . . the cancelling would be an injustice to the holders of that capital. . . ."

This is just one, if an important, detail. More weighty and significant still are the three main reports, from which substantial quotation cannot be avoided if the contribution of Raffles is to be properly appreciated. The first is quoted, without a date, in Lady Raffles' *Memoir*.

". . . Independently of the native agents employed to convey to the eastward favourable intimations of our intentions, I deemed it necessary to dispatch directly to the Isle of Bali in the first place Lieutenant Smith in the 'Arethusa' cutter and afterwards Greigh of the brig 'Minto'. . . . The Rajah of Bali Baliling, with whom I first opened a communication, has not only on all occasions exhibited the greatest demonstrations of friendship towards the English, but zealously co-operated with me in conveying letters and intelligence to the Eastern Chiefs, with whom I have found it most difficult to open a communication. . . . The Sultan of Carang Asam[1] and Lombok, to whom I had not addressed a letter . . . as soon as he was informed of our intentions of invading Java, came immediately forward and offered his services in the most friendly manner. . . ."

He then gave historical and other details about these and other native territories, showing an amazing grasp of Eastern politics. Turning to the military state of the island, he wrote:

". . . The most active and unremitting exertions appear to have been made by Marshal Daendels towards securing his defences, and the fall of Mauritius has no doubt fully confirmed his apprehensions of the nature of the intended attack. It seems currently believed in Java that the Marshal expects almost immediate assistance from France; and the circumstances of his being able to hoist the French flag at such a critical moment, and with so little opposition, strongly indicates that he relies on more than ordinary means of defence, and confides in resources which render the sentiments of the Dutch inhabitants . . . of comparatively little importance. . . . Rumours of strong private discontent have, however, reached Malacca, though there is no reason to think that any concert prevails among the individuals concerned in them, or that anything of the kind will show itself openly until we appear in force in Java. . . . The intimation of your Lordship's intention of accompanying the present expedition to Java, of which I have taken care to convey them notice, will, I have no hesitation to say, tend materially to tranquillize the minds of the Dutch inhabitants, and to determine the part which they will take on the appearance of our armament. . . .

"On the whole, it appears absolutely certain that Marshal Daendels is concentrating his best troops on the Western part of the Island and in the vicinity of Batavia. As to Batavia itself, it obviously holds no consideration, either in the civil arrangements of the Marshal, nor in his intended plan of defence. It has been dismantled of all its fortifications; its public stores, ammunition, and archives have all been removed, and every means have been employed to induce the inhabitants, both European and native, to desert it entirely. The temporary seat of Government is established at Weld de Wreeden [Weltevreden], where the public functionaries of every description are obliged to reside for the present; but arrangements are making for the transfer of the whole administration to Buitenzorg, at the distance of about 35 miles from Batavia in the vicinity of the Blue Mountains. Weld de Wreeden, the first military post of importance on the rear of Batavia, can only be considered as a fortified camp; Cornelis at the distance of a little more than five miles from Batavia is the first fortified post of importance; it consists of a Fort which stands on the

[1] Karang Asam ("Sour Reef"), eastern Bali.

centre of several batteries, the front covered by a canal and the flanks by a river, while a battery placed on a rising ground commands the rear. . . ."

He went on to describe other fortified posts, from which he deduced that the Marshal "does not seem to intend to stand a regular siege in any one place, but trusts to prolong the campaign by a war of posts, till the setting in of the rainy season or the arrival of his expected succours from France. This mode of warfare, it must be allowed, is well adapted to the nature of the country, provided he could depend on the fidelity of his troops, and the attachment of the Princes of the interior, particularly the Susuhunang [of Surakarta] and the Sultan of Mataram."

He then described the measures he recommended to detach the princes and others from the Marshal, and concluded his letter with a warning about the conduct of the invading forces towards the native inhabitants.

". . . The Dutch have always spread the most unfavourable notions as to the character of the Malays, and it is certain that they will have given to the Malays a most unflattering account of the English. Those untoward prejudices will certainly be attended in the ensuing campaign with very unpleasant and troublesome consequences, unless proper precautions be taken to guard against them from the very first landing in Java . . . for a tame submission to personal injury is certainly not characteristic of either the Malays or the Javanese. . . ."

The second of these reports was dated 4th May, while Lord Minto was still at Penang. It opened with the all-important question of route, having disposed of which, Raffles proceeded to deal at length with the prevalence of piracy and the causes of it. Then he turned to Kedah and the imminent invasion of that country by the Siamese, and concluded with a comprehensive sketch of the political situation in Achin, Sumatra.

The final report, and by far the most important, was that of 10th June. It opened with a detailed account of the island of Borneo and the history of the failure of both the Dutch and the British to maintain successful trading posts there. He explained, with force and example, that the two main causes of failure had been the incapacity of the men placed in charge and the want of previous examination of the place selected for a settlement. He could not resist a slight dig at the Government of Penang.

"I fear it must be admitted that the Government of Penang had not been much more active in illustrating the state of the Malay Peninsula, or even the Provinces of Mergy [Mergui] and its vicinity, to which their attention was particularly directed in instructions by the Court of Directors to the late Mr Dundas, on establishing the Presidency of Prince of Wales Island."

He next turned to Cochin-China, the Philippine Islands, Celebes and Japan. He gave a very interesting history of European connexion with Japan, but further reference to this must be deferred until we come to the attempts made by him as Lieutenant-Governor of Java to reopen trade with that difficult nation.

Passing from the particular to the general, he allowed himself to expound his theories as to the future eastern empire that lay open to the English.

"The annexation of Java and the Eastern Isles to our Indian Empire, opens to the English nation views of so enlarged a nature as to seem equally to demand and justify a bolder policy, both of a commercial and political kind, than we could lately have contemplated. The countries which must, directly or indirectly, fall under our influence and authority, form a range of possessions which, with intervals of no great importance, extend nearly from the Bay of Bengal to our Settlements on the Continent of New Holland [Australia].

"These are occupied, except where the Dutch have taken the territorial possession into their own hands, by several small groups of principalities, none of which, taken separately, have any pretensions to the rank of a powerful or independent State. The tribes of which they are composed, though varying radically in customs, manners, religion and language and possessing various degrees of civilization, have long been confounded by Europeans under the general appellation of Malays, a term which may still be retained for convenience. It may be safely affirmed that about the period when Europeans first began to frequent these countries, they were not only much more populous, but the Governments were much more strong and steady, and the inhabitants, in general, much farther advanced in civilization. The Dutch, solely attentive to their own commercial interests, have in their intercourse with these regions invariably adhered to a more cold-blooded, illiberal and ungenerous policy than has ever been exhibited towards any country, unless we except the conduct of the European nations towards the Slave Coast of Africa. . . .

"But however their policy may be characterized, I apprehend that their claims to territorial right in the Eastern Isles, in which all the nations of Europe have so long and so blindly acquiesced, will be found to be very much inferior to what is generally supposed, unless perhaps in the Island of Java itself. As their claims, of whatsoever kind, must now revert to the French nation, it will be of the utmost importance to ascertain from the original Dutch records how far their territorial cessions and exclusive privileges do actually extend; also how far these are absolute and how far revokable; and in short to obtain a complete code[1] of the Dutch Treaties with all the Malay Princes since the first commencement of their establishments in the Eastern Isles.

"The diplomatic importance of such a code will be readily recognized by your Lordship, and in the event of any future negotiations in Europe

[1] This is presumably the set to be found in the Indian Office Library.

may prove of the most essential importance. The line of policy, which on the present occasion, we ought to adopt towards the Malay States, should be as uniform in its features, and comprehensive in its extent, as possible. The various groups of States, to which, what may emphatically be termed our Malay policy, may extend, are the following:

"1st. The States of the Malay Peninsula.

"2nd. The States of the Island of Sumatra.

"3rd. The States of the Island of Borneo.

"4th. The States of the Sunda Islands, comprehending the chain of Islands which extend from the Straits of Sunda to Timor and Celebes exclusive of Java which we may except for the present.

"5th. The States of Celebes.

"6th. The States of Sulu and Mindanawi [Mindanao, Philippines].

"7th. The States of the Moluccas, comprehending Ceram and Banda.

"8th. The States of Jililo [Gilolo] or Little Celebes.

"9th. The Black Papua States of New Guinea and the Papua Islands in its vicinity.

"These States I shall only enumerate here, as requiring distinct reports of their nature and connexion with the Dutch, or as we may now state, with the French; after which it will probably appear to be our soundest policy for the most intimate connexions by Treaty with those which have indisputable pertentions to independence. This policy will, I flatter myself, appear obvious, whether we contemplate the maintaining of the Malay Isles in permanent possession, or the possible transferring of the Dutch possessions to the enemy in the event of a peace in Europe.

"In the event of the first alternative, it will enable us to turn these possessions to the greatest advantage, whether respect be had to our European trade or to the general benefit of our Indian possessions. In the event of the second, we shall secure such a footing amongst the Eastern Isles, and such a favourable regard amongst the bravest races, as will baffle all the attempts of the enemy to dislodge us. By fixing ourselves in Banca, Bali, Celebes and Jililo, we should have a chain of posts which would prevent the enemy entirely from attaining very formidable power or deriving his former advantages from possession of Java and the Moluccas; and by forming a Settlement in Borneo, connected with the interior of that country, so fertile and so rich in the precious metals, we should soon be in a condition to compete with them on equal terms.

"The whole of the States, which I have now specified, have been so much accustomed to European interference and control, that the greater part of them are by no means fitted with the enjoyment of a fair and liberal independence, nor are they likely to become so for a series of years. At the same time, the treatment which they have experienced from the Dutch, has been in general so extremely galling and oppressive, that a more liberal policy can hardly fail of conciliating their affections in a high degree; sufficiently conscious of the inability to stand alone, and warned by the breaking up of some of the most oldest and most powerful estates, they would gladly ally themselves to so powerful a nation as the English, on anything like fair and equitable terms, by which they might be secured from civil commotions, without being deprived of all their natural advantages, as under the Dutch domination.

"Now as our principal political embarrassment, with regard to Java and the Eastern Isles, arises from the danger of these being given to the enemy, in the event of a peace in Europe, I beg leave to suggest to your Lordship a method of avoiding a part of this danger, which by no means appears impossible or even arduous to carry into execution, though it is not likely to occur to the Malay Chiefs, unless it should be suggested to them. In ancient times, the Malay Chiefs, though possessing the titles of Sultans or Rajahs, and with full possession of authority within their own domains, yet all held by a superior of Suzerain, who was King of the ancient and powerful estate of Majopahit[1] on the Island of Java, and who had the title of Bitara.[2] Malacca was one of the first States that shook off this allegiance, and became in the end so powerful, as to hold a great part of the Malay Peninsula and of the opposite coast of Sumatra in a similar dependence, though the Sovereigns of these States retained their titles of Rajahs or Sultans, and exercised their authorities within their own territories. Now, though the present Malay Chiefs are jealous and punctilious in high degree about their own titles, they are by no means equally so respecting holding of a superior whose title would save their own dignity; and I conceive they must easily be prevailed upon by suggestions, to invest the Governor-General of India with the ancient title of Bitara, equivalent to Lord Protector, which has become obsolete amongst them for more than three centuries and which would not, I conceive, be reckoned injurious to the dignity of any modern Chieftain whatever titles and epithets he might bear.

"This would give a general right of superintendence over, and interference with, all the Malay States, which might be acted upon, when circumstances would then be necessary; and might be so limited by Treaty as to remove any occasion of suspicion from the native Powers. It is of importance, however, that this should appear to be the spontaneous and voluntary act of the Malay Chieftains, as by this means it would be less liable to modification in the event of any Treaty which may be concluded in Europe with the enemy; but I shall here solely confine

[1] Majapahit—"Bitter Bel"—the last kingdom of Java to profess Hinduism, overthrown by the Mahometans in the fifteenth century. Bel is the tree bearing the sweetish fruit sometimes known as the Bengal quince.

[2] *Bhatara* (Sanskrit): "Exalted".

myself to the bare statement of the idea, and leave for future consideration its different limitations, and the means which might be proposed for carrying it into execution.

"In the districts that may be reduced under the sole authority of the English, little doubt can be entertained that we shall best consult our own interests by a line of policy radically different from that of the Dutch. In all the Eastern Dutch Settlements, their favourite policy has been to depress the native Malay or Javanese inhabitants and give every encouragement to the Chinese, who are only itinerants and not children of the soil, and who follow the general practice of remitting their fruits of their industry to China, instead of spending them where acquired. . . . They have, almost from the first, been the agents of the Dutch, and in the Island of Java, in particular, they have almost acquired the entire monopoly of revenue farms and Government contracts. At present, many of the most respectable Dutch families are intimately connected with the Chinese in their contracts and speculations, and it is only very lately that Marshal Daendels sold the whole province of Pasuki [Besuki] to the Captain China, or Head Chinaman of Surabaya. . . . The ascendancy of the Chinese, whether of a commercial or political nature, should be cautiously guarded against and restrained; and this perhaps cannot be better done than by bringing forward the native population of Malays and Javanese, and encouraging them in useful and industrial habits.

"The observations, which I have suggested to your Lordship, regarding the Chinese, are in a high degree applicable to the Arabs, who frequent the Malay countries and, under the specious mask of religion, prey on the simple unsuspicious natives. The Chinese must at all events be admitted to be industrious; but the Arabs are mere drones. . . . They are also very frequently concerned in acts of piracy and great promoters of the slave trade. This class of adventurers it will be our object sedulously to oppress, but a regulated trade with any of the commercial States of Arabia as Muscat, Mocha or Jidda, may prove extremely advantageous to the Malay countries. . . .

"Let the Chinese and the Arabs, as well as the Americans, trade to the Eastward, but let their trade be regulated and above all, let them not be left in the enjoyment of exemptions and advantages which are neither possessed by the English or the Malays. Since the reduction of the influence of the Dutch in the East, several of the ports dependent on them have almost become Arab Colonies, as Palembang, Tringano and Telawany [Taliwang] on Sumbawa. The evil is obviously increasing every day, and can only be checked by encouraging the native Malays, and regulating on equal terms the duties of the Malay and other Eastern ports.

"Another class of commercial interlopers who will require our vigilant attention is the Americans. . . . Of late they have become better acquainted with many of these Islands, from their vessels having been employed by the Dutch. If such active and enterprising traders, who are certainly not particularly well affected towards the English, be permitted to trade to the Eastern Islands on equal terms with the English, it will inevitably be injurious to our commercial interests; but if they are permitted the free range of the Eastern Archipelago, perhaps it would be difficult to devise a measure more injurious to our political influence, as well as our commercial interests. The Americans, wherever they go, as they have no object but commercial adventure, and as firearms are in the highest request, especially among the more Eastern Isles, these would be considered as the most profitable articles. They have already filled the different clusters of Islands in the South Seas with firearms, and they would not fail to do the same in the different Eastern Islands. These considerations seem obviously to point to a line of policy respecting the trade of the Eastern Islands, which in some respect coincides closely with that adopted by the Dutch, while in others it differs entirely in ultimate principles.

"In many respects the commercial policy adopted by the Dutch with regard to the Eastern Islands, and the Malay States in general, was not only contrary to all principles of natural justice and unworthy of any enlightened or civilized nation, but characterized by a degree of certainty for which it was scarcely worth taking the trouble of being so preposterously wicked. Thus in the Dutch orders, respecting trade and navigation, in the very first article it is stated that 'all persons whatever are prohibited under pain of death from trading in the four fine kinds of spices unless such spices shall have first been bought from the Company.' After the enactment of a penalty so outrageously disproportioned to the offence, the authentic accounts of their attempts to destroy and eradicate, from a vast range of extensive countries, the most advantageous produce of the land, in order to favour their own petty traffic, and their burning a large proportion of the residue, in order to keep up their monopoly price in Europe on a small proportion of this produce, must be viewed by all liberal minded and intelligent men with sentiments of contempt and detestation.

"Against errors of this kind your Lordship's presence in the East will be an effective preventive, but it may still be questioned whether, in the present state of these countries, it may not be necessary, in the first instance, to retain some traits of Dutch policy. One feature of Dutch policy, to the Eastward, seems to have been the entire exclusion of all other Powers, whether native or European, excepting at certain specified ports under their own immediate influence and control. The policy was as much connected with political government of the country, as with the commercial profits of the Company; for in an archipelago of such unparalleled extent, inhabited with tribes of such various character, formidable in a very high degree for their want of civilization, it was necessary to bring forward some of the most powerful and most favourably situated of these numerous States, and to hold them answerable for the proceedings of the smaller districts under their influence.

"This policy gave rise to the establishment of certain regular and determined trading ports and the vigilant suppression of all attempts at competition and independence in the inferior States. Had this measure been conjoined with the liberal policy tending to facilitate the home trade, as we denominated, between these privileged ports established by the Dutch and the various countries under their influence, I apprehend that little doubt can be entertained that it would have tended materially to promote the civilization and general improvement of all the Eastern nations.

"Very different, however, were the Dutch agreements with the different Rajahs of the Archipelago. In some cases it was to secure monopoly of all the tin, pepper, camphor, or other saleable articles that the country produced; in another it was to bind the Chiefs of the country to destroy the only saleable articles that the country produced, lest the monopoly price of the Dutch should be injured by a greater quantity of such produce being brought to market. The Dutch genius, though exclusively devoted to commerce, has never yet been able to discover that in the long run it must be more profitable, 'to make smaller profits on a larger capital'; and their policy has not been unaptly compared to a man putting out one of his eyes in order to strengthen the sight of the other.

"Against the policy of determining certain and regular ports, as emporiums of trade, it does not appear to me that there are any valid objections to be stated; and I therefore submit this measure to your Lordship's consideration as the most effectual method of preventing the Eastern Islands from being overrun by a multitude of unprincipled adventurers, chiefly Chinese, Arabian and American, whose presence in these countries will neither tend to strengthen the interest of the British nation, nor ameliorate the condition of the natives.

"If this measure, however, should approve itself to your Lordship, it may still be proper to enquire in what respects our policy may be considered superior to that of the Dutch, and how it is calculated to promote the improvement and advantage of the Malay nations, in a higher degree than those. It must be admitted that the policy, which we have hitherto pursued with regard to the Malay nations, has been by no means of a conciliating or prepossessing nature. Our intercourse with them has been carried on almost exclusively by adventurers, little acquainted with either the country or the people, who have frequently been more remarkable for boldness than principle. Indeed the want of any settled basis of traffic, and the long indifference of the British Government to the complaints of either party, have produced so many impositions, reprisals, piracies, and murders, that it has fairly been observed that every Eastern trader must have been himself very much in the situation of a trader in spirits, tobacco and blankets amongst the Indians and North Americans.

"It was properly remarked by Mr [Robert] Farquhar, in his report on Prince of Wales's Island, that this indifference of the British Government must have originated solely for the want of information or from its incorrectness, since little doubt can be entertained that the riches of Sumatra and Borneo are equal to either Brazil or South America, and it is only from the disadvantages, under which we have hitherto entered into the competition, that these great sources of wealth have been so long engrossed by the Dutch, Spaniards and Chinese. But this previous neglect of the British Government, we may confidently expect, will form no rule for the future, and the benefits which the Malay nations may derive from a close connexion with the British Government and nation, are such that there is no probability of their ever deriving from the French or Dutch.

"The doctrine that a Colony should always be considered as a distant province of the Mother Country, could never have been received by the Dutch, and the radical want of strength in the Government of Batavia must always have prevented them from venturing to act upon it. Of course they must always have contemplated the prosperity of the Eastern tribes with the invidious regret of a rival shopkeeper, and regarded their progress and civilization with the jealousy of a timorous despot, which in point of fact we know they actually did. The power of the English in the East enables them to employ a less timid policy; humanity imperiously requires that they should employ it and fortunately their own interests coincide with these, as an additional inducement.

"The causes which have tended most to the depression of the Malays and the deterioration of their character are the following:—The civil commotion to which every State is liable from the radical want of strength in the Sovereign and the constant wars between petty Chieftains and Heads of villages and districts; the ill-defined succession to the Throne, from the doctrine of primogeniture being imperfectly recognized in the Malay States; the prevalence of piracy in all the Eastern Seas; the system of domestic slavery with all its concomitant evils . . .; the want of a generally established and recognized system of laws, regarding all questions, civil and criminal, in the Malay States; the want of a similar system of commercial regulations . . .; the discouragement given to regular trade by the monopolies of the Malay Rajahs. The redress of these evils is in a great measure in the power of the English nation; it is worthy of their general character, and there is no other nation that possesses the means in an equal degree, even if it possessed the inclination.

"With regard to the feudal wars of petty Chieftains and the civil commotions which constantly aggitate [*sic*] the Malay States, these have been greatly increased by the policy of the Dutch whose authority has been in a great measure maintained and supported by dissentions which they were in the habit of exciting in the more powerful Malay States. In consequence of this, we find that scarcely a single powerful estate now subsists which was in existence when the Dutch settled in the East. . . . This evil was prevented effectually during the Dutch domination by their assuming the paramount right of granting investiture to every Prince who succeeded to the Government of a country, and if such a plan as I have alluded to were to be adopted by the English, a similar policy, either by granting investiture, or by recognizing the heir apparent would naturally require to be followed. . . .

"Of the prevalence of piracy on the Malay coast and its being regarded as an honourable occupation worthy of being followed by young Princes and Nobles I have already had occasion to speak. This is an evil of ancient date and which has struck deep on the Malay habits. The old Malay romances, and the fragments of their traditional history, constantly refer to piratical cruises. . . .

"Connected with this evil, but of much wider extent, is the system of slavery in the Malay countries, which, to apply the energetic language of Mr Pitt to this subject, has been none of the least efficient causes of keeping down these regions in a state of bondage, ignorance and blood. On the grand evils of the system of slavery, and its necessary concomitant, the man-trade and its pernicious consequences, whether personal, civil, social or domestic, it is fortunately at the present period unnecessary to expatiate, since by the late 'Act for the Abolition of the Slave Trade' that system of crime is prohibited in all territories in H.M.'s possession or occupation. . . . The sources of slavery in the Malay countries are chiefly the following:—Piracy, captivity in war, man-stealing, and the penalites enacted in the Malay Law respecting debts and sundry misdemeanours. . . .

"Nothing has tended more decidedly to the deterioration of the Malay character, than the want of a well defined and generally acknowledged system of Law. . . . Another of the customs injurious to the Malay nations, is the trading monopoly, which in most of the Malay ports, is actually assumed, or attempted to be assumed by the Malay Chiefs. Of this monopoly there is no trace in the Undang [Law] of the Malays, or in the fragments of their history, which I have seen, such as the traditional annals of Malacca, and after an attentive consideration, I am induced to think that this pernicious practice has been entirely copied from the monopoly regulations of the Dutch. Where this system has been fully carried into effect, it has generally succeeded effectually in replacing industry and commercial enterprise; and where it has been for some time established, its evils have been felt deeply, so that there is no doubt but that the Malay Chiefs could easily be induced to relinquish it in favour of a regulated commerce. . . .

"From similar considerations, as well as in comformity to instructions issued from home, the Dutch nation appear to have pursued as a principle of policy the propagation of Christianity among the Eastern Islands. . . .

"In these observations I have in some degree avoided alluding to the advantages which may be expected to accrue to the British nation itself, and also to the British possessions in India from the acquisition of Java, and the Eastern Isles, because I am persuaded that the real advantages, which these countries possess, will be found, under a liberal and enlightened system of management, vastly to exceed any expectations which may be formed in the present state of our information concerning them. In their present state, with the exception of Java, these countries are poor in respect of general wealth, and can only pay in rude produce for the articles which they require from other countries. The rude produce, however, from the Malay countries is of various kinds, some of which are extremely valuable, and equally calculated for the European, the Indian and the China market. The intercourse between countries rich in manufacturing industry, and countries rich in raw produce is universally admitted to be of equal benefit to both. In respect of the Malay Islands, India must long be regarded as a manufacturing country and is particularly fitted to supply a variety of articles in general request among the Malays, without interfering with the industry of the Mother Country. The trade from India to the Malay countries has hitherto chiefly consisted in Opium and piece goods, to which India has chiefly received back gold-dust, spices, gums and coffee. I omit the mention of copper, as it is not a native Malay production, but chiefly derived from Japan. The circumstances, however, under which the Indian trade to the Eastward has hitherto been carried on, and the insecurity and want of protection under which it has always laboured, rendered the past no criterion of the future, and I have no doubt it may be improved to an almost indefinite extent, as the Malay countries advance in civilization. The Java sugar is at present reckoned nearly on a par with the fine sugar of Manila, and the Java coffee next to the coffee of Mocha and Bourbon [Réunion]. Either of these productions are capable of being greatly extended. . . .

"With regard to the Chinese market, the Malay countries furnish a variety of articles of the most general use and most constant demand, and which do not affect either the products or manufacture of either Great Britain or British India. Tin is one of these products, which finds a constant and almost indefinite demand in China, and which is solely produced in the Malay countries. . . . The quantity of pepper yearly required for the Chinese market has been estimated at 50,000 picules. . . .

"In the present unparalleled state of the European market on the Continent, it is hazardous to venture to allude to it. It may, however, be stated, generally, that the acquisition of the Dutch possessions in the East places the command of the spice trade, together with that of pepper and coffee, besides a variety of other Eastern produce, entirely in our hands, and that the Continent must either do without these articles, or submit to purchase them from the English. The valuable forests of Teak, and other ship timber in Java, and other Eastern Isles, are acquisitions of the highest national importance in the present state of European politics, and promise to render our Navy independent of the stores formerly derived from the precarious friendship of the Northern powers. Nor is the acquisition of a range of countries, apparently possessing the most valuable gold and diamond mines in the world, an object unworthy of our notice in our present situation, in which the drain on our specie has been great in an unprecedented degree, and when, for the restoration of the precious metals among us as a circulating medium, we are likely to be left in a great measure to our own resources.

"To dilate any further on these topics is unnecessary as, on your Lordship's approach to Java, every day will bring forward information to which it is not now in my power to allude. The suggestions, which I have already offered, may perhaps have already appeared to your Lordship unnecessarily prolix; but of putting you in possession of all the information which I have been able to obtain, and of all the views of the subject which I consider as meriting attention, I have only endeavoured to apply to that confidence which your Lordship reposed in me in appointing me your Lordship's Agent in the Malay States.

"I have now only to congratulate your Lordship on the most splendid prospect, which any administration has beheld since our first acquisition of India; the pacification of India completed, the tranquillity and prosperity of our Eastern possessions secured, the total expulsion of the European enemy from the Eastern Seas, and the justice, humanity and moderation of the British Government, as much exemplified in fostering and leading on new races of subjects and allies in the career of improvement as the undaunted courage and resolution of British soldiers in rescuing them from Oppression."

On 27th April, the Council at Calcutta had written to the Secret Committee:

"Your Honourable Committee will probably concur in opinion with us that Mr Raffles has manifested a considerable degree of Industry, Judgment and Ability, in carrying into effect the very delicate and important objects of his Mission, and that the information he has acquired respecting the state and disposition of the Native Powers of Java, and the nature and extent of the enemy's military force and defences warrants an expectation of the successful issue of the Enterprise against the enemy's possessions in the Eastern Islands."

We can agree that this opinion was not unjustified. A consideration of the voluminous information on which he must have drawn for this survey of the Far East fills us with amazement. During a residence of only five years at Penang, where he had been fully occupied as the heart and soul of the local government, and a few months at Malacca, where he was collecting an immense mass of detailed information as to the present state of Java, corresponding with numerous Malay rajas and at the same time arranging for the reception and victualling at Malacca of the fleet and expedition, he yet found time to assemble data about the Far East to a degree probably unparalleled, at that time, by any single European. Surely this was a remarkable achievement.

Chapter Nine

THE JAVA EXPEDITION, 1811

THE dispatch of the expedition from Malacca began on 11th June 1811. The troops had been reorganized ashore and, after practising field operations, had re-embarked in their assault formations. Twelve hundred sick had to be left behind, but the fifty-seven transports carried a total of some eleven thousand soldiers.

The ships were sent off in small divisions, each in charge of a frigate and attended by sloops and Company cruisers. The largest transports, carrying the horse artillery and cavalry, were in charge of Captain Christopher Cole in H.M.S. *Caroline*, this division being led by our old friend Captain D. Macdonald. They ran into a heavy sumatra (local cyclonic storm) and were fortunate not to lose any ships.

Minto and Raffles were accommodated in H.M.S. *Modeste*, commanded by George Elliot. Captain Greigh in the *Minto* was in attendance, and Leyden, to the joy of Captain Taylor, was put on board that ship. For a description of the voyage, it it impossible to improve on the brisk narrative of Minto:

"The 'Modeste' was not attached to any division, and, being sure of overtaking the earliest and swiftest, we remained at anchor till the whole had departed. The fleet consisted of 81 sail of all descriptions, and it was dispatched in many divisions because we had several narrow straits and difficult passes before us, which must have occasioned confusion, and probably accident and loss, if so large a body of shipping had kept together. This voyage is made interesting by the very positive opinions which Admiral Drury had given himself, and had managed to obtain a countenance to from several quarters of authority on such questions, that it was absolutely impracticable to make a passage to Java with a fleet of transports, if it should sail from Madras later than March 1st. It was with this opinion that I had to contend, pushing forward the Expedition in the present season, although it could not take its departure so soon as the day fixed by the Admiral, by six weeks according to my expectations, and, as it has proved on trial, by two months. The result has furnished another testimony in favour of the virtue called obstinacy, which is entitled by success to the more polite name of firmness.

"The difficulty was this. As soon as what is called the South-East Monsoon in the Eastern Seas sets in, the wind blows hard and pretty steadily from the East along the channel between the North of Java and the South of Borneo; it blows to the North-West along the East coast of Sumatra and between that coast and the Malay Peninsula; it blows to the North between the West coast of Borneo and the Straits of Malacca. So that, starting from Malacca, the wind was directly contrary in every part of the course to the Northern coast of Java.

"Besides this difficulty, there is a current in the same direction as the wind throughout. To carry a great fleet of transports, not famous in general for working to windward, a long voyage directly against wind and current, did not appear promising. It was known, however, that with a little patience a fleet can at that season make a passage down the Straits of Malacca by any one of the several passages which lead to the eastward. This is done by the help of squalls which generally blow from the northward; by occasional shifts of wind; and by alterations of tide or current, which afford a favourable start to the eastward.

"It was ascertained by investigation, enquiry and actual survey and trial recently made for the present occasion, that after making the West coast of Borneo, land winds at night and the sea breeze during part of the day, together with a slackening on the current and even a favourable current during particular periods of the tide, will enable ships to make a passage along the coast to the southward without much delay; and from the South-West point of Borneo, having the wind at East, you may stand at least as high as South to Java and make that island as far to the east as Samarang—which is more than we desire. The plan was therefore settled upon this foundation. The first object was to make the West coast of Borneo as much to the southward as we could. It was determined to go through the Straits of Singapore in preference to any of the more southerly issues from the Straits of Malacca, partly because the wind was rather more favourable and partly because it is the common way to China and better known to the Masters of ships under convoy.

"The 'Modeste' sailed from Malacca on June 18th. We soon passed a great part of the fleet and left them in the Straits of Singapore when we got into the open channel between those Straits and Borneo. The navigation so far is beautiful in the highest degree. We were always very near the Malay coast, which is richly furnished with islands of many patterns, and were often sailing in archipelagoes of them, so close and thick round us that we could not always see the way out, and at such moderate distances from the opposite shores as to allow us the full benefit of wood, mountain and all the shifting lines of land and water which make that sort of scenery interesting and picturesque to those passing quickly through it."

One fact Minto was unable to report; he was never to know of it or its significance. It so happened that Maharaja 'Abdu'l-Rahman, the Temenggong, hereditary ruler of Johore, had taken up his residence on

Singapore island only a short while before this fleet passed through the Straits. As he informed John Crawfurd many years later, he and his followers gazed on the passage of this great armada with amazement. No one in those parts could have seen such a display of sea-power before. And as the Temenggong watched wide-eyed this long procession of ships, Raffles assuredly had his eyes fixed on the ancient site of the historic Singapura, of which he had read the tragic story in the *Malay Annals*. So the two men stared in each other's direction, each unconscious of the other and unaware of the chain of circumstances that eight years later was to link their destinies together.

"We cleared the Straits", continued Minto, "on June 20, at sunset, leaving a great part of the fleet at anchor behind us, and stood across towards Borneo. We made the island off Sambas, a little to the north of Pontiana [Pontianak]. Here we came up with a division under the command of Captain Cole, which had sailed from Malacca some time before us and which was preceded by another under Captain Edgell not yet in sight. We soon, however, came up with it and had then the lead of all. On the 29th anchored close to the island of Panambangan [Penebangan], which was the first rendezvous from Malacca.

"The different divisions of the fleet came up gradually and slowly, but we saw them arrive with great satisfaction, as the possibility of working to the southward was thereby completely established and our passage to Java appeared to be secured. The 'Modeste' remained at this anchorage from June 29 to July 6, and it was the more fortunate that the situation was uncommonly pretty. The island is five or six miles long and somewhat less across. It rises into three or four hills of different shapes and of considerable height, covered as usual with wood of various sorts and dimensions. There are several snug bays, with two of which we were principally concerned. In each of these there is a waving beach of white sand, about fifty or sixty paces wide from the sea to the wood, and a nice stream of fresh water running into the sea. The scenery all round is beautiful and, while we were there, animated by tents and watering parties, boats and their crews, carpenters and their gangs felling trees for spars and planks, washermen, smith's forges, Sepoys bathing and cooking —in short, a most gay and picturesque scene. The island is uninhabited by man, and nothing more formidable was seen of the brute population than wild boars; there are deer, however, and some of the small kind called mouse deer, really not so large as a hare.

"I went on shore once, to see George and Captain Edgell's works. They constructed dams across the stream of fresh water to raise the surface higher than the tide at high water. The pond head was carried down by every shower that fell, which were not a few, but they renewed the work next morning indefatigably, having plenty of hands; and in fact their labours answered the purpose, and a full stock of excellent water was obtained. The Sepoys are particularly happy on these short visits to the land. Their religion makes it difficult to supply them with food at all on board, and it is always attended with inconvenience and privations of various sorts, the whole heightened by uneasy scruples by way of spice. When they get on shore, each man cooks his own meal according to his taste and prejudices, and they bathe comfortably both to their skins and consciences. The whole scene of black and white men, of trades and occupations, with the sort of spirit, energy and cheerfulness which belongs to British seamen, make this Panambangan beach a most lively and agreeable spot.

"From Panambangan anchorage we were to pass between that island and an adjacent one to the eastward in order to make the West coast of Borneo. But no part of this track had been examined. George accordingly sent Captain Greigh with the 'Minto' schooner to perform that service, and he made a perfectly satisfactory report before Commodore Broughton had arrived at Panambangan with the bulk of the fleet.

"Commodore Broughton, who is the most cautious navigator that ever wore a blue coat, was not satisfied to abide by Captain Greigh's report, but ordered the 'Modeste' to go ahead and reconnoitre the whole passage to the rendezvous, thinking very properly that I had better be drowned than he. As I was entirely of the same opinion, I accepted the service very thankfully. In reality I knew that George was much fitter to perform this duty than any other officer of the fleet, and I thought it would be amusing to myself. . . . We made the coast of Borneo as far to the North as we could and then zigzagged our way along the shore in five or six fathoms of water to the point proposed. . . . The Commodore had also ordered George to survey the neighbourhood of Pulo Mancap, which is situated beyond the rendezvous and is surrounded with shoals. This duty we also performed, returning to the rendezvous before the Commodore and fleet reached it.

"We had fallen in with a fleet of nine Buggese Prows when we went out towards Pulo Mancap, and from them George was informed of a shoal which lay somewhat in the course to Java. George, in communicating the rest of his information to the Commodore, mentioned this shoal. Upon this he ordered the 'Modeste' to explore it, whereupon we sailed again, but returned the second day without having found it. Immediately after, accounts were received that three French frigates, with 1,000 troops, had got into Java, and again the Commodore stood my friend and gave me the post of honour, which I accepted with real pleasure. He ordered the 'Modeste' immediately to Java. We sailed that night and fell in with the very shoal which we had missed by one mile of longitude a couple of days before. But as the Commodore would not allow us any small vessel to send back with intelligence, if we should meet with any, we could not convey notice to the fleet of this danger. However, there is little risk, for it lies further to windward than they can well keep up to. In less than forty-eight hours from Rendezvous Island, we were near enough Java to have seen the land if it had been daylight. On the next morning, July 25, we got a sight of the Land of Promise."

The passage from Malacca to Java had taken just seven weeks. Not a ship had been lost. The sick amounted to 1,500, not a very serious figure considering the times and circumstances. Thus were the promises of Raffles, and the reliance placed in him by Minto, fully justified. As the latter wrote:

"The expectations which had been formed were verified in every part of the passage and everything turned out precisely as had been foretold and proposed, with the exception of finding less difficulty than had been looked for and the voyage proving shorter than could have been hoped."

Fifty years later, George Elliot, writing in his reminiscences,[1] was to claim for himself the sole merit for the selection of the route and deny to Raffles the slightest share in it.

"Raffles", he wrote, "knew nothing of winds and monsoons in the Eastern seas, and never pretended to know; nor did he know what route it was proposed to take till he was desired as Interpreter at my request to obtain information . . . as to the winds on the West Coast of Borneo at that season, in which he totally failed."

Elliot was a conceited man and he disliked Raffles. Contemporary evidence is too strong to be rejected in favour of an old man's memories. What he could have claimed with probable truth was that his father was fortified by Elliot's knowledge and experience against the obstinate ignorance of Commodore Broughton. But the credit for the route chosen must go to Raffles and Captain Greigh.

Raffles' feelings as he watched the great fleet arriving are described in his letter off the coast of Java to William Brown Ramsay. This was one in which he spoke of "the times in which I am as happy as I think it possible for man to be". He continued: ". . . and it is one of these life-inspiring moments that I now propose passing with you *à la distance*. . . . Of the importance of this conquest, the views that naturally present themselves on such an occasion, and the share I have had in bringing the important point so near a conclusion, I need not speak; you have the opportunity of seeing Government proceedings, which will be sufficiently satisfactory. . . . I wish very much to hear what is said of my political ideas respecting the government of the Eastward. . . . I will write you more fully after we are settled. Conquer we must."

As the ships approached the shore, proclamations were ready for

[1] *Memoir of Admiral the Honble. Sir George Elliot.*

distribution to the population. These were dated 4th August "off Batavia" The one addressed to the Dutch was as follows:

"England has in every period, sometimes in concert with other powers, sometimes single and alone, been the champion and defender of Europe, the hope of those whose fate was not yet consummated, the refuge and consolation of the fallen—for France has been with equal uniformity the common enemy of all nations. Between these two the option must be made and on that question the extinction of their metropolis has left the Colonies of Holland to their own free judgment. Their Country has expired. If sentiments which his Excellency has been desirous of ascribing to them should induce them to pass cordially under the British Dominion, he offers friendship and protection during any contest which it may be necessary to maintain with those who would adhere to Force."

To the Javanese:

"The English come as friends and they expect to be received as such by every description of native inhabitant, but as they have not entered the Eastern Sea for purpose of ruin or destruction, but solely with the desire of securing to the Eastern nations the enjoyment of their ancient laws and institutions and of protecting everyone from violence, oppression and injustice, the inhabitants themselves must be aware that they cannot recommend themselves to such a Government by means of massacres and commotions. The English Government accordingly require that the native inhabitants remain for the present peaceable spectators of what is about to take place and that they on no account act oppressively or take up arms against the French or Dutch, except when expressly called upon to do so by an English Officer.

"All supplies will be paid for at full value, but you are not to supply the enemy; you are also to impede the progress of the enemy's army from one part of the country to the other. The port of Batavia is open to native traders. All prows and vessels bringing provisions and merchandise will be kindly received and protected by the English ships of war."

The landing commenced that day at Chilinching, ten miles or so east of Batavia, and was unopposed.

"Leyden," wrote the disgusted Captain Taylor, "who loved acting a part, was dressed as a pirate in a red tasselled cap, a cutlass round his waist and a pistol in his belt; he was first ashore, and bore the brunt of the attack, which came from a flock of barn-door fowls headed by an aggressive rooster."

This passive attitude on the part of the enemy may be briefly explained. Daendels had foreseen the possibility that the British would attempt to land at Chilinching, and, while he had not regarded it as practicable to prevent the landing altogether, he had planned to contain the invasion force as long as possible in the fever-ridden swamps between Chilinching

JAVA AND BALI
JAVA SEA
INDIAN OCEAN
SUMATRA
SUNDA STRAIT
JAVA HEAD
BANTAM
ANJER
WYNKOOPS B.
BATAVIA
BUITENZORG
MEESTER CORNELIS
KRAWANG
INDRAMAYU
CHERIBON
PREANGER REGENCIES
BANDUNG
CHIANJUR
TEGAL
PEKALONGAN
SAMARANG
JAPARA
JUWANA
REMBANG
BLORA
GRISEK
SURABAYA
MADURA
MADURA STRAIT
BANGKALAN
PAMEKASAN
SUMENEP
KEDU
SURAKARTA
JOKYAKARTA
MADIUN
KEDIRI
BLITAR
PASURUAN
PROBOLINGO
BESUKI
BANJUMAS
BANYUWANGI
NUSA BARUNG
BALI STRAIT
BALI
SINGARAJA
BULELENG
KARANG ASAM

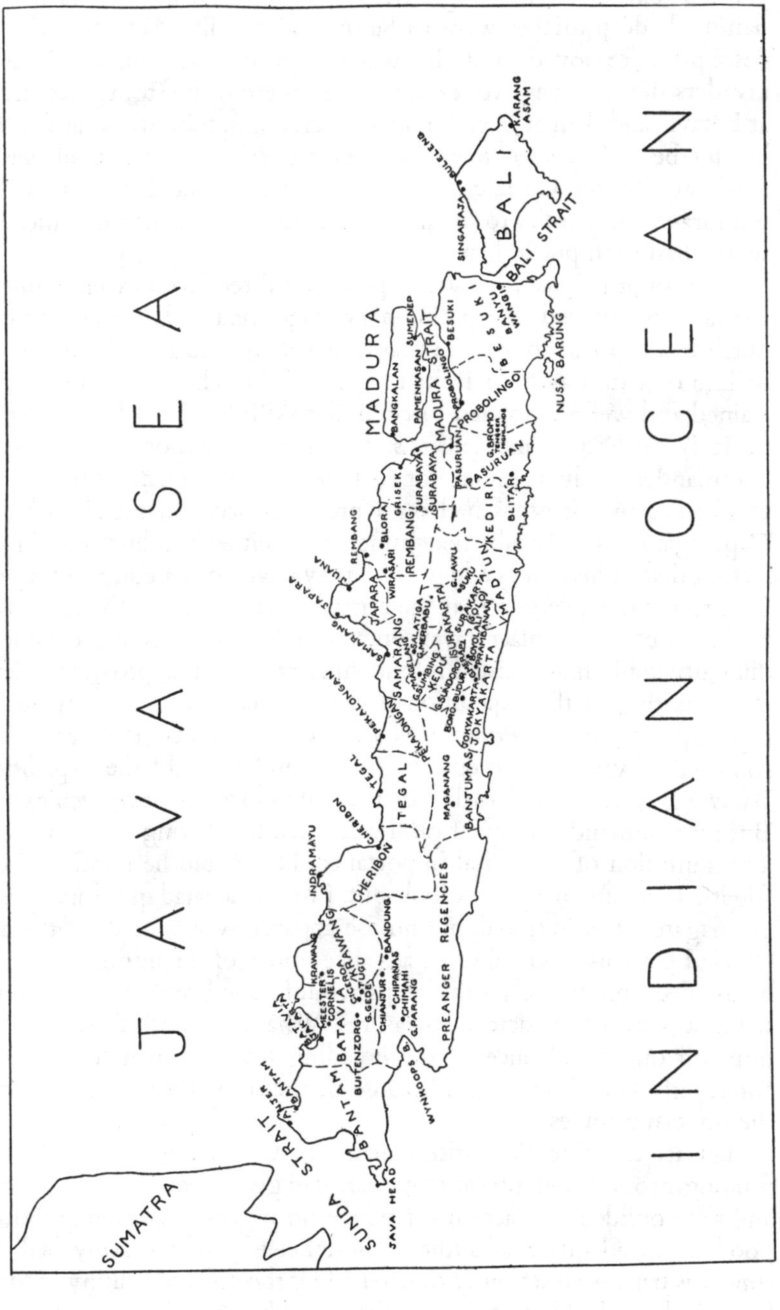

and Batavia, when losses from disease and a general lowering of morale could be expected. All bridges were to be destroyed, all rivers and creeks dammed; deep ditches were to be dug across the roads, boats of every description removed, and the water supply contaminated. When the invaders did at last move forward, they were to be stoutly resisted, first at Batavia and then at Weltevreden, all civilians, food stocks and materials having been evacuated from both places. But the real stand was to be made at Meester Cornelis. If this could not be held, the army would withdraw thirty miles to the heights of Buitenzorg, the refortification of which had been put in hand.

This in principle was a sound plan, but three factors were required to enable it to succeed: the preliminary stages had to be efficiently carried out; the army had to avoid a major defeat so as to be able to keep open its line of withdrawal to Buitenzorg; and the scheme required a highly trained and well-disciplined force, under skilful and resolute leaders.

It is easy to blame Janssens, the new Governor-General, and his commander-in-chief, Jumel, for their failure to implement the plan, and to observe that Janssens had on a previous occasion failed to hold the Cape against the British; that Jumel was neither resolute nor skilful. A lack of determination at a high level may have been a contributory cause. It is, too, almost certain that the arrival of the invasion force as to time, though not as to place, was unexpected. This was inexcusable. No difficulty could have existed in obtaining at least an approximate date for the departure of the expedition from Malacca, for its movements were reported fully in the *Prince of Wales's Island Gazette*. It is true that the route taken was not the customary one and brought the expedition to Batavia Bay very much earlier than would normally have been expected. But no commander-in-chief can be excused for relying so completely on an assumption of such vital importance. Nor could he plead the lack of frigates to maintain a proper look-out. Providence had quite unexpectedly put frigates at his disposal, but no use apparently was made of them.

Had Janssens received some advance notice of the imminent approach of the fleet, presumably some steps would have been taken to carry out the first phase of the defence measures. What real check these could have imposed on the advance of the invading force is open to question. It could only have been slight, because of the disparity in quality between the opposing forces.

Let us examine the British army first. India had proved a great training-ground, and intermittent wars had given that practical experience and self-confidence in action for which no peace-time training, however good, is an adequate substitute. The efficiency of the army had, for a time it is true, been seriously threatened by the officers' mutiny at Madras, but this threat had been successfully parried by the wise and statesmanlike handling of a very dangerous situation by Minto. This had brought him into very active association with the army, and the success of his measures had built up a bond of confidence between them. Out of evil had come good.

Two highly successful operations, Réunion and Mauritius, had come at an opportune moment to restore the army's confidence in itself. The invasion force was therefore composed of experienced and seasoned troops, well commanded throughout from the general officers down to the regimental officers. Above all, the troops respected their officers and had confidence in them. Most of them had experience of active service, many being straight from the victorious assault on Mauritius. The equipment was good; the co-operation of the navy excellent, for Admiral Stopford had hurried from the Cape and taken over the command from Commodore Broughton.

What sort of an army had Janssens to oppose this tough, highly disciplined and well-trained fighting force? Numerically the Franco-Dutch force was stronger. The exact size of it has been the subject of controversy, but 18,000 is a sufficiently accurate estimate of the total—a third more, after deducting the sick, than the effective strength of the invaders. But this advantage in strength was more than discounted by a much greater disparity in quality. The regular troops of the French army represented only a small fraction. Some had been a long time in Java and had been ruined by the climate and the lack of discipline. The rest had only just arrived. In neither case were the troops of high class. They had mostly been sent to the East after conviction for desertion or other military crimes. The officers were no better, relatively few having any qualifications for commissions. Most were promoted locally from the ranks and would have been lucky to become corporals in Europe. The native regiments were not much more than a rabble. How fine native troops can be, the British Empire has good grounds for knowing, but there are certain prerequisites: the native material must be good and freely recruited, and the European officers must possess not only high professional qualifications but also the magic power of sympathetic leadership which alone can weld a native corps into a reliable fighting force.

Janssens' native material was probably good enough, but as the "volunteers" were delivered by the French chained together in batches, they could hardly be expected to show loyalty to their officers, when their feelings were inspired by sullen resentment or active hatred. Nor would the officers have been of a quality to overcome such feelings. Few could have spoken even a smattering of the language, and their only idea of discipline was contemptuous and senseless brutality.

There was no possibility of using such troops in open warfare, or even in guerilla tactics. Only the visible leadership of their officers, and the vicinity of other European troops, could prevent them from deserting. The one hope was that behind the ramparts they would defend themselves stoutly, following the strongest instinct of the human race—self-preservation.

Two days after the landing began, Colonel Gillespie, with the advanced troops, moved forward on an armed reconnaissance up the Batavia road. Opposition was negligible and Batavia surrendered on 8th August, the main body moving in on the following day, while Gillespie advanced to the new suburb of Weltevreden.

The Dutch males had been compelled by the French authorities to leave their homes and report to an internment centre. This had led to widespread disorders among the Javanese in the capital and the surrounding districts. The looting of food stores was the principal feature, and those Dutch who were not interned frankly feared that a general outbreak against the European might develop. While, for the most part, not hostile to the British invasion, they dared not, at its inception, take any active steps to render assistance, for had it failed, their position would have been unenviable. As there was danger of real trouble with the Javanese, Minto proclaimed martial law.

Gillespie found Weltevreden undefended, but learned that Jumel was holding a strong position about a mile up the road to Cornelis. With characteristic dash he attacked at once, captured the position, and with it the French chief-of-staff, Brigadier Alberti. Thus, within a week, the road to Cornelis lay open.

The heavy batteries had now to be brought up and emplacements built. Even then, Jumel remained inactive, and it was only when the work was practically complete that he at last made use of some of his two hundred cannon. Sir Samuel Auchmuty wrote later:

"The enemy, greatly superior in numbers, was strongly entrenched in a position between the great river of Jacatra and the Sloken, an artificial watercourse, neither of which was fordable. This position was shut up by a deep trench, strongly palisaded. Seven redoubts and many batteries mounted with heavy cannon occupied the most commanding grounds within the lines. The fort of Cornelis was in the centre, and the whole of the works were defended by a numerous and well-organized artillery. The season was too far advanced, the heat too violent, and our number insufficient to admit of regular approaches. To carry the works by assault was the alternative, and on that I decided."

The British bombardment commenced on 24th August. Within two days, sufficient breaches had been opened to make possible a general assault, which was launched on 26th August.

This, while it lasted, proved a bloody affair. The enemy fought with determination, but the attacking troops, under their intrepid commander

Gillespie, who was wounded in the fighting, were not to be refused. The whole fortified zone was rapidly overrun and the French army virtually ceased to exist. Apart from heavy losses sustained in the operation, some 6,000 prisoners and the whole of the cannon and equipment were taken; only Janssens himself, with a handful of cavalry, escaped and reached Buitenzorg, where he was able to stay but a few hours, for our advanced troops were hard on his heels. Buitenzorg was occupied on 27th August, while Janssens reached the remainder of his forces, which had rallied and were holding the Gombal Hill, just outside Samarang, on the road to Salatiga.

Among the prisoners taken after the battle of Cornelis was Colonel Nahuijs. He wrote:

"The nearer I came to our taken retrenchment of Meester Cornelis, the more prisoners I met. With a feeling of shame and indignation I saw more than one officer amongst them trample on his French cockade to which he had sworn allegiance, uttering scandalous imprecations and swearing and assuring the English: 'I am no Frenchman, but a Dutchman.' I venture to say that no one took the oath of allegiance to the French colours with more aversion than I did, but no one could feel with more disgust than myself, how despicable it was, after such an oath, to behave as these officers did. When I was asked by the English officers who met us: 'To what country, sir, do you belong?' I always answered. 'Sir, I am a Frenchman from Amsterdam.' Even several weeks after, this name was given me, and I was often addressed as: 'the Frenchman from Amsterdam'."

After the landing at Chilinching, John Leyden had followed immediately behind the troops, his objective being the Dutch archives in Batavia, which he had entered as soon as the troops had cleared the road. There, according to Lord Minto,[1] in coming overheated into a cold room and spending some time examining the documents it contained, he got a chill, and fever developed. It may have been pneumonia; it may have been that the chill brought out a latent infection of malignant malaria. John Crawfurd, who had accompanied the expedition as Malay translator to the Governor-General, states definitely[2] that when he spoke to Leyden on 27th August, Leyden was suffering from malaria. Raffles described his death in a letter to William Erskine dated 10th September 1815:

"He breathed his last on the 28th August 1811, two days subsequent to the Memorable fall of Cornelis—but when, on the morning of that eventful day, I endeavoured to communicate to him the result, he was already too insensible to apprehend it. I attended him from the first to the last, and he frequently expressed his apprehension that he would not

[1] Countess of Minto, *Lord Minto in India.*

[2] *Journal of an Embassy to the Courts of Siam and Cochin China.*

survive the Attack; but as he had no deathbed accounts to settle, he pursued the same firm and unbending course which had characterized him through life."

Raffles and Lord Minto laid him in a grave in the European cemetery at Batavia. In Sir Walter Scott's *The Lord of the Isles* we find this epitaph to his old associate:

> Scenes sung by him who sings no more!
> His brief and bright career is o'er,
> And mute his tuneful strains;
> Quenched is his lamp of varied lore,
> That loved the light of song to pour;
> A distant and a deadly shore
> Has Leyden's cold remains!

Among the papers left by Leyden was a translation of the *Malay Annals*, which was ultimately published in 1821 with an introduction by Raffles. One of the main incidents described therein is the sack of the fourteenth-century city of Singapore and the rise to fame of Malacca, to which its Malay ruler had managed to escape.

To Raffles, Leyden's death was an irreparable loss. Leyden had been his first academic friend, and this friendship had grown into the closest possible bond of affection between the two men. No one ever really took his place. To no other man did Raffles expand so easily and freely. But the death of Leyden had another and from the public point of view a more serious implication. In the letter to William Erskine occurs this further paragraph:

"Never perhaps could a greater occasion have offered for the exercise of his extensive powers, and I am warranted in saying that the whole force of his mind was bent upon it. You will not, therefore, be surprised in perceiving the Situation he chalked out for himself; he was to have been my private secretary and in this capacity what would he not have done, with the latitude I should have given him?"

It was, in fact, on Leyden as an expert and trusted adviser that Raffles was relying to help him in the tremendous task of governing Java. Leyden's share would have been to carry out the research on which Raffles could base his administration and his reforms. He was already earmarked to lead a mission to Japan. With Leyden, these plans could have been discussed in every detail and without reservation. There is much truth in the saying that two heads are better than one. But now Leyden was dead, and there was no one to take his place. The whole weight of government must rest henceforward on the young shoulders of Raffles alone.

By 31st August all operations in the Buitenzorg area had ceased. On the Gombal Hill, Janssens had been joined by the Pĕrang Wedono[1] of Surakarta with 1,500 troops, and there was the obvious risk that others would follow his example, if only for their own ultimate purposes. Janssens' total force was already reported to be about 6,000 men.

Sir Samuel Auchmuty had no intention of letting such a situation develop. He ordered the dispatch by sea to Samarang of a striking force of 3,000 men, and proceeded himself with the advance party, some 1,200 men and half a dozen guns, under Colonel Gibbs. This time, unfortunately, the navy bungled the convoy arrangements. Auchmuty found himself off Samarang with only this small force, and no sign of the main body arriving within a reasonable time. He decided on 12th September to land, and fearing Janssens might recover confidence from his delay, ordered Colonel Gibbs to attack Janssens on 16th September. The attack was well conceived and boldly executed. The native troops broke and fled, and Janssens was once more a fugitive, this time to Salatiga.

Again he was called on to surrender. He endeavoured to make conditions, but when this failed he signed an unconditional capitulation on 18th September. It is perhaps worth recording that the brief dispatch reporting this to the home Government was signed on behalf of the commander-in-chief by Major William Farquhar, who had come over from Malacca with the expedition as a volunteer. He later had a lengthy correspondence with the naval commander-in-chief, who had in his official dispatch failed to give, in Farquhar's opinion, satisfactory recognition of his services. This was published by Farquhar in the *Prince of Wales's Island Gazette*, an act very characteristic of the man.

The operation, from the first landing to the capitulation, had taken just forty-five days, four days less than the passage of the expedition from Malacca. It was a great achievement, the highest praise being due to all branches of the services for their skill, gallantry and dash. Gillespie, who was always in the van, was the same brave soldier he had proved himself at Vellore.

The response from England when the news reached home was most gratifying. The Prince Regent expressed the royal gratitude in terms very flattering to the army and was graciously pleased to authorize a special medal to be struck to commemorate this signal victory. Medals were not issued with the prodigality of to-day; it was then a great honour.

But for Minto, the great architect of the plan, the man who had inspired it and taken heavy responsibilities on his shoulders, and for his chief lieutenant and planner, Raffles, whose Intelligence had been one of the chief factors for success, no such stirring eulogies were forthcoming. Minto and Raffles thought, and rightly, that the achievement was one of

[1] Commander-in-chief of the Susuhunan's forces. Wedono was the title given to senior officials not of royal blood. Hence: "War leader not of royal blood".

great importance, a whole new empire laid at the feet of England; a temporary, it is true, but not impossibly a permanent, acquisition of enormous potential value. People at home, however, were too occupied with more immediate dangers; distant victories were less exciting. This explains in some measure why a success that seemed so impressive to those who had laboured for months to achieve it created only a transitory interest in England. Then, as now, geography was not a popular subject. Few knew where Java was. It was just another island in a remote sea. Its potential wealth was not known and, in any case, political economists were already seeking to prove that colonies were not assets to the mother country, but liabilities.

But there were other and more important reasons to explain the rather cold reception of the news. As far as the Government was concerned, interest finished when it was realized that now at last the danger from French activities in the Indian Ocean were removed. The East India Company was relieved to think that its Indian properties and its India and China fleets would from now on be free from the very heavy depredations and losses to which they had been too long exposed. But satisfaction was very much modified when it was learned that, far from abandoning the island to its natural inhabitants, as originally instructed, Minto had taken possession of it and proposed to administer it, and on the Company's behalf. For this the directors had never bargained. For years they had been struggling in vain against the warlike activities of their proconsuls, who, in spite of every remonstrance, continued to add vast territories to their Indian possessions, with an expenditure that threatened the Company with financial disaster. And here they were being handed, without consultation, the whole of the East Indian assets of their late Dutch rivals. The rosy picture painted by Minto of Java's potential wealth and the immediate prospect of substantial financial surplus carried little conviction with these hard-headed merchants. They had heard that sort of story before. Moreover, if such keen men of business as the Dutch had come to appalling financial disaster over these very islands, what probability was there that the youthful secretary to the Penang Government, energetic and capable though he might be, with the assistance of a scratch lot of British and Dutch civil servants and a few officers borrowed from the army, could make a success where the experienced servants of the Dutch Company had so conspicuously failed?

In the meantime, they had no option but to accept this new asset; but they mentally determined that they would keep a strict watch to see that this young enthusiast did not try any costly experiments. The asset was in their minds already a liability. They proposed to keep that liability within the closest possible limits.

Minto and Raffles had at the moment no notion of all this. They were zealously engaged in taking the first steps for the really difficult part of the enterprise: the reorganization and administration of a new territory.

From the signature of the capitulation to the departure of Minto for India on 19th October—a bare five weeks—there was much to be done. To be sure, Minto and Raffles had gone over the ground before they had ever arrived in Java, but their ideas could be only provisional until the army had completed its task and an administrative machine had been installed to meet whatever conditions and experience should suggest.

Minto was as good as his word to the inhabitants of Java. Without waiting for the final defeat of Janssens, he issued on 11th September a second proclamation in which the broad details of the new government were set out clearly. As these formed the basis of the British interregnum in Java, they must be quoted at length.

"For the satisfaction of the inhabitants and people of Java, the following provisions are made public, in testimony of the sincere disposition of the British Government to promote their prosperity and welfare. The refusal of their late Government to treat for their interest, although disabled by the events of war from affording them any further protection, has rendered the consequent establishment of the British authority unconditional. But an English Government does not require the articles of a capitulation to impose those duties which are prompted by a sense of justice and a beneficent disposition. The people of Java are exhorted to consider their new connexion with England as founded on principles of mutual advantage, and to be conducted in a spirit of kindness and affection.

"Providence has brought to them a protecting and benevolent Government. They will cheerfully perform the reciprocal duties of allegiance and attachment.

"1. His Majesty's subjects in Java will be entitled to the same general principles as are enjoyed by the natural-born subjects of Great Britain in India, subject to such regulations as now exist, or may hereafter be provided, respecting residence in any of the Honourable Company's territories.

"2. They will have the same privilege and freedom of trade to, and with, all countries to the East of the Cape of Good Hope, and also with His Majesty's European dominions, as are possessed by natural-born subjects of Great Britain.

"3. Dutch gentlemen will be eligible to all offices of trust, and will enjoy the confidence of Government according to their respective characters, conduct and talents, in common with British-born subjects.

"4. The vexatious system of monopoly, which is understood to have hitherto prevailed, in some instances to an oppressive and inconvenient extent, will be revised and a more beneficial and politic principle of administration will be taken into consideration as soon, and to such extent, as full information on the subject can be obtained, as established usage and habit may admit, and as may be consistent with a due regard to the health and morals of the people.

"5. The Dutch laws will remain provisionally in force, under the modifications which will be hereinafter expressed, until the pleasure of the Supreme authorities in England shall be known; and it is conceived that no material alteration therein is to be apprehended.

"The modifications to be now adopted are the following:

"1. Neither torture nor mutilation shall make part of any sentence to be pronounced against criminals.

"2. When a British-born subject is convicted of any offence, no punishment shall be awarded against him more severe than would be inflicted by the laws of England for the same crime; and, in case of doubt concerning the penalty of English law, reference shall be made to the Honourable the Recorder of Prince of Wales's Island, whose report shall be sufficient warrant for awarding the penalty stated by him to be agreeable to the laws of England. No sentence against any British-born subject for any crime or misdemeanour shall be carried into execution until a report shall have been made to the Lieutenant-Governor.

"3. No sentence of death against any person whatever shall be carried into execution until report shall have been made to the Lieutenant-Governor.

"4. The Lieutenant-Governor will have the power of remitting, moderating, or confirming all penalties, excepting inconsiderable fines, short imprisonment, or slight corporal punishment.

"5. British-born subjects shall be amenable to the jurisdiction of the Dutch tribunals and to the Dutch laws, in all cases of civil complaint, or demands, whether they be plaintiffs or defendants.

"6. All British-born subjects shall be subject to the regulation of police and to the jurisdiction of the Magistrates charged with the execution thereof, and with the maintenance of peace, and with public tranquillity and security.

"7. All persons belonging to, or attached to, the Army, who are by their condition subject to military law shall, for the present, be tried for any crimes they may commit only by courts-martial, unless sent by the military authorities to civil courts.

"8. It being necessary in all countries that a power should exist of framing regulations in the nature of legislative provision adapted to change of circumstances, or to meet any emergency that may arise, and the great distance of the British authorities in Europe rendering it expedient that the said power should, for the present, reside in some accessible quarter, it is declared that the Lieutenant-Governor shall have full power and authority to pass such legislative regulations as, on deliberation and after due consultation and advice, may appear to him indispensably necessary, and that they shall have the full force of law. But the same shall be immediately reported to the Governor-General in Council in Bengal, together with the Lieutenant-Governor's reasons for passing the said regulations and any representations that may have been submitted to him against the same; and the regulations so passed will be confirmed or disallowed by the Governor-General in Council, with the shortest possible delay. The mode in which the Lieutenant-Governor shall be assisted with advice will hereafter be made known; and such regulations will hereafter be made as may be thought most conducive to prompt, pure and impartial administration of justice, civil and criminal.

"Regulations respecting the paper currency as well as the relative value of coins circulating in Java, will be published in a separate paper of this date.

"The Government shall in the meanwhile, and until the pleasure of the Supreme authorities in Great Britain shall be signified, be administered in the following manner:—All the powers of Government shall be exercised by, and all acts and orders shall be done and issued in the name of His Excellency the Governor-General of India, the Right Honourable Lord Minto, during his residence in Java.

"His Excellency has been pleased to appoint the Honourable Thomas Raffles, Lieutenant-Governor of Java, who will aid him in the execution of the said functions until his departure from the island. After the departure of the Governor-General the Honourable the Lieutenant-Governor will exercise in his own name and person the powers of Government, and will be invested with all the authorities appertaining thereto in the fullest and amplest manner."

On the same day Minto executed the commission "requiring and commanding all persons belonging to His Majesty's and the Honourable East India Company's civil, military and marine services and to every person whatsoever resident on the said Island or possession to take notice hereof and obey the said Thomas Stamford Raffles Esquire as Lieutenant-Governor of the Island of Java and its dependencies."

Minto reported to England that the title was chosen "as being more suitable than the more dignified and splendid title of Governor on the one hand, or that of mere Resident on the other". The Council was to consist of Gillespie in his capacity as commander of the forces, who was appointed senior member, H. W. Muntinghe, formerly president of the supreme court of Batavia, and Jacob Willem Cranssen, formerly president of the College of Schepemen, or board of aldermen.

Following the practice of the Dutch, which gave the eastern district of the island its own administrator, an Englishman, in the person of

Hugh Hope, was appointed with the title of Civil Commissioner "to introduce as much and as early as possible the English character into the affairs of a country which cannot become English in habits and feeling too early." Thus wrote Minto. Hope was to be stationed at Samarang, with Colonel Gibbs, as deputy commissioner, at Surabaya.

In appointing Raffles as Lieutenant-Governor, Minto had to disregard some modified obligation, which he had apparently undertaken, to give the appointment to someone else. There has been considerable speculation as to who this other person might have been. The view generally held is that it was Robert Farquhar, appointed Governor of Mauritius after its capture. That he would have been a good choice one cannot doubt, but he had already been selected for Mauritius before the Java expedition was seriously under way. This seems to rule him out. Archibald Seton and Hugh Hope have also been suggested. Seton can definitely be eliminated because, when Minto had first advised Raffles that he was bringing Seton with him, he made it quite clear that Raffles need not regard him as a rival. From other sources we also know that, before he left Delhi, Seton had struck a bargain with Minto concerning his future employment on return to India. Hugh Hope, on the other hand, seems quite likely to have been the man. To begin with, his brother, Sir John Hope, was one of Wellington's Peninsular generals and may well have solicited Minto on Hugh's behalf. That is pure speculation, but surely not improbable. But there is another and stronger argument. The Hope family had a collateral branch in Holland called van der Hoop, and Hugh himself was described by Minto as a "tolerable Dutchman". He had worked on Minto's staff in Calcutta in the Dutch secretariat. Before the exceptional qualities of Raffles had become known to him, Minto might well have thought that Hope's Dutch connexions and general qualifications made him a very suitable choice as Lieutenant-Governor of Java, and quite possibly did give him a half promise. It is also perhaps significant that the position Hope held as civil commissioner placed him next in rank to the commander of the forces. In other words he held the highest civil appointment below that of Lieutenant-Governor. If he was Minto's original selection, it says a good deal for his character that he was willing to serve loyally under Raffles throughout the British régime.

The important point for us, however, is that Minto gave the appointment to Raffles because he "could not conscientiously withhold it from the man who had won it", and he also told a friend in Batavia that it was not merely as a reward for the services he had rendered, but "in consideration of his peculiar fitness for the office".

A distant observer was to share that view. William Marsden wrote in the introduction to his *Grammar of the Malayan Language*, published in the following year, that the appointment of Raffles "to a situation of as great trust and importance as a nation can confide to an individual" justified the opinion of his talents expressed in a former work.[1]

The government was to be administered by the Lieutenant-Governor through the Council, and the orders of the government would normally be issued by the authority of the Lieutenant-Governor in Council. But the Lieutenant-Governor was also given very special powers of his own. If, for example, the Council could not agree, or there was a majority against the Lieutenant-Governor, he was empowered, if he considered the matter of sufficient importance, to enforce his own opinion. Any order passed by him in this way had the full and valid effect of an order passed by the Lieutenant-Governor in Council. When this happened, he was bound to record in writing his reason for overruling the majority of the Council, and this record had to be sent by earliest opportunity to Bengal and to London.

Raffles was to have even wider powers than those. A Secret and Separate Department was set up for the transaction of such affairs as the Lieutenant-Governor did not think fit to put to the members of the Council. Such matters would be transacted by himself individually, and separately recorded. It is important to observe that in this class were "military movements and operations of importance in time of war or internal trouble". The orders of the Lieutenant-Governor "out of Council" were as valid as those "in Council". Daendels had had rather similar powers—in fact, in the latter part of his régime he had acted almost entirely under them. As far as is known, though a great deal of business was necessarily transacted in the Secret and Separate Department, Raffles never used his powers to get his own way. On occasions, however, he clearly indicated to Gillespie that he had them if forced to use them.

Many of the public offices, including situations of the highest trust, were to be filled by Dutch gentlemen. Of that description was the *landdrost*, who conducted within his allotted territory the functions of a representative of government, including charge of the police, presidency of the court of justice, superintendence of public works, and the management of the coffee monopoly. Save where individual Dutchmen were found to be of unsuitable character or ill disposed to the British authority, they were retained in office. Apart from other considerations, this was inevitable; there were far too few English to go round.

Turning to the princes, Minto observed in his report that these were rulers of their territories only in name and in ceremonial. They were in fact completely under the control of Dutch officials known as ministers (the word is the same in Dutch), who were resident at their courts, directing their political councils, collecting their revenues, managing their monopolies and virtually reigning in their territories. By a curious

[1] *History of Sumatra*, 1811.

arrangement the ministers at the two principal courts of Solo (or Surakarta) [1] and Jokyakarta received no salaries, yet their offices were the most lucrative in Java, or perhaps—suggested Minto—in any other government in the world. The arrangement was that the ministers, now renamed Residents, should receive moderate salaries and no other emoluments whatever, except perhaps a commission on the proceeds of the various farms,[2] which would be continued for the account of the government, to stimulate their active supervision. He anticipated no difficulty with the princes if the farms were transferred from private farmers to government, because the princes always complained that the farms were sold at quite inadequate figures, while their subjects were exposed to the extortions of Javanese collectors or Chinese farmers. The princes, Minto suggested, might also be given some additional allowance from the increased revenue to be expected from this method of administering the farms.

With regard to Bantam, he contemplated maintaining the Dutch arrangement whereby the hill districts were left to the native princes and the coast was controlled by the Dutch. He proposed to retain Macassar and reoccupy Banjermasin[3] (Borneo), which the Dutch had evacuated.

In the financial field, the most urgent problem was the large amount of paper money in circulation. This, it will be remembered, had been issued by Daendels in increasing quantities in a desperate attempt to secure cash to cover his military expenditure. As a result, the currency had become so depreciated that, according to Janssens, even if the island had not been captured, the government must have ceased to function for sheer lack of funds. This problem was tackled by Minto in his proclamation of 11th September.

"The declining state of the Dutch Colony of Java and the distresses of its Government occasioned by the pressure of the war and interruption of trade had induced the Government to adopt several extraordinary and irregular means of supplying the demands of the public service and amongst other recourses a superabundance of Government paper was thrown into circulation. The excess of paper and the progressive decline of public credit had induced a gradual depreciation of the paper currency, which in the month of July and the beginning of August had fallen to the low exchange of 6½ paper Rix[4] for one Spanish Silver Dollar, making about 5 Rix Dollars in paper for the value of one Rix Dollar in silver. . . .

"The Government feels all the disadvantages of a depreciated currency

[1] Solo was the name of the original village on the site of which Surakarta was built.

[2] Not agricultural holdings, but monopolies leased out by the government. The many later references to farms and farmers should be so construed.

[3] *Banjer* is a Dutch variation of *banjir*, a flood consequent on a high tide. *Masin* means salty, so Banjermasin can be taken to mean a place flooded at high tide with salt water.

[4] The Dutch rix-dollar, worth about the same as the Spanish (or Mexican) dollar.

but on the one hand it is alive to the very general and extensive distress which the sudden extinction of so large a floating property among such multitudes must occasion, and on the other hand it cannot forget that it would be a great violation of duty to burden a new administration with the gratuitous and spontaneous restoration of an excessive currency discredited under the management of a prior Government to its original value, or rather to a value which at all time was merely nominal."

In view of these considerations, government paper to the extent of 4,500,000 rix-dollars and paper issued by the orphan chamber[1] to the extent of 4,000,000 rix-dollars were recognized as legal tender and were acceptable at the treasury on the basis of 6½ paper rix-dollars being equal to one Spanish dollar in silver. It was, however, stipulated that, till further notice, payments must be in the proportion of one-third silver and two-thirds paper. This paper was to be liquidated gradually. An annual duty of 5 per cent for restamping was to be levied on the value as now fixed, the money so obtained to be invested at compound interest. Two months were allowed for the restamping of the paper.

These decisions gave general satisfaction.

On the financial prospects of the island under British administration, Minto wrote to the Secret Committee in London on 5th October:

"The first and chief object of my enquiry has been a comparative estimate of charge and receipt... by the progress made in the investigation I am encouraged to state even now a confidential opinion that the resources will not only cover but considerably exceed the expenditure. I fear, however, that we cannot expect to realize this intention in the first year... this I can say with certainty, that the value of the island and the face of prosperity which every part of the island wears, even weighed down as it has been by a most oppressive system, and after a most iniquitous and grinding administration of Government, very far exceeds any notion which had ever been conceived by strangers.... Yet every acknowledged principle of good Government is unknown in Java and all the mischievous deteriorating and grievous maxims of a narrow monopolizing and harsh policy are in full force and vigour in every department of affairs. No man's interest in land exceeds the term of one year. This admits of a small number of partial exceptions, but is generally true. The whole surface is the property of Government, and very extensive territories are cultivated and managed on the account of Government under the direction of public affairs. Government exacts a pre-emption at an arbitrary price in the produce of many other lands. In a word, the whole system of property is vicious and adverse to the interests of Government and people.

"Revenues, &c, have long been all in farm; the farmers are universally Chinese who have no competitors, hence arises answering loss to Govern-

[1] Dutch court having jurisdiction over minors, wills, etc.

ment and pressing extortion of the subject. I have nevertheless been obliged to renew the farms for the remaining months of the present year. The change in the system of collecting will require considerable preparation both in regulation and in providing instruments who are now entirely wanting. The duties of export and import in the harbour of Batavia have further been placed in a Custom House, the collection being immediately under the vigilance of Government."

Minto cancelled the farms for gaming and cockfighting, and the duties on these were suppressed. It was decided to be impossible to abolish slavery suddenly, and in Java slavery was not so grievous to the slave as in some other countries. It was arranged, however, that the government should set an example by declining in future to purchase any slaves, and that a return should be prepared showing how many slaves the government actually possessed. If the number was not too considerable, it was proposed that these, at any rate, should be emancipated. Steps were taken to check the importation of slaves.

Such, briefly, were some of the principal activities of Minto. His general views on the island and the liberal policy he had laid down will be readily understood from the following quotation from a letter he wrote on 6th October to Robert Dundas who, in May of that year, had succeeded his father, Henry, as Viscount Melville, and was now, for the second time, president of the India Board of Control:

"I consider the main point as ascertained, and that Java will supply resources at the least for its own expenses. I need not say to you how great a benefit, not reducible to the columns of an estimate in dollars, will in that case accrue to the Company and the nation. We now know from proof that it was the policy of the Dutch to conceal the value and to exaggerate the defects of their possessions, especially of Java. This will account for the inadequate opinion entertained, at least I imagine so, at home of this island. It is now most flourishing; but the field for improvement is inexhaustible. All that I fear is the general peace."

By which he meant the end of the war with France, when Java might have to be handed back to Holland. He went on:

"This ought not surely to prevent us from beginning to perform the first duty of Governments in improving the condition of a people that has become tributary to our authority and tributary to our prosperity. All we are justified in avoiding is the prosecution in this interval of expensive works. The exclusion of European masters from Java is impossible in the present state of things. To make them richer, happier, and to give the people itself a feeling of independence which they are now totally without, would be the best receipt for making their country less accessible to European invaders. But in our own times this cannot be looked to, and the Government we have established must instantly be replaced by the French whenever it is withdrawn. The more flourishing the country may be at the time of such a revolution, the better, I think, for the nations without, although it may also be advantageous to the ruling European power within. But I feel assured that you agree with me in thinking our policy should lead to the improvement of the country, and, if not our policy, the eternal and fundamental law by which Governments and subjects are united. I think we ought to make it an English colony as soon as we can, by the introduction of English colonists, English capital, and, therefore, an English interest. This does not require the exclusion of the old Dutch, who will not bear a great proportion to the whole, and who will become English more readily as they are now without a country."

The Governor-General could not devote his whole time to these many and urgent business affairs. Celebrations on a scale to match the victory required his personal appearance. The senior officials of the old régime and leading Dutch citizens could not be neglected if cordiality and co-operation were to be established. Without these, the task of governing Java might have presented an almost insuperable difficulty.

There follows Minto's description of his first state ball in Batavia. It throws some light on the low standards of dress, morals and behaviour current in Java at that time.

"It is impossible", he wrote, "to give you anything like an adequate notion of the total absence of beauty in so crowded a hall. There never is a dozen of women assembled in Europe without a few attractions amongst them. Here there was no difference, except in some few varieties of ugliness and ordinariness of dress and manners. The Dutch did not encourage, nor indeed allow freely, European women to go out to their colonies in India. The consequence has been that the men lived with native women, whose daughters, gradually borrowing something from the father's side, and becoming a mixed breed, are now the wives and ladies of rank and fashion in Java. The young ladies have learnt the European fashions of dress, and their carriage and manners are something like our own of an ordinary class. Their education is almost wholly neglected; or rather no means exist to provide for it. They are attended from their cradles by numerous slaves, by whom they are trained in helplessness and laziness; and from such companions and governesses, you may conceive how much accomplishment or refinement in manners or opinions they are likely to acquire.

"In dancing, the young beauties seemed lame in English country dances, of which they knew neither the steps nor the figures; but in their own dance, which was to a very slow valse tune, the figure much the same as ours, with a valse embrace, however, instead of an allemande, they were at home, and not without grace; while our English damsels and cavaliers were all abroad, and about as awkward and crippled as their Dutch fellow-subjects had been before. Mrs Bunbury, the wife of an officer, a young pretty English-woman, stood up in the dance; but seeing when the first couple reached her, the Dutch gentleman take his partner fairly in his arms and hug her, as it appeared to her as a bear does his prey, she fairly took to her heels, and could not be brought back again by any means, to see or share such horror. The Dutch valsers certainly deal in very strict embraces, but our English gentlemen, to their shame be it said, appeared so entirely unpractised in that art, that their Dutch partners gave the point up as a bad job and were forced to content themselves with merely taking hands and swinging the loobies about.

"The chaperons and older Dutch ladies are a class not yet described in Europe. The principal mark to know them by is their immense size. The whole colonial sex runs naturally to fat, partly from over-feeding—partly from total want of exercise. The morning air is the grand pursuit of the English Orientalists; the Dutch of both sexes have a horror for it, and prefer their beds. In the rest of the day nobody can go out; and in the evening they think a drive in a carriage too great an effort. They pass their time as follows. There is a canal opposite to every door on the other side of the road. Each house has a little projecting gallery supported by posts in the canal. The lower part of this, that is to say, from the level of the road down into the water, is made in some small degree private, by upright bars at a little distance from each other, and with this bath the road communicates by wooden steps. Here the lady of the house, her relatives, and female slaves, lave their charms, and here you may behold the handmaids of Diana sporting on and under the wave in sight of all passing Actaeons. This is the morning scene. They have chairs brought out in the gallery above, and sit with their beaux in conversation and repose. Suppose an immense woman sitting behind a stall with roasted apples, and we have an old Dutch lady of the highest rank and fashion. Her upper garment is a loose coarse white cotton jacket fastened nowhere, but worn with the graceful negligence of a Scotch lass, an equally coarse petticoat, and the coarsest stockings, terminating in wide thick-soled shoes; but by standing behind her you find out her nobility, for at the back of the head a little circle of hair is gathered into a small crown, and on this are deposited diamonds, rubies, and precious stones often of very great value. It is well with this if they can speak even Dutch, many knowing no language but Malay."

The demand that he should be socially as well as officially available imposed a great strain on Minto; and he was beginning to feel it. On 23rd March he had reached the age of sixty, and for nearly seven months, except for periods at sea, he had been engaged on a task requiring the fullest of all his mental and physical resources. It was, too, his first experience of the enervating effect of the damp heat of an equatorial climate. We can hardly be surprised, as apparently he was, that he began to suffer from an "unusual langour", to which he subsequently attributed his failure to settle everything in detail before leaving for India. When, however, we examine the amount of business he did transact, the lines of future policy he did discuss, the dinners and receptions he did attend, we cannot feel that he had any solid ground for self-criticism.

It is characteristic of Raffles that, almost at the very moment when he assumed wide powers and grave responsibilities as Lieutenant-Governor of a country in which fighting had only recently ceased, he found time to sit down and write a letter to William Marsden dealing with scientific matters in which Marsden was particularly interested. The letter is dated 5th October 1811.

"My time", he wrote therein, "has been so completely taken up in political operations that I have been compelled for many months to leave my literary labours on the shelf untouched; but my present situation and our new conquest afford such a wide and unparalleled field of research that I should be worse than Goth or Vandal if I allowed it to remain untried even in the literary world. Lord Minto is now here and we have in contemplation to bring forward the Batavian Asiatic Society as soon as circumstances permit. I do not know whether you have heard that we held a meeting of the Asiatic Society at Malacca on our way down. I sent you from thence a paper of mine intended for the next volume of the Researches. . . .

"You will I am sure condole with me as the friend of literature and virtue in the loss I lately sustained in the death of my dear friend Dr Leyden. . . . We have lost in him a host of men. . . . Eastern literature has lost in him its firmest support. . . . I am happy to inform you that I have large and valuable collections on various points connected with your favourite studies; these I shall as soon as possible put into some kind of form. . . ."

This was the first of a long series of letters written to Marsden from Java, not only on literary and philological points but also on such subjects of natural history as the alleged poisonous attributes of the upas tree. For the first time he now had the power, besides indulging his own curiosity freely, to afford moral and financial support to research work of every description. Nor was he content to act merely as a beneficent Maecenas; he was not content to give his official blessing to the scientific work of others. Probably, if he could have chosen his path in life, he would gladly have abandoned politics in favour of science. As it was, he managed by superhuman industry to give such time to scientific studies that he became the partner, or perhaps one should say the director of researches actively pursued in the territories under his control.

Minto gave up his last night but one in Java to a farewell party.

"George sent you a history of my orgies", he wrote to his wife, "at a dinner given by me to Sir Samuel Auchmuty and the Army. The Army has since given a ball and supper to Sir Samuel and me jointly; and we entered hand in hand, like the two Kings of Brentford, smelling at one nosegay. This festival was at the residence of the former Governor-General and the decorations had been all, or nearly so, in a state of preparation for the celebration of Napoleon's birthday, which we disturbed like *trouble-fêtes* as we were, by landing and getting possession of Batavia, Government House, decorations and all, a few days before the grand occasion. . . ."

The following day, 18th October, he sent this warning to the Secret Committee:

". . . I will therefore specify two points at least of the present system in Java which in my faithful and deliberate judgment it would be prejudicial to every interest of the Company or the public in this country to alter or reverse in the present period of our connexion. First, I strongly recommend that the arrangements now established may not be superseded for the purpose of uniting the Government in the same person with the command of the Army. Secondly, that this island and all its affairs, civil and military, may be left under the superintendence of the Governor of Bengal, and not transferred to any other authority in India. . . .

"I am happy to confirm the opinion I have already submitted to your honourable Committee, that the resources of the island will assuredly cover all charges, civil and military."

Two comments at once spring to mind.

In the first place, as events were to show, Minto was undoubtedly right in stressing the importance of the government being in civilian hands. But it is doubtful if he realized the unpopularity of Raffles' appointment among the military caste, or of the efforts that might be made by it to obtain a soldier to replace him. Undoubtedly Gillespie had confidently expected that Java, if retained, would be a King's Colony. Had it been, his claims to be the Governor would have been extremely strong. The disappointment that followed Minto's decision, coupled with Gillespie's personal resentment at finding himself under the orders of a hitherto unknown civilian, fifteen years younger than himself, was understandable. But to begin with, at any rate, Minto seems to have been quite unaware of any trouble. He had, for example, reported to London that, when Gillespie lay wounded in hospital after the capture of Cornelis, he thought he had sent him "very good medicine in his appointment as Commander of the Forces". Gillespie found this only a bitter pill. It is true that before he left, Minto sensed "a shade of dissatisfaction in the Military Quarter". He attributed this to "the ungracious and unpopular principle of strict economy", but the dissatisfaction went a great deal deeper than that.

The other point is that Minto should have been so emphatic in his view that the colony would more than pay for itself. Raffles was to follow his lead in this sanguine outlook. But if the Company was sceptical at the first report, they were to become seriously angry when, year by year, these expectations continued to remain unfulfilled. They were not interested in the reasons for failure, convincing though they might be to impartial judgment. Financial loss alone was all that concerned them.

Minto's last evening in Java was reserved for Raffles. They dined alone together and had a final discussion on policy. The general line it was to follow is clear from one remark of Minto's: ". . . while we are here, let us do all the good we can". He knew that there would be no reluctance on the part of the Lieutenant-Governor to implement that policy.

Together with General Auchmuty, Minto left for India on 19th October. The embarkation of about 10,000 men for their return to India also began. Janssens and his staff, Colonel Nahuijs among them, were sent as prisoners of war to England.

It was not until some time after Minto was back in Calcutta that he received a reply from the Secret Committee to his letter of 22nd January. Robert Dundas wrote that the capture of Java was an object that they could not now abandon, unless compelled by overruling necessity.

"It is of infinite importance," he went on, "to the security of our possessions and trade in the East Indies, that no other European power, especially an active enemy, should have any establishment in those Seas. We are so strongly imbued in this country with the inexpediency of extending our Colonial possessions in India, that we shall be very unwilling to depart from the line of policy which is prescribed in the letter from the Secret Committee of the 31st August 1810. Considerations, however, which are pointed out in the letter from the Supreme Government [of India] of the 22nd January, have great weight and may possibly compel us to acquiesce in the limited establishment, which you appear to have in contemplation. . . .

"I regret very much that your Lordship should have felt yourself called upon to proceed on the Expedition to the Eastward, though I am not surprised at your having adopted that resolution. If there are to be negotiations, or complicated matters, political as well as commercial, your presence will probably be a relief to the Commanders of the Forces. I shall not be surprised to find, however, that Admiral Drury has considered himself to be tied down to the literal execution of his orders, in regard to the total expulsion of the enemy from Java and delivering over the country wholly to the natives, but as this is a matter which concerns more the land than the naval forces, he must ultimately acquiesce in your determination."

Chapter Ten

JAVA, 1811

i

RAFFLES was now *de facto* as well as *de jure* Lieutenant-Governor of Java and its dependencies.

"I am here alone," he wrote to the younger Ramsay, "without any advice, in a new country with a large native population of not less than six or seven millions of people, a great proportion of foreign Europeans and a standing Army of not less than seven thousand men. . . . I can hardly say what change has taken place in me since we parted. I feel I am somewhat older, and, in many points of a worldly nature, I am apt to view men and things in a somewhat different light, but I may fairly say that it is my belief that I am intrinsically the same. How far good, how far bad, those who know me must decide."

It is true that this letter was not written until October 1812, when he had completed a year as Lieutenant-Governor, yet the description could equally have applied to the time when he took over the reins of office. The ardent young man of Ramsay's recollection had, at least outwardly, sobered down to the dignified figure of the Honourable the Lieutenant-Governor.

The task before him in 1811 was one that might have frightened an older and more experienced administrator. The attitude of the Dutch towards the conquerors was, on the surface, friendly enough; but with the departure of more than half the expeditionary force, the policy, or even the mere fact, of an alien administration could only too easily convert cordiality and co-operation into hostility and active or passive resistance. The financial chaos alone, if not quickly and satisfactorily remedied, might well cause a violent reaction. The whole administrative machine required complete reconstruction, and when that was achieved, its successful operation must depend very largely on the efficiency and goodwill of the Dutch officials, who would necessarily predominate in all but the very senior posts. There were very few British available, a mere handful of them being civil servants, the rest borrowed from the army or obtained from various adventitious sources. Of the civil servants, few had had any experience of higher administration. The acting secretary to government was one Charles G. Blagrave. Officially on the establishment of the Moluccas, he had been on his way via Java to take up an appointment at Amboina, but Raffles, having no one else available, had retained him. Among the other British were Charles Assey, Thomas McQuoid, Hugh Hope, William Robinson, John C. Lawrence, John Crawfurd, Colonel Alexander Adams, Captain W. Robison, Captain Robert C. Garnham, Captain Thomas O. Travers and the eccentric Alexander Hare.

Raffles' two *aides-de-camp* were Garnham and Travers, the second acting also as town major of Batavia.

No less important than the need for good relations with the Dutch was the attitude likely to be adopted by the Javanese. Daendels had been remarkably successful in irritating the courts of the princes, and no less so in making his name detested in huge districts of the island by his conscriptions and forced-labour gangs. The resounding defeat of the French had no doubt made a strong impression on the native mind. But the return of so much of the British army to India would not have passed unnoticed. Might not the two great principalities of Solo and Jokyakarta find it possible for once to sink their differences and combine to expel the Europeans from Java? There were plenty of real grievances with which to rouse anti-European feeling among the common people. Raffles had his own ideas how to remedy those grievances, but he required time to study local conditions before he could formulate detailed plans, let alone bring them into operation. Meanwhile a policy of goodwill towards the courts of the princes must be adopted and perhaps some concessions granted. A mere policy of appeasement would be disastrous, however; it would naturally be interpreted as a sign of weakness. A firm attitude was essential, but this must not be of the aggressive type liable to provoke resentment. Diplomacy of a very high standard was clearly required to preserve a proper balance. Above all, if a quarrel should develop, it must at all costs be with one individual state and not a combination of states.

There were to be other difficulties, more intangible and remote than these, that were to be far more disabling than any problems of reconstruction or native policy. The first has already been emphasized: the East India Company's displeasure at this addition to its already excessive territories. The second lay in the uncertainty as to whether Java would be retained; and the third, contingent upon the second, whether it would be taken out of the hands of the Company and made into a King's Colony—or Crown Colony, as we would call it to-day.

This general uncertainty throughout the British régime has received too little attention. Apart altogether from the question whether Java would or would not be eventually restored to Holland, there was to be for three years the additional uncertainty whether a civilian or a military government would be in charge. When Minto had offered the appointment of Lieutenant-Governor to Raffles, he had made it clear that the final decision as to the form of government to be adopted must rest with the authorities in England. He had, it is true, annexed Java on behalf of the East India Company and recorded his very definite view that a civilian should remain in charge, but it was quite conceivable that the Government at home would consider that it should be a King's Colony with a soldier to govern it, as was the practice of the time.

Consequently, every official in Java knew that Raffles' chance of survival at the head of affairs was slender. This prevailing feeling had a very adverse effect on many of his subordinates. The majority of these were Dutch, and while some were to make a distinguished contribution in support of his measures, most of them, for one reason or another, made none. Some Dutchmen, perhaps not altogether unreasonably, were stoutly opposed to far-reaching innovations, which in their opinion were inappropriate to a "trustee" or "caretaker" authority, and might well later prove disadvantageous to, and be repudiated by, the Dutch régime, which they hoped to see restored. Many officials, too, and by no means Dutch only, were either lazy or incompetent; quite a number were definitely corrupt. A fire can be an admirable cloak to a storekeeper, to prevent the discovery of his peculations. A complete change of government and a general replacement of senior officials offers equally attractive possibilities to dishonest servants.

In a country of the size of Java and in the conditions under which the British assumed charge of it, the problems of administration were intricate, and were not made easier by the host of new regulations, covering almost every branch of administration, that characterized the government of Raffles. Drastic reforms offered a ready excuse for the indolent to throw up their hands and do nothing, and enormous scope for the unscrupulous to make personal profit from the complicated changes. The very fact that time and opportunity might be short encouraged embezzlement on a large scale.

Apart from this general tendency to slackness or worse, the prospect of a military régime encouraged the creation of two factions, military and civilian.

All these influences were hardly conducive to an orderly and planned policy of progressive government. With the Company in London anxious only for quick profits, its scepticism and irritation increasing when these were not speedily forthcoming, and with Gillespie and the other officers anxious only for Java to become a King's Colony, there was, as it were, a continuous thread of hostility running through the whole texture of Raffles' administration, increasing gradually in substance until finally it dominated the pattern.

But in October 1811, in his thirty-first year and full of keenness for his new task, Raffles, had no inkling of any of these things.

ii

The first step of the new government was to establish proper relations both with the Dutch section of the population and with the courts of the Javanese princes. On 21st October the Dutch were notified by proclamation that:

"All European inhabitants of the island of Java and its dependencies, late subjects of the former Government, are required forthwith to report themselves at the offices of the Secretary to Government at Molenvliet[1] and severally to state in writing whether they are desirous of obtaining permission to continue on this island or its dependencies under the British Government. All such inhabitants as may be permitted to remain will be required to take the Oath of Allegiance to His Britannic Majesty and of obedience to the Government of Java."

Except for one or two persons, the most notable of whom was Johannes Siberg, a former Governor-General of Java, there was no hesitation among the Dutch to register themselves and take the oath. Raffles reported to Minto:

". . . We have not had any unpleasant occurrences. As soon as it was known that the Oath might be taken the public offices were crowded from morning to night with the inhabitants. No order had ever been issued respecting the oaths, and yet every man of the Island has taken them; they may really be termed voluntary oaths. The late Council came forward in a body and after taking the Oath before me I am sorry to add got most jovially tipsy at my house in company with the new Councillors. . . .

". . . there is not among the Dutch the least symptom of dissatisfaction and all classes of people have come most quietly under British rule. The Colonel [Gillespie] is occasionally full of suspicions with regard to conspiracies and plots and I believe if he had his own way would send every Dutchman off the Island. He really has no consideration whatever for them. However, it is all without reason. . . ."

In marked contrast to Gillespie, Raffles deliberately set out, as a matter of policy, to establish the utmost cordiality and goodwill between the British and Dutch communities.

The arrival of the English, many accompanied by their wives, had a tonic effect. It was not that their standard was superlatively high. Society generally in the Europe of the period was, judged at least by modern taste, a curious mixture of refinement and coarseness. But broadly speaking, the British men and women who had now come to Java were of a better class socially and they had not suffered from the deteriorating effects

[1] "Millbrook," a parish of Batavia.

of long isolation from polite society. An important factor was the example set by Raffles himself, and perhaps in some respects even more potent, that set by Olivia.

As soon as he had taken over the government, Raffles moved from Ryswick, a suburb of Batavia, to Buitenzorg, the country residence of the former Governor-General. Although he did much entertaining of a formal nature at Ryswick, he regarded Buitenzorg as his home, and here he loved to entertain visitors of all sorts, as well as his personal friends. Buitenzorg—Sans Souci in French—stood in surroundings of great natural beauty, and Raffles did much to improve the house. This is his description of the view from it:

"I have now from my window a prospect of the most delightfully picturesque scenery. The descent from the house almost precipitate—in the bottom a valley filled with rice, with a romantic little village at the beginnings of a stream which rushes down by twenty torrents and roars booming over rocks innumerable; in the background a magnificent range of mountains, wooded to the top and capped in clouds, the nearest not more than 20 miles off; nothing indeed can exceed the beauty of the scene."

Travers, who went there in March 1813, wrote of it:

". . . I shall ever remember the happy days passed at this sweet place. There is certainly nothing to compare to it on this Island. The scenery is beautiful, between two rivers which have a rapid and meandering course over beds of stones in valleys abounding with luxurious verdure, and in sight of lofty mountains which may be said to lose themselves in the clouds. This is Buitenzorg, where I have passed the happiest days since I left my country."

It was the kind of life lived by Raffles and Olivia at Buitenzorg that probably did more than anything else to set a standard of dignity and decency for social relations in Java. In that charming and well-ordered house there was no place for vulgar ostentation, bad manners or slovenly dress. Not that life was at all formal. If Raffles on official occasions could act as every inch a Governor, at home at Buitenzorg he was the perfect host, ready, with his own charming manners, to put everyone at his ease, to discuss affairs of state with one and fine points of language or science with another; or to play cards or promote theatricals, if that was the general desire. Off duty he loved gaiety and happy guests.

In all these social duties he was admirably supported by the lovely Olivia. She had at first been rather shocked by the native dress that even leading Dutch ladies affected. The crude mass of jewellery, too, and above all the betel-chewing[1] offended her sense of taste. Being a sensible woman,

[1] It was the habit of the ladies to have beside them bowls into which they spat out the red mess from time to time.

she felt her way cautiously, indicated with extreme tact her disapproval, and let her own example of dress and behaviour have its own effect. Naturally her implied criticism of well-established customs was at first resented; that a foreigner should regard herself as a superior in manners was not easily borne. But her personal charm, her sweet, gentle and sincere nature, soon prevailed. Many of the Dutch women warmly welcomed a return to standards that they themselves preferred, and Olivia was as happy to have Dutch as English ladies in her intimate circle. She became the unquestioned arbiter of taste, the first lady of the land, not merely because she was the wife of the Lieutenant-Governor, but in her own right for the qualities she possessed.

The newly started *Java Government Gazette* commended approvingly on the change in ladies' fashions:

"At the entertainment recently given at Batavia it was remarked how great an improvement has been introduced in respect to the attire of the Dutch ladies since British authority has been established. The *Cabaya*[1] appears now generally disused and the more elegant English costume adopted. We congratulate our friends on the amelioration of the public taste, because we see in it the dawn of still greater and more important improvements."

It was Raffles' normal practice to come down each week from Buitenzorg to the Government House, Ryswick, Batavia, to attend Council meetings, staying at Ryswick only a day or two, according to the amount of business. The main secretariat was at Buitenzorg, but the secretary and some of his assistants usually moved up and down with Raffles, who reckoned to do the forty-mile journey, with relays of horses, in four hours.

The curse of a warm, damp, equatorial climate is "tidapathy", from the Malay "Tid' apa"—"It does not matter". In an enervating climate, even the smallest effort requires some exercise of will-power. The temptation is to let things slide, and once that temptation begins to take hold, a general deterioration sets in and with it a weakening of moral fibre. Raffles, consciously or unconsciously, was completely free from any subjection to the climate. His activity of mind and body would have been remarkable in any climate, however favourable. His habits of industry, his interest in every detail of administration, and his desire for exact knowledge in every branch of science struck the Dutch in Java with amazement.

"With a constitution already impaired by climate everyone was astonished at the exertion and fatigue he underwent; and the Dutch, who were altogether unaccustomed to witness such activity of mind and body, were unable to keep pace with him."

This is the less surprising when we learn from the same authority

[1] Usually *kabaya*, a loose cotton gown.

(Travers) that Raffles required three clerks to copy and keep up with what he wrote, and that he frequently dictated to two persons while engaged in writing letters himself. The routine of government moved with a rapid tempo and nobody was expected to lag behind.

Apart from this display of energy, he also set his subordinates an example of official integrity and business efficiency. It at once became apparent that those who were lazy or incompetent or not over-scrupulous in their official duties would have to be on their guard.

iii

After the establishment of cordial relations between the British and Dutch, on which the successful administration of Java must obviously depend, the second most urgent task was the promotion of satisfactory relations with the principal courts. These were at Surakarta (Solo) and Jokyakarta in Java, and at Palembang in Sumatra. The Javanese rulers were the more immediately important because, until Raffles could come to terms with them, the establishment of British authority throughout the island could not be completed.

Originally these two territories had been one, under the Susuhunan, who was also styled Emperor of Java,[1] but in the middle of the eighteenth century there had been a rebellion by one branch of the family. With the well-known technique of *divide et impera*, the Dutch government had played its part, with the result that in 1775 the rebel faction had settled down in quasi-independence at Jokyakarta under a separate ruler with the title of Sultan of Mataram. While Daendels had been Governor-General, there had been trouble with this sultan, and he had been replaced by a young nominee of Daendels, under a Regent. The dethroned sultan had, however, been allowed to remain in the city. His brother and nephew had been removed to Cheribon as hostages. The evasive tactics of the humane Dutch Resident had prevented the carrying out of Daendels' desire "to hear of their being put out of the way".

Raffles had had correspondence from Malacca with both these courts. After the defeat of Janssens, Sir Samuel Auchmuty had dispatched Captain Robison, an army officer, to convey to them the news of the surrender and to inform them that Lord Minto desired to maintain with Solo and Jokyakarta the same relations as had existed with the Dutch government and to give them every assurance of Minto's favour and protection. Both the Susuhunan and the Sultan (and Dutch Regent) of Mataram had in reply sent letters making a number of requests. Robison,

[1] Java was regarded by the natives as two countries: the centre and eastern end, which was called Java by its inhabitants, the Javanese; and the western section, which was known to them as Pasundan, the country of the Sundas.

whose subsequent conduct elsewhere was to involve a great deal of unnecessary trouble, had apparently given certain promises to both courts, but Raffles had so far declined to discuss their requests; before doing so, he wished to obtain more precise information as to the previous relations between the courts and the European power, and also the extent and exact object of these requests. He had, however, taken the wise step of sending back to Jokyakarta the two princes who had been held as hostages by Daendels.

On 25th October the new Residents, Colonel Alexander Adams for Solo and John Crawfurd for Jokyakarta, left Batavia by sea for Samarang to take up their posts.

Colonel Adams had distinguished himself as the commander of a brigade during the invasion of Java. Crawfurd, in view of the long association he was to have with Raffles, requires a little further description. He was born in 1783 and was therefore two years younger than Raffles. He had obtained a commission in India as assistant surgeon to the 3rd Regiment of Native Cavalry, and had arrived at Penang on 20th June 1808 as assistant surgeon to the settlement. Like Raffles, he took a keen interest in the language and customs of the country, later publishing three well-known books. Thanks to his proficiency in Malay, he had been taken on the Java expedition as Malay translator to the Governor-General. He seems to have been in some respects a difficult person, dour, narrow-minded and close-fisted, easily taking offence and very resentful of criticism. On the other hand, he was quite ready to criticize his superiors and was not even above making his strictures known to his subordinates. He was not regarded by Raffles' staff as a whole-hearted supporter of the Lieutenant-Governor, but he was unquestionably an able and well-informed young man.

Nothing could illustrate more clearly the acute shortage of trained civilian officials than the appointment of a brigade commander and a junior doctor to these two key positions. For such they were. If relations were not promptly and happily established with Solo and Jokyakarta, the very existence of the European power in Java might be in jeopardy. If the coming negotiations failed, at best a long and difficult war must be anticipated.

They were informed before their departure that the extravagant system whereby Residents had been allowed to appropriate to their own benefit the principal revenues of the country, such as the collection of birds'-nests, the farming of toll-gates and the management of opium sales, would be discontinued, and they were expressly prohibited from drawing any advantages directly or indirectly from these sources. Instead they were to receive the equivalent in dollars of £1,800 per annum in full settlement of all emoluments attaching to the post of Resident.

Their instructions had certain features in common. They were to notify the Dutch holders of the office that they had been removed from their posts. They were also given letters and presents to deliver to the Susuhunan and Sultan respectively. They were to discuss with them the possibility of all farms—that is, monopolies—being vested in the Company and administered by its officials. From the increased revenue to be expected by this method, additional allowances might be paid to the two rulers. It was intended to restrict the sale of opium, but it was left to be decided later whether the farmers at Solo and Jokyakarta should buy their opium at the Batavian sales or buy it under contract at fixed rates, with the Resident acting on behalf of the government. In general, they were to discover the exact relationship between the Dutch Residents and the Javanese courts as a basis for the future regulation of their own conduct. They were to be careful not to discuss the requests that had been addressed to Raffles until the situation had been fully clarified. This particularly referred to the Susuhunan, who was demanding that the concessions granted to the Dutch under pressure by Daendels should be revoked. Crawfurd, in his turn, was specifically instructed to report as to the advisability of restoring the sultan dismissed by Daendels. It was considered that this step would create a good impression of the justice and liberality of the British. It might, in fact, prove unavoidable, in order to preserve confidence and so ensure the tranquillity of the country. But until the general situation had been examined, discussion must be postponed.

The Sumatra commission was dispatched to Palembang on 2nd November. Its members included Willem Wardenaar, who had been a member of the Dutch supreme council at Batavia, and Alexander Hare. Their instructions were to inform the Dutch Resident, van Woortman, that the British had conquered Java and to request him to transfer the residency to Mr Charles Jackson. They were to hand the sultan a letter from Raffles, informing him at the same time of the friendly disposition of the British Government. The object of the commission was not only to install the first British Resident at Palembang, but also to enquire what assistance could be given to the sultan in suppressing pirates and all those who would intrude upon his domain; it was to negotiate with him a renewal of former contracts and discuss any other points he might wish to raise. The commissioners were made aware that the ultimate purpose of the British Government was to obtain possession of the island of Bangka by fair negotiation. If the situation seemed propitious, they were to discuss this proposition in a leisurely manner with the sultan, bearing in mind that the necessary establishment, for the purpose of occupation, could not in any event be sent until the setting in of the favourable monsoon. But Bangka was not to be discussed at all unless the commission unanimously agreed that it was prudent to do so, or some very definite indication was forthcoming that proposals would be likely to be favourably received. Should this happen, they were authorized to offer 20,000 Spanish dollars per annum so long as the English held Bangka and to promise that possession of the island would not be resigned to any other than the sultan. They were also authorized to purchase tin then ready at Palembang or Bangka to the amount of 50,000 dollars, the price to be that fixed by the Dutch contract, with a discount for transport to Batavia, as previously stipulated. They were to consider what measures could be taken to prevent private individuals of any nation participating in this tin trade. The intention was to put a small establishment at Muntok if this could safely be done, and to maintain a garrison at Palembang.

News came on 14th November from Crawfurd at Samarang. With a dispatch dated 7th November, he forwarded a report in which the acting Dutch Resident at Jokyakarta notified the resumption of the sovereign power by the dispossessed Sultan and the execution of the Radin Adipati (prime minister). Crawfurd commented that this action was in direct violation of the existing Dutch treaties, and that he interpreted it as an attempt on the part of the Sultan to assert his independence of British power. He made it clear that his attitude to the Sultan would be based on that interpretation.

This put Raffles at once in a difficulty. Crawfurd's dispatch indicated that he was proceeding at once to Jokyakarta, and there was no time to communicate with him before he left. Raffles, therefore, had no option but to await the report on the situation, which he assumed Crawfurd would send as soon as he arrived at Jokyakarta. A further dispatch, however, received on 18th November and dated at Samarang 10th November, made it clear that Crawfurd had already made up his mind on the situation before he had even gone to Jokyakarta, and as he talked of moving up troops, Raffles dispatched an express to him emphasizing that the tranquillity of the country was the first and most important object of his post. Writing to Minto (21st January 1812), Raffles stated:

"I was particular to express my sentiments in such terms on the very unseemly and hasty manner in which Mr Crawfurd appeared to have formed his opinion and to regulate his conduct as Resident, before he had ever arrived at Djocjocarta."

Raffles was not prepared to accept as proved Crawfurd's contention that the Sultan's action was a test of British strength. Quite possibly it was so, but on the other hand it was obviously a favourable moment for the Sultan to resume the authority of which he had been deprived by Daendels. Moreover, as the Radin Adipati had been concerned in his dismissal, it was not altogether surprising that the Sultan had taken his revenge. There seemed also grounds for thinking that the people were behind the Sultan in the step he had taken. Nor had Crawfurd apparently realized the grave risk attaching to an open breach with the Sultan. As he later admitted, it was very questionable whether there was in fact an adequate force available in Java to deal with the war that might well have arisen. Crawfurd's first clear duty was to take up his post as Resident, present the letter from Raffles to the Sultan and then open up negotiations on the normal official basis.

Three more letters from Crawfurd, dated 22nd, 23rd and 24th November, in which he was already making proposals for deposing the Sultan, only added to Raffles' anxiety. It had been Raffles' intention that the two released princes, father and son, impressed by such liberal treatment, would act as the eyes and ears of Crawfurd so that he might be kept fully advised of what was happening on the Sultan's *kĕratun*.[1] This should have proved useful at all times, and would now have been invaluable, seeing that by his own ill-advised behaviour Crawfurd had cut himself off from all personal access to the court. But he had been stupid enough to treat the two princes as if they were rivals to the Sultan. Instead, therefore, of getting any benefit from their presence at court, he had merely rendered the situation even more delicate than it would otherwise have been.

Raffles decided that it was necessary to go himself to Samarang and handle the crisis that Crawfurd's impetuosity had so wantonly precipitated. Apart from that pressing reason, he saw further advantages in a personal visit, as this would afford an opportunity to investigate the administrative and judicial systems with a view to possible reforms, to which end he decided to take Muntinghe with him. Meanwhile an urgent message was sent to Crawfurd, urging him to avoid any action likely to provoke the Sultan further or widen the breach. He was also warned that the latest information suggested that the Sultan was very popular and that there were afoot various native activities that indicated an attempt to stir up widespread disaffection against the European power.

They left Batavia on 28th November, on which same day Raffles, demonstrating his striking capacity of engaging at one and the same time in a variety of complex activities, made a public pronouncement on two social evils, gaming and cockfighting. These had been recognized by the Dutch government, which had farmed out annually the right to provide such amusements. Raffles now gave notice that these farms would not again be put up for public auction, as they were to be abolished throughout the island at the end of the year. The loss to the treasury was estimated to be over 100,000 Spanish dollars annually, but it was considered that the gain in public morals was more than adequate compensation. In the next century or more, it was to be argued whether suppression of gaming was good policy or not. Many experienced administrators, apart from

[1] Palace and its fortifications, described on page 199.

those specially influenced by the revenue provided by licensed gaming held that it was not. Raffles held that it was, a view that was later to cause endless argument in Singapore.

On his way to Samarang, he drafted a note for Colonel Adams on his line of policy with Solo. First of all it was desirable to impress by all possible means on the Susuhunan that the British had ample strength to enforce their demands and that any concessions they might see fit to make would be made purely of their own free will and in no sense in any recognition of the Susuhunan's power. From the outset, therefore, it would be necessary to declare to the Susuhunan that every treaty and contract made with the Dutch must be regarded as in complete force until a new treaty had been made. In this connexion, opportunity might be taken to point out that the conduct of the Susuhunan over the collection of birds'-nests and payment of tolls had been disingenuous. It should be made clear that the revenues arising from these farms would not in any circumstances be restored to him.

It was, wrote Raffles, intended to preserve Dutch practice in the matter of relations of the Resident and the Company with the prime minister, and the dependence of the prime minister on the Company would be strictly maintained. On the other hand, it might not be necessary to insist on the retention of the provinces ceded under the Dutch treaty of 1st January 1811; this cession could, perhaps, be revoked.

Raffles drew special attention to the Pĕrang Wedono, who had supported Janssens at Samarang. As commander of the Susuhunan's army, he appeared to be a more important figure than the prime minister and hitherto unfriendly to Europeans. His influence was very considerable and Raffles desired that he should be treated with every consideration. His allowance of 4,000 Spanish dollars a year should be continued on condition that he maintained his corps at a strength of 1,150 men. As he was a poor man, it might be politic, Raffles added, to make him financially more independent.

A practice that definitely had to be stopped was that of Europeans lending money to the Susuhunan. This had grown steadily; it was probably illegal and certainly impolitic. The influence of Europeans in political matters must be done away with completely. The Susuhunan's demand that the Chinese residing at Surakarta be placed under his jurisdiction must be refused.

"It is they who have by their integrity and skill produced the high state of cultivation the country about here shows; therefore the only security for the enjoyment of what they have gained lies in our protection, for what security can there be in the hands of an Asiatic despot?"

They arrived at Samarang on 4th December. Three days later, Raffles proceeded on a short visit to Surabaya. He arranged to arrive back in

Samarang by 14th December for the purpose of receiving homage from envoys of the two courts. On the 15th he would proceed to Surakarta and then, two or three days later, to Jokyakarta. Adams was requested to make the necessary arrangements and instruct Colonel Watson to move up immediately towards Solo with his regiment and a hundred of the Light Infantry battalion.

Raffles' intention was to make every effort to conclude a treaty with Solo before tackling the Sultan of Mataram. He very well realized the danger of a simultaneous quarrel with both these important states. The more difficult problem, partly but not entirely due to Crawfurd, would be Jokyakarta. If, therefore, he could complete a treaty with Solo, his chance of gaining his second and more important objective would be greatly improved. In informing Adams of his plans, he wrote:

"I have so much confidence in your exertions, discretion and judgment that I feel myself I may without difficulty effect this important object immediately on my arrival at Solo."

He warned Adams that the chief difficulties he might experience at Solo, as he himself anticipated finding at Jokyakarta, were connected with promises apparently made to these courts by Captain Robison. He informed Adams that he must flatly refuse to honour any contracts or agreements that Robison may have made without authority.

The official entry of Raffles into Solo took place on 21st December. He was received with all the honour customarily paid in the past to the Dutch Governor-General, and a treaty of many clauses was signed without any great difficulty. The Susuhunan agreed to give up the proceeds of birds'-nests and teak forests in return for a fixed money payment. A clause guaranteeing British protection to the Susuhunan was inserted to pave the way for the disbandment of the various forces maintained in his service. Having gone through every clause, the Susuhunan expressed himself as fully satisfied with the treaty. He produced a letter sent to him by Raffles from Malacca and remarked that he was now convinced that the English promised nothing that they could not perform. He also presented Raffles with a much-valued kris that had belonged to one of his own ancestors. So was the first step in Raffles' policy happily concluded.

While at Solo, Raffles made the acquaintance of Dr Horsfield, the American naturalist—the beginning of a most felicitous association. Thomas Horsfield was born at Bethlehem, Pennsylvania, in 1783. His parents were of Moravian persuasion and Horsfield continued in the same faith. After obtaining his doctorate in medicine, he went to Java in 1800 and was to remain in the Eastern Archipelago for sixteen years. It is very creditable to Daendels that, during his régime, he encouraged Horsfield and gave him all the necessary support to carry out his researches.

Horsfield left us this account of his first meeting with Raffles:

"In the course of this tour he made about the end of December 1811, a digression to the territories of the native Princes which brought him ... to Suracarta, the capital of the Emperor of Java. Being at this time established at this place in the prosecution of a series of enquiries into the natural productions of the Island under the auspices of the existing Colonial Government, I had the honour of being invited to the solemnities of the day....

"As soon as the ceremonies of reception were completed, Sir Stamford [Raffles] left his seat and saluted many of the persons convened on the occasion. He also came up to me and with an affability and suavity of manner peculiar to himself offered me his acquaintance without the formality of an introduction. On the following day after a visit to the palace he proceeded to my dwelling where he devoted several hours to a patient examination of the objects of natural history, drawings, maps and illustrations which had been collected and prepared during my excursions through the central and eastern territories of Java. He expressed his satisfaction at the result of my enquiries, determined my relation to the Honourable Company's Government and fixed the allowances for my services. He afforded me his sanction to extend my enquiries to all divisions of natural history without limitation or restriction and likewise recommended to my attention in an official communication various subjects of general curiosity and utility. Before his departure from Suracarta he favoured me with several private interviews in which he received with much interest many minute details on the subjects of my researches, he strongly encouraged me to continue my enquiries with unwearied diligence, promised me his assistance whenever I might require it and approved of a plan which I submitted to him of devoting several months to the more minute investigations of the Priangan Regencies.[1] He mentioned the vicinities of his own residence at Buitenzorg where a friendly co-operation with Dr William Hunter promised a successful result to a botanical excursion."

Dr Hunter was superintending surgeon to the Java government.

Very soon after his arrival in Java, Raffles had determined to collect

[1] "PRAYANGAN. This is a name given by the proper Javanese to certain of the Sunda districts of Java. It has been adopted by the Dutch with the corrupt orthography of Pryanger. Prayang, in Javanese signifies a ghost or wandering spirit of the dead, and Prayangan is 'country of ghosts'. The districts in question have been constituted a province by the Dutch, under the name of the Preanger Regencies. This embraces an area of 6,077 square miles.... The country ... although in picturesque beauty equal to any in the world, is very mountainous and relatively to other portions of the island, not fertile. The Preanger Regencies have been, since the first introduction of coffee, the chief locality for its forced cultivation." Crawfurd, *Descriptive Dictionary*.

The Preanger Regencies are now divided into two Residencies, Buitenzorg and Preanger, the chief town of Preanger being Bandung.

material on which to base an account of the island to illustrate its history and social customs with the ethnological, zoological and other details necessary to complete the picture. It is true that this laudable scheme was also suggested to him by his cousin, Elton Hamond, but from the reply sent by Raffles it can be clearly inferred that Hamond was preaching to the converted.

Apart from the importance that such a book would and indeed did achieve, the task of collecting and preparing the material made it essential that no aspect should be omitted. This postulated systematized enquiries and stimulated investigation in the widest possible field. This again suited Raffles' catholic taste. It is, in fact, difficult to determine which branch of science lay closest to his heart; whichever one forms the subject of a letter, that one seems to be his particular interest. Although his enthusiasm was all-embracing, he cannot be regarded as a mere dilettante, turning at random, as fancy prompted, from one subject to another. One of his special claims to recognition as a scientist is that he was an exact and systematic observer and, in this respect, ahead of his time. He applied to science the same meticulous care, the same search for facts, the same patient industry as distinguished his administration. Unlimited curiosity and insistence on actual data mark the scientist. These were the characteristics of Raffles.

It is a truism that enthusiasm is infectious. We need not be surprised, then, that Raffles collected round him a body of keen investigators. But it was Horsfield who was chosen to be his most ardent collaborator. Although his primary interest was botany, Horsfield, like Raffles, was unrestricted in his zest for scientific knowledge. Each recognized in the other a kindred spirit, and the assistance afforded by Raffles to Horsfield was to extend far beyond the formal approval of officialdom. It was a close working partnership on an entirely different and much more intimate footing than had been Horsfield's relations with Daendels. As a result of this happy union of skill and zeal, a steady stream of specimens began to flow to the Company's museum in London.

Raffles showed no less enthusiasm in medical science, which found in him a generous patron and an active leader. As in other branches, the right man had been found to take charge, and Dr Hunter has every claim to be included in the honourable roll of those who have devoted their lives to advance the practice of medicine.

To return to Raffles' trip eastward. The next step presented an immediate difficulty. How was Raffles to meet the Sultan of Mataram? Crawfurd had made himself so completely *persona non grata* that he was debarred from all contact with the court, so that it was impossible for him even to notify the Sultan of Raffles' intention to visit him. Some letters were hastily exchanged with Crawfurd to discover how this practical difficulty could be overcome. Finally it was decided by Raffles to send to Jokyakarta a mission consisting of Muntinghe, Captain Phillips and Colonel Colin Mackenzie, a very competent officer of the Madras Engineers, who had acted as engineer-in-chief to the Java expedition. They returned on 26th December with the very satisfactory reply that the Sultan was anxious to reach a satisfactory settlement. Raffles left Solo the same day and arrived at Jokyakarta on the morrow. To prevent any awkward occurrences, as well as to uphold the dignity of the British Government, an escort of cavalry was taken. This, with the troops already at Solo and Jokyakarta, made up a force of nearly nine hundred men.

At this point we can insert a description of the *kĕratun*. It is by John Crawfurd and is quoted from his *Descriptive Dictionary of the Indian Islands and Adjacent Countries*.

"In Java there are no isolated cottages or farmhouses; the whole island is an aggregation of villages, and both the capitals and chief provincial towns are but assemblages of villages, with a palace in the midst of them. For a town there is, in fact, no native name; the only terms for it being the Sanscrit words *nagara* or *nagari*, and *praja*. The palace of the prince is called *karaton*, a derivative from *ratu*, a king, and meaning the royal residence. This may be considered a walled town. The actual palace occupies the centre, and is surrounded by the dwellings of the princes, and those of attendants and retainers. The spaces unoccupied by houses contain the gardens and reservoirs of the sovereign. The principal approach to the palace is invariably from the north, and through a square or court of considerable extent called the *alun-alun*, the sides of which are adorned by rows of fig trees (Ficus benjamina), while a pair of these are invariably in its centre. It is here that the prince shows himself to his subjects with much ceremony once in every week, and where tournaments, public processions, and military exercises are exhibited. It is, in a word, the Javanese field of Mars. To the south side of the palace there is a similar court, but on a much smaller scale. After passing through the principal court we come to the actual entrance into the palace, called the *paseban*, a word of Sanscrit derivation, meaning 'place of entry', and also named *pagâlaran*, or 'place spread with mats'. It is a pavilion, forming a waiting room for the courtiers before entering into the presence. A spacious flight of stairs leads from this to a terraced pavilion, the *sitingil*, literally, the 'high ground', or terrace in which the prince gives audience on public occasions. From this spot winding passages through a variety of walled inclosures and gates lead to the different dwellings of the sovereign himself, and of the members of his family.

"The external walls of the ancient *kraton* were of hewn stone, or of excellent brick and mortar, without any other defence than round towers. At present they are imitations of European fortifications, with bastions, parapets, moats, and glacis, the forms, however, being always the same in other respects. Of the extent of these walled towns we can judge from the modern one of Yugyakarta [Jokyakarta], which is three miles in circumference, and in my time contained a population of 10,000 inhabitants, exclusive of the *kampung* or quarters—properly villages—which surrounded it nearly up to the glacis. The extent of the Hindu capital of Majapahit must have far exceeded this, for the two principal gateways, still standing, are distant three miles from each other. The residences of the governors of provinces, *kabopaten*, are counterparts in miniature of the palace of the sovereign."

The official entry into Jokyakarta was made without incident until the audience hall, packed with excited Javanese chiefs and armed followers of the sultan, was reached. Here Raffles was faced by a sudden emergency. In describing the event to Lord Minto, he merely reported that the seating arrangements on his arrival in the hall of audience were not to his liking, but were quickly put right. It is a very modest account of what happened. The Sultan, to test the sort of man he had to deal with, had deliberately arranged the seats in a way that put the Lieutenant-Governor in a position inferior to himself. There was a tense moment as the great assembly waited to see what Raffles would do. Failure to observe the slight intended, or even a momentary hesitation, might have been fatal. But Raffles was as quick to act as he was to note the arrangement and understand the implication. He refused to take his seat until the chairs were rearranged, to show the Sultan and all his supporters that he, Raffles, was the chief authority in Java and no one could take precedence of him. Probably it was at this moment (described by Major Thorn, Gillespie's biographer) that many of the chiefs present drew their krises. Any false movement by Raffles might have cost him his life.

There is no doubt that Crawfurd was right in his suggestion that the Sultan intended to take advantage of the change of government, and the return to India of some 10,000 troops, to assert his independence. His supporters had probably been encouraged to believe that this was going to happen. But the Sultan had yet to learn with whom he had to deal. Raffles, it is true, lacked those few extra inches that can give a man the assistance of a commanding physical presence, but he lacked nothing in moral stature, and there was clearly something about him that compelled respect. Whatever the Sultan had in mind—and what that was became clearer within a few months—he was unwilling or afraid to put his plans to the test at that moment, although he had Raffles and his little party completely at his mercy.

This was one of the critical moments in the story of Raffles and of the British occupation of Java. Had his personality not saved Raffles from assassination, a general uprising would almost certainly have broken out.

This would have presented a very grave problem to an officer even as gallant and experienced as Gillespie. We might even have had to abandon Java.

Raffles, having seized the initiative, proceeded to make the most of it. The treaty drawn up was the best that could be achieved at that time. He rather hoped that it might be a permanent solution, but being under no illusion as to the character of the Sultan, he described the treaty to Minto as really nothing more than an "armed negotiation", remarking that he himself had "acted not nobly, but prudently".

He set off back for Buitenzorg, travelling fast, and arrived there on the first day of the new year.

Chapter Eleven

JAVA, 1812

i

THE news that greeted Raffles on his return to Buitenzorg was very disturbing. Tunku Mahomed and Sayid Abubakar, whom he had sent to Palembang from Malacca before the expedition, had recently arrived in Java. They stated that they had reached Muntok on the island of Bangka and there had received an invitation from the sultan, Badru'd-din, to go on to Palembang, where news of the capture of Batavia had been received.

Tunku Mahomed, who with Sayid Abubakar made a deposition, claimed to have had audience with the sultan. He had pleaded that the Dutch people should be allowed to go unmolested, and had warned the sultan that, as Palembang was a dependency of Batavia, the occupation of Batavia meant that Palembang also was conquered. Badru'd-din was alleged to have replied:

"I am not like other native princes. I dread nobody, whoever he might be. I shall listen to nobody and let me not hear this a second time."

These last words he had spoken in a "terrible voice".

On 14th September he had sent some of the leading chiefs to inform the Dutch Resident of the capture of Batavia and to tell him to quit the fort. The Resident had asked for three days to prepare for departure and had requested an audience. He and some of his senior officials had been seen being conducted to the sultan by a number of the chiefs, but on the way they had been met by other chiefs, who had told them that there was no need to go to the sultan to obtain transport, for ships were ready and they would be taken to them. These men were never seen again. They and, with a few exceptions, all the other Dutch at Palembang, including their womenfolk, had been butchered.

The two Malays had abandoned their baggage and slipped away to Malacca before coming to Java, having been warned that they would be intercepted if they went direct from Palembang to Java.

Some writers have seen fit to insinuate that Raffles himself was to blame for the murders. Capital has been made out of a letter produced later by Badru'd-din as proof that he had acted only under instructions from Raffles. This and other letters exchanged with the sultan are to be found to-day in their English versions in the India Office Library. They seem to disprove conclusively the argument advanced by the Dutch writer, J. C. Baud, that Raffles deliberately encouraged the sultan to murder the Dutch garrison. Raffles was anxious to break up the alliance between the sultan and the Dutch. In his letters he encouraged the sultan to repel a Dutch fleet. It must be admitted that any attempt to stir up the sultan against the Dutch nation must inevitably have endangered the safety of the Dutch garrison, but that was a risk in war that Raffles was entitled to take. That he was aware of the risk is clear from Captain Macdonald's autobiography. He states that Raffles was nervous about what Badru'd-din might do in the event of the capture of Java, and when he was sent by Raffles on the mission to Palembang (page 122), he did, at Raffles' request, do his utmost to obtain permission to remove the Dutch garrison to a place of safety.

Raffles could hardly be blamed, therefore, for the massacre. Britain was at war with the Franco-Dutch régime in Java, and while it was the French who were the chief enemy, the Dutch made no effort to assist against them. A belligerent is fully entitled to promote risings against an occupying power. Raffles could not have been expected, much less required, to abstain from all interest in Palembang just because it might imperil the Dutch stationed there.

The news brought by Tunku Mahomed and his companion left Raffles faced with a difficult decision. His first intention was to blockade Palembang and seize Bangka, but he decided that this might be ineffective. The alternative was a punitive expedition, which would mean the dispatch to Sumatra of the major portion of the army left in Java—a serious and hazardous enterprise. The town of Palembang lay up a long winding river some sixty miles from the mouth. It was known to be heavily stockaded and defended; the banks of the river were covered with thick jungle, giving admirable cover for anyone wishing to intercept a force proceeding up it. Yet there were weighty considerations to recommend such an attack. He had staved off, for the time at any rate, possible hostilities from Jokyakarta, which, if they had broken out, might well have involved Solo also, and now any weakness towards Palembang would certainly have repercussions in Java. It seemed imperative, therefore, to exhibit the utmost firmness towards Palembang if he were not to be involved in a grave risk of hostilities nearer home. Nor could the brutal murders of Dutch men and women be allowed to go unavenged. They had been murdered after the fall of Java, and no British Government worthy of the name could leave a massacre of innocent subjects unpunished.

Before making a final decision, he waited for the return of the commission dispatched to Palembang in November.

ii

From the outset, Raffles realized that Java's future was bound up with trade recovery. The difficulties of the previous government had been due in origin to its policy of forced cultivation and monopoly, which had destroyed very largely the economic life of the East Indies. The seriousness of the situation has been aggravated by the cessation of trade with Europe and British India. All left to Java was a limited trade with America and an occasional ship to Japan.

The general lines of the policy Raffles had in mind are clear from his letter to Minto dated 12th January 1812. The only way was to give Java the means of an export cargo. The most valuable export was tin from Palembang, but the market for that was China. What was wanted was a valuable article, small in size, suitable for export to India. Most of the produce of Java was bulky, the one important exception being spices. Under the Dutch the export of these alone had maintained the balance of trade. Interference had caused an immediate export of specie, with a progressive increase in paper money. It was essential, therefore, that the Resident of Amboina[1] should be instructed to ship his spices in future to Batavia instead of Madras and Bengal. Since hostilities had commenced against Java this direct trade had become the normal one, but it was vital to reintroduce the old Dutch system to the extent that Batavia became the great emporium of local produce. Batavia could supply all the eastern isles with rice and receive in exchange the spices she could trade to India and thus balance the cash she must draw from there to finance the government and armed forces.

The first step to be taken by Java must be to encourage in every way the old inter-island trade. This meant the removal of vexatious duties and restrictions that prevented the flow of produce to Java and the supply in return of rice and other necessities. If external trade was to be concentrated on Java, the *entrepôt* for the whole area, a revision of the customs regulations was required. This Raffles set about at once.

There were, however, other obstacles to the required recovery that were not so simple. During the period of blockade that had led up to the invasion of Java, the Dutch had necessarily reduced their hold on the outer islands. They lacked the troops to garrison them, wishing to concentrate their forces in Java, which they knew to be threatened. Their sea communications had been practically destroyed by the British, and the Moluccas had been taken from them.

When the British had captured Java, they had found that the Dutch control of its old dependencies was now largely nominal. There was the

[1] The Moluccas were under the direct control of India and not subordinate to Java —a stupid arrangement.

added absurdity that the Moluccas continued to be subordinate to India, whereas common sense demanded that they should come under the direction of Batavia. Minto had instructed W. B. Martin, the Resident at Amboina, to maintain close liaison with Raffles, but this did not go so far as Raffles desired. However, one of his first actions was to abolish the duty on rice to Amboina and encourage native traders to send their prows to the Moluccas and obtain spices in exchange for rice.

To extend a similar exchange of commodities with other islands was a different matter. The local rulers, having recovered a measure of independence, regarded European overtures with suspicion. They had built up a trade with Malacca and Penang on their own terms, and were not readily disposed to divert it to Java. To insist on such a diversion might have involved military operations beyond the resources of Java, nor had Raffles sufficient armed vessels to tackle even the urgent question of piracy. Piracy was one of the fruits of Dutch monopoly, being the natural outlet for sea-loving Malays who, by Dutch regulations, had been prevented from engaging in peaceful commerce. The gradual weakening of Dutch power had encouraged piratical activity until it had reached formidable dimensions. Moreover, many of the native rulers, if not actively indulging in it, obtained much of their revenue indirectly from that source. Here clearly, then, was a grave obstacle to a revival of inter-island trading.

Apart from the direct purpose of trying to stimulate this trade, Raffles had a further objective in mind. He could never forget that Java might one day be restored to the Dutch. His ambition was, in that event, to secure at least one or two trading ports as permanent British colonies, to prevent the Dutch ever again succeeding in establishing a monopoly of the spice trade to the exclusion of all foreign rivals.

The new customs regulations were gazetted on 11th January 1812. An explanatory note from the Lieutenant-Governor in Council to the Governor-General in Council set out the principle followed.

"The duties directed to be levied at the Eastern Ports are calculated . . . on the principle that heretofore was acted upon and which it seems absolutely necessary for the security of the revenue and the general prosperity of the colony to continue, that Batavia must be considered as the principal port of trade . . . on account of the advantageous and commanding situation for the passing trade to and from China, the safety of the roads [anchorages] during the whole year, its vicinity to these districts which afford the most considerable exports to a foreign market, and its extensive population and capital as well European as Chinese dispersed in various establishments which must altogether be ruined in the event of the general trade of Java being removed to any other port were such an experiment tried and practicable."

Raffles was active also at this time in the introduction of social reforms, and ensuring that they were carried out. He had no highly trained secretariat to which to depute matters of high policy or their detailed application; experienced civil servants could have been counted on the fingers of one hand. The Englishmen holding key positions were many of them soldiers or surgeons. The success of any measure depended largely on Raffles' personal supervision. Seldom has so big a country been ruled to such an extent by a single individual.

The new arrangements for courts of justice and police were announced on 21st January. They were to come into operation as from 31st January and were subject to confirmation by the Governor-General. A supreme court of justice was constituted under the presidency of Muntinge assisted by three other members. A bench of magistrates was set up at Batavia under the presidency of J. W. Cranssen, also with three members, for the control of the city of Batavia and its environs. At Samarang and Surabaya, courts of justice under a president with two members were likewise set up and magistrates' courts instituted. It was resolved:

"That the jurisdiction of the Magistrates Court at Batavia and of the Magistrates in general over the Island, be from and after the 1st February confined to matters of Police, and that they be guided in the execution of their duty, as far as circumstances will permit, by the provisions adopted with respect to the Magistracy in the different parts of the British Empire, and which will be defined as far as practicable in the written instructions to the Magistrates, and in cases of doubt will at Batavia be referred to, and decided upon by the Honourable Lieutenant-Governor . . . at Samarang by the Civil Commissioner, and at Sourabaya by the Deputy Civil Commissioner.

"That in Civil cases the Courts of Justice conform to the same mode of proceeding as heretofore established for the said courts previous to the establishment of the British Government, but that in criminal cases they be required in the mode of proceeding to conform as much as possible to that established in Great Britain, in all cases confronting the prisoner with the evidence and a jury being called to judge of the fact on the evidence so adduced." The president and one other member of the courts of justice were to go on circuit twice a year.

"That the Land[d]rosts or Chief Civil Authorities in the different districts do form a court with the Regent, and that other native officers heretofore composing those courts for the hearing and trying of all civil cases that may arise in the district in which on both sides natives only are concerned, but they be required to keep a regular record of the same to be transmitted quarterly to the Court of Justice, and in causes where the amount exceeds 50 Spanish Dollars to submit their decisions to the Court of Justice for their confirmation previous to the award being made.

"That in criminal cases the authority of the Landrosts' Court so established is to be confined to matters of police, and in no case to exceed that of the Justices of the Peace in England except . . . where authorized by Government."

Courts of request established at Batavia, Samarang and Surabaya were to have cognizance in cases not exceeding fifty Spanish dollars, and subject to appeal to a court of justice. All officers of justice and police were restricted from compounding crimes and offences on pain of dismissal. In addition, provisional regulations in fifty-four articles were published as a guide to courts of justice and request.

Raffles wrote to Lord Minto:

". . . I think we may now calculate on the purity of the Courts and the impartial administration of Justice according to the *Colonial* law, which though as far from the Dutch as from the English is, I am decidedly of the opinion, the best that can be adopted. . . . I have the pleasure to say that it has not yet been found necessary to execute Capital Punishment. With the exception of a band of robbers in Cheribon, the country is quite tranquil. . . . In the judicial and police regulations I had not the assistance of a single lawyer's clerk. . . ."

His short experience as registrar of the court in Penang was proving of value.

In an official letter from the Lieutenant-Governor in Council to the Governor-General in Council later that month (29th), the purpose of the new measures was explained.

"These Landrosts with the native Chiefs over whom they presided and directed, were entrusted with the highest criminal jurisdiction over the natives in their districts. The irregularity and impropriety of some of their Proceedings had subjected their sentences first to an appropriation of Government and afterwards to a revisal of the Supreme Court at Batavia, but both methods were found liable not only to great inconveniences, but entirely inadequate to check the improper use of the judicial power in hands unfit for such a trust. The ill effects of the Landrosts' Courts in criminal cases was still further increased by the adherence to an imperfect code extracted from the Mahomedan Law full of barbarity and tortures, the tenure of which had only been partially investigated by the decrees of the late Government. The complete subjection, however, and the weakness of all the native Chiefs along the coast of Java made it quite practicable to subject all the inhabitants of those districts to the general law of the country, and it was therefore considered most expedient . . . to obviate this unqualified jurisdiction of the Landrosts and the still remaining use of the native codes in criminal cases by confining the first merely to the duties of police with a power of the Magistrates of England, and by abolishing the latter. . . .

"Not to lose sight of the only point which made the former courts of the Landrosts in some degree commendable, namely of bringing justice as it were to the door of every man, we have directed the Courts of Justice at Batavia, Samarang and Sourabaya to make regular circuits throughout the districts under their jurisdiction for the purpose of hearing and trying all offences and criminal cases within the same as near as possible to the spot where the offence took place. . . ."

Although every effort was being made to come as near as possible to English procedure, "we have not yet ventured to make any essential alteration in the law of this country, as the same appears to us chiefly to be a Colonial law adapted mostly to the peculiar circumstances of this Colony, and material change in which might be attended with very serious consequences. . . ."

As Raffles wrote to his old chief, Ramsay:

". . . I hope the Colony may receive all the advantages of British jurisprudence without entailing on it the disadvantages of a Judicial establishment from England, of all things the most to be dreaded for the general prosperity and happiness of the population. The British Courts of Justice fit with difficulty our permanent English establishments in India; but here their introduction would only lead to anarchy, vexation and trouble without end."

In addition to the paper currency issued in such large quantities by Daendels, there was another form of note called Probolingo paper. To raise money, Daendels had in December 1810 sold three provinces in eastern Java to certain rich Chinese, among them one Chan Pit, who had bought Probolingo and Besuki, two of the most important areas. A condition of sale had been that the purchasers should buy up every six months fifty thousand of the new notes, and to help them to pass them on to the reluctant public, Daendels had by proclamation made this Probolingo paper legal tender to any amount, with heavy punishments for non-compliance. When the time for the first instalment had come round, Chan Pit and his fellow investors had duly fulfilled their undertaking to purchase fifty thousand Probolingo notes, but had paid for them in the same worthless currency, suavely citing the proclamation that Probolingo paper was to be regarded as the equivalent of hard cash.

The question now arose whether the sale contracts of 2nd December 1810 should be honoured or not by the British Government. Eventually it was decided that they should be respected, that the lottery introduced by Daendels to liquidate this paper money should be continued and that the half-yearly lottery due to take place on 1st March should be held. The original provision of Daendels that Probolingo paper should rank with silver was revoked, except in respect of contracts entered into between the date of the proclamation of Daendels' and 14th February, the date of the British proclamation. The latter laid it down that Probolingo paper should find its own market value, which would be published from time to time in the *Java Gazette*.

It is worthy of mention that Civil Commissioner Hugh Hope won sixteen thousand dollars in the lottery, which gave rise to a jingle in the *Gazette*:

"As for the prizes great and small,
The Government was got them all,
God knows what they've been doing."

A problem that had to be faced was the treatment of creditors of the former government. These were numerous, the loans having in many cases been forcibly extracted. Minto's view was that the British Government could not be expected to pay the principal, but that it was morally bound to pay interest on the loans to all but absentee creditors. The rate was six per cent. The question had to be referred to London. If there was any reply, it cannot now be traced.

On a personal note, Raffles wrote to Minto at this time:

"For the first three or four months after the surrender with so extensive a settlement as this it became as much a matter of policy as almost necessity to bring the European population together and to make our new subjects cheerfully acquainted as well with the Government as the European subjects stationed here—by keeping a fine and open table for the first month or two I am satisfied that I have carried my principal point with Government. I have kept up good humour and good understanding until the officers of Government have fallen into their proper places—the result has been that everything is now properly arranged and there has been nothing like discordance anywhere."

This policy was certainly right, but, as Raffles very soon discovered, it was from his personal point of view extremely expensive. The purpose of this letter was to consult the Governor-General as to how far this sort of expenditure might be regarded as an accepted charge on the administration. With a house allowance of £1,000 a year, his annual salary was equivalent to £8,200. According to this letter, the financial arrangement made before Minto had left had been intended to make it possible for Raffles to "lay by £4,000/£5,000 a year". Raffles now suggested that these special entertainments should, on grounds of public policy, be debited to the treasury. To create a fund against such expenditure, he proposed that the receipts from the edible birds'-nests for the period between the capture of Java and the taking up of their appointments by the Residents of Solo and Jokyakarta might be utilized. Minto's reply is not on record, but in view of the liberal entertaining carried out by Raffles throughout the whole period, it is to be assumed that it was satisfactory.

iii

The commission that had been dispatched by Raffles to Palembang in the previous November returned to Java in March. Its members reported that their treatment by the sultan had been disdainful; he had flatly refused to make any deal over the tin. They had been "kept in a sort of confinement and restricted from a free communication with the inhabitants", but they had scented a mystery regarding the Dutch garrison that tended to confirm the various stories current in Malacca and elsewhere. Sultan Badru'd-din had claimed that he had sent the Dutch away and had razed the fort to the ground, in deference to the wishes of Raffles as expressed by his agents from Malacca long before the conquest of Java. He was therefore now an independent sovereign.

Apart from the immediate necessity of dealing promptly with the situation created by the revolt, and apart from the risks inherent in a punitive expedition of the magnitude required, Raffles saw that here was the opportunity to carry out a long-cherished plan.

He had made up his mind that he wanted Bangka as a British colony. He thought that there now was a chance not only of asserting the rights of the British to Palembang as the conquerors of Java, but also of obtaining the cession of Bangka to the British Government in perpetuity. Writing to the Governor-General on 7th March, he explained all this, and in particular the advantages to be got from Bangka as a strategic and commercial base. He emphasized that no European had yet made any claim to the island. The British Government would therefore be entitled, if it obtained its cession, to retain it even if Java were handed back. This line of reasoning is difficult to follow; having stated emphatically that Palembang was a dependency of Java and became a dependency of the British by virtue of their conquest of Java, he should logically have admitted that any dependency of Palembang was also, in the last analysis, a dependency of Java. It would seem that Raffles allowed the importance of his objective to cloud his rational judgment.

An expedition against Palembang was put immediately in hand. It consisted of eight companies from the 59th and 89th Regiments, detachments of gunners and some dismounted Hussars. There were also some sepoys and Amboynese. All were accommodated in four transports supported by two warships, a sloop, two of the Company's cruisers and two gunboats. Gillespie was in command.

In his instructions to the commander, Raffles emphasized that the possession of Bangka was to be the *sine qua non*, whether obtained by cession or by the mere act of settling there. If possible, an unqualified cession of the island to the East India Company was to be obtained.

Opposition to the occupation of Bangka was not expected, and acts of hostility on that island were to be avoided and all property respected. The provision of a fort adequate to the protection of the new establishment was to be immediately undertaken.

"In the event of the removal of the Sultan of Palembang," wrote Raffles to Gillespie, "you should . . . see that the nearest relation of the Sultan, if competent to maintain the public tranquillity, be immediately placed on the throne on such conditions as will safely prevent his ever becoming a dangerous neighbour to the British Government, taking care that the power left to him be neither too great nor reduced too low."

The sultan's eldest brother, Ahmad Najimu'd-din, seemed to Raffles to be a fit person. The Pangeran Ratu, only son of the sultan and a principal actor in the late events, was heir presumptive, but, from his cruelty and debaucheries, was obnoxious to the inhabitants. "It may become a consideration how far his character will outweigh his right by birth." In the event of any difficulties in the attempt against Palembang, Gillespie was to remember that this part of the expedition, the removal of the sultan, was not sufficiently important to justify any serious loss on our side. If the new sultan was amenable, the condition of friendship and alliance was to be the unqualified cession of Bangka and Billiton with their dependent islets. The British would make a suitable and adequate provision for the support of the sultan's rank and dignity. If the agreement was signed, envoys were to be sent to Batavia to arrange and complete a definite treaty.

The three points of the agreement were to be: first, the complete surrender of all rights in the island of Bangka and the exclusive right of the East India Company to all the mines and produce of the island; secondly, the submission of all the inhabitants and residents in the island; and thirdly, the security of property and families of all those in the dominions of the sultan of Palembang, with complete freedom to move to Bangka if they so desired.

Gillespie was to investigate rumours that some of the women belonging to the late Dutch establishment were still alive. If this was so, their rescue from the interior was to be undertaken.

The force left Batavia on 20th March, but was seriously delayed by contrary winds and did not arrive off the mouth of the Palembang river until 15th April. After various unsatisfactory delegations from Sultan Badru'd-din, Gillespie decided to abandon negotiations and proceed to the attack. It was indeed a formidable task, but resource, determination and bravery were displayed, and Gillespie himself was, as ever, at the post of greatest danger. By 28th April the town and palace were in his possession. Badru'd-din had fled with the royal treasure.

He was deposed, the Pangeran Ratu disinherited, and Ahmad

Najimu'd-din appointed sultan. By a treaty signed on 17th May, Bangka, Billiton and the depending islands were ceded to Great Britain. The government of Java undertook to pay the sultan an annual sum to support his rank and dignity, the amount to be agreed later. The sultan accepted a British agent and promised to punish those concerned in the Dutch massacre. Suitable fines were to be inflicted to be used for the benefit of the Dutch widows and orphans. Bangka was occupied on 20th May and called Duke of York Island. Muntok was renamed Minto.

The success of this expedition would never have been achieved so rapidly by a commander less daring than Gillespie. That Raffles admired him, yet at the same time found him rather an incalculable person, is made clear from a paragraph in a letter to Minto.

"It is quite unnecessary that I should inform your Lordship that I have rather a strange character to deal with; he prides himself on his quixotism but with all his irregularities is a man of so high a stamp and caste that I must esteem him. We shall never break without great concern on my part . . . but your Lordship knows his character too well to suppose it is practicable that we should both travel at the same pace. He does and will take some of the strangest starts and wildest freaks into his head that ever entered into the mind of man."

Leaving the greater part of his troops to return by the long sea passage round Borneo, Gillespie left Palembang with the remainder of his forces on 22nd May. He arrived at Batavia on 30th May, to find that Raffles had gone in haste to Samarang.

The trouble that was brewing in eastern Java was probably not unconnected with the absence in Sumatra of a large proportion of the armed forces. Whether or not that was so, it had become rapidly and ominously clear that the "armed negotiation" with the Sultan of Mataram was worth very little. Evidence was also accumulating that Mataram was trying to induce Solo to join in a revolt against the British and was achieving some success. Worse still, emissaries were reported to be visiting other princes, with a view to promoting a general rising throughout Java.

Raffles, as we have already seen, was under no illusion as to the grave situation that must arise if Mataram and Solo made common cause. In a letter dated 19th March to Adams at Solo, dealing with the improper conduct of the Susuhunan in disposing of the farms, birds'-nests and toll-gates, and criticizing other financial irregularities, we find this statement of general policy:

"As an additional inducement for continuing the most friendly line of policy with regard to the Court of Souracarta [Solo], it must be considered as an unwavering rule that measures of hostility are in no case to be contemplated against both Courts at once, and from the recent conduct of the Court of Djocjocarta and the possibility of the recurrence of similar acts on the part of the Sultan, you must be aware that the first decision of the British Government must be directed to that quarter."

The position of Adams was not easy. The Susuhunan appears to have been deliberately elusive. "With regard to forming a political interest in the Court," wrote Adams, "it is not easy, if it were possible. The Susuhunan himself has always avoided coming out in public (when I should attend him) ever since I came . . . and he has always declined every invitation I have given his Highness to the Residency, except when you, Honourable Sir, were here. Radin Adipati [title of prime minister] has been behaving in an extremely underhand fashion. Under these circumstances you will perceive the difficulty, if not impossibility, of managing affairs with this Court otherwise than by simply declaring what I know or believe to be the intentions of the British Government—a declaration which will gather more weight daily with the Susuhunan and his ministers and advisers (if contrary to his own declaration, he has any) when they perceive that I really do speak your sentiments and that their references for reversing my opinions are of no avail."

But if the attitude of the Susuhunan was evasive, that of the Sultan of Mataram was actively and dangerously aggressive. As Raffles put it in his report to Minto:

"Instead of evincing any attention to the wishes of the British Government, the Sultan availed himself of every opportunity to assert his independence. But a short time elapsed after the date of the Treaty before he directed the assassination of the father of the late Minister with whose blood he had recently stained his hands, a blameless and inoffensive old man; subsequently he caused to be strangled seven of the highest and most respectable Chiefs of the country, without even an alleged offence, men whose persons were, by the existing arrangement, under the immediate protection of the British Government; he degraded and affronted the Hereditary Prince and publicly threatened his life, which he was alone prevented from taking by the direct interference of the British Government; he refused to deliver over the lands and districts ceded to the late Government and confirmed to the present by the last Treaty; he entirely neglected and overlooked every minor stipulation of that Treaty and was eventually detected in intriguing with the Court of the Susuhunan in the violation of the most solemn and most important engagement of all the Treaties, with the avowed object of undermining and subverting the British supremacy in Java. . . . For several months he was engaged in adding to his defences by constructing new batteries, training bands of troops and latterly there arose serious apprehension with regard to the safety of the Residency and garrison."

With Olivia accompanying him, Raffles had left Batavia for Samarang on 23rd May. It had been his intention to have a force concentrated there before the end of April, but the unexpected length of absence of the expedition to Palembang had made this impossible. Time was running out. If no move was made, very soon the conflagration might start and the task of subduing it might be almost beyond his powers. The news that Gillespie had safely returned to Batavia now made it possible to take the initiative, though the forces available would be somewhat meagre, most of the troops being still on their way round Borneo.

In spite of his anxiety, he saw to it that King George III's birthday on 4th June was celebrated in Samarang with the fullest ceremony.

"At 3 o'clock an elegant entertainment was provided at the Government House at Bodjong at which the Hon. Lieutenant-Governor presided, Mr Hope and the principal civil, naval and military officers being present . . . an amiable and animated Hostess who on this particular occasion exerted to the utmost her well-known affability and pleasing manners which we never remember to have seen equalled by anyone; summoned at an early hour this thoroughly happy and Loyal Party from the friends all the officers brought to the more fascinating charms of the Fair Sex and the delights of the sprightly Dance. The Ball was opened by Mr Hope and the Lady Governess to the favourite tune of 'The Fall of Cornelis' which delightful air and the elegance and spirit with which it commenced drew forth the admiration and applause of the numerous gay and fashionable assemblage, who kept it up with uncommon spirit until 12 o'clock when supper was announced. After supper and a grand display of fireworks, the Dance was resumed and continued until long after the glowing sunbeams of the morning had made the remaining night grow dim and reminded the party that it was time to retire."

Gillespie did not stay long in Batavia. He attended the celebration of the King's birthday, himself proposing most of the fifteen toasts, then, having presided at a regimental dinner on 5th June, left overland for Samarang on the following day.

The situation that Raffles had to lay before him was—to quote his letter to Minto on 20th June—as follows:

"At the period of the arrival of the Commander of the Forces at Samarang the conduct of the Sultan had become still more daring and while he was daily recruiting his means of defence in the Kraton, the incursion of predatory parties from different parts of the territories became more frequent and alarming. Emissaries were detected, both from the Court of the Sultan and that of the Emperor [the Susuhunan] in conveying communications to the different Regents of the Company's Provinces along the coast, and to the Sultan and Prince of Madura and it was to be feared that in any protracted operations the European Government might have to cope with the whole native administration of the

Island . . . we were decidedly of opinion that the present was in all probability the only opportunity that would ever occur for the European power to exert its authority with advantage, and that in view of orders from Bengal directing the reduction of our military power, not a moment should be lost in placing the tranquillity of the Island on such a permanent footing as not to be hereafter disturbed when the means of enforcing the European authority might be beyond our might."

Instructions were dispatched to Crawfurd at Jokyakarta to secure the attachment of the hereditary prince and, if possible, to obtain his co-operation in the removal of the reigning sultan.

Simultaneously with the preparations at Samarang, Raffles had ordered a concentration of troops in the Solo area, to give the appearance that punitive action against that state was to follow the subjection of Mataram. Hugh Hope, civil commissioner at Samarang, was sent to seek audience of the Susuhunan at Solo. He informed him that, having full knowledge of the intrigues carried on with Jokyakarta, Raffles had at first determined to march on Solo, but in consideration for his Highness's feelings, had instructed Hope to inform him that he (Hope) might be the means of making such overtures from his Highness as might induce the Lieutenant-Governor to suspend the march on Solo.

Hope was able to report on 12th June that the negotiations had been finally successful.

"It was with much reluctance that I got the Emperor to accede to the request of delivering up 'all persons concerned in the correspondence' as he considered that in that was included a demand for some of his near relations. I recommended his throwing himself on your liberality as the surest means of gaining your favour."

Hope suggested that these be pardoned, as the prime minister was the real culprit.

"Respecting the payment of the sum of 200,000 dollars, His Highness agrees to it because I told him it was inescapable, but he declared his total inability to discharge the Amount . . . the disbanding of his troops to 1,000 men for his Body Guard he accedes to and to the establishment and payment of a subsidiary Force but he feels great anxiety as to the extent of the Force. He likewise acceded to the interference of the British Government in his judicial and revenue establishments as it may seem fit to the British Government. The district of Blora and Wirosobo [Wirasari] he agrees to cede immediately and such part of the Cadoe [Kedu] as the British Government may demand; as likewise any arrangement regarding the Highlands of Java he may deem necessary to make."

Raffles and Gillespie left Samarang for Jokyakarta with a small escort composed of part of the 14th Regiment and Bengal Light Infantry, the 3rd Volunteer Battalion, some gunners and two troops of dragoons. The main military force, under Lieut.-Col. McLeod, was to follow with most of the artillery. The advance party reached the Residency at Jokyakarta on 17th June. The Sultan, who was occupying a strongly defended *kĕratun*, inside and outside which were masses of his followers and plenty of guns, was not disposed to submit. On the contrary, he immediately moved part of his forces behind the Residency, cutting it off from the coast. Gillespie and Crawfurd went out in a reconnaissance with fifty dragoons. They had difficulty in getting back and there were some casualties. More awkward still, the enemy was destroying bridges, tearing up roads and putting every obstacle in the way of the main body led by McLeod. It was not easy to communicate to McLeod the grave need for his prompt arrival, but eventually a brave trooper volunteered to penetrate the enemy's lines and got through to McLeod.

The Sultan was quite confident that at last he had Raffles at his mercy. A further attempt by Raffles to obtain his submission was contemptuously rejected and a demand for unconditional surrender sent in return. One can hardly blame the Sultan for his optimism. The relatively small force with Raffles and Gillespie was confined to the Residency and its vicinity, all communication with the outside world being virtually cut off. The Susuhunan had moved his army into a strategic position to their rear.

"I should mention", Raffles wrote shortly afterwards to Minto, "that the Craton was a regular fortified position about three miles in circumference, surrounded by a wide and deep ditch, with a wall forty-five feet high, defended by well-constructed bastions, and forming ramparts all round.

"The approach to the Craton being further secured by lower walls without the ditch on the opposite side of the road, and the gates protected by drawbridges after the European model, at the period of the assault it was calculated that there could not be less than 11,000 armed men within the Craton, while large parties of one, two, three, and even four thousand occupied positions without the Craton, blocking up the main roads. . . ."

Against these, Gillespie had at his disposal "not exceeding 600 firelocks, and rather more than that number in dragoons, artillery and sepoys".

The Sultan of Mataram had yet to learn what British trained troops under a fearless commander like Gillespie could do. Discipline and firepower, bravery and leadership could afford to disregard enormous differences in numbers.

"The Sultan refusing to comply with my summons, and several of our dragoons having been cut off in detail, decisive measures became necessary; and on the 18th,[1] in the afternoon, we commenced a heavy cannonade from the fort on his Craton . . . it was immediately returned

[1] On that same day America went to war with Great Britain.

on his side, and although no further measure was taken by us during the whole of the 19th, no symptoms of concession were made by him . . . nothing remained for us but an assault. . . ."

This was launched in the early hours of the 20th.

"Gillespie was himself. The assault was made by escalade; we soon got possession of the ramparts, and turned their guns upon them. . . ."

The hereditary prince and his own personal troops kept out of the fighting, which was violent and bloody. Gillespie was wounded in the left arm. In less than three hours it was all over.

". . . at nine o'clock the Craton was ours . . . the Sultan was taken in his strongest hold; and our plan throughout was most successful; the loss to our side very inconsiderable, and comparatively nothing; on the part of the enemy dreadful . . . the person of the Sultan, as well as that of the hereditary prince, secured. . . ."

The Susuhunan's army had made no movement to assist the Sultan and discreetly withdrew shortly after the fall of the *kĕratun*, which was given over to the army to loot and produced a rich booty in which every officer and man shared in his degree. It also produced the first sharp clash between Raffles and Gillespie.

This discord, however, did not affect the unstinted praise of the Lieutenant-Governor. General orders dated at Samarang 28th June and published in the *Java Gazette* on 4th July gave, very properly, the fullest award to the personal leadership of Gillespie.

"The whole force was . . . animated by the personal example of the Commander of the Forces, who was ever foremost in danger and conspicuous in achievement. Colonel Gillespie is entitled to the full measure of admiration and applause which it is in the power of the Lieutenant-Governor to bestow; the Lieutenant-Governor requests that he will accept his best thanks for the zeal, energy and exemplary exertion which he evinced throughout and, in particular, for the personal advice and co-operation which he afforded to the Lieutenant-Governor in the political arrangements which, while it supported relations between Government and the Army, at the same time ensured to the Army in its operations the exercise of its full vigour and freedom of action. The Lieutenant-Governor laments most sincerely the wound which Colonel Gillespie received towards the close of the action. . . ."[1]

In his own dispatch, Gillespie referred generously to the merits of Crawfurd:

"I have the honour to solicit your particular attention to the valuable services of Mr Crawfurd, Resident. It is impossible I can convey to you how deeply I am impressed with a sense of his talent and excellence.

[1] Gillespie's promotion to Major-General appeared in the *Java Gazette* on 8th August 1812. It was dated 1st January 1812.

From the period of my arrival until the conquest of the Krattan he was uniformly capable and assiduous and his personal exposure in the assault on the works merits equally my thanks and commendation."

By such a decisive victory, all immediate danger to the British had been removed. With understandable pride, Raffles wrote to Minto on 25th June:

"The Hereditary Prince has been raised to the throne, all the principal Chieftains have submitted to his authority, and the country has every appearance of tranquillity. . . .

"The European power is for the first time paramount in Java. We are now able to dictate the terms of the future connexion with the British Government and the native administration. The population of no less than a million has been wrested from the tyranny and oppression of an ignorant and cruel Prince [the Sultan of Mataram]. And a country yielding to none for wealth in fertility and cultivation, offering a revenue of no less than a million of Spanish Dollars in a year, placed at our disposal. . . . The population and cultivation of the Emperor's [the Susuhunan's] dominions are not inferior to those of the Sultan and this statement alone will convey to your Lordship an idea of what has been obtained in the short space of 5 days."

It was now the task of Raffles to make such arrangements with the two Javanese rulers as would ensure against any revival of trouble. This could be done in one of two ways: by force or by diplomacy. Raffles wisely chose the second.

The treaties with Mataram and Solo were both dated 1st August 1812. One of the original copies is preserved at Auckland, New Zealand, and the text of them is to be found in the India Office Library. It will suffice here to give the comments made on them by Raffles in a letter to the Governor-General dated 8th August, a copy of which was sent to the Secret Committee in London:

"Your Lordship is fully aware of the personal character of the Susuhunan, that he is of a weak, unsteady and sinister disposition, devoted to luxury and amusements and easily persuaded towards any measure that can tend to gratify his vanity or increase his personal consequence. By the Treaty concluded with him in December last, adequate means were given him of supporting his royal dignity and rank; and I am convinced that if the change which took place in the relations of the Resident at his Court [Colonel Adams] had been more delicately managed on the part of the Resident, his neutrality, if not attachment, might at all times have been secured."

Raffles added that, although the Susuhunan had seem satisfied with the December treaty, he may have been secretly disappointed that his hopes had not been more fully realized. As for the Sultan of Mataram, the terms of the December treaty had been, if not the best conceivable, then the best possible without hostilities, which would have been most inadvisable at that time.

Of the new treaties he wrote:

"It was the policy of the Dutch Government to populate the Highlands of Java in such a manner as to sow seeds of continued dissension and discord and to encourage every symptom of animosity which might appear between the two Courts. In all their dealings with the native Princes, the success which they obtained was always by over-reaching and intrigue, and in no instance does their conduct appear to have been open and ingenuous."

It was no surprise, therefore, that the princes should have considered British liberality as weakness, all the more because British character and power had been systematically depreciated by the Dutch. A proof had now been given of British strength and determination.

The lands transferred by the treaty with the sultan included "the rich and populous districts of the Cadoe" (as Raffles later described them), north of Jokyakarta.

"By the introduction of the direct and immediate interference which is secured to the British Government by the present Treaty, Your Lordship's enlightened plans for ameliorating the situation of the inhabitants throughout the Island will be essentially promoted. . . . A settlement of the new Government in the districts not first actually transferred to the European power would present an opportunity of introducing any system which may have been decided upon for the regulation of landed property and cultivation throughout the Island and with the advantage of establishing it direct on the Javanese habits and customs without the vitiated system of the Dutch. . . ."

He drew up a report on the island of Bangka and submitted it both to Lord Minto and the Court of Directors in London. After reviewing the history of the Dutch connexion with the island, he estimated that with proper mining methods, security against smuggling and piracy, the export of tin would be found to be much greater than had previously been anticipated. He suggested that the Bangka tin might be shipped to India in payment for supplies from there to Java, or that Java should be allowed to enter on its own the trade with China. The island possessed other important advantages.

"As there is already a large town where refreshments of all kinds will be readily obtained when security of property is established and the demand for these articles is certain, this will naturally become a convenient refreshing port for ships making either the direct passage to China through the Straits of Sunda, or the eastern passage by Macasser (*sic*) . . . it being on the direct route from the Straits of Malacca through the Straits of

Dryon [Durian] or Rhio, both now generally known to be safe passages. . . ."

Another point of great importance was that Bangka had been a famous stronghold of pirates, and no better station could have been selected as a future bulwark against piracy in those waters.

Last but not least: ". . . if the course of events at home should ever oblige us to give up Java, we have in Banca a possession not 130 miles from it with all the advantage which we have enumerated to which we can lay claim, and one too that will render us so large a surplus revenue."

Minto sent his unqualified approval.

". . . I am anxious to deliver without reserve or qualifications the very high and favourable view I now have of the whole series of measures beginning with the Expedition to Palembang and ending with the arrangement of the two Courts of Solo and Djocjocarta, connected and combined with each other as these measures were. . . . Nothing can be more excellent than all your arrangements in the Eastern districts of Java. . . ."

It is interesting to note also that he agreed with Raffles that, even if Java had to be returned to the Dutch, Bangka could be retained with full propriety. Though we may not concur in this opinion, we must concede that the unbroken peace subsequently enjoyed by the British in Java is good evidence of the wisdom with which Raffles made use of his overwhelming victory.

iv

Now that hostilities in Java had been successfully concluded and treaties signed with Solo and Jokyakarta, Raffles felt that he would not be justified in delaying further a reduction in the army. India was urging the pressing need for economy, insisting that no time should be lost in obtaining the important financial relief such a reduction would afford.

The view taken by Raffles was that there was now no risk of any major internal disturbance or invasion from overseas. Gillespie held an exactly opposite opinion.

Disagreements of this kind between a civil government and its military adviser follow almost automatically after every war, but this one led to a quarrel that developed far beyond the original point at issue. The consequences of the dispute were to be of the gravest: Raffles was to come personally under a cloud of disapproval, his whole government and policy were to be seriously discredited, and this in turn was to prejudice the attitude at home towards the retention of Java.

Before dealing with the details of the quarrel, it is advisable to look at the background. There was, for example, the haughty attitude of the British army in India, which regarded itself as a superior caste, looking on officers of the East India Company and civilians alike with ill-disguised contempt. Its behaviour towards the Indian population was also apt to be high-handed and arbitrary. Even so important an official of the Company as Charles Metcalfe found himself powerless to make the army mend its ways.

"It was a shocking act of tyranny", he observed, "to throw merchants' goods out on the road because His Highness Ensign Smith desired a cart and desired it at once."[1]

Gillespie epitomized some of the best and some of the worst qualities of a professional officer of the period. Of aristocratic Irish birth and independent means, he had chosen a military career as the one most likely to satisfy his love of adventure. He was good-looking, athletic and possessed of great independence and force of character; a born leader, devoid of any sense of fear, he was determined to gain his objective, whatever it might be.

Captain Taylor recorded this engaging description of him:

"He is a fine fellow, and I do not know a man breathing whose good opinion as a soldier I would rather have, and I may say that I have obtained it. His humanity and perpetual attention to the comfort of his troops; his affable kind way of addressing them and officers of all ranks, at the same time his determination to preserve discipline and enforce orders have raised him in my opinion higher than he was before. To say he is brave to a fault if possible (for he often exposes himself needlessly) is nothing new. It is pleasant to hear the soldiers say 'There he goes—that's the boy—he's the man to follow' and all those sorts of things."

He was indeed a fine commander in the field, full of resource, initiative and bravery. On the other side of the picture, he was selfish and egotistical, impatient of restraint and unstable of character. Captain Macdonald, who greatly admired him, referred to "a haughty and over-bearing temper which it was not possible at all times either for himself or others to control". His fame as the Hero of Vellore had made him conceited and his conceit was not lessened by his additional title of the Hero of Cornelis. His attitude towards civilians would certainly have been no more accommodating than that of his brother officers, and in his eyes Raffles might well have been regarded as an upstart clerk and, as the term would have been understood in his circle, hardly a gentleman. He was also fifteen years older than Raffles, who in that year became thirty-one.

Raffles had hitherto enjoyed only a limited experience of military gentlemen. The small garrison in Penang was of insufficient standing to adopt any high tone towards the civilian population, even had it wished to do so. Colonel Macalister was not only commander of the troops, but

[1] Edward J. Thompson, *Life of Lord Metcalfe.*

a member of the Council also; he had acted for a spell as Governor. No possibility existed then in Penang of any clash between the civil and military authorities. But Raffles had already sensed, probably while in India, how easy it was to excite the jealousy of professional soldiers in all matters considered by them to be their peculiar province. While in Malacca, as we have seen, he had specifically delegated to William Farquhar the reporting of information of a purely military character, so as to avoid the risk of provoking their antagonism.

When Gillespie had come to Java, he must have guessed that his chances of remaining there in command were very good. The general officers in the expedition had good appointments in India and would certainly not have contemplated exchanging these for an uncertain period of command in Java. It could hardly have crossed Gillespie's mind that Java would not be a King's Colony, with a soldier at its head. He would almost certainly have been unaware that Minto, rating the political and commercial difficulties higher than the military, had decided not only to annex Java on behalf of the East India Company, but also to appoint a civilian as Lieutenant-Governor. When, therefore, the appointment of Raffles had been published, it must have come as a terrible shock to Gillespie, which his own appointment as commander of the forces did little to mitigate. That he should have to take second place to a mere nobody, a civilian clerk of no family and no influence, a fellow fifteen years his junior, this he must have thought a very poor reward for all his gallantry, and for the wounds and fever he had suffered.

There was worse to follow. Civilians were talking of reducing the garrison. The reason advanced was the urgent need for economy, but what if the real purpose was to reduce the status of the commander of the forces? There was, however, one bright gleam of hope: the decision of Minto was subject to home approval. No doubt those at home would soon put things right by making Java a King's Colony, so the present position had better be accepted with a good grace—provided the attempt to reduce the garrison was not pressed.

Whether this is a fair estimate of Gillespie's reactions or not, the relations between the Lieutenant-Governor and the commander of the forces were at the outset apparently harmonious. Raffles was caused some anxiety by the absurdly suspicious attitude of Gillespie towards every Dutchman. Gillespie had the proper insular contempt for foreigners, and in Java regarded all Dutchmen as actual or potential enemies, which did not help Raffles in his laudable efforts to obtain their most essential goodwill and co-operation. There was, too, an unfortunate incident when a soldier got into trouble with the authorities, and Gillespie proceeded to defy police and magistrates and everyone else. In his view, the soldier must be right, just because he was a soldier, and the Dutch with whom he had become involved were, in any event, a lot of rogues. Gillespie had to be restrained and the Dutch mollified. Raffles managed it.

During the affairs of Palembang and Mataram there seems to have been the most cordial co-operation between Raffles and Gillespie, and the praise that Raffles publicly bestowed on Gillespie was undoubtedly sincere. It is possible that Gillespie, for his part, had developed a sneaking respect for this capable little civilian who was not lacking in physical or moral courage. The harmony was somewhat impaired when the army was allowed to sack Jokyakarta without Raffles' permission. The letter he wrote to Gillespie on the matter does not appear to have survived, but Gillespie's reply is on record. It is courteous and dignified, pleading in excuse that he was incapacitated by wounds at the time. Raffles has been taken to task for complaining to Gillespie on this score and yet writing to Minto:

"The Craton having fallen by assault, it was impossible to make any provision for Government to cover the expenses of the undertaking; consequently the whole plunder became prize to the army. It is considerable, but it could not be in better hands; they richly deserve what they got. . . ."

Without Raffles' letter to Gillespie, we cannot be sure what was in his mind when he made the protest, still less how the protest was phrased. Was it that he wanted to make clear that while fighting was in progress Gillespie was in charge, but once victory had been achieved, all authority reverted to the civil power? Or had some incident occurred that made Raffles think it advisable to remind Gillespie that his powers were limited? We can but conjecture.

On the surface, at any rate, things ran very smoothly in the early stages. As a matter of policy, Raffles refrained from interfering in military matters, provided these did not affect in any way the rights or responsibility of the civil power. These he was determined to regard as his prerogative and was not going to allow them to be impaired. That was reasonable, indeed necessary, but where difficulty was bound to come sooner or later was over the question of the exact dividing line between the civil and military spheres of responsibility. Gillespie regarded every matter that concerned the military in any degree as one on which the view of the commander of the forces should prevail. Raffles considered that all questions of policy, even though involving some military aspect, must be decided by the government; while the professional views of the commander of the forces would be given due attention, the Council must ultimately make the decision or, if it failed to do so, the Lieutenant-Governor must do so, under the special authority he possessed. That this authority included military matters was definitely stated in his instructions.

When, therefore, Raffles laid before his Council a proposal to reduce the army in Java, relations between him and Gillespie suffered an immediate strain. Gillespie considered that the action of the Lieutenant-Governor trespassed on his own domain. He was, too, undoubtedly sincere in thinking that any weakening of the armed forces was far too risky.

Raffles' minute of 27th July was as follows:

"The return of the troops from Palembang and the successful termination of hostilities at Djocjocarta placing the whole of the military force at the disposal of Government, and the tranquillity of the Island and its Dependencies having been finally established on a permanent basis not likely to be again disturbed, the Lieutenant-Governor has now to request the attention of the Commander of the Forces to the orders of the Supreme Government directing the removal to India of a considerable portion of the European troops. Although the orders of the Governor-General were positive with regard to the removal of the 89th Regiment immediately after the rains, the Lieutenant-Governor felt no hesitation in detaining them until the termination of the operations in the interior, but he cannot take it upon himself for the further responsibility of detention."

The 89th Regiment should be sent away at once, and the 14th Regiment and detachments of dragoons and horse artillery as soon as tonnage was available.

To recuperate from his wound and ensuing fever, Gillespie had gone from the capital to Chipanas, in the mountains, where there were hot mineral springs. From there he replied:

"I am not desirous of detaining a larger force for the defence of the Island than is absolutely necessary. I am only anxious that we should preserve a territory which has been acquired by such considerable efforts and preserved upon the personal responsibility of that enlightened ruler who can never fail to be deeply and warmly interested in its happiness and prosperity. When the military force for the defence and security of this Island was fixed upon by the Right Honourable the Governor-General, I was compelled even then to represent the smallness and inefficiency of our establishment, but when the late accession of territory is considered and the constant reduction of our force both by sickness and the return of convalescents to Bengal, I trust I shall require few arguments to impress upon your mind the positive necessity of continuing our force undiminished."

He asked for the order to be suspended pending reference to India.

This produced a further minute from the Lieutenant-Governor.

"Under the circumstances and under a conviction as far as my unprofessional judgment is depended upon, the force fixed by the Supreme Government for the defence of this Island and its Dependencies is fully adequate, and as great as the state of the country will conveniently admit, I feel it necessary to carry into effect without reserve the orders of our superiors, notwithstanding the decided opinion now recorded by the Commander of the Forces. . . .

"When the Right Honourable the Governor-General fixed the military force to remain on this Island until after the late rains, His Lordship had in contemplation the possibility of the arrival of an enemies' force from Europe (for relief, capture not yet being known, not for recapture) which in that early stage of our possession might have endangered the tranquillity of the country; and also that an over-awing power on the Island might be useful in the first establishment of the British authority. With regard to an attack from Europe at the present date we have the authority of the Governor-General for considering such an event impossible, the maritime resources of France not admitting of the measure; and as far as regards any internal danger, I will take upon myself any responsibility that may result from the reduction of the troops. The arrest and removal of Pangerang Achmet and the establishment of a regular authority in Bantam has tranquillized the whole of that extensive province; the apprehension of Bagoos[1] Rangein and the dispersion of his party has had a similar effect in Cheribon, and our recent successes at the Courts of the native Princes have ensured the tranquillity of Java on a more permanent footing than it ever before stood. We have not a wandering banditti, much less a Chieftain from one end of the Island to the other who can give cause for the least apprehension and under the peculiar circumstances of the Island the absence of a heavy military force is rather to be wished for than its continuance when no greater political object any longer exists. . . .

"It is well known that some of the finest parts of the Island have been deserted and that others have ceased to be cultivated in consequence of the very heavy services required under the arrangements of the late Government. During the invasion and for a considerable time subsequently these demands were necessarily increased and if the whole of the force at present on the Island (not less than 4,000 European) in addition to those expected from India, it is to be feared that the inhabitants instead of deriving an advantage of the establishment under British authority, would have reason to complain of still further burdens."

Fortified by the fact that the earlier proposals of Gillespie had been rejected by the dispatch of the Governor-General on 4th June, Raffles on 25th September pressed for the embarkation of the 14th Regiment without delay. This produced a fresh protest from Gillespie.

"Convince me the French cannot land a force here and then I may acquiesce in your opinion."

He added that pecuniary considerations could not be put into competition with the general safety. To this Raffles replied that if Gillespie

[1] Bagus: "fine, beautiful", a princely honorific.

persisted in his protests the embarkation would not take place, especially in view of the alarming rate of sickness in the military force, but he called the commander's attention to the adverse effect on the finances of the government.

Further letters were exchanged. Gillespie disassociated himself from the financial aspect of the case, as the assurances made to the Supreme Government were best known to Raffles, who had the entire management of them. He was prepared to make any sacrifice to promote the interest of Java or the honour of the Lieutenant-Governor, but he maintained his military opinion and was not prepared to surrender this on any consideration. Raffles rejoined that the financial administration of the colony was either transacted in Council or known to Gillespie as a member of that Council and recalled that Gillespie himself had countersigned the first annual estimates submitted to the Government of India. Gillespie's unfortunate absence from Council meetings was not the fault of the Lieutenant-Governor, who would have welcomed his taking a more active part in the administration.

This drew from Gillespie a long statement dated 30th September as to his general attitude. Had it not been for difficulties of distance and health, he would have preferred a personal interview to discussion by correspondence. He accused Raffles of lack of frankness when they did have direct discussion. He proceeded to complain about the alleged shortcomings in the barrack department.

"Had more decision been exhibited, efficient barracks would now have been erected."

He attacked Raffles on shortage of pay for the Colonial Corps:

"In fact every representation to you Honourable Sir on the subject of the Colonial Corps has been attended by so many changes and differences of opinion on your part and want of decision, that I have been frequently at a loss to know how to act. . . . Though you may have now given orders for sending them here for organization, yet it might have been done months ago. To conclude—I again repeat that you are at liberty to act as you please as you have very frequently indeed made me know the little power I possess here, by repeating to me that your voice is decisive and having crippled me in many military points when I have given way to your opinions to avoid any unpleasant discussions."

Raffles was not prepared to accept the allegation that the delay in barrack construction lay at the door of civil administration. At a Council meeting on 19th October he stated that he was prepared to bring evidence that it lay with the military authorities and suggested that Gillespie might like to withdraw those paragraphs of his letter. This offer was ignored by Gillespie.

At the same meeting Raffles rejected a proposal put up by Gillespie on 25th August that a military board should be appointed on the lines of similar boards in the Presidencies of India for scrutinizing estimates and expenditure on military account. The reasons given by Raffles for his decision appear rational enough: there was the minor difficulty of the lack of experienced officers to compose the board, and, more serious, such an establishment for the garrison of Java was beyond the competence of government.

A lesser incident at the same date related to Captain Flint, the second husband of Raffles' sister, Mary Anne. Raffles had already recommended his appointment in some capacity relating to prize money. This had been strongly opposed by Gillespie, and when now brought forward again by Raffles was even more bitterly contested. It was eventually dropped. Flint's relationship to Raffles no doubt made the matter of greater significance than it would otherwise have been.

Gillespie at his hill station continued to brood over the prospect of a French invasion. On 28th October he addressed to the Secret Committee a letter in which the following paragraph occurred:

"I have it on undoubted authority that General Daendels will not fail of recommending to Bonaparte to send out an Expedition under his direction for the recovery of this valuable Colony and that he would direct his attacks against Samarang the centre of the Island, and aided by many of the European and native inhabitants (who do not appear to incline very cordially towards us) make an effort to get to Solo and Djocjocarta, there to join the native forces to his troops and avail himself of the resources of the Emperor and Sultan who are but too well disposed at all times to rebel and join in opposition to the existing Government in hopes of gain and aggrandizement."

The authority who gave this information to Gillespie does not appear to have been very well informed. He was, for instance, probably unaware that as soon as Daendels had embarked on the ship that took him home he had been made a prisoner, and though he was later employed again, it was far away on the Russian front. While it was doubtless true that some Europeans and some natives were ill disposed towards the English, the percentage of those who mattered must have been quite insignificant. If they were in any substantial number, they gave no evidence of this hostility. Java was to remain undisturbed by any major disorder till the end of the British régime.

While Gillespie was writing thus alarmingly to the Secret Committee, Raffles was communicating to the chairman in a more tranquil spirit:

"In the event of Java being placed under the immediate Government of the Crown, it is of importance that the Government at home should be aware of the nature and efficiency of our Colonial troops. Two Corps of this description have been raised here under the authority of the

Governor-General. The Amboinese Corps which was raised entirely from men in the service of the French Government is tolerably efficient, but with regard to the Javanese it appears that very little use of them can be made on this Island—they would perhaps make good troops if serving at the Isle of France, Ceylon, or even the Moluccas, but, while at home, they cannot be deprived of their national habits, which are in every respect opposite to what constitutes the soldier. . . . It is a fact that the natives look upon a Sepoy with more dread than upon a European and for general service they cannot be considered inferior. . . . Should the Island remain under the Company, I have no hesitation in stating my opinion that the force fixed by the Supreme Government, viz. 2 King's Regiments and 5 Battalions of Sepoys, would be fully equal to the service, and as extensive as the resources of the country in money and provisions can conveniently afford."

It is clear that the arguments of Gillespie had left Raffles unconvinced.

Another difference arose over Gillespie's residence at Chipanas. He had asked for a house to be built there at public expense. On the grounds of economy, Raffles had offered instead a government bungalow which, though not a grand residence, was apparently a wooden building quite suitable for temporary occupation. This had been curtly declined. Using unpaid native labour, Gillespie had built himself a new house on the estate, which included a coffee plantation. He then refused to pay taxes on it or to remunerate the cultivators and labourers impressed into service. The Regent of Buitenzorg complained to the Resident, Thomas McQuoid, that, as a result of the demands made upon them by the commander of the forces and his staff, the Javanese were leaving the district because they were being forced to work without wages. McQuoid reported the matter to Raffles, who, anxious not to take hasty action, asked a Dutch official to go to Chipanas, look into things, then inform him privately upon them. Not until he received complete confirmation did he lodge a formal objection with Gillespie, who was furious at this enquiry into his conduct.

No doubt this friction between the two heads had its echo in the jealousy between the civil and military departments. On 8th November Raffles addressed a letter to Gillespie, expressing disapproval of criticisms of the civil government contained in a letter received in his office from the military secretary, Major W. Colebrooke.

"A letter this day has been received", wrote Raffles, "from your Military Secretary under date 6th inst. containing several comments and observations on the conduct of the chief authority on this Island, which cannot be allowed to pass unnoticed. It is to be regretted that communications of such a nature should have been made through that channel, as it must be evident that the authority and dignity of the Government would be weakened by the admission of such occurrences; and it is also to be observed that if the Commander of the Forces thinks it necessary to question the conduct of any of the members of Government, and more especially the Lieutenant-Governor, his observations can only be admitted in a minute to be recorded in Council.

"Being desirous to preserve the cordiality so strongly recommended by the Superior Authorities and so necessary to the public interest, I have not returned this letter—and it will not at present be recorded—it remains for you to decide whether it shall be brought forward in the shape of a Minute in Council. It is my earnest wish to support the dignity and authority of the Commander of the Forces, but it is equally necessary that the authority of Government should be upheld, and as it has been proved that personal communication and discussion on every important subject are absolutely necessary to its being properly understood, and to prevent the unpleasant consequences of mutual reference, it is my intention to hold a Council at Batavia on every Friday and oftener if the public business requires it. All important military questions will then be discussed and I shall be happy to have the benefit of your personal attendance to take into consideration and decide upon whatever suggestions and recommendations you may think proper to make.

"In conclusion I must again invite you to a cordial and full communication with me on the general affairs of Government, and more especially the military branch of the service, and if any arrangements should suggest themselves to you as tending to increase that harmony and cordiality, I request you communicate them without reserve. I am sincerely desirous that all unpleasant impressions should be removed from your mind and that we should act with one accord in whatever arrangements may be adopted and it now rests with you whether the same conciliatory disposition will exist on your part."

Gillespie was little disposed to accept this olive branch. On 9th November he wrote in reply:

"On a retrospect of the various discussions which have at different times implicated us in unpleasant controversy it is a matter of serious regret to me that they have been uniformly courted by yourself, and whatever disagreeable has resulted in the progress has led to conciliatory offers on your part which would have been rendered superfluous by avoiding at first the unconciliatory measures. On the present occasion I can safely declare, and the documents will testify, that I have evinced great aversion to this discussion and except when a regard for my own authority and situation have compelled me to assert them, I have carefully avoided every remark which could tend to excite altercation. It is a source of no less regret to me that I must so often disavow any intention of reflecting upon the chief authority of this Island, an apprehension so often displayed upon your part, Honourable Sir, that it appears to employ a wish to implicate me in such a charge. . . . Had it always been your earnest wish, Honourable Sir, to support the dignity and authority of my situation, I am inclined to think the present discussion would never have commenced, and I trust it will appear sufficiently manifest that the dignity of this Government so far from being impaired has ever been supported in my proceedings . . . but I must observe that every limitation of my authority which weakens the dependence of the Army, in the same way weakens my responsibility for supporting either the authority of Government or myself.

"Your invitation to a cordial and full communication in the affairs of Government and your complaint of not obtaining the unreserved and constant advice on the progress and proceedings of the Military Department, I must consider, Honourable Sir, equally unnecessary. Have I not given detailed reports and urged the adoption of measures which have been neglected or counteracted? And have not you, Honourable Sir, obtained every information you called for from the Military Department? If not, I have no responsibility and when the suggestions and information from those Military Departments have been defective, I can only say they have been corrected when submitted through me. The military details imposed on me by Lord Minto are not the fixing proportions of Coolies or preparing minute regulations for grass contracts; these are best arranged in the respective departments, but my suggestions on real military points have been generally opposed to unmilitary objections, and if our communications have not always been cordial or arrangements adopted with one accord, it can only in fairness be attributed to the opposition and neglect my references met with or a departure from those forms and channels you now think it advantageous to observe.

"If you, Honourable Sir, are of opinion that discussion like the present should be aggitated [*sic*] in Council, you can act as you please, but I must confess my aversion of discussing points which are solely at issue between yourself and me (and which can only be determined by a higher authority) before the members who are disqualified to lend the least elucidation. Do you think it would contribute to the dignity of Government? I think otherwise, and as a reference to the Commander in Chief, my immediate head, has long appeared to be necessary to obtain a clear definition of my prerogative, it would be more judicious to await the decision that high authority will undoubtedly procure, which will promote the efficiency of the service and ensure our future cordiality. I would willingly have curtailed this discussion, I wish it had never commenced, but the imputations on your part required explanation on mine, and the correspondence has been lengthened from no indulgence of private feeling but considerations connected with the discharge of my public trust and regard for the establishment committed to my care. As for arrangements to increase our harmony and cordiality, all such as promote the service must have that tendency, and when those I have suggested are all duly appreciated it will encourage me in my efforts to that desirable end. The observations which have now reluctantly been called forth I trust are consonant with that concilation I would wish to evince, and I really think our dispositions will be best exhibited in mutual efforts of our united and distinct authorities; to enhance and elevate either in prejudice of the other only impairs the machine of Government, and I therefore affirm that a jealous anxiety in support of each other will be the best security for the authority of Government and most certain grounds for permanent concilation with ourselves."

While Raffles may have been unduly sensitive of any apparent infringement of his authority, it is clear that Gillespie took a very wide view of the responsibilities of the commander of the forces. In his opinion, no one but himself had the right or the knowledge to decide on any military question, and reconciliation with the Lieutenant-Governor, as he makes clear in his letter, was only possible if that point of view was accepted without reserve by the civil government. But such a position is not acceptable to any government and one cannot blame Raffles if it was not acceptable to him. He did, however, go as far as he could by attempting in a long letter, also dated 9th November, to define their spheres of authority, also suggesting schemes for scrutinizing and checking accounts. He invited criticism of the proposals and asked for suggestions. On 15th November Gillespie replied, declining any compromise measure and demanding the military board for which he had previously asked in vain. It is not clear if this was because he thought the scheme would not work, or if it was just out of pique, or because he thought Raffles was going to give in; but whatever the reason, the brief and uncompromising reply was unfortunate.

Notwithstanding his failure to obtain a more helpful response, and abandoning the scheme for the demarcation of authority, Raffles proceeded with his proposals for a committee to deal with military expenditure. He submitted a draft general order to Gillespie, informing him that this was a provisional measure pending the Supreme Government's approval of the appointment of a military board.

"I conceive", he wrote in his covering letter to Gillespie, "that the appointment of this committee is indispensable to preserve a due correctness and economy as well as to relieve the Government from the irksome and responsible situation of sanctioning expenses and estimates respecting the accuracy and economy of which they have not the means of judging. I therefore propose that this committee of officers be styled a Committee of Military Accounts, that their duty be exclusively confined to an examination of every estimate, contract, contingent disbursement or indent which may be referred to their consideration by the Commander of the Forces, or by Government. . . . It is left to yourself to determine what share you wish to take in its proceedings. . . ."

These proposals were approved by Gillespie and embodied in a general order dated 5th December, but Raffles' efforts to meet Gillespie's point of view had really failed, for Gillespie had informed him on 30th November, after receipt of the new proposals, that he had already written to the commander-in-chief, asking for a clearer definition of the authority invested in himself "and how far the exercise of it in professional matters for the advantage of the service can be circumscribed or controlled".

He goes on: ". . . your partial acquiescence in some measures and present attention to the forms of the service but testify the benefits that could have resulted from an earlier and more general concurrence, and although I am only enjoined to contemplate our failure in a public view, I must be allowed to deplore the least apparent interruption to that cordiality which it has ever been my most anxious desire to maintain."

Raffles wrote to Minto on 9th December:

"In the course of the correspondence with Major-General Gillespie it became necessary, in consequence of the observations made by the Major-General, to advert to several arrangements made by this Government in the Military Department, and the continued indisposition of the Commander of the Forces preventing his attendance at Council and the advantage of personal communication on the military arrangements which he deemed it advisable to recommend, the correspondence has in several instances ensued on the subjects of establishment and expenditure which was impossible for this Government to concur in consistently with the repeated instructions of the Supreme Government to avoid in the present unsettled state of Government measures of a definite and permanent nature and works on establishments involving material expense. From the several disclosures which it has become necessary in consequence to refer to the consideration and decision of the Supreme Government, your Lordship will perceive that there has throughout been a decided difference of opinion between the Commander of the Forces and myself on the system necessary to be adopted at the present moment. That the Major-General has been desirous to render the several points of our military force and position on the most efficient state possible in establishments and equipment, and that on the contrary I have thought it advisable to defer as much as possible every increase of expense and establishment, both with a view to the expected and final instructions and to the financial resources of the Colony. . . . A reference to our proceedings (Military Department) will prove that in no one instance has any representation from the Commander of the Forces been either unattended to or refused, although it must be admitted that delays in some instances occurred for want of regular estimates and plans previously required."

While this letter was being written, one was on its way from Calcutta giving the Governor-General's views on the vexed question of the military establishment:

"We are disposed to show every degree of consideration to the opinions of the Commander of the Forces on questions on which his professional knowledge and experience must be supposed to qualify him to form a judgment, but on the present occasion it appears to us too evident upon the review of the circumstances adverted to by you that our orders for reducing the military force at Java could be carried into execution without the danger of inconvenience, that we have no hesitation in expressing our entire concurrence in the decision passed on the question by the Lieutenant-Governor."

It was a victory for Raffles, but from then on he had to face the opposition of Gillespie in matters of civil administration in which hitherto Gillespie had deliberately shown no interest.

In December, Archibald Seton, Governor of Penang, was succeeded in that appointment by William Petrie, who, unlike Seton, was no friend or admirer of Raffles, describing him as the "Tide Waiter". Seton went to India and took Henry T. Colebrooke's place on the Supreme Council.

Chapter Twelve

JAVA, 1812

i

THE range of Raffles' activities in Java was so wide that, in the recording of them, strict chronology would tend to confuse the mind of the reader. The main events and military operations of 1812 having now been set down, and the early conflict of wills between the young Lieutenant-Governor and the fiery commander of the forces explained, reference can now be made to other matters falling within that year, before we go on to consider the developments in 1813.

No reform instituted by Raffles has been the subject of so much argument as his land policy. The subject is by its nature complicated, and the task of trying to assess its merits and defects is not made easier by critics having all too often been influenced by national prejudice. The tendency has been for English writers to over-praise it and for Dutch authorities to depreciate it. There is, too, the debated point whether a trustee government was entitled to introduce such a radical change, and there is a further question whether the basis of the reforms was at all in accord with Javanese customs. Finally there is the relatively minor point whether Raffles did not merely borrow his whole scheme from India instead of, as he claimed, developing it locally as the natural solution for an urgent and acute domestic problem.

On this last point, that it bore a close resemblance to the *ryotwari* system[1] in India, Raffles did not deny, but he did deny that he chose the Indian system as his model. At the time the land reform scheme was developing in Java it is doubtful if Raffles had any clear conception of current Indian land policy, though Minto may have given him some information on the subject. Minto had certainly called his attention to the need for land reform, but he had cautioned against any steps being taken without the fullest investigation. The principles of the scheme subsequently introduced had a close resemblance in many respects both to the proposals of Dirk van Hogendorp and the *ryotwari* system in India. This was to be expected, for van Hogendorp had been much interested in land policy in British India. Raffles has been accused of lack of candour in not admitting his debt to India, which is unjust. Of the committee he

[1] A system of collecting land rent or taxes whereby the government settlement is made directly with the *ryots*, the peasants cultivating the soil.

set up to collect information concerning the relations that had existed between the people of Java and the former Dutch administration, its members must have been influenced by the Indian scheme through van Hogendorp, Minto and Colonel Mackenzie, chairman of the committee. Mackenzie's views were coloured by his knowledge of the Indian policy, while the views of some of the Dutch members would have been influenced by the theories of van Hogendorp, who, in his turn, owed much to the writings of the Abbé Raynal. But how far Raffles was indebted to van Hogendorp directly is hard to decide. That he had handled a copy of the *Bericht* at Malacca seems certain, but whether he read it is doubtful, as it was written in Dutch. On his own statement, it was not till he was writing his *History of Java* that he consulted the *Bericht*. Yet plenty of persons in Java and Malacca were familiar with van Hogendorp's ideas, even before the *Bericht* was published, and his views in some shape had been circulated among his friends before he left for Holland. High among these was Muntinghe, whom Raffles came to regard as one of his most trusted advisers, particularly, as he himself stated, in connexion with land reform policy.

". . . To him I am indebted for the selection of the best talents and the command of all the information which Java afforded in the establishment of the British Government. It was Mr Muntinghe who first pointed out to me the gross errors and the still grosser corruption of the former government; and it was from a confidence in his opinion and a reliance on his unerring judgment that I first conceived it practicable to work the change. . . ."

This is a handsome testimonial to Muntinghe, but even before Raffles first set foot in Java, he had determined to abolish the abuses he believed to be inherent in monopoly, forced cultivation and other oppressive measures. Minto and Leyden had given direction to his natural liberal and humanitarian instincts, though his own researches had also revealed the disastrous results to the Dutch East India Company of the narrow policy that was one of the factors contributing to its financial ruin. Raffles had thus arrived in Java with an almost missionary zeal, and his descriptions of Dutch oppression and, by contrast, the benevolent and beneficent purposes of British rule as he conceived it, were equally coloured by his enthusiasm and must be discounted accordingly.

During the early days in Java he had discussed with Minto the policy of land reform.

"On this branch," Minto had said, "nothing must be done that is not mature, because the exchange is too extensive to be suddenly and ignorantly attempted."

With this advice in mind, Raffles set up the committee already referred to, with Colonel Mackenzie as chairman and three Dutch members,

Rothenbuhler, Knops and Lawick van Pabst. An examination of their instructions will indicate the new spirit Raffles was breathing into the responsibilities of government and will also prove what has not been so widely admitted, that he took immense trouble to build the reforms he had in mind on a sure foundation of fact as far as was humanly possible in a country only partially known to the previous government. It can be most willingly conceded that his efforts were loyally seconded by Mackenzie and his three colleagues, whose instructions from Raffles were as follows:

"The system under which the former Dutch East India Company and the subsequent French Government endeavoured to secure the revenues of Java was by monopoly, obligation on the inhabitants to deliver products at stipulated prices and contingents of rice, and of late years a tax in money was directed to be paid by the native Chiefs and Regents, leaving them the right without restriction of again taxing the inhabitants of their districts and regencies.

"Whatever reasons may be induced [for] such a system in the early state of the Dutch East India Company in Java and in the mercantile spirit which at that time animated the Government, it must be admitted that such a system is most imperfect in the present state of affairs when the Government may ascribe to itself with justice the territorial possession and sovereignty over the whole Island of Java.

"*It now becomes necessary that Government should consider the inhabitants without reference to bare mercantile profits and to connect the sources of the revenues with the general prosperity of the Colony.*"

This sentence is italicized as being worthy of particular note.

"The system of monopoly and obligation to deliver products at stipulated prices and of contingents cannot be viewed otherwise than as a check to industry and in opposition to the general prosperity of the community, and it must be equally prejudicial and dangerous to subject the Chiefs and Regents of the Javanese to an imposition of money, by which the population are exposed to any consequent levie [*sic*] of taxes which their Regents may lay upon them. It is therefore the wish of Government that this system should in process of time be abolished, and that a free trade and free cultivation accompanied by such regular and fixed taxes as may be sufficient to defray the necessary expenses of the Colony should be substituted in lieu thereof. But at the same time [as] the Government indulge the hope that such a change may eventually be made, they are satisfied that the same cannot be attempted but by degrees and a progressive system of improvement.

"With a view to effecting this general change at as early a period as practicable, and which I hope may in a few years be considerably proceeded on, I have deemed it expedient to appoint you a Committee under the following instructions, and I flatter myself that from your superior abilities and qualifications to assist Government with advice in this arduous but important arrangement, the object desired may not be found so distant as at first it may generally be supposed to be.

"It is evident that the transition from monopoly and the system of obligation to deliver products at stipulated prices and contingents to that of a free trade and cultivation cannot take place without a complete alteration in the tenure of lands, and in the services which appear now to be due throughout the Island by the common people as vassals to the Regents as their landlords. The first point in which it is necessary to proceed before any material alteration can be projected or taken into consideration, is to obtain an exact knowledge of the tenure upon which the lands in Java are at present held and cultivated, as well by the superior as by the inferior, and what are the services due to the people by their chiefs. The official information which as yet Government is possessed of concerning those points is very imperfect and it is on this account that I am desirous of a report after a full enquiry into every circumstance, and I wish that this enquiry should extend over the whole coast of Java from the eastern districts to those of Batavia (the Jacatra and Preanger Regencies included) and that all the peculiarities which may come under your observation in the one or the other of those districts should be duly taken notice of . . . whatever considerations may occur to you, either with regard to the Teak forests or otherwise, as far as the same may relate to the system of feudal services or free cultivation, will be acceptable, inasmuch as the same may tend to illustrate the beneficial or prejudicial effects of the one and other of these systems."

The members of the committee, with the approval of Raffles, decided to divide up the territory to be surveyed. Mr Rothenbuhler was responsible for the eastern districts, from the east point of the island to Tuban. Mr Knops would continue from there to Pekalongan. The area from Pekalongan to the Preanger lands, including Cheribon, was given to Mr van Pabst.

After months of investigation the last two gentlemen submitted a joint report dated 29th June 1812. They began by giving details of what they had found in the different districts, commenting that the practice in each district differed widely in many respects from that of other districts. They then made certain observations.

"The general system of the former Government", they wrote, "was exclusive culture and trade, which no doubt may be attributed to that mercantile spirit which prevailed with the first settlers of the Dutch nation on this island, and became so fast rooted that monopoly was considered as the first basis on which the future happiness and success of the Company were to be founded. To purchase cheap, and to sell at a high rate rendered a great profit, and was sufficient to blind those short-sighted rulers who received an enormous interest on the money they had ventured in the Company. As soon as the Company became possessed of territorial property, it would have been advisable to have granted free culture and trade, yet she might have reserved to herself exclusively the trade in spices and tin, the Japan trade, or particularly the Japan Copper, and the China trade. In that case, the Island of Java would in all probability have risen to the highest pitch of prosperity and welfare. It is an established maxim with the most enlightened Statesmen, that restraint in culture and commerce tends to the ruin of that country where it is enforced,[1] and Java fully corroborates the same. It is our hearty wish that a favourable change may take place under the wise direction of the British Government. . . ."

There followed their recommendations.

The limits of provinces, regentships, districts and the village communities known in Java as *desas* were so irregularly fixed that the lands of one province were frequently intermingled with those of another; that some *desas* were a very great distance from the regentship; and that pieces of ground and villages, the property of the princes, were found in the midst of the government's dominions. They should be annexed to them immediately.

All the possessions of government on the island might be divided into three provinces: Batavia, Cheribon and the North-East Coast of Java.

After new division had been made of provinces, regentships, districts and villages—this conforming as much as possible to former usages and customs, but not necessarily to extent—Regents should be appointed, preference being given to those already in office. Part of the lands should be assigned for their support, to the sultans, regents and their families, chiefs and religious authorities. The fields for the common people should be divided among the whole population of a village, and if it were agreed that some uncultivated land should be annexed to a district, those who as yet had no share should be entitled to make application for it "and such prerogatives ought to be granted to them as circumstances would allow, such as exemption from taxes on the crop for 3 years or less".

All kinds of servitude should be abolished.

The government should take into its immediate possession all the bazaars at Batavia, Cheribon and the North-East Coast of Java, together with all inland seas, lakes, fishponds and custom houses, leaving the rivers to the use of the public.

A capitation tax should be levied on all men able to work, according to their means and local circumstances. Foreigners, including Chinese (in spite of the existing Chinese capitation tax), should pay this tax also. The tax should be laid on the first crop of all kinds of produce; on the

[1] This is very much like a quotation from the Abbé Raynal.

second crop, the government should receive a fraction (half or quarter) of the levy on the first crop. Except in the coffee plantations in the Batavian regentships, owners or cultivators of ground should be allowed to plant the crops they thought most suitable. All the levies should be made by collectors appointed by the government. They should be authorized to make advances on the crop, which would contribute to the progress of cultivation, especially if no interest were charged. A sufficient quantity of paddy should be kept for seed and distributed or advanced to the poorer classes of cultivators on condition that the same be returned after the harvest.

"The Collectors are to be attentive that for the first cultivation as much land as possible be sown with paddy of the best quality. . . . For the sake of avoiding trouble and inconvenience as well as the uncertainty of the crop, we might incline to recommend a land tax; but knowing it to be the intention of Government that the new regulations should be as much as possible consistent with ancient usages, we have preferred a levy on the produce to the land tax. . . . In each Regency ought to be built proper storehouses of planks and bamboo where the people could deliver their produce. . . ."

After specific recommendations in regard to public services, which should generally be paid for, they suggested that the island of Carimon Java (or Karimunjava) should be made inhabitable by measures against pirates; that salt pans, saltpetre works, pearl reefs and birds'-nest rocks should remain in the hands of the government. The farms for salt might be abandoned in favour of free trade.

They were confident that the loss of half a million Spanish dollars in annual revenue would be more than made good, for cultivation would not only be extended under the management of individuals, but the government would also make considerable savings in servants, warehouses, etc., would increase its revenues on import and export duties, and, above all, would contribute to the welfare of its subjects.

They did not recommend the sale of districts in the southern regentships, as the population was small and the overland transport of produce expensive. They did not recommend the sale of the province of Cheribon, as the Mohammedan inhabitants were very superstitious, much attached to ancient usages, and still suffering from a spirit of disaffection.

They proposed that the entire regentship of Krawang, to the east of Batavia, and the whole of the former government province of North-East Coast of Java should, with certain minor exceptions, be sold.

As for land, they recommended that all should be allowed to buy it. This included all foreigners except Chinese, who became too powerful and numerous, were usually of the lowest type, accumulating great riches and remitting them to China. Various conditions were set out to control the purchaser. He should become entitled to all the taxes and levies formerly paid to the government by the inhabitants, could reduce these, but not increase them. He could make advances on the crop, but must conform to government regulations as to the interest chargeable. He could compel the inhabitants to cultivate their fields to produce such crops as the season, local situation and circumstances permitted and which appeared most profitable. Special conditions should be attached to the purchase of land containing coffee plantations.

Concerning the Regents, they observed that the abolition of their "contracts" in 1808 had made it clear to them that they were not feudal lords, but mere servants of government.

"Nothing is more natural than to suppose that the present Regents will be inclined to accept, and even with gratitude, the offer of Government which will not only secure to themselves a permanent subsistence, but also the future welfare of their descendants, and the succession to the Regentship to their children or nearest relations."

Lands, *desas* and people should be assigned to the Regents in such sufficiency as to secure them "an affluent support".

"The Regents in possession of their lands are to enjoy the same prerogatives as purchasers with respect to taxes, levies and other advantages. They hold their land as fief which it is not permitted to sell. . . . From the revenue of his lands, the Regent is to find all his disbursements of what name or description whatsoever they may be. . . . The Regent like landowner shall pay the people for their work and allow them a share of the rice fields."

Of external trade they wrote:

"Free trade in navigation, not speaking of those branches which the late Dutch Company reserved to herself exclusively, never existed at Batavia and was particularly limited on the North-East coast of Java with respect to places as well as merchandise. . . . That navigation comprehended Borneo, Malacca, Sumatra, Macasser [*sic*] and the Eastern Islands and was permitted to and from Cheribon, Samarang, Grisse [Grisek] and Sourabaya. . . . If no particular reasons are prevailing to the contrary, we would propose free trade and navigation to be permitted from all ports and places on this Island to other foreign parts. . . . To permission of that kind, the inhabitants will have the justiced claim, as soon as free culture is permitted of, in order that they may find means to export such articles of produce as in their opinion might be turned to a favourable account at a foreign market. . . ."

They concluded with a reference to the need for encouraging shipbuilding.

Mr Rothenbuhler's report was delayed by ill health, being dated 6th

August 1812. He commenced by calling attention to the unsatisfactory state of the native government in Java:

". . . the Regents brought up in ignorance laziness and luxury have no inclination to govern themselves much less the land and people entrusted to their care, and in consequence leave everything to their Deputies and other relations who very often are still worse. . . . The Regents and Chiefs . . . very often act under the idea that they are owners of . . . a district, who have the right, after the stipulated contributions to government are paid, to make equally such demands for their friends and relations, and to draw from the people entrusted to their care everything that can be got from them. . . .

". . . although he [the Javanese] has been conquered it is true by the greater valour and knowledge of the European, [he] has always an equal right to be treated as a man—this has always been considered in that light by the late Government and occasioned that a great number of orders and regulations have been made from time to time in order to keep the Regents and Chiefs within the limit of their duty and with the intention to guard the common man against oppression. . . ."

These, however, had been ineffective because the government had not been informed of many of the acts of injustice.

". . . it has never been possible to persuade the common people to bring in their complaints against such oppression; that is the force of the prepossession on which the Javanese has been brought up, and which makes him consider his Regent and other Chiefs as beings of a higher sphere, who have from God the means to dispose of him and his goods. . . .

"In my opinion it will be necessary in order to attain this great end that in the first place we endeavour to divest ourselves of the Regents and Chiefs as they are at present. Second, that on the whole Island of Java property in ground and free culture and trade should be allowed. Third, that at the same time every obligatory contribution and every drudging day's work should be abolished, and fourth and lastly the Javanese be allowed a proper degree of freedom and treatment. . . .

". . . it would be most desirable that the said dismission [of the Regents] was effected slowly and begun in those districts where fortresses and cities are situated, because it would be a great deal easier at such places to make the Javanese understand the necessity of such a step, and at the same time, if required, facilitate taking measures to prevent any mischief that might perhaps arise. . . . To those Regents and at least to the first Chief should be allowed a certain part of the districts that belong to them, or from other Regencies, if this is thought more proper, large enough to provide for them according to the rank they enjoy. . . .

"The allowing of ground in property to individuals will then be necessary, because otherwise Government would be obliged to have the lands administered by the Magistrates . . . or to appoint new Regents and Chiefs, or to farm them out for a certain time."

The first, considered Mr Rothenbuhler, would involve an exact register of lands and other facts, together with a large staff of officials; the second would lead ere long to new oppressions, for a farmer—that is, a tax-gatherer—looked only to immediate advantage. Private property was most conducive to active cultivation, yet:

"I am convinced that once the Javanese has a land in his possession and is left to himself without any restriction, he will not work more than is absolutely necessary for himself and his family."

Enlightenment and its new wants might make a difference, but this would take time.

"Besides this, it would . . . yet be a question whether it would answer the interest of Government to bring the Javanese to the highest degree of knowledge or not; this would also acquaint him of his own force and make him perceive at last that he could govern himself without the laws of a strange people who have no other claim upon him than that of force."

In allocating land to individuals, preference should be given to Europeans, as most likely to increase cultivation. Little if any should be given to Chinese, who, though successful cultivators, imposed on the natives and remitted their profits to China.

Coffee plantations, salt pans, birds'-nest rocks and, more particularly, sugar-cane fields should be sold if opportunity offered. Bazaars and toll-gates should be farmed out from year to year. Uncultivated land should be sold on what to-day we should call the hire-purchase system; unsold land should be farmed out annually, and the farm divided among the inhabitants of the village by the elected headman. The inhabitants should pay a duty equivalent to a share of the produce, and a poll-tax.

Purchasers should be free to cultivate whatever they liked, except the poppy. The inhabitants should be subject to the landowner in every matter of justice, but his power should not extend to punishments. He should have the right, under certain limited conditions, to call upon the people under him for such private services as the preparation of uncultivated land, but should not be allowed to introduce on his own land any monopoly or restriction of trade, or interfere with the religious customs of the inhabitants. He should be bound to keep in order public roads, bridges, etc., within the boundaries of his property, and to billet troops and provide coolies for the government.

"The lands being once sold, it is without doubt that from that time every delivery of productions for payment, or recognitions in money, services, or other obligations, to which these lands were subject before, must be reckoned to cease, in so far as their remaining not being stipulated by the conditions of sale, whether for Government use or for Regents,

Chiefs, or for whomsoever it may be. It is without doubt that hitherto Government has got much profit by these deliveries of productions and services; but it is not less sure that by sacrificing those profits, a still greater source of riches and welfare will arise which naturally will influence the happiness of the inhabitants of the Colony without the sacrifice occasioning any want."

He concluded by mentioning the need to protect the inhabitants in the possession of their property, movable or immovable, to supply means whereby complaints could be heard, and to facilitate in every possible way trade to the Moluccas and other places.

Those, then, were the findings and recommendations of the three Dutch members of the committee.

That distinguished officer, Colonel Mackenzie of the Madras Engineers, whose task it was to superintend the surveys and to compile statistics therefrom, was diverted from his task for a time by the revolt of the Sultan of Mataram. After a hasty examination of the document submitted by Knops and van Pabst, and before seeing Rothenbuhler's contribution, he made his own provisional report.

"The investigation of the late System of Administration of Finance, Resources and of Revenue in all its forms and details, the application of their results and the suggestions arising from them to be attained through the medium of a Foreign language little familiar to us, and also the difficulty of coming at the sentiments and local knowledge of the General Body of the native Javanese, from the general want of any knowledge of the language by the Dutch inhabitants, presented themselves very seriously to my views; and might have staggered my immediate resolution of using my best exertions, were I not aware that the difficulty of finding any English member at the time to act in concert with the Dutch, might in some measure atone for the temerity of my engaging in a duty so little connected with my personal habits. Yet I conceived that helping to strike out a mode of proceeding somewhat analagous to our present Indian investigations [a general survey of the country], the outlines of a plan that might be followed, at least till further experiment could improve it, was the utmost that could be expected from me, and while aided by the experience and knowledge of gentlemen selected from their actual knowledge, I trusted that hints and suggestions drawn from our practice might not be wholly useless. . . .

"However well acquainted my associates might be from local knowledge and industry to enter into the details of the late system, it was equally necessary also for them, under a limited knowledge of our language, and of the rapid progress of late years in applying the received maxims of the most eminent political economists and the mild spirit of the British Legislature to practice in our oriental possession, to have the same access to our method and some idea of our practice at hand. It could not be expected that the expanded view of things which it has occupied our Government for the last 30 years so sedulously to cultivate in our Indian possessions, could be suddenly here transferred or received in their original spirit in opposition to interests and sentiments imbibed from peculiar habits, practice or education, and so far removed from European cultivation as the Dutch Indian Settlements have been since the revolutionary war has commenced. . . . The Dutch administration of the Island has been long notorious for its defects and abuses, and the gradual decline and fall of the former Government had not yet made room for a better order of things."

He remarked that two commissions had been sent out during the period of the Dutch Republic.

". . . and in the great change to a Monarchy Instructions, founded on apparent mild principles, even appear to have been issued for correcting the evil, and establishing a system more friendly to humanity and to the general interest of the natives, when the events of the war and the consequent ruin of the finances, threw the Island into that disorder in which we found it last year with a numerous army scarcely organized, without money, credit or resources, and all its evils scarcely remedied except in the material point of the roads carried at immense expense of labour and of lives throughout this extensive island."

From documents and translations examined, it was clear "that a similar plan of statistical investigation and enquiry had in no small degree occupied the attention of the late Government".

While his work as chairman of the commission had been interrupted by service with the army against Mataram, this service had given him increased means of observation and acquaintance with native management under the Javanese chiefs. Without going into too much detail, he indicated the means whereby further exact information could be acquired.

"Whatever questions were necessary on the subject of cultivation, or indeed on any other however trivial, was necessarily addressed through the Chief and through him put round till it came to the proper person, perhaps the lowest cultivator; the answer coming in the same circuitous mode and with all the inconvenience of rendering through three different languages, Javanese, Malay and Dutch, into English. It may be imagined with how little effect any enquiry could be managed in this way, and much of the spirit and energy of the original communication must be lost. . . .

"The prejudices of caste (which in India keep for ever the great body of the people at a distance from European improvement) not existing in this Island, the education of a few select young persons in the English language, and due encouragement to the British subjects to study Javanese would in a very short time afford the means of developing those institutions and customs which have been considered to be involved in mystery and obscurity . . ."

After referring to the beauty and fertility of the country, he continued: "From every source of enquiry I could possibly refer to, it has been constantly reported, by natives as well as Europeans, that the right of property has been invariably considered solely in the Sovereign or State. . . . But it must be confessed that, notwithstanding the supreme and exclusive property of the soil recognized in the State or Sovereign and undoubtedly strengthened by the tenets of the Mohammedan Law, yet a certain right and pretension arising from occupancy and prescription appear to have been respected among the natives, and even protected by some of their institutions in certain cases in the productions and fruits of trees planted by the lower cultivators about their dwellings. The protection of these people on that soil which their ancestors had cultivated and inhabited, and the consequent increase of cultivation of produce, was looked on as the peculiar distinction of a good Sovereign; and hence a law of custom, or *adat*, was recognized, which seemed to protect them in the occupancy of the ground, and from being unnecessarily removed from the land, occupied by their families.

"As the protection of the useful body of cultivators will naturally be an object, not only of humane consideration with a British administration, but also of real importance in a political view, I doubt not that the future condition of these people will be an object of attention in whatever plan is followed and under any possible transfer of property."

He had wished to visit the island of Bali, where some institutions prior to the introduction of the laws of the Koran into Java appeared to have been retained, but he had been prevented by bad weather and the difficulty of getting into touch with the Bali chiefs.

This was Mackenzie's provisional report. Unfortunately, his final report was never completed, for he left Java in 1813 to take up the post of Surveyor-General in Madras. As he was outstandingly the most active and experienced member of the commission, this was most regrettable. He had, however, sufficiently indicated his views on the particular problem of native land tenure.

From these three reports, together with a mass of detailed information obtained from a questionnaire, Raffles had to frame his policy for this much-needed reform.

As a preliminary, the Dutch title of *landdrost* was dropped. From 15th September 1812 such officials were to be known as Residents, their duties divided into civil, military, judicial and police, revenue, treasury and collections.

"The Resident", proclaimed Raffles, "is the chief local authority in his district and will be held responsible to Government for the administration of the civil duties thereof. He will receive orders from Government and will correspond direct with the Honourable the Lieutenant-Governor and the Secretaries to Government. The Resident is also subject to the superintendence and control of the Civil Commissioner as hereafter specified."

Where there were several and distinct administrations in his district (e.g. forests and coffee culture), the Resident had no immediate authority, except in extreme emergency. Then he was to act to the best of his judgment and adopt such measures as he might deem necessary, reporting them forthwith to the government.

As he was the chief local authority, his orders were to be implicitly obeyed, but both Europeans and natives had full permission to prefer their complaints to the government, and no obstruction by the Resident would be tolerated.

The acceptance of gifts by a Resident would involve immediate dismissal. The number of his attendants and their payment were specified. No forced service by the natives, either for himself or his staff, was permitted. Any servants required must be properly paid.

Twice a week he must give audience to all who wished to see him, without distinction of rank, and he was to travel into the interior of his district at least once a month when the season permitted, to make himself acquainted with what was going on there.

He was to conciliate as much as possible the Regents and other native authorities, and to respect the habits, usages and manners of the Javanese in every instance that did not interfere with good order and the peace of the country.

He was responsible for rendering a number of returns at various intervals, covering all aspects of his district, and, in addition, to report on the arrivals and departures of all square-rigged vessels, and issue clearances. He must see that the duties of every subordinate department were conducted with regularity and correctness, and report breaches of government regulations. He must not trade or enter into any mercantile speculation.

There followed a number of regulations dealing with stores, public works and disbursements and the preparation of accounts.

Each Resident had full authority to travel over his own district whenever and wherever he thought most beneficial to the public service, but he was not permitted to quit his district without special authority. No public paper or document was to be removed from his office without the sanction of the government.

He possessed no military command or any immediate authority over regular troops stationed within his district. The Jayang Sĕkars[1] only were subject to his orders and disposal. In cases of emergency he was to apply to the senior military officer; if further force was required, to the civil commissioner. When troops were moving through his district, he would receive prior intelligence and would then have to see that the necessary vehicles and food were available, besides assisting in producing supplies for troops remaining for some time in his district and ensuring that such supplies were properly paid for.

He was responsible for the maintenance of an efficient police force, and the regular inspection of prisons. He should assist the courts in circuit in every way he could. All public institutions and charities were under his personal superintendence. He was also responsible for all public buildings, roads and bridges. He was to encourage agriculture and cultivation, especially of rice, and look after the lower classes of natives, seeing that they were not oppressed or defrauded of their proper wages. He was to promote the breeding of sheep, cattle and other domestic animals, checking their indiscriminate slaughter.

As regards the coast, he must stop all contraband trade, having under his direction the gunboats employed for that purpose. Finally, he was responsible for the collection of public revenue and the care and transference of the moneys he collected.

While these duties might seem beyond the capacity of any one man, there was hardly one that could be regarded as superfluous. With a trained staff, a Resident would have been able to implement the spirit as well as the letter of these instructions. Unfortunately the Residents had few if any subordinates on whom they could rely. Even the most zealous Resident—and all were not zealous—left many of the tasks undone. Nevertheless, the duties of a Resident, as defined by Raffles, were a model of what such duties should be. When ultimately the Dutch regained control of Java, they were continued almost unchanged.

With the land-reform scheme maturing in his brain, Raffles had an opportunity to try out his ideas on a limited scale, the experience of which was likely to prove more efficacious than the reports of commissioners, however qualified. Under the terms of the peace after the defeat of the Sultan of Jokyakarta, the district of Kedu was ceded to Britain. Crawfurd was entrusted with the task of making a special report. He described it thus in his *Descriptive Dictionary*:

"Kâdu, or in the Dutch orthography Kadoe, is the name of a beautiful, fertile, and highly cultivated province of Java. Kâdu, in Sanskrit, is 'the

[1] "Victors in their bloom", or, literally, "Conquering Flowers", the name given to the cavalry recruited by Daendels from Javanese noblemen, to provide a career for them. They had been placed under the orders of the Dutch Residents, to be employed to keep the peace and quell civil disturbances.

dragon's tail', one of the nodes of the moon in Hindu astronomy, and hence probably the designation. The province is in a valley lying between the mountains Mârapi and Mâbabu to the east, and Sumbing and Sundara to the west, the lowest of these, Mârapi, an active volcano . . and the highest, Sumbing. . . . Cadoe has an area of 631 miles. . . ."

When Crawfurd had made his report and Raffles had personally investigated the position with John C. Lawrence, who had been appointed Resident, instructions were issued for the experimental introduction of a land-rental scheme.

"The rich and populous districts of the Cadoe," he wrote to Minto, "with the other possessions transferred by the late treaty, were to be taken possession of by the European power: this act could not but be accompanied with the establishment of some system of management, and it could not be a question whether that should be introduced which in every way stood universally condemned, or one which was more congenial to the principles of the British administration in India."

An added reason for the experiment was that it could be carried out in a part of the country unaffected by any former Dutch administration.

Lawrence was instructed as follows:

"When these districts were first transferred to Government no alterations of moment were made in the general administration of the country nor in the mode of realizing the public revenue excepting as far as was necessarily occasioned by the transfer from one Power to the other: these important objects, therefore, remained to be adjusted according to the principles of the settlement which it is considered desirable eventually to introduce in the whole of the districts under the authority of Government.

"It has been a question with Government how far either the Bakals or Demangs ought to be considered in the light of land holders, as suggested by Mr Crawfurd in his report on the Cadoe; and on a due consideration of the rights and pretensions of all classes, it has been considered, that there does not exist any proprietary right in the soil between the actual cultivator and the Sovereign to establish the Bakal as the hereditary land holder. To allow him to sub-let the land of a village at pleasure, would be to grant him an authority and independence which could never have been expected, and to arm him with power prejudicial to the people and repugnant to the objects which Government have in view, in effecting the amelioration and improvement of the mass of the population.

"You will in consequence proceed to effect such a detailed settlement of the revenue as will include a consideration of the interests of every individual claimant of land in each village, and adopt as long as local circumstances may admit the principles of the ryotwar Settlement, which is understood to have been advantageously introduced in Western India. The modifications in this Settlement are of course left to your discretion and judgment.

"Under this system the Bakals, or heads of villages, may be entrusted with the police and the collection of the land rent of each village; but instead of leases being granted them as first suggested, they should receive a commission according to the form enclosed: as far as it may be found practicable, a short certificate should be given to each land holder in the village defining the extent of his property and the amount of the rent he has to pay annually. . . . As an assurance has been given that the land should be rented out for three years, the faith of Government is pledged to that measure. . . . With respect to the Chinese land holders, the leases they hold should be respected; but the new settlement must be introduced as they determine, the Resident affording every assistance in his power calculated to facilitate their making voluntary contracts [to supply rice] in lieu thereof."

In a subsequent reference to this settlement (minute of 11th February 1814), Raffles stated:

"It may be proper to observe that this was the first district in which the new revenue system was introduced; and considering the value of an experiment of which perhaps depended in a great degree the success of these important and necessary arrangements, it was considered a matter of paramount importance and to which no subordinate consideration could be put into competition, to defer as much as possible to what appeared to be the popular sentiment and opinion."

This related to the term of the tenancies, which were fixed at three years, contrary to the later practice of granting tenancies, in the first instance, for one year only. He continued:

"On reference to the documents transferred by the farmer to Government . . . the extent and quality of the lands, population and the quantity and description raised in them were clearly ascertained; and the objection which would have otherwise existed as to the paucity of information on this point was done away.

"The lands . . . were accordingly rented to the Bakals or village Chiefs for 3 years upon such terms as, considered with reference to the state of cultivation and the custom of the country were considered adequate, moderate and equitable. The Government share of the produce was commuted for a money rent regulated with reference to the average market price of grain for a certain number of years, and the Chiefs of villages were required to insert on the backs of their leases the actual number of cultivators the proportion of land held and the amount to be paid by each respectively . . . The rents have been made payable in money, but the option was allowed to the cultivators to make a proportion of their payments in rice agreeably to the custom of the country calculated at the average market price."

Raffles wrote to Marsden during the period of the experiment:

"In the provinces lately transferred to the European Government, the whole of the uncertain revenues collected by the native Princes has been reduced to a fixed land rent payable in money half yearly; and if circumstances had admitted I should have carried the same system through the country. In all changes however some difficulties are in the first instance to be encountered, and unless I felt satisfied that I could fully establish the new system before I attempted its adoption I might by a partial interference hamper and annoy the Government which is permanently to rule over the Island".

ii

With a view to supplying a need so fully established by the Mackenzie commission, Raffles proposed in his minute of 4th October 1812 that the accumulated funds of the marine school at Samarang should be used to extend the knowledge of local languages.

Another of his practical steps was to prove a lasting boon to the European residents of Weltevreden. When Daendels had decided to move the European population inland from unhealthy Batavia to the more salubrious district of Weltevreden, he had undertaken to defray from public funds the cost of a new building to re-house the old Harmonie Club. The British invasion had occurred before the new building could be completed and rising costs had brought matters to a standstill. Raffles was approached and his minute to the Council dated 17th October ran as follows:

"The Lieutenant-Governor, considering it highly conducive to the comfort and convenience of the European inhabitants of Batavia with its environs that the unfinished building . . . should be completed, and deeming it of the first importance in a public point of view to promote meetings and intercourse between the English and Dutch inhabitants, proposes that the building be finished on account of the Government. . . ."

The Harmonie was to become the acknowledged centre of social life in Weltevreden, and it was subsequently claimed for it that for more than a hundred years its doors had never been closed night or day. But for the enlightened views of Raffles as to government responsibility towards the community, those doors might never have been opened.

That same month saw the revival of the Batavian Society of Arts and Sciences. Founded in 1778 (24th April)—its motto *Tot nut van het Algemeen* ("For the Public Benefit")—it enjoyed the distinction of being the first European learned society established in the Far East, and among members were numbered men of high reputation. But, for various reasons, it had fallen on evil days. It had had its quarrels with the Dutch government, which had resented the publication of any article, however scholarly, that implied criticism of the authorities. The Napoleonic wars and the isolation of Java had also sapped interest in academic study, so that by the time Raffles arrived the Society was virtually dead.

Science to him was an essential ingredient in the life of every nation. It must, then, have given him great pleasure when the surviving members of the Batavian Society applied to him for help to revive this famous but moribund body. This was readily forthcoming; on 23rd October, thirty prominent gentlemen dined with the Lieutenant-Governor to discuss the situation. As a result, the Society came once more to life. Raffles was made president and, never too busy to find time for work that seemed to him important, he at once set about the task of overhauling the rules and objects of the Society as a first step to breathing new life into it.

iii

Many governments have come to grief over the question of finance, and it will be readily appreciated how anxiously an essentially commercial body like the East India Company viewed the acquisition of Java. The directors never wished to acquire it, and Lord Minto had deliberately disregarded his orders, which were to crush the French and then evacuate the island. Although they had to accept responsibility for Java, they did so with an evident reluctance only slightly modified by the financial prospect he held out before them. On 5th October 1811 he had written to the Secret Committee:

"... I am encouraged to state even now a confidential opinion that the resources will not only cover but considerably exceed expenditure. I fear, however, that we cannot expect to realize these expectations the first year. ..."

This sounded promising enough, but it was most unfortunate that such an expectation of prosperity should have been so early encouraged. It was nothing to the directors that the local government had to embark on two costly wars whereby the European control of the whole island of Java became for the first time a reality; nor was the potential value of Java, by reason of its essential richness and its position as the central feature of a vast archipelago, of the slightest interest to them, if the island could not pay its way. Their own finances were already seriously strained by the ever-increasing expenditure in India caused by a steadily extending control over the Indian states, an extension they were powerless to prevent. Consequently any sweeping reforms in Java, far from being welcome to them, would only increase their suspicion that the government was in the hands of a reckless man, full of wild projects and indifferent to cost.

As a result, his government, in almost every department, was to incur considerable censure, based not so much on the merits of individual reforms as on account of the annual deficit. That this was due to circumstances beyond his control and that in addition the position of Java was made even more difficult by the financial situation in India, were aspects of the case that were not even considered at home.

In spite of the obvious difficulties facing the Java government, Raffles fell into the trap of estimating a substantial balance of revenue over expenditure. In January 1812, he estimated a surplus of 705,000 Spanish dollars. This was welcome news to the Supreme Government, which was in grave financial straits, and its reply was that there would be now no necessity for the government of Java to draw bills upon Bengal during the financial year beginning on 1st May.

". . . it is expected therefore that you will refrain from drawing bills without previous intimation to this Government."

When Raffles had made his estimate, he could not have anticipated the heavy expenditure about to be incurred for operations against Palembang and Jokyakarta. On the contrary, he had no doubt budgeted for a considerable reduction in the military establishment in Java. This would have been a material help, as the troops had to be paid in silver. Still, his optimism, however justified at the time, was unfortunate and was to prove a fertile source of future trouble.

Minto went so far as to state, in a minute to the Court of Directors dated 4th July 1812, that it was only a secondary consideration that Java should yield an annual surplus.

". . . If additional and permanent security is obtained for the territory and revenue of India and for all the valuable interests for the Company and the nation in the East, without imposing anything whatever on the Company's finances, a benefit, which would have been cheaply purchased by great pecuniary sacrifices, will have been the gratuitous result of this acquisition. Had Java remained in the hands of the enemy it would not only have threatened the tranquillity of the Moluccas but have exposed our commercial profits in the spice trade to hazard and to an expense from war establishments which would have absorbed those expected advantages. . . ."

It is questionable if the Court of Directors in any way endorsed this statement of policy by their Governor-General.

By August of that year Raffles found it necessary to tackle much more drastically the problem of paper currency, which was now valued at from nine to eleven paper rix-dollars to one Spanish silver dollar, while Minto had fixed the value by proclamation at six-and-a-half to one.

In a dispatch dated 15th August he advised India of the possibility of having to substitute another paper currency for the depreciated old one, or to issue similar notes through the medium of a bank. No decision would be taken, however, until the opinion of the Supreme Government was known.

No answer was received, and by November the proportion had dropped to twelve to one. In a minute on 4th November Raffles pointed out that the situation had been made much more difficult by the demand by Bengal that no more bills should be drawn on them, and at the same time that every restriction on the exportation of specie should be removed.

"It appears imperiously necessary to adopt some decided measures both with the view to meet the wishes of the Supreme Government with regard to the exportation of specie, by allowing it to find its proper level in the market, and to prevent the ruin, which must inevitably arise to the finances of this Colony, if the depreciation of this [paper] currency is permitted to go on.

"It would undoubtedly have been more desirable to have delayed any decisive measures until the Board could have had the advantage of receiving the sentiments of the Supreme Government on the several financial statements and dispatches forwarded since the commencement of the present year, and the present uncertainty with respect to the future administration of the Colony is also a strong argument for delay, but the difficulties which arise from the present depreciation of the currency are such as might be expected to increase, if not immediately checked, and whatever might tend to restore its value must under any circumstances be beneficial. The Board therefore being decidedly of opinion that the most effectual measures only which might strike at the root of the evil can be of any permanent or real benefit, and adopting the principle that the Batavian paper currency ought justly to be supported by the internal resources of the country and not be rendered a burden on the established British possessions, no plan appears to them more advisable and effective . . . than that the whole mass of the paper be gradually withdrawn from Circulation by the sale of part of the Domains of this Island and remain in deposit in the hands of Government. . . . The sale of lands to the extent required may be readily made in the Batavia Regencies and in the environs of the towns of Samarang and Sourabaya where according to the opinion of the [land-tenure] Commission . . . such sale will not only be safe but moreover more beneficial to the future interest and situation of the Colony in general. . . .

"A supply of cash thus circulating and to be brought into the public Treasury will with the aid of Treasury notes occasionally as the state of the market require enable Government to conduct its expenses on the Island without granting any further bills on Bengal."

The Council agreed to the sale of lands to the extent of 400,000

Spanish dollars. Gillespie was not present at this meeting and later there came from the hills where he was recuperating a grudging assent.

"It might have been advisable in a public view", he wrote, "to have afforded to the Commander of the Forces sufficient light to form a competent judgment of the advantages or demerits of the arrangement, but as he had not the benefit of these, he can only now remark that as far as he is at present able to judge whatever may be the eventual good to result from the sale of lands, he has no reason to think that the alienation of so large a portion of the demains [*sic*] of the island (for some general arrangement may ere this have been decided on by His Majesty's Ministers should it have reverted to the crown) would be strictly justifiable without reference unless the Board in its mature deliberation has determined that no other expedients of less magnitude or future consequence to the state of the Colony can be adopted to meet the exigency. In that case the Commander of the Forces will not withhold his acquiescence in a limited sale, nor will he be inclined to object to the extent now proposed by the Board."

The Council, having taken note of this minute, reaffirmed the propriety and necessity of withdrawing the paper currency, and agreed to proceed with the sales, but gradually and only to such extent as was absolutely required.

It has been argued that Raffles had no right, as the representative of a trustee power, to alienate state lands in perpetuity. This contention has some validity because, if the emergency was so great that some drastic step had to be taken to prevent a financial crisis, then long leases might have been offered. It is difficult to suppose that such would not have been acceptable, and leases would have been free of the more objectionable features of outright sale.

Another criticism is that the holding of the first auctions in January 1813 followed too closely on the decision to sell and that, leaving out the question of conspiracy, the notice of auctions was too short to give firms or individuals in, for example, India time to make bids. As a result, the prices obtained from the few bids available have been regarded by some as ridiculously low.

The answer to this can only be that the emergency, if it was as grave as to warrant a sale at all, was too acute to allow of a delay of several months while notices were sent to India and the response received. As regards the prices obtained, these do seem to have been less than the value of the properties, and Dutch writers in particular have been very critical of them. That the lands became of immense value later on does not prove that, at the time of auction, they should have commanded higher prices. The situation in Java was far from settled and the restoration of her export trade by no means certain. The labour force to work the estates and the means of transport to the coast were neither in a satisfactory state. There was thus at least one element of commercial risk that might have been expected to militate against high prices, particularly with a limited number of buyers and the general state of financial stringency.

Raffles, for reasons that appeared to him adequate at the time, decided to purchase some of this land. Details of the transaction have their chronological place in the next chapter.

iv

Three problems confronting Raffles during the early months of his régime concerned opium, slavery and pirates.

The policy to be adopted in regard to opium might have appeared a purely domestic affair in the selection of a course of action that would best suit the revenue of Java and protect it from the activities of smugglers. It had, however, to be borne in mind that the policy adopted in Java might well affect the price of opium at the Calcutta sales. As the drug was deleterious to the health of the people if used in excessive quantity, Raffles was anxious to restrict imports as much as possible, which was unlikely to be popular with Calcutta merchants interested in opium, the staple of their China trade, gentlemen who were very influential in official circles.

An early declaration of policy was required because a decision had to be reached as to how the opium imported in the ships of the Java expedition should be sold. Minto had left instructions that this should be by public auction in Batavia. Raffles thought this unwise.

"After a very mature consideration", he wrote to Minto on 29th January, "of the consequences that might arise from such a plan, as well with reference to clandestine trade as to the immediate profit to Government, we have deemed it necessary for the security of this important branch of revenue to supply the retail farmer direct from the Company's stores for the ensuing year. . . .

"The general importation of opium from Bengal not being prohibited, our first object was to devise means by which the clandestine importation of Java would be prevented, and to do away with temptation, the farmers are supplied with opium from the Company's stores at the rate of 1,200 Dollars per chest, Government paying importer at the average rate of 1,100 Dollars, the chief profit to Government being thus received in the rents paid by the farmer. . . ."

This, he estimated, would bring in a clear and certain revenue of between 600,000 and 700,000 dollars a year.

"In the arrangements we have made we have been guided by the principle that this Government should interfere as little as possible with the general sales of this article in Calcutta. But we are decidedly of opinion that the greatest profit might be obtained on the portion of this valuable property consumed in the Eastern Islands by a certain quantity being annually set apart in Bengal at the disposal of this Settlement and its Dependencies, leaving this Government free in their conduct and regulations respecting the arrangements they may make regarding the importation or non-importation of opium into the Island. Such an arrangement however might greatly affect the general price on the still larger portion sent to China, and consequently it may on the whole be deemed more advisable for this Government to take means to supply itself from the market in common with other purchasers as at present.

"We deem it necessary to add that the regulations which are established for the retail vend for the consumption of opium on this Island are framed on the principle that it is most advantageous to Government . . . that the smallest possible quantity of this poisonous drug should be sold at the highest possible price, and were the article to be sold for the consumption of the Island otherwise than under these restrictive regulations, we apprehend the most fatal consequences as well to the morals of the country as to its general tranquillity. We trust that it will not be found necessary to give any assurances at the general sales at Calcutta that will interfere with the arrangements which we have adopted."

This dispatch was crossed by one from Calcutta, dated 15th February, that completely upset Raffles' proposals for the control of opium.

"It appears to His Lordship in Council to be very expedient that the wholesale trade of opium should be left entirely free, and that the opium purchased at the public sales at this Presidency should be allowed unrestricted passage to all foreign marts; and free admission into our eastern possessions to be sold in entire chests unembarrassed by pre-emption or local monopoly. . . . Notification has been made that in consequence to the late acquisitions to the eastward, the trade of opium will now be left open to Java and its Dependencies on the same footing as at Sumatra and Penang. Although it is thus resolved in no way to restrict the wholesale trade of opium, the attention of the Government of Batavia is requested to the expediency of exercising a wholesome control over the retail vend, licensing or restraining it as considerations of policy may render advisable."

This dispatch was accompanied by a personal letter from Minto dated 28th February.

". . . you will no doubt regret the loss of so material an article in the resources of the Government of Java. . . . I have concurred with my colleagues in thinking it right or rather indispensable to begin by opening the trade in that article with Java, because the Company's monopoly of opium was likely to be affected by the measure concerning Java, and although the revenue looked for from a second monopoly in that island bears a great proportion to the whole of its resources, that object is nevertheless small when compared with the opium concern in Bengal, and by aiming at the smaller object we should put a much greater hazard."

He went on to state that the scheme was entirely experimental.

"If, by opening the trade to Java, the sales at Calcutta experience a rise in the price of opium equivalent to the revenue which the monopoly at Java would yield, the system now adopted may be permanent. If a contrary result is apparent, the trial must be made in Java. . . . In the meanwhile credit must undoubtedly be given to the finances of Java for the profit which might with any certainty be made there of opium."

To this Raffles replied on 2nd April:

"After the most mature deliberation we are induced to consider the footing on which the importation now stands as almost the only one on which it is advisable to place it, as far as the interests of this settlement are concerned, and if the same materially interfered with, we are apprehensive that the important revenues derivable here will be lost without a corresponding benefit in Bengal or the chance of regaining hereafter what might be lost by failure in an experiment of the kind. Under this conviction and an impression that the very high price which opium has carried of late years at the Calcutta sales, is attributable more to the effect of the monopoly of the Dutch Government and combination of holders in China than to competition in the ultimate markets, we trust that we shall have met your approbation in continuing the regulations now in force until we can receive your final instructions after receipt of our present representation. . . .

"An idea occurs to us that . . . an arrangement might be made for gradually transferring to Bengal a proportion of the revenue on opium now derivable in Java, by the means which the possession of the long existing monopoly now places in the hands of the British Government; and that if this Government were directed to adopt the measure of raising their purchase price from the present sum of 1,200 dollars to any sum within the retail price of the farmer by degrees and as circumstances might warrant with a view to the corresponding rise at the Calcutta sales, every expected advantage might arise on the whole quantity sold in Calcutta . . . while it is not impossible that the retail price on the Island might be so regulated as to prevent much loss to the immediate revenue to be raised here through the farmer. . . ."

This brought a very frank reply.

"Looking back candidly at the opium transaction," wrote Minto on 12th May, "I fear two faults have been committed. The first—that the system was not *settled* before I left you, or, if that could not be done, that I had not left a positive instruction with you to take no definite measure till it could be concerted with this Government. The second fault was, that we pledged the faith of Government here, without being certain that some measure adopted by you in the interim might not counteract our engagement with the public."

The first fault he attributed to the distractions attending the last part of his stay in Java and to a languor he had never before experienced. In any case:

"I had confined my views and efforts to *leaving the foundations* and had early perceived the impossibility of charging myself with details. This might have diverted me from the deliberation that was due to the opium arrangement. It is true that I had adopted the opinion that Government ought to keep the opium trade in its own hands for the purpose of control as well as revenue, and I considered the opium farms, that is to say the exclusive privilege of retailing the drug granted for a valuable consideration by Government, as a settled point in the system. The exclusive *purchase* from the importer reserved to Government was a point that had not equally my notice, which I presume however was my own fault."

He stated that everything had been settled to the satisfaction of the Calcutta merchants.

"There will be some sacrifice to ransom the faith of Government but not considerable."

In his private opinion the merchants would lose nothing, but would gain by the injury of which they complained. The system to be adopted for the following year would be concerted with the Java government.

Meanwhile the merchants of Batavia, having become aware that the Supreme Government had of their own authority declared free trade in opium for Java, presented a memorial to the Lieutenant-Governor.

"Your memorialists humbly presume to advance that the paragraph (free trade in opium to Java) evidently seems to have been inserted with a view to enhance the price in opium at Calcutta by holding out to the merchant the additional mart (known to be great) of Java and its Dependencies as free and open to them which they find completely shut, being neither permitted to freely sell the article themselves nor will the Honourable Company receive it at the rate they have hitherto professed to take and have taken opium. Your memorialists . . . presume to hope . . . you will deem it but a common justice due to them to receive the whole quantity now in the market . . . at the low rate of 1,100 Spanish Dollars per chest . . . for in consequence of the encouragement held out much more has come to the mart than otherwise would have done, and this is now working to depress the article."

They also complained of high warehouse charges. The government replied:

"So far from the regulations at Batavia amounting to a monopoly, the farmer has long since ceased to receive his supply from Government . . . The Lieutenant-Governor in Council cannot but regret that you should have been induced to consider the faith of Government pledged to the purchase of any quantity of opium that might be imported. No such pledge was ever given, although Government in the wish and desire to promote the interests of the merchants have already been induced to take from them a much larger quantity than is required for the consumption of the Island."

Warehouses charges would be reduced, and new arrangements for the opium trade were under consideration.

The Supreme Government thought the merchants had some ground for complaint and agreed to grant them indemnification.

"After you shall have delivered to the farmers the quantity of opium which you may have on hand, it will be very desirable if you can get them to renounce the privilege which they now possess of being supplied by Government . . . at certain specified rates . . . in consideration of permission to purchase of any persons they may think proper.

"Among the restrictions complained of by the merchants is that of your limiting the importation of opium to the Port of Batavia. . . . To preserve our pledge to the merchants . . . it is naturally our earnest wish that they may be permitted to import their opium into any of the ports on the Island of Java where Custom Houses may be established, with freedom also to land and sell their opium at any of the Islands dependent on your Government."

This, however, was left to the discretion of the Lieutenant-Governor.

On 20th September, Raffles agreed to the wishes of the Supreme Government.

"We . . . resolved after the most mature consideration not to purchase any further quantity of opium whatsoever, and in compliance with the expectation of the Calcutta merchants and the wishes of the Supreme Government to open the ports of Samarang and Sourabaya on which the great question seemed to hinge, making the best provision on our power for the disposal of the opium already purchased. . . . In adopting these regulations, I have, however, been reluctantly compelled to have recourse to a measure which under any other circumstances might not have been justifiable after the assurance which I have already given to your Lordship with regard to the probable extent of our drafts from the Supreme Government. Your Lordship will observe that the merchants state it will be absolutely necessary for the Government either to allow the exportation of specie, or to grant Bills on Bengal, and it must be admitted that in the present state of trade, unless one or the other of these measures is resorted to the opening of the Ports can be of no real advantage to the fair trader for whom there is no corresponding export cargo. To admit the unrestrained exportation of specie would under the present circumstances of this Island be impossible for obvious reasons, and it was left to this Government either to adopt the measure of affording the means of a remittance to Bengal, or to subject the Island already suffering under a want of Specie to the effects of a clandestine exportation, which along such an extent of coast could not by any exertions be effectually checked. The measure therefore granting Bills on the Supreme Government became unavoidable. . . .

"A further experience in this Island has confirmed my opinion that so far as the Island of Java is alone concerned, any plan by which the importation or consumption of opium can be restrained will be more beneficial to the welfare and prosperity of the people, and consequently most urgent on this Government to recommend. But taking the question on a more extended view, and considering that as the habit of using opium could only be eradicated by degrees, the drug would be imported by clandestine means if ever Government prohibited its consumption, it becomes a subject of further consideration in what degree and under what regulations its use can be most effectually restricted with the greatest advantage to Government therefrom, particularly as I do not conceive the use of opium in moderation, and while confined to a certain class of people more injurious than the use of spirituous liquors in Europe on which a tax has already been considered a fair subject of revenue. It may indeed be observed with respect to opium that those who have been accustomed to make use of it cannot exist if the stimulus be suddenly withdrawn, and instances are not uncommon where its disuse has been followed by idiotism; under these circumstances, the continuance of the consumption to a certain extent becomes expedient. . . .

"The beneficial effect of this change which the restrictions and regulations of this Government have tended to continue, are evident in every part of the country where the improvement in agriculture, commerce and domestic comfort is apparent and daily increasing; the abolition of public gaming and cockfighting is universally admitted to have a principal effect in diminishing the dissipation and the consequent vices of the community; the restrictions on opium have contributed materially to the same effect, and there can be no doubt, that since the full establishment of the British Authority within the territories of the native Princes, and the consequent reduction of their irregular and disorganized troops, the population of this Island may be expected to improve rapidly in civilization, and may be found susceptible of any improvement which has been introduced within the British possessions in the East. Under the system hitherto existing, the farmer is not compelled to retail his opium at a fixed price, but is allowed to sell the same according to the circumstances of the place, Government retaining in their hands, except at Batavia (where the presence of the Chief Authority and the nature of the country and population admitted of latitude), the means of limiting the means of expenditure in each district by regulating the extent of the issue."

He made the following proposals:

"The importation of opium is to be restricted to the Port of Batavia where it shall pay an import duty of 300 Spanish Dollars per chest. That opium imported in the first instance at Batavia may afterwards be exported to any of the ports of Java or its Dependencies without payment of future duty, on certificate of having paid the import duty of Batavia. That the sale of opium to the farmers be permitted to the extent which is allowed by the terms of their contract, and that they shall supply themselves to that extent direct from the merchants without any interference on the part of the Government. That the merchants on the Island shall only sell to the farmers, and the opium imported shall be subjected to such regulations as Government may think proper for ensuring this, and for the prevention of the exportation of the specie."

Six weeks later, on 31st October, he reported to Edmonstone that all the opium in the hands of the Java government had been disposed of without any great loss, except a quantity not exceeding seventy chests, which he estimated would be sold off before the end of the year.

The Supreme Government finally capitulated in a letter dated 3rd December 1812.

"We consider the explanations furnished by you to have established in a satisfactory and conclusive manner, that the instructions imposed by your Government on the sale of the article in Java far from having been productive of the injury complained of by the merchants and others of this place, were calculated to maintain the price of the article in the Java market to the manifest advantage of the importers."

No assurances as to the arrangements in Java would be given to purchasers at the forthcoming sales.

". . . you will therefore perceive that the question is left open for your decision."

This was a victory for the Java government, and Raffles lost no time in putting matters straight. His minute and other relative data take us beyond the year at present under review, but it is as well to include them here, so that the whole question of opium as it affected Java can be considered in its entirety.

His minute of 9th April 1813 ran as follows:

"As experience has shown the disadvantages of the present system to the public revenue, and as we are authorized to adopt such measures as may be conceived most productive and suitable to the local interests of the Colony, I am decidedly of opinion that we should revert to our former system of restricting the importation of the article to the port of Batavia and of regulating the extent of its consumption by furnishing the supply required by the farmers."

Fresh custom-house regulations were published whereby opium purchased at the Company's sales at Calcutta could be imported only at Batavia, and not in less quantity than a whole chest. For consumption on the island, it could be sold only to farmers of the government. Farmers at Batavia would alone be permitted to purchase opium in the market, and for their own consumption only. All other farmers in Java would be supplied by the government at 1,200 Spanish dollars per chest. Import duty was thirty dollars a chest unless duty had already been paid at Penang or Malacca.

The prolonged argument over the sale of opium in Java is interesting not only as an example of higher authority interfering with a competent local government in a technical matter—and Raffles' competence as an administrator is well borne out in the arguments he levelled against the regulations proposed by India—but also, more particularly, as indicating the advanced views he exhibited on the pernicious effects of opium, and on the methods best calculated to eradicate the evil. Whole sentences in his dispatches find a parallel in the later dispatches of many Governors of the Straits Settlements. The arguments advanced in defence of the opium monopoly in the Straits Settlements were exactly the same as those put forward by Raffles nearly 130 years earlier. But if modern Governors have had to contend with extreme anti-drug fanaticism, which certainly did not exist in Raffles' time, Raffles had to face the fixed determination of the East India Company to make every penny it could out of the sale of opium. The Company had no thought of the possible effect that unrestricted sales might have upon the local population within its territories. The attempts, therefore, of one of its servants to limit on grounds of morality the Company's revenues from such an important source were not likely to be regarded with any marked approval.

The extent to which Raffles' policy did reduce the use of opium can be seen from the following quotation from a letter to the Supreme Government dated 10th July 1815:

"The consumption of opium on this Island has however greatly decreased, and it is the natural effect of the more industrious habits that are introduced by the system of cultivation and property that such should be the case. It is indeed the opinion of this Board that it would be neither practicable nor politic to introduce amongst the agricultural classes of the population that free and indiscriminate use of the drug which it was the interest of the Government heretofore to excite—or more properly speaking which it was the interest of the chief local authority to excite, because it was by the profits obtained by illicit trade in opium, that the principal source of its emoluments was derived—a greater and better revenue is now derived from the produce of the soil, and the Lieutenant-Governor in Council has for some time had it under his serious consideration whether it would not be more advisable on every account to discourage the vend of opium still further in the Honourable Company's districts."

Apparently he came to the conclusion that it would. On 28th September 1815 a regulation was published that "from and after the 1st January 1816, or whenever the present farm or contracts for the retail vend of opium may expire, the retail vend of that drug will be exclusively confined within the British territories on Java to the town and suburbs of Batavia".

Again, in his quarterly report dated 28th September 1815, he remarked: ". . . the abolition of its use as far as practicable will tend most considerably to prevent crime among the Javanese, and to secure the tranquillity of the country, for it has been clearly shown in the execution of the laws that those persons who indulge in the habit of smoking opium become lazy and indolent, excited by want of means to purchase the indulgence to acts of robbery, and stimulated by its effects to the commission of the highest crimes against peace and good order of society."

V

Minto, like Raffles, was a strong opponent of slavery and had instructed him to investigate the situation in Java. The problem, as Raffles quickly discovered, was by no means simple. Under Roman-Dutch law, slavery had been recognized as legal by the former European government; under Mohammedan law, by every native administration. Apart from this—apart, too, from the virtual absence of any other kind of domestic labour—the legality, under English law, of prohibiting slavery or even the importation of slaves was not at all clear.

The slave trade had been abolished by Lord Grenville's Act of Parliament in 1807, but some held that this referred to the trade from Africa to the West Indies and the local trade in the West Indies, arguing that the Act did not apply to settlements or states within the limits of the East India Company's exclusive trade, or, alternatively, if it did apply, it could be only to territories acquired by the East India Company after the passing of the Act. In Java, Minto had recognized Dutch law as applicable, pending instructions from home, and Dutch law permitted slavery. It was further argued that the slave trade in the East Indies was carried on not by British subjects in British ships, but by natives of Bali, Timor and Celebes. These were merely allies, not subjects of Great Britain. British naval captains had, however, instructions to detain any ships engaged in the slave trade in the East Indian seas. Accordingly, the Java government felt it desirable to refer the whole question to the

Supreme Government. Pending instructions from India, H.M. ships agreed to take no further action.

Raffles explained his difficulty to Minto in a letter undated, but probably 1st May 1812.

"Any interference", he wrote, "in the regulations which have so long existed in Java respecting this mode of domestic servitude is of so delicate a nature and required so much previous enquiry, caution and discretion, that I have until this date delayed addressing your Lordship fully on this subject, fearful of hazarding any information or opinions not adequately mature to form the groundwork of innovation and permanent arrangement. . . .

"With regard to slavery as it exists in the other Islands, I confess my incompetency at present to convey to your Lordship any adequate or satisfactory information and the religion and habits of the numerous states are so disposed to its encouragement, that I apprehend the evil can only in the first instance be partially removed and finally extirpated by the gradual operation of the measures that may be adopted for their general civilization."

The import duty on slaves had been doubled, and importation limited to the ages prescribed by the former obsolete regulations, but he assumed that actual prohibition of import was meanwhile impracticable, on the assumption that the British Act of Parliament did not extend to Java. The principal source of supply was Macassar.

". . . in consequence of its being the favourite source of revenues among those Chieftains, it will require much delicacy and caution in attempting any measures to restrain, where argument could be of no avail, and force would be inconvenient."

He explained that slavery also arose from war and debt, being likewise an alternative to punishment for certain crimes. Any improvement would be slow, but he did not despair of progress. He promised a further dispatch, which was very likely that dated 13th June of that year. In this he reported that the number of slaves belonging to the government was only 281, most of them employed in domestic service. If offered their liberty they would not find it worth while to accept it; the effect would be the discharge of old and trustworthy servants, with no real benefit to the persons concerned. Some slaves were employed in the departments of the magistrates and of the master attendant, but if a more liberal allowance were granted to ordinary coolies, the need for these would pass. Police regulations might be necessary to put at the disposal of the public departments, by contract or otherwise, a greater proportion of the labouring classes than was at present available. As convicts were expected from Bengal, the word could be given to them. The immediate emancipation of the whole of the coolie class was recommended.

Slavery in Java under the previous administration could, he considered, be viewed "as a regulated domestic servitude rather than a detestable system which Great Britain has to the credit of humanity so vigorously suppressed in the West Indies".

This was not strictly accurate. It was only the *trade* in slaves that had been suppressed in 1807. Slavery itself was not finally abolished throughout the British Empire until the passing of the Emancipation Act of 1833.

"Still," Raffles continued in his letter to Minto, "it is repugnant to every principle of enlightened administration."

The total number of slaves in Java belonging to individuals was 27,142, the owners being mainly European. The regulation as to importation under the age of fourteen at least avoided "the subjection of mankind after their ideas, their habits and attachments are formed—limiting the introduction to that period of life when the change cannot be felt and the misfortune is not remembered". The revival of regulations requiring Christians "to baptize and initiate their slaves in the Christian religion" would no doubt be directed by his Lordship.

The regulation that slaves guilty of insubordination could be chained and whipped, and slaves laying violent hands on their masters could be punished with death, appeared to be indispensable wherever slavery existed, and:

". . . although the mild system which is yet tolerated in Java might seem to obviate the necessity of such exclusive laws, it is to be considered that the slaves in general are led to the good conduct, which universally characterizes them on this Island, in a certain measure by this long established law, and that any serious alteration therein might lead to the most serious consequences considering the proportion which their numbers bear to the European population.

"Although with the exception of a few unnecessary and obsolete regulations the Colonial Statutes respecting slavery seem to be framed on the principles of humanity and with attention to the Christian religion, yet in consequence of the supplementary force of the Roman Law in the Dutch system of legislation, there appears to be one capital defect in the laws regarding slavery, viz., that a slave is regarded as real property incapable of personal rights . . . and although a slave under this principle may possess and obtain a portion of property for himself with the consent of his master, his possession is always precarious and his property is removable at the discretion of the proprietor."

There should be a declaration "that slaves in future shall not be considered as objects of real property, but as objects possessing of personal rights and bound only to unlimited service". They should be transferred only with their own consent; rights of punishment should be limited, and personal wrongs done to a slave should be treated as personal injuries;

slaves should have the right to acquire personal property, to purchase their freedom, and, if employed in agricultural or other labour, to be paid the same daily wages as free workers.

At the time of the arrival of the English, the only class of domestic servants in Java were slaves imported from outside, chiefly from Bali and Celebes, who had been reared in the families of the Dutch. But many English officers and others had now taken Javanese into their service, which would help to make the importation of slaves unnecessary. There were no Javanese slaves, though in some respects their condition was little better than that.

"I trust I shall not be thought altogether to have neglected the rights of private property or the advantages which this Island enjoys in its police and domestic comforts from a well-regulated system of domestic servitude —the improvements which I have suggested, I am confident may be effected by the local Government, and hereafter I feel no doubt but other arrangements and regulations arising from the same principles may eventually avert every evil of slavery and establish one of the most convenient and beneficial systems of domestic servitude advantageous alike to master and servant that is known in any dependent Colony of such importance and extent."

On 18th November a minute by the Lieutenant-Governor recorded the following:

"Very small number of vessels which have arrived with slaves during the last year, having proved that it is not so extensive to Java as might have been supposed, and the information since obtained that the principal native Chiefs are not so interested in the traffic, but that it has been carried out chiefly by Europeans, the Lieutenant-Governor proposes that with a view to extend the liberal and humane views of the British legislature to this part of the world, the further importation of slaves shall be prohibited in the Island of Java and its Dependencies after 1st January 1813, and the notice thereof be published forthwith."

This proposal was adopted. Two months later a dispatch from the Governor-General dated 17th October was received. It stated that the Act of 1807 undoubtedly applied to Java, confirming the legality of the step already taken by Raffles on his own initiative.

In December 1812 a treaty was signed with the Sultan of Banjermasin, Borneo, whereby all the privileges previously possessed by the Dutch, who had completely withdrawn from Banjermasin before the British expedition to Java, were ceded to Great Britain. Alexander Hare was sent as British representative. In addition to his official duties, Hare obtained a grant of land from the sultan and set himself up as a local chief, with a large harem as one of its most conspicuous features.

To enable the land to be developed, Hare asked Raffles if the scarcity of the local population could be assisted by long-term criminals and vagrants being sent to him from Java, to work under him for the period of their sentences. Raffles authorized this and also that the wives and families of such men, if they wished, could be given assisted passages. In principle, at such a time, there was nothing unusual about such an arrangement and, provided the conditions laid down by Raffles were observed, nothing objectionable in it. Whether, as some Dutch writers have alleged, there was in fact wholesale kidnapping into slavery and whether on arrival in Borneo these unfortunate people were brutally treated by Hare, it is difficult now to decide. A lot of capital has been made out of the incident to show that Raffles did not practise what he preached; he publicly condemned slavery and privately allowed Hare to indulge in a most vicious form of it.

Raffles had first met Hare in Malacca and, as Hare was fluent in Malay and had some acquaintance as a trader with the archipelago, had introduced him to Minto, who had taken him on the expedition. Hare was a very eccentric type, but—and this no doubt appealed to Raffles—was inspired by aspirations similar to those that were later to fire Sir James Brooke, white Rajah of Sarawak: to put down piracy and to build up prosperous settlements under British leadership. Whether, unlike Brooke, Hare proved himself as vicious as a despot as he was in private life is very hard to determine, but the evidence that he was a ruthless ruler is by no means conclusive. Raffles was undoubtedly fond of Hare, yet their friendship could not surely have continued had Raffles learned of Hare's brutality, if the Dutch stories about him were true.

It has to be remembered that contemporary accounts of Hare depend chiefly on two prejudiced sources. John Clunies-Ross, later famous at Cocos Island, worked for Hare and for some time they were friends and partners. Clunies-Ross defended Hare stoutly against Dutch abuse as long as that friendship lasted, but when they quarrelled at Cocos, nothing was too bad to say about Hare. The Dutch also had a strong political motive for discrediting Hare. They were most anxious to resume their influence in Borneo and thought they could get moral support for their claim if they argued that it was their duty to rescue the unfortunate natives from the scandalous oppression of Hare. They certainly showed no hesitation, when the time came, in making the case against him—and, incidentally, Raffles—as black as possible. But it is at least questionable whether their accusations were really founded on adequate evidence.

In *De Britsche Heerschappij over Java en Onderhorigheden*, Dr Levyssohn Norman describes Hare as "a man of the same stamp as Raffles and Brooke. He was, however, more of an eccentric Englishman than a talented statesman." We can well suppose that this is a fair description, and that Hare's vices were domestic rather than political.

The question of piracy was one that soon forced itself on the attention of Raffles. In an undated dispatch in 1812, probably June, he addressed Lord Minto on that subject. After referring to the various Dutch factories—that is, trading posts—in the eastern isles, which, though originally intended to protect the Dutch trade monopoly, were also effective for the suppression of piracy, he went on to suggest that the best method would be to establish commercial contracts between the British power and the adjoining native states.

The growth of piracy he traced chiefly to the decline of the Dutch marine and the blockade of Java. It had now reached alarming proportions and must be tackled forthwith. He suggested the re-establishment of a colonial marine force, composed of natives under European officers, with, say, twelve gunboats, three or four brigs of about 50 tons burden, and a number of small rowboats. This establishment was calculated chiefly as a defensive measure along the coasts, but would also be invaluable as auxiliary to the cruisers of the Bombay marine in any offensive operations.

"Considering the head to which piracy has grown," wrote Raffles, "it seems to require some few such as the chastisement and destructions of one or two avowed piratical States to reduce the evil within the management of the local Marine, which I have taken the liberty to suggest. It must be considered that the real strength of the British Government in the Eastern Islands is that of a mere handful of men in comparison with the military and marine which the European powers which preceded us possessed; and that it is by a political management only which may check mischief in the bud, and exhibit to advantage the power which we possess without evincing our actual force that we can expect to be respected or obeyed.

"It must also be considered that although the Malays may in military point of view possess no collective strength, such is the nature of the country and their habits that it is only by a cautious assumption and the rigid exaction of that respect for the European character which in the early times of the Portuguese and Dutch was enforced, and has hitherto been preserved from the nature of their situation. The most prominent piratical state within the immediate range of this Government appears to be that of Sambas [western Borneo]."

He also referred once more to the indiscriminate admission of casual traders, whom he regarded with disfavour, into the Eastern Archipelago. His argument was that they arrived in large ships and, being anxious to cut down the length of their stay, sold their cargoes at almost any price to the chieftains and thereby spoiled the market for the legitimate traders, whose business should be to build the trade in that area on a sound commercial basis.

In his attempts to deal with piracy, which threatened the very existence of trade, Raffles dispatched in October 1812 an expedition to Sambas under the command of Captain Bowen of H.M.S. *Phoenix*. This met with disaster, but a further expedition under Colonel Watson captured the forts, and the sultan fled into the interior.

The same year we find Raffles recommending the introduction of English cloth into Java. He wrote to Jacob Bosanquet, chairman of the Court of Directors, on 29th October:

". . . cloths from Western India have always formed an important branch in the commerce of Java, and it occurs to me that in the present state of the manufacturing interests in England, a very material proportion of this trade might with advantage be transferred to England where the cloth might be manufactured even at a lower rate than in India, it being observed that it is rather in the coarser than the finer sorts, that the bulk of the trade consists. . . . Under this idea it is my intention to send home musters of the different descriptions of cloth with the sale price in Java affixed to each with a recommendation that an adventure in the same, at least to the extent of £30,000, be made."

The first of these cloths made in the Javanese patterns were to arrive there at the end of 1814, forming the beginning of a long and prosperous British trade.

Neither Penang nor certain circles in India viewed the commercial activities of Raffles with any enthusiasm. Writing to Governor Petrie at Penang, John Palmer, the famous merchant banker of Calcutta, remarked:

"Of the narrow and perhaps interested and corrupt policy adopted to the Eastward of you, few can be more enlightened or impartial in their judgment than yourself, and I do not wonder that it should excite both your surprise and contempt as well as your scorn; and yet the Man is the Prophet and the Law with our legislation; and I apprehend that an appeal from either his presumption or dictum will be equally disregarded. But what indeed is to be expected from representation of the most flagrant grievances, when the total disregard of its own obligations has distinguished the great future of our commercial intercourse with Java."

Yet the same gentleman could write to Raffles himself a few days later:

"Some of your Penang friends carry the freedom of trade to such a glorious extent that they are irreconcilably angry with your efforts even to extirpate piracy; and wish to have been indulged in that humane and honourable intercourse with the latter race which superseded the dagger by the substitution of musketry and cannon. I have not, much as I love Penang, been hitherto convinced by their reasons nor converted by their principles, and so long as I could feel or appreciate an Universal Good I shall continue to revere the motive and the object of your undertaking."

John Palmer, one of the sons of Major (later Lieutenant-General) Palmer, confidential private secretary to Warren Hastings, was born in

1766. He occupied a unique position in India, being dubbed "the Prince of Merchants", and, as head of the greatest agency house in India, with its ramifications all over the Far East as it then was—Penang, Canton, Sumatra and Pegu, Burma—and later Java, Mauritius and Singapore, he certainly deserved the title.

vi

Not least among the important questions of 1812 concerned the immediate future of Java as a British colony and the continuance of Raffles in the position of Lieutenant-Governor. Very early in his administration there were widespread stories of his imminent replacement by a certain General Maitland. As far back as 6th January, John Palmer did not hesitate to write to his friend, the Sultan of Pontianak, Borneo:

"You will have seen, and been satisfied, that I did whatever in my power to impress the Governors of Java and Pulo Penang with the most favourable sentiments of you, and I may add, that I have not been less successful with Lord Minto. . . . I have not indeed had a favourable opportunity of stating fully to Lord Minto the great kindness of your conduct, nor have I mentioned anything about your Views and Wishes on public subjects and the affairs of your own country. I have indeed purposely abstained from this, because I learned from his Lordship that he had long ago referred whatever concerned the affairs of Borneo to Mr Raffles and that, since then, a Governor was coming from England. appointed by the King, who would be a proper person to dispose of your affairs. At present we understand General Maitland to be the Governor of Java, and that he is coming to Calcutta to make arrangements with Lord Minto. . . . I hope there will be no disappointment of General Maitland, for he is not only a friend of ours, but a great and good man besides, and will turn all his thoughts and actions to the general importance of the noble Countries which misrule and ignorance have plunged into misery, contempt and hatred."

Minto wrote to Raffles on 25th May:

"If you should be superseded I trust and believe that you will be taken the best care of that circumstances permit, and that you will always be kept harmless and free from loss. I say this, however, on the suggestion of my own mind, having received no advice from England. I do most cordially and deeply feel for your disappointment, and have only to hope that the possibility of its occurring from the beginning will have so far prepared you, as to break the blow. You will carry with you the credit of having been selected for a great trust, and of having justified the choice down to the latest period. You have many years of action and energy before you, and I trust may yet build a fair superstructure upon the foundation, which I have had the honour and pleasure of laying."

In London, the question of Java becoming a King's Colony was clearly under discussion. On 6th June Benjamin Jones wrote from the office of the India Board to Robert Dundas, second Viscount Melville, president of the Board:

"If (as I presume is intended) the Island of Java is to be transferred to the Crown, I trust your Lordship will take an opportunity, when the question comes to be considered, of recommending that its subordination to the Government of India may be preserved; that at the proper season you will exert your influence for placing the whole of the British Colonies in the East under the management of the Minister for India, which must infallibly devolve on you again."

Having presumably heard authentic news that the transfer could be regarded as certain, Minto wrote to Raffles on 9th December:

"The Subject which interests me most deeply in the affairs of Java, is the approaching change of Government, and what will be its influence on your situation and future views. It would have been very desirable to have known precisely and certainly what your wishes would point to in the event of supercession; whether to quit the Island or remain, and in the latter case, what situation you would prefer. I am not without hopes indeed of still hearing from you on this point before the arrival of General Maitland in Bengal. . . .

"If I should not receive your own ideas on the subject in the meantime my intention is, first, to bring your claims to an honourable position in the new arrangement before General Maitland as forcibly as I am able, though they can hardly be as much as they deserve. In the next place, when we come to particulars, my aim would be to place you in charge of the Residency at Solo and the general superintendence of the Eastern Provinces, subject to your approval, of course, if I should succeed. . . .

"No exertion of mine will be wanting to break a fall, which I assure you most truly I feel by sympathy, much as if I had experienced the reverse myself. . . . The appointment was originally made by a temporary authority, incompetent to ensure its permanence, and in connexion with a system equally provisional and beyond his power to perpetuate. The authorities, with whom the decision of those two points rested, have only exerted their legal powers in altering the system, with which alone your situation could stand, and selecting a person to preside in their own."

Only a week later he communicated further information that might affect Raffles' decision.

"I am inclined to doubt", he wrote, "whether you will find it advantageous to remain in Java. Gen. Maitland has, I know, made overtures to another General Officer to hold the 2nd Military Station and I should not conceive that a 3rd is likely to be employed, or if it would suit your views or feelings, to hold a Situation so subordinate."

At the end of the previous chapter mention was made of Gillespie's intervention in civil matters, in which he had formerly shown no concern. This may have been due merely to a very human desire to show the Lieutenant-Governor that, since Raffles had taken an active interest in military affairs, the commander of the forces should show an equally critical interest in civil questions. But more probably this sudden attention to the work of government was chiefly inspired by the well-authenticated report that General Maitland was actually on his way to assume charge of Java. There was no secret about this, and Gillespie must have been fully advised by his friends at home. What could be more natural than that he should now decide to take an active share in the administration so as to be able to act as adviser to the new Governor? Whether he was the other "General Officer" to whom Minto referred in his letter is not now known, yet it seems quite possible.

The prospect of a military régime also encouraged the creation of two factions, military and civilian. That, within a matter of months, the military would take over from the civilian power, inevitably tended to stimulate the arrogance of the army officers.

"I am prepared and ready", wrote Raffles to Ramsay, "to meet the change whenever it may occur . . . but I confess that I should say farewell to Java with a heavy heart."

Chapter Thirteen

JAVA, 1813

i

"AT the commencement of this month," wrote Captain Travers in his diary towards the end of January 1813, "we were looking out for the arrival of General Maitland daily as Governor-General and Commander in Chief of all H.M. Islands East of the Cape, excepting Ceylon, but on 18th we had an arrival from Bengal bringing accounts that the Board of Control had intimated to Lord Minto that it was the intention of the Ministry not to make any decision with respect to the ultimate fate of this Island until a more full and satisfactory report had been received."

It appeared, however, that Minto entertained no hope that any arguments he had urged would induce the authorities at home to maintain the present civilian government.

The sale of lands to meet the financial crisis was proceeding. With the concurrence of Gillespie, who was present at the meeting of the Council when the matter was considered, the private sale of an extensive area to Muntinghe was approved. As has been mentioned, Raffles also participated. In partnership with Nicholaus Engelhardt, he purchased at the public auction at Batavia four lots in the Regency of Chianjur, adjacent to Buitenzorg. As he lacked the necessary funds himself, he borrowed from his old Penang friend, William Robinson, enough to buy half a share, which he considered was the least amount of land he could purchase in his position as Lieutenant-Governor. The fact that he was participating was known only to a few, Gillespie among them, before the auction, though at the auction itself he made bids to stimulate prices. In this he succeeded to such an extent that he and his partner, Engelhardt, to whom the four lots finally fell, paid very much more than that Dutch gentleman had intended.

Subsequently it was found necessary to appoint a supervisor of the property. A Mr de Wilde was given the post and was allowed one-sixth share to encourage his interest. Thomas McQuoid, who had served with Raffles in Penang and was now, besides holding other offices, Resident of Buitenzorg, was, for a reason unexplained, also allowed to take up a sixth share.

Raffles' explanation of his purchase of this land was that leading

Dutchmen, Engelhardt in particular, had been hesitant to bid lest the sales should be afterwards repudiated by the Supreme Government or by some future administration in Java. No doubt participation by the Lieutenant-Governor himself constituted, in the minds of those who were aware of it, a valuable insurance against such repudiation.

The sincerity of this statement by Raffles has been questioned in the light of a letter written to him by Engelhardt towards the end of December 1812. It is quoted by Dr Sollewijn Gelpke in his pamphlet, *The Lands Sold During the English Interregnum and the Prohibition of Feudal Services Thereon*, published in 1889.

"Four months ago," wrote Engelhardt, "Your Excellency observed to me that if you quitted your present office you would be disposed to fix your residence and become a landed proprietor of Java. I one day advised you to select the site of Campong Bahrue from Mr Tency. Campong Bahrue is beautiful, but it is not equal to those lands which will be sold in the Regency of Tjandjoer [Chianjur] on account of Government, the four lands called Pegadoengan, Tjiheulang, Tjimahi and Goenoeng Parang."[1]

"I informed him", stated Raffles, "that my former observations were made in the general nature of the conversation and that I never had any serious idea on the subject."

There is no evidence to the contrary. If he ever entertained such a notion, he dropped not even a hint of it to his many correspondents. The prospect of his supersession is referred to frequently in his letters, and what the future probably held in store for him. Surely Minto was right when he expressed the view that Raffles would be unwilling to stay in Java in any position below that of chief authority. It is hard to believe that he would have chosen to remain as a private individual in a colony of which he had been Lieutenant-Governor and which, in all probability, would shortly be returned to the Dutch.

Concerning Engelhardt's suggestion, he continued:

"He became, however, exceedingly pressing, and, on the next day, submitted to me the annexed papers, showing what the estates, if purchased, might be safely bought for, the other, what he conceived they might be worth upon a speculation. Although I felt disinclined to participate in any purchase, and did not possess the funds required to meet the proposal of Mr Engelhardt, I hesitated within myself whether, after his pressing invitation, and the rumours which had been industriously spread abroad regarding the possibility and even legality of the sale, it would be prudent for me to reject them. I had heard some days before from Mr Timmerman Thyssen, a merchant of considerable respectability, and

[1] Pegadingan, Chiulang, Chimahi and Gunong Parang (Chopper Mountain). These were the four lots purchased by Raffles and Engelhardt at the Batavia auction.

strongly attached to the British Government that the reports were likely to injure the sale; and party spirit then rose so high that such surmises were readily caught at; on consideration, therefore, I thought that my acceding to the proposal of Mr Engelhardt would at once remove all doubts in his mind. This was essential, because, if he had withdrawn from his avowed intention of purchasing, the suspicions and doubts that must have arisen in the minds of others would undoubtedly have been injurious to the public interest, as well as to the credit of Government. The lands which he proposed to purchase were those adjoining to his estate at Buitenzorg. They were a convenient acquisition to the Governor, inasmuch as they would afford Europe vegetables, and enable him to establish a herd of cattle, and obtain the convenience attached to a farm, of which the Government House at Buitenzorg had been deprived by the sale of the lands in its immediate neighbourhood by Marshal Daendels. . . ."

Whatever the rights or wrongs of his purchase of land, it was to have unfortunate repercussions, which will be considered in due course.

On 16th February 1813 it was recorded that the sales of land that had taken place and those then in progress were sufficient to cover the whole of the paper currency in circulation. The Council resolved that all further sales and contracts on account of government for paper money should be avoided, and that port duties should be accepted in cash only.

The Accountant-General at Fort William confirmed on 5th February that all Batavian paper should be withdrawn. Nevertheless, the Supreme Government was beginning to show alarm and disappointment over the unexpected financial difficulties of the colony, writing in a letter dated 18th February:

"We have observed with much regret that your drafts upon this Presidency have been very considerable, although the estimates and explanations received from you gave us reason to expect, that far from requiring aid from resources of India, a very large surplus revenue would be realized by your Government, even in the present year, 1813. We are aware that you have experienced a disappointment with regard to some of your expected receipts; but the deficiencies which have occurred can scarcely have absorbed any considerable proportion of the surplus fund of 2,000,000 Dollars which you expected to have in your Treasury on the 30th April next. We have been called upon from so many different quarters to furnish large supplies in the present and in the ensuing year, and the Honourable Court of Directors have lately urged us in such strong terms to extend our remittances as much as possible for the supply of the Home Treasury, that it is become absolutely necessary that we should not permit our resources to be touched upon from quarters where funds are not indispensably required. We deem it proper therefore to enjoin in the most positive manner that you do not grant any further Bills upon the

Treasuries of India unless the emergency should be such as to involve the safety of the public interests committed to your charge; and if contrary to all expectation and to the tenure of your assurances a want of funds should be experienced by your Government, we must beg that you reduce the public disbursement in all practicable cases so as to bring the charges of the Island within the revenue actually realized by you."

Concerning a change of government, Minto wrote again on 22nd February:

". . . I have to acquaint you with an honourable retreat, if your present office should pass into other hands. Mr Parker has been compelled by ill health to quit Bencoolen. If any obstacle should arise to the views which I suppose you might entertain on Java, in the event of a change of Government, or if you should prefer the Residence of Fort Marlborough [Bencoolen] to any other situation that might be open to you in the East, my resolution is to appoint you to succeed Mr Parker; it must not be forgotten at the same time that the orders of the Court of Directors are to place a Civil Servant on the Bengal establishment in that office. That circumstance will not prevent me from appointing you, because I feel myself the claims which made so strong an impression on me will be admitted by others. . . ."

There followed reference to his own recall to England.

"If there should be any hesitation on the subject, I should feel some reliance on the early exertion I shall have an opportunity of making in person at Home, my departure from hence being fixed for next January. . . . Pray let me know your wishes on the subject of your appointment at Bencoolen as soon as possible. But I shall take care to make the office accessible to you by an actual appointment, subject to your own option, as soon as I know with certainty that the present Government of Java is to be changed. You have had, and will still have, many competitors here, and some of the very highest rank, merit and pretensions in India; but so far as the power of this Government avails, you may consider the affair as decided."

Minto had learned of the appointment of his successor before receiving any warning that his own recall was even under consideration. In that month, February 1813, he was created Earl of Minto and Viscount Melgund, not in any recognition of his great services, but merely as compensation for his supersession, arranged to suit political aims and the demands of patronage, for which the Prince Regent was probably responsible.

Two days after Minto's letter to Raffles, John Palmer, the Calcutta banker, referred again to General Maitland in another letter to the Sultan of Pontianak, mentioning some "impediment to the General's departure from England", which made the date of his arrival uncertain.

To meet the financial situation in Java, two further steps were taken on 1st March. The first was the decision to withdraw the Batavia paper currency forthwith. The second was that the Lombard Bank, an old-established institution in Batavia, should be authorized, as a temporary measure, to grant loans on the security of property and valuables to such amount as individuals might require and government approve, and should issue acknowledgments payable at a fixed date. This step was found necessary to supply a circulating medium in the absence of paper currency, for specie was practically non-existent.

Subsequently (31st March), to increase the circulating medium still further, it was decided to issue notes of small denomination, not to exceed in total 250,000 Spanish dollars. Jacob Cranssen suggested that a colonial coinage should be introduced as soon as possible, and this was agreed to, but the absence of the necessary machinery, which had to be obtained from India, postponed for some time the issue of any such coins.

Gillespie was still critical of the financial measures of the government. "... the provisional transfer of the debts due to the public by Bills drawn on Bengal would be a measure more consonant with the provisional tenure of this Government and have left the Supreme Government or the future Government of this Colony greater latitude in modifying or altering an arrangement which can only be considered provisional."

Conditions in Bantam were causing concern. During the Dutch régime it had been a source of considerable trouble to them. In November 1805 the Dutch Resident, DuPuy, had been murdered, as a result of which Daendels had annexed Bantam and deposed the sultan. In deference to native opinion, his brother had been put on the throne and given an annual subsidy, but all power had been in the hands of the Dutch Prefect. In the following April the new sultan had proved troublesome and been removed, nominal sovereignty being entrusted to two princes. Further disturbances had developed, and in August it had been decided to divide Bantam into two areas, the uplands and the lowlands, the latter becoming the sole responsibility of the Dutch, the former being allowed its own native administration under a sultan of its own choice. The coastal forts constructed by Daendels had created serious local unrest by reason of forced labour and heavy mortality among the gangs.

Satisfied that the state of affairs in Bantam was still far from happy, Raffles visited the area in person in March and negotiated a settlement with the sultan whereby the uplands also were transferred, the sultan merely retaining his official style, with an annual allowance of 10,000 silver piastres. Bantam was thus reunited, and peaceful conditions allowed the country to recover gradually from the devastation and depopulation that had ravaged it. Major Yule was appointed Resident, and the land-rental scheme extended to that district.

Another event in March was the dismissal of C. G. Blagrave, the acting secretary, for misconduct. He was succeeded by Charles Assey. Blagrave never forgave Raffles for this. He hated him, and his hatred was of a very bitter and violent type, as later events were to prove.

John Billington Loftie, husband of Raffles' sister, Leonora, had died on 12th September 1812. At Buitenzorg, on 20th April 1813 she was married to Dr Thomas Campbell Brown of the Indian Medical Service, then working under Raffles.

The first meeting of the reconstructed Batavian Society of Arts and Sciences was held three days later, when Raffles, as president, outlined the early history of the Society and sketched what in his view should be its objects and ideals. He called particular attention to what he described as the "Further East" as an area for investigation. His contribution, actual and moral, to the Society established once more its right to an honourable place in the learned institutions of the Orient and indeed the world. His achievement has been fully recognized by the Dutch as one of the undisputed benefits conferred by him on the Dutch empire in the East.

The commission under Colonel Mackenzie and the enquiring mind of the Lieutenant-Governor combined to produce an investigation into Javanese affairs of an unparalleled intensity, covering huge areas of the island which had never been surveyed in detail by the Dutch. The complete subjugation by the British of Jokyakarta and Surakarta had extended European power over the island to a degree not previously achieved, or perhaps even desired, by their predecessors. That Mackenzie should have been in charge and, from his former experience in India, been inspired with a deep interest in archaeology, were factors certain to produce rich results. In this branch he was ably supported by Captain George Baker and two young Dutch officers, H. C. Cornelius and H. W. B. Wardenaar.

In the medical field, also, Raffles was not idle. The two great scourges of Java in his time were considered to be smallpox and syphilis. To-day science would have added malaria, but no knowledge of that infection was to be acquired for another hundred years, though Jesuit's bark, which was quinine, had long been recognized as a remedial drug.

Raffles was a great supporter of vaccination, which was slowly making headway in the civilized world. It was not unknown in Java, but the novel feature of Raffles' plan was that the total elimination of smallpox, and of syphilis too, from Java and Madura should be the deliberate objective of government, and more remarkable still, that the campaign to stamp out those diseases should be waged by native assistants specially trained for the purpose, the whole cost being borne by the state.

The introduction of these benefits was entrusted to Dr Hunter, the superintending surgeon, but his death in that year—a great loss to Java—prevented the early furtherance of the reform.

The 24th April was the anniversary of the founding in 1777 of the Batavian Society of Arts and Sciences. To mark the event, Raffles delivered a discourse at a meeting of the members on that day. This is printed as an appendix to the *Memoir*, containing nothing that need be quoted here.

The success of the new Lombard Bank notes was reported to India on the same day. They had been considered more valuable than the Batavian paper currency, and since their issue, up to eight rix-dollars in paper currency had been given for one Spanish dollar note.

"They continue still to keep up their value and the absolute demand for them in the want of specie that is still felt seems likely to prevent their depreciation. . . ."

To restrict the issue of such notes and to prevent their being required in such small sums as to become a very general circulation, it was decided to establish a new paper currency to a limited extent and to assist it by the introduction of a small coinage.

Raffles, with his usual optimism, wrote to Minto on 27th April:

"The measure of recalling the Batavian paper currency by the sale of lands has been attended with every success in retrieving the value of that currency."

The new coinage became available in May and was described in the *Java Gazette* on the 9th of that month. The Java rupee, which had a Javanese inscription on one side and an Arabic inscription on the other, was of silver and was legal tender at the rate of thirty stivers (Dutch pennies) to one rupee. Tin doits (half a farthing) made of pure Bangka tin were inscribed on one side "1 Doit" and on the other "Java 1813". These were legal tender for sums not exceeding ten Spanish dollars. Two hundred and sixty-four tin doits equalled one Spanish dollar or sixty-six stivers. This made them equal to copper doits.

There was more disagreement between Raffles and Gillespie. In May correspondence passed on the embarkation of men about to be invalided home. The military authorities asked that the sick soldiers should remain on the island until a ship was available to take them to England, as Bengal would be bad for their health. To this the Lieutenant-Governor replied:

"It can hardly be supposed that a sea voyage would be likely to injure or risk their health as much as remaining on the spot where they had contracted diseases which render it necessary to invalidate them."

Major Colebrooke, the military secretary, wrote back:

". . . the Commander of the Forces would not again have urged his sentiments, did not motives of humanity impel him to entreat the Honourable Lieutenant-Governor to reconsider his decision."

Raffles gave way not very graciously.

While this amiable correspondence was proceeding, a letter dated 8th May was on its way from India, announcing the appointment of a successor to Gillespie.

"Major-General Gillespie having solicited through his Excellency the Commander in Chief to be removed from the command of the forces in Java, we have the honour to inform you that we have determined to comply with General Gillespie's request and that we have this day appointed Major-General Miles Nightingall to the command of the forces in Java."

Nightingall would be arriving in the autumn.

It is clear from his letter dated 22nd May that Minto had come to the conclusion that the situation had become unbearable for Raffles, on whose side he stood firm, and that he had used his influence with Sir George Nugent, the G.O.C., to effect this transfer, "whereby a good retreat or rather an honourable advantageous station is prepared for Gillespie, whose military character and services I shall always admire and venerate". He added: "Another desirable consequence of this exchange I hope may be the suspending of the necessity of investigating and pronouncing upon his political conduct in Java."

As for General Maitland, Travers wrote in his diary:

"Accounts from Bengal state positively that the question of this Island may not be agitated until the Meeting of Parliament . . . and the new Governor could not well be expected before June or July. Nor did Lord Wellington's unequalled success in Spain or Bonaparte's failure in Russia afford half the interest that General Maitland's holding a Command in England did. We have not long enjoyed the news when a vessel arrived from the Isle of France with news of General Maitland having passed the Cape. Thus were we at this moment teased with contradictory reports."

Lord Minto's successor as Governor-General was to be Lord Moira, a professional soldier, better known by his later title of Marquis of Hastings. In a letter dated 10th May Minto wrote to Raffles:

"Although nothing is certain, I should think, on the whole, that Lord Moira will arrive in Bengal in July, or say by the 1st August. This expectation occasions a great embarrassment and anxiety about you; for the final decision concerning Java may not be known in the country during my Government and there will certainly be a difficulty in appointing you to Bencoolen if that should be the case; for I presume you would not wish to renounce Java definitely until the necessity for doing so should be positively ascertained. What I am doing at present is to keep Bencoolen open. . . ."

Action was being taken to meet the repeated demands of the Supreme Government that Java should live within its own income. On 28th May the following minute by the Lieutenant-Governor was adopted by the board:

"I now proceed to lay before the Board the reductions which appear to me practicable in the Civil Department with a view to bring the expenses of this Island within its certain and fixed revenues, and to render it independent of distant aid and of commercial speculation for the support of its finances. . . . I believe it will be found the general efficiency of the service is not materially affected."

Of the secretary's department he remarked:

". . . this office now includes every branch of the Public Service, the Public, Separate and Military Departments, and by the establishment of the principal office at Buitenzorg where the salubrity of the climate and removal from temptation to idleness and indulgence ensure a strict and regular attendance to business it has been practicable to effect a considerable reduction without injuring the real efficiency of the Department. . . .

"Whatever it may be eventually practicable to afford under a new system of revenue collection and under the removal of those commercial restrictions that now exist, the strictest economy is at present equally urgent, proper and unavoidable."

The effect of the economies was to reduce the monthly expenditure from 69,184 Spanish dollars to 57,047. In the military department, a saving of 9,029 dollars a month was anticipated, apart from 2,000 dollars a month formerly spent on the Amboynese dragoons. Together with other cuts, the estimated total saving on the next year's expenditure amounted to 447,105 dollars.

In forwarding an estimate of receipts to India, Raffles made the confident comment:

"In the meantime his Lordship in Council will perceive that the receipts of the current year are estimated to exceed the disbursements and that thus consequently no pecuniary aid will be required from the Supreme Government beyond the sum to be drawn on account of remittances to China."

ii

Even before arrival in Java, Raffles had reported at length on Japan and had discussed with Leyden the possibility of taking advantage of the small wedge in Japanese exclusiveness that the Dutch had managed to insert by means of a small factory maintained in complete isolation at Deshima, a tiny island off Nagasaki, to which two ships went from Java once a year, going up in the south-west monsoon and returning in the north-east monsoon.

It had been planned that Leyden should go to Japan, in charge of a couple of ships, to see if the Dutch trade could not be transferred to

Britain and put on a much wider and more general basis. His untimely death had made this impossible, but Raffles was still determined to carry out his plan and was, as ever, optimistic as to the result.

Much has been written on this particular venture, and a brief summary of events is all that need be given here. The situation was complicated. Japan had shut herself off completely from all intercourse with the outside world except China and the little Dutch factory at Deshima, so Raffles planned his expedition on the assumption that the Japanese were still unaware of the change in Java. This may have been true of Deshima, for the British blockade had made any visit impossible for some years, but it seems, as Miss Hahn points out in her *Raffles of Singapore*, improbable in the extreme that the Japanese authorities had not learned of it from Chinese traders who visited Japan as freely as they did Java.

The expedition was to sail under Dutch colours, not only because the only traders officially acceptable to the Japanese were the Dutch, but also because the British were regarded with special hostility. This was due to a visit paid by Sir Edward Pellew in H.M.S. *Phaeton* to Japanese waters in 1808. He had been looking for Dutch shipping and in his search had entered Nagasaki harbour. Although he had done no harm, the Japanese had been very frightened and therefore very angry. The Dutch at Deshima had no doubt done all they could to increase this prejudice against the British.

Raffles put in charge of the expedition Willem Wardenaar, a Dutchman who had once been factor at Deshima and is not to be confused with Colonel Mackenzie's young assistant. A Scottish surgeon, Dr Daniel Ainslie, went as second in command, but was intended to take charge at Deshima if it were found possible to hoist the British flag there. Raffles described Ainslie in his report to India as "a gentleman of very superior talents and education, in whom I place the highest and most unlimited confidence for the delicate situation in which it is possible he may be placed", but Ainslie seems to have been a queer character. A later note on him by Raffles refers to him as "of uncommon talent but eccentric".

The two ships chartered for the enterprise, *Charlotte* and *Mary*, did not get off until June 1813. There had been much correspondence with Calcutta, but the blessing of the Supreme Government in the person of Minto, who had consulted J. A. van Braam, Holland's agent in India, and obtained information corroborating Raffles' advice, had been officially received. The method of approach and Wardenaar's remuneration, which was considerable, had also been approved.

The cargoes of the vessels consisted chiefly of tin, lead, sugar, pepper, cloves, nutmegs, woollens and cottons. There was also a numerous and curious collection of presents for the Tokugawa Shogun, the Emperor of Japan: a Batavian almanack, ninety-two plants, twenty sheep, four civet cats, a day-and-night spyglass, ten decanters, and a number of other articles including some pounds of Egyptian mummy, a substance used at that time as a drug. But the gift that was expected to be the key to open the door of Japanese exclusiveness was a live elephant.

After a break of five years, Hendrik Doeff, the factor at Deshima, was no doubt delighted to see two ships arrive with Dutch colours and the usual recognition signals. He sent off two clerks, but they returned with the report that there was something queer about the ships. It was not because they had English-speaking crews. The Dutch had chartered American ships before. But these visitors had brought a special letter that only Doeff was to open. This was from Raffles and contained orders for him to hand over the factory to Wardenaar and Ainslie.

Doeff seemed ready to believe that the British had occupied Java, but he declined to accept the assurance that Holland had become a vassal state of France. Eventually, in consultation with Wardenaar, whose purpose was to defeat Raffles' intentions, the decision was taken to let one of the Japanese official interpreters into their confidence. His advice was to go on with the Dutch disguise. Terrible things, he alleged, would happen if the authorities discovered the subterfuge. The ships as well as the factory would be burned, and all the Europeans killed or imprisoned.

There was certainly a considerable risk to the factory, though what effective steps the Japanese could have taken against the two ships is hard to see. At all events, Ainslie, even if he did not believe the story, felt that any refusal to comply was too big a risk and, at least, the immediate commercial purpose of the venture could go on. He told Travers later that, before he left, some of the interpreters, with whom he had become friendly, said they had guessed he was English and suspected his reason for coming. They hinted pretty broadly that if he cared to come again he would be well received, no doubt for a suitable consideration.

The return cargo secured consisted of copper and camphor—and that magnificent gift, the elephant, which it was found impossible to land and had to be taken back to Java. Nevertheless, the Japanese imagination was deeply stirred. Inasmuch as this was only the fourth time that an elephant had been brought to Japan, its arrival was looked upon as a happy omen. An unfortunate Russian envoy, detained up-country as a prisoner for daring to visit Japan, was given the most intimate details of it by his guards, and pictures of elephants by Japanese artists had a remarkable vogue. That reproduced here is taken from a small book now in the possession of Professor C. R. Boxer. It is entitled *Zen-zō katsu-gau*, which may be rendered "a quick perception of the whole elephant". Woodblock printed, presumably at Nagasaki, in the year of the elephant's arrival, it is a collection of essays and verses by local scholars, priests and poets in celebration of a highly auspicious event. On the fly-leaf of

Professor Boxer's copy, written in Dutch by the hand of Hendrik Doeff, are details and measurements of the animal brought from Java.

The *Charlotte* and the *Mary* set off back for Java, leaving Doeff confirmed in charge of the Deshima factory. Jan Cock Bloomhoff, one of his staff, returned with Wardenaar and Ainslie to convey to Raffles Doeff's terms for the continuance of these camouflaged visits.

Meanwhile in Java, Raffles, undeterred by threatened changes in the administration, was busy with his scheme of land reform. As Travers wrote:

"In obtaining the necessary information to enable him to frame such a system as, whilst it abolished the vicious practices hitherto pursued in the Island, would strengthen the resources of the Island . . . the greatest exertion was required on Mr Raffles' part, and he devoted himself with his accustomed enthusiasm to the task; night and day he worked at it. . . ."

On 14th June, satisfied with the progress of his experiments to date, Raffles laid before the board his general views on the scheme of land rents and proposed, for the board's consideration, its extension throughout the greater part of Java. The minute was of considerable length and only brief extracts can be recorded here. He began by calling attention to the abundant and authentic information then available from the efforts of the Mackenzie commission and government records. He put the disadvantages and inconveniences of the old situation as follows:

"The loss derived to the public by a delivery of produce, the sale of which may be uncertain, and the waste and expense of which is unavoidable, is not a more urgent reason for an alteration than its oppression upon the inhabitants and its discouragement to agriculture. While the Regent is bound to deliver a certain quantity of money and produce, and the feudal services of the people can be called for, to an unlimited extent, by former usage and the influence of ancient habits, there can be no security against oppression nor any excitement to industry; and the revenue of the State must equally suffer by the number of intermediate hands through whom it is collected, by the expense of subordinate officers in charge of the produce, by wastage of the produce itself, and by the irregularities and temptations to which the system gives rise.

"To the employment of the population on these feudal services which being undefined are not limited to the demands of the Government but are liable to be extended at the caprice or convenience of the local authorities, European and Native, may in a great measure be attributed the degraded situation of the lower class of the inhabitants and the emigrations which have taken place, notwithstanding the peculiar and strong attachment of the Javanese to the residence and tombs of their forefathers, to those spots in which such services were less frequently called for. In this manner the comparatively greater population in the districts of the native Princes and in the Blandong Districts[1] may also be accounted for.

"In the former, although feudal service exists in full force, the demands for it under an indolent Government who pursue no plans of internal improvement wherein labour would be required . . . are much less considerable than in the other districts where the public works conducted during the administration of Marshal Daendels became a serious drain upon a population already inadequate to the extent and fertility of the Island; while in the Blandong Districts which have been exclusively appropriated to the labours of the forests, and wherein the people have been exempted from any other service, it is known that the amount of the population has in some instances nearly doubled since the foundation of this separate establishment. . . .

"Whether therefore we view a departure from this system as it may affect an improvement in the revenue of the State or of promoting the civilization and happiness of the people and the consequent welfare and prosperity of the Colony, it appears that we are equally called upon to introduce a more liberal and beneficent system of administration; and that which has been adopted in British India, the benefits and advantages of which have stood the test of experience, presents itself on many accounts as the best which we can select for our guide. The only hesitation or doubt which can exist arises in selecting the particular principles on which it shall be carried into effect as adapted to the local circumstances of Java, and the habits, customs and prejudices of its inhabitants."

He then proceeded to deal with land tenure in Java. After quoting considerably from the report of Colonel Mackenzie, under which it appeared that all land was vested in the sovereign, he continued:

"Without at present entering into the details of the present system . . . I now proceed to state, for the consideration of the Board, the outlines of the amended system which I am desirous of introducing in its stead. As the foundation of the amended system I would propose:—1st The entire abolition of all forced delivery of produce at inadequate rates and of all feudal services, with the establishment of a perfect freedom in cultivation and trade. 2nd The assumption on the part of Government of the immediate superintendence of the lands with the collection of the revenues and rents thereof, without the intervention of the Regents whose office should in future be confined to public duties. 3rd The renting out of the lands so assumed in large or small estates according to local circumstances on leases for a moderate term.

"On the first point it is unnecessary to say more than that it is essential under any system that may be pursued, which has for its object the amelioration of the present condition of the inhabitants. . . . With the

[1] Forest country, not a place-name.

abolition of forced deliveries, the opening of free trade and commerce necessarily follows. . . . It may be sufficient . . . to observe, that, from the experience of the last years, it would seem that the produce of rice in Java is much less than the demand, and that it might even be found necessary to prohibit exportation, in order to keep the requisite quantity on the Island to guard against the possible failure in a future crop. There is therefore no doubt that in this Island a market will be found for whatever the lands produce; but it may be expected . . . that whenever the cultivator has experienced his right to the full produce and profit of his industry, that industry will increase. . . . As soon as circumstances admit, all the duties of import and export of Colonial produce should be abolished.

"By the difficulties which have for several years past existed in the exportation from Java and the arbitrary price fixed on its produce by the late Government and hitherto continued as the estimated part of the revenue, Java is in danger of losing the valuable trade in rice and salt which she formerly carried on with Malacca and the Malay Peninsula. It is well known that since this difficulty commenced, the number of Siamese junks trading to those ports has considerably increased; and that unless the Colonial produce of this Island be permitted to find its fair and relative value in foreign markets by abolishing the fixed prices which prevent its being worth the purchase of exportation, we are actually injuring the resources of the Colony, both by preventing a competition abroad, and by retaining at home a quantity of perishable produce, the value of which is only found in the estimated sales which under those circumstances cannot be effected. Thus it is that the fixed price of timber effectually deters all purchasers; and thus it would also be with rice. . . .

"Although therefore it might be advisable and necessary as a source of revenue to maintain the high price on such monopolies as may be held by Government for such part of the article as is consumed on the Island, it appears to me essential that every facility be given, by public sales and the reduction of duties, to the purchase of Colonial produce for exportation. . . .

"On the second and most important point, viz. the assumption of the immediate superintendence of the land on the part of Government . . . the only difficulty which occurs is the mode in which the Regent shall be provided for. . . . It is suggested that the Regents and the subordinate officers should be employed exclusively in police duties. . . . With regard to the employment of the Regents . . . in the interior police of the country under the immediate and vigilant superintendence of the Resident and his Assistants, it is obvious that the regulations must depend much on local circumstances. It is not intended to alter in any material degree the system or regulations of police as it exists in the interior of the country. . . .

"An arrangement of this nature may be considered a political mode of employing many persons of influence and now in authority, who would otherwise require to be pensioned, and who would not experience, under these circumstances, the disgust which might follow the removal from office. It will evidently be prudent not to abolish the rank, title or state of the present native Chiefs; but as far as practicable, it would be advisable to do away the system of paying for services by appropriations of land. The officers, generally speaking, should depend for their salaries immediately on the treasury of Government; but in cases of the Regents and some others it may be judicious to allow them to become proprietors of estates on the system now proposed. . . . It is worthy of consideration whether it would not be advisable to secure the influence of the principal Priests throughout the Island by taking them into the pay of Government. . . .

"With regard to the third point, the renting out of the lands, I conceive that the establishment of a money rent is to be always kept in view; and although the present circumstances of the Island may preclude its immediate adoption, that it should, partially and as far as practicable, be introduced. The only objection which exists, is how far the quantity of circulating medium on the Island and the actual property of the renters of the land, would admit of its being carried into effect; or in other words, whether the want of any other circulating medium or property might not occasion the lands to be rented below their value, and also diminish too considerably the amount of the existing revenue. Under these considerations, it becomes important to afford every aid to the cultivators in the payment of their rents, that can possibly be consistent with the principle now stated. It appears to me beyond a doubt that the introduction of a money rent would bring forward a large proportion of coin which at present lies unemployed, but that there does exist a necessity of receiving for some time a portion of the rent in kind. . . .

"With respect to the persons to whom the land should be let . . . I am of the opinion that the following principles may be laid down for their [the commissioners'] guidance.

> "That it is an established principle to grant the leases to persons as near the actual cultivator as possible.
>
> "That consequently in every instance where the Bakal or Head man of the peasantry is found able to rent a small lot, parcel or ground, he should have a preference; unless such preference would from local circumstances and enquiry be found to clash materially with the interests of a native with whom it is advisable to provide for on the spot.
>
> "That as it is the object and intention of Government to employ the native Chiefs as immediate officers of police, their interests and

goodwill may be conciliated, partly by the rank and ceremony which they will thus acquire, and partly by admitting them to become renters; in which case it will only be an object to render the estates personally rented by them as limited as possible.

"That where no objection exists, a preference be invariably given to the immediate possessor. . . .

"Thus the country will be divided into larger or smaller estates. . . . This arrangement of large estates might also be considered temporary and may be further modified at a future settlement when the cultivators have from the actual possession of the land, acquired some knowledge of the right of property . . . and with this view as well as to prevent the manifold and obvious objections against a perpetual settlement, arising both from the existing state of society among the Javanese, and the present circumstances of the Colony, I should propose that the land be rented for a period not exceeding three years. . . .

"It will necessarily form a part of the arrangements to be concluded, that the renter shall engage to keep the roads and bridges in repair (with the exception of the great military road), and also to furnish labour, carriages, &c, when required for the public service; but I propose that . . . the person so furnished be regularly paid for. . . .

" The Board will observe that . . . no allusion has been made to any class of people except the native Javanese. . . . I conceive the admission of Europeans to rent lands in the interior would be too great a breach of the habits and customs of the people at the first introduction of a change. . . . And the notorious extortion and manners of the Chinese . . . renders it imperiously necessary that they should be carefully excluded.

"It remains to lay before the Board my views with regard to the coffee cultivation and the Blandongs or separate establishment maintained on account of the teak forests. . . . It is evident that on the one hand the culture is under present circumstances, a very considerable loss to Government, while on the other hand, it would become a valuable export whenever the commerce of the Continent, or even that with America again opens up. . . .

"The following observations become necessary. . . . The cultivation of coffee has been carried to such extents in the Eastern Districts, that it has been forced in many instances upon soil totally unfit for it and carried to an extent which it would be impossible for Government to continue. . . . By far the greater part of these coffee gardens are not yet productive, and a large proportion of them will not yield any produce for three or four years more. . . . Nevertheless, the population has been exclusively appropriated . . . for the cleaning and preservation of these grounds . . . much labour is thereby lost which might be more profitably bestowed. . . . If these coffee gardens in the Eastern Districts were in full produce, the outlay for purchasing that produce would be more than, under the existing commercial difficulties, the finances of this Colony could conveniently be brought to support. . . . The cultivation of that plant can be considerably extended in the Western Districts if required. . . . It is clearly and decidedly my opinion that Government should cease to enforce the cultivation in those (Eastern) Districts, and restrict their measures to afford a market for such part of the produce only as cannot be sold by the renters. . . .

"I should therefore propose that the further advance of money by Government do cease in Cheribon and the Eastern Districts, and that the plantations be rented in common with other lands for a term of three years under such restrictions and regulations as would adequately provide for their preservation from injury; that the further cultivation of coffee on account of Government be exclusively confined to the Batavian Regencies in which it is not intended at present to introduce the new system; that . . . the free exportation of coffee by individuals be admitted; and provisionally, the Government should receive any that may be tendered at their stores at a price not exceeding what they pay for the same in the Regencies. . . .

"In the coffee gardens in the Western Districts disposed of to individuals by the late Government, the proprietors are only permitted to dispose of their coffee for the consumption of the Island. . . . I am decidedly of opinion that a more liberal policy should be pursued and the cultivators of coffee as well in the Western as in the Eastern Districts allowed a free exportation. . . .

"With regard to the Blandongs . . . there appears to be no objections whatever to the whole of the Blandong Districts being included in the general arrangement. By letting the whole of these lands in common with the others, by which one uniform system will be established throughout, and reserving in a clause in the Lease the right of employing such of the population as may be required in the forests on a remission of rent, every difficulty will be removed, the whole population of the country will look up to the chief authority, while such proportion only as may be required for the labours of the forest will be allotted for that service. Government will at once know the actual expense of the Forest Department and the peculiar advantages of the Blandong system, as far as it relates to the internal management and administration of the forests, will be equally well secured. . . .

"In concluding this Minute . . . I will only observe that upon a fair calculation it may be assumed, one of the Districts alone [will] eventually afford a fixed territorial revenue equal to what the whole furnish under the present system; and that the whole of the Eastern Districts taken together will produce a land rent exceeding two millions and a half of

Spanish Dollars annually instead of much less than one-tenth of that sum as at present.

"I am fully aware of the objections which may be raised against the introduction of so new and extensive an arrangement at a period when the future administration of the Colony is perhaps undetermined, and of the apprehensions which may be entertained of our proceedings fettering the future Government of the settlement . . . but on the other hand we are also to consider that the proposed arrangement has been in contemplation from the day of the fall of Djocjakarta, that it has already been proceeded on to a considerable extent, and that the minds of the inhabitants are at this moment fully prepared for the change.

"Its general adoption throughout the Island has been delayed for the last six months on the expectation of information from Europe; and the period seems now to have arrived when it must be generally introduced or dropped perhaps for ever . . . it would be highly gratifying for me to receive the recorded opinion and sentiments of each Member of the Board on the subject. These with our final resolution will of course be submitted for the consideration and orders of the Supreme Government; but if the decision is favourable to the measure itself, I do not see any necessity for delaying its execution pending a reference, during which the only practicable season and opportunity for its advantageous introduction may be lost. The Board will observe that I have not adverted to the mode in which the new system should be generally introduced, that will remain for subsequent consideration; at present I am only desirous of establishing the justice, practicability and advantage of the new system; and when this object is attained, I shall have the honour to suggest the plan which it appears to me advisable to pursue in effecting the gradual and advantageous introduction."

Captain Travers wrote:

"When first this measure was proposed, it met, if not with opposition, with at least such a cold and cautious approval from the members of Council, some of whom spoke from long experience, and a supposed knowledge of the native character, as would have damped the ardour of a less zealous mind than Mr Raffles possessed; and indeed it was the opinion of almost every Dutchman with whom he conversed, that such a system would never succeed, and that the attempt to introduce it would be attended with very bad consequences."

Muntinghe was not enthusiastic. He recorded his views on the proposals in a minute dated 28th July. After agreeing with Raffles that the objects were worthy of the British nation, he continued:

"The amelioration however of the natives of this Island, though undoubtedly a consideration of the highest moment in the eyes of humanity, seems to me to become only a secondary object in a political point of view; and with the exception of every measure contrary to the principles of justice and equity it appears to me that the safest principle that can be adopted to judge of the propriety of any Colonial regulations, or of any changes or alterations to be introduced therein is [our italics] *that every Colony does or ought to exist for the benefit of the mother country.*

"The second object proposed, namely, the amelioration of the financial state of the Colony, appears therefore to me to deserve the first consideration in a political point of view. To decide in favour of a change of so much importance as the system of land revenue, the advantage to the public finances should not only be great, but clear and certain. They should moreover be calculated in a fair manner and be drawn up after a comparison of all the profits and benefits derived from a system of monopoly with those which may be obtained by a land revenue.

"And finally to justify an operation involving so many consequences and so many chances to which a change of system must be liable, some urgent reason should exist to deviate from the present one."

He then sketched the attempts made by the Dutch to improve the position. Mr van der Hook, one of the directors at home, had shown from extracts from the Dutch East India Company's books that, from the beginning of 1700, the expenses in Java had continued to increase and to exceed the revenue. The government had been so impressed by his views that the commissioners sent out in 1793 had been instructed that the expenses must be reduced so as to equal the revenue.

The commissioners had made their report on 4th July 1796, in the year after the dissolution of the Dutch Company, which had incurred a debt it could not meet of 160,000,000 florins, partly due to losses sustained during the war from 1782 to 1786, but mainly to maladministration. The commissioners had proposed to retain the monopoly system, but to introduce reductions in expenses. Their commercial estimates had proved unreliable, and the colony had continued to be a burden on the mother country. This had made it imperative that if Holland was not to subsidize Java, the colony's revenue must be secured on a basis not exposed to the vicissitudes of trade carried on by private individuals. It had been generally considered that the charter of the British East India Company was a model to be followed, but as the Dutch Company had deliberately thrown a cloak over its own activities, it had been felt impossible to decide on a definite line of policy. Accordingly, in 1803, a committee of experienced persons had sat at The Hague to formulate recommendations.

The report of this committee, dated 4th August 1803, was opposed to any violent changes. Contingents of rice and feudal services were to be retained, together with the coffee and pepper monopolies, though free trade and cultivation were recommended for minor produce. The rest of the report dealt with general administration, the separation of government duties from the direction of trade, a board of revenue and commerce, and improved judicial and police regulations.

Public opinion had been much divided on the question of feudal services and monopoly, and in regard to the latter, the government had not followed the recommendation of the committee but had resolved that coffee and pepper were to be left to free trade and cultivation. The changes in the government of Holland had prevented any further steps being taken, and when Marshal Daendels had been appointed Governor he had merely been instructed to remove the more intolerable oppressions immediately, and to report in due course how far the Hague committee's recommendations were really suitable.

The position in Java under Britain, observed Muntinghe, was different. No longer was the colony cut off from trade with Europe or liable to the losses sustained in war; no longer was there the long history of waste and mismanagement or a pressing urgency that the colony should cease to be a financial burden on the mother country. Even assuming that under the existing arrangements and the present stagnation of trade, Java should fail to pay her way, such a loss would be more than offset by the political value of the island to Great Britain.[1] Any risk therefore to the tranquillity of the country, in whatever degree, would be proportionately less justifiable. If the new system could be introduced without upsetting the country, there were strong arguments in favour of the change. Sooner or later the system of monopoly and feudal services must produce in some degree the same evil consequences, even under the present government, quite apart from the arbitrary rule involved being completely at variance with British institutions and the privileges granted to private trade under the British charter; and though the continuance of the Dutch system for a further period might be justifiable, sooner or later it must be brought into line with British practice elsewhere.

The Lieutenant-Governor had proposed the abolition of all feudal services and forced deliveries, substituting for these free cultivation and trade, with a moderate land rent on short leases. As these proposals struck at the very root of the trouble, they appeared suitable for the purpose and were likely to be far more successful than the compromise proposals of the Hague committee, which preserved feudal services, permitting free cultivation and trade only for the less important products. At the same time, it had to be remembered that monopolies formed the backbone of the colonial revenue, so that a scheme must be produced that would create an equivalent revenue as soon as the new system came into operation.

On further analysis of the scheme, Muntinghe found it appropriate and just, yet he reflected on the effect it might create among the ruling

[1] This opinion was not supported by the East India Company!

classes, who would be deprived of much of their influence and of prerogatives based on long usage. He quoted the saying: "The breath of opinion might dissolve the British power in India."

The methods proposed for conciliating the chiefs and the gradual steps it was intended to follow seemed to him sound, but the risk remained.

"The advantages to be derived therefrom may be considered under two different points of view either with regard to the fate and happiness of the inhabitants of the Island, or with regard to the revenue and resources of Government. With regard to the inhabitants themselves it is undoubtedly as it was stated by the Honourable Lieutenant-Governor a grand object . . . to emancipate at once the whole mass of the population of this Island . . . but it might perhaps be questioned whether this object will be as fully attained as it is sincerely and humanely intended under the present system? In the first place the authority of the native Chiefs and Regents is to be continued in matters of police; and this measure seems unavoidable to prevent discontent and preserve the public tranquillity. But who is to control this power of police with regard to feudal services and other exactions, customary and usual under the former system? Who will prevent the lower class of Javanese from showing to their Regents the same veneration, the same subjection and from bestowing upon them the same services and contributions which they think it next to a religious duty to offer and perform? The system of feudal services may therefore be abolished with regard to Government, but it seems difficult to prevent its continuation with regard to the native Chieftains.

"In the second place the intention . . . is clearly that the leases of land should be granted as far as possible to the lowest class of inhabitant and to the actual occupiers and cultivators of the ground. But here another alternative seems to be unavoidable, that either the lower class of cultivators will from their poverty be unable to rent the lands for themselves, or that their petty Chief, the Bakal or Demang, renting for them their labour and produce thereof will again be at his command as under the feudal system. These Bakals and Demangs will however in all probability become the principal renters from Government. Some of them may possess on their farm one or two hundred families, and the general mass of people may therefore not derive much advantage from the change as it is really intended."

On the whole, he favoured the proposals, but considered that a more accurate financial statement, which no doubt could be based on the expected report of Colonel Mackenzie, would be required to justify the change from a financial aspect.

"The statement, however, to be fair and conclusive, should not only exhibit the loss and additional expense sustained by Government on account of the abolition of feudal services and contingents, but it should moreover include a probable estimate of the profits which in ordinary times, and on an average, were derived from the sale of coffee, sugar and other articles of trade which under a system of monopoly formed the chief resources of this Colony. Unless deceived [persuaded?] by a more accurate statement I must confess to entertain some doubts concerning the financial benefits of this system by which a number of new and additional expenses in specie will become unavoidable; or perhaps a great part of the revenue will not be receivable in money but in kind only, and while under a lease of lands exclusively to the natives the whole produce and resources of the Island will in future probably be confined to the cultivation of the favourite article of rice. And this single article, however valuable it may be for the internal consumption of the Island and for the exportation to some parts of India, does hardly appear to me sufficient to compensate the profits that may be derived from other valuable articles which the rich soil of Java may afford for a European market."

He considered, however, that the exemption of the Batavian and Preanger Regencies[1] and the acceptance of coffee freely delivered to the government at fixed rates should be sufficient to prevent this important brand of cultivation from falling into decay.

iii

It is evident that Raffles accepted Lord Minto's suggestions regarding Bencoolen. Minto wrote from India on 22nd June:

"I cannot safely wait longer for authentic accounts of the resolution taken in England concerning Java; and I have, therefore, adopted the measure of at once appointing you formally to Fort Marlborough; to take effect on your being relieved from your present office or resigning it; the allowances to commence from the time of your departure from Java. . . . I learnt with great pleasure that you have determined to accept the Residency of Fort Marlborough. When I first made this proposition I was not aware that I might soon lose the power of making the appointment. I have since felt considerable uneasiness lest I should be overtaken by an event which cannot be distant, and disabled from accomplishing an object which I have so much at heart."

A political problem inherited by Raffles from Daendels was Cheribon,[2] where there had long been complete anarchy. In July 1813 he managed to reach an agreement with the sultan whereby the management of Cheribon became the direct responsibility of the British Government, in

[1] See footnote, page 197.

[2] "The western portion of it is peopled by the Sundas and the eastern by the Javanese; and hence, perhaps, its name, correctly Charuban, which in Javanese means 'mixture'." Crawfurd, *Descriptive Dictionary*.

return for which the sultan received an annual allowance equivalent to the annual revenue he had hitherto derived from it.

"On Sunday last", we read in the *Java Gazette*, "the Lieutenant-Governor gave a déjeuner and fishing party to the Sultans of Cheribon . . . the whole party assembled about nine o'clock at the Government House and proceeded in carriages to the scene of operations, a romantic spot situated on the banks of the great river. A spacious temporary building had been constructed for the occasion, fitted up in a style which united simplicity with comfort. The first object which attracted the attention of the company on their arrival was a native band which after playing some minutes on their different instruments entirely composed of bamboo tubes, and accompanying them with their voices, commenced a Malay dance . . . breakfast was then announced, which was laid out with taste, and the Governor's band played during the repast several popular tunes and pieces of music . . . a few minutes after the company were seated at a distance of a few furlongs up the river some intoxicating vegetable was thrown into the river by which the fish become immediately inebriated and are consequently impelled by the current on the floor of the building (this was erected over the river) and become an easy prey to the persons stationed there with nets to take them. . . . After enjoying the sport for about an hour, the party returned highly delighted with the diversion of the day."

Raffles attached much importance to these official celebrations, in which both he and Olivia entertained a varied stream of guests who came and went.

The dispatch dated 8th May concerning the replacement of Gillespie by General Nightingall was brought to Java by Minto's son, Captain George Elliot, who arrived at Batavia in July. It seems that it was his added mission, at the wish of his father, to restore harmony between Raffles and Gillespie. Travers wrote:

". . . a reconciliation took place between my worthy Patron and General Gillespie which was effected through the interference of the Honourable Captain George Elliot . . . it is difficult to say how far such a reconciliation can be cordial after what has passed or what great object there could be in effecting it. . . ."

According to himself, Elliot was constantly in demand to settle disputes between these two. He wrote in his memoirs:

"During my whole stay on the coast of Java this time, which I suppose exceeded six months, I never came to Batavia (the headquarters) that I had not to make up the differences between the Governor (Mr Raffles) and General Gillespie, the Commander of the Forces and also senior member in Council. It was not possible for two such men to agree. Raffles, though a clever man, was neither born nor bred a gentleman—

and we all know that the nicer habits and feelings of a gentleman are not to be acquired—he was full of trick and not so full of the truth as was desirable, and he was the most nervous man I ever knew. Gillespie was an Irishman, a gentleman in all his feelings, but a very peppery one; a very gallant officer who utterly despised anyone who did not come up to his ideas of the necessary personal courage to constitute a gentleman—scorned trick or subterfuge or any attempt at deception; and consequently thoroughly despised the Governor. Both saw the impropriety of the two chief officers in the Island being at daggers drawn and constant variance. Gillespie was my friend and I would have done anything for him while he was at the same time ready to submit to anything that I advised. Raffles looked to me as a friend, and his having been appointed Governor by my father, I was anxious to assist him out of the foolish scrapes he was constantly getting into with Gillespie—for they were usually both in the wrong. But I really never could have any real feeling of friendship with the man, and he had a low set of people about him, all of some talent but unfit for advisers, particularly as to gentlemanlike conduct. They made up their quarrels before me with all sorts of protestations as to future forbearance and good determinations which both probably intended to adhere to; but I knew very well that within a fortnight after my back was turned there would be open war again, and so it ever was. Raffles was a very able man with his pen, and well understood the habits and peculiarities of the Eastern people; but he was unfit to govern and had the fatal misfortune of never inspiring Europeans with respect; again there was no more daring, active and zealous officer than Gillespie, but he was a hotheaded, if not a wrong headed Irishman, excellent as a second-in-command, but unfit for a chief, even as a military man, and still less calculated to take part in a civil government. They were a constant annoyance to me and I felt all along that I could do no permanent good. When Lord Hastings [Moira], the new Governor-General, put it fairly to me at Calcutta to know what could be done, I was obliged to say they should be separated, and Gillespie was given a command in India."

Nowhere else is there to be found any reference to these frequent endeavours at mediation on the part of Elliot, nor is there any other known evidence of acute differences having arisen between Raffles and Gillespie immediately after the capture of Java, the time to which Elliot refers. His memory has also misled him, for it was Minto, not Moira, who was Governor-General when Gillespie was recalled to India. At any rate, on the particular occasion when Elliot is known to have intervened, he found the situation very much better than he could have anticipated. At the ball to celebrate the King's birthday on 4th June, Gillespie had suddenly invited Olivia to lead off with him. She had accepted the invitation and, as Travers records, "such a pair were not certainly in the room". He continues:

"The apparent cordiality between the General and Mrs Raffles was attended with the best effect. On the following morning Mr Raffles visited the General and everything seemed settled to keep up appearances better in the future."

After commenting that it was the plain duty of both to do so, he cautiously adds:

"To restore the former cordiality between our Chiefs is not to be expected, but it is not difficult to soften a little the present animosity which is, I think, of importance and ought to be the object of their Staff. It is, I must declare, the wish of mine."

Difficulties concerning currency arose in that July. Muntinghe called attention to debts contracted in silver that had to be repaid in silver, government paper being legal tender only up to fifty dollars. The shortage of silver was so acute that Muntinghe considered that there should be appointed an arbitration court to arrange for payment in government paper at a suitable discount. Alternatively, in order not to discredit paper, he suggested that, if a debtor could not obtain cash for payment except at a great loss, settlement should be postponed. Further, old debts in Batavian currency had been converted into silver at the rate of ten, nine, or even six-and-a-half rix-dollars for one Spanish silver dollar before it had become known that there was to be a new government issue. Muntinghe recommended that these contracts should be cancelled to relieve the demand for silver. Cranssen expressed the opinion that such procedure would be contrary to all legal practice. At a later meeting it was agreed that, in all cases where debt was originally contracted in all Batavia paper currency and subsequently changed into silver, the certificates of new paper currency, which had been expressly issued in lieu of the former and declared payable in place thereof, could be considered available in payment. A complaint was also brought before the Council that English officers would pay their bills only at the rate of ten rix-dollars paper per Spanish dollar. The Council ordered legal proceedings to be taken against those who refused to pay their debts in a proper manner.

Probolingo paper had also to be considered in the light of recent tragic events. The two large areas of Probolingo and Besuki, which had been sold by Daendels to Chan Pit, had been exploited ruthlessly by him and were seething with discontent. Displaced Javanese had turned to armed robbery for a living, and a general exodus of the population from that part of the country threatened.

On their way to spend a day at Probolingo, Colonel Fraser, his wife, Captain McPherson and three other officers had been attacked by a large party of bandits. Fraser and McPherson had been taken prisoners and later murdered. The incident had not been a demonstration against the British; it merely illustrated the lawless state of the district. A punitive force under Major Forbes had been sent up from Surabaya, the chief of the band captured and a hundred and fifty of his followers killed in the fight.

Chan Pit was frightened. He asked the government to resume possession of the lands, and this, subject to confirmation by Calcutta, Raffles agreed to do. It was decided that treasury notes bearing six per cent per annum would be issued in exchange for Probolingo paper at the rate of forty Spanish dollars for each Probolingo note of one hundred rix-dollars.

A curious Palembang incident was to provide the third of the enemies who were later to attack Raffles in India.

Captain Robison will be remembered as having been bearer of messages from General Auchmuty to the courts of Solo and Jokyakarta announcing the surrender of General Janssens, and having taken upon himself to enter then into some sort of agreement with the courts, which Raffles had later to repudiate. Subsequently, with the rank of major, he had been appointed Resident at Palembang and his work, particularly his activities in Bangka, had won approval. On 30th July, when due to be relieved by Major M. H. Court as Resident at Palembang, he arrived at Batavia.

He then reported for the first time that he had, by friendly agreement with the sultan, Najimu'd-din, whom Gillespie had put on the throne, restored the previous sultan, Badru'd-din, who, on the capture of Palembang, had fled into the jungle and remained there. In support of his actions, Robison had brought with him the eldest son of Badru'd-din, with a number of *pangeran* (chiefs) and followers, together with various representatives of Najimu'd-din. This announcement caused general astonishment. That a Regent should depose a sultan whose installation had been a definite act of policy on the part of his government and had been ratified by the Supreme Government, and that he should have done this, not only without submitting to higher authority any proposal for the change, but also simply acting at his own discretion, this certainly was a very remarkable step. It was not, therefore, surprising that rumours soon got about that Badru'd-din had paid handsomely for his restoration. As in fact he had: Robison brought with him to Batavia the gift of £200,000 to the Java government.

The problem presented to Raffles was not a simple one. His own Resident had entered upon a specific treaty with an ex-sultan, and the reigning sultan had apparently accepted his dismissal. There was, too, considerable evidence that Badru'd-din was a much more powerful and popular figure than his brother, Najimu'd-din. He had, moreover, carried off with him the whole of the state treasure, so that Najimu'd-din had found it difficult, even with an English subsidy, to maintain himself in anything like the style of a sultan of Palembang. Lack of cash had, too, inevitably reduced his influence among the principal chiefs. Even in Batavia, quite a number of persons had expressed sympathy with Badru'd-din, being inclined to ascribe the murder of the Dutch garrison to his son. Gillespie, on the other hand, was loud in abuse of Badru'd-din.

When the Council met to consider what action should be taken, Raffles announced that the treaty negotiated by Robison must be annulled. This was agreed, and also that a commission should be sent to reinstate Najimu'd-din. Captain George Elliot was appointed leader, the other members being Court, the new Resident; Major W. Colebrooke, acting as agent for the East India Company; and Lieut.-Colonel McGregor, with a force of some four hundred European troops. The expedition left on 7th August. Robison was informed that the whole of his proceedings in connexion with the treaty were disapproved and that his conduct would be the subject of enquiry. In all these measures, Gillespie concurred fully.

Of the reconciliation between Raffles and Gillespie Travers wrote during that month:

". . . it has already been attended with one most beneficial and happy event, that of ensuring a cordial and unreserved co-operation in the measures adopted towards Palembang. . . . Had they separated immediately after the event, it would have given me sincere pleasure, but as there is some probability of the General not being relieved for some time, I must confess that I am not overjoyed at the circumstances as I know the temper, disposition and views of both parties and am very certain they cannot long remain on terms. . . ."

Later in the month, Travers made further reference to this subject:

"On the 24th the Governor and Staff dined by particular invitation with the General and to a person unacquainted with preceding events, these two characters would have appeared a second Castor and Pollux . . . a most unreserved conversation took place between these two Chiefs, the result of which was reiterated professions of unlimited friendship and goodwill."

The anniversary of the major battle in the conquest of Java was celebrated on the 26th.

"The Hero of Cornelis, the Gallant Rollo presided . . . the General gave Mr Raffles' health in proper glee and seemed to feel an interest in having it drunk with spirit and paid all respect."

During that month, Captain Robert C. Garnham, a member of Raffles' personal staff, was dispatched to Borneo with a view to further steps for the suppression of piracy. It will be remembered that an expedition under Colonel Watson had been successful at Sambas.

"The measures lately adopted against Sambas", wrote Raffles, "had in view the public chastisement of that State on account of the piracies it had sanctioned and was unconnected with every idea of the extension of territory. . . . The line of policy to be adopted with regard to the Malay States is to confine the trade to certain acknowledged and regulated ports. These on the coast of Borneo may for the present be considered Banjir Massin, Pontiana and Borneo Proper. Minor ports dependent or connected with these may hereafter be opened as the country becomes regulated and more under control. The present Sultan of Borneo Proper is understood to be well disposed and not given to the encouragement of piratical enterprise, notwithstanding that shelter is afforded to pirates in almost every river in his dominions, a number of petty states having arisen beyond the reach of his authority and control. The most prominent of these are the states of Jawaran [Tuaran] and Jampassoo [Tempasuk] to the northward of Borneo Proper. . . . It has been reported that Jawaran sends out about 50 prows in the year and Jampassoo about half that number and the number of prows belonging to these States is estimated about 150 with from one to two hundred guns. The large prows armed with guns 10 feet long probably 12 and 18 pounders their crews consisting from 80-200 men. The Lanoons[1] are the most considerable and formidable of these eastern pirates and there is little doubt that we should be justified in the immediate destruction of these prows. . . ."

At the same time, a letter was sent to the Sultan of Borneo expressing regret that several ports dependent on Borneo proper harboured pirates, and that it was the intention of the British Government to destroy every such establishment without delay. His Highness could not but be aware of the fate of Sambas, and it was the wish of the Lieutenant-Governor that Borneo proper should be warned by this example and co-operate in the suppression of piracy. Similar letters were addressed to other Malay princes.

Unfortunately Captain Garnham was unable to make much progress, owing to the advanced state of the monsoon; and before active measures could be resumed, instructions arrived from India putting a stop to the whole plan. No operations were to be made against pirates on the west coast of Borneo without the express sanction of the Supreme Government.

[1] "LANUN. This is the name given by the Malays to the boldest, stoutest, and most dangerous of all the piratical natives of the Archipelago. . . . From all accounts, the native country of this people is at the head of the great bay, which deeply indents the southern side of the great island of Mindano [Mindanao], the second in size of the Philippine group. . . . On the northern coast of Borneo, they have formed settlements, as well as on some of the smaller islands north of it. . . ." Crawfurd, *Descriptive Dictionary*.

By that time a treaty had been completed with the Sultan of Sambas. Captain Mackay of H.M.S. *Malacca* gave this report of that ruler's state visit:

"The Ship's Company were instantly drawn up under arms and I conducted him all over the ship, everyone being at their station as a mark of attention and respect. I then prepared him for a salute. Ten guns were all that could be got ready from the confined state of the decks. The Sultan, a poor half naked object, almost an imbecile, never having been visited by foreigners before, or been saluted by them; I am sure that his consequence and vanity (if he possessed any) would have been fully as gratified with five guns as with fifty, and I can vouch for his being much better pleased, for nothing but my holding him with both hands prevented him from leaping out of my cabin windows into his prow as soon as the second gun was discharged."

On 17th September Raffles was able to report to India the success of his new currency in checking the depreciation in the paper currency, which had now almost reached the rate fixed in Lord Minto's proclamation. Owing to the adverse balance of trade, the demand for specie continued, so that, until commerce improved, the only remedy was to restrict paper currency and to circulate specie in the form of coinage least likely to tempt exportation. There was a lack of equipment in the mint and it would be impossible to commence a gold and silver coinage until the new machinery arrived from Bengal. Government treasury notes issued at six per cent had continued at par; the tin doits had been a success, the demand being greater than the mint could supply. The copper doits issued by the former government had tended to depreciate, owing to too great a discrepancy between face and intrinsic value. In addition to these were lumps of copper stamped at the value of two stivers. These were popular because their intrinsic value was nearly equivalent to their face value, but this form of coinage had been subject to abuse and its value varied according to its weight.

Towards the end of September Gillespie informed Raffles that if he could take passage in the *Troubridge*, which was shortly leaving for India, he would be able to catch the winter fleet to Europe. This would mean that he must leave before his successor arrived, but Raffles readily agreed. Their relations had become increasingly friendly and they dined frequently at each other's houses in Batavia.

Raffles wrote to London on 23rd September:

". . . I have at the same time great satisfaction in adding that the difference with the Commander of the Forces to which I was reluctantly compelled to allude in my last dispatches, no longer exists—I was happy to have it in my power to return to that cordiality which was in every way desirable whenever it could be effected, without giving up the principles that appear to me to be our proper guide in the Military Department of Government. Having found the Commander of the Forces in a similar opinion I have been anxious to return to that personal cordiality which it has never been my wish to lose sight of, although a sense of public duty compelled me to think differently with regard to some of our public measures; and it affords me very great pleasure to add that the measures of Government are conducted with perfect union and cordiality."

The principal members of the Palembang commission arrived back at Batavia on 29th September and a special meeting of the Council was held on 1st October. The next day, Robison was put under arrest and, being allowed to furnish bail, was released within twenty-four hours.

Rumour became very active again, sometimes in favour of Robison, more often against him. He did his utmost to discredit every member of the commission, accusing them of suborning and browbeating witnesses and extorting evidence in every improper way. He made allegations concerning Gillespie's personal behaviour in Palembang during the previous expedition. He also entered into a very acrimonious and undisciplined correspondence with the government.

Far from demanding an immediate enquiry into these imputations, which reflected seriously on his moral character, Gillespie took umbrage at the mere suggestion of any investigation. Raffles "did not deem it consistent with delicacy to push the enquiry further than he [Gillespie], the party most concerned, deemed it proper to urge".

Meanwhile Colebrooke was preparing his report.

On 3rd October there arrived at Calcutta the ship that had brought from England Francis Rawdon-Hastings, Earl of Moira. He disembarked at 6.15 on the following morning and assumed the office of Governor-General on that day.

Then in his sixtieth year, Moira had been a professional soldier of distinction and had seen service both in America and the Low Countries. Wellington had served under him in the latter theatre. Subsequently, as an intimate member of the Carlton House circle, he had become involved in crippling extravagance and had asked the First Gentleman in Europe to use his influence to secure for him a chance to recoup his finances.

Sir Theophilus Metcalfe wrote of Moira to his son, Charles, in India:

"His debts in this country are enormous and I think his intended style of living in Calcutta will not admit of any saving of his salary."[1]

That Moira's mode of life offered a marked contrast to the easy habits of his quiet and unassuming predecessor is shown in a letter dated 17th October from John Palmer to Major O'Brien in Java.

"Lord Moira is creating to himself a vast arrear and accumulation of

[1] Edward J. Thompson, *Life of Lord Metcalfe.*

business by silly ceremonials and puppet shows, scarcely pardonable in nonage. He has not omitted, however, to assume and absorb all the Powers of the Government, civil as well as military, and professes to come to take more care of the public interests than he could of his own. He is a benevolently disposed man; and liberal to a fault, but I imagine his public extravagance will be restrained. . . . I do not imagine he is a Solomon and I consequently expect his Government will be distinguished by the views of [those] who acquire influence over him."

Minto was not to depart until over two months after Moira's arrival, so there was the unusual situation of the old and the new Governors-General being in India at the same time. Minto, however, was not the sort of person to create any difficulties. As he amusingly put it:

"I think the rising and setting suns may drive their chariots very peacefully and amicably round the Calcutta Course."

The *Troubridge* was due to sail from Java for Calcutta on 11th October. Raffles had arranged to leave Batavia for Buitenzorg before that date. On the 8th he called on Gillespie, asked if he could do anything more to assist, and offered to defer his own visit to Buitenzorg until Gillespie had left. Gillespie thanked him warmly, but said he wanted to leave quietly, urging Raffles not to upset his plans. Raffles then told Travers, in the presence of Gillespie, that he was to give him all possible help. And so they parted, apparently on the most friendly terms.

Gillespie embarked with full military honours on the 11th. Travers, who had an attack of fever, went only as far as the beach, having said his personal farewell in Gillespie's house.

"[Gillespie] took me by both hands," he wrote, "and swore eternal friendship towards me and left me in a flood of tears. Robinson, Mr Raffles' most confidential friend, embarked with him and had a long talk with him on deck, when Gillespie declared his attachment to Raffles and his positive determination to support every measure of his administration."

Thus, in a general atmosphere of goodwill, Gillespie sailed for India. A fellow passenger was C. G. Blagrave, the dismissed secretary, who, in defiance of Raffles' instructions to proceed to Amboina and take up his appointment there, was going instead to Calcutta. His presence on board was unfortunate.

Chapter Fourteen

JAVA, 1813

i

THREE days after the departure of the *Troubridge*, Captain Macdonald, in H.C.C. *Nearchus*, brought Major-General Miles Nightingall and his wife safely to Batavia.

Raffles came down from Buitenzorg to greet the new commander of the forces and gave a public breakfast at Government House, so that he could meet the members of the Council and senior military officers. General Nightingall then took the oath as Vice-President in Council.

Captain Macdonald was unfavourably impressed, describing Nightingall as "a capricious and selfish offset from a noble family (he was reputed to be a natural son of Lord Cornwallis) whose indolence and love of ease contrasted strongly with the fiery and chivalrous bearing of the gay and gallant Gillespie".

Travers, for all his admiration for Gillespie, took a much more favourable view.

". . . a steady, well informed man, a good officer and well acquainted with his duty; with no shining talents but a correct judgment and good understanding; with an anxious wish and determination to do everything proper. . . . The friendly gentlemanlike and easy salutation of the General was only equalled by the lively, affable and unaffected manner of Mrs Nightingall, who struck me as one of the most charming women I had seen in the country."

The Nightingalls stayed at Ryswick with Raffles, who had as his other guests Captain and Mrs Flint (*née* Mary Anne Raffles) and his unmarried sister, Harriet, who were leaving together for England by the *Lord Eldon* on 24th October.

It was not until late in that month that Colebrooke's report on the Palembang affair was completed. Major Robison was informed that he was to be sent to Calcutta with Colebrooke, who would take with him all the relative papers. The decision would now rest with the Supreme Government. They left Batavia at the end of the month in H.C.C. *Nearchus*.

Before this, on 14th October, Raffles addressed the Court of Directors in London, giving further details of the tin mines at Bangka, to which island Dr Horsfield had recently made an expedition. Latterly these mines had not been so productive as had been expected, partly because the easier ground had been worked out and partly because piracy had interfered with production. The legitimate export had been chiefly to Japan, but owing to corrupt native administration an illicit trade had grown up with Java, whereby tin was exchanged for opium and piece goods. A good deal of the ore was also being sent to Penang, where it formed a considerable article of export to China. The completed report of Dr Horsfield, added Raffles, established the claim of the Sultan of Palembang to Bangka, so that his right to transfer the sovereignty of it to the East India Company was unquestionable.

Two days later, on the 16th October, the introduction of the new scheme for land rent was officially made known in a long proclamation. After referring to the original instructions of Lord Minto and praising the exertions of the Mackenzie commission, Raffles announced the establishment of an improved system of political economy throughout the island, and based on the following principles:

1. The undue influence and authority of the chiefs was to be restricted. They would render important service in a department of police, being allotted suitable provision in lands and money as a reward and to stimulate their interest in the industry and protection of the inhabitants.

2. Government land would be let generally to the heads of villages, who, under certain conditions, would re-let to the cultivators. They would be held responsible for the proper management of the land, and the rent must not be oppressive.

3. Feudal services and forced deliveries were generally abolished, though in the Batavian and Preanger Regencies, a modified form of the original arrangements only had been adopted, and in the central forest districts, the Blandong system would, to a certain extent, be preserved.

4. To encourage cultivation of coffee, which would be an important export when the trade to Europe and America was thrown open to free competition, the government would purchase at a reasonable and fixed price from the cultivators any surplus that could not be sold elsewhere at a higher price.

5. To extend free trade and commerce, the bhoom[1] farms had been abolished, duties upon the principal articles of export taken off. Custom-house regulations would be amended before 1st January 1814. Toll-gate and transport duties of the interior had been diminished and would gradually be extinguished.

6. Facilities would be given for obtaining teak for shipbuilding.

7. The government had taken over the management of the salt department. An approved scheme would be introduced as soon as possible.

In continuation of this policy, the law making the importation of

[1] *Bumi*, land.

spices by individuals a capital offence was rescinded on 18th October, and the importation permitted of all spices purchased from the Company's stores.

On 23rd October recognized merchants were permitted to trade in and import spices, opium, wild nutmegs and maize, provided they produced certificates that they had been purchased from the Company's stores or obtained from places where private cultivation was permitted. As from 4th December, all salt manufacture must be on account of government, no person being permitted to manufacture it for private sale.

A long list was published of government officers forbidden either to take part in commercial speculations themselves, or to use their influence in favour of any individual engaged in the trade.

In a letter dated 1st November to the Governor-General in Council attention was called to the development of sugar plantations being handicapped by lack of capital and the necessity of supporting the cultivation of this crop.

"This could only be done by making advances in cash to them from the public Treasury, and receiving the whole produce on the Honourable Company's account, though contrary to the general principle by which we are guided of avoiding monopolies as much as possible."

Raffles briefly explained his policy in a letter, dated October 1813, to his cousin, Elton Hamond.

"A system of internal management similar to that established in Bengal has been introduced throughout the whole of this fertile and populous Island; and the revenue and police regulations have been placed on a footing to ensure to the cultivator the fruits of his industry and to the Government its just dues for the support of the State; the whole system of native management has been exploded, and the mass of the population are now no longer dependent on a Regent or other Chieftain but look up direct to the European power which protects them . . . in the first instance the lands are let generally speaking to the heads of villages as this description of people appear to me to be the resident superintending farmers of the estate. In so extensive a population there will naturally require some deviations in different districts; but the plan of village rents will generally prevail. After the expiration of one year, leases for three years will be granted; and at the conclusion of that period the leases may either be made for seven or for ten years, or the lands granted to the actual possessors in perpetuity."

In the same letter he referred to the difficulties that had arisen through the shortage of specie.

"Until the revolution in Holland and the discontinuance of communication between this Colony and Europe, large sums in silver were annually sent out to pay the establishments and purchase the investments and, generally speaking, the importations in bullion were the most considerable. The specie also when sent by the Batavian Government to British India either procured a return of silver, or the proceeds by which opium, cloths, and the principal importations required by Java could be purchased.

"For the last ten years, Java lost these advantages: and the only supply of bullion was received from the Americans, who purchased colonial produce. The blockade giving rise to extraordinary measures of defence, the whole Island was by Marshal Daendels forced to submit to military exactions; and, independent of the forced and voluntary loans obtained from inhabitants upwards of 4 millions of Rix Dollars and paper currency was thrown into the market. At the period of the establishment of the British Government, this paper had fallen in the market to the rate of 6½ rix dollars for one Spanish dollar silver.

"The public service required that, in the first instance, a supply of cash should be thrown into the Island for the pay of the troops; and for a certain time, while the Government were accumulating a small capital, a large proportion of this was kept on the Island.

"The restrictions on commerce which had heretofore existed being gradually withdrawn, the value of the silver in the market was soon ascertained. From Europe the importations of silver no longer existed. The specie with which we might have purchased the valuable articles of Indian produce required here, were no longer at our disposal, the Moluccas being a separate establishment, dependent immediately on Bengal: the consequence was natural that the silver should disappear. The small quantity imported in the first instance by the British Government was too soon soaked up in so thirsty a soil; and the circumstances above stated, added to the total want of demand of the produce of the Colony, may account for the present very unfavourable balance of trade and exchange. The coffee alone, had the American war not broken out, and the Orders of Council been revoked, would have afforded us an importation of specie of nearly 2 millions of Spanish dollars annually. At present it is literally rotting in the stores.

"The above may give you a general idea of our present situation; but as paper currency is the point on which we are speaking it may be interesting to you to be informed of an important measure which has been undertaken here. The paper currency of Batavia which was originally issued at par, amounted to about 8,500,000 rix dollars (£2,125,000 at par). At our first establishment it was respected and guaranteed by Lord Minto at 6½ for one; but in the course of a year, and notwithstanding it continued to be received in the Government Treasury at the rate originally fixed by Lord Minto, it fell to 12 and 13 for one, making a difference of near

100 per cent in its actual current value in the market. It followed, that Government must either retain it in the Treasury, or if they issued it in payments do so at the current market price of the day, at a loss of 100 per cent, for the Proclamation of Lord Minto required that they should receive it at 6½, and to the troops, or any of the fixed establishments, it could not be issued except at its value in the market. If purchases were to be made, or agreement entered into, it mattered little whether the rate of 6½ or that of 13 were stated, as individuals would take care to regulate the amount according to the current value.

"I resolve to withdraw the whole from circulation by a partial sale of lands, and by such other means as were within my reach; and I succeeded in securing the whole in the course of three months. The principle on which this measure was adopted is as follows: the amount of paper currency could be considered in no other light than a Colonial debt, the amount of which was due by Government to the public. True, it was not encouraged by the British Government, but Lord Minto had guaranteed it to a certain extent and whatever might be the eventual fate of the Colony, the burden arising from the depreciation must fall upon us. The question, therefore, was, whether we should withdraw this paper by means of British capital or by means of Colonial capital; or in other words, whether we should draw on Bengal for 1,300,000 dollars (£325,000 at par) or whether other means might not be devised that would eventually fall upon the colony. The heavy demand on the Bengal Treasury for the supply of cash to Europe, the assurance I had given on the capability of the Island to maintain itself, and the necessity of preventing the possession from becoming a drain on our more permanent possessions, induced me to devise means within my immediate reach; and I conceived it was impossible to adopt a more justifiable plan than to sell a portion of the domains of the Colony for the liquidation of the debt. I have accordingly done this, and about one-fourth of the debt may already be considered as extinct. The same principle followed up will reduce the whole in a few years, and in the meantime an issue of the Treasury notes has been made, bearing an interest of 6 per cent and payable at pleasure, which retain, and are likely to continue to retain, their original value. To meet the demand for circulation, which the withdrawing of so large a floating medium occasioned, the Lombard Bank has been authorized to issue promissory notes or obligations to a certain extent, payable in nine months; which notes are issued to individuals on the security of real and personal property redeemable at the expiration of 6 months from date of the loan. These last mentioned notes, with a small quantity of certificates issued from the Treasury, to enable the public to settle outstanding accounts in the old Batavian currency have, generally speaking, maintained their credit, that is to say, they have never been at a discount with silver of more than 20 or 25 per cent; and no extraordinary means have been taken by Government to keep them up. They have literally been left to find their level in the market.

"From these circumstances you will be able to judge the state of public credit.

"The quantity of silver is however daily becoming less. Gold has disappeared altogether and copper is the only metal in general use among the population. A general demand exists for a more extended currency; and many of the most wealthy individuals are threatened with ruin from want of means to pay their debts. In a few months, if a change does not take place, silver will not be procurable at any price; and, in establishing a Colonial currency, it becomes a question what shall be considered the standard; if silver, its price will be so high that we may expect to pay 100 per cent in addition to our fixed expenses; and if copper is made the standard we at once declare our poverty among the nations with whom we hold commercial intercourse."

Raffles wrote again on this matter to the Governor-General on 1st November. He complained of the deficiency of silver to meet the current expenses of government and the payment of the troops. Nor was the limited machinery available adequate to produce a sufficient quantity of doits required for general circulation. He was compelled, therefore, to obtain silver by bills of exchange upon India, this sum to be considered as an advance made necessary by peculiar circumstances and not a sign of insufficient resources. He estimated that 50,000 Spanish dollars a month would be needed for the troops, and proposed to draw on India to the extent of 300,000 dollars.

The distress among the people was reported to the Java Council in a memorial from inhabitants of Batavia. Owing to lack of ready money, property was being mortgaged for one sixth of its value. The Council agreed that the Lombard Bank should be authorized to issue loans to a maximum figure of 300,000 Spanish dollars on mortgages on immovable property. A proclamation to that effect was made on 3rd November. By a further proclamation, Lombard Bank notes issued under instructions dated 1st March 1813 were to count as legal tender according to the value they bore to silver in the market. In addition, the value of Spanish dollars, ducatoons[1] and other foreign coins in relation to the silver rupee of Java would be circulated and published quarterly in the *Java Gazette*.

This authorization to the Lombard Bank led to serious complications too lengthy to follow up here.

While admiring Raffles' resourcefulness in settling governmental debts by selling public land, Minto was clearly very doubtful what sort of reception this display of initiative would have in London.

[1] A Dutch silver coin worth about half a crown in English money.

"On the financial operation", he wrote to Raffles on 22nd November 1813, "of withdrawing the depreciated paper from circulation by a considerable sale of lands, the resolutions of this Government must be conveyed to you by my successor; but I am unwilling to withhold from you my individual sentiments on a measure of so much importance.

"I begin therefore by assenting without reservation to the absolute and exigent necessity which was the motive, and is the justification of the proceeding. The revenues and all the demands of government were paid in paper which could not be re-issued; there was, therefore, a virtual suspension of receipt at the public Treasury. To avoid this total loss, the paper must have been issued again, at the discount of the day, which would have discredited the currency still more, and would have involved an enormous and constantly-recurring loss. This state of things left you no option but to withdraw the paper, to make room for some better medium of circulation, and the operation of the evil was too rapid to admit of delay. The only plan for the redemption of the paper which could be found, appears very clearly to have been precisely that to which you had recourse—the sale of public property; and it must be deemed fortunate that this resource existed, and proved to be immediately available.

"I consider, therefore, your measure to have been an able expedient in a case of great emergency.

"At the same time I conceive the necessity of a prompt remedy to form the essential, and, indeed, the indispensable ground of the resolution that was taken, for I should not, I confess, have thought an extensive alienation of the public domains advisable in itself, under the particular circumstances of the Colony at the time. First, it was too important a measure to be adopted during a provisional government, the duration of which is more than precarious. Secondly, it ought (and naturally would, without the pressure of immediate necessity) to have received the previous sanction of the Supreme Government. Thirdly, although my views, as you know, lead to the transfer of public territory to the management of individual industry, and the creation of a genuine landed interest, with all its immediate benefits and ameliorating tendencies, in the room of the deplorable system of vassalage and dependence under which land is now held in Java; yet I have felt that this change could not be brought about suddenly, partly from the very nature of all extensive changes, partly from the circumstances of the Colony, which contains at present neither capital nor capitalists enough to offer a comparison between the value in the market, of land and money, either fair or at all approaching to fair. I should have inclined, therefore, to small and partial sales of land, if alienation in perpetuity should have been thought advisable at all, proportioned in some degree to the disposable quantity of money in the hands of individuals. But the general course to be recommended I conceive to be short leases, followed by longer, and ultimately by perpetuities. I touch upon these points the more willingly, for the purpose of conveying to you a caution on the subject, founded on our knowledge of the sentiments which appear to be the most prevalent at home, but which you may not be apprised of.

"There is a great division of opinion on the question of permanent settlements, and the extension of that system to the newly acquired provinces under the Presidency of Bengal, which has, in a great degree, been carried into effect during my administration.

"The introduction of that system has been gradual in those provinces, but yet more sudden than is approved at home. But Java is in a state infinitely less favourable to perpetual alienations; and you may depend upon such measures, unsupported by particular exigency, being disapproved, and, indeed, disavowed and annulled by the authorities in England."

The fears were fully justified. London roundly condemned the sales.

ii

On the night before the *Lord Eldon* sailed from Batavia for England with his two sisters and Captain Flint, Raffles gave them a farewell party at Ryswick. They left on 24th October. A few days later, Raffles took the Nightingalls to Buitenzorg for a short visit before he started with Olivia on a long-projected trip to eastern Java.

With Captain Macdonald in command, they left Batavia in H.C.C. *Aurora* on 2nd November, and, after short stops at Indramayu and Cheribon, came to Pekalongan—"Place of Flying Foxes"—whence, on 20th November, Raffles communicated to the Council the substance of the new customs regulations.

Till then, the smaller ports had been virtually excluded from trade because of heavy duties, while Batavia had no export of its own except sugar and arrack, its chief export being produce originating in other districts, particularly the Eastern Archipelago. The obstructions to trade were among the main reasons for the depression under which the island was now suffering, and the adverse balance of trade had drained the whole country of specie. The products of Java, observed Raffles, were, generally speaking, the same as those in western India, so that the demand for them must depend on the comparative price they bore—a price increased by the cost of transporting all articles to Batavia for export. As Bantam, Cheribon and the Eastern Districts now enjoyed the new scheme of land rents, they must have a market for their produce; if they did not, rent would be obtained by the government only in the form of produce, which would block up the warehouses instead of being exported overseas.

All Java's ports where duties could conveniently be collected were to be opened up, and the rate of duty equalized throughout. Vessels from western India would be restricted to Batavia, Samarang and Surabaya, as they were ignorant of local customs, but they would be allowed to proceed elsewhere on engaging to respect local authority or regulations. Vessels from Europe and foreigners, including Arabs not trading from eastern ports, must enter at Batavia.

There would be a general import duty of ten per cent on all articles for consumption in Java, but a drawback equal to the import duty would be allowed, thus freeing transit trade from duty. An export duty of three per cent would be charged on all articles exported, but this would be removed whenever the state of finances permitted. Duties on coasting trade would be abolished. The duty on goods imported in vessels not registered in any British port, except native vessels, would be fifteen per cent.

With this business concluded, the party sailed from Pekalongan to Samarang, where the arrival of the Lieutenant-Governor and "our amiable Lady Governess" produced a great outburst of social activity.

"Public breakfasts, dinners, balls and races", the *Java Gazette* reported, "follow each other in daily succession, and the happy guests quit one scene of pleasure to become actors in the next."

One of the major objects of the trip was a visit to Kedu, to enable Raffles to see for himself how far his experiment of land rents was succeeding there. The party left Samarang very early on 28th November. After breakfasting at Serondol, they climbed the lovely hill road to Banjar Kulen ("Western Range"), the country residence of Civil Commissioner Hugh Hope. They slept there and then the party divided. Olivia stayed for a few days longer, then visited Salatiga and returned to Samarang.

"On 29th November the Lieutenant-Governor entered the Cadoe [Kedu] district where they were received by Mr Lawrence the Resident. The visitors were highly gratified with the picturesque beauty and rich fertility which is said to merit the name of 'The Garden of the World'."

Raffles returned to Samarang on 1st December and spent three days of further social activity. In addition to the various banquets and receptions, he reviewed the Java Light Cavalry, and one morning attended a race-meeting at Salatiga, held, as customary in Java, before breakfast.

The next part of the programme was to be the state visits to Surakarta and Mataram. Though lacking in personal pride, Raffles had a keen perception of the dignity of his position, realizing to the full the importance of pomp and ceremony. These two visits were of the highest political importance, being the first state entries of the supreme British authority in the island into the capitals of its two greatest ruling princes. Consequently, Raffles was determined that the occasions should be marked by every detail of formality and splendour to make them memorable.

We are indebted to the "Special Correspondent" of the *Java Gazette* for the very full accounts of the proceedings on which the following narrative is based.

Raffles and his party left Salatiga on 4th December and spent the night at the fort of Boyolali, which was only eighteen miles from Surakarta. On the morning of the 5th they continued their journey as far as Assum, where they were met by the chief civil and military authorities deputed by the Susuhunan to present his congratulations and homage. With guns and an escort of fifty cavalry, the Pĕrang Wedono received the Lieutenant-Governor with the usual military honours, which included a salute of nineteen guns. A procession was formed, and about three miles farther on they were met by the Susuhunan himself, who congratulated the Lieutenant-Governor and Lady Governess on their approach to his capital.

The procession then re-formed and moved forward to Kluchu, the country seat of the Susuhunan, about seven miles from Surakarta. Here the Susuhunan and the Ratu (Empress), with the officers and ladies of the court, the British Resident (Colonel Adams) and a considerable military escort, awaited the approach of the Lieutenant-Governor, whose arrival was announced by three volleys of musketry from two hundred of the Susuhunan's guard and by the playing of the state *gamĕlans*, who performed as for the arrival of the Susuhunan himself.

"On alighting from their carriage the Lieutenant-Governor and Lady Governess conducted by the Emperor [Susuhunan] and Empress proceeded to seats prepared for them in a commodious apartment where the suite of the Honourable Governor and the officers of his staff and escort arranged themselves on one side, while the Crown Prince and the sons of the Emperor, the Prime Minister and other officers of the Court occupied the other side of the room. A table was laid in the centre covered by refreshments which were handed round by female slaves. After mutual congratulations and a few complimentary toasts, the Emperor conducted the Lieutenant-Governor to the state coach (Kia Doodoo),[1] the Empress having handed the Lady Governess to another state coach immediately preceding the Emperor's—a salute of three volleys of musketry was then fired, when the procession moved forward in the following order:—the brigade of six-pounders belonging to the Lieutenant-Governor with their waggons, sixty mounted men of the Java Light Cavalry formed in two divisions, with ranks open and drawn swords, preceded by two honorary aides-de-camp of the Lieutenant-Governor, the carriage of the Lady Governess; the state coach (Kia

[1] *Kiai Dudok*, noble seat.

Doodoo); a native commissioned officer and ten men of the Java Light Cavalry, with rested carbines drawn up in single file on each side of the state carriages as flankers; a mounted aide-de-camp of the Lieutenant-Governor attending each of the state coaches; the hussars following the state carriages in two divisions, with ranks open and drawn swords; a carriage with the wife of the Resident . . ."

The whole procession then moved on to the outer court, where the Empress and Lady Governess alighted from the carriage and moved into the hall of audience, followed by the Susuhunan and the Lieutenant-Governor. Some ceremonial toasts followed and the official arrival was thus completed.

The next morning Raffles and Olivia inspected the scientific collection of Dr Horsfield. Then Olivia held a drawing-room at the Residency. Later in the day, the Susuhunan and Empress paid their official call.

"They arrived at half past six o'clock and were received with the usual honours, after which the party adjourned to a convenient situation, from which they witnessed a splendid exhibition of fireworks. Upon their return two sets of dancing girls belonging to the Emperor gratified the company with a very excellent specimen of Javanese dancing. The dance was followed by an exhibition of sleight-of-hand, which seemed to afford considerable amusement to the Emperor and family. At half past twelve the party adjourned to the supper room, the tables of which were abundantly supplied with every rarity which the country afforded, and on the cloth being removed . . . toasts were drunk with the most animated enthusiasm. . . . The party adjourned to the ballroom, when His Highness the Emperor led off a country dance with the Lady Governess. The Honourable Lieutenant-Governor danced down a few couple with the Empress. Reels concluded the festivities of the evening."

On the morning of the 7th Raffles proceeded on horseback to inspect the subsidiary corps under the command of the Pĕrang Wedono. Later the Crown Prince arrived at the Residency in the state coach to conduct Raffles and Olivia in a final state visit to the Susuhunan. After a "tyger-fight", official farewells were paid and the visit ended.

At two o'clock on 8th December, the day on which the *Troubridge* brought Major-General Gillespie to India, the Lieutenant-Governor and party arrived at Jokyakarta. The military ceremonial was so similar to that at Surakarta that a description of it can be omitted, though it is noteworthy that Raffles' meeting with the Sultan of Mataram was reported to have been marked by the gratitude and unaffected pleasure manifested by that ruler. The usual procession formed up, but with even greater magnificence than before. It went:

". . . at a slow pace through double ranks of spearsmen amongst whom were interspersed the standard-bearers of the different Pangerangs and chieftains, to whom they belonged. The Gamelongs or bands of Javanese music, which were stationed at intervals along the road, announced the arrival of His Excellency by lively and repeated flourishes. The road from Raksanagoran to the Residency is upwards of four miles, nearly a hundred feet wide and lined on each side with beautiful rows of trees, being for a considerable distance perfectly straight, it presented on this occasion a grand perspective. Triumphant arches were erected at equal distances which produced an effect strikingly magnificent."

The next three days were spent in official calls, reviews of troops and an expedition to the south sea, followed by a sumptuous entertainment prepared by Major D. H. Dalton and the officers of the Light Infantry Volunteer Battalion. A farewell interview with the Sultan took place on 12th December, and on the following day the party returned to Samarang.

Lord Minto sailed from India for England on 11th December in H.M. frigate *Hussar*. In his farewell letter to Raffles he wrote:

"In taking leave of my public relation with you, as I must in this letter, I am at a loss how to proceed. On the one hand, there are so many points, or rather extensive subjects, on which a free communication of my sentiments is due to you, that every hour which remains of my residence in India would be too few to acquit myself of that debt. . . . On the other hand, the last, or, I may say more properly, the posthumous duties of my station in India, added to the preparations for my departure . . . leave only moments, when days would be wanted, for the demands still outstanding against me. You will therefore not impute to me want of interest in the matter I have now before me, if I aim at conciseness and brevity. . . . You will accept, therefore, what I am now able to offer, as only the friendly suggestions of the deep and lively interest I can never cease to take in all that concerns your public trust, and your personal reputation and welfare. . . . I have had an early communication with Lord Moira concerning your appointment to Bencoolen; and I have the happiness to say that he acquiesced entirely in the arrangement that was made, and specifically in the propriety of your continuing to administer the government of Java, until the future destiny of that island should be fixed by the Government at home."

So departed this friend and patron, on his way back to the wife and home in Scotland that meant so much to him.

It is not necessary to follow the rest of Raffles' tour in detail. He went as far east as Surabaya and took the opportunity while there of visiting the island of Madura. The visit has been described by Captain Macdonald, who is worth quoting, if only for one amusing anecdote.

"Attended by a numerous staff he set out for Samanap [Sumenep], the capital of this fruitful little island, and was received and entertained in the true native simplicity by that good old man—there was neither pageantry nor imposing display of any kind, beyond a few spearmen stationed round his palace, but the chiefs and people met us on the road, attired in their best, and testifying their respects in the humblest manner, while bands of music were stationed at certain distances, playing throughout the ceremony the sweet and plaintive airs of the Javanese; at the entrance stood the aged Sultan, and the members of his family, all of whom bent forward in much reverence to salute His Excellency; yet there was nothing cringing or fawning in their deportment, and it particularly struck me how anxious the old man had been to pour forth his loyalty and love for our nation; on either side of the doorway were suspended the portraits of our gracious Sovereign George the Third, and John Wilkes, who, no doubt some wag had told him, was, or had been the favourite minister of this monarch."

Olivia had not been very well and the official tour, with all the ceremonial and celebrations, had fatigued her greatly. Leaving her behind to enjoy the better air of a hill station for a few more weeks, Raffles returned overland to Buitenzorg, whither Travers had gone to meet him.

"I can scarcely express", wrote Travers, "the pleasure I felt at finding him look so well and in such very high spirits. Indeed his great success in the scheme he had formed for the settlement of the country could not fail being satisfactory. It is certainly the most conspicuous feature in his Administration; the addition of Revenue is proportionate to the general benefit the country will experience."

That Raffles had justification for his confidence that the lot of the native cultivators would be improved is confirmed by a letter published on 18th December in the *Java Gazette* by one who described himself as "Rusticus". Allowing that he might be a biased witness and that his language was of the flowery style of the period, the actual description of what he saw may be taken as substantially true, published as it was in a paper accessible to many who must have known the facts.

"Having made a tour", wrote "Rusticus", "through some of the Eastern Districts the busy rural scenes that were everywhere passing around me strongly attracted my attention. I beheld old watercourses under repair and many fields under irrigation for the purpose of receiving seed, while the hoe wielded by the brawny arm of industry rooted the noxious weeds and briars from the fertile soil of the wilderness; the clouds of smoke which obscured the sky showed that the impenetrable thicket must recede from its ancient limits and give way to luxurious crops of rice. . . . These are the visible marks of increasing industry cherished by the dawn of liberty rising on the debasing feudal system of oppression and tyranny. The inestimable boon held out by a wise and generous Government the people knew how to prize, they were delighted in having substantial property in the lands they tilled, and in being certain that they would reap the profits of their industry . . . and the lands of several districts had been let for more than double the amount they used to yield to the Government, the State having got rid of a troublesome mode of collecting revenue, and the people from a long train of petty tyrants."

One last matter must be referred to before closing the chronicle of 1813. The *Charlotte* and the *Mary* returned from their voyage to Japan on 22nd December, bringing to Batavia Dr Daniel Ainslie, Wardenaar and Doeff's assistant, Bloomhoff. Doeff's terms for the continuance of the visits of British ships disguised as Dutch vessels were conveyed to Raffles by Bloomhoff. They were no less than the acceptance of Doeff's sole control of the yearly visit to Japan in every detail. To secure himself he had arranged with Bloomhoff for a secret code of signals when the fleet arrived. Raffles took exception to this and sent Bloomhoff to Europe as a prisoner.

To make sure that what Ainslie said was discounted, Doeff stated bluntly[1] that, as Ainslie had been continuously drunk during the whole of his stay at Deshima, he had not understood what was going on there. Perhaps Ainslie had seen too much. Anyhow, drunk or sober, he had accumulated a lot of information and was able later to stand up to a lengthy interrogation in Calcutta.

Raffles was not dissatisfied. The two ships had made a successful voyage in a commercial sense and though he had probably been tricked by Wardenaar and Doeff, it might still be possible to get his hands directly on the trade. Ainslie was quite encouraging, if in fact he had been sober.

Raffles sent off a full report to Calcutta and Ainslie was dispatched there to clarify any points on which Calcutta might want further information. The commercial balance sheet submitted by Raffles showed a satisfactory result, but the prospects held out were even better. Unfortunately it was Moira and not Minto who was now in charge, and Moira was in no mood to give credit to any enterprise of which Raffles was the author. The government accountants, taking their cue from the official disapproval of Raffles, proved that the balance sheet was all wrong and that the voyage had made not a profit but a loss. The prospects in any case were quite imaginary. No trade with Japan could be good business, and copper, which was its only substantial export, would upset the old-established Indian trade.

Accordingly a letter was dispatched to Java in which the most chilling and acid comments were made on the recent venture. It need not be given in detail. It will be sufficient to observe that it opened with the assertion that Calcutta had no information on the Japan trade. Considering that the expedition had been the subject of lengthy correspondence and much reference to van Braam, all of which must have been well known to the secretariat where the files rested, this statement is a remarkable

[1] Hendrik Doeff, *Herinneringen uit Japan* ("Reminiscences of Japan").

example of governmental prevarication. The letter ended with a refusal to sanction another attempt.

Raffles, blissfully unaware of this sudden change in the official attitude, was busily engaged in his preparations for a second expedition. He sent to London for a remarkable assortment of gifts with which he hoped to coax the Japanese into co-operation with the English in an extensive trade. In forwarding the list, he wrote:

"It is unnecessary to observe that the whole of the above should be of the very first and proved quality—a deviation in this respect, even in the slightest degree, will not fail to lower the opinion of our productions in proportion."

None of these articles, however, ever reached Japan. The *Charlotte*, which was sent there during the next south-west monsoon period, was the last attempt Raffles was able to make. Doeff remained as uncompromising as before, though commercially the trip was considered successful.

It is interesting to remember that the East India Company looked on the attempt to develop trade with Japan with a much more favourable eye than did the Supreme Government. They wrote to India on 5th May 1815:

"Such an intercourse has been so long held to be unattainable and at the same time so desirable that tho' our own expectations of benefit from it either to the nation or the Company have not been great, we are disposed to regard with approbation any attempt on the part of our Government in Java which has that object for its ultimate end."

But this approval from London was to arrive too late to be of any help to Raffles. Perhaps the chief interest in the whole story is the far-sighted view Raffles formed of the Japanese.

"For a people who have had very few if any external aids, the Japanese cannot but rank high in the scale of civilization; the traits of a vigorous mind are displayed in the sciences, and particularly in metaphysics and judicial astrology—the arts speak for themselves, and are deservedly acknowledged to be in a much higher degree of perfection than among the Chinese, with whom they are by Europeans so frequently confounded; the latter have been stationary at least as long as we have known them, but the slightest impulse seems sufficient to give a determination to the Japanese character, which would progressively improve until it attained the same height of civilization with the European."[1]

We have gone beyond 1813. Travers wrote at the end of that year:

"We learned that the Company's Charter had been renewed for 20 years . . . no mention was made of Java; the general opinion in Calcutta was that the Government would be speedily upset and King's officers immediately sent out."

[1] *Proceedings of the Batavian Society*, 11th September 1815.

Chapter Fifteen

JAVA, 1814

i

BEFORE the general disapproval of India to his expansionist policy had been received in Java, Raffles had turned his attention to the Philippine Islands. He dispatched John Hunt with the following instructions, dated 20th January 1814:

"The first object of your mission is to communicate to the Chiefs of Sooloo [Sulu] and Magindano[1] the establishment of the British Empire in the Eastern Seas, the measures taken for the extirpation of piracy, and the signal punishment which in consequence thereof has befallen the State of Sambas. You will assure them that while Government are inclined to pass into oblivion the former piracies from that quarter, it is their determination to punish any State which may harbour a pirate after the promulgation of this notice. You will obtain the most accurate information regarding the extent of piratical establishments in that neighbourhood, and suggest your opinion on the best plan for adducing [reducing?] them. . . .

"You will not fail to dispose of the cargo of the Brig 'Greyhound' at Sooloo . . . and lay on her a cargo for China consisting of such articles as are ready to meet an advantageous sale in that market. . . . You will endeavour to effect an arrangement with the Sultan of Sooloo by which you may be permitted to reside in his Capital as an agent on the part of the British Government, and to open a regular and commercial intercourse."

How far Raffles' vision extended can be readily seen from this extract from his minute dated 11th February 1814, to which reference will soon again be made:

"The period is now arrived when it becomes necessary to decide upon the general policy which we shall pursue towards the different native States in these seas. . . . The policy uniformly recommended and adopted by this Government has been that of supporting the long established and acknowledged Sovereigns. . . . The power and authority of these Sovereigns is in many cases almost nominal but they are easily recognized, their rights are undisputed, and it accords as much with the justice . . . of

[1] In the south Philippines. Sir Richard Winstedt remarks: "Wallace mentions it and also 'Magindanu pirates' as if they came from thereabouts. No atlas gives Magindanu and we have no adequate works on the Philippines."

the British Government to uphold them as it is consistent with its policy to suppress the hordes of banditti who are gradually usurping the dominion of the Eastern Seas. . . .

"The population of these islands is so thin that any wandering chief collecting a few adherents among those who have no settled employment finds no difficulty in establishing himself in a wild impenetrable country and renders himself by giving encouragement to pirates independent of the real Sovereign of the country. . . . Generally speaking the natives are to be considered a mild and inoffensive race possessing some virtues . . . having no very obvious prejudices by superstition, not indisposed to industry, but being compelled by the constant state of hostility which prevails to seek for peace and quiet into the interior of the country they are little known. . . . The daring adventurous Malays and Bugguese who frequent the coast are masters of it in every direction. . . . While such pirates rule the seas only such native vessels as are armed and strongly equipped can navigate, and the small Colonial craft so essential to the prosperity of all our Eastern Settlements must of necessity cease to exist."

As an example, he quoted the case of the king of Achin, Sumatra. Traders from the Coromandel Coast (Madras) and Penang frequented every river, and the profits they derived from their dealings were an inducement to the inhabitants to throw off their allegiance. The king had made a serious attempt to recover his authority, whereupon the traders had petitioned the government to stop him levying a duty on his own account. The petition had been attended to, with the result that the king had lost not only his rights of sovereignty, but also the means of preserving his empire.

While still at Malacca as Agent for the Governor-General, he (Raffles) had satisfied himself that extensive interference of the European authority was indispensable to the regulation of the eastern seas, and accordingly he had opened communication with several of the states. At the request of the Sultan of Banjermasin, Borneo, Alexander Hare had been sent with the concurrence of Lord Minto. Pontianak and other states were anxious to obtain the protection of a British connexion and had applied for this long before our attack upon the Dutch possessions. The assurances of protection to eastern states not previously under European control should, considered Raffles, be of a permanent nature, and it would be better, therefore, if they were unconnected with Java and would thus be unaffected by any change in the ownership of that colony. The area he conceived suitable for British interests was certainly extensive.

"The great island of Borneo, the Sooloo Island, Linghen [Lingga], and Rhio, Bali, the East coast of Sumatra, Siam, Gamboja [Cambodia], Cochin China, &c, are free from all connexion with the former ruling power in these seas and want but the attention of an enlightened and liberal Government to add extensively to the commerce of India and to the permanent political ascendancy of the British influence in these seas.

"Let it not be forgotten moreover that if the moment be now lost of effecting this grand and important object it may not again be recovered."

Having submitted this minute to the Supreme Government, he addressed himself to the Governor of Penang, setting out his policy.

"Nothing can tend so effectually to suppression of piracy and to the encouragement and extension of lawful commerce and to the civilization of the inhabitants of the Eastern islands as affording a steady support to the established native Sovereigns and assisting them in the maintenance of their just rights and authority over their several chiefs, and along the shores dependent upon their Dominion. It appears to me that the adoption of this principle and the establishment of British agents accordingly at the leading ports would gradually change the barbarous and uncivilized life of the people . . . and united with the beneficial effects of the abolition of the Slave Trade would . . . gradually tend to agricultural improvement and to the prosperity and interior trade that naturally must follow.

"With a view to carry this principle into effect it seems evident that an indiscriminate resort of traders to different parts of the Malay Islands should be prevented, because it is because of the irregular traffic thus carried out that the petty Chiefs are enabled to render themselves independent of their Sovereign and to form establishments that uniformly depend upon piracy for their support. . . ."

He therefore suggested the establishment of fixed ports for European trade with customs houses to ensure regularity.

The reply of Penang was as acid and short-sighted as might be expected of that jealous government. In a minute dated 23rd July 1814, William Petrie recorded:

"It is with concern but not with diffidence that I acknowledge my dissent from the opinions of Mr Raffles and my conviction that his repeated attempts to interfere with the Malay States to the Eastward of the Straits of Malacca, these different attacks upon their rivers and Settlements, his interference in their internal Governments and regulations, will prove very prejudicial to our Eastern trade. . . . I consider Mr Raffles' plan or expectation of suppressing piracy as altogether chimerical and impracticable."

The response from India, though on a somewhat broader basis, was equally damping. It was dated 28th May and was to this effect:

". . . If Java and the other Dutch Islands should remain in the possession of the British Government there can be no motive whatever for establishing another Government in the Eastern Seas. . . . If on the other hand Java and the Moluccas should be restored to the Dutch, the introduction of a British Agency and the formation of new settlements in the immediate neighbourhood of that power would be regarded by the Dutch with extreme jealousy . . . and the consequences must be that we should be engaged in perpetual disputes, that our Commerce would decidedly be obstructed on all occasions, and that a resort to arms might become necessary . . . and if it be not politically just, or not politically expedient to attempt the formation of new Settlements after the restoration of Java . . . how can it be just or expedient to attempt their formation . . . during our temporary sway over Java? . . . The late Act of Legislature has drawn a line which excludes the Honourable Company from the acquisition of territory to the South of the Equator."

All interference in the affairs of petty independent rajas was, therefore, forbidden. Finally the Governor-General was inclined to think that the advantages to be derived from trade with Japan were greatly overrated.

The succession of Lord Moira had changed at once the attitude of the Supreme Government towards Java. Moira was not a financial expert, and on his first arrival in India he had insisted, against local advice, in remitting a large sum to London, which created a very serious lack of cash in India. He wrote on 1st February 1814[1]:

"Java is a still worse drain than the others. Instead of the surplus revenue which, for giving importance to the conquest, was asserted to be forthcoming from that possession, it could not be maintained without the Treasury, as well as the troops of Bengal. Just now, in the height of our exigencies, we receive an intimation from the Lieutenant-Governor that he cannot pay his provincial corps unless we allow him 50,000 Spanish dollars monthly in addition to the prodigious sums which we already contribute to his establishment."

On 11th February Raffles recorded his famous minute, in which he reported the success of his new policy of land rents. Of considerable length, it was subsequently printed in London for private circulation and entitled *Substance of a Minute*. After a general sketch of the history of the problem and a side reference to Mr Muntinghe's opinion that the amelioration of the finances should come before the amelioration of the condition of the people, a point of view with which Raffles himself did not agree, he went on to explain why the steps taken were essential, even though our occupation of Java might not long continue.

". . . I think myself warranted in stating an opinion that the amended system of revenue was consistent with sound policy adapted to meet the local circumstances of the Colony and necessary to the maintenance of those internal resources which it was the bounden duty of the Government to call forth as much as possible. An immediate result of this amended system must be to promote the circulation of specie by increasing its demand amongst its inhabitants in general; and to retain it on the

[1] *The Private Journal of the Marquis of Hastings.*

Island by increasing the export of produce and of promoting the circulation of specie generally in the interior trade of the country which by the abolition of transit duties is rendered free and is withdrawn from the hands of Chinese farmers and monopolists."

After dealing in detail with various points and quoting extensively from the reports of the officers charged with the duty of introducing the scheme, he concluded:

". . . the basis which I have assumed is not likely to be shaken. I have laid it as broad as practicable, and if I am not mistaken it will maintain a noble superstructure. It is due however to the caution which has been observed to notice, that neither in the arrangements which have already been made nor in those now in progress for the ensuing year has any permanent right which a just and liberal Government could enforce been given up. The Regents and Chiefs holding office at the time of the change have been allowed certain allotments of lands according to the customs of the country; but in these nothing has been foregone but the Government share of the crop, and this only provisionally. The people are equally secured in all the privileges possessed in other lands, and the general question of land tenure is in no way affected by the arrangement. . . ."

In this minute he took the opportunity to call special attention to the good services of officers who had enabled the scheme to be carried out: In Bantam, Major Yule; in Cheribon, Colonel Raban on the political side and Crawfurd in regard to land rental; in Tegal, east of Cheribon, Major Keasberry; in Pekalongan and the Kedu, Lawrence; in Japara and Juana, McQuoid, particularly in reference to the salt department; in the Surabaya districts, Colonel Adams; and in the district east of Surabaya, Mr Hopkins, who had died during the course of the settlement.

Others were also noticed, above all Muntinghe.

"I allude to Mr Muntinghe whose ability is beyond all praise and whose love of justice is only equalled by the universal benevolence of his views. To him I am indebted for the selection of the best talents and the command of all the information which Java afforded on the establishment of the British Government. It was Mr Muntinghe who first pointed out to me the gross errors, and the still grosser corruption of the former Government; and it was from a confidence in his opinion and reliance on his unerring judgment that I first conceived it practicable to work the change which has been wrought. If what has been accomplished turns out as I confidently trust it will to the general happiness and prosperity of Java, Mr Muntinghe must be considered as the link which connected all that was liberal and enlightened in the views of the former administration of the country with that simple desire of doing what was just and good which I have no hesitation in saying, vain as it may appear, has been the sole object of the present Government."

In submitting this minute to the Company, Raffles expressed the hope that early instructions would arrive, for he had had no official approval of the measures taken.

"... although I cannot but feel a most anxious solicitude until relieved by the approving voice of my superiors, I place an entire confidence in the principles which have dictated the change and which must be its justification.... Whatever must be the eventual fate of Java, whether it is decided that the Colony be attached to the Company's possessions, transferred to the Crown or even given up at a peace to a foreign power (which God forbid), the inhabitants of Java will have the happiness to bless the day which placed them under such a system of Government."

Travers recorded at this time:

"This Minute comprises a most extensive view of the former Administration of this valuable colony, the baneful effects of a misguided and ruinous policy and the inevitable and unquestionable advantages to be expected from the present system. It is at once a short but distinct history of Java, and displays a depth of understanding, a brilliancy of talent and an extent of knowledge rarely to be met with in so young a man. The work will speak for itself and will gain for him everlasting honour and renown."

Olivia returned to Batavia from the east by sea, arriving on 15th February, and the burdensome official round started again for her. The very next day she held a drawing-room, which was attended by most of the English and Dutch ladies of the capital. Raffles came down from Buitenzorg, and on the 18th, which was Olivia's birthday, William Robinson gave a grand ball and supper.

"It was now", wrote Travers, "as happy a time as I ever experienced. General Nightingall, attracted by the shining talents and ability of Mr Raffles, began to form a friendship for him, and both families began to appear as one, the utmost cordiality prevailed, and the prospect before me was a happy one indeed."

But the storm-clouds were gathering.

On the day of the ball, 18th February 1814, Raffles, having heard certain rumours then afoot in Calcutta concerning the sale of lands and his participation as a purchaser, recorded a minute in Council. It ran to forty-five paragraphs, from which quotation has already been made on page 274. He began by detailing the circumstances that had made the sales a matter of economic necessity and went on to specify the methods adopted. In the last ten paragraphs he dealt with his own participation, after pressure had been exerted on him by Nicholaus Engelhardt, claiming that the price had been pushed well above the estimate given by Engelhardt.

"I did not possess the funds required to participate in the sale, but Mr Robinson assisted me with what money might be necessary, and the share which I had in the purchase was, in fact, rather in name than reality; it was agreed that not less than one-half should stand in my name, as a smaller participation would not look well in the situation I held; but that half should be divided between us. On the sale taking place, the lots were sold for something short of 60,000 Spanish dollars, being far above the price first contemplated by Mr Engelhardt; and this high amount was bid by him in the confidence of my finding the funds for half the purchase. . . .

"It being subsequently found necessary that a person accustomed to the Javanese should be appointed to reside upon the estate to administer it, Mr de Wilde was selected; and that he might have an interest in its good management, became a partner to the extent of one-sixth; and to complete the funds requisite for the purchase, Mr McQuoid took one-sixth, but did not bid at the sale. Thus the four lots became the property of four persons, as situated in the list of purchasers."

Then he came to the vital point.

"It has been communicated to me that very extraordinary representations have gone abroad respecting this simple transaction of my participating in a purchase. I have no hesitation in stating that it was more on public than private grounds."

It was all open and above board, he stated, with the sole exception that his own participation was kept secret till the sale was completed for fear that other bidders might have been influenced had they known his prospective interest.

"I am anxious", he continued, "to court and invite the most rigid enquiry, and although, had the circumstance occurred in any other form, I should by no means have thought it wrong to purchase public property at a public sale, I could not feel satisfied to remain an interested party from the moment it had been communicated to me that the correctness of the transaction could be doubted."

Accordingly, he had requested his partners to take over his share in the property at the price he had paid for it, so that he had now no financial interest in it.

His final paragraph ran:

"I had little suspected that insinuations of the nature alluded to would have been cast, and still less that they would have been secretly transmitted, without a manly and candid avowal on the spot, which might have given occasion to explain at the moment—but it is the object of calumny to pursue its measures in secret because an open avowal might produce its antidote; and we know that insinuations often are for a time more effectual than direct accusation. I know not now the extent and precise nature of the reports but that there have been some prejudicial to my public character in this affair, I have undoubted, though unofficial grounds to believe."

Consequently he felt it incumbent on him to explain his action in the fullest detail.

"I have for the same reason to request that it be submitted to the superior authorities."

ii

The much-discussed General Maitland was still as far from Java as ever, and it was beginning to be realized that he was not coming at all. On 26th February John Palmer wrote to General Nightingall:

"I have been confounded about General Maitland. He must have humbugged my friend Cockerell to propagate a good quiz and hoax on my innocence."

Who was this General Maitland? Why did it seem so certain that he had been chosen and why, in the end, did he not come? It so happened that there were at that time no less than eleven officers of that name, at least two of them generals. An examination of their claims, however, soon makes it certain that it was General Thomas Maitland, who had resigned from the government of Ceylon on 15th March 1811 and returned to England. He had taken this step because he was ill, but there is no suggestion that he was unwilling, on grounds of health, to go again to the East. If a soldier was to govern Java, he would have been an excellent choice, though he was somewhat autocratic and of harsh temper. Yet he declined the Java appointment and accepted instead the governorship of Malta.

We can find a reason for this preference. At the time of the expedition to Mauritius and again when the Java expedition was in preparation, Minto had written to Maitland, then Governor of Ceylon, asking for some assistance. He had on each occasion received a very brusque reply. Not only had there been no help forthcoming, but Maitland had also criticized both schemes very caustically. In view of the acrimonious correspondence between Ceylon and Calcutta, we can hardly blame Maitland if he now felt unwilling to put himself under the orders of the Governor-General.

The withdrawal of Maitland, for whatever reason, did not affect the decision of the authorities to try to find a successor to Raffles. John Palmer wrote on 10th February to Sir Home Popham:

"Seton considers himself bound to support *fas et nefas* Lord Minto's arrangements for Bencoolen, and understands the Court's Order as preclusive of succession in a Bencool. servant only. What right Lord Minto had to nominate Mr Raffles prospectively, and thereby to keep the office vacant (already one year) indefinitely, nothing but the calm stoical impudence of his country can determine. Lord Moira must be an ass—as indeed I believe he is—if he does not spurn such presumption."

On 26th February, just a week after Raffles had recorded the minute concerning the sale of land, the Indiaman *Streatham* arrived from Calcutta, "bringing the most important dispatches this Government ever yet received, being no less than the impeachment of Mr Raffles by Major-General Gillespie. . . . How to account for such an act after what I have written, heard and seen I am entirely at a loss. . . ."

So wrote Travers, who was a friend and admirer of Gillespie, but to whom it seemed an act of "villainy and duplicity" that, shortly after saying good-bye to a man with so many protestations of goodwill, he should have commenced "to frame and fabricate a list of falsehoods" against him.

"The world will no doubt say that there must have been some motive for such extraordinary conduct. I can pronounce it to have originated in vanity, envy and wounded pride. Vanity because he thought his military fame was so established for his deeds on Java that, if he succeeded in effecting Mr Raffles' removal from the Government, he would be appointed to it himself. Envy because he was conscious of Mr Raffles' superior talents, which stood conspicuous on the records of Government during their misunderstanding. And his pride was hurt at his resignation having been so readily accepted, and which he tendered in the heat of passion, thinking that sooner than remove him at such a period, the Supreme Government would recommend Mr Raffles proceeding to Bencoolen and giving charge of the Government to him; in all of which he was disappointed, as he will be in his present infamous and disgraceful undertaking."

Raffles himself received this unexpected attack with characteristic calm.

"He coolly and dispassionately detailed to me", Travers recorded, "the particulars of every charge, with all their different bearings." He then passed the dispatch to Assey, secretary to the Java government, "who pledged himself after a careful perusal to refute every one [of the charges] by attested documents on oath within a fortnight. . . ."

It is not easy for the historian to offer a convincing explanation of this act of apparent treachery. Are we to assume that the reconciliation that took place just before Gillespie left Java was a deliberate fraud; that Gillespie only pretended and was already planning his revenge? We cannot believe that of him. True, a story existed that he had told his friends he would soon be back again in Java, yet he might have been referring only to the probability that Java would become a King's Colony, with himself as the new Governor. A more reasonable view is that, impetuous and quixotic as we know Gillespie to have been, he was quite sincere in his reconciliation with Raffles. The very excess of cordiality as described by Travers was characteristic of the man. Gillespie dealt only in extremes.

The real explanation of his change of heart after leaving Java should be sought in the presence on board of Blagrave, a very bitter and vindictive man, ready and able to poison Gillespie's mind. As the former secretary to the government, Blagrave could most plausibly have insinuated how Raffles had got the better of Gillespie in their various quarrels; how Raffles had made unflattering references to Gillespie, had written to Minto, had written to the Court of Directors about him. With a man like Gillespie, good resolutions would soon have withered under a steady stream of malicious innuendo.

It is known that, by the time the *Troubridge* reached Penang on her way to Calcutta, Gillespie's bitterness against Raffles had revived, for stories to that effect found their way back to Java. Gillespie received a regular ovation in Penang, and there were not lacking among the officials several who would have been only too pleased to fan his renewed resentment, so that when he arrived in India his old hatred was back at fever-point, and lacking any self-restraint, he spoke his mind loudly and savagely.

Had Minto been still Governor-General, the situation might still have been retrieved; he knew both Raffles and Gillespie and had his own views as to where lay the fault for their estrangement. Moira did not know Raffles, but as a professional soldier he did know Gillespie—if not personally, then by repute—as a very gallant officer. Moira was the natural head of the military world in Calcutta, and into that world Gillespie returned from virtual exile in Java, with all the laurels he had won there. A warm reception was assured him; all his brother officers would have been glad to see him and hear his news. In contrast to the indignities he believed he had suffered in Java, the excitement of this welcome no doubt went to his head and he said far more than a more cautious man would have allowed himself.

It seems unlikely that Gillespie had any original intention of making a formal attack on Raffles. What is more probable is that he said so much so publicly that at last he found himself unable to withdraw his words, and was then forced to make his complaint official. Blagrave, with his mind of revenge, would have been ever at his elbow, promising to produce the evidence to substantiate all Gillespie had said, and prepared, we suspect, to go far beyond anything Gillespie had ever alleged.

Gillespie's charges were first brought before the Governor-General in Council on 25th December 1813, when the matter was divided into seventeen heads of inquiry arising out of the charges. They were these:

1. The expediency of the sale of government lands.

2. Whether the sale was, generally speaking, made in the mode most conducive to the interests of government?

3. Whether the Lieutenant-Governor and Mr McQuoid and another

Commissioner became joint-owners of any of the coffee plantations; and, if so, to what extent?

4. Whether any of the plantations were disposed of by private sale to individuals; and, if so, on adequate and proper terms, or otherwise?

5. Whether an offer was made, through the late secretary to government [Blagrave], for one of the coffee plantations, of 5,000 dollars more than was actually paid by the Lieutenant-Governor and the persons united with him in purchasing the plantation?

6. The violation of the regulations of the island and the principles of policy by the union in the person of Mr McQuoid of the office of Landdrost and Resident of several Regencies.

7. The compatibility of the offices mentioned in the preceding article with the character recently acquired by Mr McQuoid of joint-proprietor of extensive tracts of land to which the influence of the above-mentioned office extended.

8. The other offices supposed to be held by Mr McQuoid and their compatibility with each other.

9. The propriety of the alteration made in the rate of profit which the holders of the coffee lands themselves enjoy; the former rate being a quarter, the present three-quarters.

10. The rate at which the coffee lands were purchased by the Lieutenant-Governor and his co-operators, with reference, on the one hand, to the intrinsic value of the lands, and, on the other, to the prices paid by other individuals.

11. The discouragement or prohibition of coffee plantations in other parts of the island, with the supposed view of enhancing the value of those acquired at the public sales, especially by the Lieutenant-Governor and his co-partners.

12. The policy of the measures adopted with respect to the Treasury Notes and Lombard Bank.

13. The expediency and propriety of the stoppage of issue of paper money from the Orphan Chamber, especially at the period when such stoppage is stated to have taken place.

14. The policy and justice of the restrictions established on the authority of the native chiefs (see Proclamation).

15. The expediency and propriety of the pledge made to receive on the part of government any surplus quantity of coffee at a nameable and fixed rate, when a higher price for it cannot be obtained in the market.

16. The conditions on which Mr McQuoid is reported to have obtained the contract for birds'-nests, and the propriety of such contract.

17. The construction of military works and application of military stores by the Lieutenant-Governor without the concurrence of his Council, and the object of such works.

So that Gillespie could give more precise information under these heads, the matter was deferred until the next week's meeting, when Gillespie attended. In his written and verbal replies, he mentioned Blagrave as one of his authorities, with the result that Blagrave was called to attend the Council on 15th January. The same day a dispatch to Raffles was prepared and sent to him with the proceedings of the Council's meeting and details of the charges—also seventeen in number—made by Gillespie and endorsed by Blagrave.

On receipt of these documents, Raffles replied immediately:

"I have this day had the honour to receive your dispatch of the 15th ult., and having carefully perused the proceedings of the Supreme Government containing the charges which Major-General Gillespie has endeavoured to fasten on my administration and character, I lose not a moment in requesting you to convey to His Excellency the Right Honourable the Governor-General in Council an unqualified assurance that I feel perfectly competent of my ability to prove to his Lordship's satisfaction that the greater part of the circumstances stated by Major-General Gillespie and Mr Blagrave are utterly devoid of foundation; that the remainder can be easily accounted for; and that the insinuations which have been made by both parties will be found to be in no way borne out by the simple facts of the case."

He returned to Buitenzorg to prepare his full reply, which was to take some weeks to complete, with hundreds of pages of text, appendixes, and data from government records. This, however, did not prevent the customary party on 14th March in celebration of his wedding anniversary.

"We sat down to dinner eighty," wrote one who attended, "after which we had a play 'Tom Thumb' performed by the guests, which went off uncommonly well. We then danced till morning and passed a most agreeable happy time. Mr Raffles was but little amongst us, because so much engaged with his Dispatches."

By a slight regrouping of the charges, Raffles reduced the number to fifteen, four of which, as distinguished by the Supreme Government, concerned the policy of his administration, and eleven his personal integrity. Of the former the subjects were:

1. The sale of lands in its relation to the redemption of the paper currency.

2. The collateral financial arrangements arising from that redemption.

3. The policy in regard to coffee culture.

4. The effect of the revenue changes on the authority of the Regents and other native authorities.

It is curious to note that Gillespie, when picking out for attack aspects of Raffles' policy, omitted to include the one fundamental point that had been most galling to himself—the policy, deliberately pursued by Raffles from the day of his first appointment, that the civil power should be the chief authority in Java. Gillespie had fought in vain against the insistence by Raffles that, even in military matters, the last word rested with him; and it was the recognition of his failure that had induced Gillespie to apply to India for a transfer. Why, then, did he not raise that issue now? Was it because, on arrival in India, he realized for the first time that his own chief, Sir George Nugent, was himself subordinate to the Governor-General and that he found no backing in India for the position he had tried to establish in Java?

The four points of policy that Gillespie did attack were certainly points of substance, and we have already examined some of the weightier arguments that could have been levelled against them. They were, however, points on which Gillespie himself, a professional soldier from his early years, was little qualified to express any expert opinion, and on all but the first he had, when senior member of the Council in Java, been discreetly silent. In regard to the sale of lands, he had been originally opposed to such a drastic measure, but had finally given way and attended the sales in person. The arguments he now enunciated were such as could be fairly used against this policy: the shortness of notice, the great size of the plots, and the general scarcity of cash. But the underlying basis of his contention was that the arguments used by the promoters of the sales were so unconvincing as to suggest that the redemption of the paper currency was not the real purpose of the transaction at all; it was merely a cloak for a scheme whereby Raffles and his special friends were to enrich themselves at the expense of the government. Gillespie cleverly avoided making any such charge openly, but the implication was too obvious for anyone to miss.

In replying to Gillespie's allegations, Raffles did not fail to appreciate the sinister picture so clearly painted. He took pains to restate the grounds on which his government had acted as it had, maintaining that no alternative was open to it for meeting a definitely critical situation. If higher authority could again be convinced, as Minto had been, that such emergency measures were unavoidable if the spectacular fall in the value of the paper currency was to be arrested, then the underlying allegation of a corrupt motive fell to the ground. Raffles was very much better equipped to marshal the arguments in support of his financial policy than Gillespie was to conduct the case against it.

In stating his further criticism of the collateral arrangements arising from the redemption of the paper currency, Gillespie was still more out of his depth. Moreover, he was foolish enough to bring forward as evidence a memorandum concerning paper currency prepared by the very senior Dutch official, van Braam. Raffles was quick to point out that, inasmuch as it had been written in England for an entirely different purpose and at a time when van Braam could not have been cognizant of Raffles' financial measures in Java, it could have no bearing whatever on the case.

Concerning the effect of the sale of lands on coffee culture, Gillespie argued that where lands had been sold the coffee monopoly had passed from the government to the purchaser. Raffles repudiated the suggestion, claiming that, under the published conditions of sale, all the rights of government remained unabated. This appears a conclusive answer, though as Levyssohn Norman has pointed out, the purchasers were dismayed at this pronouncement by Raffles, having been firmly of the opinion that they would be free to dispose of their coffee at their own discretion. This uncertainty was to continue for many years—the cause of great discontent under the restored Dutch government, which upheld Raffles' view.

To support his allegation that the new revenue instructions degraded the Regents and other native authorities, Gillespie referred to the proclamation of 16th October 1813. His views appear more fully in his written answers submitted to the Governor-General in Council on 31st December. In these he expounded what may be regarded as the standard argument of the day against any relaxation of the feudal system: that a general undermining of society would result, and that, in all probability, the Javanese, freed from feudal compulsion, would become idle and abandon cultivation altogether.

In his reply, Raffles took some trouble to explain that the status of the Regents was not affected at all by the sale of lands. Such change in their status as had taken place arose from the land-revenue regulations. This seems irrelevant, for there is nothing to show that either Gillespie or the Supreme Government had suggested that the status of the Regents was affected by the sale of lands, the reference being specifically to the land-revenue arrangements. That, however, is perhaps not very important, as the fundamental difference between Raffles and Gillespie was, on both matters, one of outlook; Raffles was an advanced liberal, far ahead of most of his generation, while Gillespie held the more conservative views of the average man of the period.

We have dealt but briefly with the first group of charges, because neither Gillespie nor Blagrave was sufficiently a master of any of the subjects to make a strong case against the Java government of lack of wisdom in its policy. At the same time, their combined charges did have the secondary effect, and one which unquestionately was deliberately intended, of throwing doubts on the purity of the motives actuating that policy. Although the Supreme Government had differentiated those acts of policy as cases where expediency only was in question, examination suggests that the first group differed from the second only in that the latter challenged Raffles' integrity openly, while the former did it by implication.

Gillespie's thirteen charges in this group were condensed by Raffles to eleven, which can be summarized thus:

1. Purchase of government land.
2. Manner of conducting the sale.
3. Underhand means to avoid paying a proper price.
4. Land purchased below value.
5. Allowing private purchases in prejudice of public sale.
6. Purchasing all coffee plantations and then discouraging the growing of coffee in eastern districts.
7. Debasing the coinage.
8. Constructing military works without consent of the Board and to assist Raffles' own coffee export.
9. The expedition to Sambas.
10. Personal indelicacy towards Gillespie, and tending to lower his dignity in the eyes of the natives.
11. The numerous offices of McQuoid, and his lease of birds'-nest rocks.

We will deal first with the more trifling accusations. Debasing the coinage sounds very sinister, but it was only a technical point—and Raffles had been against it. When the new silver coinage had been discussed, he had been in favour of a lower alloy in proportion to silver than had been used by the Dutch. The majority of the Board, including Gillespie, had voted for the same alloy as before, and Raffles had accepted this decision.

The eighth charge, which also sounds formidable, was that Raffles had undertaken military works without the consent of the Board and for the sole purpose of protecting from pirates the export of produce of his own recently purchased estate. Raffles produced evidence to prove that the works in question were constructed with the concurrence of the Board and with the knowledge of Gillespie, and that their object was to check frequent piratical raids, which were quite genuine and not, as Gillespie and Blagrave both insinuated, invented to suit his purpose. He further demonstrated that, in any event, the forts could not have been of any use for the purpose his opponents alleged, for they were sited more than two degrees of longitude distant from the estate he had purchased, and that the two districts in question were separated by impassable mountains and inaccessible shores. This charge, therefore, could not be substantiated. It is only remarkable that it was ever made.

The ninth accusation referred to the disastrous expedition of Captain Bowen, R.N., against Sambas. It was alleged that this had been planned by Raffles without consulting Gillespie, and that a hundred soldiers had been requisitioned without the latter's knowledge. Documents proved, however, that Captain Bowen had made the attack on his own initiative, and, while it was true that a hundred men had been supplied at his request to act as marines and replace losses from sickness among his normal establishment, the orders authorizing this draft had been signed by Gillespie. Moreover, as Gillespie must have known, this expedition had already been the subject of a special enquiry by the Supreme Government, and the Java Council had been advised of the conclusion, which was that Captain Bowen alone was responsible, with no reflection at all on the government of Java. Gillespie's allegations were thus definitely untrue in one important respect and unfounded in their general implication.

The last of the minor charges related to the alleged multifarious offices and extravagant remuneration of Thomas McQuoid. It is difficult to avoid the conclusion that this particular official was singled out by Gillespie to satisfy a personal spite. Apart from being an intimate friend of Raffles', McQuoid had probably, in his capacity as Resident of Buitenzorg, come into official conflict with Gillespie when the latter was at his country residence. Gillespie might, too, have had reason to suspect that McQuoid had influenced Raffles against him. The allegations now made by Gillespie were calculated to create a strong impression of gross favouritism and an improper plurality of offices. Raffles put up a spirited defence of his old Penang friend, whose original employment in Java had been at the instance of Mr Martin, Resident of Amboina. McQuoid was not, however, a private individual given employment by Raffles to oblige a fellow official, though such a practice was not at all uncommon in those days; he was on the regular establishment of the East India Company. The most telling argument used by Raffles in reply, and one that was certainly true of Java generally, was that the shortage of officials was acute. Apart from that general explanation, he made out a plausible case for the various offices held by McQuoid and explained the financial adjustments made, which would not seem to have produced, on paper at any rate, an extravagant total. Nevertheless, one cannot but feel that McQuoid, through his friendship with Raffles, got a rather bigger share of remunerative offices than was quite proper or in the best interests of Java; and, in spite of what Raffles said in support of McQuoid's ownership of land, the fact that McQuoid had been allowed to purchase and own property in the actual district of which he was Resident inevitably created a somewhat dubious situation. To-day we should feel that it was no real answer, even if true, that there was not any conflict between his public duties and his private interests, and that proof was forthcoming that the government could not have been defrauded of any revenue due to it by reason of the fact that the Resident happened to own property in his own district.

If this had been the only matter in which McQuoid was involved, the charge could have been dismissed on the ground that this state of affairs was not by any means uncommon, there being no regulation that definitely forbade it. In regard to the farming of edible birds'-nests, there seems to have been a technical breach of the rules affecting the conduct of government officials. Gillespie had informed the Governor-General in Council:

"A mountain was discovered in the Regencies to possess a portion of birds'-nests, which was advertised for sale for seven (7) years—as I have understood there was no competition, from the ignorance of persons who might have been inclined to bid—and it was accordingly purchased by Mr McQuoid for 12 hundred dollars per annum for seven years. It has been reported to me that the mountain is worth from 40 to 60 thousand dollars annually, and is within the control of Mr McQuoid, as General Resident over the Regencies."

Whether or not McQuoid should have acquired this interest, Raffles was in a position to establish that in the first year of McQuoid's tenancy the sale of nests had been less than the rent paid, and that Gillespie's estimate of the value of the property was grossly exaggerated.

McQuoid's name figured also in the sales of land, to which we must now turn.

In the dispatch dated 15th January 1813 the secretary to the Supreme Government had written:

"There is, however, one article which, above all others, requires explanation, which is the purchase stated to have been made by you, either singly or jointly with other persons, of some of the Government lands. You will consequently feel the propriety of stating distinctly whether you had any share in these purchases; and, if so, the grounds on which you conceived that such a measure could be reconciled to the faithful discharge of the high official state held by you on the island of Java."

There were three quite separate and distinct charges in connexion with these sales: the first, that Raffles himself was a purchaser of land; the second, that there had been irregularities in the procedure whereby certain favoured parties alone had been able to purchase the land privately or publicly, and in either case at prices below its true value; the third, that Raffles had been a party to those irregularities in order to further his own interests.

Leaving on one side for the moment the question of alleged irregularities, we must consider whether it was proper in principle for Raffles to purchase at a public sale any land for his own account. We have already suggested in the case of McQuoid that an undesirable situation must, in a modern view, arise when a Resident acquires a large estate in a district under his superintendence. If that is a correct view, then clearly it is no more permissible for a Lieutenant-Governor to purchase and own a large estate in the country for the administration of which he is responsible.

Further, it seems even more ill-advised that a Lieutenant-Governor, as the authority who has made the decision to sell the land, who has been responsible for the procedure whereby it is to be valued and auctioned, and who has prescribed the conditions under which it is to be sold, should himself participate as a buyer, however clean his hands and however impeccable his motives. Public opinion to-day would certainly regard that as improper, and public opinion would be right.

But it must at once be added that public opinion has advanced a long way since those days, and this principle, now so well recognized, was then far from being generally accepted. It is true that the Court of Directors ultimately held that Raffles had been guilty of a grave indiscretion, but whether they would have reached that verdict had there not been at least an element of scandal associated with the sale is very questionable. As already remarked, there was no regulation prohibiting any official from purchasing property in the country or district where his official duties lay. Moreover, while officials were not permitted to trade, some were largely remunerated by a percentage of the moneys it was their duty to collect. While this sale by the Java Council of public lands has been criticized from a number of angles, it has never been condemned on the ground that many of the potential purchasers would almost inevitably be government servants. When Penang was founded—and later Singapore—nobody questioned the propriety of the officials there taking up plots of land. Within the memory of living members of the Malayan Civil Service, officers were encouraged by official circular to buy land, not only to assist in the development of the country, but also to give confidence to the local population that British administration had come to stay.

When, then, we try to look at the question with the eyes of a contemporary, we find it difficult to believe that Raffles felt he was in any way betraying his official trust when, under the peculiar circumstances of Dutch reluctance to bid for land, he agreed to become a purchaser. Nor would public opinion generally have taken any different view. It should also be remembered, though it is often not, that Raffles had made his full statement to the Council as to why he had been a buyer, and had subsequently disposed of his interests when he had heard that opinion in Calcutta was somewhat critical. This had been before he could have had any suspicion that Gillespie was formulating specific charges. To be sensitive of criticism is not necessarily an admission of a guilty conscience. The suggestion just made that contemporary opinion might not have regarded such a purchase as improper is not negated by the fact that Gillespie attacked Raffles for being a buyer. The gravamen of Gillespie's accusations is that Raffles had not, as he had claimed, sold public land to help the financial situation; it had been a thoroughly dishonest sale and for the sole purpose of enriching himself and his friends, a very different and much more serious indictment.

In his minute of 18th February, recorded a week before the receipt of the communication from the Supreme Government, Raffles had set out all the facts. He now dealt with the specific charges, and attached the former minute as Appendix G to his dispatch to Calcutta.

Taking the second charge first, he assembled a formidable body of evidence to show that no irregularities had taken place; that Gillespie had been present at the meeting of the Council when the private sale to Muntinghe had been approved, and had also been present at the Batavia auction and acquiesced in each sale. Raffles asked, as he was certainly entitled to, why Gillespie had remained silent on these alleged irregularities while in Java, and only voiced them on arrival in India. This is a fundamental weakness in Gillespie's case; although it applies in general to the whole series of charges, it is particularly appropriate to the sale of lands.

It is always extremely difficult to prove at a later date whether a price actually obtained at an auction is theoretically a fair one or not. The later the inquiry, the more difficult the answer becomes. For all that, even allowing for the general shortage of cash prevailing at the time—and which indeed can be used as an argument of some force against the expediency of any land sales at all at that particular juncture—it is not easy to avoid the conclusion that the lands were sold at figures considerably below at least their potential value. It is no real answer that they fetched prices substantially above the official estimates, for some of these were prepared by those very persons who subsequently became purchasers. On the other hand, it is equally difficult to believe that Raffles himself was in any way party to the swindle, if swindle there was. Travers, who should have known, stated in his diary that he entertained no doubt of Raffles' innocence.

On no other occasion was Raffles' financial integrity ever questioned, and one is more inclined to the view that some of his officials put their heads together and involved him in transactions that were not at all what they might have been. It is quite possible that he was led into a false position by specious arguments, and that the speculators were afraid not that the sales would be annulled by a new government or the British authority in India, but that they might be repudiated on the grounds that competition had been bogus and the resulting prices artificially low. They might have concocted the story of Dutch fears and persuaded the Lieutenant-Governor to be a purchaser in the confident expectation that any subsequent enquiry would be prevented by him, or, alternatively, that the participation of the Lieutenant-Governor would discourage any very searching investigation by higher authority. This, of course, is mere conjecture, there being no evidence to support it. The alleged reluctance of the Dutch was not necessarily fictitious; it was quite understandable, in the circumstances.

Outwardly, at any rate, the sales seemed to have been conducted with apparent good faith, and Raffles had no reason to doubt that appearance and fact completely coincided. It is questionable whether everything was above board, yet, from a study of Raffles' character, it is difficult to conceive his doing what he knew to be wrong. We cannot but feel that he was genuinely convinced that he could be a purchaser, not only without impropriety, but also with actual advantage to the government, and was certainly guiltless of any irregularity as to the price he had paid.

The fifth charge in the second group, which was the subject of reference under the Supreme Government's fifth head of inquiry (see page 329), arose as follows:

In answer to the inquiry, Gillespie stated:

"I was informed by Mr C. Blagrave that an offer was made by letter, which came before him, from M. de Frize [Vriese] for one of the estates in the Regencies, and that he understood the sum to be 5,000 dollars more than the estimate value by the Commissioners."

Blagrave added this:

"A letter came into my possession from a M. de Vriese, assistant to the Resident of Buitenzorg [McQuoid], dated, I believe, in December 1812, offering a sum of money (to the best of my recollection, 45,000 Spanish dollars) for one of the lots in the Regencies, which letter I forwarded to the Lieutenant-Governor for his instructions, together with one of a similar nature from Mr de Wilde. As the tenders for the purchase of the Government lands were to be made through the private secretary [Assey] to the Lieutenant-Governor, I concluded that these letters would be replied to through that channel; subsequently, however, to the day of the sale (in the month of February) I was sent, by order of the Lieutenant-Governor, on a commission to Tjanjore [Chianjur] with the Civil Commissioner (Mr Hope), accompanied by Mr McQuoid. M. de Vriese, who resides at Tjanjore, joined us at the Regent's house, where we had met for the purpose of the Commission, and, entering into a conversation with Mr McQuoid respecting the sale of the Government lands, expressed himself much disappointed and dissatisfied at the treatment he had experienced. M. de Vriese observed that he understood Mr de Wilde had been accommodated with the estate he had offered for, while he (M. de Vriese), though he had tendered 5,000 dollars more for the lot he required than the amount of the estimate by the Commissioners for the sale of the land, had not even received a reply to his application. I am not aware of the sum actually paid for this by the Lieutenant-Governor and the persons who were associated or supposed to be united with him in the purchase."

This was Chopper Mountain, the estate referred to as Goenoeng Parang in Engelhardt's letter to Raffles in December 1812.

In answer to the charge, Raffles produced evidence that de Vriese's tender had been considered, but rejected as being insufficient. It had amounted to the rix-dollar paper equivalent of less than 7,000 silver dollars, whereas Raffles and Engelhardt had paid 36,500 silver dollars for that lot.

In a sworn statement dated 5th March 1814 de Vriese attested:

"To the question you have put to me concerning the sum I offered for a spot of land in the Regency of Tjanjore, which was sold with other lands in January 1813, and if I could recollect having held a conversation with you [McQuoid], in the presence of Mr Blagrave, concerning these lands, about a month after the public sale, on which occasion I remarked that, although my offer was 5,000 Spanish dollars more than the valuation of the Commission appointed to carry into effect the sale of lands, my speculation to purchase this lot was unsuccessful, I declare, and I am ready to confirm it with an oath, that I offered 45,000 rix-dollars paper money, or about 7,000 Spanish dollars silver, for a lot of land called Goenong Parang, known under No. 7, which sum appeared to me sufficient, because the land was too distant for the sale and transport of its produce to other places. I recollect perfectly well that you were at Tjipanas [Chipanas] with Mr Blagrave, but I declare that I never made a remark on the failure of my attempt to purchase the said land. I must add that I could not be deceived in this respect, however, as I was present at the sale. I had it in my power to have bid what I thought fit, but the lot having sold for 30,500 [36,500] Spanish dollars, that sum exceeded my calculations. Further, I declare that I never heard of any valuation of the lands in the Regency of Tjanjore being made by the Commissioners."

So much for the fifth charge.

The only other charge relating to the sale of lands was the sixth, which alleged that the coffee regulations had been specially amended to enhance the value of the land Raffles had bought. This is a typical example of Gillespie's inexcusable ignorance. He should have been acquainted with the regulations or, if not knowing them in detail, should have taken steps to find out before making such an allegation. Raffles had no difficulty in showing that, because of the surplus coffee already available in the Preanger districts, coffee growing had, from the very early days of the British régime, been discouraged in favour of rice in the eastern districts. This policy had been adopted before the sale of lands was ever contemplated.

The remaining charge is that of indelicacy towards Gillespie. As the whole of the charges brought by him against Raffles were undoubtedly influenced by the personal antagonism that had grown up between them, it is a little surprising that specific instances of indelicacy were not more numerous. Such allegations as Gillespie did make serve to confirm what has been suggested elsewhere, that the main causes of difference between the two men were tradition and temperament. Gillespie regarded military officers and millitary authority as, by some special right, superior to civilians and civilian power, a conviction not uncommon in his time and, indeed, for many years afterwards. Raffles, for his part, did not recognize this special distinction, taking a view of the supreme authority of civil power that was in advance of his generation. While, to begin with, he certainly made every effort to conciliate the commander of the forces, he was at the same time quite determined that the civil power should be the ultimate authority, a point of view that to-day would never be questioned. In addition, his ideas on the treatment of the local population and the preservation of their rights were not in accord with those of most of his contemporaries. High-handed action against the native inhabitants by anyone in authority, whether military or civil, caused him to intervene fearlessly.

Gillespie's main complaint under this head of indelicacy concerned the dispute over the house at Chipanas. It was alleged that Raffles had lowered Gillespie's prestige among the Javanese by causing the Regent to make the petition on behalf of the workers forced into service by the military. It is highly improbable that Raffles had done such a thing, but we can well understand how angry he must have been at this exploitation of the Javanese in complete contravention of all the regulations he had laid down.

Having given his answer to this and the various other points raised in the tenth accusation, Raffles proceeded to bring against Gillespie certain counter-charges, among them the alleged rape of a virgin from the orphan school at Samarang.

The dispatch was completed by 15th March, the day after his wedding-anniversary party, and submitted to General Nightingall. After reading carefully through it, he stated that he was more than satisfied with the answers Raffles had given, and while, on accepting the command of the forces in Java, it had been "his fixed determination to steer a single path and form no party, the present was an instance he could not have contemplated, and as he could not sit a tame spectator and see the attempts to overpower innocence and honour by falsehood, calumny and misrepresentation, aided by a little interest, he would be happy to afford his cause all the support in his power". This by Travers, who added: "Mr Raffles received these sentiments with gratitude and respect."

After some discussion, it was agreed to send Charles Assey to Calcutta, to furnish every explanation the Supreme Government might desire, and Raffles pledged himself to stand or fall by the explanation Assey would give on every point. It was further decided to send Travers to London, to afford the same service to the Court of Directors. These decisions were confirmed at a special meeting of the Council. Travers left on 29th March, Assey on 10th April. Assey was much delayed on his trip and did not reach Calcutta till June, only to find that the Governor-General was just proceeding up country. Travers landed at Plymouth on 19th September. On arriving in London, he found the East India Company friendly but non-committal, and so disinterested in Java that, wrote Travers, "dispatches from that place were not even opened in Leadenhall Street".

Raffles' dispatch was dated 25th March 1814. It was subsequently printed by him and privately circulated, consisting of twenty-one pages supported by nearly three hundred pages of enclosures and appendixes.

The answers given by him to the sundry accusations made by Gillespie and Blagrave might have satisfied the Supreme Government had he not seen fit to couple Gillespie's name with the native orphan girl at Samarang. The facts of the case are simple enough. A somewhat notorious character named Rochinet went to the matron of the school and demanded a certain girl student. The answer was a refusal. There appears to be no real evidence that the demand was made on behalf of Gillespie, or any support for the story that the girl was carried off by force to his house. It is remarkable that Raffles allowed himself to incorporate in his reply to the Governor-General a charge of this nature, made by a third party, more particularly as subsequent correspondence with India showed that the accusation, as far as Gillespie was concerned, could not be substantiated.

The matter has been dealt with at length by Major Wakeham in his biography of Gillespie, though partly with the apparent purpose of ridiculing the virtuous indignation evinced by the "Victorian writer", Demetrius Boulger, the author of the first biography of Raffles. Whether Boulger was really shocked or not, and whether morals in Java then or later were particularly lax, seems rather beside the point. Raffles was no doubt perfectly familiar with the low standards both in contemporary England and in contemporary Java and, though his own behaviour was impeccable, he would not have brought such a charge against Gillespie merely to show the looseness of his morals. Nor, again, can we believe he would have brought it at all if, when he wrote it, he had not thought it to be true.

Gillespie's morals were presumably no better and presumably no worse than those of his brother officers of the period, and indeed Major Wakeham intimates that he had had a good many affairs at home, and was separated from his wife. We know, too, that he had a local mistress in Java and had children by her. At the same time, it is not here suggested that the story concerning the orphan school was well-founded; to the contrary, it lacked probability. But Raffles took it for truth, and it must not be forgotten that he wrote his reply at great speed and in a state of high indignation, without, it is to be feared, his usual good judgment.

In making this counter-charge, it is far more likely that Raffles was influenced not by any sexual irregularity on Gillespie's part, but by the conviction that Gillespie had put himself above the law by making such a demand, worse still in respect of a native. Reference has already been made in these pages to Charles Metcalfe's comments on the cavalier treatment of Indians by British officers. Raffles had not the same experience of the military caste, but he shared Metcalfe's feelings and would therefore have felt himself as free to resist General Gillespie as he would anyone else who failed to treat the local population as he himself felt they were entitled to be treated.

Notwithstanding this, and apart from the impropriety of making a charge he could not substantiate, it was a grave error to introduce such a topic into an official dispatch. Its consequences were far-reaching. It was inevitable that Moira, with his military background, would incline to the side of a distinguished soldier in any quarrel with a civilian of whom he knew little or nothing. The general weakness of Gillespie's charges, as revealed by Raffles in his defence, would have compelled Moira to give a verdict for Raffles, notwithstanding the unfortunate purchase of land, had not this question of the orphan been introduced in his reply. That offended immediately every canon of honour and decency that the soldier Moira held sacred. Even if Raffles had been able to prove the point, Moira would still have remained deeply incensed by what he would have regarded as a grave impropriety in thus publicly compromising the dignity of a major-general. As that allegation could not even be proved, his opinion of Raffles, already weakened by the accumulated suspicion engendered by Gillespie's charges, fell to zero. Consequently his judgment of the quarrel and of Raffles' whole administration in Java became tainted by prejudice directly inspired by this particular incident.

iii

In all the biographies of Raffles, the charges of Gillespie and Blagrave figure prominently, and quite rightly so, for they proved a decisive factor in his career. But, as far as can be ascertained, no mention has hitherto been made of the curious array of charges also brought at this time by Major Robison, who, as a result of his misguided action when Resident of Palembang, had been sent back to Calcutta, there to add his strident and bitter voice to those already raised against Raffles.

If Gillespie can be described as a lion and Blagrave as his attendant jackal, Robison can be fitly represented as a hyena. The whole basis of his attack on Raffles was one of fierce personal animosity, and had his been an isolated impugnment, it would have carried no weight with the Supreme Government. But coming immediately after the allegations of Gillespie and Blagrave, no doubt it had its effect.

Raffles' spirited reply was dated 1st October 1814. There is a copy of it in the India Office Library. He began by observing that if the charges had not reached him through the Governor-General in Council, he would have "felt little inclination to have waded through and much less to have answered such a mass of absurdity and trash". As far as the charges affected his administration of Java, he pointed out that his policy in regard to Palembang and the action he had taken were well known to the Supreme Government and had had its approval, and that the conduct of Robison at Palembang had already been condemned by the same authority; that it was untrue that he himself had ever given any indication to Robison that he had approved of his policy, or had subsequently changed his mind.

There were other small points concerning Robison's arrest, the treatment of witnesses, and so forth. Raffles disproved them, and they need not detain us here. The more interesting part is the section described by Robison as "some account of the general manner of proceeding of the Java Government". In this Robison endeavoured to prove, as Raffles observed, that there was "little honour, justice or prudence in the government, and that public interests had been sacrificed to vainglory and the splendid profusion of the Lieutenant-Governor". The purpose of all this could only be "that if it was necessary he [Robison] should sink, he was determined to do his utmost that the Java Government should sink also".

Raffles dealt with the charges under eleven headings. We need but touch on them very briefly. Robison described the public officers of Java as "a set of needy adventurers, most of them taken out of the fifth class of society". In reply, Raffles gave a list of the twenty Residents, of whom fifteen were officers in the army or in the military or civil service of the East India Company, two were Dutch gentlemen who had special claims on the British Government, and three only were English gentlemen not in the regular service of the East India Company. Two of these last had been introduced by high officials of the Company, the third appointed by the late Governor-General. He then proceeded to mention a number of less senior officials, including his brother-in-law, Captain Flint, and another brother-in-law, Dr Brown of the Bengal Service, whose presence in Java had, he remarked, apparently escaped the notice of Major Robison.

Reference was also made to Mr Bingley, recently dead, who is chiefly interesting to us as the man from whom Raffles derived one of his names. Bingley had lost all his money in Europe, and Raffles had provided a minor post for him in Java. This modest case of help in an age of extravagant patronage cannot be regarded as a very heinous crime, more particularly when, as Raffles pointed out, there existed an acute shortage of competent officials available to him for maintaining the greatly extended administration of the country under the British régime. In this connexion he revealed the striking fact that there were in Java only three members of the Company's civil service. They held the three most senior posts in the island. All the other important offices were held by officers in the King's or Company's military service, much to the annoyance, often voiced, of the commander-in-chief in India.

We may pass over some ill-informed comments by Robison on the administration of the orphan chamber and go on to the "pomp and parade of the Lieutenant-Governor and his Lady", an accusation so full of "ribaldry and nonsense" that Raffles found difficulty in treating it seriously. He was accused of never going abroad without a troop of European dragoons retained solely for the purpose of "galloping before and after his or the Lady's coach", and two European messengers in "Royal liveries". He was further alleged to own "two splendid palaces"; a post establishment was maintained on his behalf at the public expense, which was alleged to cost more than double the salary of the Lieutenant-Governor; he made levies on the country to work on his estate at Buitenzorg, to complete his pet road or to help his carriage along when travelling "like a courier".

In his reply, Raffles pointed out that though from the outset the Resident had been authorized to have escorts, he himself had not had one until (a side thrust at Gillespie) the attitude of the commander of the forces had encouraged disrespect on the part of the military towards the Lieutenant-Governor. He had then been advised to have such an escort for his personal protection. Although his original intention had been to utilize native cavalry, the commander of the forces had preferred that hussars should be employed. The small contingent detailed for the purpose also found orderlies for the commander of the forces.

Robison had also levelled the grave accusation that the Lieutenant-Governor's coach was drawn by no less than six horses. Raffles mildly reminded him that all coaches in Java were drawn by four ponies (not horses) and on occasions in hilly country, by six. This was the universal practice. As for the attendants in royal livery, these were the usual door-keepers attached to public offices and "their livery is anything but royal; it is in fact the same shabby coarse dress by which they were distinguished under the former Dutch government". Regarding the two palaces, "the so-called Government House at Ryswick could not by the wildest imagination be described as a palace". It was a small house in private ownership, rented by the Lieutenant-Governor. "Government House, Buitenzorg, built fifty years before by Governor Imhoff, is certainly a more palatial place", but it was in a state of ruin and had to be repaired to be made habitable. Apart from being the only place suitable for government entertaining, it also housed the effective part of the secretary's establishment.

Turning to the post establishment, he pointed out that it was a private concern for the hiring out of horses and carriages, and "if Major Robison paid his bills before he left Java he must have known that anybody could have had the use of a set of horses for twelve dollars". The late Governor-General had never ordered its abolition, but the Lieutenant-Governor had wellnigh abolished it, because it had proved oppressive to the native population.

The story of the so-called levies on the civil population was pure nonsense. The Buitenzorg estate comprised only a small kitchen garden inadequate to supply the vegetables required; a small flower garden; and a small enclosure for deer. It was true that at one time there had been a considerable establishment of troops at Buitenzorg, and the local natives (another thrust at Gillespie) had been forced to supply a certain number of coolies to attend them. This had annoyed the local population, though the forced labour involved had been trifling compared with what had been customary under the Dutch. It had been, however, only a temporary measure, and the general policy of the government throughout Java was to abolish as far as possible all forced labour.

We need not consider all the charges in detail, but one final example must be given to show the type of accusation brought forward by Robison. It was that the Susuhunan of Solo had been obliged to "submit to the indignity, as impolitic as it was cruel, of travelling from his capital to Samarang in order to be taught the game of whist with the Lady Governess". To this Raffles answered that the Susuhunan had never been to Samarang in his life and, as far as he, Raffles, was aware, had never been taught to play the game of whist either by the Lady Governess or by anyone else.

No doubt, he continued, this fiction "afforded Major Robison such a grand close to his pathetic appeal in favour of the many thousand victims of oppression, that truth appears to have stood as little in the way of his invention in this instance as in most others".

So much for Robison's charges. Even if he had not revealed his character clearly over the Palembang affair, it is obvious from the tenor of his accusations that he was a miserable, spiteful creature, wholly irresponsible and unfitted for any major degree of authority. The chief interest in his attack lies in Raffles' answers. He supplies quite a lot of incidental information about himself not easily obtainable from any other sources.

Such, then, were the charges his three enemies had lodged against him. The verdict on them is recorded later. One must remark here, however, that, till the day of his death, Raffles was never to escape completely from the cumulative effect of these onslaughts on his administrative ability and personal integrity. Never again was he to enjoy that happy confidence given him so unreservedly by Minto. In its place there was to be the shadow of official mistrust, varying in intensity, but always present.

Whether his antagonists obtained due satisfaction from the lingering wounds their revenge had thus inflicted, who can say? Before judgment could be passed, Gillespie was dead. He was killed at Kalunga, in the Nepalese war, on 31st October 1814. Moira, writing to Lord Bathurst, Secretary for the Colonies, on 10th November, observed that the loss of such a distinguished soldier would, in any case, be a matter for deep regret, but was the greater because Gillespie had fallen in an unsuccessful attack.

"The good fortune which had attended him in former desperate enterprises", wrote Moira, "induced him to believe, I fear, that the storm of the fortress of Kalunga might be achieved by the same daring valor and readiness of resource whereby he had on other occasions triumphed. . . . The assault, in which he was killed, at the foot of the rampart, involved, as I conceived, no possibility of success."

Luck had deserted Gillespie at last. He was knighted in 1815 before the news of his death reached England.

His two supporters have no such claim on our regard and little seems to have been recorded about them in subsequent history. Blagrave, in his blind rage against Raffles, had overlooked that a violent attack on a subordinate authority might be interpreted by the higher authority as casting reflections on itself also. This was precisely the view taken by the Gevernor-General.

"The disrespectful terms in which Mr Blagrave speaks of the Lieutenant-Governor of Java" were considered in the minute of 30th January 1815 "to be very unbecoming and reprehensible, and the expression used at the conclusion of Mr Blagrave's letter is not only improper in its application to Mr Raffles, but is also disrespectful to the Government to which Mr Blagrave addressed himself."

This reprimand doubtless ruined any hopes of promotion that Blagrave may still have nursed.

By 1822 Robison had advanced one step in rank, as he was then a lieutenant-colonel commanding the 14th Foot at Poona. But his talent for quarrelling with authority seems to have remained undiminished, for he was then about to be tried by court-martial on charges of general insubordination, and in particular for writing letters to the *Calcutta Journal*, criticizing the commander-in-chief. The last trace we have of him is contained in one or two letters to him from John Palmer, in the last of which (24th August 1822) Palmer explained how he had completely failed in his attempt to persuade the Governor-General to countermand the trial.

It has not been thought worth while to pursue Robison's subsequent history. One suspects that he continued to run true to form.

Chapter Sixteen

JAVA, 1814

i

HAVING completed his reply to the charges brought by Gillespie and Blagrave and dispatched it, Raffles, like a sensible man, would have dismissed the matter from his mind. The answers he had submitted and the formidable array of affidavits that supported them must surely convince the Supreme Government that he had been the victim of a malicious and vindictive libel. Nightingall had been so impressed with Raffles' innocence that he had undertaken to use his influence with his military friends in India, a gesture of obvious advantage to Raffles. Any lingering doubts that might persist in Calcutta or London would be readily resolved by Assey and Travers.

"While you are quietly gliding", he wrote to William Brown Ramsay on 21st March 1814, "on the smooth and sunny stream of private life, it is my lot to be tossed on boisterous billows, and to be annoyed with all the clouds and evils which ensue from party spirit.

"Without family pretensions, fortune, or powerful friends, it has been my lot to obtain the high station which I now fill; and I have not been without my due proportion of envy."

He then referred to Gillespie's charges:

"The whole are, I thank God, easily to be repelled; and the closer the investigation, the purer my conduct will appear. Lord Minto is fully aware of the violent faction which has taken up arms against me, and will defend me in England. In India I have possession, and a clear character to maintain it; let Satan do his worst. . . . My enemies have said much, and written much; but, in the end, truth and honesty must prevail."

Meanwhile, the business of government required his undiminished attention.

Hunt, who had been sent to the Philippines in January, forwarded from there on 17th March a copy of a treaty signed with the Sultan of Magindanu, reporting at the same time:

"Should the Government decide on the propriety of fixing a Residency at Mindano [Mindanao] . . . it would be advisable to resolve upon it with as little delay as possible, as his power is so precarious that unless we decide upon it promptly, he will be compelled to throw himself into the arms of the Spaniards. . . . It would tend materially to establish the source of future revenues if a few experienced Chinese could be sent on from the gold mines at Pontiana [Pontianak, Borneo] to put these people in the proper way of working theirs, and a few intelligent Javanese versed in the manufacture of indigo to instruct them to make the most of a plant already luxuriantly growing on their hills."

Nearer home, the Raja of Karang Asam ("Sour Reef"), an eastern state of Bali, had made an incursion against Banyu Wangi ("Fragrant Water", i.e. of a coconut), at the eastern extremity of Java, from which Bali is separated by a narrow strait. General Nightingall left Batavia to take charge of operations. In due course he was able to report that activities had been avoided, the occupation of the town and fortress of Buleleng having caused the Raja of Karang Asam to offer submission.

Trouble of a more serious kind was developing in Celebes, where the Raja of Boni was flouting British authority.

"The restless and ambitious disposition of the native Chieftains of Celebes", wrote Raffles, "had long been a source of annoyance and trouble to the former Government of this Colony. The recent conduct of the Raja of Boni at once hostile and insulting demanded an example."

So Nightingall and his forces proceeded there from Bali.

On 13th May Hunt reported on Sulu, to which he attached importance as "one of the most fertile islands in the world", its position favourable for it to become "the great commercial mart of this vast archipelago". The people were suspicious and hostile, the authority of the sultan only nominal.

"A blow must be struck at Sooloo and the dispersion of its villainous hordes," wrote Hunt, "or the expectations of Government will be disappointed."

Needless to say, this proposal did not appeal to the higher authorities. Hunt was recalled, and in due course the Philippines passed completely under the control of Spain.

Later in May there came the exciting news that the Prince of Orange had returned to Holland, that independence had been proclaimed and that by the Anglo-Dutch treaty of 13th December 1813, all Dutch shipping was to have free access to British ports. There was no word yet as to the fate of Java.

The Dutch community naturally wished to dispatch a letter of congratulation to the Prince of Orange and applied to Raffles for permission. In the light of subsequent events his reply is worth noting.

"His heart must be cold indeed which on such an occasion is not dilated with the warmest enthusiasm and I do not hesitate to declare that I shall ever feel it as one of the proudest events of my life to have been but the channel of forwarding to so brave, to so virtuous and yet so long oppressed a Prince those ardent, soul-breathing expressions of loyalty and joy which I hear poured forth on every side . . . that Heaven may ratify the renewal of the ancient relations between England and Holland by the establishment of that uninterrupted friendship and good understanding, which has already and must always prove so essential to the happiness of both Nations, will ever be the most fervent prayer of, Gentlemen, your attached friend, T. S. Raffles."

This very cordial response, which was published in the *Java Gazette*, has been regarded merely as an example of his political chicanery.

When the loyal address was drafted at the Stad House on 3rd June, he took the trouble to attend, and, on being thanked by Cranssen, said he had come only to demonstrate his approval of the meeting and his approbation of the objects proposed.

The seventy-sixth birthday of George III, which fell on 4th June, served as an opportunity to the Dutch to celebrate the freedom of Holland from French domination.

"A royal salute announced the rising of the glorious day . . . at ten o'clock the Honourable Governor held a levee at the Government House which was soon crowded with happy faces and loyal hearts. A party of the Bengal Volunteer Battalion with band and colours lined the front porch through which the visitors passed, which was appropriately decorated for the occasion. The Audience Room was also superbly fitted up—under the portrait of the Benefactor of Java [Minto] surmounted with a canopy of yellow satin with gold ornaments was placed an elevated seat of crimson velvet, and here the Honourable Lieutenant-Governor received the following address which was read by Mr Cranssen in the name of the Dutch inhabitants.

"'Allow me, Honourable Sir, on this joyful day to congratulate you on the anniversary of His Majesty our most revered and beloved Sovereign's birthday. . . . I consider this to be the happiest day of my life, that I may congratulate you also on the great and unexpected favourable turn in Europe through which the Nederland, our dear beloved country, has been liberated from the oppression which it has been sighing under for nearly twenty years. It will be needless to assure you that I as well as all my countrymen are overjoyed with this intelligence as the sincere part which your heart takes in it, which you have amply manifested to us must convince you of our feelings—to crown this happiness the peace with England is restored and revived industry will be the share of the two countries if faithful and forever united together by sincere friendship; this wish is double on my side, as well as a native of the Netherlands as on account of my high elevation which I have the honour to hold under the British Government, which has cemented my attachment and connexion to that great nation in such a degree that I will during my whole life consider myself as well a British as a Dutch subject. . . .'

"His Excellency delivered the following elegant and appropriate reply:—'It would afford me the high satisfaction to meet your wishes when forwarding the addresses. . . . To you Mr Cranssen who have taken the lead in this enthusiastic and generous burst of feeling, and whose attachment to the House of Orange has distinguished every period of your life it must be peculiarly gratifying to reflect on the part you have acted throughout and on the example you have shown to your countrymen. . . . I am confident that the House of Orange will recognize in you one of its most faithful adherents.'"

This expectation was not realized.

Immediately following this meeting, the opportunity of the assembled crowd was taken to start a Java Auxiliary Bible Society. At Raffles' suggestion, his cousin, the Rev. Thomas Raffles, who, after two years as Congregational minister in Hammersmith, had, since 1812, been in charge of Newington Chapel, Liverpool, had sent out two missionaries, one of whom was T. C. Supper. On 29th June Supper wrote to Thomas Raffles:

". . . in the morning was a great levee at the Governor's house; many gentlemen came to congratulate the Governor and his lady; and on this occasion the Java Auxiliary Bible Society was erected, at which the Governor has been unanimously chosen to the chair, as also the Governess; and in this noble character his Excellency has been pleased to honour me with the important call to be a member of the Committee. . . .

". . . though he is in a station more brilliant, according to the outward appearance, than that of the Prince Regent is, and he receives more honour than all the Royal Family together receive in England, yet he is very humble and kind, and no reasonable man can refuse him his entire confidence and profoundest esteem. . . ."

Here is Raffles on Supper, also in a letter to his cousin:

"He is a good simple creature, rather silly, but amiable. He has unfortunately been in love, and as he made me his *confidant* I may perhaps have seen him on his weak side."

Both Thomas Raffles and Supper, whom Raffles caused to be appointed minister of Batavia, were Nonconformists. The mother of the first is said to have been converted to dissent by Wesley himself and her son had followed suit. Raffles, while definitely religious in a broad sense, found himself unable to subscribe to any particular creed or dogma. His view was that different races had evolved the special type of religion best suited to their spiritual needs; and while he deprecated certain aspects of Eastern religions, he felt that it was wrong to disturb belief in any religion when there was no certainty that Christianity would adequately fill the void thus created.

"If you will consent to leave the Javanese to their *own way* for the present," he wrote to his cousin, "I will commute with you by recommending a vigorous conversion on Borneo, almost the largest island in the world, and thickly peopled by a race scarcely emerged from barbarism."

All the same, he steadily helped missionaries in Java, provided they were men of industry and good character and were willing to master the language. There was plenty of work for them to do, apart from converting the heathen. This support and encouragement may be traced to Raffles' intercourse with Dr Marshman and others of the Baptist faith during his stay with John Leyden in Calcutta. He had learned to respect the missionary calling.

One man who greatly impressed him was William Milne of the London Missionary Society.

"We had a very good man of your caste among us some time since, the Rev. Mr Milne, who is attached to the mission in China. He is a liberal, well-informed, excellent man and I cannot say too much in his favour. . . . He is now in China, having touched at Malacca on his way. . . ."

In the evening of the King's birthday a dance was given at Government House, the room being suitably decorated with English and Dutch colours.

". . . as I had to preach my first sermon on next day," wrote Mr Supper, "I stopped only till nine o'clock in the evening. . . ."

During the ball, Olivia collapsed. Her health had for some time been causing anxiety. The arduous tour of the Javanese courts had gravely taxed her diminishing strength, and the short rest she had taken at its conclusion, before becoming engulfed once more in the hard round of official duties, had proved wholly inadequate.

On 7th June General Nightingall reported from Fort Rotterdam at Macassar, Celebes, where Captain Phillips was now Resident, that Boni had been stormed and the Raja's house burned, together with all the property it contained, "which I believe however was of trifling value". The strength of the enemy was estimated at three thousand men. Nightingall followed up this report with a more general statement on the position in Celebes.

"I flattter myself", he wrote on 21st June, "you will agree with me in opinion that it was impossible to avoid the rupture which has taken place with the Rajah of Boni, and which has terminated in the subversion of his authority at Macasser. . . . I confess it is a most fortunate event for us, as without a rupture, it would have been very difficult, if not impossible, to have removed the Rajah from this neighbourhood, nor would he have ever consented to cede any part of the territory which he occupied under the very guns of Fort Rotterdam. . . . I am not sorry that his conduct was such as to fully justify the strong measures which I adopted, as the whole of the territory necessary for our security will of course remain in our possession. . . ."

The overthrow of the Raja in less than an hour's fighting had caused the greatest sensation all over the island.

"It is fortunate for us that it is so for our power is a mere illusion, and if they were to retire to the hills and jungle and carry on a predatory warfare, they would annoy us exceedingly. . . . With 200 Europeans, 200 Sepoys and a couple of field pieces, I think the Resident will be able to maintain the British supremacy. I expect to receive an answer from the Boni people in a few days, and if they agree to the election of another Rajah and express a determination to remain on terms of friendship with us, I shall embark . . . on the 28th inst."

In reporting this to India, Raffles wrote: "A deep and lasting impression has been made on the inhabitants of the more Eastern Isles. . . ." Whether this impression was as real as he supposed is open to question.

One sad event in the June of 1814 has here to be set down. On his way from London to Scotland, struggling against ill-health to reach the wife and home from which he had been separated for so long, Gilbert Elliot, Earl of Minto, died at Stevenage on the 21st. He was buried in Westminster Abbey.

Towards the end of July, Java received a visit from Vice-Admiral Sir Samuel Hood, a cousin of Lord Hood and, since 1812, commander-in-chief of the East Indies. On the 23rd a ball in his honour was given by Mr J. S. Timmerman Thyssen, a leading merchant and magistrate of Batavia, who later became Governor of Malacca. Olivia's absence was noted with general regret.

At a meeting of the Java Council on 6th August, Muntinghe's resignation was officially accepted. He had originally tendered it just as Raffles had been starting on his tour of the eastern states, when it had not been possible to deal with it formally. Raffles referred to the matter in these words, which are quoted from the *Java Gazette*:

"My absence from the seat of Government has prevented me from laying before the Board at an earlier period Mr Muntinghe's application to be permitted to resign his seat in Council and the public employment which he has filled with so much credit to himself and advantage to the public interest. Being aware of the frequent repetition of this request that a retirement from public life was of importance to his private interests and pursuits, and that it consequently was an object to come to an early decision on the subject, I have already informed Mr Muntinghe that his resignation would be accepted, but in now directing that official communication be made to this effect I shall feel myself wanting in my public duty if I did not take the occasion to accord a just tribute to his eminent talents and abilities, and my sense of the cordial co-operation and support and the great assistance which my administration has derived from his able advice, sound judgment and clear understanding."

The vacant seat on the Council was taken by Hugh Hope.

Whether Muntinghe's resignation was due to indolence or because he thought it was time to disassociate himself from the British régime in Java is hard to say. Cornelis Elout, one of the Dutch commissioners who came out later, writing to Anton Falck, who had taken a leading part in the rising against the French and was then Colonial Minister at The Hague, described Muntinghe thus:

"There are but few good head pieces. Muntinghe, whom one might count among these, is laziness itself, and with an endless lot of trouble one gets his opinion about an important point, but after that he is inactive again for months."

As for Muntinghe's other possible reason, the news from Europe continued to be exciting. A *Gazette Extraordinary* announced on 25th August that peace had been proclaimed.

"Words are inadequate to express the feeling of delight with which we hasten to announce to our readers the blessing for which the world has for so long panted. The wished return to peace, which joyful news has just arrived by the following *Madras Courier Extraordinary* July 22nd, 1814: 'The general peace was proclaimed about the 10th April. Louis XVIII was proclaimed King of France in Paris about the same time. . . .' A royal salute has just been fired to celebrate this happy event."

The 24th was the birthday of His Serene Highness the Prince of Orange. This, with the news published next day in the *Gazette*, was a signal for further rejoicings.

"These commenced at the house of Mr Cranssen with an elegant public breakfast at nine o'clock. The Honourable Lieutenant-Governor and the Lady Governess and the chief officers of government and the principal English and Dutch inhabitants composed this party, which occupied the whole of the extensive suite of rooms in Mr Cranssen's noble mansion.

"The arrival of His Excellency was hailed by an appropriate salute and 'God Save the King' performed in great style by an excellent band. Besides the indispensables of an Indian breakfast, everything that would have been required to form a sumptuous dinner was to be found. . . ."

Of the evening events, the *Gazette* had something to say also:

"No sooner had the sun disappeared behind the horizon than the blaze of artificial light which succeeded almost compensated for his absence. . . . The illuminations here were so magnificent as to excite the wonder and admiration of the dazzled spectators. . . . The Honourable Lieutenant-Governor and family arrived about seven o'clock (they had left the morning celebrations about eleven o'clock) and after admiring the brilliant beauty of the scene the great part of the company went in carriages round the environs of the town to witness the illuminations; on their return they stopped at the Government House at Ryswick, on the lawns behind which a superb display of fireworks took place; some fire balloons were raised with wonderful rapidity and success.

"At the close of this exhibition the party returned to the original scene of festivity and soon the merry dance began. It continued with occasional intermissions until midnight when the supper was announced. It was laid out in a temporary building erected in the garden for the occasion, decorated with taste and elegance and calculated to accommodate about five hundred persons. The banquet combined delicacy, profusion and luxury. The wines were excellent and due justice was paid to the sparkling champagne in particular. . . .

"Mr Timmerman[1] again spoke for his countrymen stating that the most fortunate day which Java had ever known was that on which Lord Minto selected Mr Raffles as its future Governor; he briefly called their attention to the benevolent nature of his administration, and directed their lasting gratitude to the author of so many benefits. The Honourable Lieutenant-Governor then addressed Mr Cranssen in short but eloquent terms acknowledging the honour done to him and stating that if his administration in any way entitled him to the gratitude which had been expressed, it was owing to the ability of his advisers, on which His Excellency proposed the health of 'Messrs Muntinghe and Cranssen who by their conduct on the establishment of the British Government anticipate the gladness of this day and set an example which, for the happiness of mankind, has since been followed by all Europe'."

Not content with these festivities, Mr Cranssen gave an evening party two days later.

"The illuminations were splendid and the transparencies appropriate. In the centre before the great door was placed a transparency upon which appeared in large characters the words 'In honour of the heroes who rescued Java from the Tyrant's grasp'. On one side the arms of Great Britain and those of Holland on the other were displayed in separate transparencies. About sixty persons sat down at about seven-thirty to an excellent dinner. . . . In the course of the evening the Lieutenant-Governor and our worthy host were chaired round the room."

The *Gazette's* correspondent reported also that the toasts had been so numerous and had followed each other with such rapidity that the indulgence of readers was begged for "the imperfect list of them". One, however, is to be noted here. That day being the anniversary of the fall

1 Permanent hereditary name. It was and is a common Dutch practice to add to the father's name the maiden name of the mother or wife.

of Cornelis, Raffles proposed the toast of Major-General Robert Rollo Gillespie.

With an enthusiasm lacking in his predecessor, General Nightingall had been considering the cutting down of military expenditure. He recorded in a minute dated 14th September:

"... I have made it a particular part of my duty ... to ascertain what part of our present military establishment could best be spared, and also what description of troops could be dispensed with ... but the events which have since taken place in Europe render it unnecessary for me at present to enlarge upon the subject. Considering however the great pressure of the moment, the scarcity of silver and above all the heavy arrears of the army, I felt it my duty to begin by recommending the immediate abolition of the gun-carriage manufactory. ... Having now had an opportunity of seeing every part of the Island of Java, I do not hesitate to declare in the most decided manner that there is not a single spot of ground between Batavia and the East point of the Island where a body of cavalry or horse could act with effect."

Gun-bullock establishments were unnecessary owing to the nature of the country, he stated, and the Java Light Cavalry and horse artillery would be reduced. The Javanese Corps would be completed up to 1,200 men. The gun-carriage manufactory had already been closed down, and it had been decided to sell useless barracks.

Mr Cranssen raised objections at the meeting of the Council to the sale of barracks, also expressing the view that Javanese troops were untrustworthy, but he was out-voted.

There was still no news of the fate of Java. Raffles wrote on this matter to Lord Minto on 17th September, unaware that he was dead:

"The Dutch will feel some difficulty in resuming possession, and the transfer must occupy a considerable portion of time. On their part they will probably appoint Commissioners, but they cannot assume the reins without men and money. ... I do not think it would be possible for us to lend them any military force for a protracted period. The notions of our Officers are so high and the conduct of the Dutch in general so low, that it would be impossible to avoid contention and strife."

The news from India about his personal affairs fluctuated. At times Assey seemed to be making headway, at others hostility against Raffles and his measures seemed more intense. It was in no cheerful tone that Raffles wrote to Minto in the same letter:

"The sale of lands, the measures regarding the Paper Currency, the purchase of the Probolingo and other Chinese Estates, the Land Revenue arrangements—with every measure of the local Government—have been universally condemned, the two first principally on the grounds urged by General Gillespie, and the latter in a great measure on the extraordinary assertions of Mr Robison."

This letter was written a week before the receipt in Batavia of Calcutta's reply of 28th May to the proposals set out in his famous minute of 11th February. It was clear that Raffles' views no longer carried the weight with the Supreme Government that they had carried in Minto's day.

The chilling response to his suggestions for colonial development must have been a bitter blow to Raffles. Even before the Java expedition had sailed from Malacca, he had had it in the forefront of his mind that the capture of Java should not be the ultimate goal, for the risk that it might be returned to Holland at the end of the war was too great. The continued interest of Britain in the archipelago, which was his dearest object, must be guaranteed by alliances with the rulers of other islands. It is true that he hoped that, by some lucky turn of fortune's wheel, England might yet be able to retain Java itself, and he had devoted himself to trying to prove the intrinsic value of it, so as to secure at least a disposition in authoritative circles favourable to its retention.

Unfortunately all his attempts to demonstrate the essential fact that the island could be financially self-supporting, as Minto had too rashly prophesied, had so far failed, his chief card thus having been trumped. At the same time he felt quite confident that he had reinsured Britain's position in the archipelago by the treaties he had negotiated with neighbouring islands. These, he claimed, could not be regarded as subordinate to Java, and therefore the treaties would hold good even if Java had, in the end, to be handed back. And now the Supreme Government, influenced no doubt in its judgment by the financial burden of Java and the charges brought by Gillespie and his associates, coldly and with some logical force had blown his plans to bits.

It is to be readily admitted that India had no conception of the potential value of the archipelago. What it did understand very well was that the heavy drain on its silver resources continued in spite of every reprimand it sent, and in spite of every glowing promise it received of future financial stability. Yet it must also be admitted that the arguments advanced against Raffles' policy were not without potency. The propriety of his schemes was debatable. Was it proper for a self-confessed trustee government to use its temporary authority to build up such connexions as to depreciate in a material degree the value of the trust, if and when returned to its original owner? Certainly neither the Court in London nor the Supreme Government had felt any scruples in treating Malacca in just such a way, and it is ironical to recall that, but for Raffles, such a policy would have been carried out there, and in a fashion infinitely more flagrant than that proposed by Raffles for the outer fringes of the archipelago. Moreover, Raffles could reasonably argue that the monopoly created by the Dutch had been vicious in itself, quite apart from its disadvantages to Britain, and that the exclusive position of the Dutch in the archipelago had never been recognized by Great Britain. That it had been tacitly accepted was true enough, but this was merely because we had been busy elsewhere. There was nothing by way of international agreement to prevent us resuming an interest centuries old, even if there had been a long interval of passive indifference. It could also be argued that what England had done in the Napoleonic wars, without which Holland would still have been a subject state, fully entitled her to decide how much of Holland's colonial empire she could afford to return; that we had no need to be so quixotic as not only to hand back the islands Holland had owned before the war, but also to admit her right to exclude us for ever from any possible interest in any part of that vast area, which she would be quite unable effectively to control herself.

The propriety of Raffles' policy is a matter on which opinions differ. The practical objection, however, advanced by Calcutta was that it entailed risk of war. The Supreme Government rightly sensed that, after hostilities of unparalleled magnitude and cost, the British Government would not support any policy involving the slightest chance of avoidable warfare anywhere, and certainly not for a group of apparently unprofitable islands in the remote East. The strength of that attitude at home Raffles was to learn in due course. Meantime his most cherished plans were shattered and his labours of the last three years, in furtherance of them, brought to naught.

He wrote again to Minto on 2nd October:

"Lord Moira is obviously desirous of screening Gillespie, and I am confident that if Assey had not gone to Bengal and in some measure pushed the dispatches into notice, they would eventually have been allowed to lie on the shelf until Gillespie's as well as his Lordship's views had been satisfied. . . . Lord M. left England dissatisfied respecting Java. . . . This was to kindle the flame which Gillespie was ready to light, and to fan it by the encouragement of whatever might throw the affairs of Government into confusion—the pressure of the times afforded an opportunity to attribute them exclusively to mismanagement in Java, and that the existing System might be completely upset a general and universal censure is passed on every measure of the local Government. . . .

"That a disappointment may have been felt in the earlier expectations respecting our Resources, that some of our measures may have appeared of doubtful policy, and that in the course of an administration so extended, and I will add, so difficult, some and many errors may have been committed, I am ready to admit, but the universal censure that has been passed upon *all* our measures, plans and expectations is too general to be just, too pointed not to expose its object. . . . Of eventual success I am pretty confident, though I foresee much intermediate danger and inconvenience. . . .

"In a former letter I mentioned the different view taken by Lord M. regarding Japan; the partial success of the late Expedition tended to remove many of the Objections, but the Supreme Government now perceive that even in a commercial point of view the intercourse is injurious to the British Interest, particularly on account of the importation of Copper from Japan which would interfere with the produce of our own mines, and have directed that no further measures be adopted with a view thereto without special instructions from England or Bengal.

"At the period this decision was formed Supreme Government were not informed of the wonderful changes in Europe, and at all events the re-establishment of Holland would have prevented the prosecution of the policy which I had suggested as well in the instance of Japan as regarding the Eastern Islands generally. . . . In the meantime I still adhere to the original policy regarding our external possessions which I first suggested. I now as decidedly think it necessary that that policy should be waived under the changes which have since taken place in Europe; and the Dutch nation being contrary to all expectations restored, together with the ancient ties of Amity and Alliance, nothing ought to be done during perhaps temporary possession to injure the interests of those who may again become the permanent Rulers in these Seas. . . .

"Of the Land Revenue arrangement I have received something like a cold sanction but the opinion is so reserved that it may be rendered applicable in any way that subsequent events may dictate."

He ended the letter by saying that the final battle as to his measures would probably be fought in England, which he hoped to visit in the event of the colony being transferred to the Dutch.

"I may then either return to India[1] or embark in some other mode of active life—though I cannot as yet but feel I am only beginning [in] the world."

No further extension of the land settlement was attempted during the British régime. It was left to the Dutch to decide on the policy to be adopted.

On 5th November the account of receipts and disbursements for the year 1st May 1812 to 30th April 1813 was transmitted to India. This disclosed a total deficit of 2,216,879 Spanish dollars, which included two large items. A deficit of 476,000 dollars under the head of Teak Forests

[1] It was the custom of the period so to refer not only to continental India, but also to the whole Eastern Archipelago—"Farther India", as it was often called.

was ascribed to lack of information as to the price obtainable for teak when the estimate was calculated. The other, for 434,000 dollars, was attributed to "unexpected difficulties and disappointments attending the first establishment at Banca" and also to "the disappointment in the receipt of spices from Amboyna and of Sapan wood from Timor which had been estimated in an expectation of a more intimate connexion between Java and the Moluccas on which this trade depends".

There had been a loss by reason of the postponement of the Japan voyage, and the sale of civil stores had been lower than usual owing to the late arrival of consignments from Europe. The cost of the expeditions to Palembang and Jokyakarta had not been included in the estimates, and the excess of expenditure over revenue was due chiefly to the non-realization of commercial speculations from which substantial revenue had been expected.

"Satisfied as we are that every exertion has been made by us on the one hand to call forth all the valuable resources of the country, and on the other to restrain the expenditure within the narrowest limits consistent with the efficiency of the Public Departments and the prosperity of the country, we commend these accounts to your Lordship's indulgent consideration in the confident hope that however different the actual result may appear to the estimate, a due allowance will be made for the very unprecedented circumstances under which the estimate was formed, the want of efficient assistance in officers conversant with the English mode of keeping accounts and the distresses under which the Colony laboured from its recent conquest, and the almost total stagnation of commerce."

This dispatch crossed one from India dated 23rd June, which was received on 11th November. It enclosed a report of the Accountant-General on the 1812-13 accounts for Java up to the latest information received. Commenting on the dispatch from Raffles that had accompanied the estimates for that financial year, he wrote:

". . . it will be seen that so far from any pecuniary embarrassments being at that time apprehended, the most flattering expectations were then held out of the importance of that acquisition [Java] in a pecuniary point of view to the British Government."

From the information supplied by the Lieutenant-Governor in August and November 1812, no material alteration had taken place in the value of the paper rix-dollar in relation to the Spanish silver dollar. In August it had been eleven to one; in November twelve to one. Consequently, the Accountant-General failed to see that there had been any greater necessity to sell lands in November than there had been in August.

In regard to the inconvenience experienced by the Java government in receiving revenues in a paper that could not be reissued, it would be sufficiently evident that it was specie alone that could relieve its existing embarrassment, and it seemed to the Accountant-General a most extraordinary circumstance that the lands had been disposed of for paper, and that the Java government should receive it at a hundred per cent above its current value. The sale of lands, therefore, had been no help to the treasury, and as it had increased the shortage of circulating medium, was an inconvenience to the public.

A certain amount of the Batavia paper currency should have been left in the market. The Accountant-General admitted that this was at variance with the opinion expressed by him on 5th February 1813.

"But at the time I gave that opinion I never expected that the local Government would have a course to that measure merely for the purpose of issuing a similar currency under a different name. Neither did I apprehend that the redemption of the old paper would create the slightest embarrassment in their pecuniary affairs . . . neither in my humble opinion would it have occasioned the slightest embarrassment had proper measures been adopted at the time that paper was under a course of redemption."

He considered that the re-establishment of the Lombard Bank had been inadvisable, because the Java government had no real ground for supposing that the Lombard Bank paper would sustain its credit any better than the old Batavian currency. Lombard notes would not circulate at par, as they were payable in nine months. Provision should have been made for a percentage of revenue to be paid in silver, as had been so under the old Batavian currency.

"I am aware that the local Government attribute their present embarrassments to the interruptions to foreign trade, but their own financial measures appear to me so fully to account for the difficulties which they at present experience for want of silver, that in my humble opinion it is quite unnecessary to seek for other causes."

In the past, the farmers had at all times been able to pay one-third of their revenues in specie, and when the Batavian currency had been largely redeemed, the Java government might have secured the payment of a larger proportion of the farmers' revenues in specie, had proper measures been resorted to. In the last two years Java had cost the East India Company about 4,900,000 Spanish dollars.

The Accountant-General, it is to be noted, omitted any reference to the fact that, under the former Dutch régime, sufficient specie to pay the troops had been sent annually to the colony.

On the receipt of this dispatch, the Lombard Bank was discontinued as from 22nd December 1814, and all debts still due on pledges of movable property were directed to be recovered forthwith. Pending a further reference to Bengal, loans on mortgage of landed property were allowed to continue.

The Supreme Government continued to harp on the impossibility of supplying specie to Java, writing in a dispatch dated 11th November:

"... partly owing to the large amount of drafts lately granted by the Governor of Java the resources of this Residency have been so reduced as to render it absolutely impracticable for the Government to dispatch a supply of specie from here for the service of the Colony. The Vice-President in Council has learned with the utmost concern that the troops in Java have fallen or are likely to fall much in arrear, and that the military establishment of the Island cannot be supported without the aid of remittances from India. This fact is so much at variance with the tenure [*sic*] of the earlier representations both to the Government and Honourable Court of Directors that it was as impossible for the Supreme Government to have foreseen such a state of things and it is now impracticable for them to provide a remedy for the evil."

No mention was made of the enormous expenditure on local wars in India, or to the insistent demands of the Court of Directors for maximum remittances to be sent home.

General Nightingall's suggestions for economies in the military department were approved by the Supreme Government in a dispatch dated 3rd December 1814.

ii

The general frustration of all Raffles' plans, and the hostile attitude of India, were thrown completely into the background in November. On Saturday, the 26th, Olivia died very suddenly at Buitenzorg. Although she had had previous bouts of illness, her recovery had been confidently expected. The *Java Gazette*, framed in a deep margin of conventional black, unquestionably voiced, for all its formal and slightly stilted phrases, the genuine affection that Olivia had inspired and the no less genuine grief evoked by her death.

"The numerous assemblage of persons of both sexes to assist at the mournful ceremony of paying the last duties and honours to the deceased, and the general and marked expression of grief which was there evinced, is the best proof of the respect and regard which her benevolence and manners had acquired amongst all classes and society in Java, and her most immediate friends will justly say that, possessed in life of a heart glowing with most generous affections, and of a mind guided by the purest of principles of friendship and kindness, she lived beloved by all who knew her and carries to the grave the certainty of forever being remembered by them with a fond, devoted and faithful attachment."

She was buried in the European cemetery at Batavia, alongside the grave of John Leyden. Raffles caused a cenotaph to be built in her memory at Buitenzorg, the scene of their happiest days. On this was inscribed the verse:

OH THOU WHOM NE'ER MY CONSTANT HEART
ONE MOMENT HATH FORGOT
THO' FATE SEVERE HATH BID US PART
YET STILL FORGET ME NOT

This is the first verse of the little poem Olivia had sent to Leyden in 1808. It linked all three together in a way that only Raffles would have understood.

Under the Anglo-Dutch treaty of 1824, the Dutch assumed responsibility for the care and maintenance of the monument.

The position of a Governor's wife is never an easy one. She has her part to play, but however she plays it, almost inevitably some will criticize her—either because she does too little, or because she interferes too much. Raffles has been bitterly criticized by many writers, but Olivia has never been mentioned except with praise. She seems to have possessed that very special quality which, without apparent effort, can win universal esteem and deep affection. That even to this day the memory of her power to stir the imagination is instanced by the charming sketch, *Olivia Mariamne*, by the distinguished Dutch novelist, Johannes V. Jensen.

If a modern writer can be touched by her story, what must have been the feelings of Raffles when, with that terrible suddenness a tropical climate can inflict, she was snatched from him? She had been his beloved companion from the first moment of his emergence out of obscurity in Leadenhall Street, through the modest triumphs and irritating frustrations of Penang, till, under Minto's benevolent tutelage, he had been able to reveal his gifts in full flower in Java. She and Raffles had shared equally the love of Leyden and the affectionate regard of Minto. She had accompanied Raffles on visits of state to Javanese royalty, and her presence had lent additional grace, dignity and indeed benevolence to those occasions. She had, by her friendliness, helped in no small degree to heal the wounds Java had suffered by the invasion; she had identified herself wholeheartedly with every good cause, and by her high standards had insensibly become the model that all the women in Java had sought to follow. She had rejoiced with her husband in his successes and had shared with him in his disappointments. She had nursed him through desperate illnesses, never allowing her slowly failing strength to keep her from what she believed to be her duty.

Chapter Seventeen

JAVA, 1815

i

RAFFLES was completely overcome by the loss of Olivia. So severe was the physical shock to his already overtaxed strength that friends feared for his life. For once he suffered them to plan for him; he was too stunned to care. A short sea-trip was arranged. He tried to visit the Lampong country in southern Sumatra, but it was too rough to land. He returned to Batavia on 14th January, by which time his health was somewhat improved. To continue his convalescence, he spent some days with Cranssen at Chinsara. On return to Batavia he learned of the death of Gillespie before the fortress of Kalunga.

Worse news had come by the same mail. His loyal champion and friend, Lord Minto, was dead. It was on Minto that he had relied to counter in England the calumnies of Gillespie and the hostility of Moira in India. Now this most powerful support was denied him. In future he must fight his battles alone.

To the terrible blows he had suffered in the loss of Minto and his beloved Olivia was added another. By the death of William Robinson, who had sailed with him from England in the *Ganges* in 1805 and had served by his side in Penang and Java, an old and intimate friend and a trusted colleague was taken from him.

Once more Raffles' health seemed in danger of utter collapse. This time science was summoned to his aid. He determined to climb Gunong Gede, the mountain-peak that dominates the landscape behind Buitenzorg, which no European had yet done. It seems a queer sort of treatment for a man in Raffles' weak condition, but scientific interest was to him ever a powerful stimulant.

Armed with thermometers to ascertain the height, the party successfully scaled the mountain, which they calculated, from the drop in temperature, to be not less than 7,000 feet high.

"We had", wrote Raffles to Dr Horsfield, "a most extensive prospect from the summit—Batavia roads, with the shipping so distinct that we could distinguish a ship from a brig on one side, and Wine Coops Bay still more distinct on the other; the islands all round were quite distinct and we traced the sea beyond the southernmost point of Sumatra; the surf on the south coast was visible to the naked eye. To the eastward we included Indra Mayu[1] point in the prospect, and Cheribon Hill rose high above the rest. I think we may say that we had nearly within our range all that part of the Island which, by the former Government, was *not* called *Java*."

The interest and the effort, and perhaps the mountain air, helped to restore him, for the moment, to mental and physical equilibrium.

He arranged for a memorial to Minto to be placed on the summit of Gunong Gede. On it were recorded these words:

SACRED TO THE MEMORY OF
THE RIGHT HON. GILBERT EARL OF MINTO
WHO IN OCTOBER 1811
FIRST ESTABLISHED THE BRITISH GOVERNMENT
IN JAVA AND THE EASTERN SEAS.

In early April the island of Sumbawa was almost destroyed by a terrific volcanic eruption, the sound and effect of which were felt for miles around. Raffles at once called for detailed reports from every district and, as soon as they were received, dispatched them to Marsden for communication to the Royal Society.

"The first explosions were heard on this Island in the evening of the fifth of April. . . . The noise was, in the first instance, almost universally attributed to distant cannon; so much so, that a detachment of troops were marched from Djocjocarta, in the expectation that a neighbouring post was attacked. . . .

"From the 6th, the sun became obscured; and it had every appearance of being enveloped in fog. . . . This lasted several days, the explosions continued occasionally, but less violent, and less frequently than at first. Volcanic ashes also began to fall, but in small quantities. . . .

"This appearance of the atmosphere remained with little variation, until the 10th of April, and till then it does not appear that the volcano attracted much observation, or was considered of greater importance than those which have occasionally burst forth in Java. But on the evening of the 10th the eruptions were heard more loud, and more frequent from Cheribon eastward; the air became darkened by the quantity of falling ashes, and in several situations, particularly at Solo and Rembang, many said they felt a tremulous motion of the earth. It is universally remarked in the more eastern districts, that the explosions were tremendous, continuing frequently during the 11th, and of such violence to shake the

[1] Indramaya (now Indramayu): " The Illusion of India". Crawfurd describes Indra as "The name of the Hindu god of the air, and in Malay and Javanese that also of a class of aerial beings." Sir Richard Winstedt adds: "Indra was the leader of the gods on Mount Meru, the Hindu Olympus."

houses perceptibly; and unusual thick darkness was remarked all the following night, and the greater part of the next day. . . ."

One of the reports was based on the account of an eye-witness, the Raja of Saugar, Sumbawa:

"About seven p.m., on the 10th April, three distinct columns of flame burst forth, near the top of Tomboro Mountain, all of them apparently within the verge of the crater; and after ascending separately to a very great height, their tops united in the air in a troubled confused manner. In a short time the whole mountain next Saugar appeared like a body of liquid fire extending itself in every direction.

"The fire and columns of flame continued to rage with unabated fury, until the darkness caused by the quantity of falling matter obscured it at about eight p.m. Stones at this time fell very thick at Saugar; some of them as large as two fists, but generally not larger than walnuts. Between nine and ten p.m. ashes began to fall; and soon after a violent whirlwind ensued, which blew down nearly every house in the village of Saugar, carrying the tops and light parts with it. In the part of Saugar adjoining Tomboro, its effects were much more violent, tearing up by the roots the largest trees, and carrying them into the air, together with men, houses, cattle, and whatever else came within its influence. . . . The sea rose nearly twelve feet higher than it had ever been known to be before . . . sweeping away houses and every thing within its reach.

"The whirlwind lasted about an hour. No explosions were heard till the whirlwind had ceased, at about eleven a.m. From midnight till the evening of the 11th they continued without intermission; after that, their violence moderated, and they were only heard at intervals; but the explosions did not cease entirely until the 15th of July. . . ."

The distress under which Raffles was labouring was such that only by intense activity of both body and mind could it be borne. He was, as he wrote of himself at that time:

". . . a lonely man, like one that has long since been dead, but whom activity and the cares of public responsibility are now almost necessary for existence".

Towards the end of April he decided to make an extended tour of the island, with the particular intention of visiting those areas in which the new land-revenue system had been introduced, and also, of course, of pursuing his scientific and archaeological investigations. As Dr Horsfield wrote in his appendix to Lady Raffles' *Memoir*:

"This journey likewise afforded Sir Stamford an opportunity of examining in person those stupendous monumental remains of a hierarchy long since obsolete, which are promiscuously scattered through all parts of the island. In the dominions of the native princes they exist, however, in greater abundance, and possess a more important character. They consist of ruins of Hindu temples or pagodas, and of images, sculptures and inscriptions. . . ."

Accompanied by a small party, which included Captain Baker and Lieutenant Thomas Watson, he left Buitenzorg on 26th April, his first objective Gunong Gede.

"From Cessaroor [Ciceroa] to Tungo[1]", wrote Lieutenant Watson in his account of the tour,[2] "the road was in many places steep as to render our progress in carriages somewhat tedious, and finding our horses themselves unable to advance, we had recourse to the assistance of a pair of buffaloes yoked by means of a long rope in front of the horses."

At Tungo they mounted their horses and began to ascend the pass. Here they struck the road built by Daendels.

"As a monument of the grandeur of his design (if grandeur consist in surmounting difficulties) it must certainly claim our admiration but when we consider the dreadful sacrifice of human life it has occasioned, together with its comparative inutility, we cannot but despise the vain-glory that projected the undertaking."

After crossing the mountains, they reached Chipanas, where there was a government garden in which European vegetables were grown. At Chianjur they were met by the Regent of the Preanger lands. Later they entered Cheribon.

"This extensive district was one of the first that experienced the blessings of emancipation from feudal tyranny. On landing on the Eastern bank we were greeted by the acclamations of the inhabitants who congratulated us on entering the land of liberty crying 'Welcome to the English who have made us free and happy!'"

While at Cheribon, Raffles wrote on 4th May to the Medical Advisory Council on the question of smallpox, the campaign against which had been held up for two years, mainly through the death of William Hunter.

"My attention has long been directed to the very inefficient system adopted in this Colony for introducing the general benefits of the vaccine discovered—a misfortune to be attributed in great measure to the death of Dr Hunter, our late Superintending Surgeon—to whom I had fully communicated my views and wishes on the subject. The establishment of the detailed system of Land Revenue throughout the Eastern Districts, by enabling the Government to command the whole resources of the country and to become the direct landlords of the peasantry, seems in a particular degree to call for that paternal care and consideration which would devote a portion of the gross revenue towards general improvement. And while a part of this is set aside for increasing the means which may afford subsistence to a growing population, it becomes a still more

[1] This appears on modern Dutch maps as Toegoe—Anglice: Tugu.
[2] *Asiatic Journal*, 1816.

pressing duty to remove as far as possible those causes which cannot but reduce the population now existing."

These remarks referred only to vaccination, but, as Dr Dirk Schoute points out in his *Occidental Therapeutics*, Raffles had also in mind the elimination of venereal disease. This is clearly set out in a letter of the same date from Raffles to McQuoid.

The journey was continued on 8th May into the dominions of the Susuhunan. During that day:

". . . we performed a long and arduous journey of nearly fifty miles through the forest of Dayu-luhur, a route which has never before been attempted by Europeans. On leaving Maganang the road entered at once into a thick forest of bamboos, which grow in clumps at some distance from each other, leaving the space between perfectly unoccupied by any kind of vegetation. At a considerable height the trees branch off and meet, giving a mutual support and forming a canopy so close and thick as almost to exclude the light at mid-day. Each clump forms with the adjacent ones on every side natural, lofty Gothic arches, which, in the deep gloom that surrounds them, except from the partial light of torches, present as grand and awfully romantic a scene as can be well imagined."

After crossing in all nearly four hundred miles of wild and uninhabited country, with here and there ruined temples and other relics of the ancient Hindu occupation of the island before the Mohammedans came, they arrived at Magelang, where they were welcomed by Lawrence, the Kedu Resident. From there, on 18th May, they paid a visit to the Boro-Budur.

The Boro-Budur—the Great Buddha—is the most remarkable example of Buddhist architecture in the world. Built, according to the Javanese, in the seventh century, it stands on a hill near the river Progo and is in the shape of a four-sided pyramid, with six square balustraded platforms rising one on another to a huge cupola. In hundreds of niches in the walls stand statues of Buddha, and there are in addition over two thousand carvings and bas-reliefs.

It had been discovered by the British in the previous year. Anyone less scientifically minded than Raffles might have been content with recording its existence. To him, however, the discovery of such things was, in a sense, less important than that they should be exactly surveyed, sketched and described in detail. On hearing of the Boro-Budur, he had sent young H. C. Cornelius, civil surveyor at Samarang, to investigate and report upon it. But he was not satisfied to leave this and similar tasks wholly to subordinates. He desired to see for himself these magnificent monuments of the Hindu period of Javanese history, and no distance was too great, no fatigue too severe to prevent his going himself to inspect them, however short the time he could spare from urgent political tasks.

In two other aspects Raffles was in advance of his time: in his respect for the integrity of ancient monuments; and in his artistic appreciation of them in their natural surroundings. Too many relics of the past have been ruthlessly pilfered or completely disfigured by the selfish and acquisitive instincts of those who have discovered them, or those who have the power or the wealth to make their depredations. In Java, shortly before the time of Raffles, Nicholaus Engelhardt had earned some notoriety for the barbarous way in which images and other ornaments of such Hindu shrines as were known had been crudely hacked from their places and taken away to adorn his garden. Raffles abhorred such a practice and did his best to safeguard the new discoveries. Such samples of Hindu art as he did remove from Java were odd pieces lying by themselves and completely dissociated from a particular edifice with which they could be definitely connected.

Appreciation of natural beauty is a relatively modern development and had gained little headway in the early nineteenth century. But here is an example of Raffles' own feelings, expressed with that simple eloquence of which he was such a master:

"In addition to their claims on the consideration of the antiquarian, the ruins of two of these places, Brambana [Prambanan] and Boro Bodo, are admirable as majestic works of art. The great extent of the masses of building covered in some parts with the luxuriant vegetation of the climate, the beauty and delicate execution of the separate portions, the symmetry and regularity of the whole, the great number and interesting character of the statues and bas-reliefs, with which they are ornamented, excite our wonder that they were not earlier examined, sketched and described."

This vast structure, the Boro-Budur, only fifteen miles from Jokyakarta, had lain hidden in the jungle, known only to the natives, its existence unsuspected by Europeans, for more than a century of Dutch occupation of the island. The explanation must lie in the fact that the Dutch had never really occupied the island. They had largely confined themselves to the towns into which their original trading-posts had grown, and had been content to control activity only in those areas producing the commodities in which they were interested. Beyond this, their contacts with the Javanese courts had been for the most part limited to their official representatives, who had been backed, as occasion had demanded, by a show of force.

The party returned from the Boro-Budur to Magelang, whence they travelled on to Surakarta, where they were received by the Susuhunan, so Lieutenant Watson reported, "with every mark of respectful regard; the usual ceremonies being dispensed with as the visit was private".

"The Emperor himself", wrote Watson, "is quite a well-bred gentleman. His manners are dignified and elegant . . . his deportment with the English cordial, frank and unassuming."

They spent four days at Surakarta. Besides enjoying a series of entertainments, they made several trips in the neighbourhood, including one to—as Dr Horsfield later described them—"the grotesque antiquities at Suku, which possess a very peculiar character". These had only recently been discovered by Major Martin Johnson, the Resident at Surakarta.

On 26th May Raffles and his staff embarked on the river Solo and six days later landed near its mouth, proceeding from there in carriages to Surabaya, where the King's birthday was celebrated on 2nd June. The journey was continued on the 5th by the high road to Pasuruan ("Place of the Betel Pepper"), a distance of eighty miles, and on the 7th they made for the Tengger mountains, calling at various Hindu temples on the way. Subsequently, after a visit to the volcano at Bromo, they embarked at Besuki ("Prosperity") for Banyu Wangi, but were driven by contrary winds and currents into Buleleng—or, as Dr F. D. K. Bosch puts it[1]:

"A trip to Bali brings to a close this vice-regal tour, so full of interest from the point of view of the antiquarian."

The party arrived back at Batavia on 1st August, to find that Travers had returned from England the previous day. The meeting between Raffles and Travers was affecting. Travers, who had gone to England with such confidence, had returned disappointed, with no hint of any decision concerning the charges brought by Gillespie and Blagrave. He was shocked by the physical change in his chief, but found him unshaken in his confidence that his character would be vindicated.

More exciting still than the return of Travers was the news, just received, that Napoleon had escaped from Elba and war had broken out again. Raffles would have been a very sick man indeed if news of such consequence could not act as an effective restorative. He hurried up to Buitenzorg with the Nightingalls and there plied his pen with even more than his usual energy. To Ramsay he wrote on 5th August:

"The wonderful and extraordinary change in the politics of Europe by the reappearance of Buonaparte has with all its horrors showed one consoling ray on this sacred Isle; and Java may yet be permanently English. In this hope I have addressed Lord Buckinghamshire. . . ."

Robert Hobart, Earl of Buckinghamshire (who gave his name to the capital of Tasmania), had succeeded Robert Dundas, Viscount Melville, as President of the Board of Control. Raffles' letter to him is of the same date as that to Ramsay. After referring to the suddenly altered circumstances in Europe, he asked the question:

"What is to be done with Java and the Dutch possessions in the Eastern Seas?"

[1] *Inter-Ocean*, March 1930.

For the last twelve months he had been in constant expectation of the arrival of the Dutch fleet, and steps had been taken to enable the colonies to be handed over. As, however, there was now a faint hope that Java might be retained by Great Britain, a "plain statement of fact and some suggestions from the spot" might be useful to the authorities in London.

As the Dutch Company had gone bankrupt and the financial prospects held out by Lord Minto had not so far been realized, there was probably at home an unfavourable view of the value of Java. The collapse of the Dutch Company had been principally due, said Raffles, to the corruption of its servants, and while at first the British régime had failed to live up to its financial expectations, the situation had now changed for the better.

To support this optimism, he enclosed various abstracts calculated to show that the amount of revenue collected under the new system had equalled the estimated receipts. He then went on to claim, with an enthusiasm that led him into considerable overstatement:

". . . that the grand work of establishing the detailed system has been perfected; that every acre of cultivated ground has been measured, assessed and brought to account; that a body of information the most complete, the most valuable perhaps that any Government can boast of, has been collected; and that the revenue has been considerably enhanced, whilst the most liberal consideration has not only been paid to the rights, but to the feelings, the vanities, the wishes of those whose interests might be affected by the change."

He explained the proposals he now wished to make were entirely disinterested, because the administration he had in view was not one of which he would himself be prepared to take charge.

"It will require a person of high rank, either noble or military; and I have had too much experience already of the injuries which accrue from the want of that high rank."

Thanks to Lord Minto, he had been privileged "in some way first to point out the object, then to direct the course of measures which led to its attainment". The difficulties had been great, yet he felt that the charges entrusted to him by Lord Minto had been "administered with steadiness and uprightness: and after encountering all the storms of contending interests and unparalleled difficulties, I have the pleasure to find my vessel tight and trim and fit for any voyage. . . ."

"Like an anxious pilot I have anticipated with delight the hour when I may deliver her over to her duly appointed Commander. In October, 1816, I shall have been Governor of these Colonies five years, the usual period for which such a post is held. My health is delicate, and having completed twenty years' service in anxiety, fatigue and constant application, I would indulge the hope of some relaxation."

He would have liked to visit England, but for financial reasons would have to go to Bencoolen.

Before dealing with his main proposition he referred to the disappointment that may have been felt in England at the partial failure of expectations originally held out, his purpose being to remove "the shade which such failure may have cast on the authority and correctness of my representations".

"To meet what I conceive to have been a very unfair attack upon the character of my administration, I felt myself called upon to take a general review of all the leading measures of my Government which appeared to have excited displeasure. I am told that so little is the interest taken in Leadenhall Street that the Directors will not even read dispatches from Java. It is not possible for your Lordship to conceive the real injury to the public service, to the public character and to the national interest by the state of suspense, the indecision which has been connected with everything concerning Java affairs."

He explained the value of the Moluccas, of Bangka and the great island of Borneo.

"As rich perhaps in the precious metals as Mexico or Peru . . . these islands, my Lord, are doubtless the real Taprobana of the ancients—the sacred Isles of the Hindus!"

The East Indian tribes had a bad reputation in Europe because all that was known of them was their piracies and their deadly krises. The only thing needed was good government to direct their spirit and enterprise "in a course more consonant with our notions of civilization".

"And now may I ask what was the state of Scotland 200 years ago?"

He dealt next in detail with the type of administration he would recommend and the principles on which the government should be conducted. Only quite a modest establishment of officials would be required. The seat of government should be at Samarang, and if the Dutch were unwilling to move their offices there from the capital, they could be made a present of Batavia, which "might then be to Java what Chinsurah is to Bengal". Holland had for the last fifty years gained little value out of Java, and her colonies there had steadily deteriorated. It would be as hopeless to attempt to improve "the morals, habits and principles of a great proportion of the European colonists as it is to purify their institutions". Of the better type of Dutch, most were prosperous and financially independent. No doubt the British Government would be prepared to provide pensions for those suffering undue hardship from a transfer of the colony finally to England. As for the native population, he was convinced that they would welcome the colony becoming British. During his recent tour he had found everywhere the greatest horror at the thought of the island reverting to Dutch ownership. Finally, for the first time, a European power was now in complete charge of Java.

"The rebellious provinces have been brought into order, universal tranquillity prevails, and confidence is everywhere established. . . . Are we not in some measure bound to the native population to secure to them by every means in our power the enjoyment of that liberty and independence we allowed them to taste, or is the cup to be dashed from the lip as soon as it is touched? . . . In *one* word the Javanese are decidedly English; give but the *other word* and Great Britain produces not more faithful adherents to the Crown than Java may afford."

The same day, when forwarding estimates for 1815-16, he took the opportunity to try to convince the Court of Directors as to Java's sound financial position.

"These documents only serve to show the intrinsic value of Java itself in its own Revenues and Resources, but when viewed on the more extensive scale of which it is susceptible as the Centre and Emporium of the Eastern Islands, the surplus revenue now adduced would by no means be all that might be expected of these valuable possessions. The Moluccas would naturally fall again under the immediate charge and jurisdiction of the Island. Java would again become the principal Mart of Export to Europe, and if the monopoly of this branch of Commerce were permitted to increase, it would become the great market for the rest of the world."

The Prince Regent's birthday on 12th August brought Raffles and Nightingall down to Batavia. Weak as he was, Raffles would have felt it impossible to be absent from the official ceremonies customary on that day. He even attended the birthday ball, his first public appearance since the death of Olivia. This was held at the Harmonie, which owed its fine premises to his generous and sympathetic support. The following day he returned to Buitenzorg, only to visit Batavia again a week later to gratify van Ijsseldijk by attending the magnificent ball given by that gentleman on the 24th to celebrate the birthday of King William of the Netherlands.

Notwithstanding these public appearances, warranted only by his high sense of duty, Raffles' health continued to cause anxiety. The refreshing air and peace of Buitenzorg—"Sans Souci"—seemed to have lost their spell. Perhaps the house was too painfully reminiscent of Olivia and the many happy days thay had spent together there. A more bracing climate was recommended, and Ciceroa, a country seat owned jointly by Engelhardt, Cranssen and Pieter van Hermsted Cappelhoff, was put at his disposal. Early in September he and his personal staff moved up to the cooler climate of this hill station. How he employed his time there has been described by Lady Raffles on the authority of Captain Travers.

"He took with him several of his staff and a party of natives whose good sense and intelligence had attracted his notice, and whom he had brought with him from the eastern part of the Island. With these last he passed the greater part of every morning and evening in reading and translating with the greatest rapidity and ease the different legends with which they furnished him, particularly the Brata Yudha. His translation of this singular and curious poem will be found in his *History of Java*. It was a work requiring considerable labour and time; but it was a common remark with him that if a man were fully and seriously determined on accomplishing any undertaking within human power at all, he would succeed by diligence and attention. At this time he rose early and commenced business before breakfast; immediately after this he went through the official duties of the day; after which he devoted the remainder of the morning until dinner time to the natives who were living with him. He dined at 4 o'clock, and took a walk for the sake of his health in the evening; and until he retired to rest he was occupied in reading, translating and compiling. But his strength and health did not return, perhaps from his not being able to amuse his mind without over exertion and too much application."

At a meeting in Batavia on 11th September of the Society of Arts and Sciences, he delivered another long discourse, which began:

"A series of domestic afflictions, alas! but too well known to you all, have followed in such quick succession to the melancholy event which it has long been my duty to communicate, that, until the present hour, I have felt myself in every way unequal to the trying task of publicly announcing to you the death of our noble and enlightened patron, the late Earl of Minto; an event so unlooked for, and so painfully calamitous in its immediate effects, that, to use the energetic language of Mr Muntinghe, it '*obliged us*', as it were, '*to close our lips before the Almighty!*'

"For how difficult was it to be reconciled to our wishes, and to our natural conceptions of right and wrong, that a man of such public and private worth should have been lost to his country, and snatched away from the embraces of his friends and family, at the very moment he has to receive the only reward which, in this world, could recompense his past labours—a calm and placid recollection of the arduous, but successful career he had run! . . ."

Having then touched on a number of matters of scientific interest, including Dr Horsfield's recent survey of the island of Bangka, he stressed the importance of a friendly intercourse with the Japanese, ending by expressing the hope that "no withering policy may blast the fair fruits of that spirit of research which has gone forth from this Hall; nor continue, under any circumstances, to shut out one-half of the world from the intelligence which the other half may possess."

From Ciceroa he wrote to Marsden on 18th September:

"In my last I promised you a long account of the discoveries we had made in Java, and all our progress in the collection of materials for a Grammar and Dictionary as well as for a historical account of Java. . . . I have not failed to notice what you observe on the paucity of information respecting the Javanese language. . . . I have attempted to break the ice, but further as yet and until I can communicate with those who are acquainted with the more ancient languages of Western India, I dare not go.

"But of the ancient Kawi I have ventured to pronounce that it is almost pure Sanscrit; and in doing so I have been rather guided by the general opinion and the probabilities than by any knowledge of my own or reference to Sanscrit authority. . . . Of the present language, or rather languages, of Java my collection amounts to upwards of 7,000 words and is daily increasing. I have visited nearly all the remains of sculpture to be found on the Island; they are far more extensive than at first I had any idea of, and drawings of the different images as well as ground plans, elevations &c of the different buildings are in great progress.

"Many of the Hindu deities have been found in small brass and copper casts; of these I have a collection containing nearly every deity in the Hindu mythology. We have also discovered some very ancient coins with dates. . . . I have taken measures for collecting vocabularies of the Papua or woolly haired race. I have procured from Bali copies of all the written compositions of the country. . . . I have lately made a very considerable addition to my Malayan as well as Javanese library; and I have set, not only the Regents but the Susuhunan himself at work in compiling historical accounts of their respective divisions of the country; they will be of use in checking the general account which I had previously collected; and at all events it has given a fashion to literary pursuits which cannot fail of being highly advantageous to all parties in the long run. . . .

"The Dutch colonists accuse us of folly; and the only answer I can make to them is that I am ambitious of the title of Bitara in after days. Objects have a different appearance when received by the rising sun to what they may present under one that is setting."

It must be admitted that, in the field of archaeology, Raffles' elucidation of inscriptions and some of the identifications he propounded have not stood the test of time. He had not the accumulated knowledge of archaeological research available to the modern investigator. He had to rely on local Javanese experts, greatly overrating the extent of their knowledge and the value of their testimony. But, as he explained to Marsden in the letter just quoted, he regarded himself more as a collector than an interpreter.

"I have ventured to offer some notions of a plan of the history of Java and the Eastern Islands, rather with a view to inviting observation and discussion than as binding myself to any preconceived notion. It was necessary to say something on the subject, and at all events I can answer for its general correctness as far as Javanese data can be depended upon. . . . My object as you know is rather to collect the raw materials than to establish any system of my own; and notwithstanding I have in some instances assumed something of a hypothesis, I am by no means wedded to it or bound to support it."

The days thus occupied in this quiet and regular manner were good for Raffles, despite the fact that "my back aches from sheer hard writing". Indeed, Travers describes the time at Ciceroa as one of the happiest in his experience. But the peace was rudely shattered by the arrival of a private warning dated 17th May from young Ramsay that it had been decided "by the unanimous vote of his unworthy illiberal and unjust employers" —the phrase was Travers', not Ramsay's—that Raffles should be superseded.

To his personal staff, this decision seemed incredible, but Raffles took the news very calmly, reiterating that he was confident time would vindicate his conduct. Nevertheless, he decided to go in person to Calcutta to challenge the decision. General Nightingall, who had been officially appointed to act for the Lieutenant-Governor should he leave Java, and was entitled to be advised at once of any such intention, was at the other end of the island. Raffles sent off an express dispatch to the commander of the forces, then went himself to Buitenzorg. There he was joined by Nightingall, who, on receiving Raffles' message, had set off immediately and had covered three hundred miles in four days, a speed of travel that demonstrated the genuineness of his regard for Raffles.

Raffles was glad of this opportunity to discuss the situation with his trusted friend, who was emphatically against the proposal that Raffles should go to Calcutta. He himself was expecting at any moment to be appointed commander-in-chief at Bombay, having already received a K.C.B. in anticipation of the event, and, apart from the awkward prospect of their both being away from Java at the same time, he considered that such a visit by Raffles to the Governor-General would do more harm than good. It was finally agreed that, as Captain Garnham, one of Raffles' aides-de-camp, was soon leaving for India, he should take letters from both Raffles and Nightingall to Calcutta and to London.

The letters from Raffles were addressed to Lord Moira, the Court of Directors, and to the Earl of Buckinghamshire in person. That to Moira was dated 2nd October. After complaining of the delay over the decision on his case and the impossibility of his going to India at that juncture, he continued:

"That same confidence in my rectitude and in the high and renowned character it has been the pride of my country to attach to your Lordship's name, will be my solace pending the present reference. But it is incumbent on me to add that, with a constitution of body never very strong, my health has so materially suffered under a series of afflictions, aggravated by the horrors of that cloud which has so long been allowed to hang over my character, that it is possible that a decision may come too late to afford that consolation, which the just, considerate and noble mind of your Lordship may wish. . . .

"I have still more deeply to regret the unfavourable impressions under which it is obvious conclusions and opinions adverse to the principles and conduct of my Government were formed; for it was impossible for me to receive the dispatches, which had been forwarded from Bengal before the arrival of Mr Assey, and which contained a universal censure on all the measures, plans and expectations of the local Government, without attributing them, in some measure, to this cause; and without an apprehension or indeed the conclusion that your Lordship's communication to Europe would have been made under an equally unfavourable impression."

To Charles Grant, chairman for the third time of the Court of Directors, he wrote on 6th October:

"I am induced to address this direct communication to Europe . . . to provide for the possible contingency that the injury done to my character and reputation by the delay may be found so great, as to render it eventually necessary for me to have recourse to a higher or more distant tribunal. . . ."

Lastly, to the Earl of Buckinghamshire he wrote on 11th October:

". . . I learn, however, that in the month of April last the Court of Directors came to a Resolution, in consequence of some communication from the Earl of Moira, to direct my removal from this Government, and also to withhold from me the reversion to Bencoolen. . . . It is scarcely possible to conceive a greater degree of injustice than what I have thus received at the hands of the Earl of Moira."

It had been only on 2nd October, "after waiting a period exceeding 18 months", that he had ventured to appeal against the delay. In regard to whoever was to take his place:

"Calculating upon the same spirit of hostility being continued against all the measures of the late Earl of Minto, which has hitherto distinguished the administration of his successor, at least as far as the interests of this Colony have been concerned, it will be in vain for me to attempt more in this country than my personal justification. . . . I apprehend much and serious inquiry from the powers of the local Government being limited by the necessity of constant reference to India. . . . the circumstances and conditions of the Eastern Islands being so different from the continent of India that the former will not bear the application of the same regulations[1]

[1] It was on these grounds that British Malaya obtained its independence from the Government of India in 1867.

. . . I think I may say . . . that nothing will detain me in India beyond October next, the period at which I have already expressed my wish to be relieved from this Government."

Having completed these letters, Raffles returned with Nightingall to Ciceroa.

It was presumably about this date that the pamphlet, *Review of the Administration, Value and State of the Colony of Java with its Dependencies, as it was,—as it is,—and as it may be*, was produced. It is generally considered to have been written by Raffles or under his direction. A letter from Raffles to Thomas Love Peacock of the East India Company, undated but certainly in 1825 or 1826, clarifies the point:

". . . I also enclose a small pamphlet . . . entitled 'Java as it was, is and may be'—dated 1815 and at the period of my recall. It was never published. . . . It was prepared in Java in my office and edited by the late Mr Assey,[1] and may give you some idea of the various reforms and changes I had to make, and of the difficulties I had to contend with."

Charles Assey was a man of some literary distinction, and was, for a period, editor of the *Java Government Gazette* in addition to his duties as secretary to the Java government. This description of him was written by young George Augustus Addison, who came as a clerk to Java in 1813 and died all too soon of fever:

"I cannot say enough of him, and like him very much indeed. He is an excellent second to Mr Raffles, quite as indefatigable, and as capable. . . . Assey is uncommonly clever, quick, and well-informed; and, what is better, joining to an amicable disposition a fine manly independence of character. . . . It is no slight proof in his favour that General G., though cordially disliking him as a friend of Mr Raffles, did not in any of his attacks—and he spared few—venture a syllable against Assey.

"Of course there are constantly a crowd of visitors in the house; but the above, with a doctor, a Dutch secretary, and myself, are the only permanent members. The doctor, Sir Thomas Sevestre, is an original too; but I have not time to describe him. . . ."

Sevestre was a young surgeon on the Madras establishment. He held the Portuguese order of Knight of the Tower and Sword.

Within a fortnight of Raffles' return to Ciceroa, news of the Battle of Waterloo reached Java. It was only too obvious that the fate of the island must soon be known, and that the urgent dispatches just sent off by Raffles would arrive home too late.

Suspense was not prolonged. On 13th November details of the Anglo-Dutch convention of 13th August 1814 were received. Among its terms was the return of Java to the Dutch, which finally dashed all Raffles' hopes of its permanence as a British colony.

[1] Assey died in 1821.

On receiving this news, one of his first steps was to communicate it to the Javanese princes. Probably never before in Java had there been such a close and human contact between the chief European authority and the rulers of the states. Raffles, with his command of their language, his natural gift for making friends and his active interest in their history and customs, no less than in their well-being, had forged links that could not lightly be broken. The following is part of one of these letters. Dated 17th November 1815, it was addressed to the Panembahan of Sumenep, Madura:

"The Lieutenant-Governor has to announce to His Highness that he has just received the particulars of a convention understood to have been made between Great Britain and the United Netherlands, by which His Britannic Majesty, desirous of affording a lasting testimony of his friendship and attachment to the House of Orange, and to the Dutch Nation, has engaged to restore to Holland all the Colonies in the Eastern Seas which were possessed by that Nation at the commencement of the late War.

"The Islands of Java and Madura will in consequence revert to the Dutch Nation, as soon as the circumstances of Europe may admit of their taking possession, but it will be satisfactory to His Highness to know that by a Public Act of the Dutch Government in Europe all the arrangements made by the British Government on Java have been confirmed so that in the change of Sovereigns no material alteration is to be contemplated. His Highness cannot but be aware of the intimate connexion and good understanding existing between the English and Dutch Nations, and the proof thus given by the latter to respect the measures taken during the Sovereignty of the English on Java, cannot but be considered as an earnest on their part of the confidence and protection which doubtless will be always placed in His Highness's family by the Dutch Authorities of Java.

"The claims of His Highness's family on the protection and liberality of the Chief Authority on Java, whether English or Dutch, have been so frequently acknowledged, that it would perhaps be unnecessary again to advert to them were it not probable that a still further acknowledgment on the part of the British Government may be satisfactory to the mind of His Highness at a moment when there is a prospect of termination of the immediate connexion between the English and Madurese."

Later, in Sumatra, Raffles was accused of deliberately setting the ruling princes against the Dutch. This letter, and those in a similar strain to the sultans of Java and its dependencies, should always be remembered.

Although the official news was disappointing, things looked a little brighter on the personal side. Either Edmonstone or Seton had sent him copies of the Minutes recorded by them as members of the Supreme

Council. No one in India had a closer knowledge of Raffles, as a man and an official, than these two men, and it is a tribute to them both, as it is to Raffles, that, notwithstanding the obvious antagonism of the Governor-General, they should have delivered their views fairly and frankly.

Both minutes were dated 18th June 1815. Edmonstone's was a long and careful document in which every charge against Raffles was investigated. He completely exonerated him from every accusation of corrupt motives, but passed a more guarded judgment on the question of the expediency of some of his measures. With regard to the sale of lands:

"There was nothing unusual nor in itself improper . . . and to give it the character of expedience as an Act of Government nothing more was required than that the alleged exigency should really exist."

Seton concurred in the views expressed by Edmonstone.

"That Mr Raffles has not succeeded in his endeavours may I think be attributed to the exhausted state in which he found the Island, to the annihilation of its export trade, to a want of specie, and under the great disadvantages of these difficulties, to the fatal necessity of engaging in early and extensive wars with the Sultans of Palembang and Djocjocarta."

The purchase of land by Raffles he described as "indiscreet and injudicious".

ii

During November mutiny threatened among the sepoy battalions of the 4th Infantry Regiment. They had shown signs of discontent for some time past because of their long spell on the island, and the majority were now fully convinced that, when Holland took over Java once more, they themselves would be transferred to the Dutch army instead of being sent back to India. They were consequently ready for revolt—or any other mischief.

A small but dangerous minority in the Light battalion, which was stationed at Surakarta, conceived the alternative plan of remaining in Java and, by allying themselves with the native rulers, establishing a kingdom independent of the Dutch. As a prelude to this, they plotted a general mutiny of sepoys throughout the island and were already in touch with the two other battalions at Surabaya and Weltevreden. The signal would be the murder of the British officers at Surakarta, who were totally inadequate to maintain strict discipline, and the Chinese settlers, whose property would then be acquired.

Word of this conspiracy reached the ears of Major Johnson, the Resident at Surakarta. He reported the matter to Colonel Burslem, commander in the eastern districts, who promptly forestalled the rising by placing some twenty sepoys under arrest. On the ringleader was found correspondence from the Weltevreden battalion, which read to this effect:

"You are the Light battalion. If you mutiny or do anything first, we will join you."

The immediate danger was thus averted.

By that time General Sir Miles Nightingall had received his expected appointment to Bombay. The situation at Surakarta was well in hand, and there were no signs of possible disturbance among the Indian troops elsewhere, so he did not consider it necessary to put off his departure. After handing over to Colonel Burslem, he left for India, having pledged his word to Raffles that he would strongly support his cause.

Hardly had Nightingall sailed from Batavia when Raffles, back once more at Buitenzorg, received on 5th December alarming news as to the possible political consequences of further attempts at mutiny. His information was that the sepoys at Surakarta had been acting in concert with the court and—worse still—that Jokyakarta was involved. The one thing that it had been his consistent policy to prevent, the making of common cause by Solo and Mataram against the European power, appeared now to be a very dangerous possibility.

The court party was headed by the Empress and the Mangku-bumi,[1] brother of the Sushunan. They planned to seize the treasure and possessions of the Regent of Mataram, to murder him and the young Sultan (put in authority by Raffles in 1812) and, by placing the Mangku-bumi's son-in-law on the throne, reunite Mataram and Solo. It was the Mangku-bumi who had negotiated with the sepoys, who had been prepared to support his schemes, believing that if he succeeded they would have such influence in Surakarta as to establish their own position for the future.

The Susuhunan could not have been unaware of what was happening, for his brother would need his backing, but he had been too cautious to commit himself openly. Doubtless he had in mind that he might be able to use the sepoys to assist him in obtaining his independence when the Dutch returned to Java—or even to defend himself against reprisals for having collaborated with the British.

At an emergency meeting of the Council Raffles explained the position, which he also outlined in a letter dated 8th December to Edmonstone. He stressed the obvious danger that would arise if the three sepoy battalions were not soon replaced. One European battalion would suffice, and if the relief could be announced promptly, it would dissipate the rumour that the sepoys would never get back to India again. Meanwhile there was a further and grave risk that if the Dutch did not arrive soon, and with fully adequate forces, it might be impossible when they took over to prevent the native courts making a bid for independence. He reminded the Supreme Government that the territories of the native courts comprised three-eighths of the total population of Java. If, by the

[1] Prime minister, or, literally, "Supporter of the realm".

time the Dutch came, the sepoy battalions had not been relieved, they might well be convinced that they were to come under Dutch orders, and this would create a very dangerous situation. No reliance could be placed on the various colonial troops raised by the British, for they certainly would not fight against their own people. While, therefore, things were quiet at the moment, it would be hazardous indeed for the Dutch to return to Java without fully adequate armed strength.

Chapter Eighteen

JAVA, 1816

i

THE Java Council met again on 1st January 1816, when his colleagues urged Raffles to intervene personally. It was suggested that Hugh Hope should go with him, but as Hope had only just returned from a trip to China for the sake of his health and was still far from well, it was finally agreed that Muntinghe should be invited to accompany Raffles.

The party, which also included Captain Travers, left next day by ship, reaching Samarang on the 4th. A very high sea was running, but Raffles insisted on going ashore at once in the report boat, which came off on their arrival. Muntinghe and Travers followed a little later, but even so could not make the usual landing-place.

As soon as he was ashore, Raffles sent off a letter to Surakarta, notifying the Susuhunan of his arrival and of his intention to pay him a visit, but adding that he was unable to do so until his Highness's brother, the Mangku-bumi, was sent to Samarang.

The Susuhunan complied. The Mangku-bumi arrived under escort at Samarang on the 7th and was sent to Batavia. Raffles and party moved up next day to Serondol. Early on the 9th they set off for Salatiga. Although the weather was fine, there had been heavy rain earlier and the road was almost impassable. Large parties of Javanese, however, were stationed along the route to push the carriages. Progress without them would have been impossible. Salatiga was reached in time for breakfast with Major Johnson, who then accompanied them to Surakarta. By midday they reached the state boundary, where they were met by a number of Javanese officials and an escort of the Pĕrang Wedono's legion. The ceremonial stage of the journey now began.

"Our next place of stopping", wrote Travers, "was Souracarta, the ancient capital of the Emperor's dominions. There the Governor was received by the Crown Prince attended by the Assistant Resident [Lieutenant Hart], his brothers and all the Emperor's children who offered congratulations and homage. On the Governor alighting a salute of nineteen guns was fired, the troops at the same time all saluting, drums beating and colours flying."

A procession two miles in length was formed, and after a journey of about seven miles to Kluchu, the ruler's country residence, Raffles was received by the Susuhunan in person. When another salute of nineteen guns had been fired, the party moved to a pavilion specially erected, where the Susuhunan took his seat on the throne, with Raffles on his right and Major Johnson on his left, the rest of the company, with the exception of the Crown Prince, being seated on the ground.

After they had sat some time, wine was handed round; red for the Susuhunan, Raffles and Major Johnson, Madeira for the remainder of the company, as was the custom of that court. On the Susuhunan's drinking with the Lieutenant-Governor, "the infantry fired three volleys uncommonly well". Raffles was then conducted by the Susuhunan to "his state carriage drawn by six horses and resembling very much the Lord Mayor's coach in London". More salutes were fired, the troops took up position, and an enormous cavalcade proceeded to the *kĕratun*.

"The Emperor never moving out of a walk," continued Travers, "the procession went step by step which would have been tedious but for the novelty of the scene which greatly pleased me."

Further elaborate ceremonies took place in the hall of audience, and yet another procession was formed to escort Raffles to the Residency. Major Johnson then went back to conduct the Susuhunan there also, where he dined quietly with Raffles. Their conversation was described by Raffles in a dispatch to Colonel Burslem. He began by telling the Susuhunan that his mission was to inquire into the recent negotiations between the court and the sepoys of the Light battalion, then added that, as the Mangku-bumi had been surrendered, the Susuhunan was forgiven for any indiscretion he may have committed. By his subsequent remarks he made it very clear that he knew all about the intrigue against the Sultan of Mataram, at which the Susuhunan became visibly alarmed. Raffles reassured him by saying:

". . . that I had determined not to place entire confidence in reports which involved any question regarding his attachment; and that my object in thus informing him of the report to his prejudice was the more clearly to point out the consequences resulting from his having so far degraded his dignity as to put himself upon a level with inferior officers and private soldiers."

The Susuhunan explained that the action taken by the court of Surakarta had been prompted by fear of the Dutch and what they might do when they regained control of Java. Raffles asked if the Susuhunan would like him to make arrangements with the Dutch, to which the Susuhunan replied that he regarded the British as his friends and wished nothing more than that the terms of the treaty of August 1812 should remain in force. Raffles undertook to ensure that the treaty would be respected by the Dutch, and, after the Susuhunan had promised to reprove the Empress for having joined in the intrigue against Mataram, they parted with every expression of goodwill.

From Surakarta, Raffles and his little party went on to Jokyakarta, where more ceremonial visits and entertainments took place. There followed a tour through Kedu and a call on Resident Lawrence at Magelang. By 18th January they reached Pekalongan.

"Here", wrote Travers, "we were met by Captain Heyland who had just arrived from Bengal, and came with dispatches to meet us. They were of the most unpleasant nature, being the final notification of Mr Raffles' supersession, at the same time, however, offering him the Residency of Bencoolen. He received the information with coolness, solacing himself with the consolation that a little time would enable him to prove to the world how unjustly, nay cruelly, he was treated."

The documents relating to his recall are the dispatch from London to Calcutta dated 5th May 1815, the minute of the Governor-General dated 20th May, and finally the decision of the Governor-General in Council dated 17th October and recorded after the receipt of the dispatch from London.

After commenting with pleasure on the agreement of view between London and Calcutta that no new establishments in the Eastern Archipelago should be sanctioned, and that the plans of the Lieutenant-Governor of Java had not been approved, the Court of Directors referred to the trade with Japan with greater approbation than had been shown by the Supreme Government. Turning to the land-revenue arrangements, the Court observed:

"We have felt much uneasiness lest the new system of Land Revenue so hastily introduced by the Lieutenant-Governor of Java should have served to alienate the minds of the numerous individuals whose long-established authority has been subverted by it. We do not mean to question the propriety of attempting to correct the Revenue System . . . which we have reason to believe is not less defective in principle than oppressive in practice. But we are decidedly averse to violent and sudden changes, being convinced that even where the operations of a new system are calculated to improve the condition of the people, much of the intended benefit may be destroyed by an incautious departure from Institutions which have had the sanction of time. And we must deem such changes particularly undesirable in Countries where we have only a temporary position."

But the most important paragraph, as far as Raffles was concerned, was this:

"Of the various measures of the Lieutenant-Governor of Java which have been commented upon in the Dispatch now before us (5th August 1814) we shall merely observe that we cannot but lament that the just and accurate view of political and commercial economy that have served to detect the numerous errors that have been committed by the Lieutenant-Governor were not directed to the prevention of acts which have rendered the occupation of Java a source of financial embarrassment to the British Government. With reference to these considerations, whatever may be the result of the investigations of the charges preferred against Mr Raffles, we are of opinion that his continuance on the Government of Java would be highly inexpedient."

The Governor-General's minute was intended to be impartial, but it was clearly tinged with bias against Raffles. Moira had and could have had little knowledge of the Java government, nor had he any personal acquaintance with Raffles. He could not therefore take more than an abstract view of his replies. On the other hand, Seton and Edmonstone, particularly the former, both knew Raffles personally and were fully aware of the high opinion held of him by Minto, and indeed how far the measures adopted by Raffles had had his complete approval, even when they had not been directly sponsored by him. It is difficult to avoid the conclusion that Moira allowed his respect for the military caste in the person of Gillespie to prejudice his views on Raffles' administration. Be that as it may, his observations were as follows:

"I must confess that from the first I have never been quite satisfied of the propriety of letting this Enquiry end in the explanations which have been afforded by the Lieutenant-Governor, yet a considerable embarrassment has attended the notion of carrying the Enquiry further. To order investigations on the spot would be to impeach the Lieutenant-Governor distinctly, and when it was recollected that the transfer of the island to the Dutch would at once put a stop to the tracing of the questionable matter and leave the Lieutenant-Governor under a taint which he might not have deserved, my reluctance to institute such examination will be comprehended.

"The consideration is at this moment the stronger for our daily expectation of the order of surrendering Java. Thus debarred on satisfying myself on these points respecting which I am still entertaining doubt, I find it incumbent on me to discharge the narrower duty of pronouncing on such matters as are either admitted or sufficiently substantiated by the documents which I have perused. . . .

"Though, however, I consider it to be proper to acquit Mr Raffles as far as his moral character is implicated, I cannot hold his explanation of the circumstances attending his concern in the purchase of lands to have been at all satisfactory. His concern in the purchase has not been, nor could be justified. . . . Were there not every reason to suppose the Colony to be on the eve of passing from our hands, I should have felt disposed to have visited this transaction with Public Proof of disapprobation, combining this serious error with the frequent instances of mismanagement established in the conduct of the affairs of that Government and more especially in its financial concern; I should have conceived it essential to the well-being of that Colony as well as to our security in a time of anticipated great financial embarrassment to have proposed the removal of Mr Raffles from the Government of Java, and his being directed to take charge of the appointment still in reservation for him at Bencoolen. . . . That situation was specifically kept open for Mr Raffles by my Predecessor."

Raffles' administration, according to Moira, had been "consecutively injudicious" and he had "launched out into endless and costly undertakings" with "persevering imprudence".

"If, however," he ended, "he is acquitted of those charges in which his moral character is implicated, still there is no reason why he should not be employed in a situation of minor responsibility and of more strictly defined duties, of which description the Residency of Bencoolen may be considered."

That being his attitude, the Governor-General fully approved of the views of the Court as expressed in the dispatch of 5th May. The following minute was accordingly resolved on 17th October:

"The Honourable Court of Directors having subsequently ordered the removal of Mr Raffles from the Government of Java, and the selection of some person from among the Civil Servants of the Company . . . to whom the charge of the Colony can with confidence be entrusted, the Governor-General proposes to find some suitable person to succeed Mr Raffles."

John Fendall was selected for the appointment.

The confirmation by the Governor-General of the dismissal foreshadowed by Ramsay was a staggering blow. Till that moment Raffles had not imagined that the answers he had made to the indiscriminate and ill-supported charges that Gillespie had seen fit to level against him would not convince any impartial person. He had not appreciated how serious it was in the eyes of Moira that a civilian should behave with indelicacy towards a general officer, or that Moira would accept the word of Gillespie that Raffles had been solely to blame. It is also possible that the very complete answers produced by Raffles had created the suspicion that there was more in Gillespie's charges than actually appeared. Opinion in Calcutta at the time of the impeachment was probably accurately reflected in the remark of John Palmer to a correspondent.

"I have not yet seen General Gillespie . . . but we cannot fail to meet soon. I should be glad to hear his history, though his violence renders his testimony as suspicious as Mr R's integrity."

Raffles was not prepared to accept dismissal without a protest. Back at Buitenzorg, he wrote on 27th January:

"Although I bow with deference to Your Lordship's judgment in my case, I cannot be satisfied with the incomplete acquittal with which that judgment has been pronounced. . . . I cannot be satisfied with a decision which apparently leaves the main point still open to further enquiry, which deals out acquittal with a sparing hand, and, permit me to observe, does not grant a decisive opinion even on the charge of having alienated the coffee monopoly for my own benefit."

He advised Moira of his intention to appeal to England, and requested official copies of Seton's and Edmonstone's minutes.

Now that his dismissal had become a fact and no longer just a fear, Raffles' health, already gravely undermined by years of overwork and illness, and strained to breaking-point by the recent series of personal disasters, collapsed once more and to a dangerous degree. One of the violent attacks that excessive strain always induced in him developed and laid him prostrate. His friends persuaded him to be examined by a medical board. Its verdict was unanimous: he must leave Java at the earliest possible moment and go, if not to England, at least as far as the Cape. He wrote to Moira in February about Bencoolen:

"It is a matter of regret to me that I am not able to avail myself of Your Lordship's disposition in my favour on this occasion; but my health and constitution have suffered so severe a shock from continued indisposition and from the severe illness with which I have been lately attacked, that I am strongly urged by my medical advisers not to remain longer without a change of climate. I have in consequence been under the necessity of proceeding to sea for the Cape of Good Hope, and eventually to Europe, if I do not feel myself materially benefited by the sea voyage."

This letter disposes of the contention of van der Kemp that Raffles did not go direct to Bencoolen, but had to go first to England because he was debarred from Bencoolen until the Court of Directors had cleared him of Gillespie's charges. Van der Kemp is himself at fault when he accuses Lady Raffles of distorting the truth in writing as she did that it was illness that caused Raffles to go home before taking up the Sumatra appointment. The illness was very genuine. Raffles was confined to his room for more than six weeks.

ii

Colonel Nahuijs had obtained his release as a prisoner of war in England and had returned to The Hague, where he had found preparations being made for the embarkation for Java of the new Dutch Governor-General, Baron van der Capellen, his two colleagues, Cornelis Elout and Vice-Admiral Buijskes, and some 3,500 troops.

"As the Government of the Netherlands", wrote Nahuijs, "thought that the English authorities in Java were apprised since some time of the approaching arrival of their allies, and had therefore made every thing ready for their reception, it was considered superfluous to send out commissaries in advance, as had been the previous plan.

"Meanwhile from the letters of my friends in Batavia, it seemed very clear that the English were far from making preparations or taking measures for the reception and barracking of the Dutch troops, having pulled down several barracks, and amongst others sold the one called Ryswyk to private individuals.

"On the strength of this fact, I still requested to be sent out in advance for the accomplishment of our commission in Java. . . ."

The Dutch Government was of the opinion that these reports were exaggerated, and it was only after Nahuijs had offered to travel at his own expense that permission was given. He reached Java early in March.

"On my arrival in Java I perceived that no one knew that the English possessors were so soon to reinstate the former masters, and no one had heard that the Dutch fleet and the Dutch Commissaries-General on board had left Holland on the 29th October and was steering for Java.

"The unexpected sight of a Dutch frigate in the roads of Batavia brought a number of inquisitive English and nearly half the Dutch population on to the quay.

"Still higher rose their curiosity when they recognized in the approaching boat a Dutch officer, in my person. They scarcely gave me time to come ashore. Those on shore called out in chorus most agreeable to my ears: 'Welcome, welcome, dearest friend!' and I was literally stormed with questions right and left, about the news I had brought from Holland. 'Nothing, gentlemen,' said I, 'nothing, friends, but what you have certainly heard long ago, that every one in our country is very happy after our glorious campaign against France, and that you may daily expect the high Commission who are on their way to resume the government of all our East-Indian possessions.'

"No pen, at least not mine, can describe the impression this joyous intelligence had on the minds and spirits of my good countrymen who looked upon that ardently and long desired period as still very far distant, and naturally as very uncertain, as a newly appointed Governor-General [Lieutenant-Governor] was daily expected from Bengal in Batavia, which raised hopes in the English and fears amongst the Dutch inhabitants that the restitution of the Dutch colonial possessions to their old masters, one of the chief articles in the Vienna treaty, might have again been retracted or altered after the battle of Waterloo, or later. It seemed to me as if an electric shock had run through the assembled crowd and turned them all instantaneously mad.

"The cheering, the general hurrah! and the deafening cries of 'long live the King of Holland! long live Java! long live Nahuijs!' were unexampled, and did not cease until I had been conducted, I may say rather half carried by the people from the landing-place. . . .

"The feelings my arrival created in Java were various; as amongst my worthy countrymen they were those of unbounded delight, so amongst the civil and military servants of the English Government it created universal consternation and dejection. Many of the latter could not believe that their short reign was to end so soon, especially when three days after my arrival the newly appointed English Governor of Java, Tindall [Fendall], landed at Batavia with a newly nominated member of council, Mr Abrahams."

Raffles was still confined to his room at Buitenzorg, but special arrangements were made for him to have immediate warning when Fendall's ship arrived in the roads. This happened on 10th March and Travers went up to Buitenzorg to bring Raffles down. He was much distressed by his chief's appearance and tried to dissuade him from getting out of bed. But Raffles insisted on going to Batavia at once. He was therefore on the shore ready to greet Fendall when he landed. Although hardly able to stand without assistance, he personally presented all his staff to the new Lieutenant-Governor and entertained him and his party to breakfast. He then went back to bed again.

Travers recorded in his diary his impressions of the new arrivals.

"Mr Fendall is a man between 50 and 60 years of age, is of a mild, placid temper, gentle, easy and unassuming in his manner, with a sound mind and understanding. Mrs Fendall is also aged, but a most kind, affectionate, pleasing lady."

Their grown-up daughters and a friend completed the party.

"The interest which all the family appeared to take about Mr Raffles endeared them all to the members of his family, and the desire evinced by Mr Fendall to pay him every possible attention was extremely gratifying. . . . Mr Fendall meanwhile commenced his Government and soon evinced his determination to prosecute and follow up all Mr Raffles' plans and views."

He also caused an order to be published in the *Gazette* to the effect that Raffles should continue to enjoy the same courtesies and dignities as those that had belonged to him as Lieutenant-Governor. At Raffles request he authorized Sir Thomas Sevestre, Raffles' doctor, to accompany him to England. Also of the party were to be his two *aides-de-camp*, Travers and Garnham. It was left to Travers to find a ship.

Raffles' final letter from Java to the Court of Directors was written at Buitenzorg on the day following the arrival of the Fendalls.

"At the close of an arduous and extensive Administration which will be admitted to have commenced at a moment of peculiar financial difficulty, and to have been attended with embarrassments unusual to a new Government in consequence of the bankruptcy of the preceding Government and of a necessity having nevertheless existed of respecting in some degree the force and imperious measures to which that Government resorted in order to carry on their ordinary details; I am anxious to place in your possession a view of the present financial state of this Colony.

"This review I shall found not on estimates, but on actual records; and I confidently trust it will prove to the satisfaction of your Honble Court, that my ideas on the value and importance of this Colony have not been raised too high, but that time only was wanting, and a perseverance in principles of liberal and extended policy, to render it equal to all the extent that has either been contemplated or reported. I shall not detain your Honble Court by any review of the past financial arrangements adopted at different periods of my Administration. The opinions which have been passed upon them by the Supreme Government in India, and the explanations which we considered ourselves enabled to offer are already before your Honble Court; and my letter of 5th August 1815 will have explained the foundation of our present revenue and resources, and prepared you to expect that the general result will be more favourable since the system of administration which it has been my object to introduce into the Island in accordance with the principles laid down by the late Earl of Minto began to have effect."

He then quoted figures to show that revenue had gradually increased and expenditure gradually decreased.

"Your Honble Court will further be able to trace the rapid increase of the revenues of this Colony in comparison with the preceding Dutch Government, and it is sufficiently obvious from former reports and documents that the increase of revenue has resulted in a very principal degree from the introduction of land rental which now amounts to nearly one-half of the whole revenues of the Island, it is a fair conclusion to draw that the improvement thus effected is rendered permanent and that a very short time only has been required to repay in a pecuniary point of view those temporary and partial sacrifices which, in the introduction of a radical change that had equally in view the amelioration of the condition of the people and the interests of the Government, could not be avoided. . . .

"The possession of Banca is now complete, and its resources brought forward. The revenue derivable from them will continue undiminished as far as can be foreseen, since the tin has a ready and certain sale. . . .

"On the whole therefore I feel considerable confidence in the report which I am now enabled to present to your Honble Court. The outlay on the first establishment of this Government was great, and unavoidably so; it was in fact a complete purchase of every necessary article, even to the furniture of the public offices, and it is in this manner that the accounts with the prize agents became so extensive; but on the other hand, the particulars and the returns of that outlay will in a great degree be shown at the transfer of the Colony in the amount of stock which then will either be taken over by the succeeding Government, or be disposable to be converted into money. By the account enclosed you will perceive there remains a surplus of 378,410,416 Rupees to the credit of the Government of Java. The quantity of coffee also now in store, and which has long been waiting the necessary tonnage to be conveyed to Europe, is 60,000 peculs, which at the present market price at Batavia is equal to 1,320,000 Rupees."

Raffles was well enough to preside on 12th March at a small dinner, when "a select party" was invited to meet the new Lieutenant-Governor and his family. This completed Raffles' official duties, and his time was now occupied in getting ready for his own departure, the news of which soon became widely known, its imminence indicated by an advertisement in the *Gazette* of a large and varied assortment of his books for sale.

"The Dutch and Native inhabitants", recorded Travers, "began to evince by means the most flattering the very high respect and esteem they entertained for Mr Raffles. All the Public bodies presented him with addresses and no mark of admiration and respect was left unpaid. The British inhabitants, headed by the Military, assembled and presented the most gratifying address, accompanying with a service of plate as a token of their lasting regard. This Garnham and I were deputed to purchase and present in England."

The address of the military officers and merchants of Batavia ran:

"We, the undersigned inhabitants of Batavia, request to approach you on your departure from this Island and to offer you the warmest expressions of our respect and attachment. Placed as we have been during your administration of this extensive and valuable Colony, we have had the opportunity of observing the eminent talents of your Government and the virtues of your private character; and we feel ourselves fully warranted in expressing our admiration and acknowledgment of the ability, justice and impartiality by which you have been guided in the intricate and peculiar circumstances attending this Colony ever since it came under British Government. While we regret most sincerely the state of your health which renders your departure from India necessary, we confidently hope that your recovery may be complete, and that your life may long be preserved for the exertion of those talents and virtues which have distinguished your career in Java. As a lasting memorial of our esteem we request your acceptance of a service of plate which we shall cause to be presented to you as soon as possible after your arrival in England."

Although testimonials to departing governors can be regarded as the customary respect paid to high officials and the sincerity of the expressions can often be questioned, no one can seriously doubt that the words used in these addresses by both British and Dutch were genuinely inspired. As for the Javanese, one aged chieftain, when asked by Fendall whether his people were pleased at the prospect of Holland resuming control, replied:

"Can't you fancy a young and beautiful widow, who has been joined to a harsh and withered old man, but has lost him and is wedded to a liberal and gallant young bridegroom—can't you fancy how she will rejoice when she finds the old man returned to life again and come to claim her?"

The time for departure was drawing very near. Luckily a country-ship, the *Ganges*, had arrived at Batavia, and Travers was able to arrange accommodation. It is interesting to note the cost. For Raffles, Travers secured two-thirds of the roundhouse for £650; for himself, a small cabin in the cuddy for £350. Freight for baggage was £20 a ton. "He has brought over", wrote his cousin, Thomas Raffles, later, "Eastern curiosities and treasures to the amount of thirty tons weight, in upwards of two hundred immense packages." This, then, was no small item in the expense of homecoming.

Let Travers describe the final days.

"Mr Fendall gave a Dinner, Ball and Supper to Mr Raffles on Saturday 23rd, and Dalgairns and I gave him an entertainment on Sunday 24th; and on Monday at sunrise he embarked, the Troops all under arms and every mark of honour paid him. He was accompanied to the bank by all the respectable inhabitants of Batavia, who took leave of him with tears in their eyes, and the chief Chinese and Native inhabitants would not take leave of him till they had seen him on board, when they evinced the deepest grief on taking leave. All his intimate friends came off on board with him and here I am not capable of describing the distressing scene which took place on the separation of the Family, who had been living together like brothers for five years, and were now to part, for how long could not be known to any."

iii

It remains to sum up Raffles' administration of Java.

On the data available it is difficult to-day to form a definite view as to how far the financial embarrassment was due to government policy and how much to causes outside its control. It is no easier for us to decide how far the efforts of the government to overcome its difficulties were well directed and efficacious. The Supreme Government and the Court of Directors had answers to these questions. They held the Java government responsible and blamed it for its failure. These verdicts were pronounced from a distance. It is true that they were subsequently qualified to a considerable degree, though never enough to satisfy Raffles. By that date, however, the matter had become, as far as the Court at any rate was concerned, largely academic.

When we consider the views expressed in 1816 we must conclude that they were prejudiced by certainly three factors. The first was the Court's increasing disappointment that the optimistic promise of financial self-sufficiency held out originally by Minto, and continuously re-echoed by Raffles, was never redeemed. It was always a case of "jam to-morrow", while what the Directors wanted, and wanted badly, was "jam to-day". Secondly, neither India, after the departure of Minto, nor London at any time, had the smallest conception of the conditions Raffles had to face in Java, nor did either of them show the slightest interest in discovering what those conditions were. Lastly, there was the smoke of suspicion, remaining from the fires of complaint lighted by Gillespie and his supporters.

To-day we can see some parts of the picture more clearly: a country completely disorganized and virtually bankrupt; a mass of depreciated paper money; an almost complete absence of a silver currency or, indeed, any currency other than paper; a large army requiring payment in silver; the export trade dead and difficult to revive; an inadequate civil service of dual nationality and, on the British side at least, limited administrative experience; no authority to whom to turn for prompt guidance (Java dispatches remained unanswered for months, and in some important instances for ever). To all those difficulties had to be added two expensive wars and a general sense of uncertainty of tenure and frustration in policy. To sort out all these difficulties and restore the country to peace and prosperity in five years was hardly a possibility. Raffles had administrative powers amounting to genius, but he was faced with dilemmas comparable in essential features, though not in magnitude, to those that a post-war world is still facing to-day. The science of political economy has made vast strides since Raffles' time, and if our modern political economists cannot find short cuts to prosperity or even agree among themselves on right courses of action, we can scarcely blame Raffles if, without their accumulated experience, he too failed to find them.

Perhaps not all his measures were prudent or best adapted to the situation. It is, however, demonstrably true that almost single-handed he battled manfully with the complexities of the situation. It was not his fault that the Moluccas were under a separate administration, that Penang was unco-operative and hostile, or that India and London were more concerned with silver shipments to Europe than with the financial struggle of Java.

An impartial verdict on his financial policy must be that the measure of his success is to be assessed in relation to the immensity of the problem and on that basis his measure of success should be rated high. Had he had from India in Moira's day the sympathetic help and guidance he had enjoyed in Minto's, and above all had he had more time, his measure of success would undoubtedly have been higher still.

The recall of Minto from India in 1812 and the arrival of a professional soldier to be his successor just at the very time when Gillespie resigned in disgust and returned to India was a calamity. The attacks of Gillespie, Blagrave and Robison, though ultimately rebutted by Raffles, made his whole administration suspect and completely stultified his efforts to carry on a progressive policy. It followed naturally that the Court in London, with its preconceived ideas on Java, was only too happy to find its worst fears, as it believed, justified. The latter part of the British régime in Java was, therefore, overshadowed by general frustration of government and a sense of injustice and disappointment on the part of the Lieutenant-Governor. There was, too, the ever-present factor of uncertainty, in its different forms. It made possible, and indeed encouraged, among his subordinates an attitude of passive resistance and in some cases even definite antagonism to his policy, which Raffles, blinded by his own enthusiasm, never fully appreciated. To this undercurrent of opposition can be largely ascribed the administrative failures of some of his well-conceived reforms.

In principle, the new Dutch government of Java was by no means hostile to his land-revenue system. On 4th August 1816 van der Capellen wrote to Falck, the Colonial Minister at The Hague:

"Difficult though it may be to decide immediately what should be done in the future, and what principles of administration should be followed, yet I believe that we shall keep a great deal of the English system in respect of what they call land revenue. So far it seems to me that the cause of the frequent complaints we hear daily about it concern more the application of this new system, and one so strange to this country, rather than the system itself. Whatever may be said on the practical character of the Javanese, on his few wants, on his dislike of work even when his own interest is affected by it, I am of the opinion that now the Javanese have had a few years' experience of more liberty and less oppression, he won't easily be brought back to the earlier state of affairs, suppose one wanted, and for other reasons, to introduce less liberal measures. Certainly there is much to be improved in the system itself, once we have determined to retain it, like every other new organization; also they have certainly miscalculated the revenues resulting from it as our experience already shows."

He wrote again on 30th December:

"I am more and more convinced that the objections raised to the English revenue system concern the way it was introduced and the wrong application of it more than the system itself."

Cornelis Elout, one of the two commissioners sent out to assist van der Capellen, shared this view. Writing to Falck on 4th July 1817, he said:

"So far we have no intention at all of upsetting Raffles' system; more likely we shall keep it. I refer to the official letters in the Colonial Department so that you may acquaint yourself with the irregularity with which everything has been introduced, the inaccuracy with which it has been governed; we spend our time continually examining and where possible amending this."

According to Elout, the trouble was that Raffles kept on changing his mind, and was too susceptible to individual representations.

"Raffles had not that inflexible firmness in treating everything and everybody; he made exceptions, he responded to all sorts of inspirations, so that the subordinate authority, for example the Resident, did as he pleased, heedless of regulations. We are suffering now very much from that fault. Mr Assey himself has admitted this to me, so that people in Holland must be careful and must not themselves be carried away or scared by what that gentleman [Raffles] or Mr Crawfurd (otherwise a very capable man) or others will spread abroad, for really not everything which is printed is thereby made true, and the well-known *Minute* of Mr Raffles as well as the regulations here, of which he was the author, contain assertions, statements of fact and orders which did not take place, or not quite, or not everywhere, or not without great exceptions."

Whatever the theoretical merits of the land-revenue scheme, the introduction of it was imperfect in many respects, and it was carried on without any continuing or fixed principles. Two conditions precedent for the introduction of such a sweeping reform were, firstly, a proper survey of the land concerned, and secondly, an adequate staff of competent officials to supervise the system. Officials were few and inexperienced and they had no valid data on which to fix assessments. Each man therefore acted according to his own energy and his own ideas.

When the land-revenue scheme was introduced, but the essential collectors were not forthcoming, the Residents' task became quite impossible, so administration fell into the hands of subordinate native authorities, who exercised a tyranny only different in form from that which had been legally abolished. The whole scheme was novel to the Javanese, who probably never understood what was supposed to be happening.

The desperate financial position of the government induced Residents to fix assessments too high in order to produce a greater revenue. There was a great gap, however, between estimated and actual revenue, and when the Dutch returned they found most districts vastly in arrears with the revenue they were supposed to have produced. The system also favoured moneylenders, who advanced loans at extortionate rates to the Javanese peasantry to pay their land tax. Many European officials were corrupt, diverting to their own use money they were supposed to collect for the government.

Frankly, the whole administration was chaotic. Crawfurd, who had taken his full part in trying to work the scheme, subsequently admitted quite candidly that many mistakes were made by himself as well as others, and that Raffles saw the whole machinery break down before he left Java. It is difficult to believe that Raffles really appreciated that. If he did, his references to his reforms in his *History of Java* were singularly disingenuous. He went to great personal trouble, travelling throughout Java, to find out how the system was working, but being of an optimistic temperament, he probably saw everything in rather rosier colours than the facts warranted. No doubt, too, his officials were anxious to show him the best side of the picture as he travelled round. His last days in Java were clouded with disaster and ill-health, and it is to be doubted if he ever realized how far his great conception had failed; that it had failed is abundantly proved by the evidence of van der Capellen and Elout, there being no reason to suppose that their adverse reports were prejudiced.

This does not mean that Raffles stands condemned for his tremendous effort. He made a break with the past that his predecessors had never had quite the courage to undertake. No one can say that such a reform was not long overdue, or that Raffles personally did not take every possible step to produce a scheme consistent with both humane policy and sound economic practice. His failure was due to causes beyond his control, and the only valid criticism that can be levelled against him is that he failed to appreciate how far practice lagged behind theory. He continued to speak of his reforms as if they had proved an unparalleled success, where they fell far below what he had anticipated and what, in fact, he might have achieved had time and external circumstances not been against him. Still, nothing can dim the honour due to him for his fearless attempt to probe the source of trouble and apply a remedy.

Varied scientific interests occupied Raffles' mind, however much he might be beset by official problems. That he had any time, let alone any energy, to devote to the exacting requirements of science fills one with amazement. But it seems likely that scientific work was to him in the nature of a recreation, in the true sense of the word, even though bodily fatigue under such a pressure of public affairs and in such a climate rendered this recreation almost impossible. Apparently science was so deeply embedded in his mental make-up that he turned to it whenever the slightest opportunity offered, not only without effort, but also with a positive sense of relief. No one who had not his scientific mind would have sought convalescence after a serious illness by climbing a mountain, hitherto unexplored by Europeans, with all the paraphernalia necessary to ascertain its correct height; or, to occupy a period of rest prescribed by his doctors, translating into English verse the innumerable stanzas of a Javanese poem. But Raffles did both, and no doubt thought his actions quite normal, if he thought about them at all.

Of the wonderful archaeological discoveries that form one of the glories of the British period in Java, Dr F. D. K. Bosch remarks:

"It is no accident that it was during Raffles' régime that Borobudur was discovered; that Major Martin Johnson, the British Resident at the Court of Surakarta, heard of the existence of the Chandi Sukuh on Mt Lawu; or that Raffles' friend, Horsfield, the American naturalist, during his sojourn in the East of Java, devoted particular attention to the antiquities and wrote a finished account of the Chandi Panataran near Blitar."[1]

The campaign against smallpox and venereal disease unhappily came to naught. Dr Hunter's death put it back for two years, and when Raffles again brought it forward, his own days in the island were numbered, and his departure caused the scheme to be abandoned. Had this not happened, the practical difficulties in the way of achievement would have been enormous. Javanese resistance might well have frustrated the beneficent intentions of the government. Moreover, the scheme was to be based on information collected for the land-revenue assessment, which was found to be so defective and unreliable that it could have proved as of little value for this as for its real purpose. But the idea does Raffles honour. Had he remained in Java, his administrative genius might well have overcome even those formidable obstacles. It is a point of interest that if this scheme had come to fruition, a free medical service would have been introduced in Java in the first quarter of the nineteenth century.

It was in Java that Raffles first became acquainted with the mysteries of freemasonry. Lord Minto was already a brother of the order, and in 1812 in his presence at a small Lodge on a coffee estate, Raffles was initiated. He made rapid progress, attaining the 18th degree before he left Java, but there is no reference to this new interest in any of his correspondence.

Some Dutch authorities have endeavoured to establish the thesis that "without Daendels there could have been no Raffles". This has been echoed, in some measure, by certain English writers, who argue that Daendels, by making a complete break with the past, opened a clear road for Raffles. Further confusion has been caused by the assertion that Raffles decried Daendels to enhance his own reputation, but there is the clearest evidence that Raffles was far from being a wholly indiscriminate critic of Daendels. He spoke in high praise of some of his administrative reforms. What he condemned, and admittedly in strong terms, was the ruthlessness and inhumanity of some of Daendels' acts. Dutch historians have been

[1] *Inter-Ocean*, March 1930

equally outspoken, and it would be difficult for any impartial critic to take exception to such well-deserved strictures. The hopeless situation that faced Janssens on taking over from Daendels was largely, though not entirely, due to the combination of violence and obstinacy exhibited by his predecessor.

To recognize Daendels in the guise of an *avant-courier* for Raffles is extremely difficult. That Daendels, by his misguided activities, simplified the problem of the invasion forces is true enough. That his reforms paved the way in any material degree for those of Raffles is not so easy to establish. One may agree that Daendels initiated, at least on paper, the first centralized government in Java and organized a civil service to carry it on. In this sense he broke with the past and cleared the way for his successor. Had Raffles been merely a normal successor, it could possibly be argued with some reason that he was able to build on the foundations laid by the Dutch Marshal. But Raffles was far from being a normal successor to Daendels. A successful invasion had intervened, and nothing can furnish a more effective break with the past than the capture of a country by a foreign power. It mattered little or nothing to Raffles what his Franco-Dutch forerunners had done or not done, except in so far as he inherited some of the disastrous results of their activities. Those results were hardly such as could be readily built on. The country was seething with discontent, areas of it verging on starvation, the Javanese princes angered to the point of revolt, the treasury bankrupt and the whole administrative and economic machinery on the point of collapse.

Before he reached Java, Raffles had formulated in a general sense what British policy ought to be and what main directions reforms should take. His first step was to provide a British administration on the British model, and this was, in all the highest executive posts, composed of British civil servants, or such British officers or civilians as he could find. The Dutch were invited to collaborate and a large number of selected individuals were given offices of varying degrees of importance. Two Dutchmen, Muntinghe and Cranssen, were appointed members of the Council as a matter of high policy, as well as by reason of their special fitness for the posts. But in the administrative system set up, and in the spate of social, economic and commercial reforms that followed, one cannot trace much indebtedness to Daendels. Indeed, Raffles' reforms differed strikingly from those of Daendels, both in principle and application. It seems, therefore, abundantly clear that it was the successful invasion of Java by the British Army that, from an administrative point of view, made the real break with the past, enabling Raffles to carry out reforms already teeming in his head before he sailed from Malacca. If there was an *avant-courier* for Raffles in the political field, it was, perhaps, Dirk van Hogendorp—it was most certainly not Daendels.

The real significance of Raffles, however, is surely not limited to his administrative genius, or to the wide range of reforms he sought to introduce, important as those were. Where Raffles differed fundamentally from all his predecessors was in his approach to the problem of colonial administration. He boldly announced that the duty of a colonial government was to serve the interests of the inhabitants of the colony and not the interests of the mother country. Here, with a vengence, was a break with the past. Whether he borrowed the details of his reforms (or some of them) from van Hogendorp, or from elsewhere, is a matter of historical interest, but otherwise of only secondary importance. The skin may have been the skin, after some dressing, of van Hogendorp; but the voice was the voice of Raffles. He was the first to introduce into colonial administration the new liberalism of which, in Europe, England was the chief nursery. A chapter had been closed; it was Raffles who opened the new chapter, of which not even our generation will see the final pages.

Chapter Nineteen

ENGLAND, 1816-1817

THE *Ganges*, commanded by Captain Falconer, had a deservedly good reputation for comfort and sailing qualities. It was a curious coincidence that she bore the same name as the vessel that had brought Raffles from England in 1805 and had later been lost off the Cape.

The party travelling home was a small one. Besides Raffles, Travers, Garnham and Sir Thomas Sevestre, it included two Malay clerks, a young Javanese noble, the Radin Rana Dipura, and a merchant of Batavia named Graham, who had managed to make £60,000 in four years, a feat even for those days.

At sunrise on 25th March 1816 the *Ganges* weighed anchor and the voyage home began, with the *Auspicious* sailing in company under Captain James Neish, a close friend of Falconer's.

On the following day Raffles wrote this letter to Edmonstone:

"I cannot quit Java without returning you my warmest acknowledgements for the consideration which you have always evinced for me, and in particular for the kindness and protection with which I am confident you have endeavoured to shield my public as well as my private character in discussions in which both had been most violently and wantonly attacked. . . .

"Of the public measures in administration it is perhaps improper for me to speak; and probably it may be as well that they are left to speak for themselves. All I ask, and all I urge is that the results of my administration be not partially considered; these cannot be fairly understood nor duly appreciated until the close of the British Government, and as the Dutch authorities are now on the way out, a delay in the decision will not occasion inconvenience.

"The Court of Directors appear to me to have formed a very hasty judgment on questions regarding which it was impossible for them at the time to possess full information. The apprehension that, by the introduction of the Land Revenue System, I have alienated the affections of the people, is absurd and hardly deserves refutation. In the whole arrangements I have carried the Regents along with me; and I leave it to others to inform you of the feeling which has existed among the native population on the occasion of my quitting the Government. . . . I leave the character of my administration in general to be appreciated by my successor; and I look forward with confidence to a period when it will be proved that I have not been found wanting in the discharge of the high, arduous and responsible trust committed to my care. . . .

"My public letter will inform you of the necessity which drives me to the Cape, and eventually to Europe; and unfortunate as this unexpected circumstance must be considered, I must hope that the necessity of proceeding to Europe and of consequently giving up a lucrative employment, occasioned as it is by illness brought on by great exertions, by anxiety and a sense of injustice, will not weaken any claims which I may possess for the consideration and justice of the higher authorities."

The action taken in this matter by those higher authorities is recorded later in these pages.

He ended his letter with:

"Into the hands of Mr Fendall I resign my charge without reluctance."

A moving little ceremony was performed on the third day out, when Travers presented to Raffles privately in his cabin a farewell address composed before his embarkation by "the family", as his staff had been called. This Travers had been asked "to present to him after our getting out to sea". It ran:

"Among the varied and distinguished proofs of regard and veneration which you have received from all classes and descriptions of people in this Island, on your approaching departure, we hope you will accept from us a more silent, but not less cordial, assurance of the regret we feel at losing you; of the grateful and pleasing remembrance we shall ever entertain towards you; of the respect and affection, in short, which can cease only with our existence. . . .

"Whatever may be our future destination, and however it may be our chance to be scattered, when we return to our different fixed stations in life, we can never forget the time we have passed in Java. The public sentiment has expressed what is due there to the energies and value of your administration, which the more it is examined the more it will be admired. It belongs rather to us to express what we have witnessed and felt—to bear testimony to the spotless integrity and amiable qualities which shed a mild lustre over your private life. These we acknowledge with gratitude, and these are imprinted in our hearts too strongly to be ever erased.

"You will not receive these expressions of our regard until you have left us; and when, perhaps, it will be long ere we meet again. Accept them then, dear Sir, as the genuine feelings of our hearts. . . ."

The signatories, all members of his personal staff, were: C. Assey, Thomas McQuoid, R. C. Garnham, Thos. O. Travers, J. Dalgairns, C. Methven, T. Sevestre, J. Eckford, Thomas Watson, H. G. Jourdan and W. Cotes.

Travers has recorded that Raffles was completely overcome by this tribute and unable to utter a word. In the stress and excitement of departure, weakened by ill-health, he could have had little time to think of anything but the matter in hand, little strength to do anything not immediately necessary. But now, as he read this address, a host of memories must have crowded into his mind: the happy days of intense activity and the flowering in his grand schemes of reform; the domestic tranquillity of Buitenzorg, shared by a loving wife and a devoted staff; and then the sudden blighting of all his hopes, his own desperate sickness of heart and body; the death of his beloved Olivia, now lying in her grave at Batavia, alongside his greatest friend, Leyden; and Minto, who had been such a good friend and staunch supporter, dead too. No wonder emotion held him silent.

". . . but the moment he began to recover a little, he took up his pen, and whilst the feeling and impression was fresh, he wrote the beautiful and affectionately expressed reply, which was afterwards printed by his friends. . . ."

This is part of what he wrote:

"MY DEAR AND VALUED FRIENDS,—This last and unexpected proof of your attachment and esteem is too much for me; it is more than, in the shattered state of my existence, I can bear without an emotion which renders it impossible for me to reconcile my feelings with the ordinary feelings of consideration. You have struck chords which vibrate too powerfully—which agitate me too much to admit of any attempt to express to you what my feelings are on the occasion of your Address.

"You have been with me in the days of happiness and joy—in the hours that were beguiled away under the enchanting spell of one, of whom the recollection awakens feelings which I cannot suppress. You have supported and comforted me under the affliction of her loss—you have witnessed the severe hand of Providence in depriving me of those whom I held most dear, snatched from us and the world, ere we could look around us! You have seen and felt what the envious and disappointed have done to supplant me in the public opinion and to shake the credit of my public and the value of my private character; and now that I bend before the storm, which it is neither in my power to avert nor control, you come forward to say, that, as children of one family, you will hold to me through life. What must be my emotions I leave to the feelings which dictated your address to decide, for, in truth, I cannot express my own. . . ."

The voyage to the Cape was uneventful and the weather generally good. A continuous exchange of messages between *Ganges* and *Auspicious* was telegraphed, supplemented, when weather suited, by personal visits. Raffles in the early days was far from well, but gradually he improved and was able to devote an increasing amount of time to the writing of his history of Java. He was a good sailor, unlike his two Malay clerks, who were prostrated when the sea was at all rough.

In the evenings whist was usually played, then the party sat on the poop to enjoy the moonlight.

From a chance encounter with another ship they learned the news that Captain Falconer had been awarded by the Calcutta underwriters the sum of 1,000 guineas for his heroism in putting out a fire in the *Ganges* off Ceylon, when, but for his courage and resource, the ship and all aboard must have been lost. Raffles proclaimed this as an occasion for a bowl of punch, which he mixed with his own hands, and led the congratulations due to the commander alike on his courage and its reward.

By 13th May the Cape had been rounded successfully, and on the 18th, about three o'clock in the morning, the ship made St Helena, which Raffles was anxious to visit in order to have audience with Napoleon. Demetrius Boulger, in quoting Travers' account of this incident, states that Raffles left no written record. To the contrary, he did—in a letter to Alexander Hare dated 20th May.

"We have to thank our perseverance and the unremitting kindness of friends for obtaining an interview with the ci-devant French Emperor during our short stay of about thirty-six hours in this place, and as you are not likely while you remain in the East to receive a more authentic account of the present situation of this extraordinary character than what I may be able to give you, I am induced to give you a few particulars while the impression is alive and undiverted by other objects.

"We made the Island in the night, and by keeping close to the land escaped the notice of the cruisers till some time after daybreak, when we were brought to by several shot from the batteries—a man-of-war's boat now came on board, when we learned that it was possible we might by application be permitted to land, but that until permission was granted we could not even anchor. A letter was accordingly dispatched to the Admiral's[1] secretary, and about ten o'clock the signal was made for us to anchor. The ship was no longer under charge of the Captain, and as soon as the anchor was dropped a party of marines came up the side. In about an hour, however, Colonel Mansell, a particular friend of Garnham's, came off, and by the Admiral's permission conducted us on shore. Here we found that Napoleon's residence was at present fixed in the interior at Longwood, about eight miles from the valley, and that he was in the habit of receiving visitors, arrangements being previously made for that purpose by applications first to the Governor [Sir Hudson Lowe] and afterwards to the Count de Bertrand, Grand Marshal of the Palace, for you must know that in his own circle Napoleon keeps up all the forms of a Court. He is recognized by the English only as General Buonaparte,

[1] Sir George Cockburn.

but among his own people he assumes all the parade, &c, of Emperor—he has a circle of twelve miles around Longwood within which he may go unattended by a British Officer.

"His party consists of the Comte de Bertrand, Grand Marshal of State, the Countess with three children, a daughter and two sons—the eldest named Napoleon being godson to Buonaparte, the younger, Henry, still more nearly related by the reports of the scandalous. Count Lascasas [Las Cases], Councillor of State; Counts Montholon and Gourgaud, Marshals De Camps; Aide-de-Camp; young Lascasas, son of the Count, a boy about fourteen years of age; Page [boy] and Captain Piontowsky [Poniatowski], a Polish officer who has long followed the fortunes of Buonaparte; these, with the Countess Montholon and children and Cipriani, who has been his maître d'hôtel for twenty-five years, comprise the whole party.

"In consequence of the instructions laid down from home, private ships are required to sail the moment their wants are supplied, and on the evening of the day we landed we were apprised that the water had already been ordered, and we must embark the next morning. The Governor's permission to visit Buonaparte had been obtained, and a further application sent to Bertrand, but his reply had not arrived. However, on the next morning I waited on the Admiral and obtained an assurance that although nothing could prevent the ship getting under weigh at the appointed time, she would be permitted to lay to for me for an hour or two, which he hoped would afford sufficient time for the attainment of our object.

"We accordingly lost no time in mounting the best horses we could procure, and proceeding to Bertrand's—a hovel situated on the verge of the circle prescribed for Napoleon. We were introduced to the Count and Countess, and learnt to our great mortification that in consequence of some misapprehension it had been arranged that our visit to the great man should not take place till the following day. Bertrand having once obtained the Emperor's wishes on the occasion could not think of interfering further. However, after much entreaty, he was induced to relax, and very kindly gave us a pass permitting us to walk through the grounds, observing that as the Emperor had lately been indisposed, it was possible, as the day was fine, he might walk in the garden, and perhaps perchance we might see him. This was enough; we allowed our hopes to revive, and trusted to good fortune for the rest. We then moved on to the lodge (Longwood), and through the interest of the purveyor obtained an introduction to the family then at breakfast.

"Buonaparte was not yet up or dressed—in fact, he seldom leaves his room till four in the afternoon. I now found that great interest was taken in the family to procure me an interview, but that it was attended with great difficulty, for he had the day previous refused to receive a party according to appointment, and had resolved not to see any one on this day. My best friends were, however, the two English surgeons who attend him, and to whom I had previously been introduced by my friend Urmston; with them Buonaparte would appear to relax more than with others. In his own family he preserves all the distance of a ruling Emperor, but with them he has frequently of late spoken apparently without reserve.

"We now partook of some refreshment at the breakfast table, at which Count Lascasas presided. He spoke English remarkably well, and entered into conversation on general subjects and respecting Java. He appeared to be a man of great penetration, and conducted himself perfectly as a gentleman. In about half an hour he withdrew, and his place was supplied by Count Gourgaud, a gentlemanly young man. The Polish officer sat quietly at the table, not saying a word, and looking as inanimate and stupid as may be.

"Lascasas now returned and told me that the Emperor was well, in better health than yesterday, and that it was very probable he would see me about an hour before the usual hour of coming out, but that he (the Count) could not be certain of it. He thought it was probable that the Emperor would see me, and he hoped so. It was then about noon, and to pass the time until three or four we went over to the camp, and while at tiffin received a note stating that the Emperor was in the garden.

"Our hopes were now about to be realized, and we accordingly assembled in a room which overlooked the garden, waiting for the summons. The Count Bertrand and his lady had just arrived, and the Emperor, attended by them and the rest of his suite, had just entered the bower as we passed. I must here inform you that Buonaparte invariably receives his visitors in this bower or while walking in the garden, preferring, I suppose, the extensive canopy of heaven to the undignified appearance of a plaistered ceiling. Our first view of him was from the window across the lawn, where we beheld, not what we expected, an interesting animated and martial figure but

"A Heavy, Clumsy-looking man, moving with a very awkward gait, and reminding us of a citizen lounging in the tea-gardens about London on a Sunday afternoon. He was dressed in a large but plain cocked hat, dark green hunting coat, with a star, &c, on the left breast, white kerseymere breeches, and white silk stockings. He had no sooner passed in review than the Count Lascasas quitted the party and came to inform me that the Emperor would receive me. Now, then, behold me in the presence of certainly the greatest man of the age. I will not attempt to describe to you the feelings with which I approached him; let it suffice that I say they were in every way favourable to him. His talents had always demanded my admiration, and in the brilliancy of this side of his character. In a word, I felt compassion for his present situation.

"On my nearer approach he stopped, took off his hat and slightly bowed, then placing his hat under his left arm, commenced a string of questions, which he put in quick succession, and in a tone and manner as unexpected as authoritative. Your name? Where are you from? What country? You are from Java; did you accompany the expedition against it? Had the Dutch taken possession? How do the kings of the Islands conduct themselves? Are the Spice Islands [Moluccas] also ceded? In what ship did you come? What cargo? Is the Java coffee better than the Bourbon? Does Batavia continue as unhealthy as ever? Then, looking towards the gentlemen forming my suite, who are these? I then introduced Garnham. Your name? Your regiment? Have you been wounded? Travers was next introduced, when he was in like manner demanded his name and regiment. On introducing Sir Thomas Sevestre as a 'chirugien', he repeated 'surgeon', 'surgeon', and making an inclination to move, we mutually bowed, put on our hats, and turning back to back, withdrew from each other. Count de Bertrand followed us and invited us to partake of refreshments, which we had the honour of receiving off the Imperial silver, and then, mounting our horses, made the best of our way to the valley, which we reached just before sunset, and just in time to embark.

"Buonaparte must either be very different in his present appearance and demeanour to what he once was, or we have all been in a great measure deceived. In person he is more like old Wardenaar, of Batavia, than any man I can name. This resemblance struck us all. To be sure, he has not quite so large a belly, but in other points he does not fall short in size. His face is square, his colour sallow, and his eyes jaundiced without reflecting one ray of light. His visage in general was not unlike that of a Brazilian-Portuguese. Though still deficient in animation, his manner was abrupt, rude and authoritative, and the most ungentlemanly that I ever witnessed. While speaking he took snuff, or rather seemed to take it, for there was none in his box, and altogether treated us in the same manner, as in his worst humour he was wont to do, His Own inferiors.

"Believe me, Hare, this man is a monster, who has none of those feelings of the heart which constitute the real man. I was favourably inclined to him; I compassioned his situation, but from the moment I came into his presence these feelings subsided, and they gave place to those of horror, disgust and alarm; I saw in him a man determined and vindictive, without one spark of soul, but possessing a capacity and talent calculated to enslave mankind. I saw in him that all this capacity, all this talent, was devoted to himself and his own supremacy. I saw that he looked down on all mankind as his inferiors, and that he possessed not the smallest particle of philosophy. I looked upon him as a wild animal caught, but not tamed. He is, in short, all head and no heart—a man who may by his ability command respect, but by his conduct can never ensure the affection of any one. I am still more deeply impressed than ever with the highest opinion of his abilities. It seems as if the despotism of Europe, all the ability of other countries, were concentrated in him. He is the head of the great monster Despotism, but has no connexion with the heart. 'Tis folly to talk of this man's rising by taking fortune just in the nick of time. Fortune may in some degree have favoured his plans, but it is he who conceives them, and can show equal ability, whether fortune favour or not. There is nothing dignified either in his appearance or in his conduct. His appearance I have accurately described, and during the seven months he has been at St Helena there is not a single anecdote related that can induce us to believe that feelings of magnanimity, philosophy, or benevolence ever could enter into his heart. The alarm I felt was lest he should escape.

"Until the arrival of Sir Hudson Lowe, the present Governor, he was under the personal charge of Admiral Sir George Cockbourne [Cockburn], who brought him out from England—the charge was transferred to Sir Hudson about six weeks ago, and the change has not proved very agreeable to Buonaparte. Sir Hudson is a reserved and sour-looking man; the Admiral, mild, affable, and conciliating; Sir Hudson the reverse. Buonaparte swears that he is a Prussian, and has already told him that he wants none of his attentions or civilities."

Travers describes their reception by Napoleon as "absolutely vulgar" and adds one detail not to be found in Raffles' account: that Napoleon did not wait for the answer to one question before putting the next. Raffles' remarks on Java, however, seemed to interest him.

The *Ganges* left St Helena on 27th May and had a good run home. On 6th July, his thirty-fifth birthday, Raffles entertained the company and Captain Neish from the *Auspicious* to dinner. Reporting this in his diary, Travers added:

"Few men have pushed themselves forward with the rapidity that Mr Raffles has done and I have no doubt if his health improves but that he will shine in the world one of these days. A better or wiser stored head will seldom be found on such young shoulders."

Events were to prove this prophecy correct except in one respect: the health of his hero was not to improve.

The Scilly Isles were made at dawn on 11th July. By eleven o'clock in the morning the two Indiamen were off Falmouth, and boats came out to take off the passengers, demanding and receiving fifteen guineas for this service for Raffles and his party. As Raffles left the ship, Captain Falconer fired the salute to which a Governor was entitled.

Before being allowed ashore they had to submit to a lengthy interrogation, not because of their baggage, which contained only immediate personal requirements, for Raffles had insisted that valuables of every description should be left on board and properly recorded in the ship's manifest, but because the officials were justifiably incredulous when the members of the party testified on oath that they were in perfect health. Their thin, yellow faces hardly offered supporting evidence. Eventually, however, their word was accepted and they were permitted to land.

It was eleven and a quarter years since the young clerk had set off in another *Ganges*, and with such high hopes, to take up his appointment in the new Presidency of Penang. To-day, the one-time Lieutenant-Governor of Java stepped ashore, a wizened little man, his skin the colour of old parchment, his features drawn by sickness. Were his hopes buried in Java with Olivia and Leyden, or was his spirit still undaunted, his will to succeed unweakened by sorrow, ill-health, calumny, official strictures? Raffles himself gives the answer in a letter to W. B. Ramsay, written on board and dispatched on landing, to warn his friend of arrival.

"To be plain, I must tell you, my dear friend, that after suffering severely from an illness brought on in consequence of great anxiety and personal fatigue I embarked on 25th March last from Batavia, and am now looking for the English Coast. . . . For myself, although I am considerably recovered, I yet remain wretchedly thin and sallow, with a jaundiced eye and shapeless leg. Yet I thank God, my spirit is high and untamed, and the meeting of friends will, I hope, soon restore me to my usual health. I return to you, however, a poor solitary wretch; and the rocks of Albion, which under other circumstances would have met my eyes with joy and gladness, will not now present themselves without reflections which I cannot dwell upon. . . ."

In spite of his eagerness to reach London and forcibly appeal to the Court against the incomplete judgment passed upon him, his insatiable thirst for knowledge made the progress from Falmouth to the capital more like the sauntering of an enthusiastic tourist than the completion of an official journey. He and his party made an early start next morning and reached Truro in time for breakfast. As soon as the meal was finished, they set off to see one of the oldest and most famous copper mines in Cornwall, Wheel Busy mine, near Chacewater. In spite of the remonstrances of his friends, Raffles insisted on going down it, being also most interested in the steam-engine erected by Joseph more than one hundred years before. The quality of the copper, he thought, was inferior to that from Japan.

As they moved on towards London, sightseeing continued unabated.

A carpet factory at Axminster, the cathedral at Salisbury, the new military college at Bagshot: nothing must be missed. From Bagshot, Travers started early with the dispatches, his intention being also to find out what sort of reception Raffles was to expect.

After fixing up temporary accommodation and taking breakfast, he called at East India House, where he was greeted with great cordiality by William Ramsay senior and Thomas Reid, now chairman of the Company. Raffles arrived in London on the 16th, and Travers was able to promise him an equally cordial reception, which, even to a man of such robust optimism as Raffles, must have come as a relief. A cold welcome, after all he had endured, would have been hard to stomach.

Travers had found rooms for him at 23 Berners Street, which he made his headquarters throughout his leave. Mrs Flint and Sir Thomas Sevestre lived there also, while Travers was at number 52, on the opposite side of the street.

The following day Raffles called at East India House and was well received by the directors, who may have been shocked by his physical appearance and inclined to be sympathetic. Anyhow, it is one thing to write chilling letters of disapproval to a man at a distance of several thousand miles and quite another to stand up face to face in argument against him. Besides, the success or failure of Raffles' administration of Java had now become an academic question; if anyone was to suffer, it would be the Dutch, not the East India Company. The prestige, too, that Raffles, in spite of official disapprobation, had achieved in England, and the powerful friends he had somehow collected in advance of his return, made it no doubt politic to modify the Company's harsh attitude towards such a clever and forceful little man. He was not, however, given immediate satisfaction; the final decision remained in abeyance until the following year.

One matter was now definitely settled to his advantage: the Court withdrew, at long last, its demand for a refund of the extra pay drawn by him while secretary to the Penang government. This came as a great relief to him. The Company had taken its time. Though always leisured in its proceedings, it seems to have gone out of its way, in all its dealings with Raffles' personal affairs, to be even more dilatory than was its normal habit.

Concerning Raffles' sixteen-months' stay in England, the diary of Captain Travers is only intermittently helpful. His family lived in Ireland and he was much preoccupied with his own affairs, not the least important of which was the choice of a wife. Fortunately, to help fill the gap, we have the correspondence and reminiscences of Dr Raffles, as he later became, who travelled down from Liverpool to welcome his cousin in London.

"He did not know me," Thomas wrote home[1] to his wife on 31st July, "nor did I for a moment recognize him. . . . He had lost nothing of himself but his colour and his flesh. . . . He intends to publish an account of Java, and is very busy in getting maps, &c, prepared for the work. He has very extensive collections of Javanese literature of his own collecting. I am amazed at his industry. In one day he wrote two hundred letters with his own hand, and dictated to two secretaries besides."

Of Raffles' reunion with his mother and his youngest sister, Ann, there is no record, but here is Thomas's account of a call on Mrs William Raffles at her home in Spitalfields.

"One of his first visits was to his aunt, for they were very fond of each other. He left his equipage, which was a splendid one—and private carriages with rich liveries were not so common then as they are now, and were indeed a great rarity in the quiet corner of London in which my father lived—and, walking the length of Princes Street,[2] knocked at old No. 14, and on the opening of the door went at once into the sort of parlour-kitchen where my mother was, busied as usual about her household affairs. 'I knew well', he said, 'where at this time of the day I should find you,' and taking his accustomed seat in an old arm-chair by the fire-side, where he had often sat, made her at once, by his affectionate and playful manner, quite unconscious of the elevation to which he had attained since he had last sat there. 'Aunt,' he said, 'you know I used to tell you, when a boy, that I should be a Duke before I die.' 'Ah,' she replied, 'and I used to say that it would be "Duke of Puddle Dock",' which was a proverb in London at that day, referring to a wretched locality in Wapping, and with which aspiring lads, who had great notions of the greatness they should hereafter attain, were twitted. . . ."

Captain Falconer brought the *Ganges* round to the London Docks, where Raffles' heavy baggage, which included tons of specimens, Javanese furniture and other curiosities, were unloaded and conveyed to 23 Berners Street. The unpacking and arranging took several days, after which Raffles, accompanied by Travers, Mrs Flint and young Ramsay, went to Cheltenham, "following the fashion of the time", as William Hickey puts it, "for all those recently returned from the East, with a view of getting quit of all lurking bile". The party "had a very capital house in the Crescent N. 3 where we passed our time most agreeably". They all took the waters each morning, but Raffles appeared to benefit little from the

[1] "Returning up the hill to Mason Street, the last house but one at the southern end, on the west side, was long the residence of the Rev. T. Raffles, LL.D. . . . The house was roomy and convenient, with a large garden behind, raised up on a high terrace, considerably above the level of the street. . . ." J. A. Picton, *Memorials of Liverpool.*

[2] Princes Street is now that part of Princelet Street, E.1., stretching from Brick Lane to Wilkes Street.

treatment. During their stay they made the acquaintance of Mr and Mrs J. Watson Hull and their daughter, Sophia, of County Down, but at that time resident in Cheltenham.

Travers left Cheltenham for Ireland on 10th September and shortly afterwards Raffles returned to London, to attend the wedding of his sister Harriet, who was marrying Thomas Browne of Somerset House in October. His health continued to be very indifferent and he underwent yet another course of mercury, an excessive dose of which kept him in bed for a month.

On hearing in Ireland of the precarious state of his friend's health, Travers was so alarmed that he very gallantly postponed making his proposal of marriage to Miss Mary Lesley and started back for England on 9th November. The weather was exceptionally bad and he did not reach London until the morning of the 14th, when he found Raffles much better and in very good spirits. He had received addresses from all the native chiefs in Java. According to Travers, they were couched "in the warmest style and evince the respect and admiration in which Mr Raffles' name was held on Java; these were written and sent to Government some time after our departure from thence, and at a time, of course, when Mr Raffles's power was at an end."

This no doubt helped to hearten him in the labours of compiling his history of Java, which Messrs Black and Parry, publishers to India House, had agreed to publish. For years he had been collecting material for it and translating extracts from the Javanese, but it was not until October 1816 that he began writing it. He worked at such speed that it was written and printed in less than seven months. Lady Raffles records that the pages he wrote every morning were sent straight off to the printers, who supplied proofs the same day, which he corrected on his return from the evening's social engagement.

A short respite was provided by Christmas Day, when Raffles was the host. For this occasion he had collected every relative within reach, and thirty persons in all sat down to dinner. It must, as Travers remarks, "have afforded my worthy friend a great deal of inward satisfaction to have around him all his family who looked up to him with pride and admiration".

By the end of the year, rather depressing news was received from Java. So eager had been the Dutch to recover it that their officials and imposing armament had outstripped the instructions sent out by the British Government via the Supreme Government in India. Supported by a very considerable army, larger in fact than the British had required to capture Java in 1811, the new government had arrived with something of the air and arrogance of a conqueror, expecting Fendall to haul down the British flag forthwith and embark at once for India.

Even had Fendall received explicit instructions to act in this summary fashion, he could hardly have been expected to comply with them to the letter; we had been administering the island for five years, and the process of handing over would inevitably be lengthy and complicated. The financial settlement alone was certain to be an involved one. The Dutch, however, were so impatient, that the slightest delay to full occupation had been loudly criticized and ascribed to British bad faith. Possibly Fendall was a little dilatory, yet he could not have been as keen to hand over the colony as the Dutch had been to receive it back. Captured at a cost of many British lives and much British treasure, it had been administered with great energy and at considerable expense, for the ultimate benefit of the Dutch. The previous administration by the Dutch had not been conspicuous for success, nor their share in the Napoleonic wars conspicuous for achievement.

Godert Alexander Gerard Philip, Baron van der Capellen, was a pleasant young man, thirty-eight years of age, but lacking in experience. To guide him at the outset, two commissioners had been sent with him from Holland: Cornelis Theodorus Elout and Admiral Arnold Adriaan Buijskes, who occupied himself chiefly with service affairs. The real ruler was not van der Capellen, but Elout, whose position was strengthened by his relation by marriage to Falck, the Colonial Minister at The Hague. Eleven years older than van der Capellen, he was hard and narrow-minded, very jealous of the high standing of the English name in Java, and making no secret of his dislike of them. From the very beginning he had made it clear that those Dutchmen who had assisted Raffles' government were looked upon as having collaborated with an enemy. Cranssen was never re-employed. Muntinghe was felt to be indispensable, but his position, as we shall see, was made difficult.

Junior Dutch officials had soon seen which way the wind was blowing, and had endeavoured to ingratiate themselves with their new masters by rudeness to their former British friends, who in their turn had bitterly resented seeing their lucrative positions being handed over to the Dutch who, they had felt, had done nothing to deserve them. Some were sorry for the Javanese, now subject once more to a power that had, or so they thought, a bad reputation in colonial administration.

Whatever the causes, the friendly spirit between the British and Dutch, so successfully built up by Raffles, came to a sudden and unhappy end; and so marked was Dutch hostility that Moira had felt impelled to write a personal letter to van der Capellen, calling attention to the attitude of Dutch officials to the British, a complaint that, he had been careful to add, did not extend to his Excellency personally.

It was also reported that the Dutch were not maintaining the liberal principles of their predecessors.

"Should Java ever become free of the Dutch nation," commented Travers, "it must be attributed to the want of conduct in the Colonial Government. The path is now open to them and if they only follow the road cut open for them by the British Government, they may ensure to themselves the easy administration of one of the finest Islands in the world."

With the opening of the new year Raffles was hard at work again, but distractions continued to grow. The young Radin who had accompanied them to England had to be entertained. Some of this fell to Travers and included some hours at the Mint, where they saw new shillings struck at the rate of sixty-three a minute, and a visit to the opera to hear Madame Fodor. Raffles himself escorted the Radin to see some "electricity and galvanism", which seems to have created such an impression on the young prince's mind that he said he would not be in the least surprised to learn that in England the dead could be restored to life.

More exacting were the demands of Society. In those days, any distinguished newcomer, his entrée once achieved, was welcomed into the relatively small circle of those who could claim to be Society. Through the good offices of East India House and such distinguished friends as William Marsden, Sir Everard Home (the King's physician) and Sir Joseph Banks, president of the Royal Society and acknowledged leader in all branches of natural history, Raffles had already become something of a public figure, not only as a distinguished colonial official, but also as a savant. When word reached him during January that the transfer of Java to the Dutch had been formally completed, it must have made his time there seem like a dream—a very pleasant dream for a while, though it had ended more like a nightmare.

So we find him on 28th January in the House of Lords, viewing the opening of parliament by the Prince Regent, whose carriage was stoned, an event symptomatic of the state of public opinion at the time. On 3rd February he attended the Regent's levee, when he and Travers were presented to George Canning, who had succeeded the Earl of Buckinghamshire as president of the India Board of Control. On the 20th they both attended the Queen's drawing-room, escorting the two daughters of Sir Everard Home, and two days later Raffles married Miss Sophia Hull, whom he had met at Cheltenham.

The engagement had been kept secret, Travers and young Ramsay being among the few who knew of it. The marriage was equally quiet. Even Sir Thomas Sevestre, living under the same roof as Raffles, was quite unaware of anything unusual until he was informed that he need not wait for breakfast, as Mr Raffles had gone out to be married.

Immediately after the wedding, Raffles and Sophia left for Henley on the first stage of their short honeymoon. From there Raffles wrote on the 23rd to Thomas:

MY DEAR COUSIN,—You will, I doubt not, approve of the change I have made in my condition in again taking to myself a wife; and when I apprise you that neither rank, fortune, nor beauty have had weight on the occasion, I think I may fairly anticipate your approval of my selection. The Lady, whose name is Sophia, is turned of thirty; she is devotedly attached to me, and possesses every qualification of the heart and mind calculated to render me happy. More, I need not say. . . ."

Perhaps not, but he could hardly have said less!

Travers was favourably impressed.

"The lady has my best opinion. I think her amiable, affectionate, sensible, personable, tho' not very handsome, with a good figure and extremely well brought up and possessing many amiable qualities, both of head and heart."

A wag wrote this little jingle in a London paper:

"If Marriage a Lottery is call'd
As All Calculations it baffles;
Think of one who thus risks, unappalled,
All her future fortune in Raffles."

One may certainly wonder if Sophia might not have been appalled had she foreseen the sort of life she would be called upon to endure, the dangers and discomforts, the tragedies and sorrows. In the event she proved a devoted wife; she feared no risk and shirked no hardship to keep by her husband's side. Without her loving care he might never have won through to the days that made his fame.

They spent two days at Henley, a week at Hampstead, and then went back to Berners Street, where, early in March, a dinner was given to enable Mr and Mrs Hull and Sophia to meet some of Raffles' family and friends.

The decision of the Court of Directors, which had been made known to Raffles before his marriage, was transmitted to India in a dispatch dated 13th February 1817.

"After a scrupulous examination of all the documents . . . and an attentive perusal of the Minutes of the Governor-General and of the other members composing the Council, when it was under consideration, we think it due to Mr Raffles, in the interests of our service, and to the cause of truth, explicitly to declare our decided conviction that the charges, in so far as they went to implicate the moral character of that gentlemen, have not only not been made good, but they that have been disproved to an extent which is seldom practicable in a case of defence.

"It is not now our intention to discuss the expediency of the leading measures of the administration of Java while Mr Raffles presided over the government of the island. . . . Before pronouncing on the final operations of that Government we are desirous of fuller information and further time to deliberate. . . . But the purity as well as the propriety of many of his acts as Lieutenant-Governor having been arraigned, accusations having been lodged against him, which, if substantiated, must have proved fatal to his character and highly injurious, if not ruinous, to his prospect in life, his conduct having been subjected to a regular and solemn investigation, and this investigation having demonstrated to our minds the utter groundlessness of the charges exhibited against him, in so far as they affected his honour, we think that he is entitled to all the advantage of this opinion, and of an early and public expression of it. . . .

"On most, if not all the points at issue, we concur with Mr Edmonstone both in his reasonings and conclusion and whatever judgment may be ultimately passed on the various measures of the late Goverment of Java, which underwent review on the course of the investigation into the conduct of its head, we are satisfied, not merely that they stand exempt from any sordid or selfish taint, but they sprung from motives perfectly correct and laudable. If we notice the circumstance of Mr Raffles having been a purchaser of lands at the public sales on the island, it is for the purpose not so much of animadverting, after all that has passed, on the indiscretion of the act (for it was unquestionably indiscreet) as of expressing our firm persuasion that he has stated, without equivocation or reserve, the reasons which induced him to engage in these transactions, and that they do not at all derogate from those principles of integrity by which we believe his public conduct to have been uniformly governed."

In other words, his character had been cleared, but the Court continued to reserve judgment on the wisdom of some of his measures. Probably the directors were reluctant to express any decided views on such complicated issues. If the story is true that a great number of his more important dispatches had lain unopened on their desks for years, their reluctance showed a commendable prudence. Raffles can have regarded with little satisfaction a testimonial that vindicated his integrity without allowing his competence.

The appointment to Bencoolen was at the same time confirmed. In his letter from Henley of 23rd February he wrote to Thomas Raffles:

"They end with leaving Sumatra open to me, and as there seems an inclination to extend my political authority there, I think it almost certain that I shall go out in the course of the year. . . ."

This reference to the extension of his political authority is worthy of note.

The exhausting round of business and pleasure continued. Later in March he attended the House of Commons and heard Brougham speak for some hours on The State of the Nation. Sophia and Mary Anne Flint did their best to see what London could offer, and, as Raffles was still very much occupied with his book, Travers generally acted as escort. On 20th March Raffles was elected a Fellow of the Royal Society, among his supporters being Sir Everard Home and William Marsden. This honour must have been particularly gratifying. It also gained him the friendship of the Duke of Somerset, an active Fellow of the Royal Society, and of the Duchess of Somerset and her father, the Duke of Hamilton.

In April, after a short visit to Brighton, the social round began in earnest. Night after night Raffles was attending fashionable parties, or entertaining celebrities at his own house. The combined strain of late nights and work-filled days wore him down severely and he became terribly thin. His friends were very anxious and looked forward eagerly to the trip to the Continent that he had promised himself as soon as the book was out. The news from Java continued to be bad. There were stories of cruelty and oppression. The new Governor-General was still popular, but Elout was reported to be increasingly hostile towards the English and the Dutch who had co-operated with Raffles.

The *History of Java* was published in two large volumes about 10th April. It was tactfully, and with royal assent, dedicated to the Prince Regent. Reviews followed, some immediately. The *Quarterly Review*, in its issue for that month, gave it twenty-four pages. Apart from suggesting that the book could have been better arranged, the notice was most favourable. Even the *Prince of Wales's Island Gazette* gave its approval which, considering how unpopular the author was with the government of Penang, was noteworthy. John Crawfurd, now home from Java, was critical of it in the *Edinburgh Review*:

"The ninth, tenth and eleventh [chapters] are by far the worst and in determining the chronology great errors are being committed. There is a propensity to magnify the importance of the early story of the Javanese; and in calculating and adapting the native to Christian time, the principle has been wholly mistaken and an error of several years throughout the whole is the consequence."[1]

Elout wrote to Baron Hendrik Fagel, Dutch Ambassador to Britain, on 6th April:

"If the work which Mr Raffles is supposed to be going to publish has already come out, or is going to, it would be a great service on the part of Your Excellency, to us, to send us some copies: it can only be of the highest importance to read his information, for he is beyond dispute a clever and enlightened person, but less accurate, as it seems, in details of administration."

The book was a remarkable *tour de force*. Experts have since made havoc of its theories and historians have questioned the complete success of Raffles' reforms, some of which were admirable in intention, if they

[1] *Edinburgh Review*, Vol. 31, 1819.

hardly achieved all that their sponsor claimed in retrospect for them. But it cannot be denied that it was the first book in the English language to give a comprehensive account of Java from every angle. Perhaps no book in any language had covered such a wide field with such a wealth of first-hand information.

The position Raffles had already achieved in society secured for his book immediate success in the circles of the fashionable and the learned. All doors were eagerly opened to him. On 27th April he was invited to dinner with Princess Charlotte, daughter of the Prince Regent, and her husband, Prince Leopold of Saxe-Coburg. While in Java he had sent over to the Princess some valuable presents, particularly six fine Javanese ponies, four of which she was accustomed to drive in her phaeton. On his return to England he had sent her other presents, including some tables and chairs of *kayubuku*[1] wood. From that time on he was a regular visitor to Claremont. The Princess was expecting her first child.

Raffles was at Cheltenham when he received a command to attend a levee at Carlton House on 29th May. According to Dr Raffles:

"At the Levee . . . the Prince [Regent] took occasion in the most public and handsome manner to express his approbation of the work [the history], and also of those public acts of his administration, of which it was in fact the record. When my cousin's time to be presented came, he caused the whole process to be suspended; his attendants formed an arch [*sic*] round him, and in the presence of them all, the Regent said he was happy to embrace that opportunity of thanking him for the entertainment and information he had derived from the perusal of the greater part of the volumes; and also of expressing the high sense he entertained of the eminent services he had rendered to his Country by his conduct in the Government of Java. What he said occupied nearly twenty minutes. He then conferred on him the honour of knighthood."

"Why, Charlotte," said Prince Leopold when he heard of it, "they have made him a *knight*!"

This was said in the presence of Raffles, who, in reporting the incident to his cousin, remarked that the Prince's tone and manner had been "quite ludicrous". Many, Raffles perhaps among them, had expected not less than a baronetcy, and rumour had it at the time that he would have been so honoured had the Prince Regent not been so jealous of his daughter's friends.

It seems that thenceforward Raffles used exclusively his second name of Stamford. The explanation given by Lady Raffles is that he thus avoided any confusion with Sir Thomas Sevestre, "his body physician", as Cousin Thomas disdainfully described him. John Palmer of Calcutta attributed the change to vanity—"humble Thomas is sunk". The most

[1] *Kayu* (wood) *buku* (knot), known as Amboina wood (*Lingoum indicum*).

likely reason was that there was more than one Thomas Raffles in the family. Whatever the truth may be, he became known to the world as Sir Stamford.[1] We hope his Jamaican friend, whoever he was, from whom he derived that name, felt duly rewarded.

The Continental tour began about the middle of June, the party consisting of Raffles and Sophia, Mrs Flint, Rev. Thomas Raffles, and Sophia's brother, Lieutenant William Hull. Travers had also been invited, but his heart was in Ireland, where he was hoping to win the hand of Mary Lesley.

A full account of the tour can be found in *During a Tour Through Some Parts of France, &c*, published by Thomas Raffles. The party left from Brighton. They had to be rowed out to their ship and some difficulty was experienced in getting their travelling carriage hoisted on board. The trip to Dieppe was crowded and uncomfortable, but once they were ashore, the expedition seems to have continued without a hitch. After some little time in Paris, where the Jardin des Plantes interested Raffles, they travelled on to Switzerland, returning through Germany and the Netherlands.

The only part of the tour that really concerns us is the visit to Brussels, where they arrived on 15th July. Raffles dined with Anton Falck, the Colonial Minister, upon whom, according to van der Duyn in a letter to van der Capellen, he made a good impression. The purpose of his visit is clear from a letter he addressed to Falck on the 17th.

"The dangers to which the interests of my late colleague, Mr Cranssen, appear to be exposed in consequence of the part he has taken . . . are so obvious and great, that my high respect for his character and principles will not allow me to remain inactive in his behalf, and I trust, Sir, from the polite attention which I have had the honour to receive from you, that you will pardon the liberty which I am now taking in respectfully soliciting your particular attention to his case. . . .

"I have undertaken to assure you, Sir, that there does not exist a more true Hollander than Mr Cranssen, nor one who glories more in his Prince and the maintenance of his present dignity and authority. . . . He never could have considered for a moment, that he was acting inimical[ly] to the interests of his country. England had been no enemy to Holland; she had gone to Java as a protecting power, and until the Colony could be delivered over to Holland, it was placed partly under his charge. . . .

"Mr Cranssen is advanced in life and he cannot live in disgrace. If the commissioners continue to slight him, he will be driven to Europe, to the ruin of his property; or he will die of a broken heart, an event which I can assure you has more than once been predicted by those who have written to me concerning him. Whatever may be my claims in the

[1] Even then there was confusion. Cousin Thomas's eldest son was christened Thomas Stamford, and when, in 1864, he published the memoirs of his father, at least one library catalogued him as Sir T. S. Raffles, this nearly forty years after Raffles' death.

consideration of the Dutch Government, and I cannot but consider that I have some, I would willingly forego them all in this suit for Mr Cranssen; and as it is the only favour I should presume to ask, I hope, Sir, that I may look forward to your support and assistance in a request which I hope to be permitted personally to make to the King in his favour. It is that his conduct may be approved for the part he originally took, and that he may be protected from injury and slight on account of any share he may have had in closing the concerns of the British Government. . . ."

Four days later Raffles dined with the King of the Netherlands, formerly William, Prince of Orange, and spoke on behalf of his late Dutch colleagues and the Javanese princes. "I think I made some impression on him." Back in Berners Street, he wrote to Marsden on 27th July:

". . . although the King himself, and his leading Ministers seemed to mean well, they have too great a hankering after profit, and *immediate* profit, for any liberal system to thrive under them."

At Berners Street he found Travers, now happily engaged to Mary Lesley, and McQuoid, who had just arrived on furlough from Java, where he had set up in business as McQuoid & Co., agents.

Raffles planned to leave England for Sumatra in October, so a round of farewells had to be endured. On 11th August he and Sophia left London for Liverpool to see his cousin, and also to dine with the Duke of Hamilton. They then crossed to Ireland to say good-bye to members of Sophia's family, returning to Bristol on 5th September. After a visit to the Duke and Duchess of Somerset at Maiden Bradley, their home near Bath, they arrived in London on the 12th. A week later Raffles went alone to Bedfordshire for final talks with Sir Hugh Inglis, former deputy chairman of the Company, with whom he stayed for two days. Back in London, he presided at a dinner in the City.

"On the 23rd", wrote Travers, "we assembled a large party at the Albion[1] in the City, where we had a very famous dinner. Sir Stamford took the Chair, and Garnham and I were his supporters. We had some good singing, and a number of bumper toasts. On the Island being given, Mr Ellis arose and, in a most elegant and appropriate speech, paid Sir Stamford's Administration a very high compliment. Mr Ellis had visited Java on his way to China with the Embassy,[2] of which he was one of

[1] The Albion faced the stage-door of Drury Lane Theatre, which, having been burnt to the ground in 1809, had been rebuilt and opened once more in 1812. It was the custom of the actors and actresses to drop into the Albion after the theatre closed, and join in the smoking concerts. Two years after the dinner now referred to, Edmund Kean took London by storm at "Old Drury".

[2] Lord Amherst's mission to Peking in 1816, to urge for better treatment of British merchants. It had failed because Amherst had refused to perform the kow-tow to the emperor.

the Commissioners, shortly after our departure, and again on his return after shipwreck."

On the following day Travers left for Ireland to get married.

No doubt as a result of his acquaintance with the Princess, Queen Charlotte, consort of George III, also took an interest in Raffles, an interest heightened, it would seem, by the various presents he had given to her granddaughter. The following delightful little anecdote is from the reminiscences of Cousin Thomas:

"He told me that the Queen (Charlotte) heard so much of the curious and precious things which he had brought from India [Java], and especially of the furniture—tables, chairs, &c, which he had presented to the Princess Charlotte, made of the Kiabooka wood of India, which adorned the dining and drawing-rooms at Claremont—that she expressed the intention of coming to see him: the fact is, she also wanted to obtain some portion for herself. 'Of course,' he said, 'I could not allow the Queen of England to come to me'; but he sent word to her Majesty, by Lady Harcourt (through whom the Queen's message had been conveyed to him), that he would do himself the honour of waiting upon her Majesty, at any time and place she might please to appoint. To this arrangement her Majesty assented, and named St Leonard's, the seat of the Countess Harcourt, who was one of the Ladies-in-waiting, and one of her Majesty's personal friends, as the place of the interview. Lord and Lady Harcourt were also personal and, indeed, intimate friends of Sir Stamford. Of course, he was there in good time, and told me that, while waiting for the Queen, he talked with Lady Harcourt about me. 'And what', said I, 'could you say about me?'—'Oh,' he said, 'I told her that you were a Dissenting minister—that I had been to visit you at Liverpool —that I had heard you preach twice, long sermons, without a book.'— 'Ah,' said Lady Harcourt, 'but you must not tell the Queen that, *for she hates Dissenters!*' At length her Majesty arrived, and after the formalities of introduction, &c, it was proposed that they should take a walk in the park. But we had not gone far when her Majesty said, 'I hear wonderful things of the treasures you have brought from India, and everybody is in raptures with the beautiful tables, &c, which you have given to the Princess Charlotte.'—'Of course,' said he, 'I was obliged to say that I should be greatly honoured if her Majesty would accept a specimen of the wood for her residence at Frogmore.' The offer was graciously accepted; and he told me that he ordered a pair of tables, which were being made for Sir Joseph Banks, to be sent immediately to Frogmore. The next thing was an invitation, or rather a *command*, from the Queen, to spend an evening with her at Frogmore. There he met Lord Amherst, who was just on the point of sailing as Governor-General of India. . . ."

Lord Amherst did not become Governor-General of India until 1823.

It seems possible that during his stay in England, at some time previous to his knighthood, Raffles met Warren Hastings. No record has survived, but the suggestion that a meeting took place is found in Raffles' letter, dated "Friday", to Dr Fisher, Bishop of Salisbury:

"Mr Raffles presents his compliments to the Bishop of Salisbury and can assure his Lordship that nothing will afford him more pleasure than the honour of being personally known to Mr Hastings, and the opportunity of evincing his respect and veneration for a character so truly great. The Duke and Duchess of Somerset intend honouring Mr Raffles with a visit at three o'clock on Monday next. Perhaps that time may be convenient; if not, any more early hour on that day, Tuesday or Wednesday, that Mr Hastings will name, will be perfectly convenient to Mr Raffles.

"Mr Raffles will esteem himself honoured in the company of Mrs Fisher and the ladies."

Through the influence of Charles Grant the elder, father of the future Lord Glenelg, he was introduced to the Clapham Sect, advocates of the abolition of slavery. Grant was not only a senior member of the sect, but had also been three times chairman of the East India Company. Among the new friends this brought to Raffles was William Wilberforce, then at the height of his fame.

Perhaps to no other family in the highest ranks of Society did Raffles become more closely attached than to the Duke and Duchess of Somerset. During the remainder of his life he carried on a regular correspondence with the Duchess, who shared in his scientific interests, and these letters form a valuable source of information as to his activities and his life. As Miss Hahn observes:

"He was sensitive, eager, intellectually passionate: she was sympathetic and receptive. Because it was the duchess rather than the duke whom Raffles addressed in his letters, they were buoyant, fascinating compositions with a special flavour, and made much better reading than did the missives dealing with the same subjects which he wrote to Marsden, valued old friend as he was."

It was about this time that the portrait of Raffles by G. F. Joseph, A.R.A., was painted. In 1859 it was presented by his nephew, the Rev. W. C. Raffles Flint, to the National Portrait Gallery, where it still hangs.

Preparations for departure were now actively in hand. Besides Raffles and Sophia, the Bencoolen contingent was to include Travers and his wife, William Hull, Mrs Grimes, who was Sophia's nurse, Dr Joseph Arnold, the botanist, who had been recommended to Raffles by Sir Joseph Banks, William Watson, brother of Thomas, now Captain Watson, who had been with Raffles in Java, two lads, Walthen and Simes, who had been educated at Raffles' expense, and Radin Rana Dipura. Domestic animals, birds and a large collection of plants were also to be taken.

The East India Company had arranged passages in a new ship, called as a delicate compliment, the *Lady Raffles* and commanded by Captain Harry Auber, Sophia's brother-in-law. William R. Jennings, the acting Resident at Fort Marlborough, Bencoolen, was advised on 15th October of Raffles appointment, not as Resident, but as Lieutenant-Governor.

". . . such designation being intended as a peculiar mark of the favourable sentiments, which the Court entertain of that gentleman's merits and services. This designation is to be confined entirely to Sir Thomas S. Raffles and not to devolve upon his successor at Bencoolen."

Thus was the bitter pill sugared.

Raffles found the final farewells very trying. To the Duchess of Somerset he wrote:

"Oh! that this leave-taking was at an end. My house is filled with those who are determined to say goodbye and make me more miserable when it requires all my fortitude to keep my spirits calm and uniform."

On his last visit to Claremont, Prince Leopold said to him:

"Sir Stamford, the Princess and myself are much indebted to you for the many expressions you have given us of your regard. Allow me to put this ring upon your finger as a token of our united regard."

The Princess, looking over her shoulder, added with a smile:

"And I request you will sometimes wear it for my sake."

Thomas Raffles, recording the incident, mentioned that it was a diamond ring worth four hundred pounds.

The *Lady Raffles* was to sail from Portsmouth. Travers came there from Ireland with his bride on 19th October, to find Raffles and Sophia already installed at the George. The next day, Raffles wrote to his mother:

"It is only a little time and I will be with you again. Nothing can keep me beyond five years and I may be home much sooner . . . keep up your spirits, my dear mother, there is much pleasure and happiness in store for you. My friend Mr John Taylor will take care you want for nothing. Should any accident happen to me your £400 a year is still safe."

The ship arrived at Portsmouth on 23rd October and, as the wind was favourable, all made haste to get on board. But no sooner had she sailed than five days of gale and high seas followed, so, as Sophia and Mary Travers were both prostrate with seasickness, they put into Falmouth. Even then, no one managed to get ashore till the evening of the 29th, when they all went to the hotel where Raffles and Travers had spent their first night in England on arrival from Java. From there Raffles wrote to Falck on 3rd November:

"Before I proceed to those scenes where I am to witness the effects of your Councils at home I am anxious again to impress you with the importance of upholding Mr Muntinghe and Mr Cranssen. The last accounts from Java speak decidedly on the subject; there is an evident inclination to injure and degrade both of them, and however Mr Muntinghe may appear to be considered on the records transmitted to Europe, he has met with no personal attention or consideration of which he can speak; on the contrary he is so impressed with the conduct of those in power against him, that he now looks only for a quiet place of refuge. Ought this to be the case? Mr Muntinghe is the only man you have to depend upon in bringing about the change you desire, and if you allow him to be slighted and disgusted, you will be long before you meet with another of equal merit and capacity."

The party embarked once more on 6th November, but after a few hours' sail the pilot decided to turn back and anchor. So bad was the weather that it was not until the 9th that the travellers could land. It was then that they learned the tragic news that Princess Charlotte had died on the 5th giving birth to a still-born child.

This was a national tragedy; to Raffles it was a great personal one. It must have seemed to him that all his friends were doomed to die prematurely. Thomas Raffles wrote:

"... the loss of the amiable Princess ... touched him most tenderly, for he had a sincere regard for her, beyond any consideration of rank, or wealth, or honour, to which he might have attained, had both their lives been prolonged. There was no doubt entertained at the time that if she had survived he would have been Governor-General of India; while she would have been but too much delighted to have raised him to the peerage in that capacity."

A change in the weather on 20th November caused another start to be made. The party was a little different now. William Watson had fallen sick and had to be left behind, and the lad Walthen, not liking his experience of ocean travel to date, had bolted. In their places came Lieutenant Johnson, a half-pay naval officer, and our old friend Sir Thomas Sevestre, whose finances made an early departure from England most pressing.

Yet again, soon after leaving, a south-west gale was encountered. Captain Auber decided to put back to Plymouth, but just as the ship was once more off Falmouth, the wind veered and she was able to resume her original course. From then to the end of the month, the weather remained extremely rough, and Sophia became so weak that she could not stand. The other bride was in little better shape. But after that the weather steadily improved and the passengers were able to forget their series of false starts and harrowing seasickness, and settle down to enjoy life on board.

"You will be glad to hear", wrote Raffles to the Duchess of Somerset, "that all the individuals of the Ark are well and thriving. The cows, dogs, cats, birds, the latter singing around me, and my nursery of plants thriving beyond all expectation; the thermometer is at 70. What a waste of waters now lies between us and yet the distance daily widens, and will widen still until half the world divides us."

Christmas Day was kept with such festivity as the absence of roast beef would permit, and New Year was seen in with a dinner and dance. At the end of January there was a temporary break in the fine weather, but then the temperature rose pleasantly and winds became light. This was very fortunate, for on 15th February, when they were southward of the Cape, Sophia gave birth to a daughter. Neither mother nor child seemed to have suffered any harm from the earlier rough experiences. Captain Auber, officiating as parson, christened the infant Charlotte Sophia, and at the suggestion of the Radin, Tunjong Segara, "Lily of the Sea". Her first name was after the Princess and also the Duchess of Somerset, who was her godmother. As Travers remarked, it was odd that both Raffles and his first child were born and christened at sea.

After a voyage of 14,244 miles, with no calls at intermediate ports, they anchored on 19th March 1818 off Rat Island, about six miles from Bencoolen. H. R. Lewis, on behalf of Jennings, the acting Resident, came off to arrange for the landing on the morrow.

"The Chief Authority", wrote Raffles to the Court of Directors, "had abandoned his post some months previously and the whole arrangement of the place was in the hands of an individual [Lewis] born in the country who, though holding an inferior rank, had contrived by his intrigues to usurp the whole influence of the place."

They were taken ashore next day by Captain Francis Salmond, the master attendant. The landing took place at eleven o'clock in the morning, the troops of the garrison being drawn up as a guard of honour.

"My arrival", wrote Raffles to the Duchess of Somerset, "was not hailed by the most auspicious of omens, for the day previous to it a violent earthquake had nearly destroyed every building in the place, and the first communication which I received from the shore was, that both Government-houses were rendered useless and uninhabitable. These earthquakes are said to occur every five or six years, and they have now lasted from the 18th of the last month up to the present period, the shocks occurring within the short intervals twice or thrice a day. The most violent shock happened on the 18th, before our arrival: it occurred during the night, and, by the accounts given, it must have been truly awful. Every building had suffered more or less; some are quite ruins, others hardly deserving repair: the house which I now occupy is rent from top to bottom, there is not a room without a crack of some feet long and several inches wide; the cornices broken and everything unhinged; from some houses many cart-loads of rubbish have been cleared away, and still they are inhabited, notwithstanding they rock to and fro with every breeze."

The next day being Sunday, the whole party went to church. On Monday a levee was held, all the gentlemen of the settlement attending to meet the new Lieutenant-Governor.

Chapter Twenty

BENCOOLEN, 1818

SUMATRA, land of heavy rain, immense forests, the tiger and the gibbon, is the sixth largest island in the world. Its western side is very mountainous, the Bukit Barisan running for a thousand miles along that stormy coast, with many volcanic peaks, and lakes in the craters of extinct volcanoes. The main rivers all flow eastward. Civilized first by Indian Buddhists, it became later largely Mohammedan. The first Europeans to set up trading stations were the Portuguese, early in the sixteenth century, by the end of which they were superseded by the Dutch.

Compared with Java, the settlement that Raffles had arrived to administer was insignificant. Excluding the two small dependencies of Natal and the island of Ponchan Kechil (Little Ponchan) in Tapanuli Bay, both farther along the west coast, beyond Padang, the whole extent of his territory was only a strip along the coast, some three hundred miles in length, from Indrapura in the north to Krui in the south. Save for Bencoolen, there was not a single place that could merit the name of town. The whole of the coast, except at Bencoolen and Krui, was inaccessible to shipping on account of the heavy surf, and the rivers were all blocked by bars. No roads had ever been constructed across country, the only means of communication being along the beach to the mouths of the different rivers, where European residencies had been established for collecting the pepper brought down to them.

Padang, between Bencoolen and Natal, had been in Dutch possession until 1795, when it had capitulated to the British. It had been restored under the Treaty of Amiens, but, like Malacca, had not been reoccupied by the Dutch before the war had broken out again. When the Dutch had finally returned to Java, they had not had the ships available to resume possession, so Padang still remained under British administration.

The history of the settlement at Bencoolen—Bangka Ulu[1] of the Malays—had been an unhappy one. Established in 1685 under the mistaken impression that the best route to China was through the Strait or Sunda, it had very soon been found of little value. It represented a dead loss annually and had become a standing deterrent against the establishment of any factories east of India. The seat of government had originally been Fort York, but in 1714 Deputy Governor Joseph Collet had built a

[1] "Up-country Bangka." But this is a Malay mistranslation of the Javanese Bangka Kulun—West Bangka.

new fort some six miles to the south and named it after the Duke of Marlborough. This may well have been a healthier site, but Collet would have been better advised to go eight miles farther south to Pulau Bay, where there was a safe anchorage and a large stretch of level ground, far more suitable for a settlement than Bencoolen, which was backed by hills and ravines where water collected into marshy valleys, so productive of malaria.

Up to 1801 a system of monopoly had existed. "The Company", wrote Raffles, "reserved to itself the monopoly of the pepper trade, while the rest was appropriated by the local Government, who, under the denomination of Governor and Council, were in effect the managers of a trading concern . . . and considered the trade and resources of the country placed under their management as their exclusive property, to be divided among themselves and those whom they might patronize, that is to say, their juniors in the Civil Service."

Eventually the Court of Directors had awakened to the diminution of the pepper investment and the increase of charges, not to mention the quarrels of the local authorities among themselves, and had abolished the whole establishment, instead of undertaking the necessary reform. The management of Bencoolen had been transferred to India, and expenses drastically cut down, but the pepper monopoly had been maintained. "Unfortunately," wrote Raffles, "the reduction of the establishment and the maintenance of the pepper monopoly were two things absolutely inconsistent." The position of Bencoolen had therefore become worse than ever before.

Few places can be more depressing than a colony that has proved a failure. The people of England had long forgotten the existence of Bencoolen, if ever they had been seriously aware of it. The murder of Thomas Parr, the Resident, in 1805 had given it a slight flicker of notoriety, but this event had soon faded from recollection. The Company remembered it twice a year, when its sole export, a part cargo of pepper, arrived, and when the annual deficit of £100,000 had to be met. The district was saturated with malaria; the officials underpaid, corrupt and without hope; the Malays, suffering under the iniquitous system of forced culture, disaffected and hostile.

The total population did not exceed sixty thousand, of whom about ten thousand were to be found in Bencoolen itself or its environs. A quarter of this number were represented by the "European Establishment", consisting of "military, convicts, Caffrees[1] and Bengalese", together with some five hundred Chinese. The Asiatic population was falling steadily.

[1] Caffres, descendants of slaves originally imported from Mozambique and Madagascar.

What Marsden, who had been there from 1771 to 1779, had told Raffles about Bencoolen is not on record, but we have Raffles' own reaction to it.

"This", he wrote to Marsden, "is without exception the most wretched place I ever beheld. I cannot convey to you an adequate idea of the state of ruin and dilapidation which surrounds me. What with natural impediments, bad Government, and the awful visitations of Providence which we have recently experienced in repeated earthquakes, we have scarcely a dwelling in which to lay our heads, or wherewithal to satisfy the cravings of nature. The roads are impassable; the highways in the town overrun with rank grass; the Government House a den of ravenous dogs and polecats. The natives say that Bencoolen is now a *tana mati* (dead land).[1] In truth, I could never have conceived anything half so bad."

For a man of his ambition, this might have seemed the finish of his career; if he escaped malaria, a few dull years in which to make some money, supposing that were possible in this derelict backwater, and then home for good. But Raffles had no such defeatist ideas. He continued:

"We will try and make it better; and if I am well supported from home, the West coast may yet be turned to account. You must, however, be prepared for the abolition of slavery; the emancipation of the country people from the forced cultivation of pepper; the discontinuance of the gaming and cock-fighting farms; and a thousand other practices equally disgraceful and repugnant to the British character and Government."

To his sister, Mary Anne, he wrote at the same time, with an invitation for her and her husband to join them at Bencoolen:

"This is a miserable poor place and not to be compared to the smallest Residency under Java, but we continue to make ourselves comfortable. There is plenty for me to do for some time and after that my Dutch friends will require a little brushing up in the further East. . . . I fear I have little to give you but eating and drinking and a broken down home. You cannot conceive what a prosing, domestic couple we have become. We really want you to enliven us."

Some of the reforms mentioned to Marsden he was able to initiate without delay. There were, for example, some two to three hundred Caffres belonging to the Company. These he solemnly enfranchised at a public meeting, giving each a certificate of freedom—a step subsequently approved by the Company, which, however, expressed regret that he had been so precipitate. But indeed there seems to have been need for swift action; not only had the slave trade been made illegal in British territory,

[1] *Tana* (*tanah*), land; *mati*, dead.

but also the situation of these unfortunates was a moral scandal, "the women living in promiscuous intercourse with the public convicts for the purpose (as I was informed by the Superintendent) of keeping up the breed, and the children living in a state of nature, vice and wretchedness".

As he wrote later to Wilberforce:

"Among the more striking irregularities which I found to prevail was the encouragement and countenance given to slavery by the entertainment on the part of the Government of a gang of negroes in number between two and three hundred. This appeared to me so opposite to the Company's general practice and principles in India that I did not hesitate to take upon myself the measure of emancipating the whole and by this my first act to give an earnest of the principles on which my future government would be conducted. The provision was continued for the old and infirm as well as the children; and as the latter were numerous, no time was lost in affording them such education as might fit them for the new state and condition to which they had been raised."

The school for the Caffre children was entrusted to the chaplain, the Rev. Charles Winter.

The convicts to whom Raffles referred in his letter to Marsden numbered about five hundred, transported from India during the previous twenty-three years. These, he informed Marsden, also deserved urgent attention.

"The object of the punishment as far as it affects the parties must be the reclaiming [of] them from bad habits but I do question whether the practice hitherto pursued has been productive of that effect. This I apprehend to be in a great measure in consequence of sufficient discrimination and encouragement not having been shown in favour of those most inclined to amendment. . . . It frequently happens that men of notoriously bad conduct are liberated at the expiration of a limited period of transportation, while others, whose general conduct is perhaps unexceptionable, are doomed to servitude to the end of their lives. . . .

"It rarely happens that any of those transported have any desire to leave the country; they form connexions in the place and find so many inducements to remain that to be sent away is considered by most a severe punishment. While a convict remains unmarried and kept to daily labour very little confidence can be placed in him; and his services are rendered with such tardiness and dissatisfaction that they are of little or no value; but he no sooner marries and forms a small settlement than he becomes a kind of colonist."

Basing his reforms on this principle, Raffles divided the convicts into classes according to their characters and was able to build up a very useful body of settled labour.

Another class of person, but one more difficult to help, was the debt slaves or *menghiris*. Ostensibly these were people who had given the services of themselves or their children in discharge of a debt, though in fact such debts were never discharged. A good many imported slaves were also disguised as *menghiris*. How Raffles dealt with them will be seen later.

Discontinuance of public cockfighting and gaming was a further reform instituted at once. It meant a considerable loss to the public revenue, but Raffles realized that it was impossible to proceed with any moral or economic reforms if such inducements to vice were tolerated. Nor could he look for any sympathetic co-operation from the local chiefs unless his own government set a proper example, and it was his intention to meet the chiefs as soon as practicable with a view to deciding what action could best be taken to end forced cultivation and forced deliveries of pepper.

Before this could be done, it was essential to bring about a complete change in the relations between the Europeans and the natives. The murder of Parr in 1805 had frightened the European population of Bencoolen to a degree exemplified by the excessive punitive measures then adopted. As a result, there was a continuing state of tension. The Europeans were frankly scared of the natives, whom they regarded as hostile and treacherous. The natives, for their part, were sullen and suspicious. No real progress could be looked for until this barrier of mutual suspicion was broken down. Raffles therefore dispensed entirely with the guards and sentries who had been considered absolutely essential for the personal safety of the chief authority.

"On Sir Stamford's first arrival in 1818," recorded Sophia, "he found that every tree and shrub had been cut down (from fear of the natives) around the residence of the chief authority, which had in consequence a most desolate appearance; he immediately formed a garden and surrounded the Government House with plantations. . . ."

The local chiefs were invited to visit him at his own house, where they were always welcome. Their confidence was gradually restored and they soon began to realize that in Raffles they had a true and understanding friend. The way was thus paved for practical results when the opportunity offered.

One problem for which no real solution was open was the number of unemployed civil servants. There were at least twenty-five for whom there was no employment whatever. Removal to other areas was the only solution, but that was a matter for the Company. Meanwhile Raffles took steps to provide some measure of employment for them and so keep them out of mischief.

Such is a very brief sketch of the domestic reforms initiated by Raffles on his first arrival, some at least of them planned in England after discussion with the officials of the Company.

Before we go on to consider his other activities, three matters relating to his personal finances must be referred to, for they were to have very unpleasant repercussions. The first relates to the voyage in the *Lady Raffles* from England. This had cost £1,500, which Raffles had paid out of his own pocket. In taking over the administration of Bencoolen, he drew on Government for this amount. The second relates to his salary as Lieutenant-Governor of Java. While he had been there, half of his remuneration had, at his own request, been paid in rupees in Bengal, while the other half had been paid in Java in the form of treasury notes, which had been at a discount of from fifteen to twenty per cent. Though he could, of course, have kept them as an investment, he had been compelled to spend most of them as soon as he received them. Yet he had managed to save a considerable sum in these notes, which, when he had handed over the administration to Fendall, he had had no alternative but to sell at a loss of over 30,000 rupees. Others in that position were allowed a refund, but as the regulation had been of his own making, he had not felt it proper to take personal advantage of it while still in Java; apart from other considerations, it might have embarrassed Fendall. Now, on taking over the government of Bencoolen, he considered himself justified in drawing that also.

The third matter concerned his salary as Lieutenant-Governor of Bencoolen. Lord Minto had informed him that he would be entitled to draw the allowance of Resident of Bencoolen from the date of his ceasing to be Lieutenant-Governor of Java. As the Bencoolen post had meanwhile been elevated to that of Lieutenant-Governor, he now drew salary for one year (1816-17) at Resident's rate, and a second year (1817-18) at Lieutenant-Governor's rate, this step being taken subject to the approval of the Governor-General and the Court of Directors. The Company's custom at that time was to pay its officials only for such periods as they were at their posts, but Raffles took the view, and was reasonably confident that the higher authorities would do the same, that inasmuch as his visit to England had been largely on the Company's business, he would not have to bear the loss in salary occasioned by his two years' absence from the East.

These three items were duly set forth in the accounts of Fort Marlborough. Lest the second and third should be disallowed, he purchased Government securities to that amount and arranged for them to be deposited with the Accountant-General in Bengal.

On 22nd March he sent a memorial to the Court, asking that if his administration of Java "shall generally be proved to have been proper, and such as the circumstances in which the Colony was placed called for, the Court will award him such consideration as he is entitled to expect with reference to the general scale of his services and pretensions".

We return now to his public work in Bencoolen. It might have been thought that the reforms already described would have kept him fully occupied, but in fact, though he did not underestimate their importance, they sank, as he said himself, into insignificance by comparison with the political issues raised by the activities of his Dutch neighbours. Here it should be emphasized that he excluded Java from his interest. What the Dutch did in Java was not his business, though he had his own views as to the wisdom of their policy. His acute concern was the apparent determination of the Dutch to dominate the whole Eastern Archipelago and to restrict the British to the narrow confines of Bencoolen itself.

Writing to Ramsay on 14th April 1818—that is, within a few weeks of arriving at Bencoolen—he described the position as he saw it.

"The Dutch possess the only passes through which ships must sail into the Archipelago, the Straits of Sunda and Malacca; and the British have now not an inch of ground to stand upon between the Cape of Good Hope and China, nor a single friendly port at which they can water and obtain refreshments. It is indispensable that some regular and accredited authority on the part of the British Government should exist in the Archipelago, to declare and maintain the British rights, whatever they are, to receive appeals and to exercise such wholesome control as may be conducive to the preservation of the British honour and character. At present the authority of the Government of Prince of Wales' Island extends no further than Malacca, and the Dutch would willingly confine that of Bencoolen to the almost inaccessible shores of the West coast of Sumatra.

"To effect the objects contemplated, some convenient station within the Archipelago is necessary; both Bencoolen and Prince of Wales' Island are too far removed, and unless we succeed in obtaining a position in the Straits of Sunda, we have no alternative but to fix it in the most advantageous position we can find within the Archipelago; this would be somewhere in the neighbourhood of Bintang."

Bintang (also known as Rhio or Riau or Riouw, after its chief town, which is on an adjacent islet) is the largest island in the Rhio archipelago and close to Singapore. It will be remembered as one of the places to which missions were dispatched by Warren Hastings before Penang was finally selected in 1786. The mission to Rhio was entrusted to Captain Forrest, but when he got there he found he had been anticipated by the Dutch, doubtless forewarned of British intentions. The British interest in Rhio persisted, however, even after the founding of Penang. In a letter from Dundas to Lord Malmesbury dated 30th May 1790 it is described as outstandingly the best site as a port of refreshment for the China ships and also as the most suitable place for an *entrepôt*. It was even suggested at that time that Penang should be abandoned in favour of Rhio. However, the Dutch realized, as they were to discover again later, that a British port at the southern end of the Straits of Malacca would imperil their monopoly in the Eastern Archipelago, and declined to give up Rhio on any terms.

Of Dutch pretensions, Raffles wrote in the same letter to Ramsay:

"Prepared as I was for the jealousy and assumption of the Dutch Commissioners in the East, I have found myself surprised by the unreserved avowal they have made of their principles, their steady determination to lower the British character in the eyes of the natives, and the measures they have already adopted towards the annihilation of our commerce and of our intercourse with the native traders throughout the Malayan Archipelago. Not satisfied with shutting the Eastern ports against our shipping, and prohibiting the natives from commercial intercourse with the English, they have dispatched Commissioners to every spot on the Archipelago where it is probable we might attempt to form Settlements, or where the independence of the native Chiefs afford anything like a free port to our shipping. Thus not only the Lampong country has been resumed, but also Pontiana and the minor ports of Borneo, and even Bali, where European flag was never before hoisted, are now considered by them subject to their authority, and measures taken for their subjugation. A Commissioner also long since sailed from Batavia to Palembang, to organize, as it is said, all that part of Sumatra; and every native prow and vessel is now required to hoist a Dutch flag, and to take out a Dutch pass from Batavia for one of the ports thus placed under their influence; so that whatever trade may still be carried on by the English with the native ports of the Archipelago, must already be in violation of the Dutch regulations, and at the risk of seizure by their cruisers, who have not hesitated repeatedly to fire into English ships. The Commanders of the country ships look to me to protect their interests, and even to support the dignity of the British flag; and it is to be hoped some immediate notice will be taken by our Government of these proceedings."

Elout was in great alarm about Raffles. An examination of the *History of Java* and researches in the government archives had confirmed his opinion of Raffles' ability and knowledge and his strong antipathy to Dutch monopoly. One particular dispatch had caused him special anxiety. This was that written by Raffles on 5th August 1815, on learning of the escape of Napoleon from Elba. He had then called attention once again to the intrinsic value of Java and had pressed strongly that, if the war was to continue, the British Government should annex it. This dispatch was seized upon by Elout to prove that Fendall's delay in handing over Java had been a deliberate attempt to implement this very policy recommended by Raffles, and that Raffles' visit to England had been to aid and abet the plot.

The news that Raffles was returning to the East and would be Holland's near neighbour at Bencoolen had intensified this alarm. Worse still, van Braam, the Dutch agent in India, had reported that he had learned from good private sources (no doubt John Palmer) that Raffles had in mind the extension of British influence, particularly in Sumatra.

No time was to be lost. Every outpost the Dutch had ever occupied, for however brief a time, must be reoccupied without delay, all Malay princes being made to understand that the British régime had been an unimportant interlude. The Dutch were once again the paramount power and with very adequate forces to maintain their authority. Abandoning all interest and influence in the area, the British had sailed away.

Doubting, perhaps, the complete efficacy of these measures, Elout had revived an old project to safeguard Dutch monopoly once and for all. Holland's possessions in continental India had for a long time been of little value to her, but, thought Elout, they must be of great value to England. Accordingly, he had suggested to his government at home that negotiations should at once be opened with England whereby Penang and Bencoolen should be exchanged for the Dutch colonies in India, or Bencoolen for Malacca, thus making the equator the boundary between the Dutch and English possessions. The authorities in Holland, however, having won so much in the Anglo-Dutch settlement of 1814, were in no hurry to reopen negotiations. No doubt they were prudent in their hesitation, but it is interesting to observe that this rather hopeful proposal of Elout's was the germ from which ultimately grew the Anglo-Dutch treaty of 1824.

Among the commissioners sent out from Batavia was Muntinghe, Raffles' friend and supporter. Elout had decided that Palembang was the key position in Sumatra, so there had gone Muntinghe. We shall have early occasion to refer to this again.

While in England, Raffles had done his best to impress upon Canning and the Court the dangers that would threaten British interests in the Indies if the Dutch resumed and perhaps extended their monopoly. To Canning he had addressed a long paper called "Our Interests in the Eastern Archipelago", in which he had stressed the importance of establishing a third station in addition to Penang and Bencoolen.

"The station which I would recommend, if attainable, is the Island of Banca. Till its late surrender, it had been exclusively British. . . . Next to Banca the Island of Bintang, at the extremity of the Malay Peninsula, appears to be possessed of the largest share of those advantages which should be sought on such a Station. . . .

"The commercial ambition and activity of America, Russia, and France are daily increasing. What is to prevent them from taking possession of those advantages which the Dutch and English, in the extent of their Asiatic dominion, seem to have overlooked?

"Is not Russia extending her influence on all sides? Has not France, in renouncing the Mauritius and all rights of erecting forts on the Continent of India, acquired a fresh motive for making Establishments in the Eastern Seas? . . . The Americans have already a considerable trade with the Eastern Islands, and are favourably looked upon. Would any of these nations be desirable neighbours? . . .

"Should the attention of the British Government be directed to the importance of civilizing Borneo, or of a trade with Japan; should the independent principles now prevalent in South America extend to the Philippine Islands, and an opportunity be offered of instituting advantageous communication with them; such an Extablishment as I propose would afford important facilities, and, in the meantime, it would enable us to collect such information as might direct our judgment on all these points. . . .

"If we much longer postpone demanding that the engagements which we contracted as Governors of Java and its dependencies shall be fulfilled by the Dutch, and that the relations with the native Princes, whether of alliance or independence, which we have recognized while we ruled in those Seas, shall be maintained by our successors, our silence will be construed into an abandonment of our right to speak, we shall strengthen what appears to be the best objection that can at present be made to such a claim, viz. that it comes too late, that the Dutch have already pledged themselves to the contrary and cannot retract, especially at our suggestion, without disgrace.

"Again, the impression of British generosity in surrendering the Dutch Colonies at all is rapidly subsiding, as is also, among the native Chiefs, the impression of our power; and it is clear that, with respect to taking possession of a vacant port, or making a Treaty for privileges with an independent Chief, the prize is to the swiftest.

"But there is also a particular circumstance which requires our immediate vigilance. An extensive Marine is fitting out at Batavia, ostensibly for the suppression of piracy. Unless we go hand in hand in maintaining the general security of the Eastern Seas, and show ourselves immediately as a party interested, so as to share the influence which the display of this armament is calculated to produce on the minds of the native Chiefs, it will easily be made the means of resuming that absolute Sovereignty over the Archipelago which is the avowed object of the Dutch policy, and which [it] is so highly important to our honour and interest to prevent."

His warning bore fruit. In the instructions dated 5th November 1817, sent out to him at Bencoolen, there appeared this paragraph:

"It is highly desirable that the Court of Directors should receive early and constant communication of the proceedings of the Dutch and other European Nations, as well as of the Americans, in the Eastern Archipelago. The Court therefore desire that you will direct your attention to the object of regularly obtaining such information and that you will transmit the same by every favourable opportunity."

Subsequently the Court explained, with rather excessive emphasis, that these instructions had referred only to commercial affairs, and had no political significance whatever. They had singularly misjudged their man if they had supposed for a moment that such instructions would not be interpreted by Raffles in the widest possible sense. Had he not told his cousin Thomas that there seemed "an inclination to extend my political authority there"?

In the absence of any representative of British interests in the Malay world, he considered that it was his duty to assume this authority himself, feeling he had some sort of mandate and that his defence of British commerce would at least be in line with British policy; and particularly that it would have the support of Canning. In this he was to be sadly disappointed.

His immediate plan was to try to secure for Britain the Sumatran side of the Strait of Sunda. If the Dutch were too strong for him there, a post in the vicinity of the Rhio archipelago was to be the second string to his bow—and probably in his heart of hearts he thought it the better string.

The first step was to send an ambassador, in the person of Travers, to Batavia. Travers was to discuss arrangements for the Lampongs, the strip of land adjoining the territory of Bencoolen and stretching to the Strait of Sunda opposite Bantam. Raffles wished to establish that British territory extended as far as Semangka Bay, the most likely site, as he then thought, for the British harbour he hoped to establish in the Strait. He based his case on the article in the treaty that provided that only territory in the hands of the Dutch in 1803 had to be returned. He argued that the Dutch had not at that time been in occupation of the Lampongs, that the British flag had been hoisted there in 1811, and that, in any event, there was some doubt as to where the boundary between the original British and Dutch territories actually lay.

As for Padang, he called attention to a debt owing to the British Government for the administration of the settlement and suggested that some responsible official should be sent to Bencoolen to arrive at a financial arrangement before any attempt was made by the Dutch to reoccupy the place.

Travers left Bencoolen in the *Lady Raffles* on 3rd April and, after some troops had been dropped at Krui, reached Batavia on the 23rd. Though the situation was electric and the Dutch authorities in a state bordering on panic at the reappearance of Raffles in their neighbourhood, Travers' official reception in Java was quite civil, while he was warmly welcomed by Cranssen, whom he found living at his country house in melancholy retirement. Some of his old Dutch colleagues regarded him rather coldly, others were actively rude, fearing perhaps that any show of amity might react to their own disadvantage. Colonel Nahuijs deplored this attitude of his compatriots to their former British friends.

The Governor-General and Elout behaved to Travers with complete propriety, which was the more laudable in that they clearly observed the irregularity of an emissary being sent by a subordinate official such as Raffles to try to negotiate matters that could only properly be a subject of discussion between national plenipotentiaries.

Travers recorded his impressions of these two leading personalities: "Baron van der Capellen, gentlemanlike in appearance, and quite so in manner, rather high and formal, but always the gentleman; not a man of talent, ability or business, yet cautious and reserved in his communications; speaks English uncommonly well, as does Mr Elout, who is advanced in life, and one of the keenest, sharpest, offhand men I ever recollect to have met, and his manner is very agreeable; quick and observant, he understands your meaning before you finish half your sentence. He has a most penetrating eye and a very sensible countenance."

While being civil and friendly, they declined, and quite rightly, to give Travers more than a general negative to Raffles' proposals. A reply was sent officially. The first round was with the Dutch.

Before Travers sailed back to Bencoolen, van der Capellen and Elout dispatched a small force to Padang via Bencoolen. It left Batavia on 26th May under James DuPuy, a Dutchman with an English education who had served as assistant to Assey in the Java secretariat. His selection was represented as a compliment to Raffles, but the reason for his appointment was the same as that of Muntinghe at Palembang, to test the sincerity of his repentance for collaborating with the British during the interregnum.

Travers had been instructed by Raffles to invite Dr Horsfield to Bencoolen, an opportunity welcomed by the American, who wished to see Raffles again and to arrange with him for the transport of his large collection to England. He left Batavia with Travers in the *Lady Raffles* on 16th June.

Raffles had not been inactive during the absence of Travers. Ever since coming to Bencoolen he had been anxious to discover what sort of country lay immediately behind the settlement. Of his preliminary expedition, he wrote to the Duchess of Somerset:

"Of the country I had seen nothing and of the general character and condition of the people I then knew little. My first incursion into the interior was immediately East of Bencoolen; here I found the country in a wretched state and very thinly populated. I ascended the first range of hills and having taken up a position on the Hill of Mists (Bukit Kabut), which commands a most extensive view of the surrounding country and on which no European had ever before set foot, I determined to make it our country residence and accordingly gave orders for clearing the forest, &c. In this I have already [11th July of that year] made considerable progress. A comfortable cottage is erected and as far as we can judge the thermometer is at least six degrees lower than at Bencoolen."

This new home was at Pĕrmatang Balam—Doves' Hogs-back, or Rise.

"The only inconvenience will arise from the tigers and elephants which abound in the vicinity . . . in many parts the people would seem to resign the empire to those animals, taking but few precautions against them and regarding them as sacred . . . when a tiger enters a village the foolish people frequently prepare rice and fruits . . . they do the same on the approach of the smallpox and thus endeavour to allay the evil spirit by kind and hospitable treatment. I am doing all I can to resume the empire of man and, having made open war against the whole race of wild and ferocious animals, I hope I shall be able to reside on the Hill of Mists without danger from their attacks."

The next excursion was to the districts of Seluma, Manna and Kauer. On this occasion Sophia and Dr Arnold, the botanist, went with him. As far as Manna the route was chiefly along the seashore. Then, accompanied unwillingly by Edward Presgrave, Resident at Manna, together with six native officers and fifty coolies, they struck fifty miles inland to the country of the Pasumah tribe.

"I should not omit to inform you, that the immediate occasion of my visiting Pasumah was to reconcile contending interests which had long distracted the country. For the last ten years these people had been at war with us or rather we had been at war with them for we appeared to have been the aggressors throughout. I was assured that my person would be endangered, that the Pasumahs were a savage, ungovernable race, and that no terms could ever be made with them. . . ."

This part of the journey was extremely arduous and not without its dangers. They had to cross mountain ranges from three to five thousand feet high and in some places considerably higher. There were only a very few passes through the mountains and these were either unknown or traced with great difficulty. This was no small feat even for so active and experienced a man as Raffles, but for Sophia it was really a tremendous undertaking.

"Lady Raffles accompanied me," wrote Raffles to Robert Inglis,[1] son of Sir Hugh, "and you may form some idea of the fatigue we underwent when I tell you that for the three days we had to pass in the forest and the mountains the paths were so narrow and precipitous that it was absolutely impossible to relieve her from the fatigue of walking except by occasionally carrying her for half an hour on a man's shoulders. We walked from before daylight sometimes till nine at night and then we had to prepare our leafy dwelling from the branches of the surrounding trees. We carried a cot and bedding with us but sometimes this did not come up; and I had to select the smoothest stone from the river to serve as a pillow."

It was during this journey that they discovered the gigantic parasite known to the natives as the Devil's Betel Box. It was found to measure from the extremity of the petals rather more than a yard and was estimated to contain a gallon and a half of water. The weight of the whole flower was fifteen pounds.

"It appears at first," wrote Raffles, "in the form of a small round knob, which gradually increases in size. The flower-bud is invested by numerous membranaceous sheaths, which surround it in successive layers, and expand as the bud enlarges, until at length they form a cup round its base. . . . The inside of the cup is of an intense purple, and more or less densely yellow, with soft flexible spines of the same colour; towards the mouth it is marked with numerous depressed spots of the purest white. . . . The petals are of a brick-red with numerous pustular spots of a lighter colour. The whole substance of the flower is not less than half an inch thick, and of a firm fleshy consistence."

This flower, which issues parasitically from the lower stems and roots of the shrub Cissus, was subsequently given the scientific name of *Rafflesia arnoldi* in honour of Raffles and his botanist.

When they reached the Pasumah country Raffles felt that their efforts had met their due reward.

"No sooner had we attained the summit and bent our steps downward than our view opened upon one of the finest countries I ever beheld, amply compensating us for all the dreariness of the forest and for all the fatigues we had undergone; perhaps the prospect was heightened by the contrast; but the country I now beheld reminded me so much of scenes in Java and was in every respect so different to that of the coast that I could not help expressing myself in raptures.

"As we descended the scene improved; we found ourselves in an immense amphitheatre surrounded by mountains ten and twelve thousand feet high; the soil on which we stood rich beyond description and vegetation luxuriant and brilliant in every direction. The people, too, seemed a new race, far superior to those on the coast—tall, stout and ingenuous.

[1] Later Sir Robert; he succeeded to the baronetcy on 26th August 1820.

They received us most hospitably. . . . I was not a little gratified to find everything the reverse of what had been represented to me. I found them reasonable and industrious, an agricultural race more sinned against than sinning. . . .

"During our stay . . . the Chiefs entered into a Treaty, by which they placed themselves under the protection of the British Government, and thus all cause of dispute and misunderstanding was at once set at rest."

They started back for Manna on 24th May by a different route. Raffles and Arnold went ahead with a view to finding the river and preparing a fire. Following behind, Sophia and Presgrave missed their way and got completely lost. Then Presgrave fell into a large pit from which he extricated himself with great difficulty. It was only by a fortunate accident that they came upon Raffles and Arnold.

"Our first day's journey", wrote Raffles, "was to Camumuan which we reached a little before six in the evening after the hardest walk I ever experienced. We calculated that we had walked more than thirty miles and over the worst of roads. Hitherto we had been fortunate in our weather; but before we reached this place a heavy rain came on and soaked us completely. The baggage only came up in part and we were content to sleep in our wet clothes under the best shade we could find. No wood would burn; there was no moon; it was already dark and we had no shelter erected. By perseverance, however, I made a tolerable place for Lady Raffles. . . ."

The following day most of the journey was downstream by raft and they were able to reach Manna in about seven hours. Ultimately they arrived back at Bencoolen on 3rd June "to the no small astonishment of the colonists who were not inclined to believe it possible we could have thought of such a journey".

To Calcutta he wrote of these excursions:

"I found the country almost deserted, the remaining inhabitants in the most abject state of poverty and wretchedness. . . . I found . . . that not only were the people obliged to deliver their pepper to the Government at an inadequate price but that for the benefit of the Resident each village was obliged to deliver monthly at inadequate prices fixed quantities of rice, poultry, oil, &c, that not only all important trade was checked by the Company's officers receiving all the produce but that heavy and prohibitory transit dues on cattle, &c, levied at each river for the benefit of the Resident made it impossible for the people to carry on any important traffic.

"The southern districts were ravaged by wars with the Pasumahs and by the smallpox and there are no efficient measures to check smallpox by vaccination . . . to whatsoever immediate cause the desolation of the country may be attributable, it was clear to me that nothing but a general and radical reform in the general administration was calculated to save it from utter ruin. . . .

"The presence of the Chief Authority in the outer Residencies was an event that had never before occurred and for a moment people were excited; they looked up to me with confidence, a ray of hope seemed to animate them and they had courage to state their grievances. To have heard them and not given immediate relief might have broken their spirit for ever. I therefore listened to their complaints, treated them as people awakening from a long sleep and at once proposed to them such a radical change in their condition as was consistent with the character of the British Government and with their unhappiness. All forced services and forced deliveries of every denomination have been abolished, the cultivation of pepper has been declared free . . . all transit dues have been abolished."

To all this the Company gave its full approval.

On the same day as Raffles and his party returned from the southern districts, DuPuy arrived also at Bencoolen, having been delayed by bad weather on the voyage from Batavia. Before the discussions concerning Padang could be started, the King's birthday had to be honoured. As soon as those ceremonies were complete, the talks began. They lasted for three days, while DuPuy's unfortunate escort tossed on the dangerous swell outside the harbour.

The point at issue was simple. Raffles was asked to instruct his representative to hand over Padang at once, in reply to which he demanded acceptance of the debt to Britain, to be jointly ascertained, as a prerequisite for such an order. He was clearly evasive. His grounds for refusal were really very slender as he had no authority whatever to prevent the Dutch resuming possession of Padang. But Padang, as he had been quick to realize, was the key to Sumatra, and he was not prepared to give it up without a struggle. Technically he was correct in maintaining that it was not covered by the London convention of 1814. By a literal interpretation, it had not been physically in Dutch possession in 1803, a fact that the Dutch were compelled to recognize, if only among themselves.

When Raffles firmly declined to issue the required authority, DuPuy returned to Batavia, as he had been instructed to do. The correspondence on Padang was continued between Batavia and Bencoolen, while each made representations to its superior authority. DuPuy hinted to Elout that Raffles had tried to bribe him from his allegiance to the Dutch. In his published diary, DuPuy is more explicit. Elout swallowed the story without hesitation; anything to the discredit of Raffles was readily believed. The story, however, lacks probability. What possible advantage Raffles could have obtained by bribing a relatively junior Dutch official to join his government is hard to imagine, quite apart from the scandal it would have caused. One suspects that DuPuy was merely attempting to ingratiate himself with Elout. No one in Java was in a position to contradict him.

Angered by this revelation of a chink in their armour, the Dutch proceeded to do all they could to discredit with his countrymen the clever author of this unfortunate discovery, and Raffles gave them ample grounds on which to base their attacks.

With Travers and Horsfield aboard, the *Lady Raffles* reached Bencoolen on 29th June. As soon as Raffles heard of the attitude adopted by the Dutch over the Lampongs, he saw he had been snubbed and at once proceeded by more direct methods to obtain his object. The coast was surveyed by Sophia's brother, Lieut. William Hull, and Lieut. Johnson, as a result of which the British flag was hoisted and military posts established at Semangka and Kalambayang or Forest Harbour. The Dutch promptly set up rival posts and there the two small military groups remained side by side for many months, exchanging letters while they consulted their respective principals.

We must now revert once more to Palembang. It will be remembered that as soon as he had learned of the defeat of the French army in Java, Badru'd-din, Sultan of Palembang, had tricked the Dutch garrison into leaving their fort, had murdered the lot and declared his independence. As soon as this news had reached Java, Raffles had dispatched a force under Gillespie to Palembang to avenge the murders and also to secure the cession to Britain of the tin islands, Bangka and Billiton. Gillespie's expedition had been brilliantly successful; Badru'd-din had fled into the jungle, his brother, Ahmad Najimu'd-din, had been put on the throne, and the desired treaty signed. Later difficulties had arisen because Badru'd-din still possessed the royal treasure, being moreover a more forceful and respected person than his brother. Robison, the Resident, had taken upon himself to persuade Ahmad to withdraw in favour of Badru'd-din, who had sent a large sum of money to Java as a douceur. Raffles had rejected this solution of a practical difficulty and when the Dutch had returned to Java, Ahmad had still been on the throne, but not too happily, for his brother was in the adjacent jungle, plotting revenge.

The instructions given to Muntinghe on his appointment as commissioner are not known, but it is clear that the situation at Palembang was complicated. By the 1814 agreement the Dutch had undertaken to respect treaties concluded by the British with local powers. Probably, however, they considered Palembang a complete dependency of theirs, entitling them to resume unrestricted possession. Muntinghe would soon have realized, if he had not already been aware of it, that Ahmad was unpopular, and even if Badru'd-din had not been a standing menace to the peace of Palembang, Elout would still have regarded Ahmad with disfavour and suspicion, if only because he had been put on the throne by the British. But if Ahmad were removed, Badru'd-din was the only possible alternative—and it was he who had murdered the Dutch garrison.

As soon as he had arrived, Muntinghe had rather blatantly adopted the role of representative of the paramount power and had begun to take various steps to show his powers, including the renovation of the defences. Ahmad sent a secret emissary to Raffles asking what he should do. Raffles did not hesitate; he sent a vigorous protest to Batavia, calling attention to the British treaty. He seems to have said that, pending a reply, he would take no active steps in supporting Ahmad. Nevertheless, he did dispatch Captain Salmond overland to Palembang as a special envoy to the sultan, merely to find out, as he later stated, the facts. As the land route from Bencoolen to Palembang had never been traversed before by a European, Salmond was given a small military escort and, most sinister of all, two field guns.

Without waiting to learn the outcome of this, Raffles, as soon as DuPuy had left for Batavia, set out by sea for Padang, to explore its hinterland. No European had ever made the trip. The attitude of the inhabitants was uncertain, but believed to be hostile, yet the temptation to enter the historic country of Menangkabau, ancestral home of all the Malays, was not to be resisted, and the dangers and discomforts of the journey did not dismay him, or indeed Sophia, who accompanied him. Dr Horsfield gladly joined the party, and Joseph Arnold, who was suffering acutely from malaria, was persuaded to go with them as far as Padang, as the sea trip was thought likely to be beneficial.

The party left Bencoolen for Padang early in July on board the *Lady Raffles*. The passage was calm and the time was happily spent examining such parts of Horsfield's extensive collection already on board the ship as were available, and studying the maps, drawings and manuscripts he had assembled for transport to England. On their arrival at Padang it was found that, in spite of the explicit instructions sent on ahead, the Resident had taken no steps to collect guides or make any other arrangements to facilitate the expedition, being convinced that as soon as Raffles appreciated the difficulties and dangers the project would be abandoned. He was soon disillusioned and set about his task with such speed and efficiency that by 14th July the baggage and provisions were ready. The first party set off on that day, Raffles and Sophia remaining behind.

"This party," wrote Raffles to the Duchess of Somerset, "which consisted of about two hundred coolies or porters, each man carrying a separate load, fifty military as an escort and all our personal servants, left Padang on the afternoon of the 14th July by beat of drum, forming a most ridiculous cavalcade, the interest of which was much heightened by the quixotic appearance of my friend Dr Horsfield who was borne along on the shoulders of four of the party in order that in preceding us he might gain time for botanizing."

Raffles intended to depart himself on the 16th, but the rain descended in torrents and no one could move out of the house till after ten o'clock. The chiefs who were to accompany him appeared shortly afterwards, but declared that it was impossible to proceed that day because the river had overflowed its banks and all communication with the country was cut off. In spite of this, they managed to get away at noon, the party including a local chief, two princes of Menangkabau and about three hundred followers.

Their further adventures were described by Raffles in a very long letter to the Duchess of Somerset. A briefer account is contained in a letter to Robert Inglis, and some quotations from this can be given.

"The difficulties which were opposed far exceeded those we met with at Pasumah but determined to overcome them we accomplished our object and during a journey of fifteen days, principally on foot, we passed over a distance of at least two hundred and fifty miles which no European foot has before trodden, crossing mountains not less than five thousand feet in elevation; sometimes whole days along the course of rapid torrents and others in highly cultivated plains and throughout the whole in a country in the highest degree interesting.

"We here found the wreck of a great empire hardly known to us by name [Menangkabau] and the evident source whence all the Malayan Colonies now scattered along the coast of the Archipelago first sprung, a population of between one and two millions, a cultivation highly advanced and manners, customs and productions in a great degree new and undescribed. I can hardly describe to you the delight with which I entered the rich and populous country of Menangkabau and discovered after four days' journey through the mountains and forests this great source of interest and wealth.

"To me it was quite classical ground and had I found nothing more than the ruins of an ancient city I should have felt repaid for the journey but when in addition to this I found so extensive a population, so fertile a country and so admirable a post whence to commence and effect the civilization of Sumatra the sensation was of a nature that does not admit of description. Instead of jealousy and distrust on the part of the natives, they received us with the utmost hospitality and though their manners were rude and sometimes annoying it was impossible to misunderstand their intentions, which were most friendly. They had but one request, namely that I would not allow the Dutch to come to Padang—for the twenty-three years that the place had been in our possession great changes had taken place, new interests had arisen, children then unborn had become men and those who had become friends to the Dutch were now no more. . . .

"I did not hesitate to enter into a conditional Treaty of friendship and alliance with the Sultan of Menangkabau as the Lord Paramount of all the Malay countries, subject, of course, to the approval of Lord Hastings.[1] The state of agriculture in the Menangkabau country is far higher than I expected to find it; but not in any respect inferior to what it is in Java and in some respects superior . . . in manners and civilization, however, they are very far behindhand. Some traces of a former higher state of civilization are discernible but in general the people are little beyond what they are found to be in other parts of Sumatra. The Sovereign of Menangkabau has little or no authority and the population seem to have relapsed into the ancient divisions of tribes so general throughout Sumatra."

Raffles was under no misapprehension as to the importance of Padang. As he wrote to Marsden at that time:

"Our discoveries in Menangkabau enhance the value of Padang town; it is the key of that place and of all which is valuable in Sumatra. Without this we can do nothing—with it everything."

To the Secret Committee in London he wrote:

"In comparison with Menangkabau and Padang, Bencoolen sinks into insignificance; and it is my intention to refuse admission to the Dutch at Padang until I receive further orders from England. I sincerely hope your Honble Court will be able to effect an arrangement for its remaining permanently English."

By the end of July the party was back in Padang, to learn that Joseph Arnold had died of fever there on the 26th, the first of the many tragedies that were to sadden Raffles' time in Sumatra.

"He had endeared himself", wrote Raffles, "to Lady Raffles and myself by his most amiable disposition and unassuming manners; he formed part of our family, and I regret his loss as that of a sincere friend. To the best disposition he added a most cultivated mind; and, in a public point of view, his loss will be severely felt."

When the *Lady Raffles* arrived back at Bencoolen on 3rd August, two important pieces of news awaited the Lieutenant-Governor. The first was that when the cash in the treasury had been checked on the departure of H. R. Lewis on sick leave to Calcutta, a deficit of 160,000 Spanish dollars had been revealed. Even more disturbing was that Captain Salmond had been arrested by Muntinghe in Palembang and sent as a prisoner to Batavia.

Salmond's military escort had halted some miles from Palembang and

[1] Moira had been created Marquis of Hastings in 1817.

Salmond had gone on with a small suite. He had given Ahmad the Union Jack sent by Raffles as a token of support, and this the Sultan is said to have raised with his own hands. Muntinghe had clearly been flustered by Salmond's arrival. Like Elout he was a lawyer, but he lacked experience of practical affairs. His position as a former member of the British Council in Java made the present situation the more awkward for him, and one rather suspects that he was a little doubtful of the correctness of the Dutch attitude towards Palembang. Anyhow he had probably felt that he must show a determined front and had played right into the hands of Raffles by arresting Salmond and his suite.

Raffles decided to retailiate by moving troops into the area of the Musi river, where the great mountain range that divides Sumatra throughout its length descends towards the Strait of Sunda. The particular region was something of a no man's land between the territories of Bencoolen and Palembang. The population inclined to look more towards Bencoolen than Palembang, yet the area was unquestionably inside the boundaries of Palembang. Raffles dispatched a small force of local irregular troops, formed under the rather grand title of Sumatra Hill Rangers, with W. H. Hayes, Resident at Lais, in command, and with orders to penetrate into this area and occupy positions with a view to winning the support of the local population.

By 12th August Raffles had completed the drafting of a public protest. When Salmond and his suite were brought back from Batavia to Bencoolen in a Dutch ship on the 26th and Raffles had heard Salmond's version of Dutch activity in Palembang, he produced a second protest on 1st September. These two documents were couched in rather extravagant language, their author diplomatically disguising the political weakness of his case by the adoption of a high moral tone. The first was too long-winded to be really satisfactory, but for all that it was capable of arousing national sentiment at home, which in due course it did.

In England, interest in the East Indies had been steadily growing. During that August, for example, the commercial community had raised their voices against the new Dutch customs regulations in Java, which were held to be directed against England. Baron Fagel, the Netherlands ambassador, felt that before public opinion in England hardened against Holland a fresh move to make an Anglo-Dutch treaty of colonial partition should be initiated. He sought permission from his government to proceed.

Muntinghe at Palembang, believing the transfer of troops into the Musi area to be a projected attack on Palembang, applied for reinforcements. Various detachments were sent to him. Then followed a prolonged series of marching and counter-marching, which achieved nothing, though it cost some European lives from sickness. Muntinghe and Raffles carried on a lengthy correspondence, each trying to outdo the other on the loftiest moral plane. It would be tedious to quote their various letters. The arguments on both sides were somewhat specious, accusations and counter-accusations being made with more vigour than probability. The military forces exchanged occasional compliments, but never shots. Neither side was prepared to carry matters so far. The country was very remote and malarial, and from a European point of view very unattractive. Rice and salt for the troops were hard to get and, as most of the inhabitants had fled, porters were almost impossible to obtain. The Dutch also managed to impound most of the craft on the rivers, which made it difficult for the British to get across. The whole performance was, except for those unlucky enough to be taking part, a little ridiculous, and Raffles was ill-advised to embark on such an unprofitable adventure. It is true that he alarmed the Dutch considerably, but he also greatly increased their resentment.

"They say", he wrote, "I am a Spirit that will never allow the East to be quiet and that this second Elba in which I am placed is not half secure enough."

As he had no authority for this expedition, he put himself at a great disadvantage and reduced his chances of convincing his own authorities of the justice of his case.

Now that Ahmad had given them the opening, the Dutch exploited it to the full. He was persuaded to sign a treaty abdicating in favour of Badru'd-din. According to Raffles, it was not in fact signed and Ahmad never agreed to it. The truth is hard to discover, but Muntinghe's letter to Elout justifying the legality of the treaty is certainly involved and not very convincing. Not to be outdone, Elout wrote to Falck:

"What Raffles had been trying again will become apparent to you from the official letters. . . . The Sultan of Palembang declares for certain that he has put his name and seal on our treaty knowingly, but also that the British agents, or rather the subordinates of Mr Raffles, had given him an English document to sign which he was told was an order to feed transport troops, while on the other side, it proved to be an invented treaty!"

Badru'd-din in the meantime had sent to Batavia copies of some letters he had received from Raffles in Malacca before the invasion of Java, urging him to expel the Dutch from Palembang. These letters, so Badru'd-din claimed, proved that Raffles and not he was responsible for the murder of the Dutch garrison. These copies arrived opportunely, for they helped to salve the Dutch conscience over restoring to his throne the murderer of their compatriots.

The continued activities of Raffles, and the Dutch nervousness of Ahmad, induced Muntinghe to exile Ahmad and all his family to Java.

But peace did not come to Palembang. In promoting Badru'd-din in place of Ahmad, the Dutch soon found they had exchanged King Log for King Stork. Badru'd-din declared his independence, and the establishment of Dutch sovereignty in Palembang had finally to be accomplished by force of arms, and then only after some grave military disasters.

Chapter Twenty-one

BENCOOLEN, CALCUTTA AND PENANG, 1818

i

IN discussing Raffles' exertions in Sumatra during his early months there, we have omitted reference to the contemporary activities of Major William Farquhar, Resident at Malacca.

When Penang had first received news from Europe that peace had been signed, it had also learned with dismay that Malacca was to be restored to the Dutch. As far back as 1816, according to his own account, Farquhar had recommended that negotiations should be opened with the Raja of Lingga for the cession of Rhio to England. But, as so often happened with Farquhar's excellent ideas, nothing had come of his proposal. When, however, the return of Malacca became a matter of almost immediate realization, people in Penang began to view with increasing alarm the future of British trade in the Straits of Malacca. The commercial community was under no illusion that Malacca in Dutch hands would be a serious threat to the recent prosperity of Penang, apprehension increasing as evidence accumulated that the Dutch had returned to the East determined to reinstate in full their old policy of monopoly in any direction they could.

The new Dutch Governor of Malacca, J. S. Timmerman Thyssen, late of Java, duly arrived at Malacca with his staff, his chief assistant being Adriaan Koek, and the naval commander Rear-Admiral Wolterbeek. Arrangements for the handing back of the settlement were begun, and proved to be a more lengthy business than was approved by the Dutch.

At Penang, commercial pressure was put on old Colonel John Alexander Bannerman, who had succeeded Petrie as Governor, to persuade him that a port in the vicinity of the Rhio archipelago must be found to offset the return of Malacca to the Dutch. Farquhar was therefore instructed by Bannerman to proceed to the eastward with a view to negotiating commercial treaties with Rhio, Lingga and Pontianak, Borneo. He was also to come to a similar arrangement with the state of Siak, Sumatra. Subsequently Farquhar claimed that he himself had initiated these moves.

On the excuse that he was going in search of an English woman carried off by pirates, Farquhar left Malacca on 19th July, successfully completed a commercial treaty with Siak, then sailed to Pontianak, dropping on the way messages at Rhio and Lingga that he would be returning there shortly. At Pontianak he found he had been forestalled by the Dutch. Boekholtz, the Dutch representative there, informed him that, as all Borneo had come under their control, no other nation could be allowed to enter into any agreement with the local chiefs. Elout's son, Cornelis Pieter Jacob, who was at Pontianak at that time, wrote to van der Capellen on 25th August:

". . . Farquhar said he wanted to go to Malacca but I have reason to believe he will rather go once more to Lingen [Lingga] and Rhio, where he (I believe) before he came here, has delivered letters in passing. He is alleged to be wanting to start establishments in Little Carimon or Great Carimon and Singapore, situated South of the Malay Peninsula."

This reference to Singapore is interesting.

Farquhar was ahead of the Dutch at Lingga and Rhio. The situation there needs explanation, for it had an important bearing on later events. The genealogical tree on page 751 may help to clarify it. These two archipelagoes, Lingga and Rhio, formed part of the kingdom of Johore. Some while before his death in 1812, Sultan Mahmud of Johore had given his eldest son, Husain Muhammad, known as Tunku Long,[1] permission to live and have his seat of government at Rhio. Tunku Long's younger half-brother, 'Abdu'l-Rahman,[2] was Raja of Lingga. When Sultan Mahmud had died, Tunku Long had been away visiting his relative, Bĕndahara Tun Ali, hereditary chief of Pahang, and in his absence his half-brother had, by Malay law, been placed on the throne of Johore as Regent. The man responsible for this was Raja Ja'far, a Bugis,[3] who held the office of Yam-tuan Muda ("Young Lord") of Rhio. His sister, Tunku Hamidah, had been one of the wives of Sultan Mahmud, and he (Ja'far) had brought up 'Abdu'l-Rahman.

Communication was possible only during the favourable monsoon, so it had been nearly a year before Tunku Long could claim possession of the throne. When he had finally arrived at Rhio, where Raja Ja'far was acting as viceroy under the self-given title of Raja Muda (Crown Prince), he had been prevented by that forceful personality from succeeding to the throne and, unable to gain his rights, had gone to live on the island of Bulang, where his distant cousin, Muhammad, was Engku Muda. Muhammad, whose daughter was married to Tunku Long, had refused the title of Temenggong of Singapore, wishing to be recognized as Raja Muda of Rhio. He was of the Malay family, though his mother, herself the daughter of a Malay princess, had had a Bugis father.

[1] Tunku (His Highness) Long (the eldest born).

[2] "Servant of the Merciful", i.e. God.

[3] The Bugis pedigree is long, and therefore not included in the genealogical tree. Ja'far was the sixth Yam-tuan Muda of Rhio, an office the Bugis had hectored the Malay Sultans into giving them.

On Farquhar's arrival at Lingga, he had a meeting with 'Abdu'l-Rahman and the other chiefs. During the course of the discussions, 'Abdu'l-Rahman openly stated that he was not the Sultan and was therefore not empowered to come to any arrangement with the British. It was also apparent that he had no wish to be Sultan. Farquhar was referred to the Raja Muda at Rhio as the appropriate authority, and it was with him that the commercial treaty was concluded.

The apparently successful outcome of his mission was reported by Farquhar to Penang and Calcutta, while both John Palmer and Raffles received personal letters from him concerning his activities. On the question of forming a British settlement south of Malacca, Farquhar was of the opinion that the Carimon[1] islands, lying at the southern end of the Straits of Malacca, about twenty miles from Singapore, would be most suitable. He described them in a letter to Calcutta on 31st August as a "complete key to the Straits of Singapoor, Dryon [Durian] and Soban[2]". He even went so far as to open negotiations, on his own authority, with the Raja Muda for the British occupation of the Carimons, which also were part of the kingdom of Johore, as a commercial centre. For this unusual show of initiative, he was duly rebuked by Bannerman, but the project remained dormant in his mind.

ii

Raffles had already come to the conclusion that in Sumatra he was losing a single-handed fight. He had issued his public protest to arouse opinion at home and force the hands of ministers whose support he must have, sooner or later, for final victory. But time must elapse before his protest could reach England, and as time was the essence of success against Dutch expansion, the Supreme Government must be induced to take action at once.

On his first arrival at Bencoolen he had notified Hastings to this effect and had sought permission to go to Calcutta should the necessity arise. To this he had received a very cordial reply dated 6th July 1918.

"I have the honour to acknowledge your letter and to offer my congratulations on your safe arrival. It was painful to me, that I had, in the course of my public duty, to express an opinion unfavourable to certain of your measures in Java. The disapprobation, as you would perceive, affected their prudence alone; on the other hand, no person could have felt more strongly than I did, your anxious and unwearied exertions for ameliorating the conditions of the native inhabitants under

[1] Usually spelt thus, though Kĕrimun is more correct. Other versions are Karimon and Karimun.

[2] This cannot be identified. Farquhar was probably referring to Bulang.

your sway. The procedure was no less recommended by wisdom than by benevolence; and the results have been highly creditable to the British Government. I request you to consider yourself at liberty to carry into execution your wish of visiting Bengal, whensoever your convenience and the state of affairs in the Island may afford an eligible opportunity. The means of rendering the settlement at Bencoolen more advantageous to the Honourable Company than it now appears to be are certainly more likely to be struck out in oral discussion."

On the strength of this, Raffles decided to go to Calcutta. Ships called at Bencoolen at very infrequent intervals and it was not until the end of August that the arrival of the brig *Udney* gave him the opportunity he so urgently desired.

"Sir Stamford", wrote Sophia in the *Memoir*, "embarked in a very small vessel, which had no better accommodation than one small cabin, with only a port-hole to admit air, where centipedes and scorpions roved about without interruption; but personal convenience was never considered by him if it interfered with duty, and no better opportunity was likely to occur. . . ."

From this it might be imagined that Raffles went alone. He was in fact accompanied by Sophia, who was expecting her second child in March, and her brother, William Hull, who was suffering seriously from malaria. If Sophia made only one reference to Olivia in the *Memoir*, she was almost as reticent concerning herself, and then only made modest mention of "the Editor".

After much searching of heart, it was decided to leave little Charlotte behind, in charge of the competent Mrs Grimes and under the watchful eyes of Travers and his wife.

The *Udney* left Bencoolen on 2nd September. In the Bay of Bengal she lost a mast, and thirty-six miles below Calcutta was stranded on a sandbank by a drunken pilot and nearly capsized—Calcutta's second unkindly reception of Raffles. The party was taken off by the agent, Archibald Ritchie, and sent up in another ship to Calcutta, where, on 29th September, Raffles was able to make a dignified landing under the salute due to his rank. William Hull was put on board a ship leaving for England.

It seems reasonably certain that Raffles had little expectation of winning Hastings over to an aggressive policy in Sumatra. The more essential object of his visit was to obtain authority to establish a British post at the southern entrance to the Straits of Malacca. The proposition had already been advocated by Penang, and for once he found himself in harmony, if only for a brief time, with the government of that island, which was no more sympathetic towards him than it had been in Petrie's day. Governor Bannerman was the father-in-law of Raffles' old antagonist, W. E. Phillips, who had been acting Governor of Penang on the arrival of the new establishment in 1805, and was still there.

Raffles' plan was twofold; first, a commercial treaty with Achin, at the northern entrance to the Straits, and secondly—and much more important—the acquisition of a southern post, his idea being similar to Farquhar's that it should be in the area of the Rhio archipelago. Farquhar suggested the Carimons. To Canning, Raffles had suggested Bintang, but there can be no doubt that Singapore was also in his mind. Lady Raffles states in the *Memoir* that he had fixed upon it before leaving England, and it was certainly his objective in his discussions with Hastings. He had first become aware of Singapore—*Singapura*, Lion City, or Tumasek, as it was once called—from his reading of Malay history. Long before Malacca, it had occupied a unique position as the great Malayan *entrepôt*—just such a position as he dreamed his new settlement would occupy. And it was characteristic of Raffles that in his political planning he loved to have a historic background for his actions. What could possibly appeal more strongly to Malay sentiment than the restoration of ancient Singapore to her old magnificence?

Elout junior's letter to van der Capellen of 25th August of that year is evidence that Farquhar also had Singapore in mind, but whether of his own conception or as a result of correspondence with Raffles it is hard to say. There is no other contemporary evidence that Singapore was in Farquhar's mind as most clearly it was in the mind of Raffles.

The meeting between Raffles and Hastings was cordial. Much had happened since the Java days. Raffles had been rehabilitated at home by the Court of Directors; had been allowed to retain the rank of Lieutenant-Governor; had been knighted by Hastings' old patron, the Prince Regent; had ceased to be an official of no consequence in a remote dependency; had become a man of position, the friend of many influential persons of the first rank.

So, on 16th October, Raffles was able to write to Marsden:

"You will be happy to hear that I have made my peace with the Marquess of Hastings and that His Lordship has at last acknowledged my exertions in Java in flattering terms. This was one object of my visit to Calcutta and on it depended in great measure the success of the others. I am now struggling hard to interest this Supreme Government in the Eastern Islands; and the measures taken by me at Palembang, &c, will I doubt not lead to the advantage of some defined line of policy being laid down for the future.

"With regard to the Dutch proceedings at Palembang, of which I hope you are ere this fully apprised, Lord Hastings has unequivocally declared that his mind is made up as to the moral turpitude of the transaction and that he considers this but as one of a course of measures directed in hostility to the British interests and name in the Eastern Seas. My dispatches are now under consideration and it is uncertain what may be the immediate result.

"There is but one opinion in regard to the manner in which our interests have been sacrificed by the transfer of Java, &c, and it is clear that the Government at home will be called upon from hence to interfere for the security of our trade; but in the meantime and pending the reference to Europe I fear that nothing decisive will be done. Lord Hastings is, I know, inclined to recommend our exchanging Bencoolen for Malacca and to make the Equator the limit. . . . They possess no information which can assist the decision in Europe; what they forward will be obtained from me; and I am not aware of any advantage which will arise from delaying a decision till their references arrive. Every day, every hour, that the Dutch are left to themselves, their influence increases and our difficulties will be proportionately increased."

However sympathetic Hastings may have been in conversation, he did not forget for a moment the definite instructions he had received in England that he was to avoid at all costs a quarrel with the Dutch in the East. Their feelings had already been aroused by the outrageous activities of their unscrupulous neighbour in Sumatra, and on learning of his public protest, they wrote from Batavia to Calcutta and to their own government. Their letter to Calcutta was dated 5th October. In it they did not limit their complaints to local troubles in Sumatra, but attached copies of letters written by Raffles to encourage the chiefs in Rhio, Pontianak and Bali to resist Dutch reoccupation. Farquhar in Malacca, they said, had also been requested by Raffles to decline to hand back that place, pending a general clarification of the Anglo-Dutch situation. In their anger, the Dutch, writing to their own government, included a paragraph charging Raffles with moral responsibility for the murder of their garrison at Palembang. Such an accusation, based on copies of letters supplied by ex-Sultan Badru'd-din, seems to have been a questionable weapon. That they themselves felt some delicacy should be exercised in the use of it is shown by its exclusion from the dispatch to Calcutta. Later, however, van der Capellen, writing to Hastings on 16th April 1820, did not hesitate to blame Raffles for the massacre. Hastings was not favourably impressed.

The Batavia dispatch to Holland concluded with an urgent plea that negotiations be reopened with the British Government for an exchange of colonies and a clear dividing line between their respective spheres of interest.

In their dispute with Raffles the Dutch had, from a legal standpoint, some good arguments on their side. In equity, their case was by no means so good. The spirit that had animated them on their return to Java was in no small degree responsible for the antagonism that had developed. It was not unnatural that Raffles should resent the Dutch attitude towards the British and their interests, considering all they had done for the Dutch. Moreover, Dutch pretensions went far beyond the intentions of the 1814 treaty. They now lay like an octopus across the route to China, with sensitive tentacles stretching out farther and farther to reach to any point where Britain looked like getting a foothold. It was, in any case, unreasonable to suppose that the victors in the Napoleonic wars, and the greatest maritime power in the world, would tolerate for ever exclusion from such a vast area, more particularly as Holland was quite incapable of absorbing within a measurable time an empire of that magnitude, or even controlling it. The power of the Dutch rested for the most part on small forces dominating local rulers. Of the hinterlands of those kingdoms they had little knowledge, and over much of it less control.

But Hastings had had his instructions: the Dutch were not to be provoked. On 10th October and again on 7th November he wrote to van der Capellen, disavowing the activities of Raffles in Sumatra. This must have been made known to Raffles, for he deemed it necessary to wrote to John Adam, at that time chief secretary to the Supreme Government:

"I . . . regret most deeply that I should have adopted any measures not in consonance with the wishes of His Lordship. His Lordship in Council may be assured that my proceedings will be entirely influenced by the orders which I have now received and that in all future communications with the agents of the Dutch Government the most conciliatory and amicable spirit shall be manifested."

He went on to explain that when he had been in England he had been led to suppose that his powers at Bencoolen would be greater than they were. For example, when asked if he would accept the lieutenant-governorship of Bencoolen, he had replied that he would, "provided the political agency in the Archipelago were attached, but not otherwise". After the decision of the Court had been passed:

". . . it was proposed to designate me Commissioner and it was considered that I might advantageously take up the charge of the British Interests where the local Government of Java had left off; it was subsequently agreed that I should take the title of Lieutenant-Governor, on which that of Commissioner became unnecessary."

He was always aware that the Residency of Fort Marlborough was dependent on Bengal, but:

". . . in returning to this country I had in view a more important duty and responsibility than under any circumstances could have been called for in the limited concerns of Bencoolen. I considered it the wish of the authorities in England that I should as far as possible check the

Dutch influence from extending beyond its due bounds, and I had reason to expect that I should receive detailed instructions to this effect."

The instructions when they had arrived, had not gone so far as he had expected.

". . . but yet they gave me the range of the Archipelago for which I had all along been desirous, and which I may indeed say was a condition of my appointment. . . . I left England under the full impression that I was not only Resident at Bencoolen but in fact Political Agent for the Malay States, on the same footing as Mr [Robert] Farquhar held that appointment as Lieutenant-Governor of Penang after the Peace of Amiens."

His measures at Bencoolen and his proceedings towards the Dutch had been dictated by emergency. As an explanation of his direct communications with England he attached a copy of the letter from the secretary of the East India Company dated 5th November 1817, which had stated: "It is highly desirable that the Court of Directors should receive early and constant communication of the proceedings of the Dutch and other European Nations, as well as the Americans, in the Eastern Archipelago."

Acceptance of his arguments were recorded in the reply from Adam dated 28th November.

". . . the explanation afforded by you of the circumstances under which you have maintained a correspondence with the Honourable Court of Directors and the Secret Committee is perfectly satisfactory to the Governor-General. . . ."

Which view London was later to repudiate with emphasis.

From Calcutta, instructions were sent to Bencoolen that Padang was to be handed back to the Dutch, that all contact with Palembang was to cease, and that the parties in the Musi river area and at Kalambayang were to be called in.

On the principal matter that had brought Raffles to Bengal, the outlook was more promising, Hastings being inclined to fall in with his suggestions for negotiating a commercial agreement with Achin and forming a British base at the southern end of the Straits of Malacca—this without obtaining the previous consent of the Court of Directors.

"Sir Stamford," were Hastings' parting words, "you may depend upon me."

Captain John Monckton Coombs of Penang was appointed Raffles' fellow commissioner in the matter of Achin. Raffles was to go first to Penang, where he would be joined by William Farquhar, who, if a new settlement was established, was to be put in charge of it, taking his instructions from Raffles.

"I have now to inform you", Raffles wrote to Marsden, "that it is now determined to keep the command of the Straits of Malacca by forming Establishments at Acheen and Rhio, and that I leave Calcutta in a fortnight as the agent to effect this important object. Acheen I conceive to be completely within our power, but the Dutch may be beforehand with us at Rhio."

The news that Raffles was in Calcutta reached Penang and caused a stir in official circles there. As was remarked in the *Prince of Wales's Island Gazette*:

"This visit, the object of which has not yet transpired, has given rise to much conjecture and speculation."

John Palmer, ever jealous for his old Penang friends, regarded the intrusion of Raffles at this stage of affairs with suspicion and resentment. Writing to Captain Coombs, he warned him of the projected commission in terms very unfriendly to Raffles.

"I was rejoiced to see by your letter of the 14th that you were likely to be at Penang in all the month; for I would fain have you prepared for the due reception of our Knight, if ever he contrive to get amongst you. But I am doing what I may to spike a too rapidly revolving, noisy and I think dangerous Wheel, and do not despair of freeing the green from its impertinent Intrusion. In a recent discussion with A. [Adam] I have ventured to assume that it were the very height of injustice to F. [Farquhar] if he remained in the Straits—as he ought to do—to foist a fresh man upon the fruits of his labour; and when in Truth all is accomplished that even the eminent Endowment of Sir Knight could by possibility effect, and that if a more signal Completion of his important Arrangements were indeed even necessary, the maturity of his Judgement, of his Experience and of his Character in every Sense of that emphatic word—better qualified him for definitive measures than *any* man in Asia.

"I had proceeded thus far when I was favoured by a call from Sir Knight, who stayed a couple of hours at my Desk musing pretty largely into all Details of projected measures. I may not have an Opportunity of forwarding this by an earlier Conveyance than that which will land him at Penang; but I give it a chance that you may escape by possibility the Danger of a Surprise. If no further vacillation destinguish [*sic*] our proceedings he carries instructions of his own Drafting, to form stable Connexions, political and commercial, where F. has already put his Seal and the object of his Visit appeared to be to ascertain my notion upon the nature of those Relations. It seemed to be settled that we should neither assume nor look for Sovereignty nor any sort of domination—but maintain the Rajahs in their Authority and under their respective Banners. Passes allow the freest Intercourse of Trade with all People; he suggested a doubt whether if our Flag flew, as it must, over our Factory, &c, Americans would not be precluded by the Convention from trading to Ports in Alliance with us, but I suggested that as the restrictive Clause was expressly designed to protect the Company's Monopoly on Sumatra, and which he had by their Authority relinquished, and as the effect of the restraint forced them into Dutch and Malay Ports, it might be competent to the Governor-General to grant Licenses to all Foreigners desirous of so trading; and that with respect to Sumatra the benefits of the Indulgence would be twofold—depressing our Rival whilst it aggrandized Ourselves. He is gone to dress a Letter to the Government on the Subject in order to the securing of naval co-operation in this salutary Policy. I gave more readily into this from public motives than from private you may conclude; for so long as we must stick to the barren side of Sumatra, I hoped to elevate Tappanooly at the Expense of Padang, and so paralyze the Station between the Influence of Bencoolen and Tappanooly—which you know has one great local Advantage over all the West Side of the Island. I had in view, however, to get the Knight out of your waters, for though I fear I may not *preclude* him, I trust I may shorten his Stay among you. Acheen is obviously of minor importance as to Time and Circumstance; and as I said to A. in my note of yesterday that anybody of fair Fame from Penang could as effectually as Solomon himself carry the Governor-General's Instructions into execution there, I thought the 'Minto' should be sent after you immediately. A. writes to me that he has in detail ample and luminous what F's Letter gave me in Abstract; and I expect an unreserved Communication on the Subject from him. But in fact I have the sum and substance of all F's important Achievements—for such they are—and I don't care a Straw for details. Sir Knight has had just such another Letter from F. and is to send it to me after getting it from the P.C. and I shall thence be able to descant largely in that quarter upon the value of F's happy and critical Services. At present I do not choose it should be known I hold its Counterpart, and perhaps (as I could indeed discover) something more fully from F. himself. I have hitherto suspected, and my Conference has not much weakened the Apprehension, that the Knight is netting out for himself an Empire East of yours, hoping that Banca, by purchase, or Commutation, may be the Seal of it, and Sumatra a Dependency. This last, unless an entire and exclusive Dominion, evidently will not satisfy his Ambition; nor even yield that Occupation which a restless Mind and Frame seem to exact; and especially as it does not allow of his glutting his resentment against the Dutch—which is, I think, quite a Principle in his Politics, if it is not in his nature. I should be inclined to retaliate a spice of this Gentleman's Behaviour towards you, if I did not fear some hazard of delay and all its evils, by making on this Stage of the Mission a Stand in favour of F. or rather your Governor's Authority, for his is the exclusive merit of putting an able and active Instrument in motion, and neither Justice nor Decorum should permit his title to be disputed, or disparaged. I could urge that two efficient measures of his Government prove his vigour and capacity, and render it incumbent on the Sup. Government to leave the Selection of these for their Completions solely to him. But I dread an interruption to what is going forward, reprehensible and unnecessary as the manner of proceeding is.

"Besides I know that there exists so vast a Superiority of Judgement at Penang over Sir K. that once within your Influence he will drop into his appropriate place. I have no wish to depreciate his Talent or fitness, and but for the undeserved and deliberate treatment you experienced from him, I should have respected the Knight more upon Acquaintance than previously; he has been either remarkably candid or remarkably artful in the readiest Acknowledgment of more than one instance of erroneous Policy in Java and Sumatra and as erroneous, views of things of which he had spoken in a tone of decision. He was disposed to be a little mysterious indeed with me after having repeatedly requested my Interposition but he frankly threw off his disguise as well as his reserve, almost in the same breath; and I believe conceals nothing that he thinks I wish to know. He is a kind hearted man, a little selfish in his views of Ambition and Policy—perhaps from a conviction that the whole range of Eastern Subjects does not require the Talent of more than one ordinary man—and that man he desires to be.

"If I can get back my very crude and hasty minute or review of Sir Stam. Sketches of Arrangements—you shall have it. It successfully exposed I think the fallacy of his Southern and Eastern Line of Connexion—abandoning the Straits of Sunda and all under his Influence—and pressed the immediate dominion of your Straits and the acquisition of a Footing at Rhio and Acheen. I can see no longer, and therefore bid you farewell."

Hastings wrote to the Secret Committee on 25th November:

"It is with much regret that we have found ourselves compelled to adopt a tone of censure on the conduct of Sir Stamford Raffles in the instances now under consideration, for though we conceive him to have misconstrued his powers and to have taken an erroneous view of the procedure proper to be held in these cares, we are fully persuaded that he was influenced by motives of unquestionable zeal for the interests of the Honourable Company and the nation. So far indeed have the proceedings now adverted to been from diminishing our general confidence in Sir Stamford Raffles that we have actually entrusted to him the conduct of an important service to the Eastward to which we shall have the honour to refer. . . .

"For the present we contemplate nothing beyond the consolidation of our engagements with the independent States of Rhio and Siack and their dependencies and the formation of a connexion with Acheen. No pretext can be offered by the Netherlandish authorities against this procedure and your Honourable Committee may be assured that our first object will be to avoid any misunderstanding, or even discussion, with that power which can have the remotest tendency to compromise the existing amity between the two States."

The instructions Raffles had received from Hastings were dated 28th November and were, as Palmer observed in his letter to Coombs, undoubtedly drafted by himself. They were signed by John Adam and ran as follows:

"HONOURABLE SIR,—In pursuance of the intention signified in my letter of the 10th of October, addressed to you and Captain Coombs, I have now the honour to communicate to you the instructions of the Governor-General in Council for the regulation of your proceedings in the execution of the separate duties which it is his Lordship's purpose to confide to your management, after the conclusion of the negotiations at Acheen.

"2. The proceedings of the Dutch Authorities in the Eastern Seas, as represented to this Government by your dispatches, and those of the Governor in Council of Prince of Wales's Island, leave no room to doubt that it is their policy, by possessing themselves of all the commanding Stations in that quarter, to extend their supremacy over the whole Archipelago. The success of this project would have the effect of completely excluding our shipping from the trade of the Eastern islands, except on the terms which the Dutch Authorities might impose, and would give them the entire command of the only channels for the direct trade between China and Europe, which, under circumstances easily supposeable [*sic*], without contemplating actual hostilities, would greatly impede the prosecution of that valuable commerce.

"3. Under these impressions it appears to the Governor-General in Council to be an object of essential importance to our political and commercial interests, to secure the free passage of the Straits of Malacca, the only channel left to us since the restitution of Java and the other Dutch possessions. It is chiefly with this view that the proposed arrangement at Acheen has been determined on without further reference to the Authorities at home; but the most material point to attain, and that which will indeed constitute the only effectual means of accomplishing the object of securing a free passage, is the establishment of a Station beyond Malacca, such as may command the southern entrance of those Straits.

"4. The Port of Rhio appears, from all the information before the Governor-General in Council, to possess the greatest advantages for this purpose. Its position, just beyond the entrance of the Straits, exactly in the track of shipping passing in or out of them, enables it effectually to command both the Straits of Malacca and of Sincapore. The harbour is capacious and well adapted for the safety and supply of shipping. The

Dutch possess no right, and have as yet stated no pretension to interfere with the independence of this state, which is generally acknowledged. The disposition of the native authorities to cultivate an intimate connexion with us, which has probably been strengthened by their apprehension of the designs of the Dutch, may be inferred from the alacrity with which they entered into the engagement, lately proposed to them by Major Farquhar, under the authority of the Government of Prince of Wales's Island, while that engagement offers the most favourable opening for improving and confirming our connexion with the Government of the country.

"5. The arrangements formed by Major Farquhar might indeed suffice for all our purposes, which are purely commercial, and quite unconnected with any views of political power or extension of territory, if there were any security for their permanency against the possible designs of the Dutch. But although those engagements provide for the freedom and security of our commercial interests, they do not go to the exclusion of the political ascendancy of the Dutch, which, if once established, would speedily be followed by the annihilation of the independence of the Native Government, and consequently of our commercial privileges. The recent proceedings of the Netherlandish authorities at Pontiana, as exhibited in Major Farquhar's report, form a strong ground for apprehension that they will not hesitate to employ their preponderant naval and military power, for the destruction of the independence of any of the Malay States, where they may wish to establish a control, and that no intercourse would be permitted between the States thus falling into their power and British subjects, excepting on the terms they might think fit to impose.

"6. The maintenance of our existing engagements, therefore, with the Chief of Rhio and other States in that quarter, as well as the more general objects adverted to in this dispatch, seem to point out the necessity of supporting the arrangements made with those States, by measures of a different character from what under other circumstances would have been necessary.

"7. Of these, as already observed, the improvement of our connexion with Rhio and the establishment, if practicable, with the consent of the Native Government of a British Post there, are the more likely to answer the object we have in view, without involving us in any discussions with the Netherlandish Power.

"8. In the event, therefore, of the Dutch not having preoccupied Rhio, and its being practicable to obtain the footing required by means of negotiations with the Native Chief, it is the desire of the Governor-General in Council that measures should be immediately taken for permanently establishing the British interests at that port, and his Lordship is pleased to confide the negotiations and arrangements directed to this object to your judgment and discretion.

"9. It is expressly to be understood, and it will be incumbent on you always to keep in mind, that the object in fixing upon a Post of this nature is not the extension of any territorial influence, but strictly limited to the occupation of an advantageous position for the protection of our commerce.

"10. Your familiarity with the nature and objects of the measures in contemplation, and your intimate acquaintance with the character of the people, render it superfluous to furnish you with any specific instructions regarding the mode of opening and conducting the negotiation.

"11. The precise nature of the arrangement to be concluded is also left to your judgment, governed by the general principles already stated. His Lordship in Council is assured that you will omit no effort to accomplish the object in view, in the manner most desirable for the security of our interests, and most satisfactory to the native authority. The long experience and peculiar qualifications of Major Farquhar, the late Resident at Malacca, and his late employment at Rhio and Lingen, eminently fit him for the command of the Post which it is desirable to establish and the local superintendence of our interests and affairs. Major Farquhar will accordingly be instructed to accompany you to Rhio, and, in the event of your concluding a satisfactory arrangement with the native authority, you will leave that officer at Rhio, under such instructions as circumstances may dictate, and consider yourself at liberty to proceed to Bencoolen, where your presence will be required. Whatever troops and stores may be necessary in the first instance, are to be furnished by the Governor in Council of Prince of Wales's Island, who will receive the instructions of the Governor-General in Council on the subject.

"12. In the arrangements contemplated by the Governor-General in Council, for the security of our interests in the Eastern Seas, and of which those now directed at Acheen and Rhio form the most important that can be effected under the authority of this Government, pending the references made to Europe, it is the intention and desire of his Lordship to consider Acheen, and all interests within the Straits of Malacca, under the immediate superintendence of the Government of Penang, and to place our relations with Rhio and Lingen, and the general management of our interests beyond the Straits of Malacca, under your immediate control as Lieutenant-Governor of Bencoolen. A communication to this effect has been made to the Government of Prince of Wales's Island, from whom you will receive the most cordial assistance and support in the execution of the measures confided to you.

"13. An application has been made to His Excellency, the Naval Commander-in-Chief, that a frigate may be appointed to proceed to

Prince of Wales's Island for the purpose of conveying you to Rhio and eventually to Bencoolen, and arrangements are in progress for permanently stationing two of the Company's cruisers to the Eastward. One of these will be available for the service of the Post to be established at Rhio, but to provide against any delay in its arrival, or in that of the frigate at Prince of Wales's Island, and to enable you to dismiss the surveying vessels as already directed, you are apprised that measures have been taken for engaging and equipping a vessel in this port, which will be at your disposal for the service of the present mission, and eventually for your conveyance to Fort Marlborough.

"14. Copies of the Treaties concluded by Major Farquhar with the Chiefs of Rhio, Lingen, and Siack, and of his dispatch to the Government of Prince of Wales's Island, are enclosed for your information. Siack being within the Straits, the further arrangements with that State will fall within the province of the Government of Prince of Wales's Island, but it is proper you should be apprised of our relations with it. Lingen is closely connected with Rhio, and you will, of course, follow up the Treaty concluded by Major Farquhar with the former, by such measures as may be requisite to form an attachment at Lingen, but this is a point which must be determined by further information and observation on the spot. A very limited establishment, at all events, will be sufficient.

"15. The allowances received by Major Farquhar, as Resident at Malacca, will constitute a proper scale of remuneration for the duties which it is now proposed to assign to him. You will fix provisionally, and subject to the confirmation of the Governor-General in Council, the other salaries and establishments that may be requisite for giving effect to the several measures now contemplated, and you will be sensible of the importance of attending to economy in all the arrangements now conditionally authorized.

"16. You will receive from the Persian Secretary, credentials to the Chiefs from the Governor-General, of which English drafts are herewith transmitted. You are already provided with suitable presents.

"17. These instructions are framed under an impression that the Dutch have not formed any establishment at Rhio. In the event of their having done so at the period of your arrival, you will, of course, abstain from all negotiation and collision, and observe the same line as is pointed out in the event of such an occurrence at Acheen.

"18. A copy of the letter addressed to the Government of Prince of Wales's Island by the Governor-General in Council on the subject of this dispatch, is enclosed for your information, and you will communicate immediately with Colonel Bannerman on all points connected with the present service."

A letter was addressed on the same day to Farquhar, congratulating him on the success of his mission to Rhio and ordering him, "to secure the continued benefit of your experience and talents", to accompany Raffles to Rhio, "with a view to your remaining in the local charge of the British interests in that quarter, under the general superintendence of the Lieutenant-Governor of Fort Marlborough".

Farquhar had returned to Malacca towards the end of October and had informed Governor Timmerman Thyssen by letter of his treaties with Rhio and Siak. To this he had received a reply to the effect that the Dutch maintained their right to control the territories of the chiefs of Rhio, Lingga and Johore, as dependents of the Dutch government at Malacca, and that they were not prepared to accept the arrangements made with the princes of Lingga and Rhio. "We will not permit either of them to cede one inch of ground to the English." Admiral Wolterbeek had wasted no time in setting sail for Rhio.

Farquhar had reported this to Penang, who passed on the information to Calcutta, but it did not reach there until after Raffles' departure. Then the Supreme Government advised Penang that no doubt Sir Stamford Raffles would abandon his proposed mission to the eastward and that the question of Dutch claims would now have to be referred to London. Some rumour of the Dutch attitude must, however, have gone ahead of the official communication from Penang, for on 5th December supplemental orders were issued to Raffles as follows:

"Since the Instructions contained in my letter of the 28th ultimo were presented, it has occurred to the Governor-General in Council, that in the event of the previous occupation of Rhio by the Dutch, or other circumstances, preventing the accomplishment of our views at that port and at Lingen, it might be expedient to endeavour to establish a connexion with the Sultan of Johor on the same footing as is now contemplated with Rhio and Lingen.

"2. The position of Johor renders it nearly, or perhaps entirely, as convenient a Post for our purpose as Rhio; but the imperfect information possessed by the Government, both of the local circumstances of the town and harbour and the condition and relations of the State of Johor, induce the Governor-General in Council to prefer a connexion with the Chief of Rhio, and his immediate superior, the Raja of Lingen, if it be practicable. For the same reason it will be incumbent on us, even if we find ourselves excluded from the latter, to act with caution and circumspection before we enter into any engagements with a State of which we know so little as Johor.

"3. It will be necessary therefore, in any event, to make a previous inquiry with a view to obtain correct information on the following points:

"1st. The local capabilities of Johor for a British port, such as we are desirous of establishing at the mouth of the Straits of Malacca; the extent and capacity of the harbour, means of supply, and other points of this nature.

"2nd. The actual political condition and relations of the State of Johor, the degree of independent authority exercised by the Chief—his power of maintaining any engagements which he may contract, his relations with other States, especially the Dutch settlement at Malacca, and the Government of Siam. There is some reason to think that the Dutch will claim authority over the State of Johor by virtue of some old engagements, and though it is possible the pretensions might be successfully combated, it will not be consistent with the policy or present views of the Governor-General in Council to raise a question of this sort with the Netherlandish Authorities. You are aware also of the considerations which make the Governor-General in Council reluctant to engage in any measure that would bring us into collision with the Government of Siam.

"4. In the event of our views at Rhio and Lingen being unattainable, and of the information you may procure concerning Johor being entirely satisfactory on the points above adverted to, you will be pleased to open a negotiation with the Chief of Johor, and carry into effect at that place an arrangement similar to the one at present contemplated at Rhio.

"5. In the contemplation of your having recourse to this measure, a letter has been addressed to the Chief of Johor by the Governor-General, and amended credentials comprehending that State have been prepared. You will receive both these documents from the Persian Secretary, and will make use of them according to your discretion in the case, and under the reservations stated in this letter."

Palmer wrote on 4th December to Farquhar:

"Your kind and interesting letter of the 11th October was by some accident perdue for several days; and did not reach me until I had the advantage of reading your other letter to Sir Stamford Raffles. I was delighted to find that your whole mission had not been abortive; although the invincible supineness of our rulers merits that we should be excluded from every place Eastward of Penang. I earnestly hope that Bannerman has instantly detached a force to protect and give consequence to a small civil establishment at Rhio and Lingen, Siac, &c, for on his Promptitude, Vigour and Determination rests everything we have to accomplish in our new relations of Policy and Commerce. Sir Stamford's mission is, I conclude, too late, either from what we have already done or (from what we have not done) what Mynheer will have done ere now. The vital importance of a Chain of Ports which would secure the Straits of Malacca to us in Peace and War seems not only never to have occurred to the Public Authorities at home, as in India, nor to have been respected when forced upon their notice; and I doubt not that between the expense and trouble of repairing that Negligence the public interests will groan for years to come. However, neither expense nor trouble should be your present or our future care, for either the Dutch or us must have the mastery of those Straits and we shall not escape both or either of those Evils by submission to their pretensions.

"I do hope, my Friend, that you will be employed to complete and perfect the only substantially important measures which have been attempted since the Peace with Holland in these Seas; and that even Sir Stamford may not be used to diminish the value of your previous services, and yet I can see nothing less in his mission Eastward of Penang unless it be the certain Provocation of Mynheer to terms or counter-action. For the worthy little statesman cannot budge a peg without exciting their Suspicion and inspiring their Terror and Hatred and Hostility. This, however, like the general tenour of my sentiments upon our Eastern Policy and arrangements, is little less than High Treason; and as I don't covert [*sic*] Hostility from great or little let my Reflections rest with yourself.

"As I had heard from Bernard,[1] and you mention him in your letter to Sir Stamford, I took action to back your suit—but most superfluously, to be sure, for he was too well inclined to run before your wishes—and am satisfied that if anything is available at Bencoolen Bernard is certain of obtaining it.

"I trust you will have proceeded to Penang early in November and have had a Supplication to hang on another year and see the Issue of Events, big as they are likely to be, to the Eastward. Your idea of taking Post on Little Carimon is admirable, and with your preliminary arrangements on one of your flanks and on the rear I should hope to see the British Flag easily exploring by Dryon and Syncapore just what Seas we like to visit, and perhaps procure our friends on Borneo some mitigation of their Dependence. I am satisfied that if the suggestions thrown out about Pontiana, years ago, had been listened to, Mynheer would never have thrust his Nose among that people. I should like to know how my Samba friend will fare, though I think he would not suffer a Dutch man even to save his life. I attach no vast importance as a merchant to these States, but in Policy we should uphold every one of them not stained with Blood and Pillage; and acquire the Domains by force or those who are; for by all means we should strengthen our own hands and weaken those of our plodding Rival when nothing but defeat ever diverts from his designs. Sir Stamford thinks of circumnavigating Sumatra and I predict that he can only accomplish the voyage in safety by being on a British frigate. I won't despair of seeing you again in India, for if I can I

[1] F. J. Bernard, Farquhar's son-in-law.

think of running down to Penang, &c. I am compelled, however, to take my leave of you now, and abruptly, God bless you."

Having got his instructions in their final shape and to his own satisfaction, Raffles wasted no time. H.C.C. *Nearchus* (Captain William Maxfield) was put at his disposal for himself, Sophia, who was near her time, and the rest of his party. H.C.C. *Minto*, a name of good omen, was detailed to accompany him with a small escort on board, and Lieut. J. S. Criddle in command.

To the Duchess of Somerset Raffles wrote:

"I have now accomplished the principal object of my visit to Bengal and propose embarking once more in the course of four or five days for the Eastern Islands, which I doubt not I shall find as fresh and as blooming as ever. I yet hope to be in time for the public good, but the policy of the Dutch and the unreserved terms of the Convention preclude me from being very sanguine. My own health remains much the same as when I left England and Lady Raffles is, if anything, better. Do you not pity poor Lady Raffles and think me very hard hearted to drag her about in her present state, but she will not remain from me and what can I do? We are now about three months without any news of our dear baby, so that you see we have our minor as well as major separations.

"I have begged Lady Raffles to give Your Grace an account of the Regal State of the Governor-General, which really surpasses all I had heard of it. I take down from hence a medical man of the name of Jack, who will be entrusted with the botanical part of my researches; and I have two Frenchmen, M. Diard and M. Duvausel, the former the pupil and the latter the stepson of Cuvier; so that in comparative anatomy I shall be strong. These three *savants* with a missionary clergyman, who takes charge of a printing press, form my equipment from Calcutta, so that I hope we may do something. . . . I have full powers to do all we can; and if anything is to be done I think I need not assure Your Grace that it shall be done—and quickly done."

It had been with the help of Dr Nathaniel Wallich, curator of the Botanic Gardens, that he had secured the services of that brilliant and delightful young botanist, Dr William Jack. Georges Cuvier, later Baron de Cuvier, was the eminent French anatomist. The "missionary clergyman" was Nathaniel Moore Ward of the Baptist Missionary Society, a nephew of William Ward, who had helped Carey to found the B.M.S. in Bengal.

The two ships left Calcutta on 7th December. It was quite characteristic of John Palmer that, notwithstanding his acid comments about Raffles in his letter to Coombs, he sent a very friendly note of farewell on that same day.

"My Dear Sir Stamford,—I drop you a line to express the hope of your amendment since you embarked; and that you will gratify me by a similar missive, confirming your recovery, when the pilot leaves you. I beg you to offer my respectful compliments to Lady Raffles with my wishes for the health and happiness of each of you."

The letter continued with this interesting remark:

"I think Koek has gone directly to Johore [from Malacca], as he could scarcely be necessary as a courier to the Admiral at Rhio, &c, and it might be of some weight in the Admiral's argument, if the Principal disavowed his agents or representatives. Conjecture, however, is impertinent, as you will know in 20 days the true posture of things throughout the Straits."

The exact meaning of this paragraph is obscure, but it seems to confirm that some information as to Admiral Wolterbeek's departure for Rhio had already reached Calcutta.

If any proof is needed of the place Raffles had in mind, it is to be found in his letter to Marsden, written "off the Sandheads" on 12th December.

"We are now on our way to the Eastward, in the hope of doing something, but I much fear the Dutch have hardly left us an inch of ground to stand upon. My attention is principally turned to Johore, and you must not be surprised if my next letter to you is dated from the site of the ancient city of Singapura."

He also dispatched a note to Jennings, the Resident at Bencoolen, requesting that the battalion there, which was about to be relieved, should proceed via the Strait of Sunda, where a ship would meet it with instructions.

iii

The two survey ships mentioned in the thirteenth paragraph of the instructions received by Raffles were the *Investigator* and the *Discovery*, the first commanded by Captain J. G. F. Crawford, who was working under the orders of the famous hydrographer, Captain Daniel Ross, F.R.S., in the *Discovery*. The two ships were about to begin a survey of the Straits of Malacca, and arrived at Malacca from the Portuguese island of Macao on 17th December, to find that William Farquhar had just handed over the settlement to the Dutch and, unaware of his new assignment, was preparing to depart for Europe on three years' leave. They sailed on the 23rd, the *Discovery* to begin operations, the *Investigator* to go on to Penang to collect stores, and also to escort Farquhar in the brig *Ganges*, which was owned and captained by his son-in-law, F. J. Bernard.

Captain Crawford had been recently married, and kept a diary so that he could report his doings fully to his wife. In it he recorded that on Christmas Day he was signalled to board the *Discovery* and there received the indents for the stores he was to collect in Penang. Captain Ross mentioned:

". . . an apprehension he entertained, from some conversation with Major Farquhar, that it was not unlikely that the Government or Sir Stamford Raffles (hourly expected from Calcutta) would endeavour to detain me for other services; recommending me, if this supposition was rightly conjectured, to fight strongly against any detention. His instructions to me are to quit with all dispatch, after procuring the supplies."

The *Investigator* reached Penang on the 29th. Crawford called on the Governor, Colonel Bannerman, describing him thus:

"He is in appearance a plain, old, little man, ruddy and hale. At first sight he might be taken for a man of 45. He must be near 60 years of age, as he was a Colonel on the Madras Establishment previous to his being in the Direction."

Two days later the *Nearchus* arrived at Penang after a voyage described by Dr Jack in a letter to Dr Wallich as long, tedious and uncomfortable. "Sir Stamford was very ill part of it."

The news that greeted them at Penang was that the Dutch had occupied Rhio. At first the Raja Muda had refused them admission, but finally he had been obliged to do so and had made a treaty with Admiral Wolterbeek on 26th November. The Temenggong of Singapore had also been asked to affix his seal. This he had declined to do, but had afterwards assented, on the understanding that he was not thereby to be held party to the treaty. Tunku Long, the legitimate sovereign, had not been summoned by the Raja Muda to the conference.

"By neglecting to occupy the place," Raffles sadly recorded, "we lost Rhio."

Of Farquhar Lady Raffles wrote in the *Memoir*:

"On reaching Penang he [Raffles] found that this officer had already engaged his passage to England, in a vessel which was to sail in a few days. Colonel[1] Farquhar was, however, prevailed upon to alter his arrangements."

It was a temporary measure. Farquhar would defer his furlough until the new settlement, should one be formed, was securely established. Bannerman considered that, by accepting this prospective appointment, Farquhar had "allowed himself to be seduced and made a party in Sir Stamford Raffles's proceedings".

On that last day of 1818 Captain Crawford was bidden to dinner at Suffolk, the Government House—"not kept in that order it was when we visited it in Mr Phillips' time"[2]—and here he met Raffles, whom he had last seen in Java.

"We sat down at about 5 p.m.," wrote Crawford, "the dinner having been kept back one hour for Lady Raffles, who resides with the Governors'

[1] He was promoted shortly after this date.

[2] Phillips, of course, was still at Penang, but not now acting Governor.

family. Before taking our seats, I was introduced to the Governor's daughters, one married, two spinsters, Lady Raffles and Mrs Burney by the old Colonel, who was skipping about the room with as much agility as a boy of 18, in highest glee. We dined in the Marble Hall, had the Governor on my right and his niece, Mrs Burney, on my left. . . .

"Sir Stamford, for this is the name he is recognized by, in consequence of a gentleman with a Portuguese Order (an Assistant Surgeon on the Madras Establishment, by name Sir Thomas Sevestre) being on board the same ship on leaving England, which gave umbrage to Lady Raffles to have a man of his low rank called 'Sir Thomas'. . . . He exposed himself greatly today, when speaking of his former chum Mr Phillips, by remarking 'He was a worthy good fellow,' qualified with this observation that he did not possess capacities sufficient to set the Thames on fire; continuing his address to the Governor after a short pause, 'Well, Colonel, you know I cannot be idle, I must always be doing something.' . . .

"His personal appearance is not so good as when at Java; a courtier in action, but I believe, he is an excellent worthy man, possessing great abilities, and of a bustling active disposition. In a confab. with Ross, it appears that Sir Stamford has opened the eyes of the Marquis of Hastings to the National loss that will be felt in not having a port to the eastward of Malacca, for the encouragement of our merchants to carry on a barter with the Malays, as the wily Dutch are forming treaties and placing flags on every spot to keep us out and the exorbitant duties now levied at Batavia and wherever their colours are flying is tantamount to a prohibition from shipping. . . .

". . . we intend establishing a factory at Acheen, Sir Stamford having credentials from the Marquis of Hastings constituting him his Representative and Agent amongst the Malay Chiefs. One bone of contention between him and the Penang Government is, the inhabitants of Acheen are in a state of insurrection, two Chiefs disputing their rights to the throne, and Captain Coombs was to be dispatched to give the balance in favour of one. Sir Stamford opposes this, and intends supporting the person obnoxious to the Penang Government, and, with the authority he bears, he no doubt will carry his point. It is supposed a reference will be made to the Supreme Government.

"Sir Stamford and Colonel Bannerman are both united in opinion as to the propriety of having a Settlement to the eastward of Malacca, as the Malay trade is blocked up from the English by prohibition. Sir Stamford, at the instigation of Major Farquhar, picks on the Carimons, the Colonel is for Sumatra, but by the instructions I carry for Ross from Government he is to comply, as far as our services will permit, with the wishes of Sir Stamford who directs us immediately to survey the Carimons. I certainly think that, as Sir Stamford has the two Bengal ships under his orders, either of them might be sent for that venture, instead of diverting the attention of the China Surveying Establishment from their present employment on the Sands. By our going southward we will lose time and impede the Survey of the Straits. Governor Bannerman has taken the 'Discovery' and 'Investigator' under his orders during the time we are to remain within the range of his Government."

This step had been taken by Bannerman at the request of Raffles.

The voyage from Calcutta had been Dr Jack's first experience of Raffles, and this was his first visit to Penang. His earliest letter to Wallich from there began with a series of exciting botanical discoveries and finished with his views on the official outlook at Penang and his own estimate of Raffles.

"There does not appear to be any cordiality here on the part of this Government, nor am I much surprised. For they cannot but feel how little and insignificant they are in comparison with the energy of Sir Stamford. I cannot express to you how much I am delighted with him. He is of the *real* sterling stamp and of that active and comprehensive mind that diffuses a portion of its energy all around. Even our two *savants* feel a little of the Promethean touch, without which—it is needless to say more. Twelve o'clock—so goodnight."

The atmosphere in Penang was certainly strained. Bannerman had protested to Calcutta against the proposed mission of Raffles to Achin, claiming that satisfactory arrangements had already been made and that the intervention of Raffles would weaken the status of the Penang government. Instead of discussing the problems of Achin and Rhio, Raffles and Bannerman entered into a lengthy exchange of notes, at first fairly friendly. Bannerman began by pointing out that as the Dutch had reacted so violently against Farquhar's treaties with Rhio and Lingga, he assumed that Raffles would now abandon that part of his mission. Should Raffles decide, however, to carry out his instructions, he would have "the most cordial and efficient assistance and co-operation from the Government of this Island". To this Raffles replied that the occupation of Rhio by the Dutch had been made by a subordinate authority, and he doubted if it would be consistent with our national character and interests to permit this infraction of our rights, which was also an attempt to lower British prestige with the Malays.

"The eyes of the whole Malayan race are turned upon us at this moment and, according as we may now act, will be their future opinion of our character and power. . . . It is true that under the policy the Dutch have now adopted, it may be difficult to find even an islet throughout the whole range of the Archipelago to which they will not lay claim, but while we refrain from collision in any spot where they have troops or a station, we may safely consider ourselves, in common with every Malay or Bugguese adventurer, entitled to a footing on any unoccupied territory in which we may have the advantage of a post and accommodation for troops. The Island of Singapura or the district of old Johore appear to me to possess peculiar and great advantages in this respect. The Carimon Islands have great advantages. . . ."

He further observed that the states of "Indragore [Indragiri] and Jambi" in Sumatra were still independent. The Dutch did not appear to have put in any claim there, and Indragore was the only channel of commerce with Menangkabau.

"A station at Indragore is not exactly what we want at the present moment, but driven as we may be out of almost every more commanding station, it may deserve attention."

He added that Major Farquhar agreed with his line of action, to which Bannerman replied that Farquhar's opinion "must be received with some reserve on the present occasion when his feelings are so highly gratified by the flattering manner in which the command of the proposed establishment has been offered to him". He expressed regret that Raffles should continue in his determination, warning him that the Penang government[1] would not now feel justified in detaching five hundred men to proceed with him; the most it could offer would be three hundred and forty. Apparently he also suggested that, under his instructions, Raffles should go first to Achin, for Raffles stated in a further letter that it was left to his discretion whether he should proceed first to Achin or not. He also mentioned that he understood that the whole strength of the relieving battalion, nearly twelve hundred men, would be at his disposal. Was he to take it that the reduced number now offered by Bannerman was an indication of his refusal to co-operate?

Bannerman replied on the same day that, according to the instructions of the Governor-General, as received in Penang as well as by Raffles, Achin was stated to be the first object of the mission. If Raffles possessed any instructions not received by the Penang government, he, Bannerman, would bow to such authority. In spite of having recorded his disapproval of Raffles' proposals, he had offered co-operation in the provision of stores and men, and he suggested that the correspondence might now cease.

The Colonel then relieved his feelings by a letter to John Adam. Having reported the arrival of Raffles at Penang, he emphasized that he had impressed on him the "utmost caution and circumspection" in the carrying out of his instructions.

"The Governor in Council has conceived that every motive of duty and policy combined to urge the strong remonstrances which have been

[1] Erskine supported Raffles; Phillips supported Bannerman, or more probably dominated him.

made to counteract the determined purpose expressed by Sir Stamford Raffles of proceeding in the first instance to the eastward in preference to undertaking the mission to Acheen, which is the primary object of his instructions."

With this dispatch, Bannerman forwarded a minute dealing with Raffles' suggestions. The first plan, the purchase of Bangka from the Dutch, Bannerman declared to be inspired by "views of personal ambition, I suspect, more than the cause of our national interest". It was as chimerical as it was impracticable. The second plan, to establish a post at Johore or in the Straits of Singapore would frustrate the object of the negotiations then proceeding in Europe.

"The period for preliminary negotiation with the Malay States is past. Malacca was an annual loss to the Government, and any station near Dutch influence is bound to prove a failure."

The only merit of the second plan was that it was open for adoption at any time in the future. If Raffles persisted in it—"and I fear my remonstrance will have little effect on his restless, enterprising and ambitious spirit"—Bannerman assumed that any settlement formed would fall naturally under the control of Penang. It was his opinion that the independence of Rhio could be obtained by negotiation with the Dutch.

Meanwhile Raffles was completing arrangements for the expedition to the east.

Chapter Twenty-two

THE FOUNDING OF SINGAPORE, 1819

i

BARON FAGEL, the Dutch ambassador in London, had obtained permission from his government to enter into negotiations for an Anglo-Dutch treaty of colonial partition, his somewhat optimistic proposal being to exchange the Dutch possessions in India for Bencoolen and Penang. After delay occasioned by Castlereagh's absence from England, a meeting was held on 31st December 1818, and, as Castlereagh was indisposed, the discussion took place in his house. To Fagel's surprise, the British Foreign Secretary appeared better informed about the activities of Raffles in Sumatra than might have been expected. A further meeting was held on 12th Janaury, when Castlereagh volunteered that both he and Canning disapproved of the political adventures of Raffles.

The very next day Raffles' protest of 12th August 1818 was published in the *British Press*, one of the lesser London dailies. This was copied on the 14th by the *Times*—"a real jingo paper", according to van der Kemp—the *Chronicle*, the *Advertiser*, the *Herald*, the *Post*, and even the strong Tory paper, the *Courier*. Most of the papers carried outspoken leaders.

Castlereagh was furious, as he frankly told Fagel.

"Je l'ai trouvé," wrote Fagel to The Hague, "aussi mécontent que je pouvais l'ètre moi-meme de cette nouvelle incartade du Sr. Raffles."

An immediate enquiry was instituted in London to ascertain what, if any, political authority had been given to Raffles. Thus Thomas Courtenay, secretary to the India Board of Control, wrote to Joseph Dart, secretary to the East India Company, on 21st January:

"Sir Thomas alludes in his correspondence with the Secret Committee to instructions received from the Court of Directors and to sentiments and intentions entertained by them respecting the Eastern Seas of which no trace is to be found in the letters from the Court to Sir Thomas Raffles which have been sent up to the Board for approbation. I am therefore directed by the Board to enquire whether the Court have knowledge of any circumstances which can in any way justify or account for these allusions of Sir Thomas Raffles.

"The style adopted by Sir Thomas Raffles in some of the papers already before the Court as well as the general tenor of his proceedings being calculated to countenance a belief that he had been invested with some public character on the part of the British Government in addition to that which belongs to him as Servant of the Company, the Board think it right to express their perfect confidence that no such character has been conferred on Sir Thomas Raffles by any department of His Majesty's Government."

This letter was accompanied by a memorandum, presented to Castlereagh by Fagel, of correspondence that had passed between Raffles and the Dutch government in Java.

Dart replied to Courtenay:

"The said memorandum has been referred to the consideration of the Committee of Correspondence and I have received the command of the Court to acquaint you . . . that no instructions have been given to Sir Thomas Raffles nor are there any on the records of the Company beyond what have been officially transmitted to the Board for approbation."

On 27th January, therefore, a letter was sent to India.

". . . We think it necessary to direct you to issue positive instructions to that officer [Raffles] that he on no account conclude any treaty or engagement on the part of His Majesty or of the Company with any native Prince or State without your special authority and sanction and that he do inform the Dutch authorities . . . that they are to address to you any communications which they may have to make . . . you will understand that in the proceedings reported in the dispatches of Sir Thomas Stamford Raffles and especially in all those in which he has assumed the character of a representative of the Government of His Britannic Majesty he has acted entirely without authority, and that although in consideration of the situation which he formerly held in Java he was complimented by the East India Company with the title of Lieutenant-Governor of Bencoolen, his proper functions are those only of the Company's commercial Resident at that factory. The tone of Sir Thomas Raffles' proceedings has induced us to take this opportunity . . . to make it clearly understood that it is to Your Lordship in Council and not to the subordinate functionary at Fort Marlborough that the care of the British interests in the Eastern Seas is committed."

On 1st February Lord Lansdowne, prompted probably by Raffles' friend, the Duke of Somerset, raised the protest in the House of Lords, and though Lord Bathurst, Secretary for the Colonies, stated categorically that Raffles was merely a commercial agent and had no political authority, the debate further stimulated interest in Dutch activities in the Indies.

As Raffles wrote later to the Duchess of Somerset, the British Government "would not like the agitation of the question but they ought to have been aware that it could not be avoided, and that however easy it may be in the Cabinet to sacrifice the best interests of the nation, there are spirits and voices engendered by the principles of our Constitution that will not remain quiet under it".

The British Government continued to set its face against entanglements in the East. Castlereagh told Fagel on 10th February that he had requested the Board of Control to instruct Raffles to remodel his conduct suitably to his role of commercial agent. Four days later, Fagel received a letter from Castlereagh stating that "the acts of Sir Thomas Raffles as alluded to by His Exc. will be entirely disavowed, that gentleman being merely a commercial agent, and not having been authorized to act politically in any manner whatsoever".

Courtenay wrote to Dart on 25th March:

"The Board have commanded me to observe . . . that the conclusion without any instruction or authority whatever by a gentleman in charge of a subordinate commercial factory of a treaty by which the British Government is bound in new engagements with a Native Prince of Sumatra [Menangkabau] appears to the Board to afford a fresh proof of the inconvenience that cannot fail to result from the continuance at Bencoolen of a person, however individually respectable, who has in so many instances overstepped the limits of his duty."

The Court of Directors informed Bengal on 12th May that Raffles had entirely mistaken the nature of his position.

"In addition to the circumstances to which the Secret Committee have referred, we have to express our particular disapprobation of the reference made by Sir Thomas Raffles (in his letter to the Vice-President in Council of the 6th July 1818) to the expression of wishes which he asserts to have been communicated to him by this Court before he left England, thereby implying that instructions were given to him independently. . . . We are quite at a loss to imagine to what Sir Thomas Raffles intends to refer, but he cannot be ignorant that instructions or intimations of opinion conveyed otherwise than in a regular dispatch are of no authority whatever. . . .

"With these impressions as to the late proceedings of Sir Thomas Raffles, although sensible of his zeal and talents, we cannot but entertain strong doubts whether he ought to continue to hold the situation in which he has so widely and inconveniently overstepped the limits of his authority."

The peculiar circumstances of Raffles' appointment to Bencoolen were not to be taken "as precluding you from appointing a successor to Sir Thomas Raffles if you shall view his conduct in the same light in which it appears to us, which we cannot doubt, unless any circumstances in extenuation of that conduct, with which we are not acquainted, shall have come to your knowledge".

At the end of this communication was the significant paragraph:

"While this dispatch has been in preparation the Secret Committee have communicated another letter addressed to them by Sir Thomas Raffles under date the 1st September 1818, announcing the conclusion of another treaty with the Sultan of Palembang. This fresh instance of the disposition of Sir Thos. Raffles to exceed his instructions and powers induces us to enforce more strongly your attention to the instructions in the preceding paras."

Three months before this stern epistle left London, the bustling little man who was the object of all these strictures had hoisted the Union Jack at Singapore.

ii

"You will immediately embark on the brig 'Ganges'," ran Raffles' instructions to Farquhar at Penang on 16th January 1819, "and proceed to the Straits of Singapore, communicating by the readiest means you have in your power with Captain Ross of the 'Discovery' who has been requested to await your arrival on the N.E. end of the Little Carimon in order to submit his surveys of those islands."

Pending further instructions, Farquhar was not to found any settlement on the Carimons.

"Having ascertained the capability of Singapore and its vicinity, and the result being satisfactory, you will make such arrangements for securing to us the eventual command of that important station as circumstances . . . may dictate."

Farquhar was then to proceed to Rhio, to discover the nature of the engagements entered into with the Dutch. If the Raja Muda should consider himself competent, the right to settle at Singapore or the Carimons should be obtained from him. The sanction of the Raja of Lingga should also be obtained. In addition, he was to investigate the political situation at Johore. Tunku Long, the legitimate chief, was understood to reside in the Straits and to be well disposed to the British. Having chosen the site for his post, Farquhar was to remain there and dispatch Lieutenant Crossley with his report.

"And until I am able personally to visit the spot you are authorized to engage whatever establishment, European or native, may be required, and I place the most confident reliance on your rendering the proposed Post tenable with the least delay possible."

At the same time he notified Adam of his plans.

". . . The Island of Singapore, independently of the straits and harbours of Johore which it both forms and commands, has on its Southern shores and by means of the several smaller islands which lie off it, excellent anchorage and smaller harbours, and seems in every respect most peculiarly adapted for our object. Its position in the Straits of Singapore is far more convenient and commanding than even Rhio, for our China trade passing down the Straits of Malacca, and every native vessel that sails through the Straits of Rhio must pass in sight of it.

"The town of Johore is in the main some distance up the river, the banks of which are said to be low, but on the score of salubrity there does not seem to be any objection to a Station at Singapore or on the opposite shores towards Point Romania [Rumenia] or another of the smaller islands which lie off this part of the coast.

"The larger harbour of Johore is declared by professional men whom I have consulted and by every Eastern trader of experience to whom I have been able to refer to be capacious and easily defensible and the British flag once hoisted, there would be no want of supplies to meet the immediate necessities of our establishment. There is considerable uncertainty as to the state of affairs at Johore.

"There does not appear to be any authority of importance at Johore; the legitimate heir to the title is a wanderer and was absent when the old Sultan died. According to custom the King could not be buried till his successor was invested with the title, but ultimately the King was buried and the second son being then at Lingen assumed the charge of that Island in the name of the Sultan of Johore but his authority apparently does not extend beyond Lingen. Major Farquhar has been ordered to proceed to the Carimon Islands and to the Eastward to investigate the possibility of a Settlement."

The *Ganges* was to be accompanied by the *Mercury* and the *Nearchus*, the first two carrying troops.

While these preparations were in progress, Raffles had given it out that the commissioners, Coombs and himself, would proceed without further delay to Achin, in accordance with the wishes of the Penang government. On 18th January, as soon as the three vessels had sailed, Bannerman wrote to Raffles:

". . . the moment has now arrived . . . to entreat you will stay proceedings and suspend the prosecution of your mission to Acheen, until a reply is made to some very important references I have had the honour to forward to the Governor-General."

Dr Jack gave an explanation of these tactics in a letter to Dr Wallich:

"I have already mentioned that I thought there was no cordiality on the part of this Government towards Sir Stamford, and you shall hear presently the length they have proceeded in their spirit of jealousy. You probably know that Sir Stamford left Bengal with a commission to settle the affair of Acheen where two rivals had been contending for power, and both are desirous of obtaining our aid and protection. He has also in view to make some settlement further to the Eastward, and as these are in fact the most important, he was anxious to make the easiest possible arrangement of the Acheen affairs in order to be more at liberty in proceeding with his plans.

"Expedition however forms no part of the political code of Penang.

Besides which there has been such a scene of intrigue and, I believe I may add, corruption going on here in regard to Acheen, that it is quite disgusting. Of the two rivals whose claims are to be decided, the one is legitimate king with whom the nobles quarrelled some time since, and whose power is insufficient to preserve peace. The other is the son of a Penang merchant [Sayid Husain] who appears to have no other claim than his father's immense wealth, and the support he has, God knows why, been receiving from this Government.

"You may easily imagine that the arrival of a man like Sir Stamford to clear up such a business as this, could not be welcomed by those whose schemes are likely to be overset by the event, and they accordingly determined to throw every possible obstacle in the way, and to try every scheme that *cunning* could suggest to defeat his objects and prevent if possible their own disgrace. It would be tiresome to relate to you the artifices, the meannesses they had recourse to in the pursuit of this object. Sufficient to say their conduct was disgraceful not only to their rank and situation, but to their character as men. But they had to do with a man too much their superior.

"Sir Stamford first intended to have gone to Bencoolen, on Lady Raffles' account, and to have returned to make the final arrangements. The intrigues that are going on here, however, have rendered the execution of that plan impossible, and he was at last obliged to determine on her remaining here and going himself over to Acheen. In the meantime, that his other plans might not be ultimately suspended during the delays of the Acheen business, he employed Major Farquhar to proceed on a mission down the Straits as, tho' very desirous of it, he could not go himself. Major Farquhar sailed on 18th, and he [Raffles] was to go in a few days after to Acheen.

"Now you must know that Sir Stamford had offered to the Governor that if he wished to make any reference to Bengal on the subject of Acheen, that he should delay his proceedings till the answer should arrive and in the meantime pursue his ulterior object. But the Governor [Bannerman] was just as averse to these other views, and wished if possible to prevent him accomplishing either, declined the offer in hopes by throwing obstacles in the way, to keep him idle here. He was afraid to take any decided step to prevent his going to Acheen till after Major Farquhar should have sailed, for fear he should go away on that expedition. But no sooner was Major Farquhar's ship out of the harbour, than he addressed to Sir Stamford the most urgent solicitations he would suspend all proceedings relative to Acheen till a reply should be received to important references that had already been made to Bengal. This I suppose was considered a master stroke of policy, but *respice finem*. The moment he received this, Sir Stamford took his resolution. Major Farquhar's ships

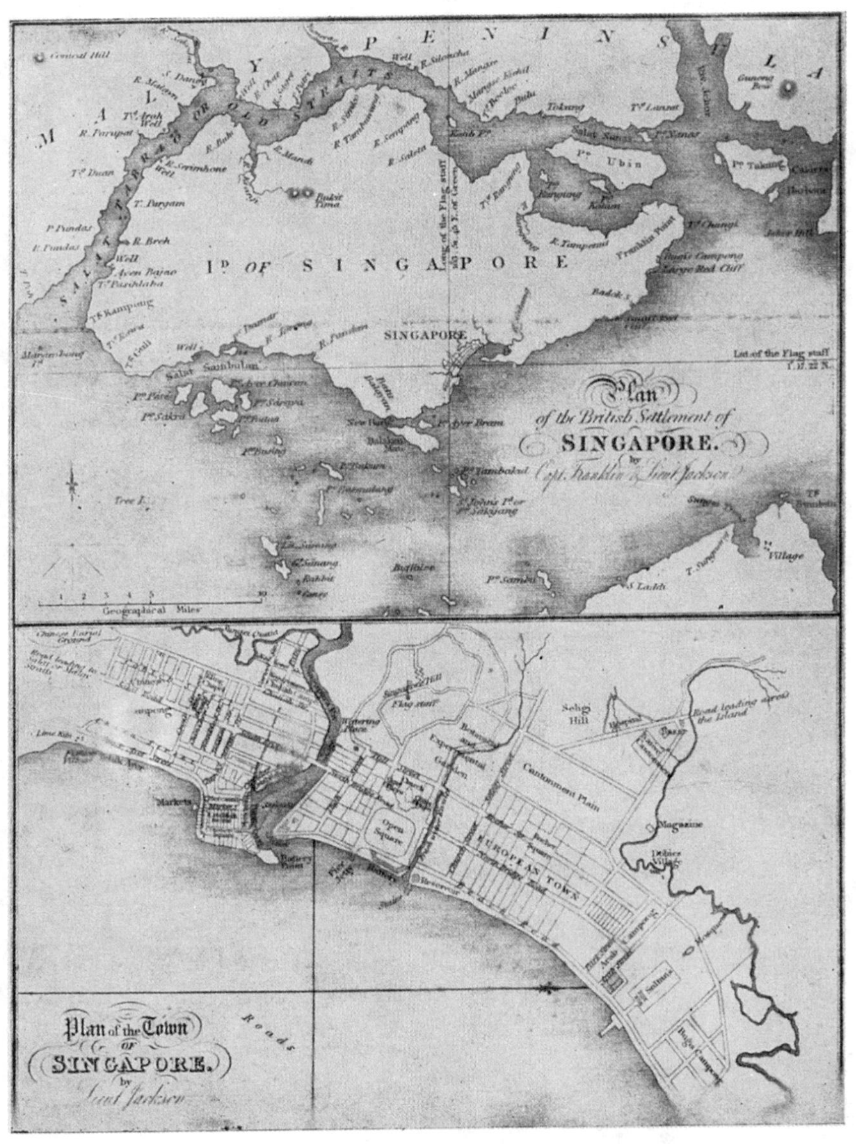

MAP OF SINGAPORE AND PLAN OF TOWN

Prepared by Captain Franklin and Lieutenant Jackson.

Reproduced from Crawfurd's "Journal of an Embassy to the Courts of Siam and Cochin China."

were but just outside the harbour and at anchor till next tide. He immediately dispatched intimation to them, ordered the ship in which he was to go to sea immediately and commenced sending everything on board. This was in the evening, and as soon as everything was arranged for his starting before daybreak next morning he wrote to the Governor to say that he had determined to meet his wishes, and comply with his request of suspending all proceedings relative to Acheen till the arrival of the expected reply, and had in consequence determined to sail next day to overtake Major Farquhar. . . . You may easily conceive the Governor's astonishment and disappointment at finding his schemes defeated, and falling into a snare of his own devising."

Bannerman had played right into Raffles' hands. After consulting Coombs as to the risk from a postponement of the mission to Achin, Raffles had written to Bannerman that, in view of the Governor's earnest entreaty, he now felt justified in meeting his wishes, more particularly as his services in the meantime could be advantageously employed in advancing the ulterior object of his mission.

"With a view to this latter object it is my intention to embark tomorrow on the 'Indiana', in the expectation of overtaking Major Farquhar. In availing myself of the opportunity thus afforded, I shall be enabled to exercise a more immediate and active superintendence over the object of his mission, while I may confidently calculate in returning to this port in time to proceed to Acheen, after affording the delay you earnestly desire."

He had seen to it that this letter reached Bannerman after he himself had sailed from Penang, leaving Sophia in the care of Dr Jack in a house he had taken. Coombs similarly only became aware, after he had gone, that his fellow commissioner was away in pursuit of Farquhar.

The names of the ships that comprised this historic expedition should be recorded. They were:

H.C.C. *Nearchus*	Captain William Maxfield
H.C.C. *Minto*	Lieut. J. S. Criddle
Ship *Mercury*	Captain J. R. Beaumont
Ship *Indiana*	Captain James Pearl
Brig *Ganges*	F. J. Bernard
Schooner *Enterprise*	Captain R. Harris

To this little fleet must be added the two survey ships, *Discovery* and *Investigator*, which were to join the expedition at the Carimons. The *Minto* went first to Pedir, Achin, to inform Jauhar al-Alam Shah[1], one of the two candidates for the throne, that Raffles would be visiting him later and that he must have nothing to do with the Dutch. This action of Raffles' was to come in for a good deal of criticism.

[1] *Jauhar al-Alam*: "Jewel of the World."

An explanation of the inclusion of *Indiana* is given by Crawford in his diary.

"The way of the transaction was a preconcerted plan. Sir Stamford, having power to do as he liked at Calcutta in the execution of the Company's pleasure, under the ruse arranged with a house of agency [John Palmer] to send the ship to Penang where he engaged to take her up on account of Government. This was readily assented to, trade being so extremely poor. To Captain Pearl, a naval officer, her Commander, it was hinted what admirable ballast bricks would make, and their dearness to the Eastward, no doubt of their answering a good speculation. He followed the suggestion. . . ."

Crawford had gone ahead of the expedition in the *Investigator* to rejoin Captain Ross, who had not been pleased at being placed under new orders. However, the two agreed "on the propriety of putting into execution the strenuous request of Sir Stamford, for he stated he would have a vessel to follow us up to the Carimons in a few days, to bring up Ross's report, whether it would be a good port for merchant vessels, and whether we might find a spot that a Town and a strong fort might be built for the defence of inhabitants and property".

The two survey vessels had arrived in Malacca roads on 17th January.

"The people of Malacca", wrote Crawford, "I find are not aware of the intention of Sir Stamford, but no doubt will soon gain indications of it from Penang, which certainly will annoy Governor Timmerman, who is very touchy on this subject, having previously a slight suspicion from some hints that fell from Major Farquhar that an attempt would be made for the establishment of an English Settlement among the Islands."

Timmerman Thyssen had more than a suspicion. Farquhar had informed him quite openly of British intentions. Nor can there have been much doubt in the minds of the local inhabitants. 'Abdullah recorded this opinion of the reason given out by Farquhar for his mission to Siak, Pontianak, Lingga and Rhio:

"It was not to look for a lady; that report was spread intentionally, so that people might not know that the English were going to search for a place to found a city."

The *Discovery* and *Investigator* reached the Carimons in the afternoon of 19th January, and the survey of the islands at once commenced. They lie about twenty miles from Singapore and are a familiar sight from there. Great Carimon is twelve miles long and five miles wide, with two peaked mountains in the centre, the higher being about two thousand feet high. The island is separated from Little Carimon by a deep and narrow gut. Little Carimon is two miles long, being dominated by a hill about five hundred feet high. Captain Crawford, after a superficial examination, came to the conclusion, as recorded in his diary, that the Carimons, while convenient for local shipping and as a port of call for Indiamen on their way to China, would require complete clearing before any produce could be grown, which he considered would be a very formidable undertaking. Moreover, there would be little shelter for the boats of shipping and for cargo to come off, as the two anchorages were completely exposed to one or other of the prevailing winds. Also the islands appeared to be hardly defensible against an enemy.

On 26th January two ships and a brig were sighted to the northward. The *Discovery* and *Investigator* weighed and proceeded to meet them. They proved to be the *Nearchus*, *Mercury* and *Ganges*.

"She sails ill," wrote Crawford of Bernard's brig, "and is dirty and uncomfortable."

As Raffles was expected soon in the *Indiana*, Farquhar persuaded Captain Ross to return to the Carimons. Next morning, parties went ashore to explore Great Carimon. Farquhar and Ross concentrated on the north side, while Crawford, Maxfield and Lieut. Henry Ralfe, the gunnery officer from the *Nearchus*, landed at the sandy bay. Being then high water, the tide had risen to the lower branches of the trees, and Crawford did not enjoy wading through water and mud up to his knees to get ashore. At dinner that night:

"Major Farquhar expressed himself delighted with this place and said that an excellent town possessing every mercantile convenience might be built, and he declared he would prefer it to any other spot. I believe no other person entertained the like sentiments of the goodness of the ground, and its exposed situation."

Had the original instructions by Raffles to Farquhar not survived, this comment would have been still more interesting in the light of the subsequent statement by Farquhar in his memorial to the East India Company.

"Having surveyed the Carimon Islands which did not afford advantages for the settlement, it was resolved to proceed to Johore but on the way at the suggestion of your Memorialist they stopped on 19[1] January at Singapore."

Dinner was hardly finished when the *Indiana* and the schooner *Enterprise* came to anchor. The whole party waited on Raffles, and in the evening he called a council, consisting of Farquhar, Ross and Maxfield, to discuss the Carimons. Crawford records that Captain Ross "pointed out on a chart a spot he considered more eligible in point of harbour, cleared of jungle and advantageous for trade to the north east of St John's Island which he had observed, on our passage to China, when it was agreed we should in the morning get under weigh and examine this port before deciding on any other".

Crawford could have put this better, but the decision reached is clear

[1] Should be 29.

enough. St John's is one of the little islands off the southern tip of the island of Singapore.

Early in the morning of 28th January the squadron sailed from the Carimons, and at four o'clock in the afternoon of the same day "anchored off the intended port of Singapore, near a fine sandy beach". No landing was made that day, but a deputation of natives came aboard. On being asked if the Dutch had attempted to exert their authority there, they replied that old Johore had long been deserted, and that the chief authority, the Temenggong, resided at Singapore, where no Dutch had ever been received. Raffles stated his intention of calling on the Temenggong. He landed with Farquhar next morning.

One eye-witness account has survived: that of Wa Hakim, who was fifteen years old.[1] Unlike Crawford's narrative, it was not recorded until very many years later.

"At the time when Tuan Raffles came, there were under one hundred small houses and huts at the mouth of the river; but the Raja's [Temenggong's] house was the only large one and it stood back from the river, between the sea and the river, near the obelisk.[2] About thirty families of Orang Laut[3] also lived in boats a little way up the river, at the wide part. About half the Orang Laut lived ashore and half in boats. . . . The place where the Orang Laut lived was called Kampong Temenggong, and it faced the river. There were a few Malays who lived near, their huts facing the sea. Our boat lay where the Master Attendant's Office now is. I myself was born in Singapore waters, and this settlement of Malays and Orang Laut was in existence in my earliest recollection. . . ."

All the accounts state that the island was uninhabited except for about five hundred Malays, most of them *orang laut* living in their boats. There were in addition, however, a number of small Chinese settlements inland, engaged in working gambier plantations.

"The men that lived in boats", continued Wa Hakim, "were the first to see Tuan Raffles coming. I remember the boat landing in the morning. There were two white men and a Sepoy in it. When they landed they went straight to the Temenggong's house. Tuan Raffles was there; he was a short man. I knew his appearance [i.e. subsequently]. Tuan Farquhar was there; he was taller than Tuan Raffles and he wore a helmet. The Sepoy carried a musket. They were entertained by the Temenggong, and he gave them rambutans and all kinds of fruit. I together with the Malays and Orang Laut followed them to the edge of the verandah. Tuan Raffles went into the centre of the house. About four o'clock in the afternoon, they came out and went on board again. . . ."

1 See bibliography, H. T. Haughton.
2 The Dalhousie monument.
3 "Men of the Sea"—sea gypsies.

The accounts all seem to agree that the first landing was made at the Singapore river, and this has been generally accepted. But there is a well-established Chinese tradition that the *locale* was not the Singapore river, but the Rochore river, farther to the east. The exact spot is not perhaps important—it was at one end or the other of the flat plain bounded by these two rivers.

Of their reception, Crawford wrote:

"Whatever the inmost sentiments of the Malays' hearts may have been, they received Sir Stamford with great cordiality and friendship, declaring that nothing could give them greater happiness than to be in alliance with the English, but stated that it did not rest with them but with higher authority, the Rajahs of Rhio and Lingen, who were the Sovereigns of this country."

Raffles had already determined to exploit the peculiar political situation in regard to the sultanate. From the Temenggong, Maharaja 'Abdu'l-Rahman,[1] he now sought confirmation of the facts. It seemed that the kingship of Singapore had descended through twenty-five sovereigns from the first Hindu prince who had established himself there. Later sultans had resided at Rhio or Lingga, exercising a certain control over those islands as also over Pahang and Johore. The Great Council of Johore consisted of four persons: the eldest son of the sultan; the Bĕndahara, chief of Pahang; the Temenggong, chief of Singapore and Johore proper; and the Indrabangra, whose title was now extinct. The second and third positions were filled, if possible, by the sons of the sultan. The Raja Muda of Rhio had only local jurisdiction. Before his death, Mahmud, the last sultan, had declared his eldest son, Tunku Long, as his successor, but, as we have seen, this had been prevented by the Raja Muda. Both the Temenggong of Singapore and the Bĕndahara of Pahang supported Tunku Long.

That same afternoon Major Farquhar sailed for Rhio with instructions to conciliate the Raja Muda. He travelled in the *Ganges*, with the *Nearchus* in company. The following day Raffles concluded a provisional treaty with the Temenggong, who, as we know, had seen the Java expedition of 1811 pass through the Straits of Singapore and had been duly impressed with the power of England. Under the treaty the English were authorized to establish a post, in return for which the Temenggong was to receive protection and an annual payment of 3,000 dollars. So long as the English remained to protect him, the Temenggong undertook to have no relations with any other nation. Pending final arrangements and a formal treaty with Tunku Long, troops and materials could be landed, and the Company's flag hoisted.

All that day and the next, troops were landed with their baggage,

[1] Not to be confused with the Raja of Lingga. See genealogocal tree, page 751.

and tents were pitched. Captain Ross commenced a survey of the harbour, while the *Indiana* made an attempt to get to Johore, "to ascertain", wrote Crawford, "the disposition of its Chief and the inhabitants regarding the British residing in their country". Wind and tide were against her, and she had to return.

"Where the tents are pitched," wrote Crawford, "the ground is level above one mile, partly cleared of the jungle, with a transparent fresh water brook or rivulet running through it. On the hill at the back of the principal village we learned that Sir Stamford had given instructions to have a fort built, and a bastion of about 12 or 16 guns on the point where the fresh water creek is. This spot of ground is the site of the very ancient city and fort of Singapore, whose sovereigns, upwards of a thousand years ago, gave laws to Java, Sumatra and their adjacent Islands and a great part of the Malay Peninsula. No remnants of its former grandeur exist, not the slightest vestige of it has ever been discovered. As for the strength of the fortifications, no remains are to be seen excepting by those possessing a fertile imagination and can trace the foundations or parts of earthen bastions in a mound of earth that lines the beach and winds round the margin of the creek. This place, once so great, once so powerful, is now a petty fishing village, until our coming here unknown in modern history or geography, for Sir Stamford found accounts of it in a very old Malay work. I sincerely hope that under these auspices of the English it will again revive to its former splendour."

These impressions were confirmed by John Crawfurd when he visited Singapore almost exactly three years later, on his way to Siam. He wrote on 3rd February 1822:

"I walked this morning round the walls and limits of the ancient town of Singapore, for such in reality had been the site of our modern settlement. It was bounded to the east by the sea, to the north by a wall, and to the west by a salt creek or inlet of the sea. The inclosed space is a plain, ending in a hill of considerable extent, and a hundred and fifty feet in height. The whole is a kind of triangle, of which the base is the sea-side, about a mile in length. The wall, which is about sixteen feet in breadth at its base, and at present about eight or nine feet in height, runs very near a mile from the sea coast to the base of the hill until it meets a salt marsh. As long as it continues in the plain, it is skirted by a little rivulet running at the foot of it, and forming a kind of moat; and where it attains the elevated side of the hill, there are apparent the remains of a dry ditch. On the western side, which extends from the termination of the wall to the sea, the distance, like that of the northern side, is very near a mile. This last has the natural and strong defence of a salt marsh, overflown at high water, and of a deep and broad creek. In the walls there are no traces of embrasures or loopholes; and neither on the sea-side, nor in that skirted by the creek, is there any appearance whatever of artificial defences."

To these two pictures can be added a little more detail. Singapore is the most northerly of the numerous islands that almost block the southern end of the Straits of Malacca, and lies about eighty miles north of the Equator. It nestles in a re-entrant of the southern coast of Johore and is separated from the mainland by Johore Strait—the old Straits of Singapore—about one mile wide for most of its length, but in places only three furlongs. At its greatest length from east to west, the island is about twenty-six miles, with a maximum depth of fourteen miles. The total area is about two hundred and twenty square miles, some seventy square miles larger than the Isle of Wight, which it resembles in general outline.

To quote once more from Crawfurd's *Embassy to Siam*:

"Viewed from a distance Singapore presents no marked elevation, but has the unvarying aspect of one continuous forest. The surface however is undulating, consisting generally of rounded hills of from 80 to 120 feet high, with narrow valleys, not above 15 or 20 feet above sea level. A chain of rather higher hills runs through the island from east to west, making the watershed in one direction to the north, and in the other to the south. The culminating point of the land is a hill, nearly in the centre of the island called *Bukit Timah*, that is 'tin hill', and this rises to the height of 519 feet above low water mark spring tides."

The island is not the same to-day as it was in the day of Crawford and Crawfurd. Apart from the almost complete clearing of the jungle, the area now comprising the city of Singapore has been vastly changed in its appearance by large reclamations along the water front. Whole hills have been tipped into the sea, and the line of the foreshore straightened out. At the time of the first settlement, the water front was far more irregular, and the bays were much deeper. The piece of level ground first occupied is now the Padang, but the flat stretch of clear land and sandy beach where Raffles first set foot extends to-day much farther seaward, and the curve of the bay has been largely flattened out.

Raffles wrote to Marsden on the last day of January:

"Here I am at Singapore, true to my word, and in the enjoyment of all the pleasure which a footing on such classic ground must inspire. . . . Most certainly the Dutch never had a Factory in the Island of Singapore; and it does not appear to me that their recent arrangements with a subordinate authority at Rhio can or ought to interfere with our permanent establishment here. I have, however, a violent opposition to surmount on the part of the Government of Penang. . . . This, therefore, will probably be my last attempt. If I am deserted now, I must fain return to Bencoolen, and become philosopher. . . ."

Tunku Long arrived on 1st February. There are two accounts of how he came there, neither source entirely reliable. The first was from the mouth of Wa Hakim:

"Batin Sapi, an Orang Laut, went to bring Tunku Long from Bulang. I think he was away four days. Batin Sapi came back first and then Tunku Long came. The English had been some days ashore and had made atap [palm-leafed thatched] houses when Batin Sapi went to fetch Tunku Long. When Tunku Long came, Tuan Raffles was living ashore in an atap house. They had a discussion first in the Temenggong's house and afterwards in Tuan Raffles' house in Padang Senar."

Mr W. H. Read has pointed out the extreme improbability of an *orang laut* being sent to fetch Malay royalty. We can assume that Batin Sapi, if he went at all, was merely a member, though perhaps the leading member, of the crew.

The second account is by our old friend, 'Abdullah of the *Hikayat*. It is only second-hand, for he did not arrive at Singapore until four months after the original landing. According to him, the messenger was Raja Embong, a kinsman of Tunku Long.

"He embarked . . . in a small boat and set sail for Rhio with instructions to fetch Tunkoo Long 'by hook or by crook' even if he had 'only one shirt to his back'."

'Abdullah goes on to tell how Tunku Long, on hearing the news, was terrified that he would be seized by the Dutch. He gave out that he was going fishing, then set out to do so, having made a secret arrangement with a friend to provision another boat and meet him at sea, so that he could continue to Singapore.

Whatever the true version, Crawford was able to write:

". . . a Rajah, as if dropped from the clouds, made his appearance in the village, declaring himself the lawful Sovereign of the whole of the territories extending from Lingen and Johore to Mount Muar near Malacca: and his uncle, the Rajah of Rhio and a young brother, the Rajah of Lingen had dispossessed him of his rights and property and usurped the throne of his father, the former placing the latter on it. A question was put to the Rajah and the natives of the village who they considered their lawful Sovereign and without hesitation they declared in favour of this man, and confirmed his story. . . ."

The claim now appeared sufficiently good for Raffles to feel that a treaty would give an indisputable title. Tunku Long, for his part, was frankly scared. He had never met Raffles before, though he did know Farquhar, having visited him at Malacca to complain of the loss of his inheritance. He must have heard of him, however, and was apprehensive. But Raffles had a way of his own with the Malays.

"Mr Raffles", recorded 'Abdullah, "then began to speak, smiling with infinite charm and nodding his head in deference, his words sweet as a sea of honey. Not only the hearts of men but the very stones themselves would have melted on hearing his words, spoken in dulcet tones, gentle enough to banish every anxiety and suspicion which might linger still in the innermost recesses of the human mind . . . as men of a sudden see the full moon shining in all its lustre on the fourteenth day of the month, so was the honesty and sincerity of Mr Raffles apparent to Tunkoo Long."

'Abdullah was not present and here relied on the account of others, or perhaps merely drew on his imagination, yet Raffles' preliminary discourse had its effect. He and Tunku Long withdrew for a private talk, during which details of the treaty were quickly arranged. Tunku Long was acknowledged as Sultan of Johore, with the title of Sultan Husain Muhammad Shah, to ensure the continuance of which dignity, he himself suggested the immediate massacre of all the Dutch at Rhio.

During the first three days of February, the survey of the anchorage continued.

"As we explore the harbour," wrote Crawford, "the more we value its goodness in affording safe, elastic, stiff holding ground and on a nearer approach to the land the bottom gently shelving to a beach of fine white sand."

The bricks bought from Captain Pearl were landed from the *Indiana*, whereby he "has deducted an excellent percentage by taking advantage of the market".

In the afternoon of 3rd February the *Nearchus* and *Ganges* returned from Rhio. Captain Maxfield gave Crawford an account of the trip.

"Maxfield informed me that the Major landed at Rhio, Malay town, with great ceremony accompanied by an honorary guard of about 40 European soldiers and sailors, and all the gentlemen on board the ships. The Dutch were alarmed at so formidable an appearance and were extremely polite, personally paying their respects to the Major, coming across the water for that purpose. As their force is so small (not more than 50 men) they hold the tenure of their rights on a slender thread from the well-known character and disposition of the Malay, and hearing of our landing at Singapore with justified alarm. . . .

"Major Farquhar proposed to the Rajah to renew the contract made a few months ago that the English should be treated in his territory equal to the most favoured nation, and requested permission to allow us to colonize Singapore. These proposals he met with coldness of demeanour (the Dutch being present) stating that he could not with honour or propriety do so, for a late treaty he formed with the Dutch was to maintain their influence over his and his nephew's (the Sultan of Lingen) territories, and further he had stipulated he would neither sanction the English or any other nation to have any factories within his jurisdiction; excepting the town of Johore or the Carimon which he reserved free from any contract and in consideration of the goodwill and esteem he had for the English. They had his warmest approbation to settle there, but he disapproved of our landing at Singapore and his word was pledged to the Java Government to keep us out of the Straits of Singapore and consequently he could not forfeit it or suffer the harmony he lived in with the Dutch to be broken. The Major, perceiving nothing favourable could result from prolonging the audience, rose to take his departure.

"Then the Rajah displayed the nature of the Malay character by inviting him into a private apartment, securing the door against intrusion and leaving the Dutch and English gentlemen to amuse themselves, the former displaying uneasiness and sulky fits of spleen, to the great amusement of the English spectators. The Major, after having thus been closeted for upwards of two hours, retired to the ships, and when on board he related the discourse he had had with the Rajah to the following purport in which this Chief evinced a decided partiality to our cause by proposing that a strong force be sent to assist him in defence of his country against the Dutch. Then he would throw off the trammels of their power, whom he reprobated and represented as cruel and tyrannical tax gatherers, and it would afford him the greatest happiness for us to keep Singapore, advising us by no means to allow the Dutch to seize it and although outwardly he must disapprove of the measure he would privately aid and assist us all in his power for the improvement of the place. He further stated that he had a delicate game to play as he dreaded both the power and the inclination of the Hollanders to injure him and he informed the Major it was necessary for him officially to protest against Sir Stamford's proceedings to the Java Government."

Raffles believed in ceremony, and though not much was possible in the circumstances, what could be done to mark the occasion and bring home its significance to the Malay audience was done. We are again indebted to Captain Crawford for a description of the proceedings.

"5th Feb.: At a late hour received notes from Captain [Lieutenant] Crossley, Sir Stamford's Secretary, inviting the Commanders and all the gentlemen belonging to the Ships, to be on shore the following day, as spectators to the signing and sealing of the Treaty between Sir Stamford Raffles and the Sultan, and requesting salutes royal to be fired from each Ship on the occasion.

"6th Feb.: The day set in with delightful fine weather, breakfasted with Major Farquhar in the 'Ganges' then repaired to the 'Investigator' and dressed ship. Proceeded to the shore accompanied by Messrs Armstrong and Crighton. At noon we all mustered round our Chief, making a decent show of about 30 gentlemen. The Ships being decorated, flags, boats, all clean and fine, serene weather, formed a pleasing picture, and must have an imposing effect on the minds of the inhabitants. On shore some field pieces were mounted, the artillery and seapoys drawn up under arms. Eight field officers and a great many private tents pitched, and the seapoy village, all gave an animating and lively sensation to my feelings, the buzzing noise, the apparent busy employment of individuals and consequential importance of others, the pretended apathy of a few, the variety of remarks, all combined to afford me a fund of amusement. In one of the tents a cold collation was provided, another was fitted up in 'State'. Chairs were placed for Sir Stamford, Major Farquhar, the Sultan, the heir apparent (his eldest son) and the Tomagan (which title is similar to our vice-roys or governors of a town). These chairs, the ground, and from the door of the tent for about 100 feet on the banks of the river were lined with scarlet broadcloth.

"At 1.0 p.m. the Sultan, on leaving the palace, fired 3 guns. This led into an error the Ships which commenced firing royal salutes, instead of, as was intended, to take up the guns fired by the artillery. The Sultan was escorted by a military guard, making a respectable appearance, their dress is rather uniform, pikes decorated with stained hair and feathers, flags white and red, the standard carried before his person was one of the last colour. His habitments were gaudy silks, inelegantly put on, his chest was exposed displaying a disgusting breast and stomach, and the nihility of his countenance did not impress on the minds of the European spectators any respect. Our troops formed lines on each side of the red carpet and presented arms on his passing between them. At the entrance of the tent he was received by Sir Stamford, who led him to the chair on his right hand, the Tomagan sitting on the Major's right hand.

"On presentation of the preliminary articles, the seapoys fired three volleys. Then Sir Stamford presented his commission from the Marquis of Hastings, a Malay translation was read by the Sultan's secretary (the best dressed man among them, a scarlet loose coat over a silk gown, a handsome cruse [kris], the coat ornamented with gold lace) in a loud voice to the inhabitants (Malays and Chinese), who had surrounded the tent and squatted on their hams, behaving throughout the ceremony with respectful decency and silence.

"The treaty was read in English by Captain Crossley, for the edification of the Europeans, English, Dutch, French and Danes, individuals of each nationality being present. Then it was signed and sealed by Sir Stamford on the part of the East India Company, and was sealed by his Malay secretary, with the seals of state belonging to the Sultan and Tomagan (Malay princes never signing). . . . Three copies of this Treaty of alliance were made out, one for the Governor-General in India, one for the Resident of Singapore (Major Farquhar) and the other for the Sultan. . . .

"After the ceremony of signing and sealing was over, presents were given, consisting of opium, arms, and woollens of a scarlet colour. During the whole of the ceremony the vulgarity of the Sultan's expression, the want of expression and the perspiration running down his face, combined with the wicked and dastardly proposal he made a few days ago, for the murder of the Dutch at Rhio, raised in the feelings of the English spectators a horrible and disgusting loathing of his person, and several in pretty audible whispers, expressing these thoughts on the occasion sufficiently loud for Sir Stamford to hear, and in which sensation I suspect he inwardly accorded. The Tomagan had a countenance more of dark cunning with some sparks of duplicity than otherwise, if I might be allowed to form an opinion of his heart from the index of his face; his certainly hard expression marked him to be fit for treasons, stratagems, war.

"We then proceeded to a bank lining the beach, where chairs were provided for the official parties on the left flank of the artillery. On these being seated, the Sultan's secretary directed a Malay to hoist the Union (which had been hauled down for the purpose), the seapoys fired a volley on the Sultan's taking his seat, and on the Flag being displayed a Royal Salute was fired by the artillery and repeated by the shipping. Then we repaired to the banquetting tent; after the Sultan was seated, the principal Malays sat down promiscuously with the English, and a few royal bumpers were quaffed off with 3 times 3, and a degree of jollity and fun went forward. . . . The party soon broke up and each returned to their respective homes about 4 p.m. leaving the Major on shore in the official position of Commandant. As Sir Stamford quitted the beach I proposed and, after a little demur it was acceded to by the party, to give him three cheers, in which the Malays joined with spirit; it was, of course, repeated by the crews of the boats. . . ."

That night Raffles gave a dinner party on board and was very attentive to Ross and Crawford. He "smoothed Ross's pride a little by rising and drinking his health". Radin Rana Dipura, who had visited England with Raffles, was also at the party. He was now a lieutenant in one of the local regiments at Bencoolen. His father had sworn him to everlasting hatred of the Dutch.

The treaty was signed by Raffles as "Agent to the Most Noble the Governor-General with the States of Rhio, Lingin and Johor" against the seal of the East India Company. It was sealed also by the Sultan and the Temenggong, and was dated 6th February 1819, which is now the accepted date for the founding of Singapore. At one time there was some confusion arising from Raffles having referred, in his *Statement of Services*, which he submitted to the Company in 1824, to his landing at Singapore on 29th February. Apart from there having been no such date in 1819, it is clear that February was a slip of the pen. Mr C. B. Buckley subsequently discovered a copy of the treaty in the Johore archives, thus settling the point once and for all. There was, in fact, all the time another copy in the India Office.

The terms of the treaty are quoted as follows in Buckley's *Anecdotal History of Old Times in Singapore*. After a description of the high contracting parties, there followed these nine articles:

"Article 1st

The preliminary articles of agreement entered into on the 30th January 1819, by the Honourable Sir Stamford Raffles on the part of the English East India Company; and by Datoo[1] Tummungung Sree Maharajah Abdul Rahman Chief of Singapoora and its dependencies for himself and for Sultan Hussein Mahummud Shah Sultan of Johore is hereby approved, ratified and confirmed by His Highness the aforesaid Sultan Hussein Mahummud Shah.

"Article 2nd

In furtherance of the objects contemplated in the said preliminary agreement; and in compensation of any and all the advantages which may be foregone now and hereafter by His Highness Hussein Mahummud Shah, Sultan of Johore, in consequence of the stipulations of this treaty; the Honourable English East India Company agree and engage to pay to His Aforesaid Highness the sum of Spanish dollars five thousand annually; for and during the time that the said Company may by virtue of this treaty maintain a factory or factories on any part of His Highness's hereditary dominions; and the said Company further agrees to afford their protection to His Highness Aforesaid as long as he may continue to reside in the immediate vicinity of the places subject to their authority. It is, however, clearly explained to and understood by His Highness that the English Government in entering into this alliance and in thus engaging to afford protection to His Highness is to be considered in no way bound to interfere with the internal politics of his States or engaged to assert or maintain the authority of His Highness by force of arms.

"Article 3rd

His Highness Datoo Tummungung Sree Maharajah Abdul Rahman Chief of Singapoora and its dependencies having by preliminary articles of agreement entered into on the 30th January 1819 granted his full permission to the Honourable East India Company to establish a factory or factories at Singapoora or on any other part of His Highness's dominions; and the said Company having in recompense and in return for the said grant settled on His Highness the yearly sum of Spanish dollars three thousand and having received His Highness into their alliance and

[1] Dato', datok. See glossary.

protection all and every part of the said preliminary request is hereby confirmed.

"Article 4th

His Highness the Sultan Hussein Mahummud Shah Sultan of Johore and His Highness Datoo Tummungung Sree Maharajah Abdul Rahman of Singapoora engage and agree to aid and assist the Honourable English East India Company against all enemies that may assail the factory or factories of the said Company established or to be established in the dominions of Their Said Highnesses respectively.

"Article 5th

His Highness the Sultan Hussein Mahummud Shah Sultan of Johore and His Highness Datoo Tummungung Sree Maharajah Abdul Rahman of Singapoora agree, promise and bind themselves, their heirs and successors that for as long time as the Honourable English East India Company shall continue to hold a factory or factories on any part of the dominions subject to the authority of Their Highnesses Aforesaid and shall continue to afford to Their Highnesses support and protection, they Their Said Highnesses will not enter into any treaty with any other nation and will not admit or consent to the settlement in any part of their dominions of any other power European or American.

"Article 6th

All persons belonging to the English factory or factories or who shall hereafter desire to place themselves under the protection of its flag shall be duly registered and considered as subjects to British authority.

"Article 7th

The mode of administering justice to the native population shall be subject to future discussion and arrangement between the contracting parties as this will necessarily in a great measure depend on the laws and usages of the various tribes who may be expected to settle in the vicinity of the English factory.

"Article 8th

The port of Singapoora is to be considered under the immediate protection and subject to the regulation of the British authorities.

"Article 9th

With regard to the duties which it may hereafter be deemed necessary to levy on goods, merchandise, boats or vessels, His Highness Datoo Tummungung Sree Maharajah Abdul Rahman is to be entitled to a moiety or full half of all the amount collected from native vessels. The expense of the port and the collection of duties to be defrayed by the British Government.

iii

To make public the English occupation of Singapore, Raffles issued the following proclamation:

"A Treaty having been this day concluded between the British Government and the native authorities, and a British Establishment having been in consequence founded at Singapore, the Honourable Sir T. S. Raffles, Lieutenant-Governor of Bencoolen and its dependencies, Agent to the Governor-General, is pleased to certify the appointment by the Supreme Government of Major William Farquhar of the Madras Engineers to be Resident, and to command the troops at Singapore and its dependencies, and all persons are hereby directed to obey Major Farquhar accordingly. It is further notified that the Residency of Singapore has been placed under the Government of Fort Marlborough and is to be considered a dependency thereof; of which all persons concerned are desired to take notice.

"Dated at Singapore this 6th day of February 1819."

His memorandum of instructions to Farquhar bore the same date and ran as follows:

"Herewith I have the honour to transmit to you one of the copies of the Treaty this day concluded between the Honourable The East India Company and Their Highnesses The Sultan of Johore and The Tummungung of Singapore and its dependencies.

"2. As the object contemplated by the Most Noble the Governor-General in Council, namely the establishment of a Settlement beyond Malacca, and commanding the southern extreme of the Straits, has thus been substantially accomplished, I proceed to give you the following general instructions for the regulation of your conduct in the execution of the duties you will have to perform as Resident and Commandant at the Station which has been established.

"3. As you have been present at and assisted in the previous negotiations and are fully apprised of the political relations existing between the States in the immediate vicinity of this Island, it is only necessary for me to direct your particular attention to the high importance of avoiding all measures which can be construed into an interference with any of the States where the authority of His Netherlands Majesty may be established. Whatever opinion may be formed with regard to the justice or nature of the proceedings of the Dutch authorities in these Seas, it is not consistent with the views of His Lordship in Council to agitate the discussion of them in this country, and a station having been obtained which is properly situated for securing the free passage of the Straits and for protecting and extending the commerce and enterprise both of the British and of the native merchants, all questions of this nature will necessarily await the decision of the higher Authorities in Europe.

"4. It is impossible, however, that the object of our Establishment at Singapore can be misunderstood or disregarded either by the Dutch or the native authorities; and while the former may be expected to watch with jealousy the progress of a Settlement which must check the further extension of their influence throughout these Seas, the latter will hear with satisfaction the foundation and the rise of a British Establishment in the centrical and commanding situation once occupied by the capital of the most powerful Malayan Empire then existing in the East; and the prospect which it affords them of the continuance, improvement and security of the commercial relations by which their interests have been so long identified with those of the British Merchant. It is from the prevalence of their feeling among the natives and the consequences which might possibly arise from it that I am desirous of impressing on your mind the necessity of extreme caution and delicacy not only in all communications which you may be obliged to have with the subject of any power under the immediate influence of the Dutch, but also in the intercourse with the free and independent tribes who may resort to the port of Singapore for the purposes of commerce or for protection and alliance. The offer which is understood to have been made to the Sultan by the Bugguese is a sufficient proof that in all communication regarding the proceedings of the Netherlands Government we should carefully guard against the expression of any sentiments of dislike or discontent, however justly these feelings may be incited, lest our motives be misconstrued not only by the Dutch but by the natives themselves.

"5. With regard, however, to those States which have not yet fallen under their authority, it is justifiable and necessary that you exert your influence to preserve their existing state of independence. If this independence can be maintained without the presence of an English authority it would be preferable as we are not desirous of extending our Stations; but as from the usual events [outcome] of the Dutch policy the occupation of Tringana [Trengganu] and the extension of their views to Siam may be reasonably apprehended, and a very limited establishment may become ultimately necessary. It is at all events of importance to cultivate the friendship of these Powers and to establish a friendly intercourse with them; and as the recent application from the Sultan of Tringana for a small supply of arms affords a favourable opportunity of advancing towards these projects you will avail yourself of the first opportunity to comply with his request.

"6. A similar line of policy in relation to the States of Pahang and of Lingin would be conducive to the maintenance of the influence and just weight which the British Nation ought properly to possess in these Seas.

As it is my intention to return to this Island after the completion of the arrangements at Acheen, I shall then be able to avail myself of the information you may have collected in the intervening period relevant to the political state of Borneo Proper, Indragiri and Jambi. In the meantime it is probable that the knowledge of our establishment at this Station will have considerable weight in preventing these Powers from falling under the influence of the Dutch.

"7. With reference to the native authorities residing under our immediate protection, it is only necessary to direct your attention to the conditions of the Treaty concluded with these Chiefs; which it will be incumbent on you to fulfil under any circumstances that may arise in a manner consistent with the character and dignity of the British Government. In the event of any question of importance being agitated by the Dutch Government at Batavia or the authorities subordinate to it, you will refrain from entering into any discussion that can be properly avoided and refer to the Authority under which you act.

"8. To enable you to conduct the civil duties of the Station with efficiency, I have appointed Lieutenant Crossley your assistant; and thereafter will conduct the details of the Pay Department, Stores and Commissariat with such other duties as you may think proper to direct. The allowances for your assistant being fixed at Spanish Dollars 400 per month subject to the confirmation of the Supreme Government.

"9. As the services of Lieutenant Crossley as my Acting Secretary will be for some time required under my immediate authority, Mr Garling of the Bencoolen Establishment will officiate until his return. In the event of it being necessary for you to leave the Station or of any accident depriving the Company of your services, your assistant is appointed to succeed to the temporary charge until further orders.

"10. Mr Bernard has also been appointed to take charge provisionally of the duties of the port as Acting Master Attendant and Marine Storekeeper, and in consideration of the other duties that may be required of this Department and the general services which this officer may be required to perform he is allowed provisionally to draw a monthly salary of 300 Dollars per month.

"11. As the convenience and accommodation of the port is an object of considerable importance, you will direct your early attention to it and to the formation of good watering places for the shipping. You will also be pleased to establish a careful and steady European at St John's [Island] with a boat and small crew for the purpose of boarding all square rigged vessels passing through the Straits and of communicating with you, whether by schooner or by a small canoe as you may find most advisable.

"12. It is not necessary at present to subject the trade of the port to any duties—it is yet inconsiderable; and it would be impolitic to incur the risk of obstructing its advancement by any measure of this nature.

"13. In determining the extent and nature of the works immediately necessary, the defence and port of the Station, my judgment has been directed in a great measure by your professional skill and experience. With this advantage and from a careful survey of the coast by Captain Ross aided by my own personal inspection of the nature of the ground in the vicinity of the settlement, I have no hesitation in conveying to you my authority for constructing the following works with the least delay practicable. On the hill overlooking the settlement and commanding it and a considerable proportion of the anchorage, a small fort or a commodious block-house on the principle which I have already described to you capable of mounting eight or ten twelve pounders and of containing a magazine of brick or stone together with a barrack for the permanent residence of thirty European artillery and for the temporary accommodation of the rest of the garrison in case of emergency. Along the coast in the vicinity of the Settlement one or two strong batteries for the protection of the shipping—and at Sandy Point a redoubt and to the East of it a strong battery for the same purpose. The entrenchment of the cantonment by lines and a palisade as soon as labour can be spared from works of more immediate importance.

"14. These defences together with a Martello tower at Deep Water Point which it is my intention to recommend to the Supreme Government will in my judgment render the Settlement capable of entertaining a good defence. The principle on which works were charged for at Malacca is to be considered as applicable to this Station and it is unnecessary for me to urge you the necessity of confining the cost of these works within the narrowest limits possible. As the construction of them however will necessarily demand a greater proportion of care and superintendence than the performance of your other duties will permit you to devote to them, I have appointed Lieutenant Ralfe of the Bengal Artillery to be Assistant Engineer. This officer will likewise have charge of the Ordnance and Military Stores and for the duties attendant on both these appointments conjoined I have fixed a salary of Spanish Dollars 200 per month to commence from the first instant subject to the confirmation of the Supreme Government.

"15. As you will require the aid of a Staff Officer to conduct the duties of the garrison, I have thought proper to authorize the appointment of a Cantonment Assistant on the same allowance as lately authorized at Malacca. As this officer may be considered your personal staff I shall not make any permanent arrangement regarding it and have appointed Lieutenant Dow to the temporary performance of its duties.

"16. The indent for ordnance and military stores which you have handed to me shall be transmitted to Bengal without delay and I request you will lose no time in the erection of storehouses for their reception. An application for the number and description of the troops which you recommend to form the garrison of the Residency will accompany the indent together with an application for provisions equal to their supply for twelve or fifteen months.

"BUILDINGS

"17. I should not think myself justified at the present moment in authorizing an erection for the accommodation of the Chief Authority but I shall take an early opportunity of recommending the adoption of this measure or in the event of the Supreme Government declining to authorize it the grant if a monthly allowance sufficient to compensate you for the inconveniences to which in the infancy of the Settlement the Resident is necessarily liable. The storehouse for the Commissariat Department is at present of indispensable necessity; and you will accordingly be pleased to erect a house of this description of such materials as can be procured and as soon as you may find practicable. A magazine built of such materials for the military stores would be subjected to some risk; and I therefore confide to your professional judgment the adoption of such measures for their security as you may judge most expedient in the present circumstances.

"18. For a very short period it may be necessary to retain the brig 'Ganges' as a store vessel but I rely on your discharging her the moment her services can be dispensed with. In the event of your adopting this arrangement you will be pleased immediately to trans-ship to that vessel the public property now on board the H.C. Hired Ship 'Mercury', whose charter expires on the 24th instant, previously to which you will accordingly be pleased to discharge her from the public service. You will inform the Commander that I am entirely satisfied with his conduct while he was under my authority and that as tonnage will probably be required to convey troops and stores from Prince of Wales Island I shall be happy in the event of his early arrival at that port to consider his request for the further employment of his ship to be entitled to some consideration.

"19. You are already apprised that the H.C. Ship 'Nearchus' has been put under your orders and the services of the schooner 'Enterprise' will be also available by you during the remainder of the period of two months for which she was engaged.

"ACCOUNTS

"20. The accounts of the Residency are those which deal with the receipt and disbursement of the public money. These are principally—

"No. 1 An Account Particulars of Military Disbursements in which every military abstract and disbursement is clearly entered.

"No. 2 A General Account Particulars which will comprise the particulars of every disbursement of whatever nature and containing also under the head of 'Military Establishments' a correct copy of No. 1, and

"No. 3 A General Treasury Account showing on the one side the general amount of the disbursements made on each particular account or head; and on the other the balance which remained on the first of the month together with all the sums which may be received during the course of it.

"21. The accounts of Commissariat can at present be arranged according to the established form. They cannot, however, be kept with correctness by Mr Garling; and I shall take care to procure and forward from Penang the necessary forms under which the First Assistant will probably be able to arrange them on his taking charge of his appointment. You will, of course, exercise a strict superintendence over this Department, no disbursements from which are to be made without your authority, and you will be pleased to examine the accounts rendered to you previously to transmitting them to Fort Marlborough.

"22. A quarterly account of expenditure and remains of military stores will be transmitted to me. You will also be pleased to forward the usual return to the Presidency of Fort William [Calcutta] agreeably to the regulations of the Service.

"23. It does not occur to me that there is any other point of importance on which it is necessary at present to give you any instructions. I shall probably return to this Residency after a short absence, and if in the meantime any important matters should occur which I have not anticipated in this letter I have the satisfaction afforded me by a perfect reliance on your knowledge, zeal and advancement of protection of the honour and interests of our Country moderated by the prudence and judgment which the infancy of our present establishment so particularly demands."

Raffles left in the *Indiana* on 7th February, nine days after landing there. Thus, in so short a period, was Singapore founded.

Claims have been advanced by Farquhar, and by others on behalf of Captain Ross, that the selection of Singapore should be credited to the one or the other. Farquhar could fairly assert that his mind was working on parallel lines with Raffles', though the Carimon Islands were his particular choice. Captain Ross, at the conference at the Carimons, undoubtedly pointed out to Raffles that the harbour of Singapore was a most suitable spot, quite unaware, we may suppose, that he was preaching to the converted. The existence of the island was common knowledge. It was well known to the Dutch, who had had many dealings with Johore, and had in their very early days (1609) considered making their chief settlement there. As late as 1808 Abraham Couperus, former Dutch

Governor of Malacca, had advised the Java government that Singapore was much to be preferred to Malacca.

Captain Alexander Hamilton wrote in his *New Account of East India*:

"In anno 1703 I called at Johore on my way to China and he (the Prince of Johore) treated me very kindly and made me a present of the island of Singapore; but I told him it could be of no use to a private person, though a proper place for a company to settle a colony on, lying in the centre of trade, and being accommodated with good rivers and safe harbours; so conveniently situated that all winds served shipping to go out and come into those rivers."

John Crawfurd, quoting this in his *Embassy to Siam*, adds:

"This remarkable description, however, was neither known to the founders, nor to anyone else at the time."

The second part of this statement is certainly incorrect and probably the first also. Hamilton's account appeared in Milburn's *Oriental Commerce*, published in 1813, which, dealing as it did with all the ports and countries in which the East India Company was interested, would surely have been read by Raffles, that ardent collector of books about the East. If he was not personally acquainted with Milburn, he had known enough about him to cause him to be elected Honorary Associate of the Batavian Society.

As for Farquhar and Ross, let each have his fair share of personal credit. But the real inspiration and the original selection belong to Raffles, and it would be difficult to imagine that, had there been no Raffles, there would have been any Singapore.

Chapter Twenty-three

PENANG, ACHIN AND SINGAPORE, 1819

i

IT was not until 31st January that Travers at Bencoolen received the first letter written to him by Raffles from Calcutta—that is, nearly five months after the *Udney* had left Bencoolen. This is a good example of how bad were the communications in those days between India and its dependencies farther east, particularly Bencoolen. In this letter Raffles had written enthusiastically of his talks with Hastings, but Travers was somewhat mystified as to what success Raffles had in fact achieved, for by the same mail came official instructions for Padang to be handed back to the Dutch and for the troops in the neighbourhood of Palembang to be recalled. These posts had cost valuable lives, including W. H. Hayes and Lieut. Johnson, and their withdrawal was regarded locally with great relief, even though these instructions from India seemed like a surrender to Dutch pretensions in Sumatra. Except from a scientific point of view, Raffles' journey to Menangkabau had consequently proved valueless. It is interesting to speculate, nevertheless, how far the subsequent history of Sumatra might have been changed had Raffles been allowed to retain Padang and develop British influence in the valuable and productive area of the Padang highlands.

In Batavia there was jubilation on the receipt of the dispatch from Calcutta in which Hastings disavowed the activities of Raffles in Sumatra; its terms exceeded anything van der Capellen had dared to hope. He was now in full charge as Governor-General, the Commission General having been dissolved on 16th January. Elout and Buijskes had left Batavia on the 28th, but there was still time to catch their ship at Anjer, the little fortress town on the Strait of Sunda. So van der Capellen, in the highest of spirits, sent Elout a copy of the splendid news he was reporting to Falck at home. This is what he wrote to Falck:

"Two days before the departure of Elout and Buijskes we received a pleasing letter from Calcutta. Nothing could conclude our proceedings in a more agreeable way than the receipt of that letter, the contents of which have surpassed my expectation. I had hardly imagined that the Bengal Government, without consulting the higher authorities in Europe, would have disapproved so positively of the behaviour of Sir Raffles and would express this so plainly. This news has generally effected a very agreeable sensation and contributes not a little to respect for Dutch authority, as already the retreating of the English under Captain Salmond from Palembang, the occupation of our former possessions in this archipelago, the existence in these seas of a respectable navy seem to have brought about with the native princes an idea that the authority of our European neighbours in this part of the world has declined in the same proportion as ours, which for a few years vanished completely, has increased."

He could not know that at this moment when he wrote so joyfully to his Colonial Minister, Raffles, who, report had said, was on his way to Achin, was actually in Singapore. Disillusion was soon to follow.

The news was received first at Malacca. To protect themselves from trouble with the Dutch, the Temenggong of Singapore and the new Sultan of Johore wrote highly diplomatic letters to Malacca and Rhio respectively. The Temenggong addressed himself to Adriaan Koek at Malacca as follows:

"Be it known to our friend that while we were living at Singapore nine vessels suddenly arrived, namely seven ships, one *kura-kura*[1] and one ketch. All of us who were at Singapore were very much startled. At last the chiefs landed and paid us a visit; they were Mr Raffles and Mr Farquhar. The latter went on to Rhio; but the former remained at Singapore and informing us that he intended to remain there proceeded to land his men and stores. We were powerless to say anything, and could neither send word to Malacca at that moment nor to Rhio.

"Just at this juncture Tunkoo Long arrived at Singapore from Rhio having heard that a number of ships had arrived at Singapore and being anxious about his son whom he came to take away. As soon as he came, he had a meeting with Mr Raffles, who forthwith laid hold of him and made him Raja, installing him as Sultan at Singapore. All this we make known to our friend. At this present time the English are establishing themselves at Singapore and are making a *loji* [factory] and so we inform our friend, assuring him at the same time that we in no way separate ourselves from the Dutch. As it was with us at the beginning so it shall be to the end as long as there are a sun and a moon."

The letter to Rhio from Tunku Long was to this effect:

"I have to inform you that the Raja of Johore came to me one night in the middle of the night and announced that there were a great many ships at Singapore and the numerous soldiers and quantities of stores were being landed. I was a good deal surprised at this news and not a little anxious and uneasy on account of my son who was there. Without taking thought of what I was doing I set off the very same night. I completely lost my head and never thought of letting you know of my departure.

"When I reached Singapore I went to see Mr Raffles who immediately

[1] A type of small ship, now obsolete.

laid hold of me and would not let me go again but insisted on making me a Raja of the title of Sultan. There was nothing else for me to do and I had to comply with what he proposed, but I pointed out I was under the [Dutch] Company. Thereupon he gave me a sealed document of appointment. These things I make known to you and I ask for your pardon and forgiveness; for it is in you that I trust for I regard you as my Father in this world and the next, and I have in no wise acted against you or abandoned you. However, Raffles has directed me to bring to Singapore the women and children of my family and I am now ordering Raja Shaban to take them there together with any property of mine."

When Captains Ross and Crawford put in at Malacca on 9th February, they found Timmerman Thyssen in an angry mood.

"He had shown himself extremely indignant over the Singapore affair and had allowed hasty and intemperate words to break out. He talks of proceeding to the new settlement with an armed force and bringing back Major Farquhar in chains."

Drastic orders had been issued to prevent any of the Malays going to Singapore, while some of Farquhar's servants, who had endeavoured to rejoin him, had been arrested and put in gaol. At dinner with the two British captains, the Governor made only one reference to Singapore. This was when he turned to Ross to drink his health and "declared that the King of Holland ought to confer on him the Order of Merit for discovering a port of such excellence as Singapore".

Clearly his Excellency did not imagine that the island would remain long in British hands.

Raffles arrived at Penang on 13th February to complete his second task: the new treaty with Achin. But before he could leave, there were letters to be written. First in importance was the official dispatch to India. This, addressed to John Adam, was a long document and much of it was merely a recapitulation of facts already set down in these pages. *Inter alia*, he expressed himself completely satisfied with the validity of the arrangements made.

"It is true that the treaty concluded by Major Farquhar, the agent of the Penang Government, was with the Raja Mooda . . . but it does not invalidate the claim of the rightful Prince. . . . The Dutch possess no authority by virtue of the new Treaty concluded with the Raja Mooda even to exercise any power or to establish any settlement either at Pahang, Lingen or elsewhere and in short have no pretensions to derive even from the vizier to any other possession than that at Rhio. . . .

"The occupation of Singapore destroys the political importance of Malacca . . . it paralyses all plans for the exclusion of our commerce and influence with the Malay States . . . the spell is broken and one independent Post under our Flag may be sufficient to prevent the reappearance of the system of exclusive monopoly which the Dutch once exercised in these Seas and would willingly re-establish. . . ."

The same day—13th February—he wrote to Bannerman, asking that two companies of sepoys be dispatched to Singapore to complete the garrison.

One might have thought that the Penang authorities, for all their personal dislike of Raffles, would have regarded the new settlement as a complete answer to Dutch monopoly—indeed as the very solution they themselves had been demanding so loudly, and would have done all in their power to ensure its permanence as a British settlement. But there proved to be more hostility and pusillanimity in Penang than anywhere else. If a reason is to be found, it was that with Singapore under the control of Raffles at Bencoolen, the position of Penang would be greatly weakened.

Bannerman flatly declined to supply any troops until he had had a reply to a letter he had just sent to India with a copy of a minute recorded at a meeting of the Council. In this last he ridiculed the claims of the newly acknowledged Sultan of Johore. The port of Singapore, he argued, would ultimately have to be evacuated, "in which case, no doubt, the smaller our military force may be at Singapoor, the greater facility will be given to the Supreme Government to order it to be withdrawn". The time having come "for throwing aside all delicacy", he proceeded to attribute to Raffles "personal ambition and a desire for aggrandizement at the expense of his neighbours" as the motives for the new colony. Lastly, and here was the rub, it would be absurd to place Singapore under Fort Marlborough, six to eight weeks distant, instead of under Penang, which was only six to eight days away.

Raffles was neither surprised nor disturbed by this attitude of the Governor. He merely reported Bannerman's refusal to Adam, adding that he proposed to order a detachment from the 20th Regiment at Bencoolen to proceed to Singapore.

On 16th February Bannerman received the first official Dutch protest. Malacca enquired under what authority Raffles had occupied Singapore. This Bannerman transmitted to Calcutta with due relish, writing to Raffles on the same day:

"I conceive it an act of duty . . . to call upon you to furnish, if you have not already done so, orders to that officer [Farquhar] by an express boat, directing him rather to evacuate the post at Singapore with his party than allow a drop of human blood to be shed in maintaining it."

Raffles ignored this hysterical appeal and contented himself with sending a formal note to Malacca that Singapore had been occupied by the British, and that the Resident there had been strictly instructed not to interfere with the politics of the adjacent islands.

To Charles Assey in England, he wrote:

"Mynheer will probably enter into a paper war on the subject; but we may, I think, combat their arguments without any difficulty. They had established themselves at Rhio, and by virtue of a Treaty, which they had forced the Raja of that place to sign, they assume a right of excluding us from all the Islands and declaring the people their vassals. The legitimate successor to the empire of Johore is with us, and on the ruins of the ancient capital, has signed a Treaty with us which places Singapore and the neighbouring islands under our protection. We do not meddle with the Dutch at Rhio."

From the Dutch, the greatest danger to be feared was obviously prompt military action to occupy Singapore by armed force, a repetition of what Muntinghe had done at Palembang, when he had arrested Captain Salmond. Had the Dutch so reacted, it can be regarded as almost certain that, beyond at most an official protest, the British Government would have abandoned Singapore and recalled Raffles. But this step, which Malacca anticipated, was precisely the one that van der Capellen decided not to take. He was so impressed with the critical attitude adopted by Hastings towards Raffles and his filibustering in Sumatra, that it never seriously crossed his mind that this far more glaring outrage would not be denounced at once by Hastings just as soon as he heard of this latest adventure of his undisciplined lieutenant. Van der Capellen therefore set his mind firmly against military action. Instead he sent to Hastings a dispatch of great length, but phrased in very moderate language. It was written in French and dated 25th February 1819.[1]

"It is extremely painful to me to find myself once again obliged to bring charges against two British officials employed by your Excellency. I am all the more distressed in that I share most cordially in the kindly and friendly feelings existing between our respective Governments, and in view of the esteem and high consideration in which I hold your Excellency personally, I am most anxious to discuss with you only those subjects bearing on a relationship I am happy to foster. . . ."

After referring to recent events at Rhio and Singapore and the treaties concluded by both Dutch and British with the Malay chiefs, he proceeded to state his case. Before the capture of Malacca by the British in 1795, it had had as its dependencies the states of Johore, Pahang, Rhio and Lingga. When Abraham Couperus had surrendered Malacca to the British, he had also withdrawn the Dutch garrisons from the other four places, which had then reverted to the Sultan of Johore without any regard for the treaty still in force. By taking this step, Couperus had exceeded his instructions, so that, although the British had occupied only Malacca, the other states had remained dependencies of that colony and,

[1] For this and other dispatches see van der Kemp's *De Singapoorsche Papieroorlog*.

with the re-establishment of the *status ante bellum*, were once again Dutch possessions. So claimed van der Capellen.

As for Singapore: "It appears that *le chevalier* Raffles and Major Farquhar were accompanied by a certain Toekoelon [Tunku Long], brother of the reigning Sultan of Linga, &c, and pretender to the throne which the latter has occupied for several years. The presence of a malcontent chieftain, surrounded by the appearance of force and supported by British officials, could have grievous consequences, and, in any case, would give those officials the appearance of wishing to ferment trouble and discord. . . ."

The Dutch Government, bound by a solemn treaty, must of necessity interest itself in all that could affect the tranquillity of the Johore states, and expected that a good and just Government such as the British would take immediate steps for the repression of the measures adopted by its subordinate agents.

Such was the first major salvo in the paper war anticipated by Raffles.

Major Farquhar wrote from Singapore to Bannerman at Penang on 1st March:

"Having obtained what I conceive authentic information that the Governor of Malacca has addressed a letter to you intimating that the British establishment recently formed at Singapore has been affected in a forcible manner without the previous consent of the Local Authorities of the country, and having at the same time ascertained that this information has been grounded on a letter from hence by High Highness the Tummung'gung to Mr Adrian Kock [Koek] of Malacca, I beg leave herewith to transmit an explanatory document signed by Tunkoo Long, Sultan of Johore, and the Tummung'gung of Singapore, which will no doubt remove every doubt which may have arisen in your mind relative to the proceedings which have taken place. . . ."

The enclosure ran as follows:

"This is to make known to all whom it may concern, that our friend Major William Farquhar, British Resident of the Settlement of Singapore, has called upon me to declare whether or not any letter or letters have been written by me to the Governor of Malacca, or to any person under his authority, or to the Raja Mooda of Rhio, intimating that the factory which the English have recently established here was forcibly formed against my will; I hereby freely acknowledge that I did write a letter to Mr Adrian Kock of Malacca, and one to the Raja Mooda of Rhio, to the above effect, but my motive for so writing arose solely from the apprehension of bringing on me the vengence of the Dutch at some future period.

"But I here call God and His Prophet to witness that the English established themselves at Singapore with my free will and consent; and that from the arrival of the Honourable Sir Thomas Stamford Raffles no troops or effects were landed, or anything executed but with the free accord of myself and of the Sultan of Johore. In token of the truth whereof we have hereunto affixed our respective Seals."

Five days later, Captain Ross called at Singapore to inform Farquhar that he had learned from an undoubted authority that Governor Timmerman Thyssen had sent a dispatch to Batavia, strongly recommending that a force should be sent to seize the English at Singapore before military reinforcements could arrive there. Farquhar wrote off by express prow to Bannerman:

". . . As you are fully acquainted with the strength of the party at present doing duty here I feel assured that you will adopt such measures as you consider the nature of Captain Ross's report and the urgency of the present case may demand. In the meantime, however, I have only to say that everything here shall be held in readiness as far as our means will admit to resist any hostile attack on the part of the Batavian Government. We are at present much in need of a supply of money and have no means of procuring any here."

Whatever faults Farquhar may have had, lack of physical courage was not one of them.

If the affair of Singapore was a matter of dissension in Penang, the much-delayed mission to Achin was also causing serious disagreement. To begin with, Coombs, Raffles' fellow commissioner, had been not unreasonably annoyed at Raffles' sudden departure in the *Indiana* for the Carimons. On Raffles' return, Coombs' feelings were still further wounded by the discovery that Raffles' had sent a personal letter to Jauhar al-Alam Shah at Achin. As Jauhar was not the Penang candidate for the throne, this letter was regarded as a piece of sharp practice on Raffles' part, a view shared by the Supreme Government when news of it reached Bengal. But if the commissioners held completely divergent opinions as to whom they should recognize as the ruler of Achin, they made common cause in resisting Bannerman, who, after refusing to send a single man to reinforce Singapore, was now trying to send a force five hundred strong with the commissioners to Achin.

They got away in the *Indiana* on 8th March, accompanied by Richard Caunter of the Penang secretariat, and, in deference to Bannerman, an escort of a hundred men.

Four days after they had sailed, Sophia gave birth to a son, who was named Leopold after Prince Leopold, and Stamford after his father.

The mission anchored in Achin roads on 14th March. The political knot they had come to untie was this:

Jauhar al-Alam Shah, who had been sultan since 1802, had gradually lost his authority, and the opposition party had decided to look for a successor. Their choice had fallen on Sayid Husain, the rich Penang merchant referred to in the chapters devoted to Raffles' period there,[1] and as this obviously suited the commercial community in Penang, there had been substantial backing there for the new candidate. In 1815 an expedition had been formed at Penang to establish the new sultan, by force if necessary. The local government had not intervened because, in the previous year, great discourtesy had been shown to Captain Canning, who had been sent to Achin to try to negotiate the protection of shipping from local piracy. The expedition had duly sailed, but no sooner had it reached Achin than Sayid Husain had claimed that he was too old to rule and that his second son must be accepted as the new sultan under the title of Saif al-Alam Shah.[2] Jauhar had retired to Pedir, where he had later been joined by Tunku Pakeh, one of the stalwarts of the Penang expedition, who had since fallen out with the new sultan. Shortly after that, Saif al-Alam Shah had found that he could not control the three great divisional chiefs, or *sagis*, of Achin, and had retired in turn to Telok (Bay) Semawe, west of Pedir. Thus, when the commissioners reached Achin, they found no sultan in residence, but the control in the hands of the three *sagis*, of whom the most dominating character was Panglima Palim.

Raffles and Coombs sent word to the *sagis* that they wished for a meeting. The only one to reply was Panglima Palim, who said that he would meet them in eight days' time. Meanwhile the mission was not allowed to land officially, though individual members could and did. It was quite clear that the atmosphere was hostile and the people suspicious that Achin was to be seized forcibly by the English. Before Panglima Palim arrived, the commissioners were warned by friends of ex-Sultan Jauhar that treachery was intended, so Raffles sent word ashore that he was ill and the meeting was cancelled. For this he was later censured by Calcutta.

At this point the divergent views of the two commissioners reached a critical stage, and for nearly seven weeks they sat on board the *Indiana*, bombarding each other with paper—"thousands of pages," wrote Raffles to John Palmer—Raffles standing up for Jauhar al-Alam, and Coombs for Saif al-Alam.

The claim of the second was, as Sophia wrote in the *Memoir*, "not a little strengthened by his command of wealth". In describing the "intrigue, trouble, and difficulty" attending "the arrangement of this disputed point", she added as a footnote:

"This was the only instance in which a bribe was offered to the Editor: a casket of diamonds was presented, and it seemed to create much surprise that it was not even looked at."

[1] See pages 49 and 132.

[2] *Saif al-Alam*: "Sword of the World."

Before recording the end of the matter, we must return to Penang, where Bannerman had received a dispatch from the Governor-General. It was dated 20th February and must have afforded Bannerman and Phillips no little satisfaction.

"Sir Thomas Raffles", wrote Hastings, "was not justified in sending Major Farquhar eastward after the Dutch protested; and if the Post has not yet been obtained, he is to desist from any further attempt to establish one."

Thus encouraged, Bannerman recorded the following minute, a copy of which he sent to Calcutta:

"I have the honour to present to the Board the letter from Major Farquhar dated the 1st instant conveying intelligence of a very extraordinary communication which the Chiefs of Johore and Singapoor appear to have spontaneously and clandestinely made to the Raja Mooda of Rhio and to Mr Adrian Kock, the senior member of the Dutch Council at Malacca. Although the circumstances mentioned in Major Farquhar's letter had previously come to our knowledge yet I conceive we are bound to forward these documents by the very first opportunity to the Governor-General. It is, however, very unfortunate that Major Farquhar's present communication instead of removing the mischievous impressions which the secret correspondence of the Chief may have excited will, on the contrary, only serve to strengthen them materiallly in the minds of the Hollanders and nowhere more so than in Europe where the inference will undoubtedly be that whilst the secret letters of these Native Chiefs were spontaneous and untutored their recantation forwarded by Major Farquhar was written under the control of that officer. There is one fact, however, deduceable from this correspondence and which I must notice as it substantiates the truth of my former assertion that the Chiefs of Singapoor and Johor are dependents of the Sultan of Rhio, &c. I can see no other reason why these Chiefs should have addressed the Raja Mooda of Rhio but that they knew they were accountable to him for their conduct and had reason to dread his vengeance just as that of the Hollanders."

At this point he added a further minute arising out of the receipt of Farquhar's urgent dispatch of the 6th.

". . . It must be notorious that any force we are able to detach to Singapoor could not resist the overpowering armament at the disposal of the Batavia Government, although its presence would certainly compel Major Farquhar to resist the Netherlanders even to the shedding of blood and its ultimate and forced submission would tarnish the national honour infinitely more seriously than the degradation which would ensue upon the retreat of the small party now at Singapoor. Neither Major Farquhar's honour as a soldier nor the honour of the British Government now require him to attempt the defence of Singapoor by force of arms against the Netherlanders, as he knows Sir Stamford Raffles has occupied that island in violation of the orders of the Supreme Government and as he knows that any opposition from his present small party would be a useless and reprehensible sacrifice of men when made against the overwhelming naval and military force that the Dutch would employ. . . .

"The question then is Shall this Government reinforce Major Farquhar and invite him to a violent opposition against the Netherlanders? Or shall it recommend him rather to evacuate the post Sir S. Raffles has so injudiciously chosen than shed a drop of human blood in its defence? After the knowledge we possess of the views and present policy of the Governor-General; after the information we have obtained of the means used by Sir Stamford Raffles to obtain the Island of Singapoor; and after the intelligence we have received of the Dutch right to that territory, admitted as it is by the secret correspondence of the Chiefs there, I am decidedly of opinion that this Government will not be justified in reinforcing Major Farquhar and inciting him to resist the Hollanders by force of arms. I had fully stated the possibility of a hostile attack from the Dutch to the worthy Major when he first lost sight of his usual prudence and allowed himself to be seduced and made party in Sir Stamford Raffles' proceedings. . . ."

After suggesting arrangements for any emergency evacuation of Singapore—"I confess the mortification to me would be infinitely aggravated if I saw Major Farquhar and his detachment brought into this port under the Dutch flag"—he concluded:

"However invidious the task I cannot close this Minute without pointing out to the notice of our superiors the very extraordinary conduct of the Lieutenant-Governor of Bencoolen. He posts a detachment at Singapoor under very equivocal circumstances without even the means of coming away and with such defective instructions and slender resources that before it has been there a month its Commander is obliged to apply for money to this Government whose duty it becomes to offer that officer advice and means against an event which Sir Stamford ought to have expected and for which he ought to have made an express provision in his instructions to that officer. My letters of the 15th and 17th February will prove that upon his return from Singapoor I offered him any supplies he might require for the detachment he had left there and also earnestly called upon him to transmit instructions to Major Farquhar for the guidance of his conduct in the possible event of the Netherlanders attempting to dislodge him by force of arms. Did he avail himself of my offer and state what further supplies Major Farquhar would require? Or did he attend to my appeal and send the requisite instructions to that officer? No. He set off for Acheen and left Major Farquhar to shift for himself. In fact he acted (as a friend of mine emphatically observed) like a man who sets a house on fire and then runs away."

In great indignation, young Dr Jack wrote to Wallich on the following day:

". . . Sir Stamford left Major Farquhar there as Resident and the company of Seapoys he had taken with him and returned here. His first care was to send a reinforcement to insure the respectability of the new station, and applied for the troops which this Government had promised to have in readiness whenever he should call for them. Would you believe that they actually refused them in defiance of their written promises and the orders of the Governor-General, and why, because they disapproved of the measures that had been taken, or in plain English, because it did not originate with themselves. There is good reason to believe that they have conveyed intimation of their hostile sentiments to the Dutch in the hope of its exciting them to exert themselves against the Settlement. I should hardly obtain credit for all the extraordinary steps they have taken to effect if possible the ruin of the Finest Settlement in the British possession. Happily, however, they and the Dutch together will only be able to create some petty obstructions which a little time will entirely obviate. I hope, too, their conduct will sooner or later meet with its due reward and be exposed as it deserves, for it is impossible to conceive anything more disgraceful from first to last. On the island there is but one opinion both of the Governor and the limb of Satan[1] who guides him and is prime mover of all the iniquity and mischief at the place. The Government must be bad indeed that cannot even command a voice amongst those most nearly connected with it and dependent on it."

Soldier though he was, Bannerman allowed himself to be so blinded by his jealousy of Raffles—that, at least, is the charitable explanation—and aided and abetted by his son-in-law, the egregious Phillips, that he wrote to Farquhar on the 16th:

"The intelligence you have thought it your duty to communicate to me, although very important, you must have been well aware could excite no surprise in my mind in as much as you were personally and distinctly apprised by me before you quitted this island that you were proceeding in an undertaking which was in violation of the orders of the Supreme Government and which would expose you to a hostile attack from the Netherlanders.

"I have now therefore to enclose for your information copies of two important letters lately received from the Supreme Government on the subject of the Dutch occupation of Rhio and a copy of the correspondence which passed between Sir Stamford Raffles and myself after his arrival from Singapoor. Although it is not the province of this Government to

[1] Presumably Phillips.

furnish you with any instructions, yet a perusal of the enclosed documents may serve to guide your judgment, how far you will be justified in shedding blood in the maintenence of your Post and particularly after the communications made to the Netherlanders by the Chiefs of Johor and Singapoor which will certainly induce them to consider every resistance on your part as adding violations to injustice.

"The Honourable Company's Cruiser 'Nearchus' and Hired Brig 'Ganges' will afford you ample means for your removing your party from Singapoor in the event of such a measure becoming in your judgment proper and necessary; but I have distinctly to acquaint you that you must not expect any reinforcements from this Government until a reply is received from the Governor-General in Council, as it is the decided conviction of this Government that any force from this island could not oppose the overpowering armament at the disposal of the Batavian Government, and would only widen the breach which the late proceedings at Singapoor have made between the British and Netherlandish authorities.

"Another European officer, however, and a further supply of cash equal to the payment of your detachment for two months shall be forwarded by the very first opportunity. I have also to acquaint you that your letter conveying the recantation of the Chiefs of Johor and Singapoor as well as your present letter shall be transmitted to the Supreme Government immediately.

"In conclusion I must beg particularly to apprise you that after the receipt of the present information respecting the views of the Governor-General and the sentiments of this Government you will not be justified in the measure of shedding blood by pleading hereafter that your honour as a soldier compelled you to make resistance. As a soldier I must unequivocally declare to you that your personal honour is in no degree implicated in the present occasion to render the shedding of blood necessary."

Not content with this, Bannerman so far forgot himself and his duty as to send next day to Timmerman Thyssen a letter that one hopes is unique in British military annals.

"Honourable Sir,—Information having reached me that the Netherlanders Government of Java are it is strongly believed preparing to send up a force with orders to seize the English detachment posted at Singapoor under the command of Major Farquhar, I conceive it is a duty I owe to you as well as to myself to apprise you immediately that the whole subject respecting the occupation of that island was referred by me to the Most Noble the Governor-General on the 17th ultimo and His Lordship's reply may be expected before the expiration of twenty or thirty days from this date.

"Pending this reference therefore, motives of humanity I hope you will allow, as well as the undoubted duty of preserving undisturbed the very friendly relations subsisting between our respective countries, call upon us to adopt ourselves and to recommend to the Netherlanders Government of Java the same moderation and goodwill as have hitherto attended the transactions between your Government and mine. With this view I have a right to expect that you will join your best endeavours with mine in deprecating any such violent measure on the part of the Java Government as would lead to a cruel effusion of blood and excite a collision between Great Britain and Holland.

"I am the more induced to make this appeal to you as Sir Stamford Raffles is not under the control of this Government, and I am really unacquainted with the nature of the reply he may have returned to your communication of the Treaty existing between your Government and the Kingdom of Rhio, &c."

To this he added the postscript:

"I have the honour to add that Sir Stamford Raffles is now absent from this settlement."

Meanwhile, van der Capellen had written to Falck on 12th March:

"According to information of March 1st from Rhio the English garrison has been staying all the time in Singapore. I will send someone to those parts to make sure of the real state of affairs. If you look at the map you will see that Singapore is situated between the island of Bintang (in which is Rhio) and Malacca. I will refrain from further remarks."

A week later he wrote again: "My official letter gives you another contribution to the acts of Mr Raffles in this archipelago where he is untiring in inventing means to prejudice us and to provoke actions which I shall fight as long as possible with might and main. His way of acting with regard to Singapore surpasses anything which he has done so far. Nothing would please him more than to make us lose our patience at last with his frantic deeds and to see us fire the first shot."

That same day, 19th March, the *Calcutta Journal* reported the conclusion of the Singapore treaty. After referring to "its very great commercial and political importance", the article continued:

"We believe and earnestly hope that the establishment of a settlement under such favourable circumstances, and at a moment when we had every reason to fear that the efforts of the Dutch had been successful in excluding us altogether from the Eastern Archipelago, will receive all the support which is necessary to its progress, and that by its rapid advance in wealth, industry and population, which in their establishment and development form the most honourable monuments of statesmen, it would attest hereafter the wisdom and foresight of the present administration and its attention to the commercial and political interests of our country.

"We congratulate our Eastern friends and the commerical world in general on the event which we this day report to them. They will rejoice in our having occupied the position which was required as a fulcrum for the support of our Eastern and China trade and from whence we can extend our commercial views and speculations. The spell of Dutch monopoly, so justly reviled and detested, and which had nearly been again established, has been dissolved by the ethereal touch of that wand which broke in pieces the confederacy that lately threatened our Continental possessions;[1] and while we are indebted to the noble ruler of these dominions for the peace and security of our homes, we have none the less reason to admire and applaud the extensive foresight by which another and nearer link has been added to connect us with China and by which our Eastern commerce has been secured."

It is not surprising that Hastings, under the most rigid instructions from London not to provoke a dispute with the Dutch, was somewhat taken aback on learning that Raffles, even with the knowledge that the Dutch had occupied Rhio, had felt himself entitled to stretch his orders far enough to risk a quarrel with them by forming a settlement on an island in such close proximity.

Notwithstanding this, the attitude of the Supreme Government was on the whole favourable. After observing in a letter to Raffles that the abruptness of his departure from Penang to the eastward was inconsistent with the dignity of the position he held, the Governor-General in Council continued:

"The selection of Singapoor for a Post is considered as to locality to have been highly judicious, and your proceedings in establishing a Factory at that place do honour to your approved skill and ability, though the measure itself as willingly incurring a collision with the Dutch authorities is to be regretted . . . your engagements with the presumed legitimate Chief of Johor and the local Government of Singapoor are provisionally confirmed. . . ."

Further information on this point was required, but:

"It is intended to maintain the Post of Singapoor for the present."

Hastings has been accused of going back on his promise, "Sir Stamford, you may depend upon me." If, however, one puts oneself in his position, the backsliding was but a modest one; in fact, except for rather irritable criticisms of some of Raffles' own personal acts, and a mild degree of general reprimand for disobeying his instructions, he did stand by Raffles very skilfully and staunchly in the storm that followed.

Van der Capellen wrote to Hastings again on 25th March, reporting

[1] The campaigns against the Mahrattas and Pindaris.

the new information he had just received from Malacca. On 4th April he wrote to Falck:

"On the receipt of this letter you will be acquainted with the occurrence in Singapore. If I had followed my feelings, I should certainly not have handled the matter with so much calmness, but I should rather have attacked Raffles as he deserved it. I imagine that he will have become known to his own Government in such a way that nobody will shield him any more. If the English keep Singapore we had better give up Malacca. The map alone will show you this clearly. Therefore with regard to this matter I hope that, during a possible negotiation and a refusal of Lord Hastings, they will not approve in Europe of a *status quo*. *They* must leave it or *we* must. You know how Elout and I, both of us, think about an exchange of Sumatra for the continent of India. It goes without saying then that I set my seal absolutely to the proposal made by you to the King concerning this matter."

Hastings was aware that London's reaction to Singapore would not be at all favourable, and that he himself might well be censured for giving the far from popular Raffles such encouragement as he had. He was, however, in no mood to receive any criticism of the policy of the Supreme Government from a subordinate authority. He would be compelled to send a diplomatic answer to the Dutch to avert any violent retaliation; the explanation to London would have to be very carefully worded: but as far as Colonel J. A. Bannerman, Governor of Penang, was concerned, no restraint need be imposed. And none was.

"With regard to the station established at Singapore," wrote Hastings on 8th April, "though we are not prepared to express our final opinion upon the determination adopted by Sir Stamford Raffles to occupy that harbour, we cannot think it was within the province of your Government to pronounce a decisive opinion upon a violation of his instructions. Commissioned and entrusted by this Government, to this Government alone he was answerable. The instructions under which he acted, and which were communicated to your Government that you might the more readily promote the object, were adapted to the port of Rhio chiefly and the probability that the Dutch might anticipate us there rendered it necessary to prescribe a line which was in that contingency to be followed with the utmost exactness. The same principle was in the subsequent instructions extended to Johor. In both cases the injunctions referred to the possible event of an apparent right having been actually advanced by the Dutch. But though the spirit of inculcation to avoid collision with the Dutch applied itself to any other possession, it necessarily did so with a latitude suited to circumstances. We think your Government entirely wrong in determining so broadly against the propriety of the step taken by Sir Stamford Raffles on a simple reclamation from the Governor of

Malacca which whether well or ill founded was to be looked for as certain. . . .

"Under these circumstances it does not appear to us that any doubts which may be excited at the present stage of the business could be a legitimate principle for your guidance so as to exonerate you from the obligation of fulfilling our directions for your supporting Sir Stamford Raffles with a moderate force should he establish a station on the Eastern Sea. So far do we regard you from being freed from the call to act upon our instructions that we fear you would have difficulty in excusing yourselves should the Dutch be tempted to violence by the weakness of the detachment at Singapore and succeed in discharging it.

"Representations will be made to this Government and investigations must be set on foot; in the interval which these will occupy we have to request from your Government every aid to the factory at Singapore. The policy of it which we lament to have been avowed and recorded would find no tolerance with the British Government should misfortune occur and be traceable to neglects originating in such a feeling. Whether the measure of occupying it should ultimately be judged to have been injudiciously reasoned or otherwise the procedure must be upheld unless we shall be satisfied (which is not now the case) that perseverance in maintaining the port would be an infraction of equity."

The receipt of this castigation must have been a mortifying experience for the old colonel. On 18th May he replied "in a hurried note" in which he explained, with due deference to his Lordship's views, "that I have received a lesson which shall teach me how I again presume to offer opinions as long as I live". After describing the course of the controversy between Penang and Raffles, and at the same time asking that if Singapore were retained it should be placed under the Penang government, he concluded his dispatch with:

"I am sorry, my Lord, to have trespassed on your time but I have a whole life of character to defend and in this vindication I hope I have not borne harder than what is necessary on Sir S. Raffles and others. I have taken particular care to have here no personal controversy or cause of personal dispute with that gentleman. On the contrary he and his amiable Lady have received from me since their first arrival from Calcutta every personal civility and attention which Your Excellency had desired me to show them. . . . Illiberal or malicious revenge I thank God my heart knows not and never has known. The revenge which may be apparent in this address is only such as justice imperiously required and morality sanctioned. Its only objects were to procure reparation for the injury I have sustained and to promote the just ends of punishment."

Having written this, he hastily dispatched two hundred men and six thousand rupees to Singapore.

Poor Bannerman. He had fallen into the same trap as had Major Robison before him: by attacking the subordinate of a higher authority, he had impugned the higher authority itself.

ii

The minor paper war between Raffles and Coombs aboard *Indiana* was won in the end by Raffles, it being finally agreed that they should go to Pedir and try to make a treaty with Jauhar al-Alam Shah. In this no difficulty was experienced; terms were completed and the treaty signed on 22nd April. The British were thereby given freedom to trade at all ports of Achin, the sultan agreeing to accept a British Resident. Achin was to enter into no treaties with any other power without permission of the British, and no foreigners at all were to be allowed to settle in Achin, British being allowed, but only with the authority of the Resident. In return, Jauhar was given bills on Bengal to the value of 100,000 rupees. Various firearms and military stores were also handed over to him. The commission then sailed along to Telok Semawe and there advised Saif al-Alam to accept Jauhar as sultan, which he did readily enough until the commission had safely left.

As was to be expected of him, Raffles had taken the opportunity to explore the neighbourhood. Of his discoveries and the outcome of the mission, he wrote later to Marsden:

"Our political negotiations were eventually successful and although I had much anxiety and annoyance I have no reason to regret my employment on the Mission. Our Government were nearly committed on the worst side of a very troublesome question; and it required no common degree of assiduity and perseverance to persuade authorities, who had previously declared opinions, that they were wrong. . . . The most important discoveries we made were in the existence of extensive teak forests near the Northern coast and the general prevalence of mutilated Hindu images in the interior. . . . There is a fine harbour on the Northern side of Pulo Way,[1] the best in the Acheenese dominions and until this period unknown to Europeans. It will be long, I fear, before Acheen will be restored to a state of complete tranquillity and confidence."

The *Indiana* arrived back in Penang on 28th April. Raffles stayed there for several weeks before leaving for Bencoolen by way of Singapore with his family, Dr Jack and the others who had accompanied him from Calcutta. They sailed from Penang in the *Indiana* on 22nd May. Two days later, in London, there was born at Kensington Palace the future Queen Victoria.

Singapore was reached on 31st May. They stayed there for nearly

[1] Pulau Wai, a small island off the north coast of Sumatra.

three weeks, Raffles' time being fully and, as wrote his wife, "most agreeably occupied . . . in marking out the future town and giving instructions to Colonel Farquhar for the arrangement and management of the new Colony". He took the opportunity to send home letters, the purpose of which was not merely to tell his friends how he was getting on, but also—and of more importance—to build up in influential quarters in England a feeling of confidence that Singapore was an acquisition of outstanding consequence, both in itself and in the final breach it constituted in Dutch monopoly.

The letters were all of similar tenor and much of each was devoted to matters already mentioned in these pages, so it is not necessary to give here more than a few extracts.

To Colonel Addenbrooke, who had been equerry to Princess Charlotte:

"Since my return to this country my public attention has been chiefly directed to the proceedings of the Hollanders who not satisfied with receiving from us the fertile and important Islands of Java and Moluccas, have attempted to exercise a Supremacy over the whole of Borneo and Sumatra and to exclude our Nation from all intercourse with the other States of the Archipelago. They have not been very particular in the means, and they seem to have considered the degradation of the English character as necessary to their own Establishment. You may easily conceive how much annoyance this has given to us, and prepared as I was to remain a quiet spectator of all their actions, I have not found it possible to continue entirely neutral. While they confined their proceedings to the Countries in which the European Authority was established, we had no right to interfere, these we had by Treaty agreed to transfer to them and they were of course at liberty to act in them as they thought proper without reference to our interests; but they no sooner found themselves possessed of these than they conceived the idea of driving us from the Archipelago altogether, and when I made my reappearance in these Seas they had actually hardly left us an inch of ground to stand upon—even our right to the spot on which I write this tho' yesterday a wilderness and without inhabitants is disputed, and in return for our unparalleled generosity we are left almost without a resting place in the Archipelago.

"But it is not *our* interests alone that have suffered by this unexpected return, those of humanity and civilization suffer more deeply. To comprehend the question justly you must consider that it has been an object of the first importance to our Indian Interest as well on account of this Commerce itself as the safety of our more extensive Commerce with China which lies beyond them and that for the last Century owing to the defects and radical weakness of the Dutch we have been able to effect this without serious molestation from them.

"The consequence of this constant and friendly intercourse [with the Malays] has been the establishment of numerous independent States throughout the Archipelago—these have advanced considerably in civilization and as their knowledge increased so did their wants, and their advancement in civilization might be estimated in the ratio of their commerce—the latter is suddenly arrested by the withering grasp of the Hollander—the first article he insists upon is the exclusion of the English and the monopoly on account of his own Government of whatever may be the principal produce of the place. The private Merchant is thrown out altogether or condemned to put up with vexations and impositions, but above all the unhealthy climate of Batavia at which Port alone the Dutch seem determined that all the trade of these Islands shall enter. Surely after the millions [that] have been sacrificed to this hated and destructive policy, they ought to have had some common feeling for humanity, some object in view beyond the cold calculations of profit and loss. Let them do what they please with Java and the Moluccas, and these contain a population of at least five millions, but with the population of Borneo, Sumatra and the other Islands which is at least equal in amount, they can have no right to interfere by restorative regulations. Let them have their own lawful subjects to what account they please, but let them not involve our Allies and the British character in the general vortex of the ruin they are working for themselves. . . .

"Our eventual object is of course to secure the independence of Bornean, Sumatran and other States with which we have been in alliance for the last seventy years, and further if practicable to regain the Settlements of Malacca, Padang and Banca. These ought never to have been transferred to the Dutch, but as they are indebted to us in nearly a million Sterling on the adjustment of their Java accounts, it is to be hoped we may yet make a compromise for their return. . . .

"[Singapore] is within a week's sail of China; still closer to Siam, Cochin China, &c, in the very heart of the Archipelago or as the Malays call it the navel of the Malay countries. Already a population of about five thousand souls has collected under our flag—the number is daily increasing, the harbour in every way superior, filled with shipping from all quarters, and although our Settlement has not been established more than four months every one is comfortably housed, provisions are in abundance, the troops healthy, and everything bearing the appearance of content. . . .

"Our object is not territory but Trade; a great commercial emporium and a *fulcrum* whence we may extend our influence politically as circumstances may hereafter require. By taking immediate possession we put a *negative* to the Dutch claim of exclusion and at the same time revive the drooping confidence of our Allies and friends. One free port in these seas must eventually destroy the spell of Dutch monopoly; and what *Malta* is in the West, that may *Singapore* become in the East. . . ."

To Robert Inglis:

". . . The free and uninterrupted command of the Straits of Malacca having been obtained, it is conceived that the Dutch Government will readily cede to us the Settlement of Malacca now useless to them and with it Rhio and the Islands lying off the southern entrance of the Straits; and these obtained our object will be to gain Banca. . . . This would of course settle the Palembang question at once; and as our Ministers can no longer be ignorant of the intrinsic value of Banca to the British Government on account of its mines and the question is thus one in which not only the National honour but the National interests are deeply concerned, it is to be hoped the best endeavours will be made. . . .

"You will have heard that shortly after my arrival at Bencoolen I had the satisfaction to establish a Bible Society. This was followed by the establishment of schools, and recently on the visit of the Bishop of Calcutta to Penang we formed a District Committee of the Society for Promoting Christian Knowledge entitled the Prince of Wales's Island and Fort Marlborough Committee. I have now with me on board the ship in which I proceed to Bencoolen a printing press with types in the Roman and native characters and have just granted permission to the Extra Ganges Mission to establish a college at Singapore for the study of the Chinese language and the extension of Christianity."

This was in response to an application received by Farquhar from William Milne at Malacca for a grant of land for the purpose of erecting "a dwelling house, schools, places of Christian worship, &c", as he was desirous of commencing a Chinese and Malay mission at the settlement as early as practicable. Milne, who had so impressed Raffles when he had visited Java, had gone out to join Robert Morrison at Canton, where Europeans could remain only during the six months of the year when the Company's fleet was trading in China. For the other six months it was their custom to go to the island of Macao. As, however, the Portuguese had withheld permission for Milne to live in Macao, Morrison had sent him to Malacca in 1815 to start the Extra—or, more properly, Ultra—Ganges Mission in that place. Milne was a fine linguist. He had a press at Malacca, where a tremendous amount of printing, mainly Chinese block printing, was done, tracts and Scriptures being circulated far and wide by junk and sailing-ship.

To the Duchess of Somerset:

"My new Colony thrives most rapidly. We have not been established four months and it has received an acquisition of population exceeding five thousand, principally Chinese, and their number is daily increasing. It is not necessary for me to say how much interested I am in the success of the place; it is a child of my own and I have made it what it is. You may easily conceive with what zeal I apply myself to the clearing of forests, cutting of roads, building of towns, framing of laws, &c, &c."

Concerning these matters he sets out further instructions to Farquhar on 25th June, two days before he sailed.

". . . Points of primary importance to be attended to should be the construction of convenient watering places and affording to ships the means of watering, ballasting as well as loading, with the least possible delay. . . . I feel satisfied that you will concur in the necessity of giving your early attention to this subject as well as to the removal of the present temporary buildings between the Stores and the river and the erection of a convenient shed or bankshaw [*bangsal*] at which Europeans may land their goods. The removal of the bazaar from its present site is indispensable. . . .

"The whole space included between the old Lines and the Singapore River is to be considered as cantonments, and of course no ground within this space can be permanently appropriated to individuals. Whenever you may have planned the lines, barracks, &c, for the troops and set apart sufficient accommodation for magazines, &c, it will be necessary to allot sufficient space in a convenient and proper situation for officers' bungalows, the extent of each to be regulated by you according to circumstances and the ground to be occupied by the officers as is usual in other cantonments. The residency of the Tummung'gung is of course to be considered the only exception. The whole of the Hill extending to the fort within the two rivers and the fresh water cut is to be reserved for the exclusive accommodation of the Chief Authority and is not to be otherwise appropriated except for defences.

"Beyond this limit the opposite point of the river including the whole of the lately cleared high ground and a space of two hundred yards from the old Lines should also be reserved entirely for public purposes and no private building whatever for the present allowed within the same. In the native town as they have been and will be marked out proper measures should be taken for securing to each individual the undisputed possession of the spot he may be permitted to occupy, which should be regularly registered in your office.

"The European town should be marked out without loss of time, and this should extend along the beach from the distance of two hundred yards from the lines as far eastward as practicable including as much of the ground already cleared by the Bugguese as can possibly be required in that direction, reimbursing the parties the expense they have been at in clearing, and appropriating to them other ground in lieu. For the present the space lying between the new road and the beach is to be reserved by Government but on the opposite side of the road the ground may be immediately marked into twelve separate allotments of equal front to be appropriated to the first respectable European Merchants. To these persons a Certificate of Registry and permission to clear and occupy may be granted. . . . Whenever the allotments may be appropriated others of convenient dimensions may in like manner be marked out inland and streets or roads formed according to regular plan. It would be advisable that a circular carriage road should be cut in each direction from the cantonments during the present dry season. A bridge across the river so as to connect the cantonments with the Chuliah, Chinese and Malay towns on the opposite side . . . should be constructed without delay, and so soon as other more immediate works are completed a good bungalow for the residence of the Chief Authority may be constructed on the Hill."

In expectation of the arrival from England of his sister Mary Anne and her husband, he reserved one of the twelve lots for Captain William Flint. A second was to be held for Thomas McQuoid, a third for Lieut. Crossley, a fourth for Messrs Carnegy & Company, a fifth for Mr Francis Ferrao, and two more for his own disposal.

"Those of Mr McQuoid and Captain Flint I would wish to be adjoining."

Raffles also negotiated and signed an agreement with the Temenggong. The details of it are quoted from Buckley's *Anecdotal History of Old Times in Singapore*.

"Article 1st

The boundaries of the lands under the control of the English are as follows:—From Tanjong[1] Malang on the West to Tanjong Katong on the East and on the land side as far as the range of cannon shot all round from the Factory. As many persons as reside within the aforesaid boundary and not within the campongs of the Sultan and Tummung'gung are all to be under the control of the Resident, and with respect to the gardens and plantations that are now or may hereafter be made they are to be at the disposal of the Tummung'gung as heretofore; but it is understood that he will always acquaint the Resident of the same.

"Article 2nd

It is directed that all the Chinese move over to the other side of the river forming a campong from the site of the large bridge down the river towards the mouth and all Malays, people belonging to the Tummung'gung and others, are also to remove to the other side of the river forming their campong from the site of the large bridge up the river towards the source.

[1] Cape.

"Article 3rd

All cases which may occur requiring Council in this settlement shall in the first instance be conferred and deliberated upon by the three aforesaid, and when they shall have been decided upon they shall be made known to the inhabitants either by beat of gong or by Proclamation.

"Article 4th

Every Monday morning at ten o'clock the Sultan, the Tummung'-gung and the Resident shall meet at the Rooma Bechara[1]; but should either of the two former be incapable of attending they may send a deputy there.

"Article 5th

Every Captain or Head of a Caste and all panghulus[2] of campongs should likewise attend at the Rooma Bechara and make a report or statement of such occurrences as may have taken place in the Settlement; and represent any grievance or complaint that they may have to bring before the Council for its consideration on each Monday.

"Article 6th

If the Captains or Heads of Castes or the panghulus of campongs do not act justly towards their constituents, they are permitted to come and state their grievances themselves to the Resident at the Rooma Bechara who is hereby authorized to examine and decide thereon.

"Article 7th

No duties or customs can be exacted or firms established in this Settlement without the consent of the Sultan, the Tummung'gung and Major William Farquhar and without the consent of these three nothing can be arranged."

With all these matters settled to his satisfaction, Raffles sailed with his party in the *Indiana* for Bencoolen on 28th June.

[1] *Rumah Bichara*, Courthouse.
[2] *Penghulu*, territorial chief.

Chapter Twenty-four

THE PAPER WAR, 1819

i

IT is never easy to discover John Palmer's personal opinions, for he varied the tone of his remarks according to the person he was addressing, but it seems reasonably clear from his letter of 18th June 1819 to Raffles that he was sceptical concerning the treaty concluded at Achin with Jauhar al-Alam Shah.

"I am favoured with your letter of the 19th ultimo and beg to accept my thanks for the promised detail of your proceedings at Acheen; and which I shall read with interest if not with pleasure; for *prima facie* I have not the satisfaction of an entire concurrence in them; and esteem the evidence of a thousand pages as extremely equivocal of a good cause. How a subject so comparatively [simple] could have produced such a waste of time and paper is to me a riddle; but it shall so remain until an honest judgment can be formed from the materials which construct the fabric of Acheen negotiations.

"I fear Jowar Allum must remain in exile without military support; and that his elected Rival may not choose to forsake his Sagies of Acheen proper; and if so that proclaimed an Outlaw, Pirate or Rebel, the old Syed's treasures will be required for the redemption of Syful Allum. If Acheen proper be of no greater importance than the rest of the Kingdom, it might be a wholesome Policy to leave it to its election of a Chief, especially if defection among the electors is more likely to aid your work than arms in favour of the ex-King. I sincerely hope, however, that from here and here only your Treaty will be acted upon; since from whatever motives I apprehend its abortion under the administration of Penang. If I could command or sway, it should be so; and the fairest play possible given to your arrangements."

Concerning Singapore he added:

"For the East all is clear and sound in Policy. Rights of either side not founded on the pleasure of the people are farcical—but the exercise of power in your hands will be benign and I hope to see Singapoor the crowded emporium of all the Eastern Seas. I have no direct recent accounts from there and await yours with the same confidence of satisfaction as impatience."

The very same day he wrote to Phillips, avoiding the topic of Singapore:

"For your letter of the 2nd April take my thanks; it met the eye of my friend Adam and makes a due impression upon the general bungle of our Eastern Politics. I think that between your communications and those of Coombs we have unmasked the artifices and Charlataneries of the Golden Sword[1] and left him his just title to repute for more Talent than integrity; and with less of that than is seen to look very diminutive in argument and reasoning when opposed to Coombs, though I regret to learn from Metcalfe that our friend's intemperance on some occasion gave the Knight an advantage of which he dexterously profited."

To Coombs, from whom he had received a number of dispatches on the matter, he wrote:

". . . the last of your communications . . . completes a mass of information developing more intrigue, artifice and fraud than any political manœuvre ever armed with before. As I have received your letters, I have submitted them to Adam; he or myself has shown them to Metcalfe with whom at this minute the greater part of your packets are deposited. I believe they ascend a step higher and partially at least reach the eye of Lord H. If they produce the effect I should hope for, I look for the redemption of your Treaty on the ground of a barefaced predilection of the First Commissioner, and the palpable contrivances he has resorted to to bolster up the cause of the ex-King; which probably comprise documentary Fabrications which could not stand up to an honest Inquisition. . . .

"Raffles professes to do you ample justice, and it consists with his Policy, having accomplished his purposes, to conciliate you and your friends; his letters to me undergo a revision by Adam and the Secretary, and will detect him in impositions if he has not acted up to his promise to write to Lord H. . . ."

The chief interest of these letters is that they reveal the extent to which lobbying could be practised in Calcutta. Raffles, no doubt, was not unaware of it and for that reason took considerable trouble to write to Palmer at length and, when himself in Calcutta, to explain his plans with apparent frankness. It must also be remembered that Palmer's friendship with the leading figures in Penang was of long standing, and his business connexions there were important to him. But the way he passed on to Adam private letters from Penang, written obviously for that very purpose, for Metcalfe or even Hastings himself to see, does not show Palmer in a very attractive light. How far his canvassing of the secretariat was responsible for the attitude of the Supreme Government is hard to assess. Certainly that attitude was not very favourable. Raffles was censured for leaving Coombs in the air and rushing off to Singapore, and for communicating on his own with Jauhar al-Alam Shah. As for the mission, Calcutta considered that if it had been thought right to summon the local chiefs to a council, then the commissioners had been

[1] One of Palmer's nicknames for Raffles.

in duty bound to attend that council. Of the treaty concluded, it was observed that the benefits were "future and precarious" for the British, but "instantaneous" for Jauhar al-Alam Shah. It was, however, decided to ratify it, inasmuch as "there would have been little use in withholding our ratification when all the obligations on our part had been nearly, if not wholly, fulfilled".

In a letter to Metcalfe, Raffles defended his action in sending Lieut. Criddle to Pedir in the *Minto*, and also for departing so suddenly himself from Penang. It was written in the following September and no doubt duly filed in Calcutta. By that time, however, interest in Achin was, like the treaty, dead. Achin to Raffles had been, one fancies, a poor second best. His real objective all the time had been Singapore, and his success there had reduced the Achin mission to the level of a tiresome duty that still had to be carried out. His sole remaining interest, we suspect, was to defeat the plan of the Penang government, and he was prepared to sit on board the *Indiana* for nearly seven weeks in Achin roads to achieve his purpose. One unexpected value the treaty did ultimately have. In the protracted negotiations that finally culminated in the Anglo-Dutch treaty of 1824, it served as a useful counter in the hands of the British plenipotentiaries.

ii

Bathurst's reply to Lansdowne in the Lords was welcomed with great enthusiasm in Java.

"I rejoice not a little," wrote van der Capellen to Falck on 22nd June, "and all right minded people with me, at the news received from England, and to see Raffles called in Parliament Commercial Resident is something of what he deserves."

Raffles own comment was: "Ministers must be very hard pushed or made of strange materials when they can screen themselves under misrepresentation and falsehood."

Van der Capellen's letter of protest to Hastings in February brought an extremely diplomatic reply. It was dated 26th June and ran to sixty-one paragraphs. Extracts from it follow.

"3. The spirit of aggrandizement evinced in the proceedings of the Commissioners-General of His Netherlandish Majesty, and their manifest endeavours to establish the absolute supremacy of the Netherlands in the Eastern seas, made it necessary for us to adopt precautions with a view to avert the injury and degradation, which could not fail to ensue from a listless submission to the unbounded pretensions displayed on the part of your nation.

"4. That our views relative to those seas have been ever confined to the security of our own commerce, combined with the freedom of that of other nations, is a position which does not need demonstration. Its undeniable truth is shown by the whole series of our conduct in the Eastern seas, during the period, when our power in that quarter was unrivalled and unassailable. We might then without difficulty have made arrangements for the establishment of our supremacy and might have stipulated for the preservation of those arrangements at the general peace of Europe. Instead of which we shunned the ready means of aggrandizement and restored to your nation its noble colonies, without having made any step towards the increase of our own power, during the long interval in which no nation of any quarter of the globe could have impeded its extension.

"5. In restoring your colonies with unlimited confidence and without any literal restriction, we had not to expect that you would assume as restored what we never received from you, and never occupied ourselves. We little thought that some of the first acts of your Government after the restitution would be to reduce to vassalage the States, which we had treated as perfectly independent, and to impose Treaties on those States, having for all of their principal objects the exclusion of our commerce from all ports, except when admitted by your permission. . . .

"10. Sir T. S. Raffles, on his arrival at Prince of Wales' Island, found that the agents of your nation had anticipated him at Rhio. He therefore very properly avoided that port.

"11. He proceeded to Singapoor and there formed a treaty, with a chief, whom he described as the rightful sovereign of Johor, as well as with the local Government, which he represents as being independent of that established at Rhio. A copy of the treaty is annexed for your Excellency's information.

"12. Sir T. S. Raffles has not sufficiently explained to us why he proceeded to Singapoor, after learning the extent of the pretensions advanced by your agents at Malacca. A strict attention to our instructions would have induced him to avoid the possibility of collision with the Netherlandish authorities on any point. And so sincere is our desire to bar the possibility of any altercations with your Excellency's Government that the occupation of Singapoor has been to us a source of profound regret.

"13. In fact, after becoming acquainted with the extent of the pretensions advanced on the part of your nation, and before we knew of the establishment of a factory at Singapoor, we had issued instructions to Sir T. S. Raffles directing him, if our orders should arrive in time, to desist from every attempt to form a British establishment in the Eastern Archipelago.

"14. These orders did not however arrive early enough to prevent the establishment of a factory at Singapoor; and the question for our consideration now is, whether we shall maintain the establishment, which has been formed, or carry a complimentary deference for the Netherlandish authorities so far as to withdraw it. . . .

"19. Let us be convinced that, in establishing a factory at Singapoor, we have intruded on any right possessed by your nation or any claim which we are bound in equity to respect. In this case we should immediately withdraw our establishment from Singapoor, fully recognizing your title to expect that course of conduct from us.

"20. On this point we at present entertain the strongest doubts, which we proceed to explain most frankly to your Excellency, in order that your Excellency may favour us, if it be in your power, with such proofs and arguments as may tend to remove them.

"21. Your Excellency claims Rhio, Johor, Pahang and Lingin as dependencies of Malacca. But, when our Government was established at Malacca, the Dutch authorities at that place, in pursuance of the declared intentions of their superiors, the Government of Batavia, had withdrawn their establishments from Rhio, the only port in their occupation and declared the independence of the Chief of that country. On the strength of that public and conclusive transaction we have always considered and treated Rhio as an independent State, and never exercised over it any act of supremacy.

"22. When we restored Malacca to you, we could not restore that which we did not receive from you. We did not restore Rhio, Johor, Lingin and Pahang as dependencies of Malacca, because (not having obtained them from you) we did not possess them as such. We restore to you what was transferred to us in 1795 and nothing more. That transfer did not include Rhio, Johor, Lingin and Pahang, and this seems to be admitted in your Excellency's letter to which we now have the honour to reply.

"23. Under these circumstances we do not conceive that your Excellency can justly appeal to any connexions, whatever they may have been, which may have existed before 1795, but which were not included in the transfer made to us in that year.

"24. Such connexions were abrogated by the official acts of the representatives of your country on that occasion. We did not reap the advantage to which we should have been entitled, if those connexions had been declared to be in existence; and the subtraction of those advantages from us, had there been a title to them, would have been a fraud of which your nation was wholly incapable. . . .

"25. If, as we hold to be the case, you have no just claim founded on engagements, which may have existed before the transfer of Malacca in 1795, your only right depends on the Treaty concluded at Rhio on the 26th November 1818. . . .

"27. Major Farquhar's Treaty was settled with the Government of Rhio, not as a dependency of Malacca, but as an independent State, purposely with a view to the validity and value of the connexion, after the restoration of Malacca to your nation. . .

"29. If our previous Treaty, which contained nothing injurious to any foreign nation, was not entitled to respect from your nation, we do not know by what reason your Excellency can expect us to acknowledge and respect your subsequent Treaty, tending manifestly to our injury and annulling engagements previously existing between the State of Rhio and our Government.

"30. The only rights of possession in the Eastern Archipelago, which we are bound to acknowledge as vested in the Netherlandish nation, are derived from the Convention of the 13th August 1814, between our respective Sovereigns, in which it was settled that we should restore, with certain exceptions, the Colonies, Factories and Establishments possessed by Holland on the 1st January 1803.

"31. The possessions to be restored under this Convention are of two descriptions. Those which were actually in the possession of Holland on the 1st January 1803, and had been captured by us between that time and the general peace, and those which, though restored at the peace of Amiens, had not actually been occupied by Holland before the renewal of hostilities in 1803.

"32. With regard to either description we engage to restore such Colonies and dependencies as actually came into our possession at the respective periods of acquisition.

"33. Java was in the possession of Holland on the 1st January 1803. When Java came into our possession the only dependencies beyond that island attached to that Government were the Residencies of Macassar on Celebes, and Copang on Timor, and the Factories at Palembang and Japan, and these only are we bound to acknowledge as the proper dependencies of Java reverting to your Sovereign with that Colony by the Convention of August 1814. When your Excellency carries your pretensions further, as we have a deep interest, so we possess an indisputable right to examine into their foundations.

"34. Malacca was not actually in the occupation of Holland on the 1st January 1803; but has nevertheless been restored with the only dependency which came into our hands along with that Settlement [Padang].

"35. According to this interpretation, if we had received Singapoor as a dependency of Malacca in 1795, if at that time the Dutch authorities had made over to us any Factories or Establishments of any kind at Singapoor, if they had even asserted an acknowledged right to that place as a dependency, we should now, notwithstanding the lapse of so many years during which it has been independent, be disposed to recognize your claim. But the Dutch authorities which transferred Malacca in 1795 declared that Rhio and Johor, Pahang and Lingin, through the first of which you claim Singapoor, were not dependencies of Malacca.

"36. We observe . . . that you are disposed to argue that the withdrawing of the Dutch Establishments from the States of Johor, Pahang, Rhio and Lingin, and the declaration by the Dutch authorities at Malacca of the independence of those States, were measures not approved by the constituted authorities of the Dutch East India Company.

"37. We entreat your Excellency to consider that, supposing this to have been precisely as stated to your Excellency, we were nevertheless acting under those declarations, which were to us authentic and sufficient during twenty-three years of possession, throughout which time not a single effort was made to undeceive us, either in war or peace. . . .

"38. If we could agree to consider Rhio as a dependency of Malacca, it would still remain to be shown that Singapoor is a dependency of Rhio, or of the Principality of which the Government resides at Rhio. . . .

"45. We shall endeavour to ascertain to our own satisfaction whether or not the Netherlandish Nation possesses a right tc the exclusive occupation of Singapoor, and if that point be decided in the affirmative, we shall without hesitation obey the dictates of justice by withdrawing all our Establishments from that place. We most cordially invite your Excellency to furnish us with proofs of the justness of your pretensions. . . .

"46. In a like manner we shall endeavour to ascertain whether or not the Chiefs of Singapoor with whom Sir T. S. Raffles has concluded engagements, possessed a right to enter into those engagements; and if it should appear that the right of the Government of Lingin or that of Rhio, or of any other native Power, has been violated, our respect for the rights of every Power will induce us instantly to abandon Singapoor, on the requisition of the injured Power. . . .

"48. If the result of our enquiries and deliberations be to confirm our present apprehensions and to convince us that the Netherlandish Nation has not any right to exclude us from Singapoor, and that the persons who have signed the Treaty with us are the legitimate rulers of the country, we must in this case hold Singapoor, till we know the result of the reference which we have made to Europe, as we have already had the honour of intimating to your Excellency.

"49. The result of that reference, we trust, will be either to define the respective limits of the rights and power of the Netherlandish and British Nations in the Eastern Archipelago, or to establish a liberal and friendly policy for the guidance of the local Government on a footing of cordiality, equality and reciprocal benefit. . . .

"53. We beg leave to refer your Excellency to the language addressed by your agent at Pontiana to Major Farquhar, requiring the latter to refrain from attempting to form any connexion with any of the Chiefs of Borneo, on the ground that the whole of that country had come under your control. In a similar manner you now claim the right of excluding us from all the countries of Johor, Pahang, Rhio and Lingin. . . .

"57. The measures pursued by the Netherlandish Government since its re-establishment in the Eastern Archipelago leave us only the choice of one of three modes of acting. To submit implicitly to all your pretensions, which our interests and our honour alike forbid. To oppose them by systematic counteraction and resistance, which friendship and courtesy prohibit. Or to refer all questions for the decision of our respective Governments in Europe, which is the course we have adopted. . . ."

iii

However critical John Palmer had been of the Achin affair, he was sufficiently clear-sighted to grasp the significance of Singapore. To David Brown, a leading business man in Penang, he wrote with cautious optimism on 27th June:

"I attach great importance to the acquisition of Singapoor, until your principles of Policy are honestly recognized by both States; but on any terms I look to an extension of British Commerce from that Possession; and to the increasing consequence of Penang if, as it ought to be, Singapoor is under your authority. Malacca is in principle sealed up; and may be had for a Song if we are justified at Home, but I am less sanguine of the favourable reception of our recent measure than I was, from the tenor of my communications down to the end of February. The nearer objects at Home seem to occupy the whole eye of the Government."

iv

Two days out from Singapore, the *Indiana* ran aground while passing through the Straits of Rhio during the night.

"It was feared", wrote Sophia in the *Memoir*, "that she would not be got off and a small boat was prepared to convey him [Raffles] back to Singapore with the Editor and their child, an infant four months old; but just as they were leaving the vessel hopes were entertained that by throwing all the water overboard to lighten the ship she might be got off, and before morning the attempt succeeded. It was then considered fortunate that the accident occurred so near a European settlement. . . ."

According to the *Prince of Wales's Island Gazette*, the Dutch Resident at Rhio replenished the water—at least, that was the account received from there. Sophia had a different story to tell.

". . . but on stopping at Rhio and sending in a boat stating what had happened and requesting a supply of water the Dutch Resident refused all intercourse, asserted that Sir Stamford went as a spy and would not give the assistance solicited; it was therefore with considerable anxiety that the voyage was continued; fortunately in passing through the Straits of Banka a good Samaritan appeared in one of the beautiful American vessels so numerous in these seas, when the Captain generously and at considerable risk, for the wind was strong and in his favour, stopped his course and with great difficulty, by means of ropes, conveyed some casks of water and went on board himself to enquire into the cause of distress; the Captain's name is forgotten but his kindness has often been acknowledged with gratitude and praise."

After that the voyage was uneventful and delightful.

"It is difficult to convey an idea of the pleasure of sailing through this beautiful and unparallelled archipelago in which every attraction of nature is combined; the smoothness of the sea, the lightness of the atmosphere, the constant succession of the most picturesque lake scenery, islands of every shape and size clustered together, mountains of the most fanciful forms crowned with verdure to their summits, rich and luxurious vegetation extending to the very edge of the water, little native boats often with only one person in them continuously darting out from the deep shade which concealed them, looking like so many cockle shells wafted about by the wind."

So wrote Sophia, who came with the others in the *Indiana* safely to Bencoolen on the last day of July. It was a happy reunion with Charlotte, already a toddler and "the most gentle, timid being in existence". Bencoolen, too, offered a more smiling welcome than on their first coming there. Of the trees and shrubs replanted around Government House, Sophia wrote:

"As a proof of the luxuriance of the vegetation in these islands, it may be stated that during his absence of eleven months the casuarina trees had grown to the height of thirty or forty feet; and he had the pleasure on his return to see the house encircled by a shrubbery of nutmeg, clove, coco and cassia trees; the place seemed to have been changed almost by magic from a wilderness into a garden."

Raffles' own feelings for the place had also undergone a great change. His first impressions had caused him to speak disparagingly of Sumatra. No doubt the immediate territory under the control of Bencoolen, had it been typical of Sumatra, would have warranted such a poor opinion, but the expeditions he had managed to make into the interior had opened his eyes to the attractions and potentialities of this huge island.

For the moment there was little to be done in the political field in Sumatra. Resistance to the Dutch there had been castigated at home in terms as thoughtless as they were unjust, and Raffles was specifically confined to Bencoolen itself, for fear that, by wandering afield, he should give offence to his neighbours. There was now nothing to distract his mind from the pressing needs of Bencoolen, with ample scope for his reforming zeal.

V

After receiving the stern reproof from Hastings, Governor Bannerman had been misguided enough to send copies of all the correspondence to London, together with a dispatch in which he had stated at length the various arguments he conceived to weigh against the occupation of Singapore. At the same time he has sent letters to the chairman and deputy chairman of the Company, explaining once more that his policy had been uninfluenced by jealousy of Raffles. If Calcutta had been severe, London was hardly less so, his attitude being considered "totally irreconcilable with every principle of public duty". Bannerman did not live to receive this final blow. He died of cholera on 8th August, and Phillips acted as Governor in his place. This was the fifth time Phillips had served in that capacity.

In England, public opinion against the Dutch was again stimulated by the publication that summer of a pamphlet by Charles Assey entitled *On the Trade to China and the Indian Archipelago*. Its sub-title, "The Insecurity of the British Interests in that Quarter", indicated its general purpose, and its reference to Bintang and Raffles' mission to the Rhio archipelago was a foretaste of things to come. The Dutch were furious. Falck called it "Assey's libel".

In official circles, however, the diplomatic exchanges were pursuing their leisurely and discreet course when, at the beginning of August, like a bombshell, arrived the news that Raffles had contrived to obtain by treaty with some local Malay authority the ancient port of Singapore. The British authorities were quite as angry as the Dutch. When the first information of the eastward mission had been received, London had immediately replied that it strongly disapproved, particularly as Sir Stamford Raffles had been placed in charge. It is not surprising, therefore, that the dispatch of 14th August, after receipt of the news of Singapore, was in a very irritable tone and emphasized that "any difficulty with the Dutch will be created by Sir Stamford Raffles' intemperance of conduct and language". The Secret Committee went on to state:

". . . a definitive judgment upon the conduct of Sir T. Stamford Raffles in respect to Singapore must be delayed until the receipt of the Governor-General's opinion as to the manner in which His Lordship's instructions have been executed, more especially as the objections founded by the Governor-General on the written instructions in question were answered by Sir Thomas's assertion that he was wholly entrusted with discretionary powers; an assertion which brings to mind one of a similar sort as to the tenor of the communications made to him in a conversation before he left England.

"With respect to the written instructions furnished to Sir Thomas by the Governor-General in Council, they have unquestionably been contravened both in letter and in spirit; in letter by his proceeding to the Eastward before he visited Acheen and by communicating privately with the King of Acheen before he went to the seat of the Acheenese Government; and in spirit by risking a collision with the Dutch in the Straits of Malacca.

"The false steps taken by Sir Thomas in concluding Treaties with the Chiefs of Sumatra, in instigating a spirit of resistance to the Dutch, and assuming the title of Agent to Great Britain in the Eastern Seas, rendered doubtful the expediency of employing him at all in any negotiation or undertaking in the Eastern Seas. No time is to be lost in disavowing the Treaties concluded by him with the Chiefs of Sumatra; and if Sir Thomas Stamford Raffles should evade an order to this effect the duty of disabusing the said Chiefs must be confided to the Government of Prince of Wales Island.

"His Majesty's Government were about to propose an amicable discussion with the Netherlands Government . . . when intelligence of the acquisition of Singapore arrived. If the discussion is to be interrupted by the intelligence of fresh feuds and violence in the Eastern Seas it seems quite hopeless to begin the work of amicable adjustment. . . . If the Dutch should forcibly expel our garrison at Singapore we must either submit in silence or demand reparation at a hazard of war which may involve all Europe. . . .

"The doubt stated by the Government of Prince of Wales Island as to the competency of the East India Company under the new Charter to make conquests to the Southward of the Line is considered as being well founded.[1] Sir Thomas Stamford Raffles cannot presume to suppose that he has been empowered by His Majesty's Government to make such acquisitions on behalf of the Crown. He has by no means made out the title of the Chief from whom he has obtained the cession of Singapore; and as the Dutch had asserted a previous claim to Singapore founded on grants from the Sultan of Rhio he was bound by his instructions so far to respect such claim as to make its validity a matter of discussion and to refer that discussion to Bengal. He has thought proper to act in direct contradiction to those instructions and has chosen to presume that the discussion will go more favourably to this country if, instead of the tedious

[1] The Secret Committee seemed equally unaware that Singapore lies north, not south, of the Equator.

process of investigating the title of the Dutch Government to all they claim, His Majesty's Ministers shall have only to maintain Sir Stamford Raffles in possessions which he has thought proper to occupy."

But diplomats of the calibre of Castlereagh never allow their feelings to guide their policy. Having expressed his annoyance in no uncertain terms, he did not forget the policy he had laid down in regard to the East Indies. On 13th August he wrote to Lord Clancarty, the British ambassador at The Hague:

"There are two principles from which the British Government can under no circumstances be expected to depart; the one is, they cannot acquiesce in a practical exclusion or in a mere permissive of British commerce throughout the immense extent of the Eastern Archipelago; nor can they consent so far to expose the direct Commerce of this Country with China to all the obvious dangers and disadvantages which would result, especially in time of war, from all the military and naval keys of the Straits of Malacca being exclusively in the hands of the Netherlands Government."

The dispatch of the Secret Committee to Calcutta therefore ended by saying that it had been decided to await the explanations of the Governor-General "before retaining or relinquishing Sir Thomas Raffles' acquisition at Singapore".

C. A. Grey, writing to Assey at this time, remarked:

"I am entirely out of the way of learning what effect the receipt of these dispatches has had, but I was informed that Ministers were about ten days ago in consultation with regard to the interests of this country in the Indian islands; and it is to be hoped that the actual arrival of this moment, when the encroachments of the Dutch had very nearly come to the point of shutting out our trade from every port between Penang and the Moluccas, will induce Ministers to adopt a decided policy . . . but unless the public voice declare against it, I fear that the welfare of millions in that part of the world will weigh but little in the scale against the convenience and policy of European Continental objects. Would it be possible to interest the commercial world also and to unite in a general feeling towards the Eastern Archipelago? I can't help thinking that some of the members of the Administration are aware of the importance of the moment, and that Mr Canning would be disposed to listen to the suggestion of his Liverpool friends on this subject."

Boulger quotes this letter as written by Assey, but the copy among the papers of Dr Thomas Raffles gives Grey as the author. Assey passed it on to Dr Raffles on 9th August, when he also forwarded the letter from Raffles mentioned on page 506.

While Castlereagh may have been impervious to commercial influence Canning was not. Before becoming president of the India Board of

Control, he had been returned to Parliament by the commercial vote in Liverpool, and was therefore keenly interested in the views of business men. It is to be suspected that he was early determined to keep Singapore. His correspondence with the Special Select Committee, set up to produce factual evidence of Dutch monopoly in the East Indies, suggests that he was prodding that committee to supply him with ammunition to fight the battle.

Assey had hoped that his specialized knowledge would be called into use, and he had tried to obtain the appointment of secretary to the British delegation that would negotiate with the Dutch. Unfortunately for him Castlereagh had strong views—as indeed had Falck—on the undesirability of local experts participating in the discussions, on the grounds that negotiations were liable to become clouded by too much local detail and too many personal views. After prolonging his stay in England as long as he could afford, Assey eventually abandoned his hopes and returned to India, where he resumed his medical profession. It was a pity that his services were not directly utilized, for he was well equipped for the task. But his published writings and his private conversations had had their effect.

The Dutch Government, having so recently received from the British Government such a complete disavowal of Raffles, whose status had been described to them as scarcely higher than that of a commercial agent, looked with confidence for an immediate and no less complete disavowal of this fresh outrage perpetuated by this apparently minor official, an outrage, too, that put all his previous enormities in the shade. There was indeed no small possibility that the British Government, infuriated by this further and much graver act of insubordination—for such at first it appeared to be—might have repudiated out of hand the acquisition of Singapore.

This was exactly what the Dutch hoped would happen. While, however, it had been easy to disown Raffles, playing a lone hand against the Dutch in Sumatra, particularly as his operations there did not happen to suit the policy of the British Government, it was not quite so easy to follow the same technique when he was acting under the instructions, even if he had stretched them a little, of the Governor-General in Council. Moreover, public opinion against the Dutch had now been seriously roused in England, and while it was still Raffles who was making trouble, the Government could not afford to ignore public opinion entirely, even though it was only commercial opinion. If the man and the deed could be kept separate—if, that is, attention could be focused on the importance of the acquisition of Singapore, and the fact that Raffles had been responsible for it could be conveniently forgotten, all might be well.

Instead, then, of truckling once more to Dutch remonstrances, the

British Government on this occasion was content to share their indignation—and temporize. From that moment the future of Singapore was virtually assured. The diplomatic struggle that followed resolved itself into an argument as to what price should be paid for it.

We are able to follow the general course of the negotiations by studying the correspondence between the two foreign ministers and their ambassadors. The principals at the outset were Castlereagh and Canning in London, Baron van Nagell[1] and Falck in Brussels, where Britain was represented by Lord Clancarty. The Dutch ambassador to Britain was Baron Fagel.

In his letter of 13th August, to which reference has already been made, Castlereagh instructed Clancarty to suggest to the Dutch Government that they should "appoint one or more plenipotentiaries to meet in London in the month of November next for the purpose of amicably discussing and regulating the rights and interests of the two States in the Eastern Seas". This interval of time would give an opportunity for discovering what measure of success had been achieved by the orders sent out by Great Britain and Holland to the East, to prevent disputes and provocative action on the part of their respective officials, and also for us to ascertain the exact extent of Dutch pretensions there, whether in the form of strict possession or by concession from native princes; and finally, what the attitude of the Dutch Government itself was towards the freedom of subjects of other powers to frequent those seas.

After laying down emphatically the two principles from which the British Government could not depart, Castlereagh invited attention to the conciliatory attitude of the British Government, as displayed by the Governor-General in his "prompt and unsolicited disavowal of the unauthorized treaties of cession and occupations of territory, which, under a mistaken view of his powers, were made by the Lieutenant-Governor of Bencoolen". In return the Dutch Government "must leave open to Great Britain such commercial facilities, including the residence of commercial agents, as may satisfy the fair pretensions of His Majesty's subjects".

British requirements were commercial and not political, and if the Dutch Government thought it could "establish the same exclusive dominion over the islands, which we have gradually acquired over the continent [of India]", they had better consider the difficulties involved, and what a hazardous and impracticable policy this must prove.

Clancarty replied on 18th August. After referring to various conversations, he reported the private view of van Nagell, who "professed himself as agreeing entirely in all that I said and stated that he himself believed

[1] Anne Willem Carel, Baron van Nagell van Ampsen, known by his main surname, van Nagell. Formerly Dutch ambassador in London.

that the King had no desire whatever to adopt the mad policy of exclusion; that all he understood his Majesty to wish was to enjoy in full sovereignty those settlements which had been ceded to him, and those which had prior to the war been so enjoyed by his Nation . . . that it should not be their policy to render these factories exclusive, either with or without the sanction of the native princes; indeed he seemed surprised that such a line of policy could have been suspected as having been adopted by them and still more that they should ever have been supposed mad enough to have conceived the idea of possessing themselves of all the keys and shutting up the double entrance to the Eastern Seas through the Straits of Malacca and those of Sunda". Clancarty wrote that he had explained in reply that he had observed that their recent settlement at Rhio, in addition to their possession of Java and their claim to the Lampongs, "presented something upon which the suspicion of such a policy might not be deemed unreasonable" and that, to support his contention, he had also pointed out the positions on a map. Van Nagell "allowed it might be so, but deprecated, nevertheless, its being for a moment supposed that they could ever have entertained so absurd a project of risking the enmity of Great Britain and everyone else trading in that area".

Two days later Clancarty wrote again to Castlereagh, reporting a confidential talk with Falck, carried on with the full authority of the King. It appeared that a meeting of plenipotentiaries in November would be acceptable to the Dutch, but that the extent of ground to be covered was not so easy to agree. Falck had been somewhat evasive, expressing his anxiety to await the arrival of Elout, now hourly expected from Batavia. Clancarty had endeavoured to explain the British point of view.

"M. de Falck stated that some difficulty might arise: for, tho' as far, as their claims were founded on strict possession in acknowledged sovereignty, as in the case of Java and Banca, &c, he did not conceive there could be any doubt that such claims would be admitted as entire and absolute, to be regulated by their sole will and decision (to which I did not object); yet to what extent their views should be carried, as founded upon concessions from native princes; how far they should conceive it requisite to seek the exclusion of others from the settlements, they should thus form; how limited in point of space, or how far they should seek to exclude the residence of the commercial agents of other Powers at them, these were questions, upon which he had not yet made up his mind: neither could he determine upon them, till after conversation with M. Elout. . . .

"I told him I was sorry to find there could exist on the part of any member of his Government, even for a moment, any doubt of rendering the fair and friendly participation in the commerce of the Eastern islands open to all, but was sure that upon consideration of the pernicious results, which must arise from such policy, his more mature opinion would coincide with ours upon the subject. . . .

"I conceive the leaning of M. de Falck's mind to be in favour of exclusive commerce, under concessions from native princes, and fear this leaning is rather likely to be strengthened than relaxed by consulting with those, who may have imbibed local prejudices. What is the King's opinion upon this point? Maybe I have no means of yet knowing; but as far as that privately confirmed by M. le Baron de Nagell is concerned, and may have weight, I have reason to know it coincides entirely with ours. . . . I believe myself that all our difficulties with the Dutch in those parts have originated from Sir Stamford Raffles. His conduct excited, as it appears, the jealousy of M. Capellen (who very happily is a man of good sense and fully imbued with the opinion of the closest connexion with us being requisite for his country), hence grew several of the establishments made by them, and thence the necessity of making others on our part appeared to our Government at Calcutta."

Baron van Nagell wrote to Fagel on 31st August:

"I cannot disguise the fact that Sir Stamford Raffles has, up to a certain point, achieved his aim and has alarmed the British Cabinet as to our views; it is essential to work to remedy these false insinuations, and to convince them that we have not got any of that dominating ambition, which the said Sir Stamford Raffles attributed to us; this man is a Herostrate,[1] and seeks to cause a stir to make himself of importance, and if I may be permitted to hazard an opinion, I believe that when one wishes to be listened to with confidence one must always avoid employing agents of that kind."

This letter and its enclosure were passed on by Fagel to Castlereagh on 7th September. Castlereagh wrote back on the following day:

"I return you with many thanks the confidential communication with the enclosed letter from M. de Nagell. The reply to Lord Clancarty's 'note verbale' is, perhaps necessarily, obscure upon the mode of interpreting general principles applicable to the relative position of our interests in the Eastern Seas; but as we are agreed in the policy of some clear friendly understanding, I willingly accept M. de Nagell's assurances as auspicious harbingers of our future hopes, and doubt not the same temper which has carried us successfully through other matters of greater importance will bring us upon this subject also to an early and satisfactory settlement."

The article that had appeared in the *Calcutta Journal* concerning the importance of the Singapore acquisition was reprinted on 7th September in *The Times*.

[1] Herostratus burned down the Temple of Artemis at Ephesus in 356 B.C. for the sole purpose of immortalizing himself.

vi

The Marquis of Hastings was busy seeking facts. On his instructions, Metcalfe wrote to Raffles on 21st August, sending a copy to Farquhar:

"Having recently received a dispatch from the Netherlandish Governor-General at Batavia dated the 25th March, in which he stated that the Prince, whom you represent as the legitimate Sovereign of Johor, was lately residing at Rio under the care of the Vice Roy or Rajah Moodha and at the cost of the Sultan reigning at Lingin, I am directed to request that you will without delay furnish particular explanations on this point.

"You will be pleased to report the precise nature of his situation at Rio, if the fact of his Residence be established; as well as the duration of his Residence and the exact period and immediate cause of his withdrawing from Rio. His Lordship in Council also wishes to learn whether any overtures were received by you or Major Farquhar from the Prince, whom you consider as the legitimate Sultan, and whether you had any communication with the Chief previously to the 1st February, the date on which he is said to have arrived at Singapoor. I am desired to point out the importance of your transmitting a full and distinct exposition of all circumstances preceding the conclusion of the Treaty with that person, in order to enable this Government to justify the procedure of its Agents against the charges advanced by the Netherlandish Government of Batavia. His Excellency in Council will anxiously await your report, in the hope that it will remove from the transaction the uncertainty and ambiguity which at present attach to it."

On the same day Hastings sent a long dispatch to van der Capellen in answer to the equally lengthy one from Batavia of 25th March. All that need be quoted here is a reference to the arrangements made by Raffles with Tunku Long and the Temenggong:

"Our accounts do not admit of the belief that any compulsion or menace was used in the Treaties which they entered into, or that those were concluded otherwise than with the most perfect goodwill on their part."

Farquhar's first report on Singapore to Raffles was dated 2nd September:

"In spite of very wet weather, roads have been mended and the clearance of woods in the vicinity of the Settlement is progressing. The Chinese Town on the S.W. side of the River is becoming extensive, new streets have been laid out to meet the steadily increasing population. A new bridge has been formed over the Freshwater Stream and a commodious Reservoir and Aquaduct constructed near the foot of the Hill from which ships can at all times be supplied with excellent water."

A good harbour had been found "near the middle of the small Strait formed by the Singapore Shore and the Adjacent islands" and both entrances could be easily defenced. Farquhar omitted to mention that the discovery was made by Captain Maxfield. It is known to-day as Keppel Harbour.

The continued occupation of Singapore by the English was causing van der Capellen grave concern. As he wrote to Falck on 23rd September: "We are heavily compromised in the eyes of the native princes. The Viceroy of Riouw is constantly asking the Governor of Malacca, whether a decision has not yet been reached upon the Singapore affair, and whether the English will be staying there. They don't understand how it can be possible that we don't expel them. It makes a very unfavourable impression upon them, and this has been still further increased by the occurrence in Palembang. The whole archipelago became instantly aware of that and the success of the expedition is, particularly in these circumstances, mostly necessary. . . .

"I repeat what I have written to you in my previous letter; if we leave the English in the possession of Singapore, we must not imagine that Malacca can be of the slightest importance to us. We keep the Princes, subjected to us, still true to us with beautiful words, though it is not always easy, but when they see that we really do give up Singapore, they will desert us and regard our authority as crippled and subjected to that of our jealous neighbours. We must remember this before committing a mistake on that point."

Chapter Twenty-five

BENCOOLEN AND CALCUTTA, 1819

i

APART from his natural desire to see Bencoolen happy and prosperous, Raffles nursed the hope that if he could build up a model colony there, his success might, even at that late hour, convince his masters at home that, having thrown away Java, they could possess in Sumatra a greater prize still.

On his first arrival he had taken immediate steps to curb the more obvious abuses. Slavery, as far as the Company was concerned, had been abolished, as also had forced cultivation; Bencoolen had been declared a free port, and the currency regulations adjusted on a fairer basis. All these were relatively simple issues, readily dealt with by administrative action. But the mere repeal of unjust legislation could not by itself solve Bencoolen's problem; it was only the first, if the most essential, step. If the settlement was to be restored to prosperity, far-sighted planning was also required.

Being a realist as well as an idealist, Raffles needed to be assured that his policy would be soundly based. To arrive at the facts, he set up a number of committees. Collection of information was their primary concern, but they had also two secondary objects. In the absence of a Council, there was no official body whom he could consult, so it was highly desirable that an informed public opinion should be created, this being achieved by the selection of prominent officials and others to participate in the investigations. Secondly, there was a plethora of redundant officials with no duties whatever to perform.

Of the two most important committees, one dealt with the causes of the deplorable state of the settlement and what could be done to improve it; the other was required to suggest how schools could be established for the education on simple lines of the children. Both these committees were entrusted to the chaplain, the Rev. Charles Winter. On the first, which had the wider scope, he was assisted by Dr Jack and Captain Cathcart Methven, who had been transferred from Java; on the second by Dr John Lumsdaine, Captain Watson and the young Baptist missionary, Nathaniel Ward, who also ran the printing-press.

Charles Winter had already started a school for the Caffre children in the settlement, and the committee was now requested to consider how education could be extended to include not only all native children in

Bencoolen, but also those in the interior. The principle of education that Raffles had in mind was that adopted by the national schools in England.

Travers refers in his diary to these committees, of some of which, though apparently not the two most important ones, he himself became a somewhat unwilling member.

"Upon these I stood conspicuous and had various intricate and puzzling reports to make out, which were the more annoying as I knew they were likely in many instances to become public. However, I did my best and satisfied Sir Stamford in all that I was concerned with."

The two main committees made their reports at the beginning of October. After a general description of Bencoolen and the districts under its immediate control, the first report referred to the prevailing belief that the steady fall in population was due either to the ravages of smallpox or to the extreme unhealthiness of the territory (both of which the committee questioned) or to the unproductive nature of the soil (which, in the committee's view was, at least in the interior, as fertile as the richest parts of Java). The truth was, suggested the committee, that the people were extremely poor and deficient in industry.

"In no part of our Indian possessions we believe shall we find them so far back in this respect."

For an explanation, they felt they must examine the historical background.

"We shall for the sake of illustration suppose that at the first settlement of the British in this quarter people were in much the same condition as at the present moment, and it will subsequently appear that they could not have been lower, and were probably higher. What then could have been the consequences had they been left to themselves to pursue their own course of improvement? The valuable productions of their country would in that case either have furnished the inhabitants themselves with the means of commerce and of acquiring wealth on which all the natural consequences would have attended, improvements in the arts of life, a taste for its luxuries and a more regular and organized system of things; or another effect might have been produced, the people continuing divided into small societies without much power of means of resistance would have tempted the rapacity of some enterprising individual, the country would have been subdued and order established by the strong arm of power. . . . Many temporary disorders would have taken place but the progress of things though slow would have been sure.

"Different from either of these has been the effect of British influence. We appeared on their shores in the character of traders not of conquerors; of traders, however, possessed of power much superior to that of the people whose productions we desired. Our first contacts were made with the chiefs for the delivery of a stipulated quantity of produce, but as their power was yet inconsiderable irregularity in the fulfilment would be likely to occur from a variety of causes. Wars and disputes among the people would further tend to the interruption of our commerce and a certain interference in the affairs of the country. To preserve tranquillity and enforce the existing agreements would appear not only for our own interest but for that of all parties. When a powerful nation once interferes in the concerns of a weaker, it is impossible to fix the limits of its authority. Every such interposition would operate to weaken the power of the native chiefs, and as it fell . . . the more the irregularity in the fulfilment of their contracts. . . .

"The presence of an agent in each district would be found advisable; a closer inspection would bring to light the petty oppressions exercised by the chiefs and it would at length appear a salutary measure to interpose our authority in favour of the people. . . . The interference of the agents of the Company in their internal administration and the restriction so imposed on the authority of the native chiefs, struck at the root of civil society. . . .

"There is nothing perhaps more difficult than to draw a true and accurate character of a people nor shall we pretend to do so, but we think the observations we have offered will justify the opinion we have expressed that under prudent and judicious management there exist qualities and powers which may be expanded and directed and a foundation on which a better order of things may be established."

Although Raffles was critical of certain points in this report (the copy in the India Office Library has marginal notes apparently in his hand), there is no doubt that he was in general sympathy with the views of the committee. As soon as he had had opportunities of visiting the interior, he had quickly grasped that Sumatra presented an administrative and political problem totally different from the one he had had to tackle in Java. Here, he felt, there was need for the establishment of a despotic authority.

"In order to render an uncivilized people capable of enjoying full liberty," he wrote to his friend Thomas Murdoch, "they must feel the weight of authority and must become acquainted with the mutual relations of society. . . . Power we do and have possessed; we have employed it in the most arbitrary of all modes, in the exaction of forced services and in the monopoly of the produce of the country. While as if in mockery we have professed to exercise no interference with the native administration of the country, we have made ourselves the task masters of the people and with a false humility have refused to be their governors. Ought we not to discard this empty pretence; the people are now living without a head to direct them for we have destroyed the power of the native Chiefs; both reason and humanity would urge us to take the management into our own hands and to repair the mischief of a hundred years by affording them a regular and organized government. . . . Tyrants seldom want an excuse and in becoming a despot I am desirous to give you mine. . . ."

The regulations introducing these reforms, and also the new legislation regarding *menghiris* (debt slaves) were not published until the following year,[1] but for convenience can be referred to here. The principles outlined in the former were as follows. The European establishments having been withdrawn from the outstations, it was necessary that the administrations in those districts should be explained and understood. It was consequently declared:

"1. That it is the desire of Government to give the utmost freedom to cultivation and by promoting a spirit of enterprise and speculation among individuals to extend the commerce of the country and advance the interests and happiness of the people at large.

"2. That in order to ensure to the cultivator the fruits of his industry enquiry has been made into the nature of the tenure of lands and it has been found that a permanent interest in the soil is not inconsistent with the native institutions of the country.

"3. That it is in consequence the intention of Government to respect and confirm these rights by acknowledging the different Chiefs as proprietors of the land over which their several jurisdictions extend and to consider the villagers as holding it from them."

The order then explained the duties of the various types of native authorities, of which the principal ones were to be called "Officers of Division". They would be held responsible for the general superintendence of their respective divisions, receiving their orders direct from the Lieutenant-Governor.

"To this officer does the Government look not only for the vigilant administration of Police but for the zealous execution of every measure conducive to the prosperity and improvement of the country. He will especially have the control and management of the bazaars and will be responsible for the roads, bridges and ferries, for keeping an uninterrupted communication throughout the country and for preventing any undue exaction or restriction which can in any way interfere with the freedom of trade and uninterrupted disposal and transport of the produce of the country."

In regard to slaves and *menghiris*, the new regulation observed that experience had proved that "the present system of slave-debtors is at variance with the principles of good government inasmuch as it affords

[1] "New Regulations for the Management of the Outstations" (May 1820), "New Regulations Regarding Debtors and Slaves" (November 1820), printed as Appendix F and Appendix G in *Proceedings of the Agricultural Society Established in Sumatra* (1821).

the means of evading the rules for the suppression of slavery and encourages a spirit of gambling and idleness to the ruin of the character and morals of the borrower as well as the interests of the lender". The basis of the reform was that a slave-debtor could work off his debt and that the period must not in any case exceed ten years. During the period of debt-service, certain conditions as to payment and clothing had to be observed. On the other hand, if the slave-debtor failed to carry out his part of the contract, he could be punished by the court. It was still lawful for a man to give his service to discharge a loan or debt, but this could only be done for one year unless with the approval of a magistrate and under a proper record of the contract. On reaching the age of fourteen, children who, because of the poverty of their parents, had been handed over to others as debt slaves must be brought for registration before a magistrate, who would decide at what age each child became free of debt slavery, taking into consideration the length of time the child had been maintained by the employer. As for slavery in general, those who were actually in that condition would be recognized as such, but they had to be registered, and once the register was completed, no other person whatever could be recognized as a slave. The regulation was designed to prevent fresh slaves being brought surreptitiously into the settlement.

The other main committee had tackled its problem. Education of the adult population was possible only within limits, for they were too set in their ways to be capable of radical improvement, but if the children could be influenced at their impressionable age, then the future might be bright indeed. In his early consideration of this question, Raffles had realized that children were of use to their parents in various ways, such as guarding cattle, and as the parents would be unlikely to appreciate the benefits their children would derive from education, some inducement, in the form of allowances of rice for regular attendance, would have to be contemplated. As one immediate step, he had suggested for the committee's consideration that a prospectus in Malay be circulated. This proposal had at once been accepted, and by this means it had been made known that under the proposed scheme children would be taught to read and write their own native language, would be instructed in the elements of general science and in the principles of practical morality. It had been emphasized that there would be no interference with their religious beliefs. The ages acceptable would be from three to sixteen years. At this stage, at the suggestion of Raffles, four Sumatran chiefs had been added to the committee, which, after consultation with these, was able to give its report on 2nd October.

After a lengthy sketch of the primitive degree of civilization to be found in the settlement and the reluctance commonly exhibited to undertake any continuous physical or mental exertion, the committee affirmed that "the prospective advantages and felicitous results to be expected from the establishment appear beyond measure momentous". The method it was proposed to follow was that laid down in the Lancasterian system,[1] and the progress to be followed from the infant stage upward was explained in some detail. Apart from its value as an educative process, the committee thought that the Lancasterian system was bound to have "a beneficial influence on the morals of the children and a powerful tendency to produce good and useful habits".

"Its leading features, self tuition, or the mode of conducting the school through the medium of the scholars themselves, the rules with regard to precedence and classification proportioned under their respective attainments, the peculiar nature of the awards and punishments . . . are calculated in an eminent degree . . . to excite a generous spirit of emulation."

Notwithstanding the strong feelings of its members as Christians, the committee definitely set its face against any inculcation of Christian doctrines, hoping that if the children "can be brought to love the precepts of morality and virtue, they may become gradually enamoured of our Religion".

And so the school was started.

"Such portion of my time", Raffles wrote home in October, "as is not taken up in public business is principally devoted to Natural History. We are making very extensive collections in all departments; and as Sophia takes her full share in all these pursuits the children will no doubt easily imbibe a taste for these amusing and interesting occupations. Charlotte has her lap full of shells and the boy is usually denominated 'le jeune Aristotle'."

In the midst of all these beneficent activities the brig *Favourite* arrived at Bencoolen on 2nd October, bringing news of Bannerman's death. According to Travers:

"Whilst at Calcutta the Marquess of Hastings told him [Raffles] that he thought the Government of our Eastern possessions should be placed under one head, and that no man was better qualified for the situation than Sir Stamford and that on the removal or going away of Colonel Bannerman he would certainly recommend the measure."

Raffles decided to write at once to Hastings. Travers pointed out that it would not be easy to dispossess Phillips, who "had been so often superseded", and that if there were to be any prospect of success, another visit to Calcutta was essential. Eventually Raffles came round to this opinion, though he was reluctant to leave Sophia behind, the brig being

[1] In 1801 Joseph Lancaster established in the Borough Road, London, a school in which the elder children were set to teach the younger. This developed into the Royal Lancasterian Institution, which in 1814 became the British and Foreign School Society.

very small, its limited accommodation quite unsuitable for a woman. Sophia readily accepted the decision, and Raffles left in the first week of October, taking with him Dr Jack and Captain Watson, who had been long waiting to get to India. On the same day, Methven left for Penang, whence he proceeded to Singapore. He had got into serious trouble in Bencoolen, being described by Travers as an "efficient and able assistant led astray, I fear, by too great a love of money; this led to irregularities in office".

After a rough voyage the *Favourite* reached Calcutta about 12th November, and it was not long before John Palmer was reporting to Phillips:

"The Golden Sword came here posthaste on the alleged report of your demise, ten days after the good Colonel's. He comes on public grounds to show his Pretensions to your Government, having disinterestedly proposed long ago to the Court to reduce the Government to a Residency and consolidate everything Eastward in one Hand. I told him that I knew you had anticipated him full seven or eight years in the first suggestion; and that I had been turning Heaven and Earth to procure the confirmation of your Pretensions here and at Home. He is sanguine the Mission to Acheen having, as Assey writes me, recovered him Caste with his old Friends and slackened the enmity of his Opposers; and the success of both Services being likely to restore him to the greater zeal of his Friends. It may be so, but whilst Lord Castlereagh and the D. of Wellington are for maintaining European Relations, I fancy Singapoor will not be made a Bone of Contention."

The general plans laid by Raffles before Hastings can be gauged from the long memorandum quoted by Lady Raffles as an appendix to the *Memoir* under the title "Administration of the Eastern Islands in 1819". It opened with an explanation of why the high hopes that had caused Penang to be elevated to a Presidency in 1805 had come to be disappointed. While allowing that too great optimism may have been in part the reason, the main cause had been the lethargy of the local government and the contentious spirit of the members of the Council, "which made as many parties in the Settlement as there were opinions in the Council". Raffles then proceeded to review adjacent countries: the Burman empire, Siam, Cochin-China, Sumatra, Borneo, the Dutch East Indies, New Holland (Australia), the Malay Peninsula and China. From there he proceeded to divide his subject under three main headings:

"1. The high importance of our connexion with these countries, whether considered with reference to the national interests in general, or to those of British India in particular.

"2. The nature of our connexion which is and ought to be purely commercial, and our interference, politically, no further extended than to secure the general interests of that commerce.

"3. The object of our connexions being purely commercial our establishments should be conformable and our relations with the native states conducted exclusively on that principle."

The supremacy of Great Britain having now been established in India: ". . . it remains to draw forth the resources of the country and to open and secure the channels through which it must flow. To ensure a market for the manufactures of India and thus promote its industry and prosperity, and to give an advantageous and beneficial direction to the energies of its people, becomes an object of great and increasing importance."

The extraordinary advance of British manufactures had closed the European market, and it was to the East that we must now look for a permanent demand for Indian products.

Of territorial possessions in the East, England had more than enough already. To build up establishments on other than purely commercial principles would be courting disaster. The financial failure of Bencoolen and Penang were due to deviation from such a policy.

"The true and vivifying spirit of Commerce is one which tends as much to raise and excite the energies of the cultivator who sells, as to promote the interest of the merchant who buys and is directly opposed to that system of forced cultivation and undue monopoly, which while it destroys every motive to exertion must eventually defeat the object of those by whom it is enforced, and thus, even as a simple matter of calculation, turn to the loss of both parties."

He mentioned the principles on which this commerce should be based. "Our establishments should be directed to no partial or immediate views of commercial profit but to the preservation of a free and unrestricted Commerce, and to the encouragement and protection of individual enterprise and the interests of the general merchant."

Trade in the eastern islands had always flourished where protection had been given and political obstructions had not interfered.

"The events of two centuries have necessarily effected a considerable change in the course and channel of this Commerce . . . but the principle remains unaltered. . . . Thus although Bantam and Acheen may have long ceased to be two of the principal emporia, the place of the former has been supplied by Batavia, while the trade of the latter now centres in Penang. Dutch policy destroyed the emporium of Malacca which had by political necessity been transferred from Singapore, once the great emporium of these Seas, whose history is lost in the mists of antiquity, but whose greatness and importance are still preserved in the records of tradition. The more Eastern emporium of the Moluccas has shared the fate of Malacca and the object of the Dutch Settlement at Macasser [*sic*] is solely to prevent its rise."

But it only required the influence of an opposite policy for trade to flow to an *entrepôt* again as it always did in the past.

"Thus by the possession of Penang and Singapore . . . we have the means of reviving and re-establishing at least two of the ancient emporia."

This without interfering with the Dutch centre of Batavia. Penang, like Singapore, should now be treated as a purely commerical establishment under the general superintendence of the Supreme Government. Modest establishments only should be maintained there and at Bencoolen. The present practice of maintaining in each place a regular civil establishment "from writers [junior clerks] to the highest offices" was now shown to be wrong. While the system worked well in large territories, it was a failure in small ones.

"The number is too limited to admit of competition, or selection, and the narrowness of the field is too apt to contract their ideas to the local habits and prejudices of the place."

What advantage would the Company be likely to reap from such a policy?

"Heretofore the Company's trade in this quarter has not only been a losing one to themselves, but has tended to the depression of industry among the people, and to the exclusion and discouragement of the private merchant. This has been in a great measure owing to the mode in which it has been conducted, and to the erroneous system of combining the speculations of commerce with the powers of Government . . . of monopoly it may be said as of slavery, that it is twice cursed; that its effects are not less ruinous to those who enforce it, than to those who are subjected to it."

It could no longer be the interest or duty of the East India Company to carry into its Indian administration that vision of monopoly and coercive exertion that had so long been exploded as impolitic and unjust. It now stood on a higher and more exalted footing; the strongest bulwark of its constitution would be found in the attention it paid to the improvement and happiness of its subjects, and in the sacrifice of pecuniary interests it was always willing to make when those appeared to stand in the way of the civilization and advancement of the human race. The time was past when the Company looked for its profit from the sale of a yard of broadcloth or a pound of nails: it now acted in a more extended sphere, its principles expanding with the growth of its empire. It now looked to the wealth and enterprise of those whom it governed as the sure and only sources of its own financial prosperity. While these had not existed, it had necessarily been left to the Company to supply the wants of its Indian population, in detail; but now it must look to its trade in the Indian empire being conducted on the same principles as in the mother country. If the Company was to interest itself in commerce, it should only do so on a grand scale.

"Thus her capital would be employed to open new channels of trade, to encourage industry, and by diffusing wealth and exciting enterprise, tend to promote the best interests of mankind, and would resemble those sea-born clouds, which descending in showers on her Indian mountains, return in a thousand fertilizing streams to the source from whence they rose."

The copy of this memorandum preserved in the India Office Library contains a paragraph omitted by Lady Raffles. It deals with Cochin-China.

"Since that period an event has tended to estrange the Cochin-Chinese still further from our interests; a contract having been entered into by a mercantile house at Madras to supply the King with a large quantity of arms, they were found on examination to be of inferior quality and payment refused on these grounds."

The arms had been retained and the merchants had received only partial payment through the medium of our ships of war. The Cochin-Chinese were laying the blame and discredit on our Government. It seemed probable that French emissaries had been concerned in this incident. The memorandum continued:

"The views of the French in this quarter are not likely under present circumstances to be foregone and in proof of this it deserves notice that an Association or Company was lately formed in that country with a view to such an Establishment and that three ships belonging to this Association actually arrived in one of the ports of Cochin-China during the last year and proceeded from thence to Manilla."

In the India Office Library there is also a letter from Raffles to Holt Mackenzie, secretary to Government at Calcutta. It is dated 20th December 1819 and incorporates the substance of the memorandum. It would appear that the memorandum was drafted by Raffles as an *aide-mémoire* from which he composed the letter to Holt Mackenzie. While he advances much the same arguments in both documents, the letter includes one important variation that suggests a greater degree of devolution than does the memorandum.

"The residence of the superintending authority would not necessarily be fixed on either, he would occasionally visit them all and his principal residence would of course be in that which united the most advantages for his superintendence and for communication with the higher authorities."

The organization of the Incorporated Settlements (the original title of the Straits Settlements) followed the principles laid down here by Raffles.

It is impossible, in an abbreviated précis such as the foregoing, to do justice to this memorandum, which is over fifteen thousand words in length, or to the enlightened policy it advocates—the very policy, in fact, that, in modern times, has been the pride of the British Empire, however imperfect at times has been its execution.

Hastings reception of his ideas was very cordial.

"The consolidation of our Eastern possessions", he wrote on 27th November, "into one Government subordinate to the Supreme Authority would unquestionably be a desirable arrangement. I think it likely to strike the Court of Directors in consequence of the various documents which have within the last two years been transmitted to them. Their judgment possibly may not determine the point, for the consideration of the subject will be complicated with the result of discussions between the Courts of London and Brussels. I fear we shall have but a patchy determination. Till a decision shall be signified to us it would be premature to fashion, even provisionally, any plans; but it is always expedient to scrutinize in the interval all particulars so as to be prepared to act upon the principle which may be dictated to us."

Other major matters discussed by Raffles with Hastings were education and the prospect of retaining Singapore. The former was the subject of another very long memorandum, but consideration of it can be deferred, as one of its principal features, the proposal for a native college at Singapore, can be more appropriately dealt with among the activities of Raffles during his final visit there. In any event, it was intended to postpone its application until the retention of Singapore had been confirmed.

Hastings himself remained firmly in favour of Singapore and showed himself a loyal supporter of Raffles. At the same time, he enjoined the utmost economy in expenditure, not only, we may suppose, for fear that the island might ultimately be given to the Dutch, but also, and perhaps more important, lest the East India Company might utilize the expense incurred at Singapore as an argument against its retention.

What the decision at home was likely to be, no one could more than guess.

ii

The discussions between the Dutch and British plenipotentiaries, which had been arranged for November, were deferred. On 3rd December Clancarty reported to Castlereagh details of a private conversation he had had with Elout, who had been selected as Fagel's colleague in the Anglo-Dutch negotiations.

"In general terms M. Elout disclaims any desire on the part of the Netherlands to set up a system of exclusion or one of permission, as emanating from them, in the Seas within the Straits of Malacca and Sunda and yet, and notwithstanding the same disclaimer by MM. Falck and Nagell, the pretensions of this Government, as I had in some degree apprehended, amount, according to M. Elout, to nearly the same thing. The native Princes, with whom they had treaties prior to the war of the Revolution, they look upon as their feudatories, deprecating their being considered as independent, admitting that of none others, and consequently asserting their own sovereignty over them, and although they profess to disclaim exclusion, or to set up their permission as a requisite to authorize the tráde to other European States, they object to the residence of Commercial Agents of other Powers with those Princes; thus rendering the trade of all other countries, in fact, dependent upon their Residents.

"Such is the nature of M. Elout's pretensions, when fairly examined. I am however far from thinking that he will not be ready to modify, or even forego them. He appears to me to be a fair man fully impressed with the necessity of an arrangement with us, and anxious to promote it; and that the principal ground of his pretension to this kind of supreme Authority over the Native Authorities arises from apprehension of the Consequences of admitting their independence, and their objection to the residence of the Commercial Agents of other Powers from the danger of divided Authority, the possibility of intrigues . . . and the Collision which might thus be engendered between the Governments."

Much the same was happening in the East. Undeterred by Hastings' firm reply to his first letter of protest, van der Capellen wrote to Calcutta again on 16th December, attempting to demolish the arguments advanced by Hastings. He began by strongly repudiating the allegation made once more by Calcutta that the Dutch Government was pursuing a monopolistic policy. All that it was doing was resuming its old possessions. The extension of Dutch interest to Borneo had been for precisely the same reason as had induced Raffles, when Lieutenant-Governor of Java, to concern himself with that island—the prevention of piracy. In support of this, van der Capellen quoted Raffles' proclamation of 9th August 1813 and accused him of inconsistency in charging the N.E.I. government with illegal aggrandizement. It was true that when Farquhar had visited Pontianak in 1818 he had received advice from the Dutch representative that might have created a contrary impression, but Boekholtz had not been abiding by his instructions, and his expressions had been unfortunately worded.

Van der Capellen then developed the history of Dutch relations with Johore, starting with the treaty of 1784, and dealt with the positive declaration of Dutch officials in Malacca, when the British had occupied that place in 1795, that Rhio was not a dependency of Malacca. It was true that that statement had remained uncontradicted for twenty-three years, but, he somewhat naïvely enquired, "When and at what period is it affirmed that we could have asserted our claim?" He argued that between 1795 and 1818 there could have been no question of enlightening the British Government. But, he went on, the rights of the Dutch over the Kingdom of Johore were indisputable, and Singapore was unquestionably a part of Johore. He expressed surprise that anyone should question that the Sultan of Lingga was the rightful Sultan of Johore. An uninterrupted reign of nine years surely proved the fact, and till Raffles had come along and sought means to establish a title to Singapore, no one had ever suggested that Tunku Long was the rightful sovereign. He produced various letters, including one from Raffles himself when Lieutenant-Governor of Java, that proved by their mode of address that no one, not even Raffles, had ever questioned the authority of the Sultan of Lingga.

A Dutch garrison, he went on, had originally occupied Rhio as far back as 1784, though a year later Rhio had been seized by pirates and the Dutch had withdrawn. The English, when they had held Malacca, could, had they so wished, have occupied Rhio also, yet they had taken no interest in the place until Malacca was about to be returned to the Dutch, when, with suspicious haste, Farquhar had hurried off to Rhio to make a treaty with the Raja Muda, who, poor man, had had no idea what the Dutch wanted and had probably thought that the Anglo-Dutch treaty, under which Malacca had been returned to Holland, had provided some special exception for Rhio. As soon, however, as he had heard from the Dutch that he had been imposed upon by Farquhar, he had promptly denounced the treaty entered into with that gentleman.

In passing, van der Capellen did not see fit to mention the considerable Dutch force that had visited Rhio on that occasion.

'Abdu'l-Rahman, he continued, had probably been selected as Sultan because of his legitimacy, in support of which van der Capellen enclosed a document as evidence. He doubted if Tunku Long could produce equivalent proof.

This long dispatch concluded:

"I protest that it is not my fault and that I consider Sir Stamford Raffles as the sole author of all the disputes which have arisen between us and which I should be happy to see at an end as soon as possible."

He hoped, therefore, that the Governor-General would order the evacuation of Singapore without waiting for orders from home.

"It is not the honour of Britain which is or will be compromised, if Your Excellency gives the order to evacuate Singapore, but it is the honour of Holland which will be compromised, if the present situation is allowed to continue."

On 31st December van der Capellen wrote to Falck a letter containing this significant comment:

"The activities in Singapore prove that they don't contemplate ever leaving the island."

iii

In response to Raffles' invitation to join them in Bencoolen, his favourite sister, Mary Anne, arrived in Calcutta with her husband and their baby boy, Charles,[1] early in December. This cheered him a little, yet he was suffering from an unusual fit of depression. As he wrote to the Duchess of Somerset on 17th December:

"I do all I can to raise myself above these feelings in the hope that there is even in this world more happiness than we weak mortals can comprehend. I have had enough of sorrow in my short career; and it still comes too ready a guest without my bidding; but I drive it from my door and do my best to preserve my health and spirits that I may last out a few years longer and contribute as far as I can to the happiness of others. But away with this melancholy strain. I fear I am getting almost as bad as those to whom I would preach, and in truth I am at this moment heavy and sick at heart. I could lay me down and cry and weep for hours together and yet I know not why except that I am unhappy. But for my dear sister's arrival I should still have been a solitary wretch in this busy capital. I left Lady Raffles and my dear children at Bencoolen three months ago; and I have no one here of congenial feelings with whom I can communicate."

Foreseeing an early end to his public life and his return to England, he wrote to the same correspondent on 28th December:

"I must look out for some cottage or farm and profiting by the distresses of the great landowners endeavour to sell butter and cheese to advantage. Do you think this would do?"

The state of mind described in the first of these letters was doubtless the first symptom of one of those severe bouts of illness to which he was so frequently subjected. This one struck him down and kept him in bed a month, seriously delaying his return to Bencoolen. The sad thing was that, both then and on other occasions, his medical advisers attributed his chronic pains in the head to digestive disorders, whereas his head was the true seat of the trouble—and the disease was slowly getting worse.

[1] This was William Charles Raffles Flint, born on 31st March 1819. The first child of the marriage, Stamford Raffles Charles Flint, born on 16th September 1812, had died on 7th April 1816.

Chapter Twenty-six

BENCOOLEN, 1820

i

BEFORE the first month of 1820 was out, Farmer George, King of Great Britain and Ireland, died at Windsor. On or about the same day Raffles left Calcutta in the *Indiana*, accompanied by the Flints, Dr Jack and Captain Robert Hull, Sophia's soldier brother, who was going on sick leave to Bencoolen after hard campaigning in India. A fortnight later, while they were still at sea, Raffles wrote to the Duchess of Somerset:

"I have been ill—very ill, so much so that for the last month of my stay in Calcutta I was confined to my bed and forbidden to write or even to think. I was removed from my room to the ship with very little strength but I am happy to say that I am already nearly recovered; the sight of Sumatra and the healthy inspiring breezes of the Malayan islands have affected a wonderful change, and although I still feel weak and am as thin as a scarecrow, I may fairly say that I am in good health and spirits. I am beginning to turn my thoughts homewards and shall very soon ask your advice on a thousand pursuits."

London's reaction to the acquisition of Singapore became known in Calcutta in mid-February. John Palmer wrote off immediately to Raffles:

"I do not find that the September ship has brought any letters for Lord H. but the 'Augustine' conveyed him satisfactory replies touching our Eastern acquisitions and arrangements; and that Ministers will insist upon the independence of our Trade and of our commercial Relations in these Seas not in actual abrogation of any acknowledged right or title of the Dutch. The delays which Elout is exposed to for papers elucidatory, as they pretend, of all the Dutch pretensions, may prove unpalatable to our Ministry; but I think from the tone assumed by Mr Canning that we shall not wait. All Points were in discussion; and I shall not be surprised at their adjustment before the doughty Commissioner gets to Holland. He is known to be of the Napoleon leaven; and is probably as little estimable on that account with his Royal master as in the British Cabinet.

"I regretted to learn that a strong Prejudice still prevailed against you; but you will probably have heard that the Marquis has been trying to mitigate impressions and from his Influence at the juncture we may conclude not ineffectually. Your Plans speak for themselves; and if not adopted, some other cause than your *mauvais odeur* with Ministers must be assigned for their Rejection; the love of Patronage, Power and

Ostentation will long influence all Governments against the sense of their immediate Interests, if old habits have not been frequently assailed and shown in their deformity.

"I hear good accounts of Singapoor to the middle of January; but from Penang ominous tales of commercial Impediments. Bernard is said to enjoy the whole Trade preclusively; but I do not believe it or see how Farquhar after his Letters to me could suffer restraint upon any man's concerns or show an injurious Partiality towards his own connexion. . . . I learn that our Import Duty on British Spices is cancelled. Very much hurried, have only time to wish you Health and Prosperity. Remember me to Flint."

The news from London must have been very comforting to Hastings. No hasty decision was to be taken. Time at least was available to show whether Raffles had been wrong or right in the action he had taken over Singapore. Feeling a growing confidence that London was becoming increasingly favourable to the island's retention, he carried on the exchange of letters with van der Capellen, meeting argument with argument and steadily refusing to give the Dutch Governor-General any real satisfaction. No one was better able than Hastings to carry out this delaying action.

During the return voyage in the *Indiana*, Raffles took the opportunity of calling at the island of Ponchan Kechil, in Tapanuli Bay, which was reached on 23rd February. Here, where there was a British post, contact could easily be made with the Bataks, who inhabited the adjoining mainland also. Raffles was very interested in these people, particularly in their cannibalistic habits. This subject seemed to have a fascination for him, partly because the existence of cannibalism in Sumatra, originally alleged by Marsden, had been stoutly denied by others in England. He was anxious to confirm Marsden's report and also to ascertain the circumstances in which the rite was practised. His findings are contained in two letters, both written after departure from Tapanuli. That to the Duchess of Somerset is dated 12th February. The first part of it, dealing with his illness in Calcutta, was doubtless written on that date, but the rest of it cannot have been set down until after the *Indiana* had sailed for Bencoolen by way of Natal.

"I have just left Tappanooly, situated in the very heart of the Batta country, abounding in camphor and benjamin and full of interest for the naturalist and philosopher. If you have occasionally looked into Mr Marsden's History of Sumatra you will recollect that the Battas are cannibals. Now do not be surprised at what I shall tell you regarding them for I tell the truth and nothing but the truth."

After quoting some of the earlier evidence, he proceeded:

"It was with the knowledge of these facts regarding the Battas that I paid a visit to Tappanooly with a determination to satisfy my mind most fully in everything concerning cannibalism. I had previously set on foot extensive inquiries and so managed matters as to concentrate the information and to bring the point within a narrow compass. You will see now here the result; but before I proceed I must beg of you to have a little more patience than you had with Mr Mariner. I recollect that when you came to the story of eating the aunt you threw the book down. Now I can assure Your Grace that I have ten times more to report and you *must* believe me."

He then gave examples of the evidence he had collected.

"On expressing my surprise at the continuance of such extraordinary practices, I was informed that formerly it was usual for the people to eat their parents when too old for work. The old people selected the horizontal branch of a tree, and quickly suspended themselves by their hands, while their children and neighbours, forming a circle, danced round them crying out, 'When the fruit is ripe, then it will fall.' This practice took place during the season of limes, when salt and pepper were plenty, and as soon as the victims became fatigued and could hold on no longer, they fell down, when all hands cut them up, and made a hearty meal of them. This practice, however, of eating the old people has been abandoned, and thus a step in civilization has been attained, and, therefore, there are hopes of future improvement.

"This state of society you will admit to be very peculiar. It is calculated, that certainly not less than from sixty to one hundred Battas are thus eaten in a year in times of peace.

"I was going on to tell your Grace much about the treatment of the females and children, but I find that I have already filled several sheets, and that I am called away from the cabin; I will therefore conclude, with entreating you not to think the worse of me for this horrible relation. You know that I am far from wishing to paint any of the Malay race in the worst colours, but yet I must tell the truth. Notwithstanding the practices I have related, it is my determination to take Lady Raffles into the interior and to spend a month or two in the midst of these Battas. Should any accident occur to us or should we never be heard of more you may conclude we have been eaten. I am half afraid to send this scrawl and yet it may amuse you; if it does not, throw it into the fire; and still believe that though half a cannibal and living among cannibals I am not less warm in heart and soul. In the deepest recesses of the forest and among the most savage of all tribes my heart still clings to those afar off, and I do believe that even were I present at a Batta feast I should be thinking of kind friends at Maiden Bradley. What an association! God forgive me and bless you all. I am forming a collection of skulls, some from Battas that have been eaten. Will Your Grace allow them room among the curiosities?"

To Marsden on 27th February he naturally wrote a more detailed and official account. The quotations that follow indicate his attitude to cannibalism, which he clearly regarded from the detached viewpoint of a political philosopher.

"It is the universal and standing law of the Battas, that death by eating shall be inflicted in the following cases.

"1st. For adultery.

"2nd. For midnight robbery; and,

"3rd. In wars of importance, that is to say, one district against another, the prisoners are sacrificed.

"4th. For intermarrying in the same tribe, which is forbidden from the circumstance of their having ancestors in common; and,

"5th. For treacherous attack on a house, village, or person.

"In all the above cases it is lawful for the victims to be eaten, and they are eaten alive, that is to say, they are not previously put to death. The victim is tied to a stake, with his arms extended, the party collected in a circle around him, and the Chief gives the order to commence eating. The chief enemy, when it is a prisoner, or the chief party injured in other cases, has the first selection; and after he has cut off his slice, others cut off pieces according to their taste and fancy, until all the flesh is devoured.

"It is either eaten raw or grilled, and generally dipped in Sambul (a preparation of Chili pepper and salt), which is always in readiness. Rajah Bandahara, a Batta, and one of the Chiefs of Tappanooly, asserted that he was present at a festival of this kind about eight years ago, at the village of Subluan, on the other side of the bay, not nine miles distant, where the heads may still be seen.

"When the party is a prisoner taken in war, he is eaten immediately, and on the spot. Whether dead or alive he is equally eaten, and it is usual even to drag the bodies from the graves, and, after disinterring them, to eat the flesh. This only in cases of war.

"From the clear and concurring testimony of all parties, it is certain that it is the practice *not* to kill the victims till the whole of the flesh cut off by the party is eaten, should he live so long; the Chief or party injured then comes forward and cuts off the head, which he carries home as a trophy. Within the last three years there have been two instances of this kind of punishment within ten miles of Tappanooly, and the heads are still preserved.

"In cases of adultery the injured party usually takes the ear or ears; but the ceremony is not allowed to take place except the wife's relations are present and partake of it.

"In these and other cases where the criminal is directed to be eaten, he is secured and kept for two or three days, till every person (that is to say males) is assembled. He is then eaten quietly, and in cold blood, with as much ceremony, and perhaps more, than attends the execution of a capital sentence in Europe.

"The bones are scattered abroad after the flesh has been eaten, and the head alone preserved. The brains belong to the chief, or injured party, who usually preserves them in a bottle, for purposes of witchcraft, &c. They do not eat the bowels, but like the heart; and many drink the blood from bamboos. The palms of the hands and the soles of the feet are the delicacies of epicures.

"Horrid and diabolical as these practices may appear, it is no less true that they are the result of much deliberation among the parties, and seldom, except in the case of prisoners of war, the effect of immediate and private revenge. In all cases of crimes, the party has a regular trial, and no punishment can be inflicted until sentence is regularly and formally passed in the public fair. Here the Chiefs of the neighbouring kampong assemble, hear the evidence, and deliberate upon the crime and probable guilt of the party; when condemned, the sentence is ratified by the Chiefs drinking the *tuah*, or toddy, which is final, and may be considered equivalent to signing and sealing with us.

"I was very particular in my enquiries whether the assembly were intoxicated on occasions of these punishments. I was assured it was never the case. The people take rice with them, and eat it with the meat, but no *tuah* is allowed. The punishment is always inflicted in public. The men alone are allowed to partake, as the flesh of man is prohibited to the women (probably from an apprehension that they might become too fond of it). The flesh is not allowed to be carried away from the spot, but must be consumed at the time.

"I am assured that the Battas are more attached to these laws than the Mahomedans are to their Koran, and that the number of the punishments is very considerable. My informants considered that there could not be less than fifty or sixty men eaten in a year, and this in times of peace; but they were unable to estimate the true extent, considering the great population of the country: they were confident, however, that these laws were strictly enforced, wherever the name of Batta was known, and that it was only in the immediate vicinity of our settlements that they were modified or neglected. For proof, they referred me to every Batta in the vicinity, and to the number of skulls to be seen in every village, each of which was from a victim of the kind.

"With regard to the relish with which parties devour the flesh, it appeared that, independent of the desire of revenge which may be supposed to exist among the principals, about one-half of the people eat it with a relish, and speak of it with delight: the other half, though present, may not partake. Human flesh is, however, generally considered preferable to cow or buffalo beef, or hog, and was admitted to be so even by my informants.

"Adverting to the possible origin of this practice, it was observed that formerly they ate their parents when too old for work: this, however, is no longer the case, and thus a step has been gained in civilization.

"It is admitted that the parties may be redeemed for a pecuniary compensation, but this is entirely at the option of the chief enemy or injured party, who, after his sentence is passed, may either have his victim eaten, or he may sell him for a slave; but the law is that he shall be eaten, and the prisoner is entirely at the mercy of his prosecutor.

"The laws by which these sentences are inflicted are too well known to require reference to books, but I am promised some MS. accounts which relate to the subject. These laws are called *hukum pinang án*, from *depang an* [*di-pangan*], to eat—law or sentence to eat.

"I could give you many more details, but the above may be sufficient to show that our friends the Battas are even worse than you have represented them, and that those who are still sceptical have yet more to learn. I have also a great deal to say on the other side of the character, for the Battas have many virtues. I prize them highly. However horrible eating a man may sound in European ears, I question whether the party suffers so much, or the punishment itself is worse than the European tortures of two centuries ago. I have always doubted the policy, and even the right of capital punishment among civilized nations; but this once admitted, and torture allowed, I see nothing more cruel in eating a man alive than in torturing him for days with mangled limbs and the like. Here they certainly eat him up at once, and the party seldom suffers more than a few minutes. It is probable that he suffers more pain from the loss of his ear than from what follows: indeed he is said to give one shriek when that is taken off, and then to continue silent till death.

"These severe punishments certainly tend to prevent crimes. The Battas are honest and honourable, and possess many more virtues than I have time to put down.

"I have arranged to pay a visit to Tobah [Toba] and the banks of the great lake, in the course of the next year, and my plan is to go into the interior by way of Barus and return by way of Nattal, taking the longest sweep where our influence will be most felt. Lady Raffles will I hope accompany me and I shall endeavour to give up a full six weeks for the trip. I am perfectly satisfied we shall be safe and I hardly know any people on whom I would sooner rely than the Battas."

In an earlier letter (13th February) he had sent Marsden some details of the fanatical Mahommedan sect known as the Padris. As their militant activities were soon after to cause considerable alarm to both the English and the Dutch, a short extract from his report can be inserted with advantage here:

"It occurs to me that an account of the Orang Putis[1] or Padries might well be introduced into the account of our journey to Menangkabu, and I have already collected some very interesting information respecting these people who in many particulars seem to resemble the Wahabees of the desert. They have proved themselves most unrelenting and tyrannical but their rule seems calculated to reform and improve, in as much as it introduces something like authority, so much wanted all over Sumatra."

Crawfurd, in his *Descriptive Dictionary of the Indian Islands and Adjacent Countries*, has this to say of the Padris:

"About the year 1807, there sprang up in Menangkabo a new and conquering religion, being a professing reformation of the Mahommedan. It is called that of the Padris, or Rinchis, names given to the parties who first propagated it, and who were three native pilgrims recently returned from Mecca. The first name mentioned is evidently the Portuguese designation of the Roman Catholic ecclesiastics, and the last is an abbreviation of Korinchi, the district in which the reform first sprang up. The converts to the new sect were called by the Malays *orang putih* or 'white men,' in reference to the dress they wore. The following account is given by Mr John Anderson of this singular religion. . . . 'The Rinchis', says he, writing in 1822, 'are the chiefs of a religious sect in the kingdom of Menangkabo in the interior of Siak, who have been gradually extending their power and their influence during the last twelve or fifteen years. They are most rigorous in preventing the consumption of opium, and punish with death all who are detected in this indulgence. They prohibit coloured cloths of any description from being worn, and allow only pure white. Tobacco and betel, articles in such general use in all Malay countries and considered so essential to comfort, are not permitted. Every man is obliged to shave his head and wear a little skull-cap. No man is permitted to converse with another's wife, and the women are obliged to cover their faces with a white cloth having only two small holes for their eyes.' . . ."

Raffles referred in his letter to Crawfurd's forthcoming book, *History of the Indian Archipelago.*

"I am looking forward with anxiety for Crawfurd's work. From the time he has taken to arrange and polish I feel no doubt of its value. I expect from him a somewhat new view of the literature, history and antiquities of Java as he appears in his review of my work [*History of Java*] in the 'Edinburgh' to have thrown a cloud over that part of my story. I shall be happy to stand corrected where I am wrong and to acknowledge my error; but I hope he will give something more than assertion as to

[1] *Orang Puteh*, white man, i.e. man dressed in white.

the dates which he disputed. I have obtained some new lights in these since my return to this country."

The *Indiana* reached Bencoolen on 11th March, but the wind was so strong and the sea so high that the passengers could not land in Bencoolen roads and had to be taken on to Pulau Bay. Carriages were sent round to meet them there, and all the "family" dined that night at Government House.

On hearing Raffles' comments on his visit to Calcutta, Travers noted in his diary:

"From his own account it would appear that the Supreme Government entirely approved of the plan of placing all our Eastern possessions under one Government and giving it to him; and the business had been recommended in the strongest terms to the authorities in Europe. But it would, of course, take considerable time before any decision from home could be received and during this time it was Sir Stamford's intention to remain quiet at Marlborough."

The missions to Singapore and Achin had not been carried through without considerable personal outlay by Raffles, for he had "not only to provide for the whole of the paid establishment at Bencoolen during my absence, but to pay and entertain an extra establishment while in the Straits of Malacca and Singapore, hired only for the time, and consequently at high rates". As Agent to the Governor-General, he had been authorized by Bengal to draw expenses in addition to those to which he was entitled as Lieutenant-Governor of Bencoolen. On his return, therefore, he drew on Government to the extent of 27,766 rupees—about £2,600—in accordance with the account of disbursements kept by his acting secretary, Lieutenant Crossley.

While Mary Anne and her infant son remained for the time being in Bencoolen, Captain Flint left to take up his appointment as master attendant at Singapore. On his way he touched at Batavia, with the intention of transacting some business at Samarang with Deans, Scott & Co., merchants. When he sought official permission to do this, he received this reply from J. E. Brand, secretary to the Java government:

"The Resident of Batavia having laid before his Excellency the Governor-General your application for leave to proceed to Samarang, I am directed to inform you that, under existing circumstances, no person who may any ways be supposed to be connected with Sir Stamford Raffles and his views, either avowed or concealed, can be allowed a free ingress into the Island of Java, and that your request to be permitted to proceed to the eastern districts cannot therefore be acquiesced to."

It was only after Flint had protested against this suggestion by implication that an officer in the British Navy should "act so degrading a part as that of a spy" that he was given the permission he had sought.

ii

In answer to Calcutta's earnest request for more information concerning the right of Tunku Long to the throne of Johore, William Farquhar wrote briefly on 8th February by a ship on the point of sailing for India, promising to write more fully within a few days.

"I shall, however, briefly note in this place that Tuankoo Long, the present Sultan of Johor, residing here, addressed several letters to me whilst in charge of the Govt. of Malacca, subsequent to the death of his Father, Sultan Mahomet, setting forth his distress, and soliciting the assistance of the British Government in his behalf, authentic copies of which I shall have the honour to transmit."

This he did four days later, apologizing for the loss of some of the correspondence, which had taken place between 1813 and 1815.

"I trust that those [letters] now transmitted will be sufficient to show the nature of the overture made to me by that Prince at that time, and beg to observe that in consequence of the general instructions I had received from Government to avoid as much as practicable any direct interference with the disputes or internal arrangements of the neighbouring Malay States, my answers to the different appeals made to me by His Highness Tuankoo Long were dictated according to the spirit of this Policy. At the same time that with respect to the justice of his claims to succeed to his Father's Throne as his eldest son, I never entertained a doubt. The statement No. 4, which I have herewith the honour to transmit under the Sultan's seal, as well as those of His Highness the Tummagong and Tuankoo Kuseman, who are both well acquainted with the circumstances, is a brief but clear exposition of the Sultan's situation and the events which happened to him from the period of his quitting his Father's house to proceed to Pahang to the time of his finally quitting Rhio to reside at Singapore. The correctness of this account cannot, in my opinion, be called in question.

"The Most Noble the Governor-General in Council will observe by the Documents now transmitted that Sultan Mahomet some time previous to his death allowed his eldest son, Tuankoo Long, to select his place of Residence and seat of Government, which he did by fixing on Rhio and that Lingin was in consequence of this selection made the Residence of the younger brother. The death of Sultan Mahomet having occurred during the absence of his eldest son at Pahang, the Rajah Mudah of Rhio, together with some of the Chiefs in authority at Lingin, deemed it expedient, in comformity to the Malay custom, to place the Younger Brother of Tuankoo Long, then present, for a time on the Throne as Regent in order that the Corpse of Sultan Mahomet might be interred, which ceremony could not have taken place during the interregnum. But on Tuankoo Long's return from Pahang to Rhio he found the Local Authorities, both there and at Lingin, were from self-interested motives not disposed to attend to his claims of succeeding to his Father's Throne; and that notwithstanding every effort on his part to obtain his just and legitimate Rights he had in the most vexatious manner been put off from day to day and year to year with evasive answers and feigned difficulties about assembling the Chiefs of the Empire to Crown him, in consequence of those Chiefs finding it to their interest to keep the Empire as long as possible in its present disorganized and divided state that they might continue to exercise uncontrolled Authority within their respective countries, permitting Tuankoo Putrie[1] (who resides at Rhio), one of the widows of Sultan Mahomet but not the mother of either Tuankoo Long or his Half Brother, the Rajah of Lingin, to retain to this day possession of the Regalia of the Empire without which no Sovereign of Johore can be regularly Crowned.

"I must beg leave to state that during my Mission to Lingin in August 1818 that the first Public interview I had with the Rajah when all the Nobles and Chiefs were assembled he publickly declared that he was not Sultan and requested that I would not address him so, which clearly proved that the title had been forced upon him by the Rajah Mudah and others interested in keeping him on the Throne and not with his own consent. The two brothers in question have always continued on terms of strict personal friendship to this moment and as neither the Bandahara of Pahang or Tummagong of Singapore, the only hereditary Grand Chiefs of the Empire, appear to have ever sanctioned or in any way publickly acknowledged the present Rajah of Lingin as the legitimate Sultan of Johor, it clearly follows that the title has been usurped and forced upon the younger brother to serve the views of the Rajah Mudah and his adherents at Lingin, who by this means have engrossed the Authority and Revenues of both Rhio and Lingin amongst themselves to the exclusion of the rightful Heir now residing at Singapore with whom the late Treaty was concluded by the Honble Sir Thomas Stamford Raffles. His Highness Tuankoo Long resided at Rhio[2] from the period of his return from Pahang where he subsisted on a portion of the Revenues of his Father's Dominions but acknowledged no obligation or Superior Authority to his own. He came over immediately to Singapore on hearing of Sir Stamford Raffles' arrival there in order to obtain an interview with him and claim his rights."

In a further letter, dated 23rd February, Farquhar supplemented the information he had already supplied.

[1] Tunku Putĕri, ruler's consort when of royal blood.

[2] More exactly at Bulang, one of the islands of the Rhio archipelago.

"It may be proper also in this place to explain the circumstances relative to the commercial Treaty concluded by me at Rhio on the 19th August 1818 having been executed by the Rajah Mudah there in the name of His Highness Abdul Rahman of Johor and Pahang whilst that Prince had previously disavowed his right to the title. The fact that I found the Rajah Mudah of Rhio to be the only Chief at that time in Power with whom the requisite Treaty could be formed, and that as he deemed himself sufficiently warranted in making use of the name of His Highness Abdul Rahman as the Sovereign of Johor, Pahang and dependencies, notwithstanding the Public Declaration to the contrary made by the Prince himself in my presence, I did not deem it expedient under the existing circumstances to throw difficulties in the way which could only have led to unpleasant discussions tending to procrastinate if not to occasion a total failure of the objects of the Mission."

Mindful of the fact that Farquhar was still waiting for the home leave that had been promised him, Raffles, on the day following his return to Bencoolen, offered Travers the post of Resident at Singapore. It was accepted with alacrity and confirmed by Raffles in writing.

"Major Farquhar having earnestly requested to be permitted to avail himself of his leave of absence from the Madras Government to proceed to Europe, I have thought it expedient to appoint you to succeed him provisionally as Resident and Commandant at Singapore and you will accordingly be pleased to proceed to that station without delay."

There followed a number of instructions, only one paragraph of which need be quoted here. It resulted from information received by Raffles from John Palmer, who had himself received it from Penang, that the acting master attendant, F. J. Bernard, had not strictly complied with his instructions.

"It has been represented that contrary to the wishes of Government various small duties and exactions have been enforced on native prows; you will enquire into this and in order that the intentions of Government may not be misunderstood or departed from cause the Port Regulations to be affixed at the wharf in the English and native languages."

Travers sailed for Singapore with his wife and child at the end of March, bearing a letter from Raffles to Farquhar.

"I have the honour to inform you that in consequence of your repeated and earnest request to be relieved of the charge of the Settlement of Singapore in order that you may avail yourself of your permission from the Madras Government to proceed to Europe and the impossibility of my visiting Singapore myself for some months, I have appointed Captain Thomas Otho Travers, my acting second assistant, to succeed you as Resident and Commandant, and that officer has accordingly been directed to proceed to Singapore forthwith.

"On delivering over charge to Captain Travers and closing your accounts to that date, you will of course be at liberty to proceed to Europe and I shall take an early opportunity of informing the Supreme Government thereof. . . .

"On the occasion of your relinquishing the charge of Singapore, I again request to offer you my warmest acknowledgments for the zeal and ability with which you have devoted yourself to the prosperity of the Establishment and for the prudence and judgment which you have displayed under circumstances of considerable difficulty. I shall not fail to express these sentiments to the Supreme Government and I doubt not that you are to receive from that high authority the due measure of this approbation."

When Travers arrived at Singapore, Farquhar was surprised to see him. He pointed out that it was impossible to go home just then, for there was no means of doing so. It was eventually agreed that he would leave by the China fleet, Farquhar assuring Travers that he would definitely hand over the settlement on or before 1st September. Farquhar wrote to Raffles, thanking him for "the considerate motives which have influenced you on the present occasion", and expressing the hope that there would no be objection to the suggested deferment of the transfer of authority. Pending his departure, he added, Captain Travers had volunteered to assist him. He concluded:

"It may not be improper to state that the news of my projected departure having excited a very general feeling throughout the various classes of inhabitants who have become Settlers here under the British protection, they have been induced as well as the Sultan and the Tummongong to solicit that I would convey to you their united suggestion that you would, if possible, grant them a visit previous to the period fixed upon for my departure, in which solicitation I most cordially join them . . . as it becomes a duty of the first importance to strengthen by every possible means the present ardour of feeling; increasing confidence and attachment towards the British Government and Nation which has hitherto so happily prevailed . . . not only in this Settlement, but throughout all the surrounding countries."

Travers settled down in a small bungalow owned by Farquhar, and found Singapore much to his liking.

"The place is in every respect most delightfully situated; an extensive plain on the sea beach affords ample space for the troops; at the rear stands a hill commanding a most extensive and beautiful prespect to which the vast number of small islands is a most pleasing addition. . . .

"The population has increased beyond all expectation and was found on the first of this month [May] to exceed six thousand, including Chinese, Malays, Bugguese, Hindostanies, Chuliahs, &c, &c, which is immense considering the short space of time during which the Settlers have come here. The arrivals of ships and boats are numerous and will increase I have no doubt to the very great annoyance of the Java trade. The total exemption from all duties is a strong temptation and will, of course, bring the trading prows here in preference to Malacca, Penang or Java."

iii

Raffles' interest in scientific pursuits was still as keen as ever. In Java his activities had been hampered by the overwhelming demands of public and political life, but things were very different at Bencoolen—so much so that it caused him some concern.

"We have", he wrote, "literally nothing for the civil servants to do at Bencoolen, and idleness is the root of all evil; they ought to be transferred to some other settlement and not to be obliged to waste their time, life and health here."

Now, then, for the one and only time in his life, he was able to allow full rein to his passion for natural history. There was nothing to prevent him from devoting an ample share of his time to a scientific survey of such parts of Sumatra as came within his range. Much of the country was, from the scientific angle, indeed from every angle, completely virgin soil. The wealth of material was such as to satisfy even the most ardent and indefatigable naturalist.

"I have thrown politics far away; and since I must have nothing more to do with men have taken to the wilder but less sophisticated animals of the woods. Our house is on one side a perfect menagerie, on another a perfect flora; here a pile of stones, there a collection of seaweeds, shells, &c."

Dr Thomas Horsfield who had been at Bencoolen since June 1818, left there in March with his extensive collection. Raffles wrote to his friends in England to ensure that the American naturalist should receive there the warm welcome he deserved. The two French zoologists, A. M. Diard and A. Duvausel, though competent and active enough, had proved selfish and not at all co-operative. At the end of the trial period, Raffles dispensed with their services. There remained that brilliant young botanist, Dr William Jack.

To Marsden, Raffles wrote on 14th March:

"I shall have the opportunity of writing to you very fully by the 'Mary' in the course of a few days. In the meantime it may be interesting to you to know that I purpose sending by her the whole of our zoological collection, among which are beautiful specimens of the tapir, rhinoceros, kijangs [barking deer], &c, stuffed, in skeleton and in spirits. It will, I think, be as important and interesting a consignment as was ever sent home.

"I have had, as you may suppose, a great deal of trouble. The term of their engagement is now concluded with my French naturalists and they are pledged by duty and honour not to publish until the collections arrive and are noticed in England. I find the krabut or great flower to be much more generally and more extensively known than I expected. . . . The further enquiry respecting the tunnu [*tĕnok*—tapir] and babi-ala[1] induce me to believe that there is still some large animal in our forests not inferior in size to the tapir, marked with a narrow band of white round the belly and back . . . the chungkor[2] of Palembang may be a third animal. I have a long list of animals of which nothing yet is known beyond the name and description . . . the duyong[3] which I sent to Sir Joseph Banks will, I hope, have arrived safe. I have the skin and another complete skeleton here; also one about four and a half feet long preserved in spirits. . . ."

So many collectors in the past have been so careless in their recording and slipshod in their facts that the value of their collections have been gravely affected, but, as F. N. Chasen, late director of the Raffles Museum, has written, the "zoological specimens collected in Sumatra under the immediate superintendence of Raffles would do credit as a collection made under modern conditions and facilities".

No one can read Raffles' private letters without realizing how deeply love for nature and for her secrets was buried in his heart. His references to natural history are written obviously in such high spirits and often in such a jocular strain that one can feel the happiness such subjects afforded him. And few men can have had greater need for the solace in misfortune that such wholehearted enthusiasm could offer.

His children were another unfailing source of delight. To his mother he wrote on 14th April:

"Charlotte, I can assure you, is not a little proud of Grandmama's finery. She has just come in to show me the dress you worked for her. She is the sweetest and best tempered little darling eyes ever beheld. Leopold is as quick and bold as a lion. He has had a good deal of pulling down with his teeth but is getting stout again."

Then to the Duchess of Somerset a few days later:

"Your Grace will, I doubt not, be happy to hear that our prospects, even at Bencoolen, are improving; the place no longer has that gloomy and desolate appearance of which I first complained. Population and industry are increasing; the inland merchants begin to bring down the gold and cassia from the interior, and a stranger would hardly know the place again, so much is it changed from what it was two years ago. We

[1] *Babirusa*, the hog-deer.
[2] *Chĕngkau*, a monkey (*Presbytis cristata*).
[3] Dugong (Malay *duyong*), the sea-cow, an aquatic herbivorous mammal.

have a good many comforts about us, and we shall really regret any political necessity which obliges us to remove from what has now become our second home. We have a delightful garden, and so many living pets, children tame and wild, monkeys, dogs, birds &c, that we have a perfect *règne animal* within our own walls, to say nothing of the surrounding forests now under contribution. I have one of the most beautiful little men of the woods that can be conceived; he is not much above two feet high, wears a beautiful surtout of fine white woollen, and in his disposition and habits the kindest and most correct creature imaginable; his face is jet black, and his features most expressive; he has not the slightest rudiments of a tail, always walks erect, and would I am sure become a favourite in Park Lane.

"Not long ago I gave your Grace a short account of my Batta friends. I am now much engaged in obtaining particulars of a very extensive and interesting population in one of the larger islands lying off Sumatra, Pulo Nias.

"The Nias people believe in one Supreme God, Lora Langi, but they do not pay him any kind of public worship. Below him is another God, called Batu Ba Danaw, who has charge of the earth, which they say is suspended from a stalk, or string, as an orange from the branch of a tree. This is, perhaps, as happy an idea as the double-headed shot of Lord Erskine, and perhaps his Lordship may avail himself of the hint in the next volume of *Armata*. The world they suppose to have seven stages, or gradations, inhabited by as many different orders of beings. The stage immediately under us is possessed by dwarfs. The heavens, or sky above us (Hili Yawa), are peopled by a superior order of men (Barucki), of a most beautiful form and appearance. These are gifted with wings, and are invisible at pleasure, and they take an interest in all that passes on earth; they are governed by kings of their own: the one at present reigning is called Luo Mehuhana; there were four kings who ruled before him, and from whom he is descended.

"'The people of the earth', they say, 'had for a length of time continued in a state of the grossest ignorance and barbarism; they neither lived in houses nor tilled the ground, but wandered about, subsisting on what the earth spontaneously produced. At last, the wife of Luo Mehuhana took pity upon their miserable condition, and ordered one of her subjects to descend to the earth, and teach its inhabitants the arts of civilization. He accordingly descended on Pulo Nias, and instructed them how to till the ground, to live in houses, to cook their victuals, and to form societies. He taught them also to speak, for hitherto they had not possessed even this means of communication.'

"Their laws are remarkably severe. It is death to touch any part, even the finger, of an unmarried woman, or the wife of another man; but notwithstanding this, I do not learn that they are particularly chaste. The wives are bought from the parents, as in Sumatra; and a man may have as many as he can afford to pay for. . . ."

Raffles never abandoned his hope of bringing prosperity to the British sphere in Sumatra, and it was in pursuit of this aim that he extended British interest to include Nias, which lies about thirty miles off the west Sumatra coast, being about sixty-five miles long and seventeen miles wide at its broadest point. It was densely populated and was regarded as having reached a much higher state of civilization than was to be generally found on the island of Sumatra. This superiority was ascribed to the high fertility of the soil and the skill of the inhabitants in irrigation, which enabled them to grow heavy crops of rice, cotton and other produce.

"They dwell in excellent and commodious houses, the interior of which are laid out with neatness, not devoid of elegance; streets are regularly formed and paved, with avenues of trees, and stone stairs to the pinnacles of the different hills, on which their villages are mostly situated, embosomed in the richest foliage imaginable. The slopes of the hills and the valleys are covered with one continued sheet of the richest cultivation, and there is not a forest tree standing on the island; all have disappeared before the force of industry. To each village are attached stone baths, appropriated to the different sexes, which remind us of Roman luxuries. They wear a profusion of gold and other ornaments, than which nothing can be conceived more original."

The greatest menaces to the security and happiness of the people of Nias—"the finest people, without exception, that I have yet met with in the East"—were pirates and slave-traders.

"It was notorious", wrote Sophia in the *Memoir*, "that Pulo Nias, although for a long period of years nominally enjoying the protection of the English flag, was still the most abundant, and almost the only source of the supply of slaves on the coast, and that notwithstanding the prohibition against importation at Bencoolen and elsewhere, it was impossible to prevent it entirely."

An appeal by the islanders in 1811 to be taken fully under British protection had been rejected with the complete approval of the Court of Directors. Fresh representations having now been made by the chiefs, Raffles had sent Dr Jack and John Prince, Resident at Ponchan Kechil, on a mission to Nias. From their report it appeared to Raffles that possession of the island offered three definite advantages: its surplus rice would be most welcome to Bencoolen; there was great scope for missionary enterprise; and a severe blow would be struck at the slave trade. The abolition of this last, apart from removing "so dark a blot on the history of our government", would be a major step forward in the civilization of the country and would remove the greatest check on its industry; it would put an end to insecurity and diminish tribal hostility and this would encourage a taste for imported goods, which in turn would stimulate production. Also, as he reminded his superiors, Nias had been regularly used by enemy cruisers as a port for refreshment and refitment, and as a base that commanded the whole coast of Sumatra. Its possession by Great Britain would, therefore, be of immense value in time of war.

With all these considerations in mind, Raffles assumed the sovereignty of Nias on behalf of the East India Company. Calcutta appears to have given its general blessing to this step, but sought the confirmation of the authorities in London.

iv

Whatever the views of Penang were towards Singapore, and however much these were intended to belittle its importance, it is quite safe to say that they had no effect on the ultimate decision. No more damning criticism of the ineptitude and parochialism of that authority can be passed than that the opinions of the fourth Presidency, situated as it was within four hundred miles of the new settlement, and on a question of such vital consequence to it, were neither canvassed nor regarded by higher authority. The sole result of its narrow and jealous outlook was to be that Singapore was put under the direct control of Calcutta, to avoid the risk of its being crippled by the attitude of the Penang government.

If Calcutta officially ignored the views of Penang, John Palmer continued to receive a stream of letters from Phillips, Coombs and other correspondents. Palmer had his own ideas about Singapore and, though he may not have liked Raffles, he was never slow to promote his own business interests. Early in 1820 he had sent his natural son, Claude Queiros, to open up an office there, and had written to both Farquhar and Raffles to obtain their goodwill towards that unsatisfactory and tiresome young man. Not that Palmer was too happy about the prospect of Singapore being retained. The fluctuation of his hopes and fears is revealed in his correspondence. We can quote at this point from a letter of his dated 21st April 1820 and addressed to J. A. van Braam, formerly Holland's agent in India and now back in Java. Palmer was on very close terms with van Braam and used this friendship to try to sweeten relations between the British Indian Government and the Dutch East Indian Government, not without an eye to his own financial interests in Java, which were considerable.

"I do trust, my dear friend," he wrote, "that Affairs respecting our Relations in Asia will be soon settled between the Cabinets at Home upon some liberal and unchangeable Basis; and an end be thereby put to all feverish Sensations and little Jealousies between us. The best policy would perhaps consist in leaving a general Intercourse with the Natives of all the Eastern Islands, Java and the Moluccas excepted, equally free to both Netherlanders and British, for the exclusive possession or Dominion is certainly not worth contending for; if even there was no reason for consolidating the Friendship of our Nations.

"I fear you do not concede enough to Circumstances and Times and are too tenacious of Principles and indeed of Systems no longer applicable to your old Dependencies and Connexions. Heartily do I pray that all our Contests may be reduced to Paper and be explained and settled by personal Discussions; and not less that you may be sent here to regulate all local Concerns."

In a different strain he wrote to Clubley at Penang:

"As a thorn in the side of Mynheer and as an Instrument for contrasting our System of Commerce and Policy with His, Singapore is a precious Jewel to us, and I can't but think that its position gives it vast advantages as a subordinate Settlement; but I trust that neither in local, commercial or political importance it never can supersede Penang. Indeed I am disposed to think it augments the weight and value of Penang and renders the preservation of a Government there more essential than ever. It manifestly must owe its support and safety to Penang, for it is too distant for our Protection, even if hostile Positions did not intervene. . . ."

V

At Bencoolen, in the month of May, Sophia gave birth to another son, who was christened Stamford Marsden. Another addition to the family party was Sophia's younger brother, Lieutenant Nilson Hull, whom Raffles took on his personal staff.

Sophia has left a moving account of their home life at that time.

"Perhaps this was one of the most happy periods in Sir Stamford's life; politically he had obtained the object which he felt so necessary for the good of his country. He was beloved by all those under his immediate control, who united in showing him every mark of respect and attachment, and many were bound to him by ties of gratitude for offices of kindness, or private acts of benevolence and assistance which he delighted to exercise towards them.

"The settlement, like many other small societies, was divided into almost as many parties as there were families on his first arrival; but these differences were soon healed and quieted and a general interchange of good offices had succeeded. The natives and chiefs appreciated the interests which he took in their improvement and placed implicit reliance upon his opinion and counsel. The consciousness of being beloved is a delightfully happy feeling and Sir Stamford acknowledged with thankfulness at this time that every wish of his heart was gratified.

"Uninterrupted health had prevailed in his family, his children were his pride and delight and they had already imbibed from him those tastes it was his pleasure to cultivate; this will not be wondered at, even at their early age, when it is added that two young tigers and a bear were for some time in the children's apartments, under the charge of their attendant without being confined in cages, and it was rather a curious scene to see the children, the bear, the tigers, a blue mountain bird and a favourite cat all playing together, the parrot's beak being the only object of awe to all the party.

"Perhaps few people in a public station led so simple a life; his mode of passing his time in the country has already been described. When he was in Bencoolen he rose early and delighted in driving into the villages, inspecting the plantations and encouraging the industry of the people; at nine a party assembled at breakfast but separated immediately afterwards; and he wrote, read, studied natural history, chemistry and geology, superintended the draughtsmen, of whom he had constantly five or six employed in a verandah, and always had his children with him as he went from one pursuit to another visiting his beautiful and extensive aviary as well as the extraordinary collection of animals which were always domesticating in the house.

"At four he dined and seldom alone, as he considered the settlement but as a family of which he was the head. Immediately after dinner all the party drove out and the evening was spent in reading and music and conversation. He never had any game of amusement in his house. After the party had dispersed he was fond of walking out with the Editor and enjoying the delicious coolness of the night land wind and a moon whose beauty those only who have been in tropical climates can judge of; so clear and penetrating are its rays that many fear them as much as the glare of the sun.

"Though scarcely a day passed without reptiles of all kinds being brought in and the cobra de [di] Capello in numbers but the Editor never remembers these pleasures being interrupted by any alarm.

"Amidst these numerous sources of enjoyment, however, Sir Stamford never forgot that the scene was too bright to continue unclouded and often gently warned the Editor not to expect to retain all the blessings God in his bounty had heaped upon them at this time but to feel that such happiness once enjoyed ought to shed a bright ray over the future however dark and trying it might become."

These warnings were tragically prophetic.

For all his domestic felicity at that time, Raffles did not forget the desperately impoverished and apathetic people for whom he was responsible. The population was falling steadily, partly owing to the occasional epidemics, which they had little reserve of strength to resist, but in general to the emigration of the more active and younger men and their subsequent marriage outside their own area.

The surest remedy was to increase the production of food. So, on 31st May, an Agricultural Society was established for the promotion and encouragement of agriculture.

"However ill judged", Raffles observed in his presidential address, "may have been the selection of Bencoolen for our principal Settlement and however arduous the task of improvement, let us recollect it is the place where we can be most practically useful and that the greater the difficulties the greater will be the credit of overcoming them. You have already done wonders in the introduction and establishment of the spice cultivation and have succeeded against almost every possible obstacle that has been opposed to you. This will be sufficient to prove what can be done by the zeal and perseverance of a few individuals and to encourage your future exertions.

"I think there is much to condemn in the choice you have made in the soil and in the mode of manuring but I trust your intelligence when concentrated by the means of this Society will lead you to the correction of these errors and render the returns of the gardens more adequate to the capital, zeal and industry bestowed upon them. I cannot help thinking that had you selected an alluvial soil instead of the barren and unproductive hills on which your plantations now stand you would have saved yourselves much unnecessary expense and labour and succeeded more effectually in spreading the plants over the country. . . .

"The recent orders issued by Government will go some way towards the improvement of your plantations by directing your attention to the necessity of supplying your people and cattle with food, and I should hope it would not be long before each plantation has its farm and raises its own supplies within itself. I am more anxious however to impress on your minds the greater importance of the grain cultivation of the country as generally carried on by the native inhabitants. It is on this that everything must depend, for until a sufficient quantity of rice is raised for the consumption of the country it would be idle to talk of prosperity. All our efforts must be directed to the attainment of this one great object and this once attained the others will, I trust, follow easily."

This presidential address was used as an introduction to the *Proceedings* of the Agricultural Society, the first and only volume of which was printed by the Baptist Mission Press, run by Nathaniel Ward. A study of the various reports and appendixes printed in the book shows the practical purpose of the society. Apart from statistical tables dealing with population, fruit crops and other relevant matters, much excellent advice is given in regard to the production of rice, coffee, pepper and nutmegs. Attention is called to the advantage of growing guinea grass, successfully achieved by the president, as food for cattle, and also to replace the widespread and destructive lalang, the coarse grass that flourishes in the Malay Archipelago. The importance of proper manure is stressed.

"The present mode of obtaining manure by keeping cattle solely for the purpose appears extravagantly wasteful and far from creditable to the agricultural skill of the planters. Were the cattle well fed and employed during proper hours in ploughing the ground on which grain and guinea grass might be raised for their consumption, not only would a great saving of expenditure be effected but the condition of the cattle improved and the quantity and quality of their manure increased. Attention is also drawn to an artificial manure used by the Chinese, oil cake made from the residue of the katchang tana[1] after the oil has been extracted."

According to his usual practice, Raffles was also anxious to encourage in others an interest in scientific matters. The smallness of the European population in Bencoolen precluded the creation of anything on a par with the Batavian Society of Arts and Sciences, but the presence of a printing-press enabled Raffles to have published a series of papers dealing with geographical and scientific subjects. The first volume of *Malayan Miscellanies*, as they were called, was published by the Baptist Mission Press in that year.

In many ways Raffles' life at that time resembled that of a cultured landed proprietor at home (like, for example, that of his friend, the Duke of Somerset), dividing his time between his family, his agricultural properties and his scientific and benevolent interests. As he put it to the Duchess in his letter of 2nd June:

"I am no longer striding from one side of India [the Indies] to another, overleaping mountains or forming new countries. I am trying to do the best I can with a very old and nearly worn out one. My life is at present rather monotonous, not, however, unpleasantly so, for I have all the regular and substantial employment of domestic comfort in the bosom of a happy and thriving family; and in the daily pursuits of agriculture and magisterial duty I find abundance to interest and amuse. . . . I am busily engaged in taking a census of the population and enquiring into the processesses of husbandry and the village institutions, but I think you would be amused to see me amid my rude and untutored mountaineers, collecting the details and entering into all the particulars, as if they were the peasants of my own estate. I am becoming so attached to these pursuits and find them so much more satisfactory than political discussion that I believe I should be sorry to change this mode of life. Allow me, therefore, to indulge my whim for a short time longer and then I shall be able to carry home such a weight of experience as may perhaps bring all your barren lands into cultivation. If I am not rich enough to have a

[1] *Kachang China*, of the peanut family.

farm of my own I shall wish to become a farmer on your lands and then. . . ."

Towards the end of June he wrote to another correspondent:

"I no more trouble my head about the Dutch. I have turned farmer and as President of the Agricultural Society find more real satisfaction than is to be derived from all the successes that could attend a political life."

To Marsden, godfather of his younger son, he wrote on 27th June:

"My three children, Charlotte, Leopold and Marco Polo, as so he is still called although he was christened Stamford Marsden,[1] are certainly the finest children that were ever seen; and if we can manage to take them home in about four or five years we hope to prove that the climate of Bencoolen is not so very bad."

On natural history, he had this to report in the same letter:

"As there was no chance of a direct opportunity I have sent by the 'London' duplicates and even more complete sets of the quadrupeds and birds than those sent by the 'Mary', numbered, named, and ticketed so as to correspond with my catalogues. I am at this moment superintending a complete set of the drawings to be forwarded by the present opportunity via Calcutta. I fear there will hardly be time for completing the duplicates of the catalogue of birds. My writers are now engaged upon it and I will do my best to send it by the present conveyance . . . we are now busy in arranging the reptiles and crabs of which we have a very large collection."

As a trading concern, the East India Company was not interested in these activities. Its only comment on the collections sent home to Sir Joseph Banks in the *Mary* and the *London* was a prohibition on any further expenditure of its funds in this manner. These two consignments were by no means the whole of Raffles' collection; the rest he intended to take home in due course under his own supervision, together with many irreplaceable Malayan manuscripts, books, pictures, and his own exhaustive notes and observations on all the islands of the Eastern Archipelago.

A month later he wrote of his family to his friend, Thomas Murdoch:

"You will, I am sure, be happy to hear that we continue in excellent health and as yet unaffected by climate and other drawbacks. Lady Raffles looks better at present than I ever knew her and my three children are everything that the fondest parent could wish. Charlotte and Leopold (your godson) are both running about and are as blessed in intelligence as disposition. Charlotte is all mildness, *Leo* all boldness; the youngest, who is called Marco Polo after his godfather, Marsden, bids fair to follow in the same steps; and we are as happy a family as you can well conceive."

Frequent reference to the children are to be found in his letters to the Duchess of Somerset. Here is one of them:

[1] Marsden had written a book on Marco Polo.

"Leopold is the wonder of all who see him. Charlotte speaks English very distinctly, and finds no difficulty in Malay and Hindustanee, and it is curious to observe how she selects her language to the different natives. To us or her nurse [Mrs Grimes] she always speaks English; to a Malay she is fluent in his language, and in an instant begins Hindustanee to a Bengalee; if she is sent with a message she translates it at once into the language of the servant she meets with. She is only two and a half years old; such is the tact of children regarding languages. She always dines with us when we are alone and the cloth is no sooner removed than in bounces Master Leopold singing and laughing and occupying his place. Mr Silvio, the siamang, is then introduced and I am often accused of paying more attention to the monkey than to the children. This last gentleman is so great a favourite and in such high spirits that I hope to take him to England with the family. . . ."

On a more serious note, he wrote to another correspondent:

"I learn with much regret the prejudice and malignity by which I am attacked at home for the desperate struggle I have maintained against the Dutch. Instead of being supported by my own Government, I find them deserting me and giving way in every instance to the unscrupulous and enormous assertions of the Dutch. All however is safe so far, and if matters are only allowed to remain as they are, all will go well. The great blow has been struck, and though I may personally suffer in the struggle, the Nation must be benefited—and I should not be surprised were the Ministeries to recall me though I should on many accounts regret it as the present moment. . . .

"Should Mr Grant come into the chair [of the Company], there is still a hope that all may be right. I am not, however, very sanguine, and shall be prepared for whatever ignorance, injustice or party-spirit may dictate.

"I have lived long enough in the world to appreciate what is valuable in it; and the favour of Ministers or Courts never appeared to me equal to the conscientious conviction of having done one's duty—even the loss of fortune, honours, or, I might add, health. I have more satisfaction in what I have done since return to India than with all my former endeavours; and the more I am opposed, the more my views are thwarted, destroyed, and counteracted, the firmer do I stand in my own opinion; for I am confident that I am right, and that when I appear at home, even those who are opposed to me will be the first to acknowledge this. They do not, and will not, look at the question in its fair and true light; and such appears to be the spirit of *persecution*, that it would be idle to oppose it at this distance. I shall, therefore, bend with the blast, and endeavour to let the hurricane blow over me: the more violent it becomes, the sooner will it expend itself, and then it will be time for me to raise my head, to show the injury and devastation which has been spread abroad, and the folly of the course which has been pursued.

"The only mischief in this line of policy is this, that it will force me to become a more public and prominent character than I would wish. My ambition is to end my days in domestic peace and comfort and literary leisure. A busy scene will oppose this, and though I may become a greater man, I perhaps may not become a happier one. . . .

"After all, it is not impossible the Ministry may be weak enough to abandon Singapore, and to sacrifice me, honour, and the Eastern Archipelago, to the outrageous pretensions of the Dutch. In this case, I may be recalled sooner than I expect, perhaps immediately. This I am aware of, but I should be best contented with things remaining *even as they are* for two or three years to come; I should then be better prepared for the contest; for a contest it must come to, sooner or later, and the longer the adjustment of our differences with the Dutch, on a *broad* and *just* footing, is delayed, the better must it be for our interests. . . ."

And so he remained quietly at Bencoolen, "confined to Marlborough", as he wrote to Marsden on 27th August, "on account of the positive orders of the Court of Directors", his longest journey the ten miles or so to his country home at Pĕrmatang Balam.

vi

Meanwhile the negotiations between Great Britain and Holland hung fire. Lord Clancarty had reported from Holland in January that the Dutch wished to postpone the discussions till April, as Falck had been detained at Vienna. The discussions were further postponed till June. Even this date was not very convenient to the Dutch, as Elout made clear in his letter dated 20th May to Fagel from The Hague.

"I continue to regret the absence, far too long for me, of M. Falck. It certainly is for both of us a matter of no small moment that we cannot see the head of the Department of the Colonies and consult him, before, and during, the conference on points as delicate as those, which have to be discussed by us with the British Government. On the other hand, I feel not only the impropriety of keeping the British Commissioners, and with them the British Government, waiting any longer, but also that it is important to our King that our mutual relations be speedily settled on a fixed basis."

He therefore expressed himself ready to cross to England by the proposed date. In the same dispatch he made some critical observations on Raffles.

"There has been much, and very recent, news from Java, also from M. van der Capellen, both official and private letters. In all of them they are pressing hard for an arrangement with England, to set bounds to the misbehaviour of the British agents, especially Raffles, who is very ill-disposed towards us. He has been able to convince the Bengal Government over the occupation of Singapore by all sorts of specious and false arguments.

"That Government in a letter to the Governor-General, van der Capellen, states that they cannot believe that what he writes to them is not true, because, in that case, they would have been horribly misled and deceived by their own agents. But how is it possible to reconcile the close friendship of the two countries in Europe with the fact that the Bengal Government employs for a mission, like this one, in the area of Malacca, a man whose deeds and actions in the Lampongs, at Padang, in Palembang, they had come to understand and had disapproved of in the plainest language?

"Raffles has to be removed from that part of the world or there will be no peace for the Dutch Government out there. Many, and among them respected and sensible Englishmen, disapproved of his behaviour. In the newspaper of Penang his behaviour is sneered at and blamed (as they tell me). It is a pity the British Governor of that establishment has died: he was never willing to have any share in Raffles' shameful behaviour, but always opposed him. Now that man is dead, and so for the unwearying and restless Raffles every obstacle from that side is removed. Raffles is now, or has been, in Calcutta, and was trying, they say, to obtain the government of Penang, and to get within that province every British possession in that part of the world. God grant that he won't succeed."

Fagel replied on 30th May. He agreed that the negotiations should not be postponed beyond the end of June.

"The coronation of the King [George IV] fixed for the first August (after which date neither Ministers nor Members of Parliament will stay any longer in town and everybody will rush to the country) is already limiting the time that will be available to us far too much. With regard to the spirit and attitude to be introduced into the conference by us, I share your Honour's opinion as to the necessity of removing Raffles from those parts, if the Dutch Government is ever to be at peace over there."

It was not until July that discussions actually began, Castlereagh and Canning representing the United Kingdom, and Elout and van Nagell the Netherlands. Great Britain was still waiting for a full report from Hastings as to the legality of the occupation of Singapore, but according to the British résumé dated 4th August, some progress was made. The chief difficulty was that the Dutch plenipotentiaries, to establish the strength of their argument, had produced to Canning van der Capellen's letter to Hastings of 16th December 1819. Opinions may well differ as to the validity of the case presented therein. Some may think it a most convincing one; others may regard much of the evidence as being of doubtful value and a good part of the argument vitiated by special pleading. Elout, at any rate, was delighted with it, considering it an impeccable statement of the Dutch case. When he had shown it to Canning, it had made a considerable impression, so disturbing Canning and Castlereagh that they felt they could not continue negotiations until they had received a copy of Calcutta's letter in reply.

That Singapore must be maintained and the extravagant and monopolistic claims of the Dutch in the East Indies must be checked was the firm opinion of leading business houses in the City. Submissions by delegations of a very representative character were presented to Castlereagh. Before a committee of the House of Lords, Charles Grant gave this evidence:

"I consider the possession of Singapore, and the occupancy of that place, to be very important to the British interests; and I heartily wish it may be found consistent with the rights of the two nations that Great Britain may keep possession of it. I think it is remarkably well situated to be a commercial emporium in those seas. I have no doubt it would very soon rise to great magnitude and importance; and if I may be permitted to allude to the conduct of any individual on this subject, I must say that I think the whole of the proceedings of Sir T. S. Raffles have been marked with great intelligence and great zeal for the interests of his country. I remember well being struck with how much has been done in a very short time at Singapore, both as to the resort of people as settlers and of shipping for trade. It should be remembered that it was quite an unoccupied spot when he took possession of it."

Grant followed this up with a letter to Raffles on 19th July:

"You will easily conceive that it has not been possible for me to enter fully with you into the various subjects of the letters and papers you have sent me. I have, however, done all that I believe you expect from me, that is to uphold your views of what our national policy ought to be with respect to the Eastern Archipelago. . . . You are probably aware of the obstacles which have been opposed to the adoption of your measures and even threatened your position in the Service. Your zeal considerably overstepped your prudence and the first operation of it became known at an unfavourable juncture. It was thought that the state of affairs in Europe required that they should be discountenanced.

"The acquisition of Singapore has grown in importance. The stir made here lately for the further enlargement of the Eastern trade fortified that impression. It is now accredited in the India House. Of late in an examination before a Committee of the House of Lords I gave my opinion of the value in a moral, political and commercial view of a

British establishment in the locality of Singapore under the auspices of the Company. From all these circumstances and others I augur well as to the retention and encouragement of this Station your rapidity has preoccupied."

Grant did not as Raffles had hoped, again become chairman of the Company.

vii

Both Farquhar and his son-in-law, Bernard, had written to John Palmer upon the arrival of Travers at Singapore. Palmer wrote to Bernard on 6th June:

"I was a little surprised by your letter of the 20th April announcing the Colonel's relief by Captain Travers; for, although when Sir Stamford was here, I knew that in deference to the Colonel's wishes he meant to give him a successor, I concluded he would await his specific call for one, and not take him at a moment when he could not get a passage Home. I trust indeed that he is in no manner hurried, and will only resign when he is quite prepared to quit the Settlement. I hear of its Prosperity with great pleasure, and am glad to receive the Document you sent me in refutation of the alleged obstructions on the Trade. It was not indeed to be credited by those who knew the Colonel, and it was found, therefore, necessary by the cavillers to assign a new Motive for his assumption of new Powers, and that was nothing less than your usurped influence over him for selfish purposes in pursuits interdicted to you ostensibly by your official Station. These were current whispers here which might be owing to the jealous uneasiness of Penang, but I could never trace them to an authentic Source, and their impression was soon lost."

Twelve days later he wrote to Farquhar:

"Although I can scarcely hope that this will find you at Singapoor, I take the chance of that desired Event since I am not of the Chorus which hope for a change there. I did not require the proofs which young Bernard has handed me of the fallacy of the Rumour about restricted Trade and the like, for I had evidence to the contrary in the countless Vessels resorting to Singapoor and in the facility enjoyed by my *protégé*, Queiros, and others. I conclude that Raffles will have repaired to you on your Summons, but I do not know what he could have had to do to anticipate it, for it was his professed Purpose when here that it was due to you and himself as well as the Public Interest that he should have personally relieved you of your Charge; and to regulate all our bearings with the principal Native Authorities.

"You have two Consolations of which nothing can deprive you if you live to the age of Methuselah—first the conviction of your own Conscience that your whole soul has been bent upon the Welfare of the people under your paternal Sway; and last you have witnessed its efficiency. Let us pray that Singapoor may under the influence of your Principles continue increasing in Prosperity and Happiness.

"The Policy pursued by this Government in relation to the Dutch having been highly applauded in the Cabinet at Home, let us hope that the redoubtable Elout will not turn us from our high Pretensions.

"I do not know what Raffles can do for Bernard, except keep him in his place, but he has probably heard, as I had, that B. interfered with and monopolized the Trade; and that Rumour is probably among the causes of this projected transfer to Bencoolen. It is possible that a Mas. Atten. may abuse his station in that way, but he ought not to be condemned unheard. Raffles told me, however, that he had from the first reserved the berth for Flint as a *pis aller*, and perhaps he can do nothing better for him. I understood that he had so explained himself with you when Bernard was appointed.

"Nothing appears to have been settled about Penang, but I hear that the Temper about Raffles at Home denies him any chance of a succession, and that will probably drive him Home. Even the whole Eastern Government would be insufficient for Raffles, whose Genius and Talents and restless Spirit require a larger and busier Theatre."

The allegations that his son-in-law was monopolizing the trade of the port were repudiated by Farquhar with his usual warmth of feeling. Having convened a committee, which reported that the allegations were unfounded, he wrote to Raffles "with feelings extremely wounded at the idea of complaints so injurious to the character and conduct of the authorities being clandestinely circulated", but as there was no immediate opportunity of forwarding this letter and a copy of the committee's findings to Bencoolen, he wrote also to Calcutta, adding that "during a period of nearly twenty-nine years of uninterrupted service in India the present is the first instance to my knowledge that even suspicion of negligence or misconduct has attached to any public act of mine".

No wonder Palmer remarked that "Farquhar seemed very sore".

By 28th June Palmer was feeling less confident about the future of Singapore. To Phillips, congratulating him on being confirmed as Governor, he wrote:

"Lord H. told me yesterday, not consequent to this recent Dispatch by the 'D. of York', that he expected Singapore would be given up. I can't reconcile this to the public Approbation of his line of Eastern Policy, but I can't suspect the accuracy of his information. I don't suppose that the Golden Sword will vex these parts much longer."

Travers recorded in his diary in July:

"The confirmation of Mr Phillips as Governor of Penang was announced this month and consequently was a severe disappointment of

Sir Stamford's prospects, who has now but little chance of succeeding for some considerable time. The appointment of Mr P. appears to have given very general satisfaction, having acted so often, not less I believe than seven different times."

Calcutta had not been satisfied by Farquhar's answers on the subject of Tunku Long, writing on 3rd April:

"The information which those dispatches contained is deficient on the points noted in my letter to Sir T. S. Raffles of the 21st August last, especially with regard to the Enquiry whether any overtures were received from Tuankoo Long or any communication held with him immediately prior to his arrival at Singapoor."

To this Farquhar replied on 4th July:

"1st. That Tuankoo Long was residing at Rhio when Sir Thomas Stamford Raffles arrived at Singapore but not under the care of the Rajah Mudah or Viceroy nor living at the cost of the Sultan reigning at Lingin but enjoying in his own right a certain portion of the Revenues accruing from the Possessions of his late Father at Rhio and he was a perfectly free Agent.

"2nd. The precise nature of his residence as far as I have been able to ascertain is as stated above and the duration of it about eight years. The immediate cause of his withdrawing from Rhio was in the first instance for the purpose of obtaining an interview with Sir T. S. Raffles, and his having subsequently fixed his residence here arose out of the Treaty which was entered into by Sir Stamford with him and His Highness the Tummongong.

"3rd. No overtures whatever were made by Tuankoo Long immediately prior to his coming to Singapore nor did I hold any communication directly or indirectly with His Highness at that period, and further, to the best of my knowledge and belief, the Tuankoo Long made no overtures to Sir T. S. Raffles or received any from him during the period alluded to. It has, however, been ascertained that His Highness the Tummungong soon after the arrival of Sir T. S. Raffles at Singapore deemed it expedient to dispatch a Messenger to Rhio in order to acquaint Tuankoo Long with this event, which was the cause of that Prince immediately determining to quit Rhio for the purpose of holding a conference with Sir T. S. Raffles at that place."

John Palmer wrote to Captain Flint at Singapore on 16th July:

"It seems to be the opinion of a very high authority [Hastings] here that we shall relinquish Singapoor but I have been unable to discover on what grounds his inference is formed. It is, however, cause enough for great circumspection in the settlers, for even if it should happen that the Island is only abandoned, and not surrendered to the Dutch, I apprehend that it would be imprudent to form establishments or engage in distant speculations. I am therefore inclined to recommend to you and Friend D.[1] a certain abstinence in your undertakings and let them be of prompt and easy adjustment, if I receive better information, pro or con, you shall have it. . . ."

By the beginning of August it had become obvious that Farquhar had no intention of leaving Singapore voluntarily at the end of that month.

"The fact is", Travers recorded, "that the Colonel on my appointment to succeed him had I believe made up his mind to go home at the time fixed upon by himself. But on finding the place daily improve and likely to become of considerable importance he changed his mind and hoping to have an opportunity of providing for his large native family[2] he determined if possible to remain, little caring with regard to me what inconvenience he subjected me to and having possession and being my superior officer he had, of course, every advantage over me, as a reference to the superior authority would be attended with a delay which would, of course, be ruinous to me."

Relations being now strained, Travers felt compelled to leave Farquhar's bungalow.

Eventually Farquhar wrote Travers an official letter, promising to hand over the settlement without any further delay on 1st October. Travers agreed to this. On 1st September the schooner *Frolic* "arrived from Bencoolen bringing Mrs Flint and child and Captain McKenzie[3] to succeed me in the Government".

"This", Travers went on, "created a new stir. It appeared that Sir Stamford, calculating on my being in charge had appointed McKenzie to succeed and sent him via Singapore to Bengal with dispatches. The plan was for him to return to Bencoolen and so to arrive at Singapore about the time when the China ships would be there next year in one of which it was my wish to go home. And this would have met my wishes extremely well but Colonel Farquhar interposed and holding still by his wish to remain construed a complimentary expression in one of Sir Stamford's letters as a kind of request to continue in charge."

Travers had almost made up his mind to go to Calcutta when news arrived of a good ship, *Minerva*, being due from Java shortly and bound for Europe direct, so he decided that he would abandon the argument and go home.

While the British officials and merchants in Singapore might behave, whatever their private thoughts, as if there was no doubt that the colony would be retained, Sultan Husain Muhammad, more often referred to in these pages as Tunku Long, and the Temenggong were by no means

[1] Deans, of Deans, Scott & Co., in which Flint had an interest.
[2] Farquhar's wife was a Malay.
[3] Captain William Gordon Mackenzie.

happy in their minds. It was true that the action of Raffles had not resulted, as it might well have done, in the violent seizure of Singapore by the Dutch. The two chiefs had guarded themselves against such a contingency by writing diplomatic letters to the Dutch authorities. When the Dutch had taken no military action, they had recovered their courage and had been prepared, under some pressure possibly, to recant. But when Dutch resistance to British penetration in Sumatra had been crowned with complete success, and time had gone by with no news of any decision concerning Singapore, it was not surprising that, with political pressure from Java continuing unabated, their fears returned. Apart from losing the lucrative offices that had descended upon them like gifts from heaven, they would have to face the anger of the Dutch should the sovereignty of Holland be admitted by Great Britain. So in September the Temenggong sent this letter to Farquhar:

"We, Sultan Hussein Mohomed Shah . . . and the Tummung'gung, Maharajah Abdool Rahman . . . conjointly with every inhabitant residing on the Island, Malayans, Bugisses, Arabs, Chinese and natives of the coast of India [Chuliahs], having heard with dread and dismay reports which, although we believe them to be vague and without foundation, and disseminated by weak, foolish, fearful or wicked men who have beheld with an evil eye our prosperity and happiness, or it may be at the instigation of the Dutch (from whose sway God defend us) yet which naturally fill our zealous hearts with terror and anxiety as well on account of ourselves as for the sake of generations as yet unborn, request Colonel Farquhar, Resident of Singapura, to state decidedly whether or no anything definite has been arranged with respect to the Island of Singapura for we one and all feel extremely desirous that the English Company should not set aside the Treaty they have made with us, we have all been very happy during the period of our abode here in this centre of all the Eastern Islands the celebrated residence of our ancestors.

"We have none of us heard whether the Governor-General in Bengal has received any intelligence from England respecting this place, and this is a point we feel most anxious about, for we most sincerely trust that we may not be placed in the same melancholy predicament with the people of Java, Palembang and Banka, who were highly satisfied with the English Government at Java when unexpectedly an order was received from the King of England directing that the Island be given up to the Dutch. . . .

"We therefore, the inhabitants of Singapura, fearful of a like occurrence, desire some definite information respecting ourselves, and if none as yet should have been received we earnestly beg Colonel Farquhar and Governor Raffles to enquire and ascertain the point from the Governor-General in Bengal."

After explaining that the whole of the inhabitants, already amounting to many thousands, had been put to considerable expense in building houses, and that they had come together at Singapore because of their great confidence "in the rectitude and support of the British Government, many having quitted Father, Mother, houses, villages, and even wives and families to come and reside under the fostering care and protection of the British flag", they expressed the strong hope that the British would not abandon them.

"If the Settlement be relinquished we can only attribute it to the acts of the Rajah Muda of Rhio, who in the first instance concluded a Treaty with Colonel Farquhar and afterwards on the arrival of the Dutch, lost sight of that Treaty and attached himself entirely to the Dutch; this was exclusively an act of his own policy."

Nevertheless they looked to the British Government to continue to support them, "as the British have now no other Settlement to the Eastward, except Singapura, than which we believe there is not a country possessing more substantial advantages in all the Eastern Islands". Should this flourishing settlement be abandoned, the British Government would not only lose a most valuable possession, but also by that act "all further confidence between the English and Malay States would be greatly impaired, if not totally destroyed".

This letter was signed by Sultan Husain Muhammad, the Temenggong and six chiefs on behalf of their various communities. It was accompanied by the request that it be entrusted to Captain Mackenzie, "he being a man well acquainted with the language and customs of the Malay nations, so that he personally could lay it at the feet of the Marquis of Hastings, the Governor-General of all India, whose palace is at Calcutta in the Kingdom of Bengal, the fame of whose greatness of mind, love of justice, magnanimity and virtue have reached to the ends of the world".

The *Minerva* arrived at Singapore on 17th October. She was a "free-trader" and not up to the standard of an East Indiaman, but Captain Flint thought well of her. For accommodation for himself, his wife and child and four servants, Travers obtained three cabins for £300, which he considered cheap. The *Minerva* was due to sail on 1st December.

On 24th October, at Bencoolen, Captain Robert Hull died after a severe illness lasting only five days. This was a sad blow to Sophia, though she was fortified by the presence of her younger brother, Nilson.

From Calcutta, John Palmer wrote to Farquhar on 30th October:

"I hear that the Dutch are confident that we shall be ousted; but to this hour nothing decisive nor even indicatory has occurred; they have the advantage in the Commission, although Crawfurd, who is said to be its Secretary, is almost a match for Elout. Mynheer, however, has only to frighten Field-Marshal Wellington and Lord Castlereagh with 'disturbing the peace of Europe' and our pretensions sink; for the Duke knows how cheaply he won his Laurels, and Castlereagh does not wish the fragility of his Treaty to be tested. Entre nous, I doubt whether Singapoor is even worth your struggle for it. Still I will battle and bustle all in my power for its retention, because I think it is the first firm step in the civilization of the Eastern Tribes. . . ."

As the various routine reports from Singapore continued to arrive at Bencoolen, Raffles was able to appreciate the magnificent start made by the new settlement. In his statement dated 13th May, less than fifteen months after the founding, Farquhar had reported that the inhabitants, excluding the garrison and camp followers (640), had already reached a total of 4,727, which included nine European settlers, 2,851 Arabs and Malays, 556 Bugis, 1,159 Chinese, 132 Chuliahs and twenty Portuguese. The houses constructed had numbered five hundred and six. On 8th November he was able to give a very encouraging report on trade for the first twenty-one months.

"It affords me the greatest satisfaction that . . . the trade of the Port already far exceeds what Malacca could boast of during the most flourishing years of its long continuance in our possession. Upwards of a hundred sail of Bugis Prows alone have already arrived here (and some are still expected), many of them being of the most valuable class. The harbour is likewise crowded with various other trading prows and junks from Borneo proper, Sambas, Pontiana, Java, Lingen, Rhio, Jambie, Tringanu, Pahang, Siam, &c, &c, in short this seems to be the favourite rendezvous for all description of Eastern traders. . . .

"The trade to Siam by means of junks promises to become of the first importance as well as that to Cambodia, Cochin-China and China itself, and I might I think venture to add Japan also, although no direct intercourse has as yet been established with this interesting kingdom, still the difficulties which have hitherto prevailed against opening the trade might, I conceive, by means of China junks be gradually overcome. Singapore is so admirably situated in every respect for becoming a grand commercial depot and port of transfer trade that too great a value can scarcely, in my opinion, be placed in the possession of it by the British Government."

Writing to Phillips at Penang on 20th November, John Palmer, in referring to Singapore, touched on a matter that had caused such excitement in England earlier in the year: Queen Caroline's return from exile in Italy and George IV's attempt to gain his freedom from her.

"Of its [Singapore's] retention or fate, nothing is yet known, and Lord H. infers, on grounds he does not disclose, its surrender to the Dutch but until the Queen is beheaded I conclude the question of Singapoor will sleep soundly enough. All the Council think if it were retained it must go to Penang; and so the Golden Sword thought, whilst aiming at your supercession."

The next day he wrote to David Brown:

"Singapoor is *in statu quo* and so it must remain until the new whale, the Queen, a loose fish according to some, gives place to some other Monster. In the meantime we ought to be riveting our position and procuring the Malays to protest against, and even to prevent our Retreat, if we are directed to abandon the Island. . . ."

To Raffles, on 22nd November, he wrote one of his more flattering letters. After various references to Raffles' activities in Sumatra, he continued:

"No progress appears to have been made at Home on Eastern discrepancies but *you* will not despair of a Cause which is in the hands of a man [Crawfurd] who, in addition to his own brains, has helped himself to yours. It was said that Crawfurd was Secretary to the Anglo-Netherlands Commission and we may hope almost as much from his knowledge and ability as from Assey's, had he condescended to be our Friend's jackal, and perhaps we may expect more from a certain Character of Vigour and Array against Mynheer.

"Lord H. continues to think we shall recede but he has never said why nor quoted his Authority; we may, however, suppose it was Canning; for a Director [of the East India Company] would know as little of the views of the Cabinet as you or I. All here imagine that, if we retain Singapoor, it will be brought under Penang; abating your feeling under the Dismemberment of Dominion I think you should rejoice at the Loss, for even in such a theatre conflictions start up. Our friend F[arquhar] has, from some want of prevision, evidently involved you and himself in distress and trouble, but I shall not be at all surprised that he holds his Charge until its end is decided by the Authorities at Home. But this Merry Queen of ours absorbs the whole faculty of the kingdom; divorced or acquitted, such affairs as our Eastern Relations will not occupy much of the Ministers' attention."

Though the *Minerva* was due to sail from Singapore on 1st December, her departure was delayed. On that very day Travers received a letter from Raffles, "informing me that the Marquess of Hastings had fully approved and confirmed everything connected with Singapore and my appointment and giving me various instructions as to my future administration". This was passed on to Farquhar, who flatly declined to hand over charge of the settlement until he had received a reply to his own letters to Calcutta. After much searching of heart, Travers decided to stick to his plan, and on 2nd December he and his family embarked, his departure being "sincerely regretted by every person at Singapore with the exception of Colonel Farquhar, who was no doubt very glad to see me off". His long official connexion with Raffles thus came to an end and with it the invaluable background afforded by his diary.

After waiting for some time for a copy of Hastings' reply to van der Capellen's letter of 16th December 1819, without which the Anglo-Dutch negotiations could not be continued, a rather peevish letter was sent from London to Calcutta on 20th December.

"Your discussions with the Netherlands Government of Java", it ran, "have been the subject of other dispatches. We are extremely sorry that the observations which we have made upon your delay in transmitting documents to us are applicable to those which have passed upon this important subject, especially the letter from the Baron van der Capellen to Lord Hastings on the 16th December 1819, and the reply which we know, through private channel, to have been made to that letter. It would be no easy matter to convey to you a correct notion of the awkward embarrassment under which His Majesty's plenipotentiaries have been placed by this delay in the pending negotiation, and of the advantage it would have given to the plenipotentiaries of the King of the Netherlands had they insisted upon availing themselves of it."

The negotiations thus interrupted were not renewed until 1824, and and then once more on British initiative.

Towards the end of 1820 a copy of Crawfurd's *History of the Indian Archipelago* reached Raffles at Bencoolen.

"Crawfurd's work", he wrote to Cousin Thomas, who in December of that year became LL.D. (Aberdeen), "is written in a very popular style. . . . It has all the characteristics of the author, that is to say considerable talent, an imposing manner, much assurance and assumption and very little principle. It does not contain one fact that is new to me and most of the reasoning and conclusions are founded on partial views. . . . He is a clever fellow and will I doubt not have his day, and I should be sorry to check the interest of his work by any severe criticism. . . ."

He then proceeded to censure the book even more freely. Later he had twinges of conscience.

". . . whatever his faults he has devoted his mind exclusively to objects in which my heart and soul are deeply interested. Let Crawfurd have his swing and the more extended the better; in the present times we perhaps require such bold and fearless men. The cloud of ignorance which still hangs over England with regard to the Eastern Islands cannot be dissipated by ordinary means or by dint of reason; it requires the agency of some of those elements which, while they disperse, cannot avoid partially destroying. Where we differ we shall explain and longer and cooler heads may light their matches from the sparks which we strike out. Two of a trade, they say, can never agree; and Crawfurd and I are perhaps running too much on the same parallel not now and then to be jostling each other but if in following my steps he profits by my errors and experience it will be a satisfaction to me."

Notwithstanding this, he wrote a highly critical report on Crawfurd's book. It was subsequently published (October 1822) in the *Quarterly Review*.

Chapter Twenty-seven

BENCOOLEN, 1821-1822

i

FROM his relations with his constituents, Colonel William Farquhar can be adjudged a man of little discretion, but of much self-importance. His behaviour towards Travers was curious enough; towards others it was no less so. When Richard Reed declined, on grounds of religious scruples, to attend the services of the Baptist missionary, Samuel Milton, Farquhar peremptorily suspended him from all official duties pending reference to Bencoolen, notwithstanding the fact, later pointed out by Raffles, that Reed was holding a civil post, so that garrison orders were inapplicable to him.

Again, when a number of merchants headed by A. L. Johnston wrote calling attention to the excessive presents demanded by the Temenggong, to the arrest by the Temenggong's orders of a Chinese junkmaster who had declined to comply, and to the discouragement to native traders that such action was likely to create, Farquhar replied in a most bureaucratic style:

"It is not without feelings of surprise and regret that I perused the letter you deemed it advisable to address to me . . . on a subject which in no way required the interference of the Body of European Merchants residing here. . . . I cannot for a moment admit of the propriety or expediency of interposing uncalled for their collective voice in any measure having a political tendency."

Not content with so treating responsible merchants like Johnston, who later under Raffles enjoyed the status of what may be called the first "unofficial", by which abbreviation unofficial members of Council in modern times are commonly known, Farquhar fell out with Captain Flint, the master attendant. The cause was Flint's practice of flying a white ensign over his office to proclaim its whereabouts. Farquhar ordered its removal on the grounds that only the Resident was permitted to fly a flag, to indicate that he was the chief authority. Flint countered this by demanding power, refused by Farquhar, to insist that ships should not wear pennants when at anchor in the harbour, a practice forbidden by the Admiralty and one against which their specific orders had only recently been repeated.

Somewhat arbitrary action by Farquhar against a shipmaster named Gillon provoked a very stern rebuke from Calcutta. Captain Gillon commanded the brig *Adventure*, chartered by Claude Queiros, a natural son of John Palmer, who had sent him to Singapore to act as his agent there. Some of the crew petitioned against Gillon and, after hearing the case, Farquhar arrested him and dispatched him under escort in his own ship to Penang for trial. As Penang had no court to deal with such a case, Gillon was sent on to Calcutta. After a lot of correspondence, Calcutta, while disposed to agree that Gillon's account of his personal treatment was exaggerated, added:

". . . the view which his Lordship in Council took of your conduct in precipitately apprehending and sending Mr Gillon for trial to Prince of Wales's Island and of the injurious consequences of that procedure to him is still unchanged. . . . His Excellency in Council therefore cannot exonerate you from the responsibility to which in the judgment of Government you are justly liable."

This was a mortifying experience for Farquhar, but he had only himself to blame. By nature rather a weak man, he was not infrequently unhappy in the choice of occasions on which to demonstrate his authority. Also he was conceited and all too ready to look for affronts or what seemed to him attempts to flout his authority. He had been a successful administrator at Malacca, but that was a small and peaceful settlement, where important problems requiring his decision had seldom arisen. The situation at Singapore was different. A new settlement provided endless problems of every sort, and its development depends materially on their successful solution. Farquhar lacked the character and the experience essential to the task. Raffles, on the other hand, was in his element when coping with such difficulties. The clash that later developed between the two of them was, in these circumstances, almost inevitable.

Two other sources of trouble were beginning to appear. The first was the expenditure on public works, the growing cost of which, under the uncertain tenure of the colony, was criticized by the Supreme Government; the second was the allocation of land to individual applicants. As to the former, it is sufficient to quote the explanation afforded by Farquhar to Raffles in his letter dated 17th April 1821. After referring to the instructions he had received from Raffles on the first establishment of the factory and the need "to afford every obtainable facility consistent with a due regard to economy in promoting the trade of the port, and affording every practicable convenience and facility to those merchants, both European and native, who were desirous of taking up their residence at Singapore", he gave details of what he had done.

"The whole face of the country, as you well know, on our first arrival at Singapore presented nothing but a vast forest of the largest and most impenetrable kind reaching in every direction to the virgin sea, a small green flat along the edge of the beach, barely sufficient to admit of our pitching the tents of our small detachment, was the only ground so far clear as to admit of being occupied.

"On your departure from hence on 6th February 1819 I lost no time in commencing to clear the ground to be appropriated for a Cantonment which I deemed, of course, to be the first undertaking which called for immediate attention both as connected with the health of the troops and security of our Post. The mode of conducting and charging for the public works having been settled by you on the same principle as obtained at Malacca during the period I presided over that Settlement, as subordinate to the Government of Penang, viz. that they should be performed under my own immediate superintendence on trust, the charges being attested on honour, and a Field Officer's, and 8 per cent. allowed to be drawn on the amount disbursed. On which system the whole of the extensive fortifications of Malacca were demolished by me."

Farquhar then proceeded to particularize the various works carried out, explaining that in the first instance few labourers could be obtained, so troops off duty had been used. The labour forces thus assembled had been mustered in the presence of himself and Lieutenant Ralfe every morning and checked again every afternoon. Labour costs at first had been high, but as the population had increased, wages had fallen to the level prevailing at Malacca. It would probably fall below that in due course.

After clearing the site of the cantonment, the old lines of Singapore had been connected together and batteries established. After this the very arduous task of clearing Singapore Hill had been undertaken, and drainage and road work put in hand so as to provide space for the various contingents of natives arriving to settle. Most of this work was done by contract, the lowest tender being accepted. No roads not absolutely necessary to the settlement had been laid. Although the building of a bridge across Singapore river had been authorized, this had not yet been put in hand, though the materials had been collected and were in store. Ferry boats provided an adequate service. Considerable expenditure had been incurred in providing a reservoir, the watering of ships being considered of first importance.

Nothing, he submitted, had been done that was not imperiously necessary for the success of the settlement, and if, notwithstanding his explanations, he was considered to have been extravagant, he could but state that the utmost economy had been practised, the money had been actually expended, and at the time when the major works had been put in hand there had appeared no prospect of the settlement being given up. The allowance of 8 per cent. on the cost could not be regarded as excessive, for no substantial allowances were granted to him at Singapore. His remuneration as Resident and Commandant did not exceed what he had drawn at Malacca, where he had had comparatively little to do, and where his expenses had been less than half those at Singapore. Even the Resident's bungalow had been built at his own expense.

The next matter he raised was one that was to cause keen friction between him and Raffles. It concerned the allocation of sites. He explained that as the northern bank of the river was the only eligible ground for building substantial warehouses, the land on the south bank being low and marshy, some European merchants had been allowed to occupy small portions of ground on the north bank, but had been warned that it might still be required by the Government.

Having denied that any favouritism had been shown in allocating sites, he concluded:

"It may not be foreign to the subject to remark that in consequence of the facilities which have hitherto at a very considerable expense been afforded to the native settlers, so rapid an increase of trade and population has taken place, that the few allowances granted last quarter for the retail of prepared opium, spirits and tax on gaming yielded nearly 2,000 dollars per mensem, a sum sufficient of itself (if ever but in part applied to that purpose) to liquidate in the course of a short period charges hitherto incurred on account of clearing lands, buildings, &c, &c."

Raffles was clearly uneasy as to the method employed in the allocation of sites. We find Farquhar giving later, at his request, a list of allotments; later still, which hills had been granted to which persons: but as the whole question was to be a subject of serious criticism by Raffles when he returned to Singapore in 1823, it can be left till then.

ii

Ella Sophia, fourth child of Sir Stamford and Lady Raffles, was born at Bencoolen on 27th May. The event is briefly touched upon in Raffles' letter to the Duchess of Somerset two days later.

"God willing," he wrote, "we hope to embark from this for England, if not in 1823, certainly in 1824; I am not aware of any changes which are likely to protract my departure. On the contrary, everything seems to concur in proving the necessity, to say nothing of the inclination to return: political events may hasten, but cannot well retard it; and my presence in England may soon become indispensable in support of what I have been trying to do in this part of the world. It is hardly possible for you to conceive how much I have suffered for opening so important a channel for trade as has been effected by the establishment of Singapore: everything is condemned. But a truce to politics: I have other reasons to urge me home. Neither my health nor that of Lady Raffles is very good; I never was strong, and during my first residence in India [East Indies] the climate made a considerable inroad on my constitution. I have had two or three severe attacks since my return, and am now under the necessity of being very careful. I really do not think I could last out above two or three years more; and certainly ambition shall not weigh with me one moment against life. Besides this, my dear little rogues will be rapidly expanding. Charlotte is already as advanced as most children of five years old: she takes an interest in every thing that is going forward, and is really becoming quite a companion. In two or three years both her mind and body will require a colder climate, and to send her home for education, as people usually send their children from this country, is out of the question; we have determined to take her and all the children (for we have now four born in as many years), and to time our departure with reference to their health and happiness. Leopold also will, in two or three years, have grown beyond my management, and it will be time to commence upon the rudiments of a better education than I can give him. I believe people generally think I shall remain longer, as they hardly suppose in such times, and with an increasing family, a man will be inclined to forego the advantages of the field before me; but they know me not. I have seen enough of power and wealth to know that, however agreeable to the propensities of our nature, there is more real happiness in domestic quiet and repose, when blessed with a competence, than in all the fancied enjoyments of the great and the rich.

"Of public news I have very little to communicate, and perhaps none that will be interesting. The Dutch you know are still at war with Palembang, and they have lately fitted out a *third* expedition, consisting of upwards of 3,000 Europeans, fresh from Holland; poor fellows! They are determined on vengence. No quarter is to be given, and dreadful will be the massacre if they succeed, which God forbid! . . ."

Not long after this word was received from Batavia that Sir Joseph Banks had died on 9th May 1820. To Raffles his loss seemed irreparable. Banks had been the very soul and mainspring of the Royal Society, and Raffles feared that his death would take the heart out of the scientific work for which Banks had made the Society famous. The new president of the Society was Sir Humphry Davy.

Then from India came the news that Charles Assey had died on 24th March at Kidderpore, a village on the Hooghly, south of Calcutta. He was about the same age as Raffles, and in the dark days in Java no one had been a more loyal or a more trusted friend. Later in England he had valiantly championed the causes Raffles had at heart. Only recently Raffles had received from him the detailed sketch of the British administration in Java, which Assey had worked up at his request. And now Assey was dead.

But death was soon to strike much nearer home. The very first victim of an epidemic that now swept over Bencoolen was little Leopold, who, after a very short illness, died on 4th July.

"My heart has been nigh broken," wrote Raffles, "and my spirit is gone; I have lost almost all that I prided myself upon in this world and the affliction came upon us when we least expected such a calamity. . . . Had you but seen him and known him you must have doted—his beauty and intelligence were so far above those of other children of the same age that he shone among them as a sun enlivening and enlightening everything around him. I had vainly formed such notions of future happiness when he should have become a man and been all his father wished him that I find nothing left but what is stale, flat and unprofitable."

Before he and Sophia had time to recover from this terrible blow, Sophia's brother-in-law, Captain Harry Auber, who had brought them out from England in the *Lady Raffles*, was carried off by a violent attack. His brother Peter was then assistant secretary to the East India Company. Writing to him on 12th July, Raffles managed somehow to realize that the death of Harry would mean more to Peter than the death of his own son.

"I little thought a week ago when overwhelmed with grief by the loss of our dear and eldest boy Leopold who was snatched from us after a very short illness that I should so soon have been called upon to report another, and to you, my dear friend, a still more severe loss. The vessel leaves this port immediately and bad news flies fast. Cruel as must be the stroke and ill qualified as I am at the present moment to break it to you with the tenderness and caution I could wish, I must perform the duty; I must rend your heart by telling you that our dear friend and your brother is no more! He breathed his last yesterday and was carried off in a few days by a series of apoplectic fits which baffled all the powers of medicine. He has just been buried and I snatch a moment from the time I am obliged to devote to Sophia to send you the melancholy intelligence. . . . I shall not trouble you with our grief, you will have enough of your own. . . ."

Sophia was prostrated.

"Whilst the Editor", she wrote, "was almost overwhelmed with grief for the loss of this favourite child, unable to bear the sight of her other children—unable to bear even the light of day—humbled upon her couch with a feeling of misery—she was addressed by a poor, ignorant, uninstructed native woman of the lowest class (who had been employed about the nursery), in terms of reproach not to be forgotten:—'I am come because you have been here many days shut up in a dark room, and no one dares to come near you. Are you not ashamed to grieve in this manner, when you ought to be thanking God for having given you the most beautiful child that ever was seen? Were you not the envy of every body? Did any one ever see him, or speak of him, without admiring him; and instead of letting this child continue in this world till he should be worn out with trouble and sorrow, has not God taken him to heaven in all his beauty? What would you have more? For shame, leave off weeping, and let me open a window.'"

By 10th November, Raffles was able to write:

"Sophia has at last undertaken to write to her mother. She is getting better and I am happy to say the children are well; for myself I am at this moment under the operation of mercury and maintain but a crazy kind of existence. I sometimes think it very doubtful that I shall ever reach England again: at other times I rally a little; but on the whole I begin to be more indifferent as to the result than I used to be."

The precaution had been taken of inoculating their other children, and they hoped that nothing would touch them, but on 10th December, Raffles wrote home:

"We are at this moment in great alarm for our dear Charlotte, who labours under a violent dysentery. Sophia has not left her for three days and nights and our almost only hope is now in effecting a salivation with mercury. So severe has been our affliction in the loss of poor Leopold that we are not capable of sustaining a second shock of the kind just now. The younger children have also been seriously ill but are getting better.

"We have at any rate resolved to send all we have left as soon as a ship going direct may be procured; I have half made an agreement with the Captain of the 'Borneo'[1] for the purpose and they will probably sail in February. What a severe reverse is this! But the other day we were alarmed lest we should have too many, now all our anxiety is to preserve some even of those we have. The change of climate may do wonders, and we shall hope to follow them in a year or eighteen months. I keep to my present resolution of going to Singapore in the course of the present year; some change will be necessary for Sophia."

iii

"I returned to India", reads the opening paragraph of John Crawfurd's *Journal of an Embassy to the Courts of Siam and Cochin China*, "in the month of May 1821 and in September was nominated by the late Marquis of Hastings, then Governor-general of India, to proceed on a mission to the Courts of Siam and Cochin China. . . . My companions were Captain Dangerfield and Lieutenant Rutherford, of the Indian army, and Mr Finlayson, of His Majesty's Medical Service. Captain Dangerfield was appointed my assistant, and to succeed in case of accident; Mr Rutherford

[1] A little ship of 428 tons, built in Borneo and jointly owned by Alexander Hare and John Clunies-Ross.

commanded our small escort of thirty Sepoys; and Mr Finlayson was attached to the mission in quality of medical officer and naturalist. . . . The 'John Adam', an Indian-built ship of about 380 tons burthen, was appointed for the accommodation of the mission."

The instructions conveyed to Crawfurd by George Swinton, secretary to the Supreme Government, were, briefly, that he was to attempt to resume friendly intercourse with those countries and regain the lost trade with them. ". . . during the first half of the last century, that trade became extremely inconsiderable, and during the last seventy years may be looked upon as having altogether ceased". This from Swinton.

"Having received my instructions," continued Crawfurd, "and being charged with letters from the Governor-general to the Kings of Siam and Cochin China, accompanied by such presents as are required by the usages of the East, we embarked, on the 21st November 1821, and dropped down the river with the ebb-tide. . . ."

iv

The new year brought no respite for Raffles and Sophia. During the night of 3rd January little Marco Polo died of dysentery. Charlotte continued ill.

"All our hopes", Raffles wrote next day to Mary Anne, "depend on our being able to get her off early to England."

Ten days later he added the postscript:

"I open this letter to add that our dear Charlotte has just been snatched from us. I have nothing to add."

To a friend he wrote on 15th January:

"We have this morning buried our beloved Charlotte. Poor Marsden was carried to the grave not ten days before, and within the last six months we have lost our three eldest children; guess what must be our distress. This is a melancholy day and I have turned my thoughts to serious subjects: among the rest to the risk we run by remaining longer in this country. I have therefore taken the first step towards going home by sending in my resignation. On referring to my commission I find that I am not allowed to leave India without permission from the Court under the hand of thirteen or more directors. . . .

"We have now only one child left, the little Ella, still an infant. Thank God she is apparently well and it is our determination she shall go home in the 'Borneo', in which ship I had engaged accommodation for the three. I shall not attempt to convey to you anything like an idea of poor Sophia's sufferings. Charlotte had attained that age when she was quite a companion and of all the misfortunes likely to happen this was the last looked to, yet severe as the dispensation is we are resigned to it;

we have still reason to thank God. I still propose visiting Singapore about September next but to return here the following May. By 1st January 1824, God willing, we hope to be on our way home".

His letter to the chairman and deputy chairman of the Company ran thus:

"During the last year my constitution has suffered so severely from repeated attacks of illness that I can no longer look forward with confidence to protracted residence in an Indian climate. Under this circumstance I am reluctantly compelled to apprise the Court of Directors of my desire to be relieved of my present charge at the close of the next year, beyond which period I fear that it will be impossible for me longer to administrate their affairs in this quarter. . . .

"I shall not on the present occasion enter upon any review of the very peculiar and distressing circumstances under which I have been lately placed or refer to the disappointments I have experienced. I am satisfied that I have honourably and zealously discharged the public trusts which have been confided to me and that eventually I shall find in the Honourable Court every disposition to view the circumstances under which I have been placed and my services and claims generally with justice and liberality."

To this these two gentlemen were to reply in due season:

". . . We take this opportunity of expressing our regret at the circumstances which have induced you to come to this determination. Although we have had occasion strongly to express our disapprobation of some of your proceedings at Fort Marlborough, we are disposed fully to acknowledge your integrity, zeal and ability. We are your loving friends, &c."

This was honourable recognition of his services. Justice and liberality were not to be so freely dispensed.

Outward bound for Siam and Cambodia, the *John Adam* called at Singapore on 21st January and was delayed there by adverse winds for nearly a month, during which period Farquhar managed to persuade Crawfurd, possibly without much difficulty, that it had been he, not Raffles, who had been responsible for the original call at Singapore, thereby insinuating that the choice of the settlement had been his. This myth was later given support by Crawfurd when he included an account of Singapore in his *Embassy to Siam and Cochin China*.

During February, Raffles wrote home:

"I have been desperately ill and confined to a dark room the last ten days but thank God I am better."

Again on the 26th of that month:

"As the 'Borneo' will be off in a day or two I sit down to give you something of a general letter but I am too ill and weak to write much and you must excuse repetition should I fall into it. For the last three weeks I have been confined to my room by a severe fever which fell on the brain and drove me almost to madness. I thank God, however, that I have now got over it and am on my legs again; but I am still weak and unable to converse with strangers.

"The first and most interesting subject is our dear child. Our little darling is under the immediate charge of Nurse Grimes. She leaves us in excellent health, and we indulge the hope that by the strong measure we have taken of sending her to a healthier climate we may be spared this one comfort to solace and enliven our declining days. Sophia's health, though it has suffered severely is, I thank God, improving, and if it is the will of God that we even continue as well as we are we hope to be able to stand out another year or two with tolerable comfort. . . ."

Then comes a touch of the old Raffles:

"I fancy I shall find plenty to do at Singapore . . . the place thrives wonderfully . . . there is sad confusion at Penang, first among the Governor and his Councillors and next with the Siamese, who have burnt and sacked Queda and obliged the King to take refuge at Penang. You, of course, are aware of the history of these proceedings; it is a result that has long been anticipated but need not now have been brought to issue. Had the Government of Penang possessed sufficient foresight to have supported the King by sending him a force when he was still in his capital it would have averted the storm."

To Cousin Thomas he wrote on 17th April:

"We now pass our time in great retirement. I have lately completed a very comfortable country house and much of my time is taken up in agricultural pursuits. I am by far the most active farmer in the country and as President of the Agricultural Society not only take precedence at the Board but in the field. I have a dozen ploughs constantly going and before I quit the estate I hope it will realize a revenue of two or three thousand a year besides feeding its population. It is an experiment: but it will encourage others and as it is a property which belongs to the Company no one can accuse me of interested views in the efforts I am making. It is possible that in England I may look with interest to the returns in money which my oats and barley may afford, but here I am quite satisfied with seeing and collecting the produce of my industry and exertions, keeping my mind and hands clear and clean from any pecuniary consideration whatever. I am cultivating and improving for the mere love of the thing, and the desire of employing my time advantageously for others."

News reached Bencoolen that India was to have a new Governor-General. Hastings' powerful lieutenant, Charles Metcalfe, had at last succeeded in smashing the firm of Rumbold & Palmer, thus breaking its unholy stranglehold on the finances of the State of Hyderabad. While not financially interested, Hastings had maintained throughout a close friendship with Sir W. Rumbold and, feeling himself compromised, had decided to resign. Canning, President of the India Board of Control, was reported as his successor. It should be added here that John Palmer was in no way connected with Rumbold & Palmer, though William Palmer of that partnership was his natural half-brother.

Raffles had a high opinion of Canning, whose influence in Eastern affairs was great. He referred to this prospective appointment, together with other matters, in a further letter to his cousin, dated 25th July:

"I am sure it will be satisfactory to you to know that both Sophia and myself have become ourselves again: not that we can forget our past and heavy afflictions or cease to mourn over them; but we can now again enjoy the present hour and look forward with steadiness and satisfaction. . . .

"We have had a very sickly season and among the casualties are our Chaplain[1] and Doctor; Jack has also been obliged to fly to Batavia for change of air, and deaths are of daily occurrence in our small circle: but notwithstanding we still look up; therefore with the blessing of God don't despair of seeing us in 1824.

"I have long looked for the appointment of Mr Canning as Governor-General and upon the whole I augur well of his Government, not from any personal views as to myself but with respect of the public interests to which I cannot but look with anxiety. My life has hitherto been a public one; and long habit if it is nothing else has made the public will as interesting to me as my own personal prospects ever can be. Without attending to it I should lose half the interest of my life so that you must not be surprised if I still hold on the same course even though I may not be able to prove that my interests are advanced by it. To these I never looked *primarily* and God grant that I never may. I believe, paradoxically as it may seem to say so, I should lose my identity were I to cease to love other things better than myself. It may be a wrong turn of mind but such is the twist of it and matured as it now is by forty years growth I fear I must change myself ere I think or act otherwise. Do not, however, do me the injustice to suppose that I am overweeningly attached to the things of this world—am in love with ambition or suppose I can reform the world by my endeavours. I think I know myself better. I would rather be the simple *unit* with the united *few*, who act rightly and on principle, than a blazing cypher acting for self and my own nothingness, but a truce to this. I hope to be at Singapore by the time Canning arrives so that he will find me at my post of danger and yet I hope of honour too."

But George Canning was not destined to become Governor-General of India. On 12th August Robert Stewart, Viscount Castlereagh, com-

[1] Charles Winter. On his death, his widow and family returned to England.

mitted suicide at Foots Cray, his home in Kent, by cutting his throat with a penknife. Canning succeeded to the post of Foreign Secretary, Lord Amherst being appointed Governor-General of India. The new president of the Board of Control was Charles Bathurst.

It was Raffles' intention to visit Singapore towards the middle of September. At the end of August Dr Jack returned from Java no better in health than when he had departed. It was decided to send him to the Cape. On 15th September Raffles had to take up his pen and write to Dr Wallich:

"We were to have embarked this morning for Singapore but the wind has proved foul and it was ordained that we should remain another day to bury our dear and invaluable friend William Jack. Poor fellow! A finer head or heart there never was; and whether as a bosom friend or as a scientific assistant he was to me invaluable; he had been ill long and returned from Java about a fortnight ago after an unsuccessful visit for change of air: we embarked him yesterday in the 'Layton' for the Cape and he died this morning before the ship weighed her anchor.

"I am so depressed in spirits and altogether so incompetent to the task of writing to his father at this hurried moment when all is confusion for my embarkation that I must postpone it but I beg you to assure him that the loss is as deeply deplored by his friends here as it is possible it may be by his family at home; and that for myself I am so overwhelmed by the misfortune that I cannot command myself to enter into particulars...."

Accompanied by Sophia, young Nilson Hull, Captain Salmond and Dr Lumsdaine, he managed to get off on 17th September. He had remained at Bencoolen for an unbroken period of over two and a half years. That he should have been content to do so and should have thought it unnecessary to visit his new settlement during all that time is surely remarkable. It was not that he had lost interest in it. In spite of the appalling lack of communications he still insisted on being the controlling authority, and the unfortunate Farquhar, compelled occasionally by force of circumstances to comminucate with the more accessible Calcutta, was liable to be censured for not addressing himself to his immediate superior in Bencoolen.

What is the explanation of his long residence at Bencoolen? No single factor gives the answer, various circumstances combining to keep him there. In the first place it is quite understandable that he should have been unwilling to accede to the request of Farquhar and the Malay chiefs to visit the settlement before Farquhar's then intended departure. He had only recently arrived back in Bencoolen from Calcutta, where he had been desperately ill. He hated travel by sea. Moreover, there had been little to do at Singapore beyond simple pioneering work, which Farquhar was well qualified to supervise. His major scheme for the centralization of all authority in the Eastern seas could not possibly be realized for some time. Again, Hastings had enjoined the utmost economy, the future of the island being by no means secure. From Bencoolen, Raffles had at least been able to help by keeping up a steady pressure on his influential friends at home.

It is true that he had been "confined to Marlborough on account of the positive orders of the Court of Directors", but even that would not have kept him prisoner in Bencoolen for over thirty months without moving farther from it than Pĕrmatang Balam, had there not been a marked decline in his physical strength. Though he had talked again and again of a trip to Lake Toba and the Bataks—and with Raffles talk and action had always been almost simultaneous—nothing had come of it.

We see too a marked change in his ideas of how long he could remain in the tropics. Not long before, it had been five or six years; now it was a matter of two at the most—indeed some doubt existed in his mind whether he would even live to return home; not that he thought it mattered very much. This physical lassitude was directly due to declining health and, while it was unaccompanied by any slackening of his mental activities, it predisposed him to let things slide along, to wait on events rather than force the pace and make events wait on him. His life at Bencoolen had been in many ways Arcadian and he might have decided to prolong his stay there had not Arcadia almost overnight been turned into a charnel-house. Tragedy heaped on tragedy galvanized him into one supreme effort of activity at Singapore. Then home to England.

By 1st October the ship was in the Straits of Bangka, whence he wrote to Cousin Thomas:

"Death, as if he seemed determined to glut himself to the last, snatched from us two days before we sailed another member of our family, my invaluable and highly respected friend Dr Jack; he had supplied the place of Dr Arnold and all my future views in life were intimately blended with the plans and projects which we had formed. He was to have accompanied me to England and his death has left a blank which will not be easily or speedily filled up.

"I am now on my passage to Singapore accompanied by Sophia and her youngest brother; and my plan is to remain there about six months with the view of arranging and modelling something like a constitution for the place and transferring its future management to a successor. Should God spare our lives we then look to return to Bencoolen for the purpose of winding up; and then about the end of the year if it be not too presumptuous to look forward so far after what has passed we contemplate the prospect of revisiting old England. . . ."

Singapore was reached on 10th October.

Chapter Twenty-eight

SINGAPORE, 1822-1823

i

WE can readily imagine with what eager interest Raffles studied the approaching shore as the ship neared Singapore. It was now a vastly different place from the primitive encampment he had left in February 1819, just over three years and eight months before. In 1819 John Palmer had written with his usual acidity:

"He talks of the prosperity of his new Settlement as if years had rolled over our possession and Agriculture and Commerce had grown with population; when I believe fifteen hundred square feet have not been cleared away for the kitchens of our troops."

Yet Raffles' confidence had not been misplaced. On the day following disembarkation he wrote:

"The coldest and most disinterested could not quit Bencoolen and land at Singapore without surprise and emotion. What then must have been my feelings after the loss of almost everything that was dear to me on that ill-fated coast? After all the risks and dangers to which this, my almost only child, has been exposed, to find it grown and advanced beyond measure and even my warmest anticipations and expectations, in importance, wealth and interest—in everything that can give it value and permanence?

"I did feel when I left Bencoolen that the time had passed when I could take much active interest in Indian affairs, and I wished myself safe home; but I already feel differently. I feel a new life and vigour about me and if it please God to grant me health, the next six months will I hope make amends for the gloom of the last sixteen. Rob me not of this my political child and you may yet see me at home with all wonted spirits and with an elasticity about me that will bear me up against all that party spirit can do to depress me."

To the Duchess of Somerset:

"Here all is life and activity; and it would be difficult to name a place on the face of the globe with brighter prospects or more pleasant satisfaction. In little more than three years it has risen from an insignificant fishing village to a large and prosperous town, containing at least ten thousand inhabitants of all nations actively engaged in commercial pursuits which afford to each and all a handsome livelihood and abundant profit. There are no complaints here of want of employment, no deficiency of rents, or dissatisfaction at taxes. Land is rapidly rising in value and in respect of the present number of inhabitants we have reason to expect that we shall have at least ten times as many before many years have passed. This may be considered as the simple but almost magic result of that perfect freedom of Trade which it has been my good fortune to establish. . . .

"I am at present engaged in establishing a constitution for Singapore, the principles of which will I hope ensure its prosperity. . . . In Java I had to remodel and in doing so to remove the rubbish and encumbrances of two centuries of Dutch maladministration. Here I have an easier task and the task is new. In Java I had to look principally to the agricultural interests, and the commercial only so far as they were concerned with them; here on the contrary commerce is everything, agriculture only in its infancy. The people are different as well as their pursuits.

"I assure you I stand much in need of advice and were it not for Lady Raffles I should have no counsellor at all. She is nevertheless a host to me, and if I do live to see you again, it will be entirely owing to her love and affection: without this I should have been cast away long ago. . . ."

This third and last visit of Raffles to Singapore was by far the longest, lasting nearly eight months. It was to be one of intense activity, notwithstanding the serious bouts of illness that assailed him from time to time. In fact, the fear that he might not be spared to carry out the plans germinating in his brain was to act as a sharp edge to his labours, imparting to them a sense of special urgency.

He and Sophia stayed at first with the Flints.

"There was no house belonging to the Government," Raffles explained to the Court in a letter to which we shall have occasion to refer again, "and I did not intrude on the accommodation of the Resident, who occupied his own quarters. The most reasonable that offered was the upper part of a house occupied by the master attendant, which was engaged at 150 dollars per month, and for the most part occupied by the writers and servants of the establishment. . . ."

Whilst at Bencoolen, he had been kept generally informed of the activities of Farquhar and there was not a little that had made him uneasy. Now that he was on the spot, he was determined to see that his own ideas prevailed. If Farquhar obstructed him, then Farquhar would have to go. The issues at stake were far too important for any indulgence in sentiment.

One of the chief causes of anxiety had been the planning of the town. Raffles had suspected that Farquhar lacked method, and there had been grounds for fearing that Farquhar's friends had been favoured. In the previous April he had called for a full report. This Farquhar had sent, but Raffles had withheld comment, pending his own arrival at Singapore.

The very first thing he had then seen was that his positive instruction, that the land on the north bank of the river should be exclusively reserved for the government, had not been carried out. Already there were commercial buildings appearing in the reserved area.

Farquhar explained that no European would build on the south bank because the land there was low-lying and liable to flooding. The first step, then, was to ascertain whether in fact it was physically impracticable to utilize the south bank. On 17th October, just a week after his arrival, Raffles appointed a committee of disinterested persons to advise him. Its members were Dr Lumsdaine, Captain Salmond and Dr Wallich, who, convalescing from fever contracted in Nepal, happened to be on a visit to Singapore.

These three gentlemen made their report on 23rd October. After explaining that they had consulted "every source of authentic information that appeared in any shape to bear upon the main question", they observed:

". . . the tract of land at the back of the southern bank of the river is in general lower than that of the opposite side and for the want of a proper embankment is commonly overflowed during the height of the spring tides. There can be no doubt, however, that on raising and draining it by means of a strong piece of masonry along the river side, not only will extensive grounds be rendered permanently dry and salubrious but they will become available for all purposes of building and cultivation . . . from a careful personal examination of the site of the proposed buildings we feel warranted in giving it as our decided opinion that the plan is fully practicable."

After giving various details, the report ended:

"Upon the whole, therefore, we are of opinion that the projected plan of constructing warehouses on the south bank of the river and of draining the low ground in the rear of it is not only highly expedient and perfectly practicable but under existing circumstances the most advantageous and fittest that could be adopted in accomplishing the grand objects in view."

Raffles proceeded to follow the advice of the committee. The river was bunded on the south bank, and a small hill standing on Singapore Point was tipped into the swamp to make a reclamation where approximately stands Raffles Place to-day. 'Abdullah has left a vivid account of how the task was accomplished.

"The next day there came a man whom those two gentlemen [Raffles and Farquhar] had sent to engage Chinese, Malay and Tamil labourers, about two or three hundred men at a rupee a day, and they were told to dig away the earth and carry it off; and there were some men breaking the rocks, for there were a great many large rocks there, and everyone had his work to do; there were dozens of overseers, and it all looked like people at war. Labour became dearer every day, and in the evening the money was brought in sacks to pay the men. Thrice every day Mr Raffles went there to supervise the men's work, and there were a number of men superintending the workmen, besides which Mr Farquhar did not fail to go every morning on horseback to measure out the land. . . ."

Meanwhile Dr Wallich suggested that a site should be provided for a botanical garden. This Raffles warmly welcomed and apportioned an area of about forty-eight acres on the north-east side of Fort Canning, giving the maximum variety of soil and elevation. Dr Wallich considered it "in the highest degree satisfactory".

The garden thus created is not to be confused with the modern Botanical Gardens, which only date from 1860. The original garden was abandoned in 1829, presumably under a false idea of economy. By 1835, George Windsor Earl wrote in his *Eastern Seas*:

"At the foot of the hill lies the botanical garden which is now overrun with weeds, though several nutmeg trees planted by the founder of the Settlement flourished and bear fruit without any care or cultivation."

The suitability of the south bank having been confirmed, Raffles had but one other major problem to solve before he could complete his reconstruction of the settlement: to discover under what terms and conditions the settlers of different races had been permitted to occupy land. A lengthy and increasingly acrimonious correspondence ensued between Raffles and Farquhar, the first determined to discover the exact conditions, the second trying to explain the somewhat vague terms under which various individuals had been allowed to take up land and build on it.

Raffles did not wait to get the position clarified. It was a matter that would not become urgent until people were compelled to shift their quarters and demanded compensation. Meanwhile he had no intention of allowing anything to delay the planning of the settlement on a scientific basis, and those of whatever race who found themselves in the wrong area would have to move. To act so drastically required considerable courage, and only a man of dynamic energy combined with great personal influence and good sense could have carried it through without so alienating public opinion as to jeopardize the rising prosperity of the infant settlement. In the event, one or two persons proved contumacious, more particularly Queiros and Cathcart Methven, late of Bencoolen. The more responsible Europeans realized that Raffles' decision was unavoidable in the long-term interests of the colony and they accepted the orders to move, and the modest compensation offered, with a reasonably good grace. Had Raffles shirked the problem, it would soon have become beyond the power of anyone to tackle it successfully.

The working out of the plan was entrusted, according to his normal practice, to a committee. This was called the Town Planning Committee and consisted of Captain C. E. Davis as chairman, George Bonham, a civil servant, and A. L. Johnston, the leading merchant to whom reference has already been made. It is interesting to observe that in this committee, as in a subsequent committee charged with the task of implementing its recommendations, Raffles saw to it that one of Farquhar's relatives was included. Captain Davis was Farquhar's son-in-law, as was F. J. Bernard, member of the second committee.

The instructions issued to the Town Planning Committee on 4th November, less than a month after Raffles' arrival, were lengthy and comprehensive. They ran into thirty-two paragraphs, but the general purpose of the committee's task was clearly set out in the first paragraph.

"It has been observed by the Supreme Government 'that in the event of Singapore being permanently retained, there seems every reason to believe that it will become a place of considerable magnitude and importance', and it is essential that this circumstance should be constantly kept in mind, in regulating the appropriation of land. Every day's experience shows the inconvenience and expense that may arise out of the want of such a forecast and in this respect an economical and proper allotment of the ground intended to form the site of the principal town is an object of first importance, and one which under the present circumstances will not admit of delay."

Proceeding from this thesis, the instructions dealt first with the "extent of the town generally", next with the "ground reserved for Government" and the "European town and principal mercantile establishments", and thereafter, under the general heading, "Native divisions or campongs", with the areas to be reserved for the Chinese, Bugis, Arabs, Chuliahs and Malays.

Provision was to be made for markets and a marine yard. The whole space along the frontage of the town, between the sea and the road running parallel to it, was to be reserved for the use of the public. As far as practicable, streets were to be laid out so that they ran at right angles, and they were to be grouped into three classes, each with appropriate frontage charges. For each class of road a minimum width was to be fixed. All houses constructed of brick or tile should have a uniform type of front, each having a verandah of a certain depth, "open at all times as a continuous and covered passage on each side of the street". Proper spaces were to be reserved for police stations. When fixing sites for the principal church, theatre, etc., "care should be taken that it be in a central and open position and that a considerable space be kept clear in the vicinity".

Whilst the general planning of the European town was of great importance, of no less moment was the planning of areas to suit the different Asiatic communities. The Chinese clearly required special consideration, because from the large number of them already in the settlement and "the peculiar attractions of the place for that industrious race it may be presumed that they will always form by far the largest portion of the community".

This prophesy has been fully substantiated.

"In establishing the Chinese campong on a proper footing, it will be necessary to advert to the provincial and other distinctions among this peculiar people. It is well known that the people of one province are more quarrelsome than another and that continued disputes and disturbances take place between people of different provinces; it will also be necessary to distinguish between the fixed residents and the itinerants—between the resident merchants and the traders who only resort to the port for a time. On the latter those from Amoi [Amoy] claim particular attention and it may perhaps deserve consideration whether on account of their importance it may not be advisable to allot a separate division for their accommodation. . . .

"It being intended to place the Chinese population in a great measure under the immediate control of their own Chiefs you will fix up such centrical and commanding sites for the Residence of these Authorities and appropriate to them such larger extent of ground as may tend to render them efficient instruments of Police and at the same time raise them in the consideration of the lower classes. . . .

"The concentration of the different descriptions of artificers such as blacksmiths, carpenters, &c, in particular quarters, should also be attended to."

The other communities were less difficult to accommodate.

"In the allotment of the Bugis town it will be equally necessary to attend to economy in the distribution of ground by laying regular streets inland towards the river and obliging the inhabitants to conform thereto. . . . The Arab population will require every consideration. . . . No situation would be more appropriate for them than the vicinity of the Sultan's residence."

For the Chuliahs a division of the town up to the Singapore river would be the most appropriate in view of the "necessity of their residence being in the vicinity of the place where their services are most likely to be called for". As the Malays were principally attached to the Temenggong or engaged in fishing, it was probable that the former would settle near Panglima Pĕrang's[1] on the upper banks of the river, while the latter would doubtless find accommodation for themselves in the smaller bays and inlets beyond the part of the beach reserved for the town. At the

[1] Panglima (leader) Pĕrang (war).

same time, the committee was to satisfy itself that adequate provision was made for this important section of the population.

While the members of the committee, with the assistance of Lieutenant Jackson, the garrison engineer, were wrestling with the problems thus set before them, Raffles was equally busy trying to sort out the tangled skein of land appropriations. The correspondence between him and Farquhar does not appear to have survived in its entirety. The letters in the Singapore records are chiefly replies from Farquhar, though not exclusively so.

The first, from Farquhar, is dated 5th November 1822 and addressed to Nilson Hull, who was acting as Raffles' secretary. It was in reply to the comments made by Raffles, on his arrival at Singapore, on Farquhar's letter of the previous 30th April. After explaining that, however much he might differ from the Lieutenant-Governor, he was prepared to carry out cheerfully whatever he might decide, Farquhar requested indulgence for the difficulties he had encountered and the deviations he had made from the instructions given him in June 1819. He then pointed out the formidable obstacles that the first settlers had had to surmount and "the extraordinary energy and enterprise shown by them, without which the Settlement would never have attained its present unrivalled state".

"If blame is therefore to be thrown on the Chief Local Authority for having under existing circumstances afforded such facilities to the various classes of inhabitants as the place at the time was best calculated to afford, and that in place of reserving for the eventual and exclusive purpose of Government the whole of the available and suitable ground for mercantile concerns, he permitted individuals at their own personal risk and responsibility to erect such houses as they might deem best calculated for the immediate protection of their valuable property, under a full and specific understanding that the ground they might then occupy is claimable by Government whenever circumstances might render it expedient to do so, I must candidly confess that the weight of responsibility . . . is not of a nature to induce me to regret in the slightest degree that I have incurred it."

He proceeded to argue at considerable length why it had not been possible to carry out Raffles' instructions and in particular that no one would have voluntarily gone to the south bank because the task of draining and embanking it would have been too great for any individual to undertake. Moreover, he would not have felt himself authorized to displace, without the fullest compensation, the Chinese already on the south bank of the river to make room for Europeans, "as many of them have been obliged by Government to remove thither from the Cantonment site where the China Captain and his followers were established even prior to the formation of the British factory".

With respect to the ground fit for warehouses on the south side of the river in the vicinity of the Point, "it was by the instructions of the Lieutenant-Governor of the 25th June 1819 expressly directed to be all reserved for Government purposes which was carefully attended to until the arrival of Captain Flint who informed me that he had the Lieutenant-Governor's permission to occupy the same, which was, of course, permitted accordingly".

Emphasizing once more that no one had been given any permanent appropriation and that no one had any legal claim to be reimbursed if made to move, he then pointed out that the spots occupied by the settlers were in fact the only available pieces of ground suitable for mercantile purposes, and had settlers not been able to utilize these, "Singapore in place of attaining to the importance it has done would I fear have completely withered in the bud".

This reply failed to satisfy Raffles, and Farquhar wrote again on 14th November:

"In reply to your letter of yesterday's date requesting me to explain . . . the distinction between ground *permanently* enclosed and that on which buildings have only been allowed to be erected at the personal *risk* and *responsibility* of the parties as alluded to in my letter to Captain Methven of 15th October 1821, I beg you will be pleased to inform the Lieutenant-Governor that Captain Methven and Lieutenant Crossley obtained leave from me to erect a warehouse of certain dimensions at their urgent solicitation, on the same terms that any other certificates of occupation were granted, although no written document was given on the occasion. . . . With reference to the expression used in my letter to Captain Methven above alluded to that 'I perceived he was enclosing permanently that space of ground at the north of his present residence', was merely intended to indicate that he was enclosing it in a substantial manner and bore no allusion whatever to his assuming any permanent title to it."

The correspondence continued, on this and on other matters, with increasing acerbity, Farquhar being egged on by a faction headed by Claude Queiros to stand up to Raffles and exert his alleged powers as Resident of the settlement against those of the Lieutenant-Governor. This faction was bitterly opposed to Raffles and always intriguing against him.

The vigorous attempts by Raffles to instil into the administration of Singapore some regularity and system in place of the casual and haphazard practice followed by Farquhar had gone a long way to confirm Raffles' opinion that Farquhar was unfitted to be the Resident of a rising colony. There was one incident in particular that completely undermined his confidence in Farquhar—the discovery that slaves were being landed and sold in Singapore. What gave point to the incident was that the slave-dealer was so confident that he could land and sell his slaves with impunity that he sent Raffles as well as Farquhar one or two slaves as presents. Raffles enquired of Farquhar whether he realized that in a British colony slave-dealing was a felony. Farquhar replied that he was not unaware of that fact, but in a young colony like Singapore he had thought it unwise to be too particular. Such a reply was hardly likely to satisfy Raffles, though, as he wrote subsequently, he did not take immediate action, out of deference to Farquhar's position as Resident.

Another incident, though of less importance, gave Raffles a clear insight into the Resident's narrow viewpoint. Farquhar proposed that merchants should be forbidden to have any direct dealings with the native states. Raffles replied tartly that, as every shipmaster has always been allowed perfect freedom in this respect, he saw no reason to deprive Singapore merchants of similar facilities.

All this intense activity involved Raffles in another of his serious attacks of illness, which he fought with his usual courage. Sophia nursed him with loving care and did all she could to spare him any avoidable exertion. Some of her notes to Wallich have survived.

"Sir Stamford has passed an uneasy night, his head, however, is better but he feels terrible, nervous, wretched sensations. These I hope will subside and that he will feel better than he does at the present moment as the lassitude decreases."

Again: "Sir Stamford, I am happy to say, has passed a tolerably good night and is pretty well this morning. I might say quite well, comparing his present feelings with those of the past two days. We shall be most happy to see you at any time and at all times and you will not, I hope, forget that you have promised to take your farewell dinner with us."

On 17th November, in the midst of all the new activities at Singapore, John Crawfurd arrived back there from his mission to Siam and Cambodia, which had proved unsuccessful. He stayed less than a week. Wallich, to whom he offered a passage back to India, had hoped he would remain longer, but Crawfurd was anxious to get to Calcutta before Hastings left for home. They sailed on the 23rd, reaching Calcutta on 29th December, only just in time for Crawfurd to make his report in person to Hastings.

It may be safely assumed that before Crawfurd had left Singapore, Raffles had told him that he was proposing to resign on health grounds and that, as he did not intend that Farquhar should remain as Resident, someone else would have to be found to take charge of the colony, which he was going to recommend should be put directly under India. That he went so far as to indicate that he would be very happy to see Crawfurd given the post is to be inferred from his letter to Wallich of 13th January 1823.

"If you see Crawfurd," he wrote, "tell him I have sent up my resignation and recommendation for the relief of the present Resident and that I am anxious to get away before May."

Another question with which Raffles concerned himself was the allocation of hills. Singapore is dotted with low ridges and small hills, which clearly offered the most attractive building sites. Much correspondence passed between him and Farquhar on this matter. Raffles' standpoint is made quite clear in the concluding paragraph of a letter to Farquhar from Nilson Hull.

"It further appears to the Lieutenant-Governor that there are but two ways in which individuals can be accommodated with the ground they require, either by favour or by fair and open competition and he is desirious of adopting the latter method."

He maintained that Farquhar and Bernard had taken up excessive tracts. Farquhar denied this bitterly, and did not fail to invite attention to the much more extensive and valuable tract acquired by Flint. He also persisted in his arguments concerning the sites on the north bank of the river.

"I beg to state for the information of the Honourable Lieutenant-Governor that although I have already, I hope, very fully explained every point as far as the local Government is concerned relative to the occupation of lands at Singapore, still there are most unaccountable and extraordinary assertions set forth in the several letters under consideration and I feel myself imperiously called upon to declare once more in the most unequivocal terms that I am ready to take the most solemn oath that I never issued any permanent grants of land nor ever directly or indirectly pledged any assurance to any individual in the Settlement that in the event of Government requiring the ground on which their houses or godowns stand that they would be indemnified for them."

It is impossible to assess the rights and wrongs, but the correspondence does suggest that the whole question of allocation of lands was in a complete tangle. This may not have been entirely Farquhar's fault, yet the fact remains.

There were quarrels on many other subjects, as friction continued to grow, Raffles thoroughly dissatisfied with the measures Farquhar had taken in many parts of his administration, Farquhar loudly protesting that he had done all that was possible. For example, Farquhar had, without authority, abolished the commissariat department. This drew from Raffles the rebuke:

"That it is manifest . . . the objects contemplated by Government have been in a great measure defeated by the arrangements you have adopted and that he regrets that on this as well as other occasions which have recently occurred he has found you more inclined to argue in support of your own measures which have been disapproved than to afford that due assistance in furtherance of his order which he has a right to expect."

To this Farquhar replied to Hull: "Although, of course, bound to obey every legal order given by him as holding superior controlling power to myself over this Settlement, yet I can by no means admit that I am in any degree bound to submit in silence to whatever censures he may be pleased to pass on my public conduct particularly when I am conscious of not meriting them; and therefore if this system is to be persevered in I must in defence of my own character and proceedings have recourse to a public appeal to the higher authorites to judge between us."

The threat left Raffles unmoved. He merely caused a reply to be sent to Farquhar that any appeal would be forwarded to Calcutta by the earliest and quickest opportunity.

"Since you left us," wrote Raffles to Wallich on 8th December, "I have been compelled to some rather sharp correspondence with the King of Malacca,[1] of which, and other things, he will I doubt not complain abroad, but I am happy to say that personally we remain as you left us and that I perceive symptoms which induce me to believe that he now takes a different view of my measures to what he did at first. I have, I trust, completely upset the system of favouritism and partiality and established the principle of fair and open competition in its room. But of this more in my next. Lady Raffles continues to improve and though I am still annoyed with my headaches I am upon the whole better than when you left us. I marked out the site of a small bungalow where you threw the stone that night and in three weeks we hope to think about you there in our evening prayers."

The month of January 1823 saw the beginnings of a constitution and a code of law for the settlement. The first step was the issue of a proclamation, which was in two parts. The first part explained that, to avoid all such misunderstandings as had occurred in the past, future orders of government would be printed for public information, and translations in Malay would be posted up at convenient points. Further, it would be the duty of the registrar to ensure that, whenever the Asiatics were affected by a new regulation, the terms of it were fully explained to the various headmen, and they in turn were to make sure that it was thoroughly understood by the communities for which they were responsible.

The second part of the proclamation announced that, until a court of judicature was established, all regulations affecting property or persons would be drawn up in a regular form, serially numbered, printed with a Malay translation attached, and registered. How these judicial regulations

[1] Farquhar had been known to the Malays as "Raja Malaka" when Resident there.

were to be administered by the Resident and what assistance he would require for that purpose would be announced later. Meanwhile, so long as the Lieutenant-Governor was in residence at Singapore, all regulations under his signature would have the force of law as soon as they had been registered.

This proclamation was dated 1st January 1823, the way thus being made clear for legislative action.

Regulation I dealt with the urgent question of the proper registration of land. It established a land registry, which was to apply to all land, irrespective of whether it was retained by the Sultan or the Temenggong, or ceded to the British Government. In future, no title to land would be recognized unless it had been properly registered, and all those then in occupation of land had to register their lots before 1st February. If they did not do so, the land in their occupation would be considered as having reverted to the Government, and no claim in respect of it would subsequently be admitted.

Regulation II opened with the categorical statement that "the Port of Singapore is a free Port, and the trade thereof is open to ships and vessels of every nation free of duty, equally and alike to all". Instructions followed as to the entering and clearing of ships, the information required as to cargo and passengers, and a scale of maximum rates for "boat hire, wooding, watering and ballasting". It was, however, added that "nothing contained in these regulations shall be construed to operate against the most perfect liberty of ships to wood, water and ballast with their own boats".

Regulation III was a longer and more complicated document dealing with the "Establishment of a provisional Magistracy and the Enforcement of a due and sufficient Police at Singapore with certain Provisions for the Administration of Justice in Cases of Emergency". The regulation observed, by the way of preamble, that the extent of population and capital already accumulated at Singapore required "provision for the preservation of order and the protection of person and property", and regulations drawn up with the concurrence of the Sultan and Temenggong, being "consonant with British principles and adapted as far as consistent to the usage of the native settlers", were introduced as a provisional measure.

To provide a magistracy, a list would be drawn up of "the several British inhabitants of interest and respect in the Settlement and who may be considered competent to act as Magistrates". They would be selected in rotation three at a time to sit every quarter day.

"They will jointly try cases which are beyond the competence of a single Magistrate as quarter sessions do at home. Their authority will be similar to that exercised at home by a Justice of the Peace. Warrants issued by them against British subjects unless apprehended *in flagrante delicto* must be countersigned by the local Chief Authority. All persons in the Settlement will be under the jurisdiction of the Magistrates, with the exception of the Armed Forces, for whom special provision is made. The subjects of the Sultan and Temmungong are not excepted, but the Resident must be consulted as to the procedure in such cases. When crews of ships visiting the port are involved, the Master Attendant will sit on the Bench in his magisterial capacity."

Under the magistrates there would be "one native Captain or Headman with one or more Lieutenants or Assistants over each principal class of the native inhabitants who will be invested with especial authority over such class and held responsible for the general conduct of the same".

For cases of major importance, the Resident would hold a court as circumstances might require, assisted, when natives were involved, by the Sultan and Temenggong. In criminal cases, or civil cases in which large sums of money were involved, the general practice should be for the parties to be sent to Penang or Bengal, where competent courts existed. When civil cases were so remitted, suitable security would have to be lodged by the plaintiff.

With the work of reclamation progressing, Raffles was able to write to Wallich on 5th January:

"The lots along the south bank of the river, eight in number, with thirty or forty lots of ground along the north beach, were put up to auction on Saturday and a sum of no less then $50,000 were [*sic*] bid in the course of an hour, although each lot was put up at only $1 and the public informed revenue was not wanted and the object of the sale was only to allow everyone a fair chance, it being simply declared that Govt. preferred the system of fair and open competition to that of granting lots by favour."

When John Palmer heard about this, he wrote to Farquhar (19th February):

"R's resignation has I hear come up; and he shows an acquisition of $50,000 by the sale of Lots. God have mercy on the purchasers if they pay for their Lots, for it must take 50 mille more to make them dry and waterproof; and then perhaps Mynheer will be found entitled to them."

Events were to prove that Palmer's pessimism was, in both respects, unfounded.

Raffles' preoccupation with the administrative problems of Singapore had not for a moment caused him to forget his long-cherished scheme of a Malay college, which he felt would be the crowning monument of his new colony. While he had been planning the town, he had kept his eyes open for a suitable site, and on 12th January he wrote to his cousin:

"I have selected a spot for my intended College; and all I now require is a good head-master or superintendent. It is my intention to endow it with lands, the rents of which will cover its ordinary expenses."

The objects intended to be fulfilled by the college had been set out fully by Raffles in a minute written in 1819 and taken with him on his last visit to Calcutta. In the Governor-General he had found an unexpected ally—unexpected because Raffles doubtless regarded Hastings much as many others have been inclined to do: as a very capable soldier, but a man who liked Court life and was, perhaps, a little too impressed with the trappings of high office; not, in fact, the type of man one would expect to find endued with liberal principles. Yet in the *Private Journal* are to be found two striking passages that reveal a very different side of his character. The first is his entry for 17th December 1816.

"It is surprising," Hastings wrote, "how frequent are the occurrences in this country which bring home to the mind the irresistible refutation of the hypothesis maintained by some able men in England that it is inexpedient to enlighten the lower classes. Their assumption is, that by letting men in humble stations see too distinctly the advantages of higher positions in life you make them discontented with their natural occupations. . . . With regard to the imagined morality attendant on narrow information, every day's experience here contradicts the notion."

His views were recorded at greater length on 17th May 1818, thus:

"Let this be the answer to those who contend that it is unwise to disseminate instruction among the multitude. Absence of instruction necessarily implies destitution of morality. . . . It is befitting the British name and character that advantage should be taken of the opening which we have effected and that establishments should be introduced or stimulated by us which may rear a rising generation in some knowledge of social duties. A time not very remote will arrive when England will, on sound principles of policy, wish to relinquish the domination which she has gradually and unintentianally assumed in this country, and from which she cannot at present recede. In that hour it would be the proudest boast and most delightful reflection that she had used her sovereignty towards enlightening her temporary subjects so as to enable the native communities to walk alone in the paths of justice and to maintain with probity towards their benefactress that commercial intercourse in which we should then find a solid interest."

That Hastings should have held such views at such a date is surely a remarkable testimony both to his liberal outlook and to his political foresight. For our own immediate purpose it is equally remarkable that he should, as will be seen on a later page, have thus anticipated the views of Raffles and, by a strange coincidence, should have expressed them in words so similar to those used by Raffles in the peroration of his minute.

The success of the free-port policy was amply demonstrated in a letter Raffles wrote to Marsden on 21st January.

"By a statement I forwarded to the Court of Directors in February last it was shown that during the first two years and a half of this Establishment no less than two thousand eight hundred and eighty-nine vessels entered and cleared from the Port, of which three hundred and eighty-three were owned and commanded by Europeans and two thousand five hundred and six by natives and that the united tonnage was one hundred and sixty-one thousand tons. It appeared also that the value of merchandise in native vessels arrived and cleared amounted to about five millions of dollars during the same period and in ships not less than three millions, giving a total amount of about eight millions as the capital payment.

"This statement I thought very favourable; but I have now the satisfaction of forwarding to the same authority official statements from which the following results appear for the year 1822, a detailed and accurate account having been kept during that period of the trade of the place. Total amount of tonnage importing and exporting one hundred and thirty thousand six hundred and eighty-nine. Total value of imports and exports in the year 1822 eight millions five hundred and sixty-eight thousand one hundred and seventy-two.

"Nearly the whole of this trade is carried on by borrowed capital for which interest is paid from nine to twelve per cent per annum; and it is not a little remarkable that since the establishment of the Settlement now four years ago not a single ship has arrived from England notwithstanding European goods are in constant demand. All British manufactures that heretofore found their way into the Settlement have come by circuitous routes and with heavy charges of freight and duties at other ports added to their invoice value. No less than four free traders loaded home from Singapore last year; and the 'Venelia', by which I send this, now goes home with a full and valuable cargo of sugar, pepper, tin, tortoiseshell, &c; and we could load half a dozen more ships in the course of the season were they here."

He wrote in the same letter:

"We have lately built a small bungalow on Singapore Hill, where, though the height is inconsiderable, we find a great difference of climate. Nothing can be more interesting and beautiful than the view from this spot. I am happy to say the change has had a very beneficial effect on my health, which has been better the last fortnight than I have known it for two years before. The tombs of the Malay kings are however close at hand; and I have settled that if it is my fate to die here, I shall take my place among them: this will, at any rate, be better than leaving one's bones at Bencoolen. If it please God, we still live in the hope of embarking for Europe towards the end of the year. I am laying out a botanic and experimental garden and it would delight you to see how rapidly the whole country is coming under cultivation. My residence here has naturally given much confidence, and the extent of the speculations entered into by the Chinese quite astonishes me."

That the move to the top of Singapore Hill was in the nature of a desperate search for some means to save his life, and that it was a fight against time, emerges from a letter written two days later to the Duchess of Somerset.

"Since I last wrote to your Grace about a month ago, I have had another attack in my head, which nearly proved fatal, and the Doctors were for hurrying me on board ship for Europe without much ceremony. However, as I could not reconcile myself to become food for fishes, I preferred ascending the Hill, where if my bones must remain in the East, they would have the honour of mixing with the ashes of Malayan kings; and the result has been that instead of dying, I have almost recovered. I have built a very comfortable house which is sufficient to accommodate my sister's family as well as our own; and I only wish you were here for half-an-hour, to enjoy the unequalled beauty and interest of the scene. My house, which is one hundred feet front and fifty deep, was finished in a fortnight from the commencement. When will your Cottage be done?"

The new bungalow was made of wood, with rough plank walls and venetian windows. The roof was thatched with palm leaves. But the structure was so fragile, and the position so exposed, that whenever a tropical storm struck Singapore, everyone instinctively looked up to the hill to see if the house was still standing.

Singapore Hill had, as Raffles remarked, been the site of the royal palace until Singapore had been sacked. It was still called the "Forbidden Hill", and when Farquhar had first tried to mount some guns on the top, no local Malay had dared to ascend it. In the end, the road had had to be cut, and the guns dragged up, by the Malacca Malays who had followed him to Singapore.

The Government House estate and the botanical garden marched together. Raffles asked Wallich to send him two hundred head of spotted deer.

"If you use expedition, they may be here in three months, and by that time I shall have my fence up. Fear not for your garden, as I am constructing a fence round it which they cannot leap."

Raffles had already written to inform Calcutta that if the Governor-General decided that the two offices of Governor-General's Agent in the Eastern Seas and Resident of Singapore could now be conventiently united in one person, he would be prepared to wait till a successor more competent than Farquhar could arrive to take charge. Fearing, perhaps, that he had not been sufficiently explicit concerning the unsuitability of the present Resident, he wrote again on 27th January, and did not mince matters.

"I feel myself called upon to state in general terms that I consider Col. Farquhar to be totally unequal to the charge of so important and peculiar a charge as that of Singapore has now become. However competent that officer may have been for the charge in the earlier stage of the Settlement, it is obvious that it has for some time past grown beyond his management and that he neither entertains such general views nor can enter upon those principles of general government which now mark the character of the British Indian Administration.

"Having passed nearly the whole of his public life in the Dutch Settlement of Malacca, his views are confined to his experience of that place, where the duties were insignificant and where, from long neglect of the higher Authorities, little like regular government existed except in the forms of a Dutch Court, and the partial continuance of regulations established in the plenitude of the Dutch monopoly. The circumstances of Singapore are perfectly incompatible with these and the consequence is confusion and general dissatisfaction."

He then touched on the undesirable situation arising from Farquhar's having taken a native wife.

"The Malay connexion in which Lieut. Col. Farquhar is involved and the general weakness of his administration afford an opening for such an undue combination of peculiar interests as not only to impede the progress or order and regularity but may lay the foundation of future inconvenience which it may hereafter be difficult to overcome."

After repeating his request that a more competent officer should be appointed to succeed in the office of Resident, he added that Farquhar had formerly said that he might be willing to remain in the East until 1822, but that time had now passed and there was still no decision as to the future of Singapore.

He did not disclose to Farquhar the terms in which he had written to Calcutta, but he did warn him that his temporary charge of Singapore was drawing to a close. This roused Farquhar at once. The last thing he now wanted was to leave Singapore, nor had he any intention of doing so except under compulsion. He replied to Raffles on 29th January:

"I have the honour to acknowledge the receipt of your letter under yesterday's date intimating 'that the period for which I requested permission to postpone my departure for Europe having expired you deem it proper to apprise me of the same in order that I may be prepared to deliver over charge of the Civil Duties of the Station whenever a successor may be appointed'. In reply I beg leave to state that I never made any official application to Government for leave to relinquish the situation I have the honour to fill at Singapore and to which I stand appointed by the Supreme Government; that my having formerly specified a period to which I wished to postpone my proposed departure for Europe was certainly never intended to be binding on me under every circumstance so as to occasion a positive relinquishment of my appointment here at the expiration of any stated time; more particularly as in a subsequent reference made to me on this subject as contained in Acting Secretary Halhed's letter dated 1st May 1821 (a copy of which is herewith enclosed), I replied on 19th September following 'That I would wish under existing circumstances to defer coming to any determination on this point until such time as definitive arrangements shall have taken place respecting the permanent retention of this Settlement.'

"As no official information from the Government at home or the Supreme Government of India, decisive of the above point has as yet been received and having very potent reasons for not wishing to secede from the performance of my Public Duties, either Civil or Military at this particular time, I must beg leave to recall any implied applications which may be supposed to exist for leave to resign my situation, trusting that, whilst I continue to perform the duties thereof in an honourable and satisfactory manner, I shall not be subject to any sudden ejection which, without implied misconduct or where the services of the Individual may be otherwise called for by Government, I believe to be altogether unprecedented in India."

As far as can now be ascertained, this letter was left unanswered.

Early in February, Sultan Husain Muhammad (Tunku Long) informed Farquhar in writing that a party of Dutch and Malays from Rhio had arrived in Johore. Farquhar reported this to Raffles, adding:

"I have reason to believe the intelligence contained in the Sultan's letter is correct, having received a similar flying report a short time ago, which I communicated to His Highness the Tummungong and recommended his keeping some confidential People on the look-out, in order to afford the earliest movement of the Dutch alluded to in his letter."

On Raffles' authority, the British flag was forthwith hoisted in Johore, which was to lead to a fresh outburst on the part of van der Capellen.

ii

London wrote to Calcutta on 13th March reporting the continued suspension of negotiations and seeking information as to whether there had been any further incidents with the Netherlands Government in the East. If, said London, any representations were made by the Dutch authorities, Calcutta was to reply that the matter was still under consideration by the British Government, and that any communication the Dutch authorities might wish to make would be sent on to London. The dispatch also included this important paragraph:

"You will continue to occupy Singapore and to report to us the progress of that settlement in population and commerce. You will apprise us whether there has been any communication on the part of the Sultan of Johore or any native chief to deny the validity of our title to the island: any such pretension coming directly from the native prince you will receive with attention and fairly investigate, but you will not receive any such claim which will come through the channel of the Netherland authorities, nor from a native who shall be under their control."

Four days later in Singapore, great alarm, amounting almost to panic, seized the European community when the news spread through the settlement after nightfall that Farquhar had been stabbed by a Malay. As the attacker had been cut almost to pieces by the Resident's peons and could not readily be identified, everyone assumed that he was an emissary of the Sultan or the Temenggong. Guns were trained on the Sultan's palace, and it was only the timely arrival of Raffles that prevented Captain Davis from opening fire.

From 'Abdullah's vivid account it is evident that the only person who did not lose his head was Raffles.

"Leaping out of his carriage he sought Colonel Farquhar and when he saw that he was not killed he then went to see the corpse of Sayid Yasin. At the same moment a person was bringing fire with the intention of taking it into the Pangeran's [Resident's] court. He stumbled over the legs of the dead peon which was lying at the front gate. There was on this another hubbub about his death. Now Mr Raffles took a candle to view the corpse of Sayid Yasin and he asked of the people assembled 'Who is this?' But no-one knew him. . . . I perceived that Mr Raffles had first suspected that the Temmungong's followers had stabbed Colonel Farquhar. Captain Davis now came several times to Mr Raffles asking for sanction to fire the cannons but he was ordered to wait. Mr Barnard [Bernard] now came running from the other side and when he saw the peon's body, then he recollected of his having been sent with Sayid Yasin to see the Pangeran. He then hastened to see the corpse of Sayid Yasin when he sickened at the fault he had committed. So he went forward to Mr Raffles and saluting him told him that the corpse was that of Sayid Yasin, adding 'He a short time ago asked me to allow him to see the Pangeran about his debt when I consented, the peon being in charge.' But when Mr Raffles heard this his eyes flashed fire with rage and clenching his fist in the face of Mr Barnard so as to knock off his hat, he said

'Have you a care, Sir? If Farquhar dies I shall hang you in Singapore.' At this Mr Barnard bent before him and asked his forgiveness."

The simple facts were these. Sayid Yasin had been sued for a large debt and, being unable or unwilling to pay the amount fixed by Farquhar, had been put in prison. As a Sayid he had considered himself intolerably insulted by this treatment, a state of mind so likely to lead to an *amok*.

Raffles caused the corpse of Sayid Yasin to be put into a sort of cage and exposed to public view. For this he was blamed by many who thought that it would antagonize the Malays and endanger the lives of the Europeans. Raffles took the opposite view, it seeming to him necessary that a murderous attack on an English official must be followed by some exemplary punishment. The European community was a very small one, the Asiatic population very large. If, thought Raffles, it was not brought home to the people that an attack on a European would entail the most dire consequences, no European's life would be safe. After a short time he allowed the body to be buried and the grave became a place of pilgrimage for the Malays.

Farquhar's wound, though it led to a considerable loss of blood, was not serious and he soon recovered.

At a meeting of the Council on 21st March[1] in Calcutta, where John Adam, pending the arrival of Lord Amherst, was acting Governor-General, the appointment of Crawfurd to Singapore was confirmed. It was also decided that Singapore should come directly under Calcutta and not be subordinate to Penang. Captain Mackenzie, instead of going to Singapore, was to succeed Raffles at Bencoolen.

"On the occasion", read the resolution, "of relieving Sir Stamford Raffles from the Superintendence of Singapore, the Governor-General in Council deems it an act of justice to that gentleman to record his sense of the activity, zeal, judgment and attention to the principles prescribed for the management of the Settlement which has marked his conduct in the execution of that duty."

On that very same day, in a dispatch to Calcutta, London tardily recorded its opinion of Raffles' action in taking possession of Nias.

"We have learned with strong feelings of surprise and displeasure of the measures which had been pursued by Sir Thomas Raffles in regard to the island of Pulo Nias. In proceeding to occupy that island and in concluding treaties with several of its chiefs without the previous sanction of your Government, Sir Thomas Raffles has acted in a manner unsanctioned by law and in direct opposition to our positive and repeated instructions. . . . We should have been disposed to have visited this fresh instance of disobedience of our positive orders on the part of Sir Thomas Raffles with some severe mark of our displeasure had we not been

[1] Buckley gives this incorrectly as 29th March.

informed by his letter of the 12th September 1822 that it is his intention to return to Europe at an early period; however, we have no hesitation in declaring that his proceedings in regard to Pulo Nias are deserving of our decided reprehension."

This violent reaction demonstrated the hostile attitude that still prevailed there against Raffles. It is only to be explained by the ever-present alarm that his activities in the East would jeopardize an Anglo-Dutch settlement in Europe by which the British Government set such store. Even so, the severe tone adopted was hardly warranted.

Two days after the meeting in Calcutta, Palmer wrote to Flint's partner, J. Deans:

"Crawfurd is appointed to Singapore and going down in a week with Neish. He is a lucky fellow. I hope he may be useful to you, and believe he is so inclined."

He followed this with a letter to Phillips in Penang.

"Late arrangements East of you will excite surprise. Raf. and Lushington,[1] through the latter, have made A[dam] forget a sort of pledge to Mackenzie and the encouragement of Coombs, but if Raf. declared them both unfit, and more he would never leave Singapore again under F[arquhar], and if Monsr. l'Embassadeur[2] was ready to push a concerted measure with his knaving ways, was it not natural that, like My Lord Amherst, he should be consoled for an abortive mission . . . so have a care of your neighbours."

This comment was singularly wide of the mark. Mackenzie's succession to Bencoolen had already been decided upon, and it could hardly have been imagined that Coombs was qualified for the Singapore post, or that Adam and Raffles had forgotten Coombs' intrigues over the mission to Achin.

In that month of March Singapore received a visit from China of the eminent Robert Morrison, of the London Missionary Society, who, in 1818, had founded the Anglo-Chinese College at Malacca. His presence, and that also of the Rev. Robert S. Hutchings, chaplain at Penang, decided Raffles to seize the opportunity to launch his scheme for a Malay college at Singapore. On 1st April he convened a meeting at his house on Singapore Hill. All the leading members of the community were present, including Sultan Husain Muhammad and the Temenggong.

The proceedings opened with the reading by Raffles of the minute originally written in 1819 and now for the first time made public. It ran to nearly ten thousand words and is printed in full as an appendix to Sophia's *Memoir*. Here a few extracts should suffice to show the greatness of Raffles' conception, the statesmanlike purpose inherent in the minute,

[1] James Law Lushington, director of the Company in India.

[2] Crawfurd. His mission to Siam had failed, as had Amherst's to China.

and the eloquence and sincerity with which it was presented. The theme was introduced in these words:

"It is the peculiar characteristic of Great Britain that wherever her influence has been extended it has carried civilization and improvement in its train. To whatever quarter of the world her arms or policy have her it has been her object to extend those blessings of freedom and justice for which she herself stands so pre-eminent. Whether in asserting the rights of independent nations, whether in advocating the cause of the captive and the slave, or in promoting the diffusion of truth and knowledge, England has always led the van. In the vast regions of India, where she has raised an empire unparalleled in history, no sooner was the sword of conquest sheathed than her attention was turned to the dispensing of justice, to giving security to the persons and property and to the improvement of the conditions of her new subjects. . . .

"A desire to know the origin and early history of the people, their institutions, laws and opinions led to associations expressly directed to this end; while, by the application of the information thus obtained to the present circumstances of the country, the spirit and principles of British rule have rapidly augmented the power and increased the resources of the State, at the same time that they have in no less degree tended to excite the intellectual energies and encrease [*sic*] the individual happiness of the people.

"The acquisitions of Great Britain in the East have not been made in the spirit of conquest; a concurrence of circumstances not to be controlled and the energies of her sons have carried her forward on a tide whose impulse has been irresistible. Other nations may have pursued the same course of conquest and success but they have not like her paused in their career and by moderation and justice consolidated what they had gained. This is the rock on which her Indian empire is placed; and it is on a perseverance in the principles which have already guided her that she must depend for maintaining her commanding station. . . . While we raise those in the scale of civilization over whom our influence or our empire is extended we shall lay the foundation of our dominion on the firm basis of justice and mutual advantage instead of the uncertain and unsubstantial tenure of force and intrigue.

"Such have been the principles of our Indian administration wherever we have acquired a territorial influence; it remains to be considered how they can be best applied to countries where territory is not our object but whose commerce is not less essential to our interests. With the countries east of Bengal an exclusive commercial intercourse has always been carried on and our influence is more or less felt throughout the whole from the banks of the Ganges to China and New Holland. Recent events have directed our attention to these, and in a particular manner to the Malayan Archipelago, where a vast field of commercial speculation has been opened, the limits of which it is difficult to foresee.

"A variety of circumstances concurred to extend our connexions in this quarter. . . . Our connexion, however, with them stands on a very different footing from that with the people of India; however inviting and extensive their resources it is considered that they can be best drawn forth by the native energies of the people themselves uninfluenced by foreign rule and unfettered by foreign regulations and that it is by the reciprocal advantages of commerce and commerce alone that we may best promote our own interests and their advancement. A few Stations are occupied for the security and protection of our trade and the independence of all the surrounding states is not only acknowledged but maintained and supported by us.

"Commerce being, therefore, the principle on which our connexion with the Eastern states is formed it behoves us to consider the effects which it is calculated to produce. Commerce is universally allowed to bring many benefits in its train and in particular to be favourable to civilization and general improvement. Like all other powerful agents, however, it has proved the cause of many evils when improperly directed or not sufficiently controlled. It creates wants and introduces luxuries; but if there exists no principle for the regulation of these . . . sensuality, vice and corruption will be the necessary results. Where the social institutions are favourable to independence and improvement, where the intellectual powers are cultivated and expanded, commerce opens a wider field for their exertion, and wealth and refinement become consistent with all that ennobles and exalts human nature.

"Education must keep pace with commerce in order that its benefits may be ensured and its evils avoided; and in our connexion with these countries it should be our care that while with one hand we carry to their shores the capital of our merchants, the other should be stretched forth to offer them the means of intellectual improvement. Happily our policy is in accordance with these views and principles and neither in the state of the countries themselves nor in the character of their varied and extensive population do we find anything opposed. On the contrary they invite us to the field and every motive of humanity, policy and religion seem to combine to recommend our early attention to this important field."

After this preamble, Raffles proceeded to survey the nature and extent of this field. Taking the narrowest limits, it would embrace the whole of the huge archipelago stretching from Sumatra and Java to the Pacific islands and from there to the shores of China and Japan. From this area, ancient Rome had drawn many of its luxuries, and in more modern times successive European nations had gained importance and wealth from its resources.

"It has raised several of these from insignificance and obscurity to power and eminence and perhaps in its earliest period among the Italian states communicated the first electric spark which awoke to life the energies and the literature of Europe."

Taking a more extended view, "the rich and populous countries of Ava [Burma] and Siam, Camboja [Cambodia], Cochin-China and Tonkin" must be included.

"And if to this we add the numerous Chinese population which is dispersed throughout these countries and through the means of whom the light of knowledge may be extended to the remotest part of the Chinese empire and even to Japan it will readily be acknowledged that the field is perhaps as extensive, interesting and important as ever offered itself to the contemplation of the philanthropic and enlightened mind."

He then discussed at some length the characteristics and state of civilization of the various peoples.

"Such", he went on, "is the range of enquiry open to the philosopher; but to him who is interested in the cause of humanity, who thinks that the diffusion of humanizing arts is as essential to the character of our nation as the acquisition of power and wealth and that wherever our flag it should confer the benefits of civilization on those whom it protects it would appear no less important that in proportion as we extend the field of our own enquiry and information we should apply it to the advantage of those with whom we are connected and endeavour to diffuse among them the light of knowledge and the means of moral and intellectual improvement.

"The object of our Stations being confined to the protection and encouragement of a free and unrestricted commerce with the whole of these countries . . . no jealousy can exist where we make our enquiries. When the man of science enquires for the mineral or vegetable productions of any particular country or the manner in which the fields are cultivated or the mines worked no motive will exist for withholding information; but if in return we are anxious to disseminate the superior knowledge we ourselves possess how much shall we increase this readiness and desire on the part of the natives and what may not be the extent of the blessings we may in exchange confer on these extensive regions? How noble the object, how beneficial the effects to carry with our commerce the lights of instruction and moral improvement. How much more exalted the character in which we shall appear, how much more congenial to every British feeling. . . .

"The native inhabitant who will be first attracted by commerce will imbibe a respect for our institutions and when he finds that some of these are destined exclusively for his own benefit, while he applauds and respects the motive he will not fail to profit by them. . . . And shall we who have been so favoured among other nations refuse to encourage the growth of intellectual improvement or rather shall we not consider it one of our first duties to afford the means of education to surrounding countries and thus render our Stations not only the seats of commerce but of literature and the arts?

"There is nothing perhaps which distinguishes the character of these islanders from the people of India more than the absence of inveterate prejudice and the little influence Mahommedanism has had over their conduct and mode of thinking. With them neither civil nor religious institutions seem to stand in the way of improvement, while the aptness and solicitude of the people to receive instruction is remarkable; and in the higher classes we often find a disposition to enjoy the luxuries and comforts of European life and to assimilate its manners and courtesies."

Having then developed this point, he turned next to the consideration of "the advantage and necessity of forming under the immediate control and superintendence of Government an institution of the nature of a native College which shall embrace not only the object of educating the higher classes of the native population but at the same time that of affording instruction to the officers of the Company in the native languages and of facilitating our more general researches into the history, condition and resources of these countries. . . .

"The position and circumstances of Singapura point it out as the most eligible situation for such an establishment. Its central situation among the Malay states and the commanding influence of its commerce render it a place of general and convenient resort, while in the minds of the natives it will always be associated with their fondest recollections as the city of their ancient government before the influence of a foreign faith had shaken those institutions for which they still preserve so high an attachment and reverence. The advantage of selecting a place thus hallowed by the ideas of a remote antiquity and the veneration attached to its ancient line of kings, from whom they are still proud to trace their descent, must be obvious.

"The objects of such an Institution may be briefly stated as follows:

"*First*. To educate the sons of the higher order of natives and others.

"*Secondly*. To afford the means of instruction in the native languages to such of the Company's servants and others as may desire it.

"*Thirdly*. To collect the scattered literature and traditions of the country with whatever may illustrate their laws and customs and to publish and circulate in a correct form the most important of these with such other works as may be calculated to raise the character of the Institution and to be useful or instructive to the people."

The initial establishment suggested by Raffles to implement these proposals was very modest: one European superintendent with an assistant, three Asiatic professors or head teachers and a few Asiatic assistants. The immediate expense was not considered likely to exceed ten thousand rupees for the construction of the building and a thousand rupees a month for the running of it.

"In the formation of the establishment the utmost simplicity will be necessary as well with a view to economy as with reference to the character and circumstances of the people. The rules for its internal discipline will be few and obvious and the means of exciting emulation such as may be best suited to the condition of the students. The establishment proposed will include a native professor in each of the principal languages, Malay, Bugies and Siamese with an assistant in each department and four extra teachers in the Chinese, Javan, Burman and Pali languages.

"The course of education will be the acquirement of such of the above languages as the students may select together with Arabic to which the same professors will be competent; and in the higher classes the Roman character and English language will be taught, together with such elementary branches of general knowledge and history as their capacity and inclination may demand. The extra number of Moonshees are intended to afford instruction to the Company's servants and others; and it will be the duty of the Superintendent and native professors to form the collections and carry into effect the third and last object under such directions as they may from time to time receive.

"The more immediate effects which may be expected to result from an Institution of this nature have already been pointed out. . . . Native schools on the Lancast[e]rian plan[1] have already been established at some of our Stations and may be expected to spread in various directions; connected with these an Institution of the nature now proposed is calculated to complete the system and by affording to the higher classes a participation in the general progress of improvement to raise them in a corresponding degree and thus preserve and cement the natural relations of society. . . .

"The weakness of the Chiefs is an evil which has been long felt and acknowledged in these countries and to cultivate and improve their intellectual powers seems to be the most effectual remedy. They will duly appreciate the benefit conferred and while it must inevitably tend to attach them more closely to us we shall find our recompense in the stability of their future authority and the general security and good order which must be the result.

"There are, however, some results of a more distant and more speculative nature which it is impossible to pass over unnoticed. These relate more particularly to the eventual abolition of slavery, the modifica-

[1] Hastings was also a great admirer of this system, as emerges from the *Private Journal*.

tion of their more objectionable civil institutions, particularly those relating to debts and marriages, and the discontinuance of the horrid practices of cannibalism and man hunting but too prevalent among some of the more barbarous tribes as the Battas and Alfoors.[1] . . .

"From this it will appear how much more extensive are the advantages to be obtained from educating the higher classes, to whom alone we can look for effectually promoting the progress of improvement among the lower orders, and for extending the benefits of civilization to the barbarous tribes, which would otherwise be entirely beyond the sphere of our influence, than could be obtained from any scheme which should reverse the order and commence instruction from the bottom rather than the top of the scale. In every country the lights of knowledge and improvement have commenced with the highest orders of society and have been diffused from thence downwards. No plan can be expected to succeed which shall reverse this order and attempt to propagate them in an opposite direction; and more especially in countries where the influence of the Chiefs from the nature of the Government must always be considerable."

To the Chinese settled in the East Indies, the college would be of special benefit.

"Many of these, if not possessed of the advantages of birth, have raised themselves by their talents to opulence and a respectable rank in society. These men at present frequently send their sons to China for education, for want of an Institution of this nature which would supersede the necessity. A recent establishment of the kind has been formed at Malacca under the superintendence of an enlightened Missionary [Milne] and a branch of it already extended to Singapore.[2] It has been attended with considerable success but must necessarily be limited in its operation by its more immediate and direct object being that of religious conversion. . . .

"The advantage of extending the plan on a broader and more general principle is acknowledged by those under whom it is conducted and they may be expected, if not to combine their labours with the plan now proposed, at least to give it all the aid in their power. The expense of this branch of the Institution will probably be borne principally by the Chinese themselves who are wealthy enough to do so and are sufficiently aware of the advantages of education.

"Having now shown the extent and objects of the proposed Institution, the field presented for its operation, and pointed out some of the advantages which may be expected to result it will be sufficient in conclusion to remark that the progress of every plan of improvement on the basis of

[1] Alfuros, aboriginals of Celebes and the Moluccas.

[2] Under Rev. C. H. Thomsen.

education must be slow and gradual; its effects are silent and unobtrusive and the present generation will probably pass away before they are fully felt and appreciated. Few nations have made much advance in civilization by their own unassisted endeavours and none have risen suddenly from barbarism to refinement. The experience of the world informs us that education affords the only means of effecting any considerable amelioration or of expanding the powers of the human mind.

"In estimating the results of any scheme of the kind the advantages must always be in a great measure speculative and depending on the concurrence of a variety of circumstances which cannot be foreseen. This is admitted to apply with its full force to the Institution in question; but when it is considered that education affords the only reasonable and efficient means of improving the conditions of those who are so much lower than ourselves in the scale of civilization that the want of this improvement is nowhere more sensibly felt than in the field before us and that the proposed plan has the double object of obtaining information ourselves and affording instructions to others, it will be allowed to be at least calculated to assist in objects which are not only important to our national interests but honourable and consistent with our national character. The outlay proposed is moderate when considered even with reference to the immediate advantages, to say nothing of those which are of a more remote and speculative nature. . . .

"It may be urged that the Institution here proposed is too limited in its extent and too inadequate in its means to embrace the vastness of the object contemplated . . . the objection is in some respects just; an establishment on a much more extended scale would certainly have been desirable but many obstacles have presented themselves to the immediate adoption of any very expensive plan. The object has been to bring it to the very lowest scale consistent with efficiency in order to avoid the chance of failure were too much attempted in the beginning. . . . The noblest institutions of mankind have arisen from small beginnings and where the principles are sound and the benefits of unequivocal application such a commencement is perhaps better than one of more boastful pretensions. . . .

"We know the readiness and aptness of the people to receive instruction; we know that they have had similar institutions of their own in happier and more prosperous times and that they now lament the want of them as not the smallest of the evils that has attended the fall of their power. It is to Britain alone that they can look for the restoration of these advantages: she is now called upon to lay the foundation stone and there is little doubt that this once done the people themselves will largely contribute to rearing and completing the edifice.

"But it is not to remote and speculative advantages that the effects of such an Institution will be confined; while the enlightened philanthropist will dwell with pleasure on that part of the project, the immediate advantages will be found fully proportionate. To afford the means of instruction in the native languages to those who are to administer our affairs and watch our interests in such extensive regions is surely no trifling or unimportant project. In promoting the interests of literature and science not less will be its effect. . . . Many of the researches already begun can only be completed and perfected on this soil; and they will be forwarded on the present plan by collecting the scattered remains of the literature of these countries, by calling forth the literary spirit of the people and awakening its dormant energies. The rays of intellect now divided and lost will be concentrated into a focus from which they will be radiated with an added lustre, brightened and strengthened by our superior lights. Thus will our Stations not only become the centres of commerce and its luxuries but of refinement and the liberal arts."

He concluded this long minute with a fine peroration, so reminiscent in some of its phrasing of Hastings' entries in the *Private Journal*:

"If commerce brings wealth to our shores, it is the spirit of literature and philanthropy that teaches us how to employ it for the noblest purposes. It is this which has made Britain go forth among nations, strong in her native light, to dispense blessings to all around her. If the time shall come when her Empire shall have passed away, these monuments of her virtue will endure, when her triumphs shall have become an empty name. Let it be still the boast of Britain to write her name in characters of light; let her not be remembered as the tempest whose course was desolation, but as the gale of spring, reviving the slumbering seeds of mind, and calling them to life from the winter of ignorance and oppression. Let the Sun of Britain arise on these Islands, not to wither and scorch them in its fierceness but like that of her own genial skies whose mild and benignant influence is hailed and blessed by all who feel its beams."

When Raffles had finished reading, both Mr Hutchings and Dr Morrison addressed the gathering, the second suggesting that the Anglo-Chinese College at Malacca should be removed to Singapore and fused with the Singapore Institution, as Raffles proposed to name his new college. The subscription list was then opened by Raffles, who subscribed on behalf of the East India Company four thousand dollars and on his own behalf two thousand. Sophia gave a personal subscription of five hundred dollars. Dr Morrison subscribed twelve hundred and intimated that another four thousand would probably be forthcoming from the sale of the buildings at Malacca. Farquhar put his name down for a thousand dollars, and all the leading Europeans subscribed according to their means.

'Abdullah left an amusing description of the scene when Raffles turned to the Sultan and Temenggong and enquired what their contributions were to be. Some time before, Raffles had endeavoured to persuade the Sultan to send his son to be educated in India, but this the Sultan had consistently refused to do, giving as his excuse that his wife would not part with the lad; but that if there were a school in Singapore, she would allow him to go to that.

"Now when Mr Raffles had announced that the East India Company would subscribe $4,000 and that he himself would give $2,000 on his own account he asked with a smile what the Sultan would give: shall it be $2,000 also? But he replied with a loud exclamation and a laugh that he was a poor man, so where would he get $2,000? To this Mr Raffles argued that he should give more than he gave, as the undertaking was of immediate utility to the Malays, and greatly more so than to the English; but let it be a thousand dollars."

He then put the Temenggong down for a thousand also. In all, some seventeen thousand dollars was raised, a truly magnificent sum when one considers the value of money in those days and the smallness of the European community. It also shows how Singapore merchants were prospering. Raffles promised an annual grant of three hundred dollars from Government funds, with a further grant of twenty-five dollars for the library. Various members of the local community were elected as trustees, and patrons also nominated, among them Wallich, Wilberforce and Dr Thomas Raffles.

On 8th April Raffles promised the lease of a site, and on the 15th the trustees held their first meeting, when J. A. Maxwell was appointed honorary secretary, and the firm of A. L. Johnston & Company honorary treasurers. Sums were allocated for the various projects: for the Institution in general, $9,670; for the scientific departments, $1,075; for the Malayan college, $6,750. Lieutenant Jackson, the garrison engineer, produced a plan of the building he proposed to erect. His estimate of cost was fifteen thousand dollars and the time to build it, one year. This was approved.

This modest start was, in the opinion of Raffles, only the first step towards the realization of a project of almost unlimited scope.

"I trust in God", he wrote to Wallich on 17th April, "this Institution may be the means of civilizing and bettering the condition of millions; it has not been hastily entered into nor have its possible advantages been overrated. Our field is India beyond the Ganges, including the Malayan Archipelago, Australasia, China, Japan and the Islands in the Pacific Ocean—by far the most populous half of the world. Do not, my dear friend, think that I am led to it by a vain ambition of raising a name—it is an act of duty and gratitude only. In these countries has my little independence been gained. In these countries have I passed the most valuable if not perhaps the whole period of my public life. I am linked to them by many a bitter, many a pleasant tie. It is here that I think I may have done some little good and instead of frittering the stock of zeal and means that may yet be left me in objects for which I may not be fitted, I am anxious to do all the good I can *here* where experience has proved to me that my labours will not be thrown away.

"Ill health forces me to leave Singapore before even the material arrangements are made for its prosperity; but in providing for its moral improvement I look to its more certain and permanent advance. Would that I could infuse into the Institution a portion of that spirit and soul by which I would have it animated as easily as I endow it with lands, &c. It will long be in its infancy and to arrive at maturity will require all the aid of friends and constant support. It is my last public act and rise or fall, it will always be a satisfactory reflection that I have done my best towards it. I pray you befriend it. . . ."

Chapter Twenty-nine

SINGAPORE, 1823

i

ON personal grounds, Raffles felt keenly Sayid Yasin's murderous attack on Farquhar, and it might well have led to a reconciliation and a better understanding. Unhappily, this did not come about; relations between the two men, far from improving, steadily deteriorated, and it soon became obvious that a break was inevitable. It might almost appear as if Raffles, doubtful if his proposals for the relief of Farquhar would be accepted by Calcutta, was determined to ensure that Farquhar put himself so far in the wrong that his resignation would become unavoidable. On the other hand, and Buckley shares this view, it is more likely that it was Farquhar who provoked the final clash by allowing himself to be led into active opposition to Raffles by Queiros and other disaffected persons.

Towards the end of March Raffles had called the attention of Farquhar to "his departure from the usual etiquette in dispensing with the Military Dress of his rank". As it was not Raffles' custom to interfere, if he could avoid it, in military matters, Farquhar must have got into some very slack habits. After some exchange of letters, Raffles advised Farquhar on 23rd April that as he considered Farquhar's practice to be "irregular and improper", he had written to the Governor-General in Council, in order that the views of the commander-in-chief might be obtained. This did not please Farquhar, who replied that he ought to have been consulted before any such enquiry was addressed to India. He requested that the commander-in-chief should be advised that his "military dress was dispensed with only when not in the performance of any duty connected with my office of Commandant of the garrison". He was informed in reply that no further communication was being sent, but that he was at liberty to address the commander-in-chief direct if he so desired. Three days later, Raffles abruptly relieved Farquhar of the office of Resident.

This decision was communicated by Nilson Hull in a letter dated 28th April:

"Inconvenience having arisen from your exercising the Office of Resident during the personal residence of a higher Authority at Singapore, I am directed to acquaint you that the Lieut.-Governor has deemed it necessary to relieve you from the performing of all duties attached to that office from the 1st proximo and during his continuance at this Settlement or until further orders. In consequence of this arrangement the Lieutenant-Governor will take upon himself from the 1st May proximo, being the commencement of the official year, the direct exercises of all the Civil Duties of the Station, agreeably to the enclosed General Orders of this date which you will be pleased to publish without delay."

The enclosure read: "The Lieutenant-Governor having deemed it expedient to take upon himself protemporary [*sic*] from the 1st proximo the personal exercises of all the duties heretofore performed by the Resident, all Reports and Communications are from that date to be made direct to the Lieutenant-Governor in whose Name and under whose Authority all future Orders will be issued. Lieutenant-Colonel Farquhar will continue to command the troops."

According to Buckley, the cause of this sudden decision was an unexpected demand by Farquhar for Raffles to produce his authority for sitting in the Resident's court. Perhaps Farquhar took this step as a trial of strength, to show his own independent powers as Resident. He now challenged Raffles as follows:

". . . In reply I beg leave herewith to transmit a copy of an official Letter to my address from Mr Secretary Adam under date the 28th November 1818, appointing me to the charge of British Interests in this Quarter under the General Superintendence of the Lieutenant-Governor at Fort Marlbro' and it does not appear to me that any other authority than that of the Supreme Government can legally supersede or suspend me from the Civil Charge of this Residency. Under these circumstances previous to delivering over Charge I feel called upon in justice to myself and the situation I have had the honour to fill since the commencement of this Establishment (I trust without reproach) to request to be favoured with your authority for superseding me in the Civil and Political duties of this Residency as well as any Commission vesting in you the right to assume the local charge of the Settlement yourself."

Raffles caused Farquhar to be informed that the letter from Adam submitted by Farquhar provided the answer to his question.

"I beg to state", wrote Farquhar in reply, "that the general superintendence vested in you by the Supreme Government over the British Interests in this quarter at the time the Establishment was first formed does not in my opinion vest in you any legal right whatever to interfere directly with the Local details, especially entrusted to the Resident by the Governor-General in Council, far less to suspend the functions of that authority for the purpose of assuming them yourself. I therefore feel myself compelled in consequence of the tenor of the General Orders of yesterday's date to enter a direct and solemn protest against the same being carried into effect and I hereby protest against it as illegal and unauthorized. That under this view of the said order and the peculiar circumstances attending I conceive I should be fully borne out by the Supreme Government in refusing to yield compliance thereto.

"Still, as an act of resistance on my part would be the means of occasioning interruption and inconvenience to the Public Service, I shall therefore conform to the Instructions I have received until such time as a public appeal on the subject shall have been made to the Honourable the Governor-General in Council. I have therefore to request that an authenticated copy of this Letter together with copies of all the correspondence which has passed relative to my suspension from the Charge of this Residency may by the earliest opportunity be laid before the Supreme Government for their consideration and decision.

"In conclusion I have to remark that as this Settlement will become subsequent to the 1st proximo entirely a dependency on the Presidency of Fort William, it naturally follows (in my opinion) that the authority hitherto exercised by you as Lieutenant-Governor of Bencoolen over Singapore ought necessarily to terminate."

It would appear that Raffles had no legal power to dismiss Farquhar and, in fact, later received a qualified reprimand from India for having done so; but Farquhar bowed to his authority, pending a reply from the Supreme Government, and there the matter rested for the moment.

ii

There had been a lull in the correspondence between van der Capellen and the Supreme Government. The excuse for a renewal of letters was the news that the British flag had been hoisted in Johore. On 6th May van der Capellen addressed himself to India. After emphasizing yet again the forbearance of the Dutch authorities during the negotiations in Europe, his dispatch continued:

"It was reserved for Sir Stamford Raffles, the author of so many difficulties, to disturb once more this tranquillity and to compel me to revert to a subject which has already furnished much matter for a fruitless and painful correspondence. . . . I do not attribute those acts to your Excellency in Council but on the contrary I expect more than ever to see them disavowed and explained, as soon as they shall have come to their knowledge and the fact shall have been established. . . . Towards the close of the month of February or the commencement of March last, a British flag was hoisted at Djhor [Johore], which is situated on the south-east point of the peninsula of Malaka and the principal place of the province of that name, dependent on the Sultan of Djhor, Lingin, Pahang, &c; that this flag was brought to Djhor and delivered to the Pangholoe [Penghulu] of that place by Rajah Lachja, brother-in-law of Toenkolong, and by order of that *soi disant* Sultan!"

Calcutta did not reply to this complaint, but in a confidential dispatch to Singapore (21st May 1824) ordered that the flag should be taken down. It is not easy at this date to determine the truth of the story as reported to Farquhar. It is possible that, becoming anxious as to their position, the Sultan and Temenggong had invented it for the purpose of inducing the authorities in Singapore to allow the British flag to be hoisted in Johore.

Two days after his first letter, van der Capellen wrote again to Calcutta, in a rather plaintive style.

"For the three years that the result of the negotiations opened in London for the settlement of our differences and the supreme decision have been awaited with so much impatience, no measure has been adopted or demand made calculated to produce any change or modifications in a state of things so incompatible with our rights and injurious to our interests," yet Raffles was still making trouble.

He did not think necessary to include in his dispatch any reference to the forcible seizure by the Governor of Malacca of the Johore regalia from Tunku Putĕri, the widow of Sultan Mahmud, which had recently taken place. Presumably this act was intended to destroy the British contention that no one had been officially installed sultan, as the regalia had not been used.

In the third week of May Farquhar obtained private news that Crawfurd had been appointed Resident of Singapore. The source of his information was almost certainly John Palmer, but no letter of the appropriate date can be traced. He did, however, write to Deans at Singapore. Farquhar promptly wrote (20th May) to Raffles:

"Having yesterday received with extreme surprise authentic accounts of the appointment by the Supreme Government of Mr Surgeon John Crawfurd to relieve me as Resident of Singapore, without any official application having been made by me to resign my present situation, I have to request to be informed whether my removal from Office in this very abrupt and unusual manner has been occasioned by any representation made by you to the Supreme Government relevant to my conduct in office and, if so, that you will be pleased to direct that I may be forthwith furnished with authentic copies of all such official correspondence as may have in any way led to the adoption of a measure so deeply affecting my character."

When Raffles received this letter, he was still without any official information from Calcutta. The answer sent by him through Nilson Hull to Farquhar was, therefore, given in rather general terms.

"I am directed by the Lieut.-Governor to acknowledge the receipt of your letter of yesterday's date relevant to the appointment of Mr Crawfurd to relieve you as Resident of Singapore, and to observe to you in reply that the application which it contains would be more regularly made to the Authority of whose act you would appear to complain. The Lieut.-Governor at the same time desires me to state that he sees nothing in this appointment or in the manner of it that is unusual or that might not have been expected. Your appointment was of a temporary nature and it is some time since you were informed that arrangements were in progress for relieving you. . . .

"In this case it may be supposed that the Supreme Government have on this occasion considered all the circumstances of the Settlement, and deeming it advisable to combine in the office of Resident the duties heretofore exercised by the Lieutenant-Governor with the assistance of the Local Resident, have nominated Mr Crawfurd on this footing and in appointing him to the office have selected the person whom they deem most competent to be entrusted with these important duties.

"At any rate the Lieutenant-Governor feels satisfied that no reflection is intended to be cast on your Character and that you may rest assured of your general Merits and Services being as duly appreciated by the Supreme Government as they have at all times been by himself. The Lieutenant-Governor has not yet received any official information on this subject."

Considering the observations on Farquhar sent by Raffles to Calcutta, the penultimate sentence was somewhat equivocal.

Before Farquhar could reply, the official dispatch arrived. Hull wrote to Farquhar on the 22nd:

"The Lieutenant-Governor having received a dispatch from Bengal subsequent to my communication of yesterday's date I am directed to inform you that the Hon'ble the Governor-General in Council resolved on 21st March last that the resignation tendered by you in your Letter to the Secretary in the Political Department of the 23rd October 1820 be accepted from the date of your receiving an intimation of that resolution, and further that Mr John Crawfurd be appointed Resident of Singapore and directed to repair thither without delay. You will in consequence be prepared to deliver over charge to Mr Crawfurd on his arrival, from which date his allowances as Resident are to commence and those drawn by you are to be discontinued."

Acting on this authority, Raffles informed Farquhar that he was now also relieved of the command of the troops. Farquhar declined to accept orders in this connexion from anyone other than the commander-in-chief. Raffles was no doubt getting tired of Farquhar. On his instructions, Hull wrote to Farquhar, this also on the 22nd:

"I have received and laid before the Lieutenant-Governor your letter of this date in which you state that unless the Lieutenant-Governor can produce sufficient authority from the Supreme Government or His Excellency in Chief removing you from Command of the Troops you must decline relinquishing the same to any Senior Officer while you continue here. And in reply I am directed to convey to you his *positive Commands* that you forthwith publish the General Order of this date and obey them to the Letter—the contrary at your peril. On the arrival of Mr Crawfurd you will be relieved from all further duties at this Station and struck off the Strength of the Garrison from that date."

Farquhar replied next day: ". . . I beg to observe that although you have not deemed it expedient to furnish me with the authority requested by me in my letter of yesterday, I have been induced to comply with your *peremptory Commands* rather than occasion any inconvenience to the Public Service; at the same time I have to acquaint you that I intend to make a public appeal to the Supreme Government and His Excellency, the Commander-in-Chief against the tenor of the said Letter and Order in as far as it appears to me without any *precedent* that an Officer of my rank and standing in the Service against whom a shadow of a complaint has never been urged should, in the most peremptory abrupt, harsh and degrading manner be commanded to deliver over charge of the Troops in the Garrison under his Command to a Junior Officer previous to his having obtained any opportunity whatever of quitting his Station. It certainly never could have been in the contemplation of the Supreme Government that the relinquishment of my Command here would be carried into effect with such unheard of severity and even disgrace. To the highest Tribunal in India, therefore, will I make a solemn appeal under a confident hope that ample redress will be sooner or later afforded me for all the severity and injustice I have experienced at your hands."

Instructions were now issued to Farquhar to be ready to hand over his civil duties to Crawfurd when he arrived. Farquhar replied:

"I beg to state that as the Duties of Resident have been assumed by yourself since the 1st instant I cannot under existing circumstances consider myself as having any civil charge of the Settlement to deliver over to Mr Crawfurd."

Not interested in quibbles, Raffles caused a sharp rejoinder to be sent. Farquhar wrote back:

". . . I have only to remark that as my Public Duties as Resident have been entirely suspended by your Orders and the charge of the Public Treasury transferred to a subordinate Committee and all reports directed to be made to you, I certainly could not, under such circumstances, consider myself as any longer holding the situation of Resident."

There followed a tilt at Raffles for having refused some time before an application to enlarge the establishment of the Resident's office.

"With reference to the Public Records and the office not having been delivered over I beg to state that from the total insufficiency of the Resident's Office Establishment and the great accumulation of business, the Letter Books have unavoidably fallen several months in arrears so that a considerable time will still be required before they can be regularly transferred. It was not, I presume, at all necessary to point out to me the necessity of the performance of a Public Duty of Respect and Courtesy towards Mr Crawfurd on his landing here as I cannot accuse myself of having ever been deficient on such occasion."

Crawfurd arrived in the *Hero of Malown*, under Captain Neish, on 27th May. Defending himself to the last, Farquhar wrote to him:

"It may be necessary previous to your relieving me in charge of this Residency to inform you that I wish it to be clearly understood that I do not resign my situation voluntarily but in conformity to the Orders of the Hon'ble the Lieutenant-Governor, having in a Letter addressed to him under date the 29th January last recalled any former applications I might have made to relinquish my present situation."

During May, Raffles completed the steps he had taken in January to provide a skeleton constitution for Singapore. Regulations IV and V dealt with two major subjects, gaming and slavery, both of which were to be outlawed in his new colony. While gaming was prohibited as a public amusement, private gambling was not interfered with, the magistrates being instructed to suppress the former "as far as possible without trespassing on the free will of private conduct as long as it may not be injurious to society in general". Public gaming was then and for the next half century or longer a highly controversial issue in Singapore, opinions for and against being held and voiced with equal strength and confidence. The argument commonly used in favour of its continuance was not based on any moral considerations, but on the alleged impossibility of suppressing it and that the police charged with that task would be subject to grave risk of corruption—a much greater evil than gambling itself.

Regulation IV was in due course approved by the Supreme Government. When Crawfurd reversed Raffles' policy, Calcutta hedged, maintaining its principles, but allowing the local authority discretion to permit gaming, provided the results to the community were not injurious. Raffles learned of this retrograde step while still in Bencoolen and protested against it, but without success. Whether in fact, in the early stages of the colony with but a small force of inexperienced police, public gaming could have been successfully prevented is perhaps open to question, but when, as late as 1885, it was still maintained that prohibition was impossible is more difficult to understand. There will be few to-day, whatever their views about betting and gaming, who will not subscribe to the principles that guided Raffles in 1823.

The suppression of slavery in Singapore raised no such controversial issues. The colony was too young to have any substantial interest in the perpetuation of it. True, a certain number of slaves had been imported with the knowledge of Farquhar, but the majority of these seem to have been women, who supplied the deficiency in the female population and probably in the main became the concubines, if not indeed the wives, of leading Chinese and others. Their lot as slaves was very likely much better than that of most. It must, however, have given Raffles the keenest pleasure so to order matters as in effect to abolish the state of slavery once and for all in Singapore, the first colony where abolition obtained.

The main provisions of Regulation V were these. The Acts of Parliament prohibiting the slave trade from being carried on with or in any British colony or by any British subject must be considered to apply to all persons who had obtained a fixed residence—that is, a continued residence of twelve months—in Singapore since British authority was established. Consequently all persons who had been imported, transferred or sold as slaves or slave-debtors since 26th February 1819 were entitled to claim their freedom on application to the magistrates, and in the future no one could be imported, transferred or sold as a slave or slave-debtor "under any denomination, condition, colour or pretence whatever". The magistrates were empowered to examine each case when emancipation was claimed and, where the slaves were minors, they could be bound as apprentices to their present masters if unobjectionable, but only for a period not exceeding three years or until the minor attained the age of thirteen. If the slaves were adults, their present masters might, in certain circumstances, be entitled to continue the use of their services, but here again only for a period not exceeding three years. As Sultan Husain Muhammad and the Temenggong had "evinced their desire to aid the benevolent objects of the British Government", the regulation was to apply to their subjects also, but with the exception that the personal establishment of their Highnesses, who, not being in a position to be bought or sold, could still be registered as slaves. To native chiefs or traders resorting to the port but not having a fixed residence at Singapore the regulation did not apply, except that they were prevented from selling their slaves to anyone in Singapore. This prohibition applied also to slave-debtors, who could not be purchased from visiting ships. Raffles' regulations concerning slave or bond debtors followed the general line of those he had already introduced at Bencoolen. All slave-debtors had to be registered and their period of service was strictly determined by law.

Finally, to round off his work, Raffles issued Regulation VI. This contained additional provisions for the magistracy and administration of justice at Singapore, amending and elaborating Regulation III. Under the new regulation, instead of three magistrates being appointed each quarter, twelve were to be appointed each year. The powers and proceedings of the Resident's court were also defined, and regulations laid down for their procedure. The details need not concern us. More interesting are the principles propounded for the guidance of those whose duty it would be to administer justice. Such importance did Raffles attach to these that he issued an explanatory minute of no less than twenty-five paragraphs. In this minute he explained that Singapore presented a peculiar problem.

"As the population of Singapore will necessarily consist of a mixture in various proportions of strangers from all parts of the world . . . though chiefly of Chinese and Malays, it would be impracticable for any judicial authority to become perfectly acquainted with the laws and customs having the force of law which are acknowledged in their own countries respectively . . . under these circumstances nothing seems to be left but to have recourse to first principles, to use every precaution against the existence of temptation to crime, that is found consistent with the perfect liberty of those who have no evil intention, and when these precautions fail, to secure redress . . . and such punishment as will be most likely to prevent a repetition of the crime. . . . Nothing should be endured in the Settlement, however sanctioned by the local usage, which is likely to endanger safety or liberty, and no one of whatever country is to be debarred by any legal formalities from obtaining substantial justice so that legal and moral obligation may never be at variance."

Taking this as the fundamental principle for the laws of the settlement, he presumed that no local regulation would be enacted that society, left to itself, would not wish to see carried into effect. The people would thus support the Government and not feel that they were being tyrannized by it. At the same time, it had to be strongly emphasized that while people were fully entitled to protect themselves against injury, the *redress* of wrongs could not be obtained by the individual except through the agency of the law. No one could be a fair judge of his own case, and no one could be allowed to revenge his own quarrel. As the carrying of lethal weapons was a source of great temptation to do so, this habit, particularly among the Malays, must be stopped.

As gaming, cockfighting and intoxication were all likely to promote crime, the two first were absolutely prohibited in so far as they formed a source of profit to the individual, and the last must be checked, as far as possible, by suitable punishment. Where concubinage was generally accepted, it was very difficult to devise suitable laws against prostitution.

"The unfortunate prostitute should be treated with compassion and every obstacle should be thrown in the way that her services should be a profit to anyone but herself."

It must be found necessary to make specific regulations for the protection of the community against fire. Other measures would be required to prevent various types of fraud. All householders should be registered, and auctioneers and pawnbrokers licensed.

"With respect to the employment of informers, it may be observed that Magistrates must have information; but no bad passion should be elicited in the procuring of it: no temptation to lead others to vice for the sake of reward for informing; no inducement to betray confidence; and the act of giving information should be treated as a public and honourable duty."

He turned next to the question of what were to be considered crimes, what should be the appropriate penalties and how should injuries be redressed. Under the constitution of England, the absolute rights of the subject were firstly the right of personal security in the physical sense and personal reputation in the abstract sense; secondly the right of personal liberty; and thirdly the right of property.

"There seems no reason for denying corresponding rights to all classes of people residing under the protection of the British flag at Singapore."

In the enactment of laws for securing these rights:

". . . legal obligation must never supersede or take the place of or be inconsistent with or more or less onerous than moral obligation. The English practice of teaching prisoners to plead not guilty . . . is inconsistent with this and consequently objectionable."

The denial of a crime increased the offence. Sanctity of oaths should also be more upheld than in the English court. This might be done by administering oaths only as a last resort.

"Truth, however, must be required under pain of punishment in all cases of evidence before a Court of Justice."

Turning to punishments, he expressed this opinion:

"The imprisonment of an unfortunate debtor at the pleasure of the creditor, by which the services of the individual are lost to all parties, seems objectionable in this Settlement . . . the rights of property may be sufficiently protected by giving to the creditor a right to the value of the debtor's services for a limited period."

Care must also be taken in fixing penalties for Asiatic offenders. It was well known that the Malay race were sensibly alive to shame and preferred death to ignominy.

"This is a high and honourable feeling and ought to be cherished. Let great care be taken to avoid all punishments which are unnecessarily degrading. Both the Malays and Chinese are a reasoning people. . . . Let no man be punished without reason assigned. Let the principles of British law be applied, not only with a mildness and a patriarchal kindness and indulgent consideration for the prejudices of each tribe as far as substantial justice will allow but also with reference to these reasoning powers."

He would like to see certain axioms adopted.

"Let native institutions, as far as regards religious observances, marriage and inheritance be respected" when these were not inconsistent with justice, humanity or the wellbeing of society. "Let all men be considered equal in the eye of the law. Let no man be banished the country without a trial by his peers or the due course of law. Let no man be deprived of his liberty without a cause and no man be detained in confinement beyond forty-eight hours" without the right to demand trial. "Let the public have a voice through the magistracy, by which their sentiments at all times may be freely expressed."

The concluding paragraphs deal with the grading of punishment to suit the crime.

Such were the principles that Raffles hoped would guide the course of justice in his settlement, and no one can suggest that the attention he had given to the securing of substantial justice to all of every race had been misapplied. The principles he enunciated might well serve as a model for those responsible for the administration of justice in a mixed community where the superior authority is of an alien race and much farther advanced in civilization and coded law than the subjects for which it is responsible.

Raffles went to great pains to try to secure the support of the Supreme Government in these regulations, which he explained and justified in a dispatch to Holt Mackenzie. One extract alone need be given here; it related to the magistrates sitting in the Resident's court.

"I am satisfied that nothing has tended more to the discomfort and constant jarrings which have hitherto occurred in our remote Settlements, than the policy which has dictated the exclusion of the European merchants from all share, much less credit, in the domestic regulations of the Settlement of which they are frequently its most important members. Some degree of legislative power must necessarily exist in every distant dependency . . . even the Governor-General in Council . . . is hardly competent . . . without the assistance of local advice."

All who have had experience of Crown Colonies will endorse that opinion.

The visit to Singapore was now drawing to a close. Raffles and his party, which was to include little Charles Flint, was due to return to Bencoolen on 9th July in the *Hero of Malown*. As Captain Neish had some cargo to deliver at Batavia, they would have to touch there first, which was not greatly to the liking of Raffles, who made it publicly known that he had no intention of landing.

Four days before their departure, Crawfurd presented to Raffles a memorial signed by the whole of the mercantile community, both European and native.

". . . At such a moment", it ran, "we cannot be suspected of panegyric when we advert to the distinguished advantages which the commercial interests of our nation at large and ourselves more especially have derived from your personal exertions. To your unwearied zeal, your vigilance and your comprehensive views we owe at once the foundation and maintenance of a Settlement unparalleled for the liberality of the principles on which it has been established; principles, the operation of which has converted in a period short beyond all example a haunt of pirates into the abode of enterprise, security and opulence. While we acknowledge our own peculiar obligations to you, we reflect at the same time with pride and satisfaction upon the active and beneficent means by which you have promoted and patronized the diffusion of intellectual and moral improvement and we anticipate with confidence their happy influence in advancing the cause of humanity and civilization. We cannot take leave of the author of so many benefits without emotion, or without expressing our sorrow for the loss of his protection and his society. Accept, Sir, we beseech you, without distinction of tribe or nation, the expression of our sincere respect and esteem and be assured of the deep interest we shall ever take in your own prosperity as well as in the happiness of those who are most tenderly related to you."

Raffles' reply was of some length and need not be quoted here. It contained, however, an important statement of his views. After mentioning that his own personal connexion with the establishment of Singapore made it impossible to be indifferent to any of its interests and not least its commercial interests, he observed:

"It has happily been consistent with the policy of Great Britain and accordant with the principles of the East India Company that Singapore should be established as a *Free Port*; that no sinister, no sordid view, no considerations either of political importance nor pecuniary advantage should interfere with the broad and liberal principles on which the British interests have been established. Monopoly and exclusive privilege, against which public opinion has long raised its voice, are here unknown and while the free port of Singapore is allowed to continue and prosper as it has hitherto done, the policy and liberality of the East India Company, by whom the Settlement was founded and under whose protection and control it is still administered can never be disputed. That Singapore will long and always remain a free port and that no taxes on trade and industry will be established to check its future rise in prosperity I can have no doubt. . . ."

On the following day, Raffles laid the foundation stone of the Singapore Institution. 'Abdullah describes the ceremony thus:

". . . the Europeans, also the Sultan and Temmungong. assembled, together with all the Malays, where there was a squared stone with a hole made in it closed with iron. This they placed before the door; on which Mr Raffles arrived and the people then collected around him. He then took out a golden rupee from his pocket and put it in the hole. The European gentlemen also put in dollars to the amount of 80. The Chinese artificer then fixed the fastenings with lead to prevent its being reopened. So they laid the stone below the door and as they raised it erect a salute of twelve guns was fired on the hill. And hereupon Mr Raffles named the building 'Institution'."

When, on 20th May, Raffles had reported the founding of the Institution to Calcutta, he had been careful to explain the urgent reasons for inaugurating it without obtaining the prior approval of the Supreme Government. In the first place, his friends at Singapore had expressed a strong desire that before he left he should lay the foundation stone. Secondly, and perhaps more important, there had been the accidental arrival of Robert Morrison from China with the proposal that the Anglo-Chinese College in Malacca should be moved to British soil in Singapore.

"The interests of the Anglo-Chinese College required an immediate decision and the necessity of Dr Morrison's early return to China did not admit of distant reference, while the accidental presence of the Rev. Mr Hutchin[g]s, Chaplain of P. of W. Island, well known for the interest he has always taken in Malay literature, and the general feeling of the community combined to render the present moment peculiarly advantageous. . . . Accordingly after much deliberation and communication with Lieut.-Col. Farquhar and the Reverend Mr Hutchins it was agreed that the Anglo-Chinese College should be removed to Singapore, there to be united with a similar Establishment for the Malayan Department, including Siamese, under a general designation of the Singapore Institution."

Had Hastings still been Governor-General, the response might have been warmer. Official opinion in India was not enthusiastic. Unconvinced by the arguments advanced by Raffles, Calcutta replied (6th November) that it disapproved of this hasty action, since the fate of Singapore was still undecided. Moreover, money grants should not have been promised without previous authority. Having said this, the dispatch gave grudging approval to what had been done. Raffles had left Singapore some months before this letter arrived, but the discouraging tone of it was a foretaste of the fate that was to befall this magnificent project.

John Palmer, though for a very different reason, was also cautious about committing himself—still more his cash. When Raffles had been in Calcutta in 1819 he had discussed his scheme with Palmer, who had then given his warm approval. But when the prospectus reached him towards the end of 1823, the first shadows of financial disaster were falling on the house of Palmer. In his reply (31st January 1824), Palmer refers openly to this.

"I thank you for sending me the Prospectus of the Singapore Institute which unhappy circumstances deny me the privilege of supporting as I intended when all was Sunshine with me. This change in my capacity ought to deter me from adverting to that in my view of your benevolent and enlightened purposes. But I owe to myself, and more especially to you, not to conceal a sentiment under the force of circumstances which in no manner bias it. I have feared the precosity of the Scheme as to the People; and the effects of its abrupt transfer from Malacca upon the feelings of our Neighbours. But these would not deter me from liberally supporting your Institution to the extent of affording it a fair trial; for besides my wish to contribute to the success of so generous an Undertaking, I should never oppose my judgment to yours even in matters of which we might possess a common knowledge. If things improve with me—as they must if I can hold on for a few years longer—I shall be conspicuous on your lists at Singapore."

With the stone safely laid and the building design approved, Raffles felt, no doubt, that the Singapore Institution was as good as in being. Crawfurd, however, had no such enthusiasm for the project. His attitude was described by Palmer in a letter to van der Capellen dated 18th January 1824.

"Like the liberators of countries long sunk in slavery, Mr Crawfurd is said to have discovered that the Malays of the Archipelago are not inceptively capable of estimating the great Blessings designed by Sir S. Raffles in his magnificent Institutions and Public Works; and I hear he is contriving that all should be retrograding until it meets that point of Improvement of which the Malays are capable. These changes are by wicked People ascribed to Sir Stamford's criticism in the Quarterly Review of Mr Crawfurd's book. So one sees on what flimsy filaments of old rivalries hangs [*sic*] the Destinies of an interesting People. There may be more malice than art or truth in the Inference but if Sir Stamford's views were really Utopian, a temperate and sober man might reasonably expose them without indulging an author's sensibilities. All is at all events in suspense until Mr C. has time to investigate the utility of such enlarged Projects."

Bearing this comment in mind, one is not surprised to read this description recorded less than ten years later by George Windsor Earl in his *Eastern Seas*:

"In the centre of the *Marina*, close to the sea shore, are the ruins of a large building called the Singapore Institution, and being an object which generally catches the eye of a stranger on entering the harbour, many are inclined to doubt that the settlement can be so young as it is represented. This edifice was founded by Sir Stamford Raffles soon after the establishment of the British on the island in the fond hope that, by means of natives educated therein by European teachers whom it was proposed to appoint, knowledge and civilization might be widely disseminated throughout the Further East. The building was nearly completed on his official departure from India and negotiations were in train for embodying with it the members of the Chinese College of Malacca but when the master-mind was gone the Institution and its objects were neglected and the building fell into decay."

The *Free Press* also observed: ". . . for several years it has been an eyesore to the inhabitants of the Settlement from the desolate and neglected appearance of the building and premises; and latterly it has become a nuisance in some degree as it affords a convenient shelter for thieves, a class of being whom the benevolent founders of the Institution never contemplated should be supported on its foundation."

Yet, if the original project died an untimely death, the Singapore Institution managed to rise again in the guise of a very flourishing school.

Sir Andrew Clarke, one of the ablest Governors of the Straits Settlements, wrote in 1874:

"More than half a century has elapsed since Sir Stamford Raffles conceived the idea of establishing an institution in Singapore for the cultivation of the languages of China, Siam and the Malay Archipelago, and for the improvement of the moral and intellectual condition of the inhabitants of these countries. His idea—which for the grandeur and comprehensiveness of its design has seldom been excelled—Sir Stamford Raffles submitted to a public meeting in the form of a Minute which would endure in the literature of these Settlements, a lasting memorial of their illustrious founder."

To-day the school is still proudly called the Raffles Institution, and the recent creation of a University of Malaya gives hope that what Raffles planned in the first quarter of the nineteenth century may yet come true in the third quarter of the twentieth.

It was the last of Raffles' public acts.

"Then on a certain day," recorded 'Abdullah, "Mr Raffles said to me 'Tuan, I intend to sail in three days hence, so collect all my Malay books' and when I heard this my heart palpitated and my spirit was gone. So I asked him where he was going and he told me he was going to Europe; and when I heard this I could bear it no longer, I felt as if I had lost Father and Mother—such was my condition that my eyes were bathed in tears. When he perceived this his face became flushed and wiping his tears with his hankerchief he told me not to be disheartened for if he lived he intended to return to Singapore. . . . He then called me into the room and told me that there were three presses filled with Malay books and to wrap them up well in wax cloth and pack them in hair trunks, four in number. There were also Javanese instruments and various other articles; and when he had shown me all these he went out, so with my own hands I packed up all the books, histories and poems. Of these there were three hundred bound books, not counting the unbound ones and scrolls and pamphlets. There were three hair trunks full, six feet in length, of Malay books only. Then there were two trunks filled with letters, Javanese, Bali and Bujis books and various images, paintings with their frames, musical instruments, inscriptions and lontar leaves.[1] Of these there were three or four boxes. Besides this Javanese instruments with their equipment were in one great box, and there were many thousands of specimens of animals whose carcasses had been taken out but stuffed like life. There were also two or three trunks full of birds in thousands and of various species, and all stuffed. There were also several hundred bottles of different sizes filled with snakes, scorpions and worms of different kinds. The bottles were filled with gin to prevent corruption. The animals were thus like life. There were also two boxes filled with coral of a thousand kinds; also shells, mussels, and bivalves of different species. On all these articles stated above he placed a value greater than gold, and he was constantly coming in to see that nothing was hurt or broken. And when they were all ready they were shipped by a lighter; and when they were all safely on board, he called me into his office saying, 'Tuan, take this letter and keep it with care—it is to the same effect as the one I gave you at Malacca—and when English gentlemen arrive here show it to them and they will have regard for you.' . . . I was silent when I took the testimonial, my eyes flowing with tears from grief; the day was as if my Father and Mother had died."

The original treaty with Sultan Husain Muhammad had not proved entirely satisfactory, so a fresh one was negotiated on 7th June.

"Their Highnesses the Sultan and Temmungong," read the preamble, "having solicited that the Lieutenant-Governor would, previous to his departure, lay down such general rules for their guidance as may be most conducive to the general interests of Singapore and at the same time serve to define the rights of all parties that there may be no dispute hereafter:

"The following rules are laid down by the Lieutenant-Governor and concurred in by Their Highnesses to form the basis of the good understanding to be maintained in future."

The seven subsequent paragraphs prescribed that, from 1st June, the Sultan should receive 1,500 dollars and the Temenggong 800 dollars to provide for their comfort and respectability, and also to afford them compensation for advantages either had expected, or forgone by them, on account of port duties, tribute or profits on monopolies found to be inconsistent with the principles maintained by the British Government. These included monopolies on certain types of wood in Singapore and the

[1] Used as a substitute for paper. The tree is the palmyra palm.

adjacent islets, as well as all claims to presents or customs on Chinese traffic.

All land within the island of Singapore and the islands immediately adjacent, with the exception of the land actually appropriated to their Highnesses for their respective subjects, was to be entirely at the disposal of the British Government. The Resident would be authorized to advance such further sums of money as might be required to complete the mosque near the Sultan's dwelling, and also to assist the Temenggong in moving to the new site of his house. The Sultan and Temenggong were relieved from further attendance each Monday at the court, though they would be entitled to seats on the bench if they ever wished to attend.

"For all cases regarding the ceremonies of religion of marriages and the rules of inheritance the laws and customs of the Malays will be respected where they shall not be contrary to reason, justice or humanity. In all other cases the laws of the British Authority will be enforced with due consideration to the usages and habits of the people."

Finally, the British Government would not, for the present, interfere in the local arrangements of the countries and islands subject to the Sultan's authority beyond Singapore and its adjacent islets, except to afford them general protection as theretofore.

Raffles had been instructed by Calcutta to give Crawfurd general advice as to the administration of Singapore. This he did in a long letter of the same date.

"Having communicated so fully with you personally, on the affairs of Singapore and our interests to the Eastward, and so entirely concurring as we do in general questions of policy relating to them, it is only necessary that in transferring to you the future administration of this Settlement, I should advert to such points of detail as may require to be particularly defined."

We need quote but a few of the paragraphs that followed:

"12. By the accounts of the Town Committee just delivered, you will perceive that the amount advanced by Government as compensation for removing these houses to make room for the Commercial establishments, on the opposite side of the river, will be dollars 10,259 for the China campong and dollars 1,704 for the Chuliah campong, and enclosure No. 4 contains the plan proposed by the Town Committee for recovering those amounts from the parties who are now enjoying the benefit of it. You will adopt this or such other arrangement as you may deem most just and proper and at the same time calculated to meet the convenience of the parties.

"18. The ground plan of the town and its vicinity with which you have been furnished, with the explanations which I have personally given, will have placed you fully in possession of the arrangements I have had in view in this respect, and for all further details and information, I refer you to Lieutenant Jackson, the executive officer, who fully comprehends them and will be able to give you every satisfaction.

"19. In laying out the town, I particularly recommend to your attention the advantage of an early attention [not only] to the provision of ample accommodation for the public service hereafter whenever it may be required, but to the beauty, regularity, and cleanliness of the Settlement; the width of the different roads and streets should be fixed by authority, and as much attention paid to the general style of building as circumstances admit.

"23. Their Highnesses the Sultan and Tumongong seem to be under some misapprehension regarding the safety of Johore, Rajah Moodah of Rhio, under the direction of the Dutch authorities, having made several attempts to enforce his authority there. You are recommended to take an early opportunity of conferring with their Highnesses on the subject, and adopting such provisional arrangements for the security of the place as may be prudent, without involving us in any new question with the Dutch.

"27. Having given you these instructions as far as regards your situation as Resident of Singapore, I am desirous also of calling your attention, on some points, to the line of policy which it appears to me advisable for you to pursue more generally in your political capacity in the Archipelago. On this subject one of the most material points is our political relations with Siam and the Malayan States said to be tributary to it. On this point it is incumbent on me to state with candour that the policy hitherto pursued by us has in my opinion been founded on erroneous principles. The dependence of the tributary States in this case is founded on no national relation which connects them with the Siamese nation. These people are of opposite manners, language, religion and general interests, and the superiority maintained by the one over the other, is so remote from protection on the one side or attachment on the other, that it is but a simple exercise of capricious tyranny by the stronger party, submitted to by the weaker from the law of necessity. We have ourselves for nearly four years been eye-witnesses of the pernicious influence exercised by the Siamese over the Malayan States. During the revolution of the Siamese government these profit by its weakness, and from cultivating an intimacy with strangers, especially with ours over other European nations, they are always in a fair train of prosperity. With the settlement of the Siamese government, on the contrary, it invariably regains the exercise of its tyranny and the Malayan States are threatened, intimidated and plundered. The recent invasion of Quedah is a striking example in point, and from the information conveyed to me it would appear that that commercial seat, governed by a Prince of most respectable a character, long personally attached to our nation, has only been saved from a similar fate by a most unlooked for event. By the independent Malayan States, who may be supposed the best judges of this matter, it is important to observe that the connexion of the tributary Malays with Siam is looked upon as a matter of simple compulsion. Fully aware of our power and in general deeply impressed with respect for our national character, still it cannot be denied that we suffer, at the present moment, in their good opinion by withholding from them that protection from the oppression of the Siamese which it would be so easy for us to give; and the case is stronger with regard to Quedah than the rest, for here a general impression is abroad amongst them, that we refuse an assistance that we are by Treaty virtually bound to give, since we entered into a Treaty with that State, as an independent power, without regarding the supremacy of Siam or ever alluding to its connexion for five and twenty years, after our first [establishment at Penang]. The prosperity of the Settlement under your direction is so much connected with that of the Malayan nations in its neighbourhood, and this again [so much depends] upon their liberty and security from foreign oppression, that I must seriously recommend to your attention the contemplation of the probable event of their deliverance from the yoke of Siam, and your making the Supreme Government immediately informed of every event which may promise to lead to that desirable result."

The man to whom these instructions were addressed was of a very different type from either Raffles or Farquhar. In ability he was probably not much inferior to Raffles, and much superior to Farquhar, but he lacked the kindly qualities that had made the other two so popular—not only with Europeans, but also with Asiatics. He was conceited and rather narrow-minded, and also had the reputation of being close-fisted. 'Abdullah described him thus:

"On looking at Mr Crawfurd's disposition, he was impatient and of a quick temper; but in what he engaged he did slowly and not immediately. However, it should be perceived that he was a man of good parts, clever and profound. Yet it was equally true that he was much bent down by love for the goods of this world. His hand was not an open one, though he had no small opinion of himself. Further, his impatience prevented him from listening to long complaints and he did not care about investigating the circumstances of the case. As sure as there was a plaint he would cut it short in the middle. On this account I have heard that most people murmured and were dissatisfied, feeling that they could not accept his decision with good will but by force only."

With Singapore handed over to Crawfurd and all other necessary tasks completed, Raffles and his party boarded the *Hero of Malown* on 9th June. Let 'Abdullah tell the end of the story:

"Mr Raffles and his Lady embarked, followed by hundreds of people of all races, myself among the rest, as far as the ship; and when they had ascended the ship's side and the crew were raising the anchor Mr Raffles called me to him and I went into his cabin where I observed that his face was flushed as if he had been wiping his tears. He told me to return and not be distressed: 'If it is to be I will see you again.' His Lady now came and gave me twenty-five dollars, saying 'I give these to your children in Malacca,' and when I heard this my heart burned the more by this act of grace. I thanked her very much, clasping them by the hand in tears, and then descended to my sampan and when I had been off some distance I turned round and saw Mr Raffles looking out of the window when I again saluted him. He raised his hand to me. This was just as the sails were being hoisted; and the vessel sailed.

"Such was my separation from Mr Raffles. I was not distressed about my livelihood or because of his greatness or because of my losing him; but because of his noble bearing, his justness, modesty and respect to his fellow men. All these I remember to this day. There are many great men besides him, clever, rich and handsome, but in good disposition, amiability and gracefulness, Mr Raffles had not his equal, and were I to die and live again such a man I could never meet again, my love of him is so great."

Chapter Thirty

BENCOOLEN, 1823-1824

i

"I HAVE not as you may suppose", wrote Raffles off the coast of Borneo on 12th June, "remained at Singapore eight months for nothing; two-thirds of the time have no doubt been spent in pain and annoyance from the dreadful headaches I am doomed to suffer in this country, but the remaining third has been actively employed.

"I have had everything to new-mould from first to last; to introduce a system of energy, purity, and encouragement; to remove nearly all the inhabitants, and to re-settle them; to line out towns, streets, and roads; to level the high and fill up the low lands; to give property in the soil and rights to the people; to lay down principles, and sketch institutions for the domestic order and comfort of the place, as well as its future character and importance; to look for a century or two beforehand, and provide for what Singapore may one day become, by the adoption of all such measures of forecast as reason and experience can suggest.

"That I have not forgotten the moral interests and character of the Settlement, the establishment of the Singapore Institution will be the best proof. I have given it as free a constitution as possible; and Singapore is now, perhaps, the only place in India where slavery cannot exist."

Two days later, still off the coast of Borneo, he wrote to Dr Thomas Raffles:

"We left Singapore on the 9th and, are thus far on our return to Bencoolen, with the intention of touching at Batavia on the way. My time was so fully occupied while closing my administration at Singapore, that I really had it not in my power to sit down, as I ought to have done, to thank you most sincerely for your letter announcing the arrival of our dear little Ella; it was the first account we received, and I need not attempt to express the joy and gladness which it diffused throughout our domestic circle. Sophia's patience was almost tired out, and the news has given her almost a new life."

Ella had gone to the home of Sophia's parents at Cheltenham.

"Mr Crawfurd is now the Resident at Singapore and in anticipation of my return to Europe at the end of the year I have resigned all further charge of the place. It is a most promising Settlement and is fast realizing my most sanguine views regarding it. I have had a great deal of trouble and annoyance in the details owing to the imbecility and obstinacy of the local Resident, Col. Farquhar, but as Crawfurd has relieved him and all my measures and plans are approved of and supported by the higher Authorities, I have great reason to be satisfied with the result upon the whole.

"We have under our charge for Europe my sister Mary Anne's little boy Charles, and are thinking of preparations for the voyage home, which, with the blessing of God, we hope to commence with the new year, touching at the Cape and at St Helena on the way, so as to be with you in May or June. My health has now become worse, but Sophia's is much improved. She is in the family way and hopes to be confined in October, so that we shall not be without our cares on the voyage.

"You know by experience the misery of shipboard and will therefore not expect that I should, in such a situation, write you a very long or very interesting letter. I write these few lines with a very unsteady hand and giddy head, but as I may have a chance of sending them by some vessel about to sail from Batavia, I am unwilling to lose the opportunity of writing at all."

To Wallich: ". . . I am forced to touch at Batavia on my way to Bencoolen, very much against my will; but the Captain has goods to land, and no other opportunity was likely to offer of getting round. The Dutch will be a little astonished, but I cannot help it; I do not intend to land."

The *Hero of Malown* anchored in Batavia roads on 25th June.

"Had Buonaparte returned to life and anchored in the Downs, it would not have excited greater agitation in England, than my arrival has done here, though the sensation might have been very different. Here fear and apprehension are everything, and to these all courtesy, principle, and interest give way."

As soon as the ship had anchored, Raffles sent Nilson Hull ashore with a note to his old friend, Thomas McQuoid, and an official letter to the Governor-General.

"My arrival here", ran the note to McQuoid, "will no doubt surprise you and many others—but it has been a matter of necessity, no other opportunity offering by which I could return to Bencoolen and Neish being under an obligation to touch here on the way to land some consignments for the Government and others. This will be delivered to you by Captain Hull whom I request to introduce you. I have given him a letter to the Governor-General informing him of my arrival and mentioning the delicate state of Lady R.'s health which makes it highly desirable she should land during our detention here, which is not expected to exceed two or three days. For my part I had determined not to land and should be still anxious to adhere to this resolution, if I could induce Lady R. to go on shore without me, but I have not been very well myself and she feels some alarm about the fever affecting me. In either case however, whether one or both land, it is my wish to make free with your quarters . . . and as a final requisition I beg of you to send us off a loaf of bread without delay. . . ."

Sophia went ashore on the same day and was made welcome in McQuoid's home. Her brother duly presented Raffles' letter to the Governor-General. It was as follows:

"I have the honour to inform Y.E. of my arrival in the Roads of Batavia, the ship 'Hero of Malown' on which I am returning to Bencoolen being under the necessity of touching at this port for the purpose of delivering some consignments from Bengal. I trust our detention will not exceed two or three days, but as Lady Raffles is in a very delicate state of health, and suffers much at sea, the advantage of going on shore even for that time will be a great relief to her. Captain Hull of my personal staff will have the honour of delivering this letter."

Van der Capellen was so flustered by Raffles' unexpected arrival that his sense of official responsibility overcame his better feelings. Without asking a single question or even stopping to read the letter carefully, he dismissed Nilson and sent a curt verbal message through McQuoid that permission for Raffles to land could not be given. The next morning, he apparently decided that a written answer was called for. This he sent in French, of which the following is a translation:

"I have received with great surprise the letter which Captain Hull has handed to me on your behalf.

"I have instructed M. McQuoid to give you my reply verbally and I have no doubt but that he will carry out this commission with exactitude.

"However, I should like to add to that which he will tell you from me, that I was far from expecting to see you at Batavia after all that has happened since 1818.

"You cannot ignore, Sir, that such a visit, which you could have avoided, could only prove extremely disagreeable to me.

"The indisposition of Madame Raffles is, however, a motive that I respect too much to oppose your stay in Batavia for a few days.

"I regret, Sir, after all that has taken place, not to be able to welcome you, for I always consider it a duty and a pleasure to receive the officials of a Government so intimately associated with that which I have the honour to represent here.

"You know the state of things too well, Sir, for me to need to tell you that all communication or personal contact between us must be avoided. I can only repeat once more the whole series of complaints that I have believed it my duty to address to my Government, as to yours, for several years, against a large number of your actions directed against the interests of my Sovereign; such a communication could offer no pleasure either for you or for myself."

Raffles found this "rather amusing". He replied:

"Y.E.'s letter was deliverd to me during the night.

"I am sorry that what was intended merely as a mark of respect, should have given rise to the extreme surprise which you express. I felt it right to inform Y.E. of my being in the Roads of Batavia, and I stated the circumstances which had led to it.

"You would appear to have been misinformed in supposing that it was my intention or my desire to land or court a personal interview. My landing in Java, while under Y.E.'s government, could only have been attended with painful feelings, public as well as private, and there certainly has been nothing in the conduct of Y.E. which could have rendered me particularly desirous of personal communication or acquaintance.

"I caused it to be publicly known before I embarked, that I neither intended nor wished to land; and under these circumstances, I trust you will admit that the proscription you have thought proper to issue might, in common courtesy, have been delayed until a solicitation on my part might have called for it.

"Y.E. also appears to have been misinformed, when you state that I might or should have avoided touching at Batavia, knowing how disagreeable it would be to you. I can assure you that it was a matter of absolute necessity, in every way against my wishes and feelings; tho' I must say, I never for a moment supposed it would have given rise to any apprehensions or unpleasant feelings on your part.

"You have, Sir, thought proper to refer to political differences, and to the complaints which you have thought proper to make against my proceedings, which you considered to be directed against the interests of your Sovereign; and which it is necessary to recall to your recollection, that I have at least had similar grounds for complaining of some of the proceedings of your government; and that the very acts which you call in question arose solely from a conviction that such proceedings on your part were directed against the interests of my country. The decision as to whose views have been most correct remains with higher authorities and while I cheerfully give Y.E. the credit of having acted as you deemed best for the interests of your own country, I hope you will judge equally charitably of the motives which may have dictated my conduct.

"I have thought the above explanation due as well to Y.E. as to myself, as I should have presumed you to have been incapable of offering a personal incivility, as I am of receiving one, without noticing it as it deserves.

"I did not, Sir, consider it necessary to request your permission for Lady Raffles to land, as I could not suppose it necessary in the present state of civilized society, but I have now respectfully to request that as she is on shore in extreme delicate health, and far advanced in her pregnancy, Y.E. will ensure her a safe passport to the ship whenever she may be desirous of re-embarking."

In reporting this incident to Falck, van der Capellen seems to have had some qualms of conscience.

"I am willing", he wrote, "to leave the decision to your judgment whether I could have acted otherwise than I have done, and whether I shouldn't have, by a greater politeness to Mr Raffles, compromised the dignity of the Dutch Government. Mr Raffles ought to have foreseen that he wouldn't have been received by me and ought to have avoided Batavia for the reason. You will learn from the letter by his successor at Singapore that R. intended right enough to touch at Batavia on his return journey to Bencoolen. I have heard that he is not yet gone ashore, probably the result of my letter."

It may be added here that official dispatches from Raffles and Crawfurd to the Governor-General, reporting that Raffles had resigned and that Crawfurd had been appointed in his place, were returned to Raffles, as van der Capellen declined to accept any communications from Singapore officials.

If van der Capellen had in mind that by confining Raffles to his ship, intercourse with persons ashore would be prevented he must have been disappointed. As soon as the news got about that he was in the roads, people flocked to the harbour to see him and all the time the *Hero of Malown* was in port he held every day a sort of levee. It must have given him enormous pleasure to realize that in spite of everything he was still remembered with respect and affection.

"Sophia", he wrote, "is now under the hospitable roof of McQuoid where she is gaining health and strength to enable her to get through the remainder of the voyage. . . . For myself I remain on board according to the resolution I took on embarking. I have however had an opportunity of seeing all the English gentlemen, and have no particular cause to regret the necessity which forced us to touch here, as I have been able to see the sort of *material* of which the Dutch Governor-General is made."

In the end, the *Hero of Malown* spent a whole week in Batavia, so that Bencoolen was not reached until 17th July.

Raffles had asked for a ship to be sent out to take him, his family and his vast and valuable collection back to England. The reply was that no vessel was available to come direct, but that H.C.C. *Fame* could be expected by the end of the year. Apart, therefore, from the tasks of sorting and packing his scientific specimens, his portfolio of maps, his books, pictures and papers, of preparing a large-scale map of Sumatra, and of arranging how the administration of Bencoolen was to be carried on after his departure, he did not anticipate that he would have much more to do than wait with what patience he could for the arrival of the *Fame*. In this he was to be disappointed. This last period on "that ill-fated coast" was to be busy, long drawn out, and saddened by a series of personal tragedies—a repetition, albeit on a smaller scale, of the grim days of two years earlier.

At first all went well. In the middle of September Sophia gave birth to a daughter, who was called Flora. Sophia rapidly recovered from her confinement, and Raffles was able to write, "Our little Flora expands daily." Then Sophia was attacked with fever and was soon desperately ill.

"It was only last night," Raffles wrote to Wallich on 1st November, "that we were forced to apply thirty leeches and have recourse to warm baths and laudanum to keep down inflammation."

In the same letter he wrote:

"I lament to observe by the papers that poor Finlayson [who had accompanied Crawfurd on the embassy to Siam] breathed his last on the way home. Poor fellow, I never had much hope that he would be spared; yet his death has been to me a severe shock, admiring and valuing, as I did, his talents, disposition, and principles.

"It is only a week ago that we had another death in our family: Mr Drummond, a gentleman who had come out to us highly recommended from home, and was embarking largely in our agricultural pursuits, was carried off in less than twelve hours. I know not how it is, but these continual breaches in our domestic circles seem to be sad warnings.

"I had hoped to have got away by the end of the present year, but an accumulation of details, and the arrival of a detachment of troops most unexpectedly sent by the Bengal Government to the northern part of the Island, may keep me for some time. My health for the last week or two had rather improved, but I am still subject to the same attacks which so often and so completely overpowered me at Singapore."

To Thomas Murdoch he wrote on 14th November:

". . . Lady Raffles had hardly recovered from her last confinement when she was attacked by a violent fever which has hardly yet left her, and she is still confined to her couch. I am scarcely able to hold up my head two days together; but yet we hope that our period of banishment is nearly terminated, and that we may, with the blessing of God, see you in the course of next summer.

"What may be my future plan of life is still more uncertain; but if I am fortunate enough to reach England alive, I am certain that no inducement shall ever lead me to revisit India. I have already passed nearly thirty years of my life in the Company's service, and have always been placed in situations of so much responsibility, that my mind has always been on the stretch, and never without some serious anxiety.

"I naturally look forward to retirement, when these anxieties may cease, and I can enjoy that serenity which is above all things necessary for the peace and comfort of this life. Accustomed, however, to activity, and necessarily to habits of business, I am aware that I cannot be idle and happy at the same time, and therefore I shall be ready to enter with some degree of zeal upon any pursuits that appear to promise eventual satisfaction.

"I enclose you a copy of the address presented to me by the merchants of Singapore, on the occasion of my resigning charge of that Settlement, preparatory to my proceeding to Europe, and hope that, in the pledge which I gave them, of the *permanency* of the freedom of the Port, without dues or restrictions of any kind, I shall be supported and borne out by the authorities at home. I cannot but think that we have now taken too firm a root at Singapore, to render it even possible that it should be delivered over to the Dutch. . . .

"I notice what you say regarding the publication of some account of the establishment of Singapore, with a map annexed, and thank you for the hint. I have little to say on the subject, more than has been repeated over and over again in my official dispatches, though perhaps in different words; but as these are likely to moulder away in Leadenhall Street, without perhaps being twice read, it may be useful should I attempt a more public exposition of my sentiments and views. Indeed, after what has taken place, and particularly with reference to the extraordinary assertion of Lord Bathurst as to the nature of my appointment, something of a public nature will be required from me; and although I am far from wishing to obtrude myself or my proceedings on the public, I feel confident, that the more my conduct is investigated and known, the more credit will at any rate be given to my motives; that that, in this point of view, I have rather an inducement to publish than otherwise.

"Should, therefore, my health admit, I shall probably devote a few hours in the day, during the voyage home, to condense into a convenient space what I think may be interesting on the subject, to be revised after my arrival in England, according to circumstances. It is not my wish, any more than my interest, to run counter to the authorities that be; but, as a public man, I hardly know how I can pass over the direful sacrifices made by Lord Castlereagh without remark. My sole object, in a political point of view, is to do justice to the cause I have undertaken, and I think it only requires to be fairly and honestly stated, to make its way wherever it is known. . . .

"You will hardly believe, that at the close of my administration of that Settlement, I received the unreserved approbation of the Government of Bengal of all the measures of a public nature that I had adopted. I have, however, been opposed throughout in establishing the *freedom* of the

Port, and anything like a liberal code of management, and not only by the Penang Government, but also in Bengal. The Bengal merchants, or rather one or two of them, whom I could name, would have preferred the old system, by which they might have monopolized the early resources of the place, and thus checked its progress to importance. My views have been more enlarged, and as the authorities at home have fortunately not interfered with the details, I have taken upon myself to widen the base, and to look to a more important superstructure. I have given the place something like a constitution, a representative body, and fashioned all my regulations more with reference to the pure principles of the British constitution, than upon the *half-cast*[*e*], *or country-born* regulations of our Indian administration, which, however well they may be suited to the circumstances of continental India, are altogether inapplicable to the state of society in the Eastern Islands. This has brought upon me what may be called a local opposition-party in Bengal, and I must be content to look for the just appreciation of my views and plans rather in England than India. . . ."

And next day to Dr Raffles:

"Sophia about two months ago presented me with another girl which will help to supply the melancholy blank in our domestic circle. The child is extremely healthy and doing remarkably well, but I regret to say Sophia herself has since been attacked by a very severe fever from which she is only slowly recovering. This circumstance, added to the state of my own health, makes me extremely anxious to quit a place where we can look back with so little satisfaction or forward with so little confidence. . . .

"I have heard nothing more of the question with the Dutch, but I doubt not that it will be agitated on my arrival in England. I rely more upon the support of the Mercantile Community than upon any liberal views of the Ministry by whom I have been opposed as much throughout as by the Dutch. Of this place I have nothing at present very particular to communicate or that will not as conveniently be left for personal intercourse, but it will be satisfactory to you to know that we are doing wonders with our schools and that our Bible Society is not inactive: the two Missionaries whom we have here, Messrs Robinson and Ward, are very zealous; and Reports are now framing to be laid before the General Meeting on the 1st of January, which will, I hope, prove that we have not been inactive; and that the results are as great as we could rationally have expected in so short a time. . . ."

On 18th May 1820 an examination of the pupils had been held in the presence of the native chiefs and the parents, and twenty-two prizes—pieces of velvet or chintz—distributed among the first and second pupils in each of the eight classes who most distinguished themselves in reading, writing and spelling. The success thus achieved had encouraged Raffles to advocate (7th August 1820) classes for children of appropriate ages in simple technical subjects, so as to assist them to obtain a respectable livelihood on leaving school. Carpentry, joinery, braziery, mat-making and pottery were the crafts he had suggested.

The success achieved by Robinson and Ward, notwithstanding the great scarcity of school-books and other handicaps, had been so considerable that not only had donations of rice to encourage attendance no longer been necessary, but it had been found possible to charge a small fee. The Supreme Government had recorded its "cordial approbation" of the proposal "to extend the means of Instruction to the inferior classes of the Native Community in the immediate vicinity of Fort Marlborough". His Excellency in Council had given thought to "the practicability of a further diffusion of the advantages of Education on the Island of Sumatra" discussed by the Bencoolen committee "with great ability zeal and intelligence", yet, while the prospect was "interesting", no expense beyond that already agreed to for the enlargement of the Caffre school in Bencoolen itself could be approved; and now that rice was no longer required as "an indispensable enticement to attendance" no more such donations should be authorized!

Robinson and Ward had reported in September 1821 that, with the help of Church funds:

"Native schools have been established in the bazaars of the Settlement and in most of the villages in its vicinity; several of the boys from the parent school have been employed in these as monitors and teachers, and have proved valuable assistants in introducing the system of education."

They had put forward at the same time a proposal to extend the advantages of education "to the descendants of Europeans who are many of them hidden from superficial observation by their conformity to the natives in dress, habits and manners, and who being viewed as outcasts by all parties are left to vegetate spontaneously in the depravity of human nature, exposed to the action of the ignorance, vice and superstition which surround them". They had then pointed out that they could not furnish money to meet this extension; they were already dipping too heavily into their Church funds and could not continue to do so. If Raffles came to any decision, it is not now to be discovered, but one suspects that the demands for the strictest financial stringency prevented this extension of education, laudable as the proposal had been.

A second volume of the *Malayan Miscellanies*, printed by Ward, had been published in 1822. A third volume was projected, but, as Raffles himself anticipated, it was never published. His own absence in Singapore and the death of Dr Jack, who, under Raffles, had been the moving spirit, offer sufficient explanation.

We return to Raffles' letter to his cousin.

"Considerable interest", he continued, "has lately been excited by the progress in Sumatra of the Mahomedan sect, usually termed the Padries, or more particularly the Putcho [*Puteh*] or Whites, in opposition to the Elaws[1] or Blacks, by which latter term they designate all who do not embrace their doctrine.

"It was to the ravages of these people that I alluded in my account of the journey to Menangkabu, as having repeatedly pillaged and burnt the capital of that celebrated seat of the Malay empire; and it is with them that the Dutch, since their occupation of Padang, have been involved in a desperate and relentless war, neither party giving quarter, and prices being set upon the heads of the principal Chiefs. The first notice of this powerful sect, which had its origin near Mount Ophir, was about ten years ago; but it has been during the last three, and principally since the occupation of Padang by the Dutch, that it has become formidable, and occasioned alarm for the safety of the European Settlements on the west coast of Sumatra.

"The policy of the British Government has hitherto been that of neutrality, considering that the question related principally to peculiar doctrines of Mahomedanism, in which the natives might be best left to themselves: but the success of the Padries during the last year, in which they have overrun nearly the whole of the rich and populous countries of the interior, has at length called for measures of decision even on the part of the British authorities. A considerable force was detached from Bengal in September last, direct to Nattal; and measures are in progress for the adoption of offensive operations, should negotiation fail. The tenets of the Padries require, that all Mahomedans shall refrain from the use of opium, from cock-fighting, and other Malayan vices—that they should wear a peculiar dress, and submit to ecclesiastical authority. The Malays, who form the population of the coast districts, are averse to this change, as altering their habits, and departing from their native customs; and the European Governments are actually employed in protecting them against the improvement which would necessarily follow from their adoption of the tenets of the Padries.

"It is not to be denied that, with people of so low a state of civilization as those in the interior of Sumatra must be, success will too often make them wanton; and that their practice is frequently inconsistent with their doctrines—this is naturally expected—and the love of plunder and thirst of revenge over those who are obstinate in resisting them is too often predominant.

"The resources of these people seem considerable; and their engage-

[1] The word appears thus in the *Memoir*, evidently a misprint for Etams. The Malay word for "black" is, as now spelt, *hitam*.

ments with the Dutch have taught them to know their own strength. Their power in the interior of Sumatra may now be considered as completely established, and various speculations are formed as to the result.

"We thus see one of the finest islands in the world, on which we have had Establishments for upwards of a century, without once venturing to improve the condition of the people, or to send one Christian Missionary among them, giving way before the desolating influence of the false prophet of Mecca, and becoming rapidly a strong Mahomedan resting ground, with our eyes open, and with scarcely one effort made by ourselves to oppose them by a purer faith. The Missionaries we have lately employed in Sumatra are too few in number to do much. That they will do good, as far as their influence reaches, there can be no doubt; but that influence will long be limited to our immediate Stations, unless we increase their numbers. Instead of three missionaries, we ought to have three hundred; and the object of these three hundred should be to initiate three thousand of the natives to act as Missionaries in the interior. There are yet hundreds of thousands, perhaps millions in Sumatra, who at this moment possess no religion at all, among whom we *may* include the Battas. The Padries are now on their very borders, with the Koran in one hand and the sword in the other; and the only Missionary whom we have is an isolated individual, residing under the protection of the British Factory at Tappanooly, but who has not the means of penetrating into the interior. This individual, however (Mr Burton), has translated part of the Scriptures into the Batta language, and his success in this respect is highly praiseworthy to his application and character; but alone he can do little beyond the influence of his own Factory, which does not extend one mile inland. . . .[1]

"It would be useful to draw public attention to this subject now, particularly as it has excited much interest in India; and is the only cause likely to detain me here longer than I could wish. I cannot well leave the coast till some decisive measure is adopted: and yet in politics who can see the end? My desire is to avoid all involvement as much as possible; and if our measures are likely to be of a protracted nature, I shall not think of waiting the issue."

There was still no precise news as to when the *Fame* might be expected to arrive, and as the number of deaths in the settlement continued to rise, anxiety grew daily more acute. From Pĕrmatang Balam, Raffles wrote to a friend, probably Peter Auber, on 23rd November:

"This is a most melancholy day. One of my last letters informed you of the death of poor Drummond after a few hours' illness; one of the Mr Days died about the same time. Two days ago Mr Halhed was carried

[1] Both Richard Burton and his wife, "after having laboured diligently for several years, and succeeded in establishing schools . . . fell a sacrifice to the climate" (*Memoir*).

off; and I have just received information that my dear and valuable friend Salmond is no more.

"This last blow has been almost too much for us, for Salmond was as dear and intimate with us as our own family. I have just opened his will, and find he has nominated me as his sole executor in the following words:—'I appoint my *only* friend Sir Stamford Raffles to be my executor, and I pray to God he will take charge of my estate and children.' The loss of poor Salmond is quite a death-blow to the Settlement. How is it that all those we love and esteem, all those whose principles we admire, and in whom we can place confidence, are thus carried off, while the vile and worthless remain?

"Sophia is recovering slowly from her late illness, but she has suffered severely. I am much the same in health, but we are both low in spirits. Would that a ship had come out as I wrote for direct, that we might have been off!

"We have as yet heard nothing of the 'Fame', nor is there any opportunity besides her likely to offer."

Three more letters continued the tragic chronicle. The first was to Wallich, 24th November.

"You will grieve to hear that we have just lost our worthy, inestimable friend Captain Salmond; he is the second in our family, and the fourth in our small society who has paid the debt of nature within the last month! Would to God we were ourselves fairly out of the place! Sophia recovers but very slowly from her late dangerous illness, and these events cast a sad melancholy gloom over everything. I write these few lines at her very particular request, to remind you of my picture. Whether I go home or not, I must, if Lady Raffles survives, send her home by an early opportunity."

The second was also to Wallich, 10th December.

"We are, I am sorry to say, in great distress, having lost several friends during the last month, but the worst of all has been the loss of our only remaining child in this country, at a time when Lady Raffles was herself dangerously ill with fever. The shock has been too much for us, and I hardly expect she will get over it. We have indeed been severely afflicted, and what is worse, we are both so ill ourselves that neither of us dare quit the room. . . ."

The third was to an unknown correspondent, 20th December.

"You will grieve to hear that we have had another affliction in the loss of our dear babe, whose birth I formerly announced.

"She was carried off very suddenly, and at a moment when we were least prepared to meet such a shock. The death of poor Mr Drummond, besides several other deaths in the Settlement, has cast a gloom over everything, and Sophia was but very slowly recovering from a severe inflammatory fever which nearly proved fatal. The loss of an infant only a few months old is one of those things which in itself might soon be got over, knowing how uncertain life is at that period, but this loss of our fourth and only remaining child in India has revived all former afflictions, and been almost too much for us. Fortunately Sophia's fever has not returned since the event, and upon the whole she is in better health than she was preceding, but she has not yet left the house; her spirits, as well as my own, are completely broken, and most anxious are we to get away from such a charnel-house, but here we are detained for want of an opportunity. How often do we wish the 'Fame' had come out direct—we might have saved this last misfortune—but we have neither seen nor heard of her, and God only knows when the day of our deliverance will arrive. Either I must go to England or by remaining in India *die*. . . .

ii

After Raffles had left Singapore, Farquhar had sent him a long letter in vindication of his conduct.

"With reference to what you are pleased to remark as to your considering my appointment as Resident and Commandant of this Settlement to be of a temporary nature, I am altogether at a loss to understand what possible grounds you could have for drawing such a conclusion, since nothing contained in Mr Secretary Adam's letter to my address of the 28th November 1818, directing me to take charge of the British Interests in this quarter, appears to place the appointment on the footing implied by you, but to the contrary. In the said Letter, the Supreme Government are pleased in the manner the most gratifying to intimate to me that 'they have perused with some satisfaction and approbation the reports of my negotiations with the Chiefs of Rhio, Lingin and Siack, that it is the wish of His Lordship in Council to secure the benefit of my experience and talents in confirming and approving the relations thus established through my Agency and that His Lordship in Council therefore hopes that my arrangements will admit of my undertaking the charge proposed at least during the Infancy of the Settlement'.

"Surely then an appointment conferred by the highest Authority in British India under such flattering circumstances cannot be said to be merely of a temporary and transient nature, at least the period of its duration seems evidently to be left optional with myself, and therefore I never did or could have anticipated under such circumstances any sudden or peremptory ejectment from office without an adequate cause being assigned for the adoption of such a measure, and feeling as I do that my conduct in office will bear the strictest scrutiny, that nothing has been wanting on my part to advance the prosperity of this Settlement by every means in my power, that our Political and Commercial relations with all the surrounding Native States throughout the Eastern Archipelago, the Malay Peninsula, the Eastern coast of Sumatra, together with the kingdoms of Siam, Cambojia and Cochin China, have been supported, cultivated, and improved, both by extensive epistolatary correspondence as well as every other suitable and available means within my reach to which circumstances may in a great measure be attributed the origin of that extensive commerce, which is now carried on at this Settlement, whilst at the same time the establishment generally during the period I have had the honour to direct its affairs, has attained to a height in population, wealth and general prosperity I may venture to say quite unrivalled.

"I must, of course, acknowledge that it appears by the Resolution of the Governor-General in Council of the 21st March last that I am relieved from my Duties here in consequence of a tender of resignation made by me in the month of October 1820, but having in two subsequent letters to your address intimated my wish to cancel the aforesaid application, and from the length of time which had elapsed since the date thereof, I could not consider the intimation alluded to in any other light than that of a Dead Letter. I therefore can only attribute the measure of the Governor-General in Council in relieving me either to an ignorance of my real intentions and wishes or that clandestine misrepresentations have been made to my prejudice which have tended to deprive me of that confidence and good opinion of Government which I have so long had the honour and happiness to enjoy. . . .

"In conclusion I must profess my entire ignorance of the nature and extent of the responsibility which you represent as falling on you unless it be with respect to your own immediate measures for which as a matter of course you must be held accountable. Saving these I am not aware of any you have unburthened me of and I may in this place, I trust, be permitted to observe that had a more mature, deliberate, judicious and economical System been pursued in the late arrangements for laying out the Town and native campongs, &c, the ultimate advantages derivable to the community would have been at least equal to what they now are, whilst the very heavy expense which has been so profusely and hastily incurred on account of indemnifications, &c, to individuals for the removal of their Houses might in a great measure have been rendered quite unnecessary."

As far as can be ascertained, this remained unanswered—indeed it seems improbable that Raffles would have thought it worth a reply. Nothing shows Farquhar in a clearer light than this letter. It was the free-port policy that had made Singapore the remarkable success it was, not the "extensive epistolatary correspondence" of Farquhar to the wide range of countries he listed. Nor would the expensive resettlement of the population have been necessary had Farquhar, during three and a half years as Resident, taken more trouble to plan the settlement's development. At the same time, one cannot help but feel sorry for Farquhar. The task had been quite beyond his capacity, but he had no doubt done his best according to his lights. Raffles was unquestionably sorry for him. As he wrote to Wallich in his letter of 1st November:

"God knows I have had but one object in view—the interests of Singapore—and if a brother had been opposed to them, I must have acted as I did towards Colonel Farquhar, for whom I ever had and still do retain a warm personal affection and regard. I upheld him as long as I could and many were the sacrifices I made to prevent a rupture, but when it did take place I found it necessary to prosecute my cause with vigour and effect."

Farquhar remained in Singapore until the end of the year, occupied, one supposes, in bringing the correspondence books of the Residency up to date. When the time for his departure drew near there was, according to 'Abdullah, some difference of opinion among the merchants of Singapore as to whether or not he should be presented with a piece of plate and testimonials. Fortunately better counsels prevailed, and at a meeting of the inhabitants held on 27th December "it was resolved that on the approaching departure of Lieutenant-Colonel Farquhar it is our anxious wish to mark our sense of his private worth and uniform kindness and hospitality during the period of his Residence at Singapore by requesting his acceptance of a piece of plate of the value of three thousand sicca rupees". 'Abdullah has described his departure:

"So when Colonel Farquhar had dressed and eaten in his house, he embarked in a ketch and thousands of people followed him from his house to the sea shore, each and every one bidding him goodbye and offering their respects; and in receiving each he was detained two hours before he could get into the vessel, his tears flowing. He then took off his hat and bid them goodbye, this four or five times to the crowd. Hundreds of prows that were waiting now followed him with loud acclamations. This astonished him so much that he bent himself down. The people in the prows now fired cannons, guns and crackers, some sang, some fiddled, each to their notion—the Chinese in the fashion of Chinese, the Malays in the fashion of Malays, the Klings[1] in the fashion

[1] "The name given by the Malays and Javanese to the Telinga nation of southern India, and which appears to be a corruption or abbreviation of the genuine name of the country of this people, Kalinga. Being the only Indian nation familiarly known to the nations of the Archipelago, the word is used by them as a general term for all the people of Hindustan, and for the country itself." Crawfurd, *Descriptive Dictionary*.

They were known to Europeans as Chuliahs.

of Klings—making the whole sea resound. This went on till he had arrived at the ship, which he ascended. The prows now surrounded the ship and the crews now also boarded to say goodbye. He received each with kind words which consoled them, counselling them with much eloquence. The appearance of the scene was as a father amongst his children, till all were weeping; he wept also."

"Sĕlamat!"[1] they cried. "Sail with a good wind that you may arrive at your country to see your parents and relatives! Sĕlamat again! Long life to you that you may come back to be our Governor!"

Then Farquhar left Singapore. He made a short stay at Malacca, where, according to the *Prince of Wales's Island Gazette*, he was well received.

"At Malacca, where he had formerly been Governor for the long period of nearly twenty years, we are happy to hear he was received and welcomed by the authorities of the Netherlands Government under the Salute due to his Rank and with the most distinguished respect. The Inhabitants of every description recollecting his many private and amiable virtues and his long, equitable and paternal rule over them evinced the most cordial regard and attachment to him."

A very friendly reception awaited him also at Penang, perhaps none the less warm because it was known that he had been dismissed by Raffles. When he re-embarked for Calcutta on 20th January in his ship *Alexander*, a salute was fired from the fort and he was "accompanied to the beach by the Governor [Phillips] and staff, Commander of the Forces, the officers of the 20th Regiment N.I. and the principal gentlemen of the Settlement".

iii

The British Government was sincerely anxious to achieve a final settlement with the Dutch, and a correspondence was still passing between the Board of Control and the Secret Committee to clarify the British case. For example, the Secret Committee wrote to Canning on 24th December 1823:

"We concur generally in the tone of the Committee's letter of September 20th, 1820, but so long a period has elapsed since then that the negotiations may almost be deemed to commence *de novo*. . . . With regard to the conduct of the Dutch . . . they do not relax in their efforts to engross the trade of the Archipelago whilst . . . the forcible seizure of the regalia of Johore by the officers of the Netherlands Government at Rhio evinces a spirit entirely at variance with the profession contained in the note of the Dutch plenipotentiaries of August 1820."

On 2nd January 1824 Charles Watkins Williams Wynn, now president of the Board of Control, wrote to the Secret Committee in regard

[1] "Farewell!"

to its proposal that a line of demarcation between the Dutch and English spheres of influence should be drawn from north to south through the Straits of Malacca and between Singapore and Rhio.

"Are we", asked Wynn, "to be precluded of any settlement South of the line to be drawn between Singapore and Rhio and how far is that line to extend Northward and Eastward?"

It would be very dangerous, he considered, to leave such vast territories open to Dutch expansion. In regard to the exchange of Bencoolen, the value of Bencoolen lay not so much in what the Company would lose as in what the Dutch would gain. In political value Bencoolen would be much more important to the Dutch than anything they might be willing to cede us in Malaya.

Negotiations were reopened soon afterwards, Great Britain now being represented by Canning and Wynn, and the Netherlands by van Nagell and Falck. It had been Falck's ambition to take a leading part in the Anglo-Dutch negotiations.

"From the moment", he wrote, "that Elout had obliged the King in taking over the Finance Department, I had set my heart on going to London in his place when the time should have come to resume the negotiation ssuspended in 1820. . . . It roused my ambition to be the signatory of a treaty which would settle so many outstanding interests on fair terms. I did not doubt in the least the possibility of bringing about such a treaty in spite of all that people round about me told me and proclaimed about the imperious character of the English, especially in Colonial matters, about their jealousy of our growing trade, about the impression which the reports of Raffles—hostile to the Dutch—had made, &c. . . ."

Falck's original idea had been a general exchange of territories. He had had in mind that Penang might be transferred to the Dutch, but had been warned by Fagel that the British attached great value to Penang and that there would not be the slightest chance of their giving it up. This had become even slighter when, through the "neglect of our people to occupy Singapore", the British had gained also this fresh settlement in the Straits of Malacca. He fully appreciated, too, the extent to which public opinion in Great Britain had been roused, mentioning Assey's pamphlet as one of the contributory causes. Falck was quite convinced in his own mind that no settlement was possible unless England retained Singapore. His difficulty had been to mould public opinion in Holland to the acceptance of that unpleasant fact.

Accordingly, the delay had been welcome to both sides. From Falck's point of view, it had given his compatriots time to get used to the idea that Singapore would necessarily remain in British hands; from the British point of view, it had given time for Singapore to establish its intrinsic value. The only question, therefore, was the price to be paid.

Here difficulties arose. The British case for a comprehensive settlement in the East included a demand for a cash payment by Holland of £100,000 to cover the period when Java had been administered by Britain. Canning was quick to realize that nothing is more difficult in international negotiations than to secure payment of cash. As he wrote to Courtenay, secretary of the Board of Control:

"I have according to your desire pencilled a few observations in the margin of your paper. You will perceive by the general tenor of them I am very desirous to conclude. I wish on that account (I profess) that a pecuniary claim should not be pushed too hard because I know of no difficulty in negotiation so great as obtaining payment of money; if we make our claims so high that we must insist upon them, I fear the whole may go off without settlement. Would it not be better than this to conclude the political part and leave the pecuniary as was once intended to a commission? (Of which I beg not to be one.) But Falck's objection appears to be not to paying much but to paying at all. If this be so, may he not be driven 'ad absurdum' in so stating it, by leaving off to combat him upon items, letting him assign pretty much his own balances, and then driving him to say in what terms he thinks it possible for a British negotiator to say that he will not ask to be paid? We may be conscious of a claim and yet not press it: that is intelligible, but to abandon a claim admitted to be well founded in so many words, and still more to make a treaty for the express purpose of recording our abandonment of it, would be a degree of complaisance such as no individual or nation has ever exacted of another. This I think is our main difficulty and our situation is one altogether whimsical. We have a good claim of money and a doubtful one (to say the least) of territory. We carry our doubtful case and are foiled upon our clear one."

Prolonged argument between the plenipotentiaries followed.

iv

"We have entered the New Year," wrote Raffles from Bencoolen on 4th January, "and as yet no account of the 'Fame'. You can hardly imagine to yourself the serious disappointment to all our hopes and plans which this occasions. We begin to think we are doomed to end our days here and there is something like a spell upon our movements. After Sophia's severe illness and our last affliction, the delay of a day is most serious, and night and day we cannot help regretting that you have not assured a ship on the strength of my letter to you. I relied exclusively on what you would do, and still have no other hope than that the 'Fame' will be in time to save our lives, though we have very little confidence that this will be the case."

Sophia, in quoting this letter in the *Memoir*, described it as "To ——". There is good reason to believe that it was Peter Auber, assistant secretary to the Company. This omission to take out an insurance in England, for Raffles could not do it in Bencoolen, meant that his property, valued at something over £25,000, would be shipped at owner's risk.

Shortly after this the little *Borneo* arrived at Bencoolen to load pepper for England. She was really too small and too inconveniently constructed for Raffles and his party, but, despairing of the *Fame* ever arriving, he decided to charter the *Borneo* as the sole means of getting home. Just before the arrangements were completed, the *Fame* appeared, which was considered at the time a very fortunate circumstance. Events were to prove otherwise: the *Borneo* was to make a safe passage to England; the *Fame* was to suffer disaster.

There was now intense activity while all the collection was loaded, and the *Fame* was made ready to take home Raffles, his wife, her brother, little Charles Flint, and a certain Dr Bell.

"I have, before I embark," wrote Raffles to England on 14th January, "to wind up all my affairs.

"God grant that we may have a happy and satisfactory meeting in old England, for which I may in truth say my heart yearneth much indeed and sadly.

"We are such poor creatures, that, like the aspen leaf, we shake with every breath of air, and are daily treading on the edge of eternity."

Recent news from Singapore was not very satisfactory. There was reason to think that Crawfurd was inclined to try to belittle the work Raffles had done there. The two had never got on very well together, and Crawfurd was perhaps jealous of Raffles. Now the impetuous Flint had managed to get at loggerheads with Crawfurd, just as he had done with Farquhar. Raffles referred to this in a farewell letter to Mary Anne, written on 17th January.

"I am sorry Crawfurd does not give as much satisfaction as I could have wished, and that he is not superior to the influence of personal feelings in his public administration. I never placed much confidence in his judgment or experience, but I hoped from his *public* professions that he would have taken a different course. . . . Above all things I beseech you not to let Flint have any personal quarrel or discussion with him—on whatever subject it may be, you may be certain of one thing that it will end in Flint's discomfiture. . . . He is dealing with one who will not give him fair play—but it cannot be helped. . . . Look forward to better times—he is now in office and may mend, at all events Mrs Crawfurd's attention to you deserves our acknowledgement and I hope her influence will keep him within decent bounds. . . .

"And now my dear Pussy I must say Good-bye. I am about to separate from you to a great distance but I will neither forget you nor love you the less. . . . My wish is that you should all consider yourselves as still under my protection. I have not deserted Singapore, and never will, and perhaps one day when you least expect it better luck may happen to the place than any of you dream of."

On 30th January, three days before they sailed, Raffles wrote a long letter to the Court of Directors. It resulted from a refusal to allow his claims for (*a*) salary for the years 1816–18, and (*b*) discount on paper money on termination of his services in Java. The Court had called for a refund of these amounts drawn on Government at Bencoolen. In anticipation of the need to reach a settlement on arrival home, he now wrote:

"Previous to the close of my Administration on these Islands and the ultimate adjustment of my *Accounts*, I feel it to be a duty which I owe to myself and my family once more to bring to your notice the hardship and apparent injustice to which the operation of the Orders of the Supreme Government under your Authority is calculated to subject me with regard to my personal Allowances and the absolute loss that will accrue to me unless a more liberal and considerate view is taken of the peculiar circumstances of the case."

He argued that, at the time of his appointment as Lieutenant-Governor of Java, Lord Minto had stated that the salary allotted to the post, which was equivalent to that of the Governor of Penang, was inadequate. Daendels and Janssens had each received a salary of two lacs of rupees (200,000) per annum. His own salary had not only been substantially less, but had been further reduced in two ways: half had been paid in Bengal at an exchange of two rupees to the Spanish dollar, whereas the actual rate was two and a quarter to the Spanish dollar, while the balance had been paid in Java in the form of treasury notes, which had been frequently at a discount of from fifteen to twenty per cent. He conceded that the payment of his salary in Bengal had been at his own wish, "but then it had to be recollected that I was forced to obtain extensive supplies from Bengal and was compelled either to accept such terms as the Governor-General in Council might think proper to grant, or to enter the market at Batavia as a competitor for Bills when I required them". This latter method had been, he submitted, clearly inadvisable.

"In the negotiations with the public for the extensive supplies of cash required in exchange for Bills on Bengal to be drawn by myself at such rates as I deemed most advisable, I considered it essential to the purity of my Administration that in a Department so open to abuse there should not exist the slightest ground on which the shadow of a doubt could be cast where personal interests were for a moment concerned."

The Supreme Government had pointed out "that the same means were open to me for obtaining remuneration for the loss I experienced in receiving Paper at a discount as was allowed to others" and that no subsequent claims could be admitted. It was true that private persons could have kept the notes as an investment, but he had been constantly compelled to spend most of them just as soon as he had received them, "and though I might have availed myself of the mode of compensation with regard to the remainder which was granted to Mr Hope and others . . . I felt a diffidence in taking advantage for my own personal benefit of a Regulation which I had deemed it just to make in favour of others".

"The unfortunate circumstances under which I was relieved of the Government of Java made me more particular in this respect than I otherwise might have been and I was reluctant to bring any further claim forward before my Successor at the moment of my departure. I relied so fully upon a liberal consideration of the Supreme Government and on the justice of my Claim that I thought it sufficient to state the facts and transmit the necessary certificates to the Supreme Government in order to obtain the compensation due."

As regarded the drawing of his allowances as Resident of Bencoolen before he reached there, he based his claim on "the resolution of the Governor-General in Council and the letter from Mr Secretary Ricketts communicating my appointment in which it is expressly stated that I am to be entitled to draw the allowances of Resident of Bencoolen from the date at which I shall cease to draw those of Lieut.-Governor of Java". This arrangement had been expressly made by Lord Minto in view of the heavy expenses Raffles had incurred in Java, and was to secure him from loss when he quitted the island. When he had first applied for the allowance, Lord Minto had expressed himself perfectly satisfied with the justice of the claim and had stated that he would commend it to the favourable notice of the Court.

"The objection which is so forcibly stated as a bar to what I consider my just due in this instance, namely my having proceeded to Europe in the interim, which act by the provisions of the Legislature for the management of the Company's Territories in India is considered an absolute avoidance of Office and Salary . . . cannot legally be considered to apply to possessions altogether beyond the limits of their Charter, and to possessions held entirely on a political and provisional basis. It cannot be held that the laws and regulations of the Company for British India could apply to Dutch India."

He therefore appealed for an enlightened view of his case, and hoped for a "more favourable and satisfactory decision".

It can be added here that of the £1,500 paid out for the voyage in the *Lady Raffles* from England, the Company had refused to allow more than £1,000, so the balance of £500 had to be borne by Raffles.

At last all was ready. Raffles' collections and valuables, all uninsured, occupied nearly a third of the *Fame*, which carried also a cargo of saltpetre. Ill-health had prevented Captain Mackenzie from succeeding Raffles at Bencoolen, so the settlement was transferred to the charge of John Prince. There was the usual public address presented by the residents, after which Raffles and Sophia embarked, thankful to think they were saying farewell to the place where four of their children and many of their friends lay buried. With forty-one souls and an assortment of live animals aboard her the *Fame* sailed at daybreak on 2nd February, with a fair wind and every prospect of a quick and comfortable passage to England. Let Raffles tell the story of what befell. Two days later, he wrote:

"The ship was everything we could wish; and having closed my charge here much to my satisfaction, it was one of the happiest days of my life. We were, perhaps, too happy; for in the evening came a sad reverse. Sophia had just gone to bed, and I had thrown off half my clothes, when a cry of fire, fire! roused us from our calm content, and in five minutes the whole ship was in flames! I ran to examine whence the flames principally issued, and found that the fire had its origin immediately under our cabin. Down with the boats. Where is Sophia?—Here. The children?—Here. A rope to the side. Lower Lady Raffles. Give her to me, says one; I'll take her, says the Captain. Throw the gunpowder overboard. It cannot be got at; it is in the magazine close to the fire. Stand clear of the powder. Scuttle the water-casks. Water! water! Where's Sir Stamford? Come into the boat, Nilson! Nilson, come into the boat. Push off, push off. Stand clear of the after part of the ship.

"All this passed much quicker than I can write it; we pushed off, and as we did so, the flames burst out of our cabin-window, and the whole of the after part of the ship was in flames; the masts and sails now taking fire, we moved to a distance sufficient to avoid the immediate explosion; but the flames were now coming out of the main hatchway; and seeing the rest of the crew, with the Captain, still on board, we pulled back to her under the bows, so as to be more distant from the powder. As we approached we perceived that the people on board were getting into another boat on the opposite side. She pushed off; we hailed her: Have you all on board? Yes, all, save one. Who is he?—Johnson, sick in his cot. Can we save him?—No, impossible. The flames were issuing from the hatchway; at this moment the poor fellow, scorched, I imagine, by the flames, roared out most lustily, having run up on the deck. I will go for him, says the Captain. The two boats then came together, and we took out some of the persons from the Captain's boat, which was overladen; he then pulled under the bowsprit of the ship, and picked the poor fellow up. Are we all safe?—Yes, we have got the man; all lives safe. Thank God! Pull off from the ship. Keep your eye on a star, Sir Stamford. There's one scarcely visible.

Loss of the *Fame*

"We then hauled close to each other, and found the Captain fortunately had a compass, but we had no light except from the ship. Our distance from Bencoolen we estimated to be about fifty miles in a south-west direction. There being no landing place to the southward of Bencoolen, our only chance was to regain that port. The Captain then undertook to lead, and we to follow, in a N.N.E. course, as well as we could; no chance, no possibility being left, that we could again approach the ship; for she was now one splendid flame, fore and aft, and aloft, her masts and sails in a blaze, and rocking to and fro, threatening to fall in an instant. There goes her mizen mast! Pull away, my boys! There goes the gunpowder! Thank God! thank God!

"You may judge of our situation without further particulars. The alarm was given at about twenty minutes past eight, and in less than ten minutes she was in flames: there was not a soul on board at half past eight, and in less than ten minutes afterwards she was one grand mass of fire.

"My only apprehension was the want of boats to hold the people, as there was not time to have got out the long-boat, or to make a raft. All we had to rely upon were two small quarter-boats, which fortunately were lowered without accident; and in these two small open boats, without a drop of water or grain of food, or a rag of covering, except what we happened at the moment to have on our backs, we embarked on the ocean, thankful to God for his mercies! Poor Sophia, having been taken out of her bed, had nothing on but a wrapper, neither shoes nor stockings; the children were just as taken out of bed, whence one had been snatched after the flames had attacked it; in short, there was no time for any one to think of more than two things. Can the ship be saved?—No. Let us save ourselves, then. All else was swallowed up in one grand ruin.

"To make the best of our misfortune, we availed ourselves of the light from the ship to steer a tolerably good course towards the shore. She continued to burn till about midnight, when the saltpetre she had on board took fire, and sent up one of the most splendid and brilliant flames that ever was seen, illuminating the horizon in every direction, to an extent of not less than fifty miles, and casting that kind of blue light over us, which is of all others most horrible. She burnt and continued to flame in this style for about an hour or two, when we lost sight of the object in a cloud of smoke.

"Neither Nilson nor Mr Bell, our medical friend who had accompanied us, had saved their coats; but the tail of mine, with a pocket-handkerchief, served to keep Sophia's feet warm, and we made breeches for the children with our neckcloths. Rain now came on, but fortunately it was not of long continuance, and we got dry again. The night became serene and star-light: we were now certain of our course, and the men behaved manfully; they rowed incessantly, and with good heart and spirit, and never did poor mortals look out more for day-light and for land than we did; not that our sufferings or grounds of complaint were anything to what has befallen others; but from Sophia's delicate health, as well as my own, and the stormy nature of our coast, I felt perfectly convinced we were unable to undergo starvation and exposure to sun and weather many days, and aware of the rapidity of the currents, I feared we might fall to the southward of the port.

"At day-light we recognized the coast and Rat Island, which gave us great spirits; and though we found ourselves much to the southward of the port, we considered ourselves almost at home. Sophia had gone through the night better than could have been expected, and we continued to pull on with all our strength. About eight or nine we saw a ship standing to us from the Roads; they had seen the flames on shore, and sent out vessels to our relief; and here certainly came a minister of Providence in the character of a minister of the Gospel, for the first person I recognized was one of our Missionaries. They gave us a bucket of water and we took the Captain on board as pilot. The wind, however, was adverse, and we could not reach the shore, and took to the ship, where we got some refreshment and shelter from the sun. By this time Sophia was quite exhausted, fainting continually. About two o'clock we landed safe and sound, and no words of mine can do justice to the expressions of feeling, sympathy, and kindness with which we were hailed by every one. If any proof had been wanting, that my administration had been satisfactory here, we had it unequivocally from all; there was not a dry eye, and as we drove back to our former home, loud was the cry of 'God be praised'.

"But enough; and I will only add, that we are now greatly recovered, in good spirits, and busy at work getting ready-made clothes for present use. We went to bed at three in the afternoon, and I did not wake till six this morning. Sophia had nearly as sound a sleep, and, with the exception of a bruise or two, and a little pain in the bones from fatigue, we have nothing to complain of.

"The loss I have to regret, beyond all, is my papers and drawings—all my notes and observations, with memoirs and collections, sufficient for a full and ample history, not only of Sumatra, but of Borneo, and almost every other Island of note in these Seas;—my intended account of the establishment of Singapore—the history of my own administration;—Eastern grammars, dictionaries, and vocabularies;—and last, not least, a grand map of Sumatra, on which I have been employed since my arrival here, and on which, for the last six months, I had bestowed almost my whole undivided attention. This, however, was not all;—all my collections in natural history—all my splendid collection of drawings, upwards of *two thousand* in number—with all the valuable papers and notes of my friends, Arnold and Jack; and, to conclude, I will merely notice, that there was scarce an unknown animal, bird, beast, or fish, or an interesting plant, which we had not on board: a living tapir, a new species of tiger, splendid pheasants, &c, domesticated for the voyage; we were, in short, in this respect, a perfect Noah's ark.

"All, all has perished; but, thank God, our lives have been spared, and we do not repine.

"Our plan is to get another ship as soon as possible, and, I think, you may still expect us in July. There is a chance of a ship, called the 'Lady Flora', touching here on her way home, and there is a small ship in the Roads which may be converted into a packet, and take us home, as I have a Captain and crew at command.

"Make your minds easy about us, even if we should be later than you expected. No news will be good news."

Sophia wrote this in the *Memoir*:

"A striking proof of the attachment of those who had no longer any interested motive to influence them deserves to be recorded. After the boat which contained Sir Stamford and his family got within sight of the shore, the numerous little native craft, which were all in requisition at the moment, approached in every direction with great velocity, and the people put, without exception, this one question: 'Is the Tuan Besar (the great man) safe?' Receiving an affirmative answer, they darted off as if there was no other point of interest to them."

The loss of the *Fame* was reported by Raffles to the Court of Directors in a letter dated 8th February.

"The fire", he wrote in this, "had its origin in the store-room, immediately under the apartments occupied by myself and family, and was occasioned by the shameful carelessness of the steward going with a naked light to draw off brandy from a cask, which took fire; but I am bound to speak in the highest terms of the conduct of the Captain, officers, and ship's company, who spared no exertions to save the ship, and when that was found impracticable, to secure the lives of all on board, acting throughout with the utmost coolness and self-possession which such a moment would admit of."

Of the crew, Sophia had to say:

"When Sir Stamford first got into the boat, and they were requested to move to a little distance, a slight murmur took place at the idea of deserting their comrades, but on being assured that the only object was to choose the easiest death, they one and all yielded in perfect silence, and calmly watched the success of an effort to lower another boat; nor did they afterwards indulge in any complaint, but toiled with the greatest good humour, sometimes laughing at the Purser and the Steward, on whom they laid the blame of the accident; sometimes expressing pity for '*the lady*', and comforting themselves with the idea that *they* were not much worse off than they were before. When the boat approached the shore, they entreated that they might be indulged in the pleasure of landing the party in safety, only requesting first—to have some water; and when a large bucket full was lowered from the side of the vessel which came to meet the boats, the eager rush with which they plunged their heads into it will easily be imagined when it is recollected that they had been working for eighteen hours, without intermission, against a strong current, and in a tropical climate. Some idea may be formed of the danger which the boats were in, when it is stated that there was no handle to the rudder; and that the only way of stopping the aperture in the bottom of the boat was by one of the men keeping his thumb in it; as he often fell asleep and forgot his office, the water would rush in, and the boat was frequently nearly filled with water and in a sinking state. So crammed was it with people, that none of those who were not engaged in rowing could, during these many hours, move either hand or foot."

We returned to Raffles' report to the Court. After describing the catastrophe, he continued:

"Submitting, as it is my duty to do, with patient resignation to this awful dispensation of Providence, I make the following statement, not in the spirit of complaint, for I repine not, but simply as illustrative of my personal circumstances and prospects, as they stand affected by this dire and unlooked-for calamity.

"After a service of nearly thirty years, and the exercise of supreme authority as a Governor for nearly twelve years of that period, over the finest and most interesting, but perhaps least known countries in creation, I had, as I vainly thought, closed my Indian life with benefit to my country, and satisfaction to myself; carrying with me such testimonials and information as I trusted would have proved that I had not been an unprofitable servant or a dilatory labourer in this fruitful and extensive vineyard.

"This lovely and highly interesting portion of the globe had, politically speaking, long sunk into insignificance from the withering effects of that baneful policy with which the Hollanders were permitted to visit these regions, when it fell to my lot to direct the course of the British arms to the Island of Java, and there on the ruins of monopoly, torture, and oppression, in all its shapes, to re-establish man in his native rights and prerogatives, and reopen the channel of an extensive commerce. Political events required our secession from that quarter, but the establishment of Singapore, and the reforms introduced on this coast, have no less afforded opportunities for the application and extension of the same principles.

"In the course of those measures, numerous and weighty responsibilities became necessary; the European world—the Indian world—(the continental part of it at least)—were wholly uninformed of the nature of these countries, their character, and resources. I did not hesitate to take these responsibilities as the occasion required them; and though from imperfect information many of my measures in Java were at first condemned, I had the satisfaction to find them in the end not only approved but applauded, far beyond my humble pretensions, and even by those who at first had been most opposed to me. I need refer to no stronger case than that of the Marquis of Hastings.

"During the last six years of my administration, and since I have ceased to have any concern in the affairs of Java, the situations in which I have been placed, and the responsibilities which I have been compelled to take in support of the interests of my country, and of my employers, have been, if possible, still greater than during my former career: I allude to the struggle which I have felt it my duty to make against Dutch rapacity and power, and to the difficulties that I had to contend with in the establishment of Singapore, and the reforms which have been effected on this coast.

"In addition to the opposition of avowed enemies to British power and Christian principles, I had to contend with deep-rooted prejudices, and the secret machinations of those who dared not to act openly; and standing alone, the envy of some and the fear of many, distant authorities were unable to form a correct estimate of my proceedings. Without local explanation some appeared objectionable, while party spirit and Dutch intrigue have never been wanting to discolour transactions and misrepresent facts.

"It was at the close of such an administration that I embarked with my family on the 'Fame', carrying with me endless volumes and papers of information on the civil and natural history of nearly every island within the Malayan Archipelago, collected at great expense and labour, under the most favourable circumstances, during a life of constant and active research, and in an especial manner calculated to throw light not only on the commercial and other resources of these islands, but to advance the state of natural knowledge and science, and finally to extend the civilization of mankind.

"These, with all my books, manuscripts, drawings, correspondence, records, and other documents, including tokens of regard from the absent, and memorials from the dead, have been all lost for ever in this dreadful conflagration; and I am left single and unaided, without the help of one voucher to tell my story, and uphold my proceedings, when I appear before your Honble Court.

"It has always appeared to me that the value of these countries was to be traced rather through the means of their natural history, than in the dark recesses of Dutch diplomacy and intrigue; and I accordingly, at all times, felt disposed to give encouragement to those deserving men who devote themselves to the pursuits of science. Latterly, when political interests seemed to require that I should, for a time, retire from the field, and there was little more to be done for this small Settlement, I have myself devoted a considerable portion of my time to these pursuits, and in forming extensive collections in natural history: my attention has also been directed in a particular manner to the geography of the Island of Sumatra.

"To be brief, I may sum up the collections and papers which I have had the misfortune to lose, under the following heads. They were carefully packed in no less than one hundred and twenty-two cases, independent of those for immediate reference, but which last are also lost, not one scrap of paper having been saved, or one duplicate left:—

"*Of Sumatra.*—A map on a large scale, constructed during a residence of six years, from observations made by myself and persons under my authority, European and native, calculated to exhibit, at one view, the real nature and general resources of the country, on a very different scale to what was formerly supposed; together with statistical reports, tables, memoirs, notices, histories of the Battas, and other original races, native and European vocabularies, dictionaries, and manuscripts in the different languages, contained in several cases.

"*Of Borneo.*—A detailed account of the former history, present state, population, and resources, of that long-neglected island, already drawn out to the extent of upwards of one thousand pages of writing, with numerous notes, sketches, details of the Dayak population, their government, customs, history, usages, &c, with notices of the different ports, their produce, and commercial resources.

"*Of Celebes.*—Nearly a similar account.

"And of *Java* and the *Moluccas.*—The whole of the voluminous history, as carefully abstracted from the Dutch archives while I was in Java, with careful translations of the most valuable native books, vocabularies, memoirs, and various papers intended principally to assist in a new edition of my History of Java.

"*Of Singapore.*—A detailed account of its establishment; the principles on which it is founded; the policy of our Government in founding it; the history of commerce in the Eastern Islands; its present state and prospects; the rapid rise of Singapore; its history until I gave over charge; with all the original documents connected with the discussion with the Dutch, and every voucher and testimony which could have been required to make good the British claim, and uphold the measures I had adopted.

"*In Natural History* the loss to myself and to science has been still greater. The choicest, the cream and flower of all my collections, I retained to take under my personal charge, together with the manuscripts and papers of my invaluable deceased friends, Drs Arnold and Jack. Among these also was that invaluable, and I may say, superb collection of drawings in natural history, executed under my immediate eye, and intended, with other interesting subjects of natural history, for the museum of the Honble Court. They exceeded in number two thousand; and having been taken from life, and with scientific accuracy, were executed in a style far superior to anything I had seen or heard of in Europe; in short, they were my pride: but as man has no business to be proud, it may be well that they are lost. Cases of plants, minerals, animals, &c, &c, I shall not name.

"Indeed it would be endless for me to attempt even a general description of all that has perished; and I will only add that, besides the above, all the papers connected with my administration of Java, as collected and arranged by my deceased friend and secretary, Mr Assey, have also been lost, with all my correspondence.

"A loss like this can never be replaced, but I bow to it without repining.

"In a pecuniary point of view, my loss has not been less extensive, as may be perceived by the annexed statement, in which I have assumed the actual cost of the principal articles which have been sacrificed. Most of them are what no money can replace: such as the service of plate presented to me by the inhabitants of Java; the diamonds presented to my family by the captors of Djocjocarta; the diamond ring presented to me by the Princess Charlotte on my embarkation for India, a week before her death. These and many other tokens of regard, friendship, and respect, during an active and varied life, can never be replaced. Money may compensate perhaps for other losses, but no insurance was, or could be, effected from home. It rests solely and exclusively with the Court to consider in how far my claims, on account of services, may be strengthened by the severity of misfortune which has latterly attached itself to my case.

"The anxiety and fatigue occasioned by the calamitous event which I have detailed have been such, that however much I may feel desirous, from motives of pecuniary necessity, to prolong my stay in India, in the hope of replacing, in part, some of the personal property which I have lost, I dare not look forward to such a measure, and I am under the necessity of taking advantage of the first opportunity that offers of proceeding to Europe, where I shall throw myself on your Honble Court to enable me to end my days in honourable retirement, trusting to an all-bounteous Providence to restore me and my family to health and peace in my native land.

"In the meantime I have thought it my duty to resume charge of the

Company's affairs on this coast, and have advised the Supreme Government accordingly.

"With a former letter I had the honour to submit a copy of the address which was presented to me on the occasion of my departure for Europe, with the reply which I have felt myself called upon to make on so favourable an expression of the public feeling; and it is now with satisfaction that I transmit, for the perusal of your Honble Court, the address of condolence which was presented to me on my unexpected return under such a sad reverse of fortune.

"In expressing my deepfelt gratitude to the inhabitants of this Settlement, for their sympathy in our sufferings, and genuine hospitality, I can only say, that having been thrown back on their shores most unexpectedly—We were naked, and they clothed us—hungry and athirst, and they fed us—weary and exhausted, and they comforted and consoled us; and I pray to God that your Honble Court, as the immediate guardian of their interests, will bless this land of Sumatra in return, even for their sakes."

He did not know that at that moment Bencoolen was in the process of being handed over to the Dutch.

His personal loss by the fire he estimated as between twenty and thirty thousand pounds. In a later letter (12th March) he stated that he had spent 10,666 rupees in refitting out himself and his family.

"In the amount of gold and jewels estimated, a considerable portion was intended by way of remittance and was in fact the property of others for whose estates I had of necessity become responsible."

"So heavy a misfortune", wrote Sophia, "was sufficient to have depressed the spirit and damped the ardour of the strongest mind; but it seemed to have no other effect on that of Sir Stamford than to rouse him to greater exertion. The morning after the loss of all that he had been collecting for so many years, with such unwearied zeal, interest, and labour, he recommended sketching the map of Sumatra, set all his draughtsmen to work in making new drawings of some of the most interesting specimens in natural history, dispatched a number of people into the forests to collect more animals, and neither murmur nor lamentation ever escaped his lips; on the contrary, upon the ensuing Sabbath, he publicly returned thanks to Almighty God, for having preserved the lives of all those who had for some time contemplated a death from which there appeared no human probability of escaping."

The news of the disaster was received in the different Eastern ports with deep regret. The *Prince of Wales's Island Gazette* observed: "The loss of these curiosities which have cost so much labour and expense in compiling is very deeply to be deplored." But no one was more heartbroken than 'Abdullah.

". . . And when I heard this news I was breathless, remembering all the Malay books of ancient date collected from various countries—all these lost with the wonderful collection. As to his other property I do not care, for if his life was spared he could reinstate them. But the books could not be recovered for none of them were printed but in manuscript—they were so rare that one country might have two of them; that is what distressed me. I further remembered his intention of composing a work on these countries and his promise to put my name in it. All this was gone. When I thought of him I was the more grieved because it not only was a great personal loss to him but to Europe in as much as he had material for several histories—one on Celebes, one on Borneo, one on Singapore, besides many other subjects—but the material of all these was now gone. My thoughts then turned to the origin of his taking them but I consoled myself that he himself was saved; in this there was praise due to God Who orders to be and not to be and acknowledgments are due to His power over His slaves."

At Bencoolen, every effort was made to secure another ship for the passage home. The first offered was the *Wellington*. Raffles took her up and preparations were being made for the party to embark, when "the Commander most suddenly and unexpectedly went out of his mind and is now raving mad". They waited for the next opportunity.

While Raffles was thus buffeted by fortune, the business of the outer world proceeded.

First, there was the matter of Farquhar. He had at Calcutta a good friend and a warm supporter in John Palmer, but Palmer realized only too clearly that Farquhar had little prospect of getting any redress from the Supreme Government, for it was the Supreme Government that had dismissed him and it was unlikely to take any action that would now reflect on its own decision. Palmer made this clear in a letter he had addressed to Farquhar to meet him on arrival.

"If I condemned you not coming at first, you may judge how happy I am that you are coming at last. Expecting you daily, I drop this in the Kedjree Post Office that you may know my happiness at your approach; and infer my conviction of your honourable and exemplary Acquittal from the Charges preferred against you. Redress you may not obtain here for your Judges are *particeps criminis*. I hope to see your Papers before you get up; and (using the words of a high Authority in regard to them) that I hope they will, and I believe will, prove perfectly satisfactory."

On 11th February Palmer wrote to Coombs in Penang:

"Poor Farquhar's case is still to be considered and will yet be unredressed, flagrant as his wrongs are. Indeed the Government must condemn itself to do him common Justice, but how it is to surmount the miserable subterfuge it assumed in his supercession I cannot comprehend for it alleges only his own wish to retire as the occasion of removing him."

In London the Anglo-Dutch talks went on, the British eventually relinquishing their claim for £100,000. A treaty was signed on 17th March 1824. Its main features, so far as concerns us here, were the cession to Great Britain of the Dutch possessions in continental India, and of Malacca and Singapore in the Malay Peninsula, in return for which we withdrew all interest in the East Indian Archipelago and Sumatra, though Achin was excluded from Dutch influence in Sumatra. In other words, the British sphere of interest was the whole of the Malay Peninsula, and the Dutch sphere of interest was what became known as the Netherlands East Indies.

Some may think that Great Britain, anxious to bolster up Holland, was unduly generous in the settlement; that we might, for example, have retained the island of Sumatra as part of the bargain, or at least the Rhio archipelago and the other islands in the Straits of Malacca within sight of Singapore. There was indeed, almost at once, a dispute whether or not the Rhio archipelago was a dependency of Malacca. The Dutch had always argued that it was, so it was now claimed that since Malacca had been ceded to Great Britain, the Rhio archipelago had automatically been ceded also. This point was settled in favour of the Dutch. Later the Dutch claimed that a British settlement in Cocos Island was an infringement of the treaty, but this time Great Britain stood firm, refusing to accept the Dutch view.

The greatest pressure for the return of Singapore to the Dutch had come from the Netherland authorities in Java, but even in the East at least two Dutchmen took a realistic view. For example, de Kock, commander-in-chief in Java and deputy Governor-General, made this interesting observation to Falck in a letter dated 19th June 1824:

"I can't hide from Y.E. that my opinion has always been that we made rather too great a fuss about our pretended rights over Singapore."

And that good Dutch patriot, Colonel Nahuijs, who visited Singapore in that same summer, had this to remark:

"I believe that no person with any feeling can help being impressed when setting foot in Singapore because he can now see as a seat of European trade and industry the place which only five years before was a cavern and hiding place for murderers and pirates. The impression, it is true, is considerably dimmed for the Hollander by the thought that the English are settled in a place to which only his nation had a right, but as a friend of humanity he must prefer seeing this island in the possession of civilized Christians to it being in the hands of pirates and murderers, who made the journey through the Straits of Malacca exceedingly dangerous. And let me ask you, Would Singapore not still have been to this date the same den of murderers, as it was in the past, had it not been taken over by the English? . . .

"If the British Government, instead of entering into their contracts (valueless in themselves) with the son of the King of Johore and the head of the pirates, had driven the latter from Singapore by armed force and had established itself there, then the title of possession would have been based on the Right of War and our Dutch Government, which had left the pirates so many years in the undisturbed possession of Singapore, would certainly not have all these strong and convincing arguments which we can now bring forward. As I, however, well know the discernment and good judgment of the British high official, to whom the English East Indian Government is indebted for Singapore, I believe I should do him an injustice if I did not add here as my feeling that the above remarks probably did not escape his wise insight and that it was due to great necessity, perhaps to the impossibility of obtaining the necessary military strength and armed vessels, that it was not taken by military force."

If we may here look still farther ahead, we can gauge Raffles' own view of the Anglo-Dutch treaty from a letter written to him by Canning on 11th October 1824.

"Far from thinking", wrote Canning, "that the letter which you have done me the honour to write to me requires any Apology, I assure you that I am greatly pleased and gratified to learn that the treaty with the Netherlands Government respecting our interests in the Eastern Seas appears to you to be just in its principles and satisfactory in its terms. There could not be a more competent judgment than yours on such a subject, or one which I should have been more desirous of having in favour of our mode of dealing with it. I cannot deny that your extreme activity in stirring difficult questions, and the freedom with which you committed your Government without their knowledge or authority to measures which might have brought a war upon them unprepared, did at one time oblige me to speak my mind to you in instructions of no very mild reprehension, but I was not the less anxious to retain the fruits of your Policy which appeared to me really worth preserving, and I have long forgotten every part of your conduct in the Eastern Seas except the zeal and ability by which it was distinguished."

With his usual political sagacity, combined with his clear appreciation of what was practicable, Raffles was probably satisfied that the treaty left the gate of the Far East wide open to his countrymen. But for his single-handed endeavours, that gate would have been firmly closed. British interests in the East Indian Archipelago would never, in all probability, have extended east of Bencoolen and Penang, even if those posts had not been finally abandoned as unprofitable outposts. Even the China trade would have been lost.

v

Meanwhile, at Bencoolen, Raffles managed to engage the *Mariner*, a small Botany Bay ship, to take home himself and his party, together with the crew of the *Fame*. As he wrote to Wallich on 28th March:

"... God grant we may be more successful in her. We hope to embark on her in the course of the week, and once more to trust ourselves to the mercy of the elements. . . . Lady Raffles sends thanks for having kept my picture so long, as it otherwise would have been lost, with everything else, by the 'Fame'."

Just before he sailed, Raffles received a letter from Lord Amherst, the new Governor-General. After observing with regret that Raffles was going home, his Lordship continued:

"It would have afforded me pleasure to have found myself in correspondence with you and to have received advantages from those services which have already been so beneficially exerted in this part of our Empire."

The party embarked in the *Mariner* on 8th April, and on the morning of the 10th sailed for England in company with the *Lady Flora*.

Four days later, Farquhar left Calcutta for home in the *Maitland*. Having failed to obtain satisfaction in India, he was taking his grievances to England, with what consequences to Raffles will be seen later.

vi

Raffles had had his dreams of Sumatra's becoming "a colony which to a commercial nation like England should eventually surpass all others". In 1820 he had written to Murdoch:

"Palembang still remains independent though the Dutch blockade the river's mouth. Let the independence of this State be established: we want no more. Palembang is able to govern itself—the people are nearly as far advanced as those in Java and recent events are fast consolidating them into a great and powerful nation. Let the Dutch resign Padang as not strictly coming within the terms of the Convention which should refer to the status quo ante bellum of 1801 and not of 1795, and I ask no more than a carte blanche for five years to make Sumatra more important—more valuable to England than even Java could have been. I would spend no more money in effecting this than is now annually thrown away at Bencoolen and I would lay the foundation of a Colony which to a commercial nation like England should eventually surpass all others.

"By opening the communication between Bencoolen and Palembang the great navigable river [Musi or Palembang] of the latter place would be the outlet for all the rich produce of the interior including the spices of Bencoolen. The Jambi, Siak and other rivers to the northward would be opened as the great channels of trade while our Stations on the West Coast, which I would still maintain, would be our military posts whence all the rivers and all the interior of the country would be commanded. I would open a highroad along the centre of the Island from one end to the other and the rivers should be my transverse pathways. I would assume supremacy without interfering with the just independence of other States. I would be the protector of the native States. I would in fact re-establish the ancient authority of Menangkabu and be the Great Mogul of the Island. I would without much expense afford employment for twenty or thirty thousand English colonists and I would soon give employment to as much British tonnage and as many British seamen as are now engaged in the West India trade. In short what would I not do were I free to act and encourage rather than abuse?

"This I am willing to admit is all very speculative and I am sorry to be obliged to add very visionary, for there is no chance of my ever attempting anything of the kind—the time has gone by when I had the spirit for it. I have met with so much injustice and ill usage on the part of the authorities at home that the charm is gone, my confidence is lost and I can only think of these changes as what might have been had circumstances been more favourable. I am now confining myself strictly to my own petty States on the coast and surely what I am doing in them is rather practical than speculative. What I am doing will not only benefit these districts immediately but may enable some subsequent authority less harassed by an unconfiding Government to attempt to enlarge the sphere for the extension of British principles: I shall be content with what is immediately practical. . . ."

We have an eye-witness account of the transformation brought about by Raffles in Bencoolen. It is from the pen of our friend Colonel Nahuijs, who visited there at the end of 1823, when Raffles was waiting to depart. First let us recall Raffles' description of the settlement as he found it in 1818.

To Marsden: "This is without exception the most wretched place I ever beheld. I cannot convey to you an adequate idea of the state of ruin and dilapidation which surrounds me. What with natural impediments, bad government and the awful visitations of Providence, which we have recently experienced in repeated earthquakes, we have scarcely a dwelling in which to lay our heads, or wherewithal to satisfy the cravings of nature. The roads are impassable; the highways in the town overrun with rank grass; the Government House a den of ravenous dogs and polecats. . . ."

To the Company: "Although the insignificance of the place could not have been unknown to me, I was by no means prepared for the wretchedness and poverty which met me on my arrival . . . the public buildings had been allowed to go to ruin; the streets and highways were covered with high grass and jungle, nuisances met the eye in every direction, robberies and murders were such constant occurrences that scarce any enquiry was made into them. . . ."

Colonel Nahuijs wrote on 10th December 1823:

"A great variety of broad good roads make attractive the neighbourhood and surroundings of the establishment . . . a very attractive road twelve miles long runs from Fort Marlborough to Pamattanbalan, a Government coffee, nutmeg and clove plantation. Lieutenant-Governor Raffles has here a very good country house where he sometimes stays. Everything that grows here is in perfect order, neither pains nor expense are spared. Coffee thrives here most luxuriantly but what care is not bestowed on it! I have seen numerous young trees which are protected by attap screens against sun and wind.

"Every possible encouragement is given by the British Indian Government to the agricultural development of this establishment. Anyone willing to open an estate can get the land for a very small sum and as I have already mentioned a number of workers free of charge. The produce of the planters is free of all export duties and is admitted in all harbours of British India without payment of import taxes. . . ."

From Nahuijs we have the testimony of an independent witness to the genuine success of a scheme of native education one hundred and thirty years ago.

"What could be done for the moral improvement of the people has certainly been tried here by the able Mr Raffles, who has therein been helped in an appreciable manner by conscientious missionaries and with the co-operation of European settlers. In all places and districts, where the English have any influence and say, native schools have been established where the youth has been instructed in reading, writing and arithmetic and in useful general knowledge. The school in the principal place, Marlborough, in which I met the Head and Supervisor, a missionary, Mr Ward, has already more than 160 pupils. The order, regularity, cleanliness and propriety which I have noticed there exceed everything that I have seen of this kind and do the greatest credit to the founders and those who are carrying on the work. The tuition is that of the Lancaster School. The Malay scholars are divided into ten and the Bengalese into three classes."

It can be added here parenthetically that, after the departure of the British authority from Sumatra, Nathaniel Moore Ward laboured on there for the Baptist Missionary Society until 1850, when his correspondence ceased, and he was never heard of again.

Impressed as Nahuijs was with the orderly appearance of the Bencoolen plantations, he was somewhat sceptical as to whether they would prove profitable. Raffles, discussing the subject with him, had frankly admitted that the cost of production substantially exceeded the price obtained for the crops, and that the Company had been critical on this very point. The Company had gone further, observing on 26th January 1822 that it was a mistake to encourage planters to cultivate sugar. Sugar and rum, like spices, could be sold in London only at a substantial loss. The only thing that could be sold at a profit was cloves, and it was a pity that Sumatra could not grow cloves. No doubt the Company was correct, but surely it was a very short-sighted policy. It was quite conceivable that, as efficiency increased, costs of production would have fallen. In any event, the loss on sales in England could have been more than offset by economies in the administration of Bencoolen had the host of idle officials been transferred, as Raffles had so strongly recommended, to other stations where they could have earned their pay. Moreover, Bencoolen was then a British responsibility, and a defeatist policy was morally indefensible.

Raffles was later to be accused from quite a different angle, in that he had encouraged planters to indulge in false hopes. A certain Dr Tyler addressed a long letter to Canning from Calcutta on 3rd January 1825. After a general attack on the Anglo-Dutch treaty, he went on:

"Subsequent to November 1823, viz. in January 1824, when he must have known of the conclusion of the treaty, Sir Stamford Raffles did everything in his power to remove suspicion from the minds of the people of Bencoolen regarding this impending and terrible calamity . . . so effectually that no suspicion of the treaty's existence was present till the notification was announced."

Dr Tyler proceeded to condemn Raffles' administration, which he described as exhibiting "one continued scene of misrule and misdirection", then ended with:

"I conclude it will not be thought otherwise than that Sir Stamford Raffles should be brought to answer for his conduct at the Bar of the House of Commons."

It is quite true that Raffles had been fully aware, as had been most people in the East, that an Anglo-Dutch agreement was under discussion in Europe—had, in fact, been under discussion for nearly four years—but there is no evidence that Raffles had been given any intimation before he left Bencoolen that the signing of the treaty was imminent, let alone informed as to its principal clauses.

There is one other flaw in Dr Tyler's case: the treaty had not been signed until 17th March 1824, yet he suggested that Raffles should have heard about it in the previous January.

Certainly Raffles had visualized that under such a treaty, if concluded, Sumatra might well pass to the Dutch, but as the negotiations had taken so long, he may well have thought that the treaty would never be signed at all. In the meantime, he had done his utmost to make a success of Bencoolen, to reduce the risk of all Sumtara being handed over to the Dutch. Even if it were, it was at least possible to suppose that if Bencoolen had become prosperous under the British, it might remain so under the Dutch. If Raffles thought this, he was over-optimistic, for after the cession of Sumatra, Dutch interest was centred on Padang, and Bencoolen soon reverted to a *tanah mati*. But Raffles could hardly be blamed for that.

Chapter Thirty-one

ENGLAND, 1824-1825

In spite of his poor state of health and all that he had recently endured, Raffles was determined that the time entailed by the long voyage home should not be wasted. As recorded by Sophia, he drew up a memorandum setting out exactly how each day was to be spent, "so that I may hold the rule as inviolable as I can and, by frequently recurring to it, revive my sleeping energies, should I at any time be inclined to indolence". The programme he set himself was certainly a formidable one.

"Breakfast being fixed at 9 and dinner at 4, I appropriate, before breakfast, from 7 to 9 . . . . hours 2

"Between breakfast and dinner, from 10 to 1 and from 2 to 4 . . . . „ 5

"In the evening, from 8 to 9 . . . . . . „ 1

hours . . . . „ 8

"Before breakfast.—One hour mathematics or logic—one hour Latin, Greek or Hebrew.

"After breakfast, from 10 to 11.—In committing to paper and arranging and reviewing what I studied before breakfast.

"From 11 to 1.—Writing an account of my administration in the East.

"From 2 to 4.—General reading and reading out to Sophia.

"In the evening for one hour.—Reading a play of Shakspeare's, or other entertaining productions.

"By this arrangement, I have, in the morning, by rising at 6, one hour for exercise before breakfast, and half an hour for the same after breakfast. One hour from 1 to 2 for tiffin and exercise, and after dinner from 5 to 7, two hours for exercise or relaxation in the cool of the evening. As the servants are always behindhand in furnishing the meals, I may freely trust to their affording me time for dressing by such delays, which will only eventually break in on the proposed three hours' relaxation for the evening, a portion of which may well be spared; or half an hour may be added to the day by going to bed at half past 9 or 10, instead of nine as proposed."

This programme was to be adhered to "as far as circumstances admit", and it is much to be feared that the appalling weather experienced round the Cape interfered sadly with his laudable intentions. He wrote at St Helena on the day of their arrival:

"25th June 1824.—Arrived at St Helena on the afternoon of the 25th of June, after a passage of eleven weeks from Bencoolen, and encountering constant and severe gales off the Cape of Good Hope during three weeks of that period. The gale was so severe, that during this period we were unable to leave our cots, the sea poured through the decks into our cabin, and the war of the wind was such that we could not hear each other speak. Lady Raffles, though boarded up in her couch, was obliged to have ropes to hold by to prevent her knocking from one side of it to the other: the ship lay like a wreck upon the ocean at the mercy of the winds and waves, and we resigned ourselves to the feeling that our pilgrimage in this world was soon to close."

Sophia added to this: "Those who have never experienced such a scene can form no idea of the severity of the gale. Captain Young, who had passed the Cape nineteen times, declared he had never witnessed anything like it; nor can the Editor ever forget one night, on which Captain Herbert (for all on board were worn out with fatigue and watching), as he retired to take a little rest, desired the officer on the watch to observe in one particular direction, and call him the moment he saw the smallest speck in the horizon; the Captain then came to tell Sir Stamford that the ship still held well together. It was a dreadful night, the sky appeared a heavy dense arch, threatening to fall with its own weight, and crush everything beneath it, save on one spot, where a full moon of the deepest blood-red shed an unnatural crimson hue that just rendered the darkness visible. It was not long before the expected mark appeared, and before the Captain could get on deck, the fury of the wind was sweeping all before it."

At St Helena they were most hospitably received by the Governor, General Walker, and his wife, with whom they stayed at Plantation House until the ship sailed. One piece of sad news awaited Raffles there. He referred to it in a letter he managed to write to the Duchess of Somerset on the 26th.

"Thank God we are once more on the right side of the Cape of Good Hope, with a fair prospect of a favourable passage home. After being eleven weeks at sea, and suffering a dreadful gale of three *whole* weeks off the Cape, we landed here last night.

"I have neither time or spirits to say more than that we are alive and tolerably well, and have a hope to reach England in August. My health and strength are entirely gone, but I trust I have yet enough spirit to bear up for the voyage. To complete our sorrow, I have just received an account of the death of my dear mother, an event for which I have some time been prepared, but which has been a sad stroke at such a moment, just as I felt the possibility of once more embracing her, and cheering her latter hours: but God's will be done.

"We propose, wind and weather permitting, to land at Plymouth, and from thence to cross the country, through Exeter and Bath to Cheltenham, where Lady Raffles' family are at present residing.

"I mention this, because, next to the duty and inclination I feel to place my dear wife in the bosom of her anxious family, I am led to look towards you and yours.

"Pray excuse this hasty scrawl; my eyes are quite blinded with tears, and my hand is so nervous that I can scarcely hold my pen."

The *Mariner* left St Helena on 3rd July, crossed the line nine days later and, after an uneventful voyage reached Plymouth on Sunday, 22nd August 1824.

By a fortunate coincidence Dr Raffles was preaching that day at Devonport. He wrote off at once to his wife:

"I have literally but a moment to tell you that our dear friends Sir Stamford and Lady Raffles arrived safely at Plymouth this morning. Lady Raffles looks better than I expected to find her, but my cousin is very much reduced and exceedingly weak. I have just returned from seeing them, and after Service this evening I go to Beechwood, the seat of Mr Rosdew the Banker, where we are all to sleep to-night."

The following morning Raffles and Sophia left for Cheltenham, whence Raffles wrote on the 24th to the Duchess of Somerset:

"We were most anxious, as you may well suppose, to throw ourselves into the arms of our family as soon as possible . . . but what with assizes, horse-races, air-balloons, and other festivities of the season, we got on so slowly for the first two days, that I was obliged to push the post-boys from Bath to this place at about thirteen miles in the hour, until our front wheel caught fire, in order to satisfy Sophia's impatience to see her child. This has rather fatigued us; but you will, I am sure, be happy to hear that we have found her all that our fondest wishes could have desired. . . .

"Of my future plans in life I cannot say that I have fixed any. . . . I confess that I have a great desire to turn farmer, and have the vanity to think I could manage about two hundred acres as well as my neighbours. With this, I suppose, I should in time become a country Magistrate, an office of all others which I should delight in; and if I could eventually get a seat in Parliament, without sacrificing principle, I should be content to pass through the rest of my life without aiming at anything further, beyond the occupation of my spare time in promoting, as far as my humble means and talents admitted, the pursuits of knowledge and science, and the advancement of philanthropic and religious principles.

"Your Grace will, perhaps, say that I have chalked out for myself a very varied and diversified course; but what is life without variety? and what is existence without occupation?"

At Cheltenham, Raffles took "a snug house, number 2 Wellington Place", with the idea of "giving the waters a fair chance". These seem to have done some good, for, by the second week of September, they both felt sufficiently recovered to undertake the fatigue of a visit to London, where they spent ten very strenuous but, as Raffles hoped, not unprofitable days. He had some personal issues to settle with the East India Company, having been long dissatisfied with the attitude it had adopted towards his own activities in the East, which he felt to be unjustifiably critical.

"I was enabled to see the Chairman and Deputy of the E.I. Company and most of my best friends. The feeling, I am glad to say, seems very general in my favour, and I trust that before Christmas something will be done by those in power to acknowledge my past Services and remunerate me for my losses. I have delivered a short statement to the Court and shall await their decision with patience. I have not appealed to them *in forma pauperis*, tho' it would be affectation in me to say that my future plans in life will not materially depend on the assistance I receive from them."

This was to Dr Raffles, on his return to Cheltenham. To the Duchess of Somerset he wrote while still in London:

"The Directors are a large heavy body and move slowly. Therefore I must not complain of their delay. I am very anxious they should look into the subject before they decide, but this I fear they will only do cursorily. . . . It has been represented to me in confidence that they are fearful of bringing this matter before the General Court . . . in fact they are afraid of exposing their own mismanagement, misconduct, inattention and, I may say, shameful treatment of all my representations. It is hard however that I should suffer for this, but *n'importe* . . . I shall not be the first public servant who has been neglected by the higher powers."

They were back at Cheltenham on 24th September.

One thing that particularly impressed them both was the astonishing kindness with which they were everywhere received. The tragic story of the *Fame* had become well known. Writing to Mary Anne, Raffles described it thus:

"Our reception in England was most gratifying—nothing could equal the attention of all classes of people. . . . Our misfortunes had opened the hearts of all, indeed it seemed to be a pleasure to the people to look at us. In some places they crowded round the carriage, at others they would not receive payment for the Tavern Bill. Even in London Sophia gave her name when the shopman said 'Lord, Ma'am, you ain't the lady that was burnt in the "Fame"?' It is quite ridiculous to think of the scenes we have experienced on this account and yet is all from such kindness of feeling that I can hardly keep my eyes dry."

The Duchess of Somerset wrote to say that her son was proposing to call at 2 Wellington Place before going up to Oxford. Raffles replied on 2nd October:

"We shall be delighted to see Lord Seymour. . . . Would that I were going on with him to Oxford: and were I not a married man, I should be half inclined to study for a Bachelor degree to make up, even at this time of life, for the sad omissions of my youth. . . . In returning to the civilized world I feel like a Hottentot.

"At the suggestion of my man of business I have made a very moderate statement of my claims, in the hope that the Court of Directors may be induced, for their credit and my quiet, to grant me such compensation for my services and losses as the case may merit, but I own I have not much faith in what they will do, and if they do not act handsomely I shall be inclined to carry the matter further."

The visit of young Lord Seymour was somewhat spoiled by Raffles' ill-health. Writing to the Duchess again on the 23rd he said:

"Your Grace will have been surprised at my long silence; I have been ill and confined to my bed almost ever since I received your last letter, and I am only able to-day to refer to the date, and apologize for not acknowledging it. When Lord Seymour was with us I had entirely lost my voice from a violent cold; so that we had some difficulty in communicating; but he had hardly left us when I had one of those severe attacks in my head that nearly deprived me of reason; and I began to think I must bid you a long farewell. Thank God, however, I am better; though I am hardly able to hold my pen, and which I dare not trust except within very close limitation; for I believe that it was in consequence of using it too much on the paper I was drawing up that I have to attribute this unfortunate relapse; which has thrown me back in point of health at least two months; and as winter is fast approaching time is precious. I have finished the paper I was writing some time ago and it is now at the printers'—it is not exactly what I could have wished, and the state of my health obliged me to contract it within very narrow limits, and bring it to a conclusion rather suddenly and with less spirit than I could have wished. Such as it is you shall have it in a few days."

The document to which he here referred was his *Statement of Services*, which was being printed, for private circulation, by Cox and Baylis. He pinned his hope on this document proving the justification of his actions. This meant in effect that the Company would have to retract many of its criticisms, and no official body is usually anxious to do anything of the kind.

In the latter part of October a welcome visitor arrived at Cheltenham. Travers, hearing that his old chief had reached England, came straight over from Ireland to see him.

"Unfortunately poor fellow was sadly afflicted this day with Headache which confined him to his bed. But I had a most affectionate greeting from Lady Raffles who was looking uncommonly well. Indeed I was surprised at her appearance. She complained of loss of weight but I never saw her look better. I remained with her all day and after dinner my worthy friend Sir Stamford expressed a wish to see me. The meeting was a tender scene. Poor fellow, he was looking sadly altered but his spirits were yet good. He rallied after a short time and became quite energetic—so much so that I was obliged to leave him for fear he would over excite himself. I left him early and retired with much upon my mind and very fearful that my valued friend's constitution was too much undermined to ever get properly re-established. He seemed a complete Skeleton with scarcely enough skin to cover his bones—his head tormenting to a sad degree.

"The following day my friend Sir Stamford was much better and came down to dinner. He was well inclined but not allowed to talk much so I left early."

A room was now available and Travers moved in for the remainder of his stay. As Raffles' health improved, Travers enjoyed himself greatly.

"We were alone and when he was able to go out I accompanied. We talked over past and happy days and were never a moment idle in bringing past scenes to recollection. Indeed we had much to talk about and he had many papers to show me. His losses p. 'Fame' he spoke of like a Philosopher and really they seemed to make no impression nor did Lady Raffles speak of them but with a seeming religious thankfulness at having escaped with her life. She seemed to dwell more upon the wretched state they were in when off the Cape, coming home in a continual Gale of Wind for a fortnight, expecting every moment to founder. In short their misfortunes would serve to fill a colume and much to the credit of both they seemed to have left only an impression worthy of praise and admiration. I know not when I passed a more agreeable time than with these valued friends whom I parted from with great regret."

Raffles referred again to his *Statement of Services* in a letter to the Duchess of Somerset on 2nd November.

"I have corrected the proof of the paper which I am sending in to the Court of Directors, and have desired a copy to be sent to you. I am afraid you will not find it very interesting; but as it takes a general view of my services and the situation in which I have been placed, it may amuse you for half an hour during a dull November day. You must bear in mind *to whom* it is addressed, and the necessity of my keeping within bounds; as well as with reference to a body so constituted as on account of my own health, which does not admit of my enlarging on the subject. You will see that I have pledged myself to give the public a memoir on Singapore. I hope you will not disapprove of my taking so much blame to myself as I have been willing to do. I am ready to justify every act of my administration, and feel perfectly easy on that score, but it is for others to judge—not me; and all I am anxious to do is to get the question agitated, as I am ready to stand or fall by the result.

"I am very sensible of the Duke's kindness, and am only sorry that I give you so much trouble and so little satisfaction. Time was when I wanted not strength to second my will; but I am now, alas! shattered, and altogether unequal to one thousandth part of all I would wish or desire to do. . . ."

It would seem that Raffles' desire to enter Parliament, which he had mentioned casually to the Duchess, was in fact a very real one. He had consulted his cousin to discover what prospect there would be of his following Canning's example and standing for a northern constituency in the commercial interest. Dr Raffles wrote to him on 2nd November, giving him such advice as he could. As he said, he had kept himself "so much aloof from all political matters" out of "consideration for my clerical character" that he had felt it desirable to consult better-informed friends. The resulting advice is not very easy to follow, and is not of a conclusive character, yet it did seem possible that the Liverpool Corporation, being somewhat dissatisfied with General Gascoigne, one of their two members, might be willing to consider another candidate for the next election. Alternatively, Raffles might stand as an independent, but that would be extremely costly, and as the support he might expect would come chiefly from the radicals, he would be branded as one himself, which presumably he would not approve. The only thing that clearly emerged from the reverend doctor's letter was that the chance of a seat was a slender one.

Raffles continued to make various enquiries, but when these seemed abortive, temporarily abandoned the project, which, as he was coming to realize, might in any event be frustrated by the state of his health. It is interesting to speculate if, had he achieved his ambition, he would have obtained any satisfaction from it, or if he would have found, as other great public servants have done, that the political atmosphere was far from congenial.

A more urgent question was where to live. It did not suit him to make his headquarters indefinitely at Cheltenham; all his interests were in London. To provide immediate lodging, he rented a furnished house, 104 Piccadilly, to which he removed with Sophia, Ella and Charles Flint on 17th November. He wrote on the following day to his cousin:

"We arrived in Town yesterday afternoon, all well, and as you may suppose are in no small confusion. The house that has been taken for us, though well situated, is by no means equal to our demands for room and I fear we shall have ere long to move to another. Nevertheless we are well enough housed for a few months and I need not say how happy we shall be to see you under our roof such as it is. We breakfast at nine and dine at five, with a determination to preserve early hours as long as we can. . . . I am not allowed to be out after sunset, but in the mornings, when the weather is fair, I have abundance of visits to pay. Therefore, that I may not miss you, drop a line by the post saying when you are likely to call. Sophia is but delicate, but we are both wonderfully recovered."

On arrival in England, Colonel William Farquhar had wasted no time in placing his case before the Court of Directors. Hearing of the discussions that followed in East India House, Raffles wrote to Mary Anne on 18th November:

"Colonel Farquhar has had a very *long* and of course a very hard case before the Court. It was my wish, poor man, that he should be let off as easily as possible, but he seems to have failed in all he attempted."

He then referred to the relief of Crawfurd at Singapore by John Prince, who had succeeded himself at Bencoolen.

"Both he and Farquhar are now *hors de combat* and God grant that you may do better under a new dynasty. You will at all events have something *Princely* to commence with, and it has been said that he is not only a Prince by name but a prince by nature too . . . and it may prove so to you and all."

The change-over at Singapore did not take place until August 1826, when Crawfurd was appointed civil commissioner at Rangoon and, later, ambassador to Burma.

One of the first visitors at 104 Piccadilly was, apparently, the Duchess of Somerset, to whom Raffles wrote on 9th December:

"I have been following your kind advice, idling and playing the fool with my time as much as possible. We are beginning to get a little more to rights than when you left us but I have only been able to unpack two cases out of one hundred and seventy-three in course of transport to the house."

To this the Duchess replied[1]: "I will thank you for yours of the 9th tho' I fear to write to you lest by so doing I shd. make you take up the pen when you ought not. . . . I am glad you are getting a little to rights but pray do not unpack too much, that is an exertion—Be idle and out a great deal when it is fine."

Meanwhile he had been negotiating with his friend, Sir Humphry Davy, president of the Royal Society, to acquire his house, 23 Lower Grosvenor Street. On 31st November he was able to report to his cousin that the deal had been completed and that he proposed to move in on 1st February. The Hulls also moved to London, renting a house at Hornsey.

[1] The letter is undated, but clearly belongs here.

On 1st December Raffles wrote again to Dr Raffles. This passage appears in the letter:

"Mr Canning detained me so long yesterday evening that I was precluded from attending the Royal Society. He received me most cordially and promised me the most friendly support in all my plans. We parted under the understanding of becoming better known to each other, and I think I may fairly calculate upon his influence as far as I may require it."

Raffles' interest in Singapore had by no means diminished, and his activities on its behalf were considerable.

"There is as you may suppose," he wrote to A. L. Johnston on 2nd January 1825, "a lively interest taken in its future welfare and you may rest assured that I am not lukewarm. . . . On the subject of the clause in the Treaty which restricts Americans from visiting Singapore nothing can be more ridiculous. I have conferred with the American Minister and our authorities on the subject and I hope I shall succeed in removing this bar to your commerce. . . . I am sorry to observe your Resident has had recourse to so vicious and objectionable a mode of raising a revenue as the establishment of Gaming Farms. I think it likely the subject will attract public attention here and become matter for discussion in the Court of Proprietors, if not in a higher Court. My sentiments on the subject are now on record and I see no reason to alter them, and whenever the fit time comes, I shall be prepared to support them. . . . The overflow of capital in this country has occasioned a degree of gambling that some steady people think will end in something like the South Sea Bubble. . . . At the present moment public attention is principally attracted to the *Locomotive Steam Engines* which are to propel carriages without horses from one part of the country to the other at the rate of ten to twelve miles an hour! A considerable opposition is expected on the part of the holders of canal shares. . . ."

About this time the Court of Directors provided Raffles with a copy of the memorial submitted by the aggrieved Farquhar.

". . . Under a deep sense of the injury he has received as a high public functionary and as a soldier, your Memorialist throws himself upon your Honourable Court, and he solicits your patient attention while detailing at some length a series of acts of the most flagrant injustice and tyranny on the part of the late Lieutenant-Governor of Fort Marlborough, contrasted, as he flatters himself, by a forbearance on the part of your Memorialist, even in cases of strict right, where he felt that personal considerations might interfere with a paramount interest of the Company. . . ."

Farquhar claimed that the settlement of Singapore had been "formed at his own suggestion and matured under his personal management", in support of which assertion he referred to his own representations made to Governor Petrie of Penang as far back as 1816 in the following terms:

"'In the event of Malacca being delivered up to the Dutch, I think it would be extremely desirable if a new British Settlement could be formed in some convenient spot near the south-east entrance of the Straits, so as to be as nearly as possible in the way of shipping passing to and from China and the Eastern Archipelago. The port of Rhio, formerly a dependency of Malacca, would, if not repossessed by the Dutch, be a very desirable place for us to occupy, being at present a Settlement of considerable trade, and, although properly appertaining to the Rajah of Lingen, arrangements might be made, without much difficulty, I conceive, for the transfer of the Government to us. . . .'

"When the time approached", continued Farquhar, "for surrendering Malacca, the importance of this measure became more sensibly felt, and in the year 1818 your Memorialist was selected by the Honourable Colonel Bannerman . . . to proceed on a public Mission to the States of Siack, Rhio, Lingen, and Pontiana, for the purpose of endeavouring to establish commercial Treaties with such of the Malay powers as were at the time considered to be independent.

"In the short space of six weeks your Memorialist completed the objects of his Mission. . . .

"During the negotiations which took place with the Commissioners of the King of the Netherlands upon the surrender of Malacca, your Memorialist discovered that it was the intention of the Dutch Government to establish a Factory at Rhio, and to extend their influence to the utmost of their power among the neighbouring States as soon as the British force should be withdrawn; and as the circumstances would allow no delay, your Memorialist, on his own responsibility, dispatched an agent to the Rajah Mudah, or Viceroy of Rhio, to represent to him the advantage which would be derivable from the formation of a British establishment at the Carimon Islands, in the Straits of Malacca, and your Memorialist succeeded in obtaining permission to surveying the Carimon Islands for the purpose of forming a British Settlement. . . .

"Your Memorialist had obtained permission to be absent on a visit to Europe for three years, and on his return to Penang after the surrender of Malacca at the close of the year 1818, as above mentioned, he was making his arrangements for availing himself of this permission, when Sir S. Raffles arrived at Penang as Political Agent to the Governor-General. . . .

"Having surveyed the Carimon Islands, which did not afford the advantages for the settlement, it was resolved to proceed to Johore, but on the way, at the suggestion of your Memorialist, they stopped on the

19th [29th] January at Singapore, then the residence of a native Prince called the Tumung'gong of Johore, and the local advantages afforded by it being immediately discovered, your Memorialist on the following morning proceeded to Rhio, where he succeeded in obtaining the sanction of the Government in the formation of a British Settlement at Singapore. On the 5th of February your Memorialist returned to Singapore, and on the morning of the 6th the British flag was formally displayed. On the following day Sir Stamford Raffles left the Settlement, after having placed your Memorialist in charge as Resident and Commandant, leaving with him a Letter of General Instructions. . . ."

Farquhar then explained that, although the orders for him to proceed with Raffles to take charge of the intended settlement had shown "that his stay in India was at that time considered important", he had not abandoned his intention of going to Europe; "but circumstances occurred, occasioned by this delay, which rendered it less an object of importance". On 23rd October 1820 he had written to the Governor-General, stating "that as the same urgent call for his proceeding to Europe on furlough did not then exist, he was desirous of postponing his departure from India until the ensuing season of 1821-22". There had been no reply to this letter from Calcutta, but on 1st May 1821 Fort Marlborough had written "requesting him to specify, for the information of the Lieutenant-Governor, the period for which he was desirous of remaining in charge of Singapore; and your Memorialist, on the 19th September, replied to that latter, that he should wish to defer coming to any fixed determination on the point, until definitive arrangements should be made respecting the permanent retention of Singapore by the Company; and your Memorialist is assured that your Honourable Court will well appreciate those feelings of interest excited in his mind in regard to a Settlement selected and founded by himself, and which he was anxious not to quit until he was assured of its permanent prosperity."

Then came the crux of his complaint.

"In the month of October 1822 Sir Stamford Raffles visited the Settlement at Singapore, and though in the commencement he expressed high approbation of the Measures of your Memorialist and satisfaction with the state of the Settlement, it was not long before, finding his opinion clash with that of your Memorialist in various local questions, he commenced a course of conduct which, to an officer of your Memorialist's rank and experience in the affairs of the Company, could not fail to be in the highest degree offensive. . . .

"Your Memorialist has been thus minute because he cannot acquiesce in the Justice of the charges made against him by the Lieutenant-Governor on any of these points. But your Memorialist has no claim to exemption from the common infirmities of human nature. He may have been mistaken in point of fact, he may have erred in point of Judgment, but he may confidently say that he must have been more than man who, placed for four years in an arduous command, where his acts were reported to the Supreme Government by (to say the least) no friendly medium, and with little or no opportunity afforded of explanation on his part, could have avoided giving some excuse for complaint; but the sweeping charge of incompetence, now for the first time brought against your Memorialist, is one that the services in which he has been engaged and the opinions of those under whom he has acted for a series of years forbid him to concede.

"The facts are obvious, the explanation which would carry conviction upon the subject is long and complicated, and requires a painful degree of attention. Your Memorialist feels that the only mode of restoring that credit and reputation of which he has been unjustly deprived, is by allowing him to return, with the sanction and approbation of your Honourable Court, to that Command from which he was improperly removed."

Raffles' reply to this, dated 25th January 1825, is of very considerable length, as his letters were inclined to be. Boulger remarked that the full text of memorial and reply amounted to 33,000 words.

"I beg to return my acknowledgments", Raffles began, "for the opportunity which your Honourable Court have been pleased to afford me of perusing the statement made by Lieutenant-Colonel Farquhar, in which I am charged with 'a series of acts of the most flagrant injustice and tyranny', a charge which cannot but have had the effect of creating an unfavourable impression towards myself, and which has been presented at a moment of all others the most likely to prejudice my interests with reference to the Appeal which I have had occasion to make to your Honourable Court.

"I will admit that I regret that Lieutenant-Colonel Farquhar should have been advised to adopt this course because it compels me to advert to points which necessarily involve the character of that Officer in the discharge of his duty at Singapore, and which from motives of personal consideration towards him I preferred leaving to the Judgment and decision of the Supreme Government.

"Much of Lieutenant-Colonel Farquhar's Statement relates to services and questions long antecedent to the period at which he became connected with me in the establishment of Singapore. . . .

"The Statement of Lieutenant-Colonel Farquhar is so diffuse and violent that it is difficult to trace the exact grounds on which he prefers his charge, but it may perhaps be resolved into the three following heads, on each of which I beg to offer explanations:—

"First, the credit assumed by him for having suggested, nurtured, and matured the Settlement of Singapore to its present state of unexampled prosperity;

"Secondly, the acts of flagrant injustice and tyranny with which he so unreservedly accuses me; and—

"Thirdly, his removal from the charge of Singapore.

"On the credit assumed by Lieutenant-Colonel Farquhar for having suggested the Establishment of Singapore I will observe that this is the first time I ever heard of the circumstance, and that on reference to the Public Records I find nothing to support it. The circumstances under which the Settlement was established will fully appear in my correspondence with the Supreme Government at the time, and I can hardly suppose that a serious refutation of this part of Colonel Farquhar's Statement can now be necessary. The selection of Singapore is admitted to have been judicious, and God forbid that I should deprive Colonel Farquhar of any just credit which may be due to him in the establishment of it. But a regard to truth compels me to deny in broad terms that he ever suggested or, to my knowledge, knew or stated anything with regard to the formation of a Settlement at Singapore until I communicated to him the authority with which I was invested to form a Settlement there. It is true he had suggested to Colonel Bannerman the advantage of a Settlement at the Carimons; but when I arrived at Prince of Wales's Island, the unanimous and unqualified sentiment of the Penang Government was against the possibility of the British Government in India executing any advantageous political arrangements with the Malay States. 'Rhio and Lingen,' they say, 'being in possession of the Dutch, the Southern entrance of the Straits of Malacca were considered as hermetically sealed against us; the execution, therefore, among these States of any political arrangement as a counterpoise to the influence of the Dutch, it is needless to disguise, is now beyond the power of the British Government in India.'

"With regard to the Carimon Islands, when, out of deference to the opinion of Colonel Farquhar, I proceeded to examine them, they were proved to his own conviction to be altogether unfit for the proposed Establishment, and this fact is admitted in his present Statement.

"Lieutenant-Colonel Farquhar would infer that our Settlement at Singapore arose out of the numerous measures adopted by him at Rhio, and his negotiations there. So far from this being the case, it must be notorious to every one who knows anything of the matter, that Singapore was not taken possession by me under any authority or negotiation with the Chief of Rhio, but in *direct opposition and altogether independent of that State*, and had Colonel Farquhar adverted to the terms of the Treaty with the Sultan and Temmungung of Singapore and to the main argument in our subsequent discussions with the Netherland authority, viz.

that Singapore was independent of Rhio, he might have avoided this mistake. . . .

"Lieutenant-Colonel Farquhar has further taken great credit to himself for his management of the Settlement and its progressive advancement. On this point I should be sorry to detract in any way from his just due. I have always been ready and anxious to acknowledge the assistance he rendered to me on the first establishment of the Settlement, but when Lieutenant-Colonel Farquhar goes further, I must beg leave to refer to the sentiments of a higher authority on the subject and to quote the opinion of the Governor-General in Council as conveyed in their dispatch of the 20th September 1821:—

"'Indeed the Instructions which you furnish to that Officer for the formation of the Settlement seem to have been generally well-suited to the circumstances of the place, and the arrangements adopted by the Resident (Colonel Farquhar) would appear to be injudicious in proportion as he deviated from your directions.'

"On the second head, viz. the series of acts for which I am accused by Lieutenant-Colonel Farquhar of flagrant injustice and tyranny, I request to observe that I am not aware of having any personal question with that Officer. He can therefore only advert to the Public Acts of my Administration and as these are to be found on the Public Records, I appeal to them in refutation of the charge; I am satisfied it will thence be found that, so far from my treatment of that Officer being unjust or tyrannical, I deferred to him the utmost personal consideration which a sense of Public duty and the paramount Interest of the Public admitted.

"In support of this assertion I entreat your Honourable Court will do me the justice to peruse the correspondence which took place between Lieutenant-Colonel Farquhar and myself, and the Reports and Proceedings of the Governor-General in Council thereon, from the first establishment of the Settlement until the period of Lieutenant-Colonel Farquhar's departure for England.

"Not to detain your Honourable Court with minor questions, in which I had occasion to complain of the maladministration and imbecility of Lieutenant-Colonel Farquhar, I shall confine myself to the following points:—

"His irregularity in the construction of Public Buildings and appropriation of the ground expressly reserved for public purposes for the benefit of a few favoured individuals, which added to the mode followed in the disposal of Lands generally, in contravention of his instructions and to the manifest injury of the Rights of Government, whereby the whole plan and order of things directed on the first establishment of the Settlement were so far deranged as to render it indispensable that his Proceedings should be disavowed, that the Town should be removed and that the whole of the Land should be resumed at great expense to Government and no less loss to individuals.

"'It is from such an error on the part of Lieutenant-Colonel Farquhar that the Governor-General in Council now finds himself under the necessity of incurring a considerable expense, which, under the present circumstances of the Settlement, he was naturally anxious not to incur, or of allowing the Public Service to continue exposed to serious inconvenience and embarrassment for an indefinite period of time.'

"I will only add on this subject, that it became my unpleasant duty to undo almost everything Lieutenant-Colonel Farquhar had done, and this under circumstances of no ordinary difficulty; I had certainly a right to expect that after the subject had been deliberately viewed in all its bearings, and all that Lieutenant-Colonel Farquhar had to say in his justification had been considered, and the Orders under which I was bound to act were peremptory, I should at least have had the advantage of his personal assistance and support in remedying the evil which had been occasioned by his departure from my instructions; but in this, I am sorry to say, I was disappointed. On communicating to Lieutenant-Colonel Farquhar the Instructions for new Modelling the Town &c, and for the Establishment of a more regular Police, above alluded to, for his suggestions or corrections, that Officer returned the Draft to me without an Envelope, declined to have any personal communication on the subject; and from this period I may date the commencement of a course of opposition to every measure which I deemed it my duty to carry into effect for the general benefit of the Settlement."

After referring to the establishment of gaming and cockfighting, which had been authorized by Farquhar in contravention of his own positive orders, and which he, after much opposition had felt it his duty to abolish, he quoted a letter of 22nd April 1824, in which the Governor-General in Council "fully concurs in the sentiment expressed by you, and highly approves your determination to abolish the Gaming farms at Singapore".

As for the slave trade at Singapore:

"On this point I certainly did not give any particular instructions to Colonel Farquhar because I never could have supposed that a British Officer could have tolerated such a practice in a Settlement circumstanced like Singapore and formed after the Promulgation of the Act of Parliament declaring it to be a Felony. I need hardly therefore say how much I was shocked in hearing the cries of a female, shortly after my landing in Singapore in 1822, proceed from a vessel in the river whose principal Cargo was female Slaves for the Market of Singapore.

"On so serious a subject, however, it was my most anxious desire to proceed in a manner that would least involve Lieutenant-Colonel

Farquhar, who in the opinion of many seemed to have exposed himself to penalties of the law against the Slave Trade, and my sentiments on the subject being well known, few or no subsequent importations took place during my Residence. It was not therefore until the Public Appeal was made to me by the Magistrates of Singapore for instructions how to act in cases which came before them, I took up the subject publicly. To this representation, and to the correspondence which passed with the Resident at Singapore on the subject generally, I must request to make particular reference, because it will at once show the different views which I was induced to take on the subject from those entertained by Lieutenant-Colonel Farquhar.

"I will not detain your Honourable Court by going into further particulars. I have said enough to show that the conduct of Lieutenant-Colonel Farquhar was called in question on many of the most essential parts of his local administration, and a perusal of the correspondence will prove that he was afforded every opportunity of explaining and justifying it. In every case his own statements were transmitted to Bengal, and, if an unfavourable judgment has been passed, he can in no way complain of unfairness on my part.

"In conclusion, I beg to express my regret that I should have had occasion to trespass on your Honourable Court with such a lengthened statement, in which I trust it will appear that in the outset of my Mission to the Eastward I maintained the character of Lieutenant-Colonel Farquhar against the opinion of the Authority under whom he had previously so long acted; that whilst I have acknowledged the zeal of Lieutenant-Colonel Farquhar in the aid which he afforded me in the prosecution of my Mission, I have at the same time shown that his claim to the credit of having suggested the formation of the Settlement of Singapore or its ultimate acquisition has no foundation; that in the Administration of the Affairs of that Settlement most of the measures which he adopted were at variance with the instructions which he had received for his guidance, and that consequently many were reversed by order of the Supreme Government at a considerable cost to the East India Company and detriment of the Settlement, whilst others were denounced as unworthy [of] the character and rank of an Officer in his station; that so far from my having any personal hostility against Colonel Farquhar it must be evident to your Honourable Court that in every step I took to remedy the inconvenience occasioned by his measures, much personal trouble and annoyance was occasioned to myself, whilst every disposition was shown to carry the same into effect with consideration to Lieutenant-Colonel Farquhar's feelings; that upon each point my views and proceedings were supported by the Bengal Government and that lastly, whilst that Authority questioned the necessity of my taking upon myself the temporary direction of the Settlement without their previous Authority, they had already appointed a Successor to Lieutenant-Colonel Farquhar upon the ground that a reference to his measures 'indicated to us at least a degree of facility and want of discretion not calculated to inspire any confidence in the administration of Lieutenant-Colonel Farquhar when left without a local control'."

Farquhar, on receiving a copy of Raffles' reply, made a brief rejoinder on 2nd April, but left out any reference to Singapore and made no further claim that the choice of the settlement had been his. It need not, perhaps, be added that his request to be restored to Singapore was not granted, and it would appear that such compensation as he received for the loss of his civil appointment was made in the form of military promotion; he reached ultimately the rank of major-general.

It remains to be considered how far Farquhar's complaint against Raffles of a tyrannous attitude was justified. It must be admitted that Raffles had not only claimed in full the powers to which he believed his superior position as Lieutenant-Governor entitled him, but had also, with increasing tempo in his last six months there, dictated the policy and, indeed, controlled the administration of the colony. But, considering the issues at stake, had he had any alternative? He had known he had but a few months at his disposal—on the assumption that his health would not completely collapse—and during that time he had to plan the layout of what he believed would at length be a great city, and take the essential steps to ensure that at least the skeleton outline was actually in being before his final departure. For more than three years Farquhar had sat relatively idle in Singapore, haunted by no vision of the future city. All Farquhar had seen was a trading centre, another, if perhaps on a larger scale, Malacca, where he had spent fifteen years so happily and peacefully. Farquhar, too, had been doubtless handicapped by his Malay connexions; although such affairs were not uncommon, it seems not improbable that his position had been weakened by his domestic life. Being by nature a weak man and an indolent one, he was unable to take up a strong and definite line of policy, his instinct being to let things slide, and to fall in with the wishes of those with whom he was closely connected.

On the other side of the picture it is fair to add that his mild and honest rule in Malacca had greatly endeared him to the Malays, and his presence in Singapore as Resident from the outset had attracted to the place many who might have hesitated to come had the Resident been a stranger. It is also right to remind ourselves that he had had many difficulties to overcone—not only practical difficulties on the spot, but also those arising from his having been subordinate to a supervising and highly critical authority so inconveniently far away as Bencoolen. This does not, however, alter the fact that in all the qualities required for the task of modelling a new colony on lines suitable to future greatness, a task that had to be accomplished with speed and decision, Farquhar was as wanting as Raffles was superlatively equipped.

When the clash of temperaments had made a final solution imperative, Raffles had had no option but to take the drastic step of removing Farquhar from his position as Resident. With his usual skill he had managed to keep technically within the law and had achieved his object by the simple method of suggesting that the resignation originally tendered by Farquhar in 1818 should be accepted in 1824, but he had overstepped his powers in dispossessing Farquhar before Crawfurd had arrived. As he himself observed in his reply to Farquhar's memorial, the Supreme Government had criticized this step, but as they had taken no further action, it is clear that the sheer necessity of the step had been fully recognized in India.

Raffles was under no illusion that Farquhar's attack on him in London could hardly have been launched at a more unfortunate moment, yet one is reluctant to think that Farquhar deliberately chose it out of malice. He was smarting under a sense of injury, quite understandable in the circumstances, yet he was a decent, kindly man, and one cannot imagine that his intention was so much to discredit Raffles as to vindicate himself. However that may be, Farquhar's action provided ammunition for Raffles' enemies at East India House, for almost certainly he had enemies there as well as friends. He had never completely lived down the undoubted stigma that had attached to him from the successive allegations of Gillespie, Blagrave, Robison and Bannerman. Here was yet another attack, not this time involving any major moral issue, but if soundly based, definitely affecting his character. Were Farquhar's charges all well founded, Raffles had at least been guilty of exaggerated claims to his own credit; also, and perhaps more important, his methods had been dictatorial. This latter allegation was particularly damaging because the Company had itself had frequent occasion to complain of his disregard, or at least evasion, of its positive orders, and Raffles had, in the directors' own experience, claimed on occasion powers to which, in their view, he had not been entitled. The fact that his independence of action had won a victory for England of a most far-reaching nature, in spite of all that the Company could do to stop him, had not added to his popularity. The atmosphere, then, in which his conduct in his Eastern career was to be reviewed, and his claims for financial indulgence or assistance, were now to be examined was not likely to be very favourable.

Thus, throughout the year 1825, the question of his claim for a pension remained unsatisfied. This had a restraining effect on other matters, such as the Singapore Institution.

"In consequence", he wrote to his cousin on 9th March, "of my having a *personal* question before the East India Company, I have refrained from Correspondence with that body on that subject, and as yet I have not moved much in the affairs of the Institution; but I propose after Easter to take it up and will then write you more fully. It will, I think, be advisable to move in the first instance in London where I propose appointing a Committee. Dr Morrison does not seem sanguine about Public Meetings and seems to think we can do more by committees."

It should be added that Robert Morrison had returned from China, proposing to remain for a time in England. He was living at Hackney, where he lectured twice a week and gave instruction in the Chinese language.

In the same letter, Raffles reported:

"We are now, I am happy to say, quietly settled in our new house [23 Lower Grosvenor Street] of which I have taken a lease for thirty years. It is not very large but in every way more comfortable than the house in Piccadilly. On enquiring respectg. the house you mentioned from Henley we found the tenure dependent on two lives, and otherwise inconvenient, and we are now in treaty for a place in Surrey near Godalming, a beautiful and romantic country and a tolerably comfortable house with an extensive manor. I shall not however fix in the first instance for more than a year or two, but as far as I can at present judge, I think it likely to answer our purpose permanently. My health has improved but I am still delicate and *unsound*, so much so that I am still unable to bear the fatigue of going into the City or attending to anything like business. I look forward with no little anxiety to May and June when we hope to quit London and ruralize."

"I am much interested at present in establishing a grand Zoological collection in the Metropolis with a Society for the introduction of living animals, bearing the same relation to Zoology as a science that the Horticultural Society does to Botany. The prospectus is drawn out and when a few copies are printed I will send some to you. We hope to have two thousand subscribers at 2*l* each; and it is further expected we may go far beyond the Jardin des Plantes at Paris. Sir Humphry Davy and myself are the projectors; and whilst he looks more to the practical and immediate utility to the country gentlemen, my attention is more attracted to the scientific department. More of this, however, hereafter."

It seems highly likely that this project had first entered his mind when he had visited the Jardin des Plantes during his Continental tour in 1817. Certain it is that in 1825 he constantly measured his proposals against what was to be found in Paris. Sophia stated in the *Memoir* that he had discussed the scheme with Sir Joseph Banks before leaving England for Sumatra. No written evidence exists to confirm this, but it is far from improbable that he had talked about such a scheme to Sir Joseph Banks or to the Duke of Somerset, or that when Dr Horsfield had come to England from Bencoolen with an introduction to Banks he had advised the Royal Society how the plan was developing in Raffles' mind. That Raffles and Horsfield had never discussed such a project seems unlikely. This, however, is purely speculative; what is certain is that, even before his arrival in England, Raffles had been so closely identified with the scheme that, at a meeting held in London in July 1824 "of friends of a proposed Zoological Society", he had been appointed chairman of the committee then set up to proceed with the scheme, although he had not yet reached home. No doubt the date of the meeting had been fixed in anticipation that the *Fame* would have arrived by that date. His appointment in absence postulates his knowledge of and his interest in the project. Among the members of this committee were the Duke of Somerset, Sir Humphry Davy and Dr Horsfield, who became for a time vice-secretary of the Society.

The prospectus mentioned by Raffles in his letter to his cousin was dated 1st March 1825. Three paragraphs only need be quoted here.

"It has long been a matter of deep regret to the cultivators of Natural History, that we possess no great scientific establishments either for teaching or elucidating Zoology; and no public menageries or collections of living animals where their nature, properties and habits may be studied. In almost every other part of Europe, except in the metropolis of the British Empire, something of this kind exists: but though richer than any other country in the extent and variety of our possessions, and having more facilities from our Colonies, our fleets, and our varied and constant intercourse with every quarter of the globe, for collecting specimens and introducing living animals, we have as yet attempted little and effected almost nothing; and the student of Natural History, or the philosopher who wishes to examine animated nature, has no other resource but that of visiting and profiting by the magnificent institutions of neighbouring countries.

"In the hope of removing this opprobrium to our age and nation, it is proposed to establish a Society bearing the same relation to Zoology that the Horticultural does to Botany, and upon a similar principle and plan. The great objects should be, the introduction of new varieties, breeds, and races of animals for the purpose of domestication or for stocking our farm-yards, woods, pleasure-grounds, and wastes; with the establishment of a general Zoological Collection, consisting of prepared specimens in the different classes and orders, so as to afford a correct view of the Animal Kingdom at large in as complete a series as may be practicable, and at the same time point out the analogies between the animals domesticated, and those which are similar in character upon which the first experiments may be made.

"To promote these objects, a piece of ground should be provided in the neighbourhood of the metropolis affording sufficient accommodation for the above purposes; with a suitable establishment, so conducted as to admit of its extension on additional means being afforded."

During the same month Raffles and Sophia were invited to visit Wilberforce and his wife in their "lowly retirement" at Uxbridge Common.

"You will, I trust," wrote Wilberforce, "allow me to receive you without ceremony which is only of use where we wish to keep people at a distance, whereas I trust that between us there is a mutual disposition to render our connexion close as well as lasting."

On 28th March Wilberforce recorded in his diary:

"Sir Stamford and Lady Raffles and Dr Morrison, the Chinese scholar, came between one and two—Lord Gambier called and we had an entertaining confabulation. . . . Singular criminal law of Batas by which persons committing great crimes sentenced to be eat up alive, the injured party having the first choice, the ear claimed and eat, &c, until the mass fall on. The coup de grâce, except in strong cases, given early. When Sir Stamford contended against the practice the people urged 'What defence can we have for our morals?'"

The proposed Zoological Society bulked large in Raffles' correspondence during this period. He wrote to Sir Robert Inglis on 28th April:

"As Sir Humphry [Davy] has gone out of Town leaving with me the list of names &c to add to the names of as many of my friends as might be desirous of promoting it, I am induced to ask if I may have the honour of putting down your name. Mr Peel's[1] name is at the head of the list and those of Lord Spencer, Lord Lansdowne, Lord Stanley, Mr Heber[2], and many others of weight follow. When the list is completed to a hundred, which I conclude it will be in a day or two, it is proposed to appoint a Committee when the objects of the Society will be more clearly defined. In the first instance we look mainly to the country gentlemen for support, in point of numbers; but the character of the Institution must of course depend on the proportion of men of science and sound principles which it contains. I look more to the scientific part of it and propose, if it is established on a respectable footing, to transfer to it the collections in Natural History, which I have brought home with me."

To his cousin he wrote on 18th May:

"The few copies of the Zoological plan which were struck off were soon dispersed; I did not think of sending some to you until I found I had not *one* left for myself. Some idea has been entertained of throwing

[1] Peel was then Home Secretary.

[2] Reginald Heber, second bishop of Calcutta, author of "From Greenland's Icy Mountains" and many other hymns.

the prospectus into a new form; and at this very time I am a little at issue with Sir Humphry Davy as to the share which science is to have in the project. . . ."

Much as he enjoyed the pleasures of the capital, Raffles' heart was in the country.

"My health, thank God," he wrote in the same letter, "is upon the whole improved, and I am happy to say both Sophia and my little one are quite well. Necessity has compelled me to go much into Society and I am almost surprised that at this gay season of festivity I have been able to carry on the War. Seldom a day passes without an engagement for dinner, and for many weeks I have not been able to command an hour's leisure. It is true I have not attended very closely to anything, but all is so new, varied and important in the Metropolis of this great Empire, after so long an absence in the woods and wilds of the East, that, like the Bee, I wander from flower to flower and drink in the delicious nutriment from the numerous intellectual and moral sources which surround me.

"As yet we are unsettled as to our Country residence, but I am in treaty for a place which will bring us nearer to you by about eleven or twelve miles. My attention was turned to it by our revered friend Mr Wilberforce who has just purchased a property at Hendon, and the place to which I am looking adjoins his property. They ask £20,000 and I have offered £18,000, so you may judge how the matter stands at present."

In spite of uncertain health, he had not yet abandoned the idea of standing for Parliament, and referred to the subject in the same letter; but only a few days later came a sharp warning that his hope of an active life was but slender. On his way home from calling on his friend, Murdoch, he was seized with a fainting fit. Luckily a doctor happened to be passing, and carried him to his home. In reply to an enquiry from his cousin, who had heard of this sudden attack, he wrote on 24th May:

"Thank God I can return a tolerably satisfactory answer to your kind enquiry by saying that tho' still rather weak and nervous, I am again getting about. My attack was sudden and unexpected, but fortunately was not apoplectic as was at first feared. I was inanimate for about an hour, but on being bled got better, and have had no return. It has reminded me, however, that I have been quite long enough in London and its dissipations and excitements, and we are now making arrangements for retreating as soon as we can. Nothing has yet been determined respecting the property at Hendon, but we are still in treaty, the difference being about a thousand pounds. Sophia is quite well and desires her kindest love. . . . The dear children are in excellent health and spirits. They went to Hornsey yesterday to remain till we join them on the 15th proximo. I am afraid of writing much as my head is not quite what it should be."

There seems little doubt that he had suffered a mild stroke. It was high time he left the excitements of London for the quiet of the Hulls' home at Hornsey.

He wrote again to Dr T. Raffles on 6th June:

"I sent you by coach of Saturday a few of the copies of the Prospectus of the Zoological Society. It is a subject on which much has been said, and more might be written; but it has been thought best, in the present state of the speculation, to confine the notice to a few words. The names are coming in fast; and I shall be happy to receive a list of any of your friends at Liverpool, who may be desirous of becoming subscribers. The amount of the sum will not ruin them, neither will they find themselves in bad company: and no pecuniary call will be made until the plan is advanced, and we can show them something for their money.

"It is proposed to have a general meeting of the subscribers who may be in Town, in the course of the present month, in order to appoint a Committee, and proceed to business.

"We expect to have at least 500 members to begin with, and that Government will provide us with ground, &c.

"I am happy to say that I continue tolerably well; although the last serious attack, in reminding me of my mortality, has thrown me back considerably both in strength and spirits; so much so, that I am obliged to forego Society in a great measure, and to come to the resolution of quitting London almost immediately. We have fixed on the 15th to move to Hornsey, for a week or two, whence we shall remove to our new dwelling at High Wood. This place I have just purchased, and we are to have possession at Midsummer. It is in the parish of Hendon, and on the borders of Hertfordshire, but in Middlesex, eleven miles from London, and three from Barnet, so that we shall be at least ten miles nearer to you than we are in London. The house is small, but compact, and the grounds well laid out for appearance and economy. The land, 112 acres, in grass; and, as I have taken the growing crops, I must begin haymaking while the sun shines. There is a very good farming Establishment on a small scale, and I am now rejoiced that I can offer you and Mrs Raffles and the children comfortable beds and accommodation, whenever you can spend a few weeks with us. I anticipate, with the blessing of God, great advantages from the change of air and occupation. We have now been nearly eight months in London and most heartily am I tired of it; indeed I don't think I could stand a month longer at the rate we have been obliged to live, without quiet or retirement for a day. . . . The last attack has so shaken my confidence and nerves that I have hardly spirit at the present moment to enter upon public life, and prudence dictates the necessity of my keeping as quiet as I can, until I completely re-establish my health; a few months in the Country and on the farm may set me up again. You will probably have heard of the melancholy loss I have sustained in the death of my poor Sister Ann; she was carried off by a rapid Consumption and died at her cousin's Mrs Wise at Edinburgh. I was too weak to bear the journey or should have been on the spot at the time."

He ended with this postscript:

"I am not sure that I mentioned in my former letter that my attention was directed to High Wood in the first instance by our respected friend Mr Wilberforce who has purchased the Estate adjoining so that we are to be next door neighbours and to divide the Hill[1] between us. I am happy to say his health is improving. Do you not almost envy us such a neighbour?"

The move to High Wood was planned for the beginning of July, but there was some delay in making out the title. When Thomas McQuoid arrived from Java with his wife and two children in the middle of that month, they were still at Hornsey.

"Our plan", Raffles wrote to McQuoid in the 20th, "is to go to High Wood in the course of the week, either Thursday or Saturday, and at any time after the latter day we should be happy to receive you there with a hearty welcome and to give you a glass of home brewed. The house as yet is not furnished, but beds have been sent off and though we may delay for a few days removing the children, we shall be able to accommodate you as a bachelor for as many nights and days as you can afford to stay with us. Your best plan will be to take a chaise from whatever part of London you arrive at—if at the West end the best road is the Edgware Road going out at Tyburn Turnpike, the end of Oxford Road [Street], and proceed along the Road till you arrive at Edgware about eight miles from Town. About the middle of Edgware turn off to the right and the distance from there to High Wood is about 3 miles. If you start from the City you must go by Hampstead and Mill Hill, but the road is very hilly and, though pleasant, not so short as that by Edgware. . . . A Stage goes at 4 in the aft. from the Bank and another from Tottenham Court Road, but few prefer that conveyance, it is uncertain if you can get a place, and I hardly recommend it."

Mrs Arbuthnot refers in her *Journal* to the heat wave in London at that time. Raffles reported to McQuoid that Sophia was overcome by it.

"Everything as you may well suppose is burnt up here. In the country the Lakes and Ponds are rapidly becoming dry."

He ended: "Believe me sincerely yours in truth and *much* warmth."

McQuoid & Company had been instructed by Raffles to transmit his property—something over £16,000—to England through his London agents, Fairlie, Bonham & Company. As he had not yet received the Court's decision on the outstanding question of salary, the Government securities purchased in that connexion remained deposited with the Accountant-General in Calcutta.

[1] Highwood Hill.

It would appear that the move into High Wood took place at the end of July. The house in Lower Grosvenor Street was kept on. Sophia recorded the happiness that country life at once afforded her husband. When in Bencoolen, he had always looked forward to it, and for once his anticipations of pleasure were fully realized.

"To Sir Stamford the enjoyments of country life were peculiarly delightful, indeed almost necessary; and when he found himself once more at liberty to cultivate his garden, to attend to his farm and to interest himself in those simple pleasures in which he had always delighted, he hoped to regain that health and strength which alone were wanting to his happiness. Here he could indulge the fullness of his heart without restraint; and it was his intention, had not God ordained better things for him, to have passed the greater part of his time in the happy retirement which the spot he selected for his residence promised to secure him."

Here is Raffles' description, in a letter to his cousin on 15th August:

"I farm the ground, 111 acres, myself, and Sophia takes charge of the Poultry and Pigs. We brew our own beer and bake our own bread and lead an entire Country life. The change of air, scene and interest have already worked an amendment in my health, and as this is the first point to be attended to I devote my time almost exclusively to the farm and grounds. . . . Our excellent friend Mr Wilberforce has not yet been able to enter on his residence in consequence of the alterations it is undergoing, but we have reason to expect him shortly after Michaelmas. He is at present with his family at Sandgate and in better health than usual. . . .

"I have invested upwards of twenty thousand pounds in this place, and I hope it will yield me something better than 3 p. Cent and I have no other property which I should wish to tie up. What the East India Company may do is uncertain but if their liberality keeps up with their delay I ought to expect something handsome, though I confess I do not look for much."

That all was not going well in Leadenhall Street, Raffles was only too well aware. He wrote on the matter of his pension in a letter to Murdoch in October. After mentioning that William Astell, retired chairman of the Company, was favourable to his claims, he continued:

"However, his view of the case was not to look into any public proceedings but simply to propose a pension of 500*l* a year for my losses by the 'Fame', observing that Java was an old story and could not be gone into. . . . I certainly looked to something more both in money and in words. . . . I surely can hardly reduce my expectations below the retiring allowance of a General Officer or Bengal Civilian after 22 years service, and in looking for not less than 1,000*l* per annum I do not think I can be considered as unreasonable. Nevertheless, had the 500*l* been offered to me last year, I do not say I should have refused it."

The letter ends with a request to Murdoch to use his influence with Sir George Robinson, who was to be the new chairman of the Company, to press his case for him. He had also canvassed other powerful friends for support. They all with one accord made different excuses. For example, Hastings, who, for financial reasons, had been glad to accept the governorship of Malta after his return from India, replied from Malta:

"You will not, I am sure, doubt the satisfaction I should have in bearing the fullest testimony to your zeal and exertions. The doing so, however, in general terms would appear irreconcilable to the Records which exhibit instances where the Indian Govt. whilst I was at the head of it had not approved some of your measures. On the strange terms existing between me and the India Office such an inconsistency would not fail to be taken up and distorted. . . . It would rejoice me to be serviceable in any way not involving this dilemma, tho' I fear I have at present little influence capable of being so employed."

Neither Wynn nor Canning was any more helpful. Wynn wrote from the Board of Control on 7th October:

"You appear to be unaware that in the rewarding of services rendered to the Company we possess at the India Board only negative power; we can revise or curtail but we cannot originate or increase. This is the extent of our *legal* power, and I can assure you that there is seldom a disposition to allow us by our recommendation *practically* to exceed these limits."

Canning wrote on 27th November: "I will with great pleasure write or speak to Sir G. Robinson in the best manner that I can. But I can by no means answer for his compliance with any wish of mine upon a subject which he will certainly consider a matter of public duty. I have no reason, however, to apprehend that he thinks less favourably of your services and of your claims than I do."

Having paid a visit in September to Sir Miles Nightingall in Suffolk and to other friends in Norfolk, Raffles wrote to his cousin in October from High Wood:

"Poor little Charles narrowly escaped with his life by my horse running away with us and giving him a severe kick which has slightly fractured the skull. But he is doing well—so am I from the effects of a severe bruising and exertion on the same occasion."

In November his uncle, William Raffles, died. On hearing of this, Raffles wrote to his cousin:

"I have been confined to bed the whole day with one of my most violent headaches, and am therefore only able to say that if it pleases God I will most certainly be with you on Monday to assist in the mournful ceremony and pay the last tribute of respect and duty that is in my power. . . . Had I been able to move I should on the receipt of the first letter . . . have gone instantly to Spitalfields to offer what personal aid and consolation I could. I propose returning on Monday to High Wood direct from Spitalfields, and as we are obliged to leave Town on Friday perhaps you may still accompany us."

Dr Raffles did return with him to High Wood, and sent his wife a description of the house in a letter dated 14th November:

"The house is a modern edifice, but it is built upon the site of the old mansion which was formerly a seat of the Russells. And—what renders it peculiarly interesting—it was the residence of the patriotic Lord Russell from which he was taken to the Tower and thence to the scaffold. Many of the letters of Lady Russell which have been published are dated from this place, though called by her 'Totridge', for it was at that time in Totteridge parish. The views are most extensive and beautiful, and the diversity of hill and dale, wood and lawn truly delightful. My cousin takes great delight in the place and has already derived incalculable benefit to his health from the air and exercise which it gives him."

In his reminiscences, Dr Raffles observed:

"Wilberforce and Sir Stamford were friends, and at length came to be next-door neighbours, dividing Highwood Hill, near Barnet, between them. The village at the top of the hill was also pretty equally divided between them, Sir Stamford owning one half and Wilberforce the other. Each portion had a public house in it, and he used to laugh and say, 'Wilberforce has the "Crown", and I the "Rising Sun".' Each had an excellent house, unpretending, but very convenient. My cousin's amount of land was about one hundred and twenty statute acres, yielding enough for all purposes, with a considerable amount for sale. In fact the family lived upon it—house and stables. Lady Raffles told me that she bought nothing but wine and fish. She fed her own mutton and veal and poultry, and exchanged with the butcher for beef. . . .

"Before he [Wilberforce] came to reside at Highwood, he left the laying out of the grounds contiguous to the house to the taste of Sir Stamford. He [Raffles] took me in with him on one occasion to show me what he was doing; and I well remember the glee with which he said, taking me to a long mound which he had raised and planted with shrubs and flowers, 'There, I have raised this mound that the little man may enjoy his daily walk, sheltered by it from the north winds, which would otherwise be too severe for him.' Alas! How brief was the period allowed for the happy intercourse he thus anticipated! . . ."

As soon as his cousin had left High Wood, Raffles went to stay with Lord Harcourt at Nuneham Park, Oxford.

"About this time", wrote Travers in December, "a wonderful Commercial shock or convulsion was felt throughout the Kingdom. In London the chief and most respectable Banking houses were obliged to suspend payment and of course such a panic could not be confined to London.

Every day brought accounts of Country Banks failing and the want of commercial confidence was most generally acknowledged . . . the issue of such a great paper currency was . . . the chief source of the evil but many circumstances besides contributed."

It was almost a matter of course that that habitually unlucky man, Thomas Stamford Raffles, should be one of the sufferers. He mentioned it in a letter to Sir Robert Inglis on 31st December. Reference was made in the same letter to two other problems that had engaged his attention on return from Nuneham. One was how he could obtain a commission as a magistrate, and the other was a proposal to build a chapel of ease. It seems that the vicar of Hendon was far from well disposed to Raffles and Wilberforce because of their views on the slave trade; apparently he had investments in the West Indies, and was not at all enthusiastic about the emancipation of slaves. Neither Wilberforce nor Raffles was anxious to attend his church, and it was because of this that they had decided upon a chapel of ease, an offshoot of the parish church.

"The application I am about to make to you", wrote Raffles to Sir Robert," will be the best proof I can give that I am recovering my health and feel some confidence in my future exertions. My neighbours here have urged me strongly to act as a Magistrate, and the necessity of such an authority is unquestionable. We are more than four miles removed from our parish church and the exercise of anything like police; the consequences are as might be expected: the poorer classes left to themselves without control in this world, and neither checked by moral or any other authority, are in a sad, degraded and irregular state. We are just on the borders of another County not famous for the moral character of its inhabitants, in the vicinity of Barnes and Whetstone, which is a further reason for my undertaking the office.

"We are now concerting a plan for the erection of a Chapel of Ease; and the next object is an efficient Magistracy; for some time I resisted the entreaties of my friends that I should endeavour to get into the Commission, not feeling my health equal to the duties, and apprehensive that although during the longest part of my public life I have been acting on the principle and directing others how to execute similar offices, I might myself be deficient in the details; but from the improvement of my health and from a desire to be useful to the extent of my ability, added to the consideration that it may afford me a means of becoming *practically* acquainted with the real state of our society and of much regarding our laws and usages which it is impossible for me to know otherwise than theoretically, I no longer hesitate. . . . I have in a great measure recovered my health by being quietly in the country and avoiding public or large parties, and the benefits of a pure air; but we propose going into Town in the course of a few months."

Chapter Thirty-two

ENGLAND, 1826

"I HARDLY know how to account", wrote Raffles to his cousin on 7th February 1826, "for not having written to you since you left us. I was then very ill, but thank God I have upon the whole very much improved in my general health since, and am at present, barring occasional attacks, in better health than I have enjoyed since my return to England. Sophia has also improved and the Children, with the exception of Colds, are doing well. I have however had, and still have a good many annoyances and inquietudes which have occasionally disturbed my peace of mind owing to the misconduct and distresses of friends—but I hope these will soon be over. I go into Town to-morrow, and Sophia and the children follow me in the course of the week for the Season so that the House is quite dilapidated, carpets being taken up &c. We propose residing there till the end of May when we hope to return to the delights of a Country life. I look forward with dread and anxiety to the late hours and bustle of a London life. Nevertheless, I feel myself compelled to re-embark in it for a few months, and if I find my health seriously affected I shall without hesitation fly from it to this retreat.

"Of our Chapel I am sorry to say I can as yet make no very favourable report. We have not yet come to any conclusion and the difficulty seems to rest with our Vicar who is of a very peculiar character and on bad terms with most of his Parishioners. Mr Wilberforce being Evangelical is a great stickler for Mother Church, so that I anticipate we shall not be able to proceed without the aid of the Bishop and our ecclesiastic local. His [Wilberforce's] son, Robert, is just about taking Orders and if anything offers he would be gratified that his son performed the duties. My recommendation is to set about building the Chapel itself and discuss the government of it afterwards. . . .

"Our plans for the Summer are not yet fixed and will not be for some months. I do not find myself so much given to travel as formerly, but Liverpool and the North constantly attract my attention. And I need not say how anxious I am to visit the former.

"The East India Company are now talking of taking up my case and granting me an annuity, but I fear it will be very moderate, and 500*l* a year is the largest amount I hear of. This, had I the means of living independent of them, I should not be inclined to accept, but necessity and consideration for my family must predominate and I must e'en be content with what I can get. I have unfortunately been a considerable loser by the cession of Bencoolen—some thousands. My Bankers have failed here and altogether my prospects are not as comfortable as they were. But the pressure is I hope only temporary, and I trust all will be right again and that I shall not be obliged to seek a tropical clime again in search of *filthy lucre*—but nothing else would, I think, tempt me to venture."

Another meeting of the Zoological Society was held on 26th February, when there were present, as the still-existent manuscript records, "Sir T. S. Raffles (in the Chair), His Grace the Duke of Somerset, Earl Darnley, Sir Humphry Davy, Bt., Sir Everard Home, Bt., Davies Gilbert, Esq., Joseph Sabine, Esq., N. A. Vigors, Esq., Dr. Horsfield, and, visitors, Lord Auckland, Sir Robert Inglis, Bt., and Dr Harewood".

Joseph Sabine and Nicholas Aylward Vigors were treasurer and secretary respectively of the Society.

At the meeting it was resolved *inter alia* "that it be designated the Zoological Society and that an application be made to Government for an allotment of ground in the Regent's Park suitable to the purposes of the Institution".

"A Deputation consisting of the Earl of Darnley, Lord Auckland, Sir Humphry Davy and Sir Stamford Raffles is appointed to wait on the Earl of Liverpool [Prime Minister] in order to ascertain the disposition of Government and to apply for a grant of the ground required.

"Sir Humphry Davy being already in communication with Mr Peel, who has shewn a favourable disposition to support and patronize the Society, he is requested in the first instance to confer with him and obtain his advice and if possible his assistance in attaining the object desired.

"It being considered advisable that the objects and pursuits of the Society should be clearly defined in a Prospectus, and that a plan for the formation of the Society should be framed, a sub-Committee consisting of Sir Stamford Raffles, Mr Sabine and Mr Vigors is appointed for the purpose."

Lord Auckland and Raffles made an inspection of the piece of ground offered by the Commissioners of Woods and Forests. They wrote to one of the Commissioners on 17th March:

"We yesterday visited the piece of ground abutting the Regent's Canal, and we are of the opinion that from its great publicity, the expense of fencing, its extreme narrowness and nearness to the road, it was liable to many objections, and that it was possible upon further consideration that the Crown might be induced to let us have ground still more adapted to our purpose. . . ."

They asked for a plot of five or six acres in a more central position.

"We would also suggest our wishes that this grant should be open to further extension hereafter as the Society may require it. . . . It has not escaped us that some objection might possibly arise from Mr Jenkins [a nurseryman], the present Tenant at Will of the ground in question, but we have no doubt that an arrangement could be effected with him by which we could offer him compensation for the removal of plants from the land which it may be necessary immediately to clear, and by giving him the superintendence of our ornamental pleasure ground, and that upon consideration of new attractions to the neighbourhood of his garden he will be led at once to acquiesce."

The Commissioners were not in favour of this. Apart from other considerations, Jenkins had "rented the ground on the understanding that he should continue to do so unless the land should be required for building ranges of dwelling houses, and that as he had expended heavy sums in bringing the ground into a high state of cultivation he would require adequate compensation".

The Society then applied for "twenty acres in the north-eastern corner of the Park". Before a reply was forthcoming, Raffles received in March a letter from Thomas McQuoid, reporting that his business house in Batavia had failed and that he was bankrupt. This was a terrible blow to Raffles, for he lost thereby the £16,000 or more that McQuoid & Company had been instructed to remit to London. It represented the greater part of his remaining capital. Travers also was involved, but only to a small extent. Raffles seems to have received this news with his usual philosophic calmness, and without reproaches; but he wrote at once to Travers, suggesting that he came over to England to attend the meeting of creditors.

"Knowing full well the nature of all Dutch Institutions," wrote Travers, "and greatly apprehensive of the property of McQuoid & Co. falling into their hands I thought it best to proceed without delay to London to make the best arrangements possible to secure our property from getting into Dutch hands."

Travers and his wife Mary arrived in the second week in April and took apartments in South Audley Street.

"On Monday morning I went at an early hour to 23 Lower Grosvenor Street to find my worthy and esteemed friends Sir Stamford and Lady Raffles in perfect good health and looking extremely well. I remained with them, and returned [to South Audley Street] with Sir Stamford who wished to see Mary and we were soon joined by Lady Raffles who was most affectionate and kind. We passed all the first day with the Raffles's [*sic*] who were fortunately disengaged, and we enjoyed an evening together not a little. One striking difference in my friend Sir Stamford I perceived during the evening. Although his spirit and animation was great, his articulation was at times heavy, thick and inarticulate. . . .

"We passed a very pleasant morning at Hornsey returning a visit of

Mr and Mrs Hull. We found all the family excepting Mr Hull at home, and little Ella looking charming well. . . . On returning, Sir Stamford and I stopped in Regents Park, went to visit the Diorama and walked to view the numberless new buildings which astonished me to see erected in so short a space of time."

That evening was spent at Covent Garden, where "Oberon" was being performed.

"We soon commenced business and a day was appointed for our meeting the creditors in England of Mess. McQuoid & Co. when we had much tedious discussion but at length came to one determination that of sending out Powers of Atty. to Mess. Milne & Heswell to act for and secure for us all the property within their reach.

"Poor McQuoid and his poor wife passed a day with us, he looking the picture of misery and she bearing up extremely well. Never was a more distressing scene to me. Relief of any kind I was unable to offer. Even advice on such an occasion is difficult to give. It struck me and I am still of the same opinion that nothing is so likely to suit his present situation as a return to India, either to Pinang, Calcutta or Java. I can see no chance of [his] doing any thing in this country.

"The Affairs of the house appear to me to have been but indifferently managed and I fear my friend McQuoid is but ill calculated for a merchant. . . .

"McQuoid is amongst my earliest friends for whom I had a sincere affection and to see him at the close of his days bereft of all the comforts to which he had been so long accustomed was indeed a severe blow. His return to this country was most truly unfortunate—in short every circumstance attended to render his fall heavier, but we must not repine. . . .

"Our next trip was with the Raffles to High Wood to see Sir Stamford's seat with which I was much pleased. . . . The place adjoins a very much inferior Estate belonging to Mr Wilberforce which we went to visit. Sir Stamford seemed to enjoy seeing every part of the place and I was greatly pleased at all I did see. He was engaged to dine out and we returned about six, the distance not being more than Eleven miles."

At long last the East India Company recorded, on 12th April, its official recognition of Raffles' public service.

"Of Java.—The Court admit, that the success of the expedition to Java was promoted by the plans and information of Sir Stamford Raffles.

"That the representation of Sir Stamford Raffles as to the financial embarrassment of Java on the outset of his government is correct.

"That those financial difficulties were enhanced by the inevitable hostilities with Palembang and Djojocarta.

"That of the measures introduced by Sir Stamford Raffles for the removal of the financial embarrassments; viz. the sale of lands, withdrawal of Dutch paper currency, and a new system of land revenue:—

"The sale of lands is considered to have been a questionable proceeding.

"The entire series of measures for the reform of the currency are conceded to have been well adapted to their object.

"With regard to the system of revenue introduced by him, the Court state that they would have been inclined to augur favourably of the success of his measures, and consider it highly probable that the colony would have soon been brought at least to liquidate its own expenses by the lenient and equitable administration of Sir Stamford Raffles' system.

"The regulations for reform in the judicial department and police, the court consider entitled, both in their principles and in their details, to a considerable degree of praise.

"On the measures respecting Borneo, Banca and Japan, the Court remark, that, under a permanent tenure of Java, and a different system of policy, the measures in question (promoting intercourse and enlarging the British power) would have been valuable service.

"SUMATRA.—The measures of internal reform introduced by Sir Stamford Raffles are generally approved.

"In his political measures he incurred the strong disapprobation of the Court; but the motives by which he was actuated were unquestionably those of zealous solicitude for the British interests in the Eastern Seas, and form a part of a series of measures which have terminated in the establishment of Singapore.

"SINGAPORE.—It is allowed that Sir Stamford Raffles developed the exclusive views of the Dutch, and the measures ultimately carried into effect are to be attributed to his instrumentality; and to him the country is chiefly indebted for the advantages which the settlement of Singapore has secured to it. The Court consider this to be a very strong point in Sir Stamford Raffles' favour, and are willing to give him to the full extent the benefit of their testimony respecting it.

"His administration of Singapore has been approved by the Bengal Government."

The Court's opinion of Raffles' general services was summed up thus:

"The Government of Sir Stamford Raffles appears with sufficient evidence to have conciliated the good feelings of, at least, the great majority of the European and Native population; his exertions for the interests of literature and science are highly honourable to him, and have been attended with distinguished success; and although his precipitate and unauthorized emancipation of the Company's slaves, and his formation of a settlement at Pulo Nias, chiefly with a view to the suppression of a slave-traffic, are justly censured by the Court, his motives in those proceedings, and his unwearied zeal for the abolition of slavery, ought not to be passed over without an expression of approbation."

There was no mention of a pension. Instead, on the very same day, the Company demanded immediate repayment of £22,272.

The claim was set out thus, except that the rupees were worked into sicca rupees before being converted into pounds sterling:

	Rupees	*Pounds Sterling*
Salary as Lieutenant-Governor at Bencoolen, February 1817 to March 1818	36,284	
Interest, $5\frac{1}{8}$ per cent.	4,959	
	41,243	£3,864
Loss in respect of discount	31,435	
Interest, at 5 per cent.	3,929	
	35,364	3,313
Salary as Resident, 1816–1817	30,687	
Interest, at $4\frac{1}{4}$ per cent.	1,413	
	32,100	2,919
Commission on exports	73,792	6,914
Extra charges at Acheen and Singapore	49,840	4,670
Total		£21,680
Add balance of proceeds of spice, per Borneo		592
Grand Total		£22,272

According to the biographer H. E. Egerton, Raffles had received a warning from the directors in a letter dated 22nd February that the claim would be made. Whether or not this had been so, his feelings can be imagined. The original sums included in the statement had been the subject of intermittent discussion over a number of years, and just before he had left Bencoolen he had written at length upon the unfairness of them. But nothing he had written then or said since had produced the slightest effect. The only new feature was that interest was now charged on the major amounts outstanding and had since 1816 reached a very substantial figure. At any time during those ten years the Company had had it in its power to exact repayment.

Boulger suggests that the dispatch of the official approbation at this particular juncture was intended to show that the financial demand implied no reflection on Raffles' personal character, or on the merits of his services. If such was the intention, it must have gravely miscarried; we can only suppose that Raffles would have regarded it as a piece of gratuitous cruelty, for such it surely was. He replied to Joseph Dart, secretary to the Company, on 29th April:

"I have the honour to acknowledge the receipt of your letter of the 12th inst., and to request that you will assure the Honourable Court that I should have lost no time in complying with the requisition it contains, had not a most distressing and unlooked-for event, which occurred at the moment, deprived me of the means.

"The event to which I allude is the insolvency of the house in India, which was intrusted with the remittance of my property to this country, by which I have suffered a loss exceeding £16,000, with little or no chance of recovering any part. For the particulars of the calamity I request to refer to Messrs. Fairlie, Bonham, & Co., my Agents in this country, through whom the remittance was to have been made. Thus circumstanced, I have no alternative but to place the Honourable Court in possession of the fact, and to throw myself on their liberality.

"I have already stated to the Honourable Committee of Correspondence, that I was prepared to meet the two first and most important items by giving an immediate order on the Accountant-General and Sub-Treasurer in Bengal, to the extent of the Government securities deposited in their hands, with an order on my Agents for the balance, and I trust that, as the money was placed there for the especial purpose of meeting this emergency, the Honourable Court will not, under my present circumstances, object to this arrangement.

"On the third and next important item, viz. the amount drawn as commission on exports, while I express my readiness to bow to the decision of the Honourable Court, and to abide by it without demur, I beg respectfully to offer the following explanation:—

"It may naturally be asked why in this case I did not take the same precaution as I did in the former, by placing the amount on deposit pending the reference to Europe. To this I reply that, considering the length of time which had elapsed, the ground of the Bengal Government having sanctioned it, subject to the approval of the Honourable Court, and the non-expression of the Court's dissent to the sums drawn, I was led to infer the same was not objected to by them.

"I will only add that the delay in the Court's decision on the question has subjected me to a total loss of the amount by the present failure of my agents; for, had the Court's definitive reply reached me while at Bencoolen, I then had the funds at hand awaiting their orders.

"I would not urge this explanation with a view to any evasion of the orders now received, but simply to account for not having made any provision to meet the present contingency, and as a ground on which I venture to hope that, if still insisted upon by the Honourable Court to its present extent, I may be allowed the indulgence of time to enable me to raise the sum necessary. At present I have no other means of doing so but by disposing of my India Stock, and the sale of the little property I had set apart as a provision for my family after my death. In making this appeal to the Court, I do so in the hope that they take into consideration a life actively and most zealously devoted to their service."

The "house in India" mentioned in the second paragraph is stated by Boulger to have been "the great house of Palmer, of Calcutta and Hyderabad". He thus falls into a double error. John Palmer of Calcutta had no direct connexion with Rumbold & Palmer of Hyderabad. The latter had been forced into liquidation by Metcalfe before Raffles had left the East. John Palmer also failed, but not until 1830, and for a very different reason. Boulger was no doubt misled by the use of the word "India", which was at that time used generally for "the East". The "house in India" was McQuoid & Company of Batavia.

The first general meeting of the proposed Zoological Society was held on the same day at the Regent Street headquarters of the Horticultural Society. Among the forty-eight who attended were Raffles, the Marquis of Lansdowne, the Earls of Darnley and Egremont, Lord Auckland, Lord Clinton, Lord Stanley, Sir Humphry Davy, Sir Everard Home, N. A. Vigors and Dr Horsfield. The chair was taken by Raffles. After the adoption of a number of resolutions, it was moved by the Marquis of Lansdowne, seconded by the Earl of Darnley, and carried by acclamation "That Sir Stamford Raffles be appointed president of the Zoological Society". The vice-presidents were to be the Duke of Somerset, the Marquis of Lansdowne, the Earl of Darnley and Lord Auckland.

Earlier in the proceedings a letter from the Commissioners of Woods and Forests had been read. It was dated the previous day.

"My Lord and Sirs,—The Commissioners of His Majesty's Woods, Forests, and Land Revenues, having laid before the Lords of His Majesty's Treasury your applications, on behalf of the Zoological Society, for a grant of land in the Regent's Park, for the purposes of the Society's intended establishment; I am commanded to acquaint you that their Lordships have been pleased to authorize the said Commissioners to let to you, as Trustees for the Society, on a yearly tenancy, a plot of land not exceeding five acres in the whole, partly on the situation marked No. 8 on the accompanying Plan of the Park, and partly on the opposite side of the adjoining road, at a yearly rent calculated at the rate of £6, 6s. per acre for so much as shall be within the Park, and at 8s. per foot on the frontage of so much as shall be on the north-east of the said road; with the option on the part of the Society of taking a Lease at the end of five years for such further term as may be agreed upon, and at such rent as shall be equal to the rent paid by other Lessees of land designed for sites for villas in the interior of the Park, and upon the usual conditions.

"The Society is to fence and lay out, plant, keep, and occupy the ground within the Park in such manner as shall be previously approved by the said Commissioners, who are to be at liberty to require the removal of any animal which may be brought upon the premises by the Society, and which may be deemed likely to become a nuisance or objectionable in the neighbourhood. . . ."

The site is clearly defined in the *Centenary History of the Zoological Society of London*, published by the Society in 1929, the centenary of its incorporation by Royal Charter in 1829.

"The plot of land on the south side of the Outer Circle roadway, not exceeding 5 acres, was approximately the area enclosed in a line from the present Main Gate by the Terrace Walk to about the beginning of the Great Lawn, then turning at right angles to meet the Outer Circle again, near the Old Tunnel, and on the North Side, the strip exactly opposite, between the Outer Circle and the Canal, but continued to the west about the same distance. Any buildings were to be confined to the land between the Outer Circle and the Canal."

For this description and other details concerning the formation of the Society, we are indebted to Sir Peter Chalmers Mitchell, C.B.E., D.SC., F.R.S., author of the history and also to the Zoological Society.

Raffles did not survive to see the Society in active existence, but, in the words of Sir Peter Chalmers Mitchell, he did live "long enough, not only to establish the Society, but to stamp its future with his strong personality". The bust of Raffles, as founder of the Society, is familiar to all visitors to the Lion House in the London Zoo.

Feeling perhaps that an appeal *ad misericordiam* was likely to avail him little with the East India Company, Raffles followed up his first letter to Dart with another, which was dated 16th May and dealt in detail with the several claims of the Company.

"As it may be more regular", he wrote, "that the explanations referred to in my last letter should be forwarded to you instead of the Auditor, I have now the honour to submit them.

"In explanation of the sums drawn as Extraordinary Charges at Acheen and Singapore, amounting to Rs.49,840, I request to observe on the first item, viz. 'In 1819-20, charge as Agent to the Governor-General, Rs.27,766.'

"This disbursement was incurred and charged under the authority, and consistently with the orders, of the Supreme Government, and independent of the personal allowances of the Resident of Bencoolen.

"It occurred under the following circumstances:—Inconvenience had arisen from the mode in which former Residents had drawn their personal expenses, and it was on my suggestion directed that in future I should be allowed to draw monthly the average of the former charges on this account, reference being at the same time had by the Supreme Government to the increased expenses which must necessarily be incurred by me as Agent to the Governor-General, and otherwise in moving from place to place. It was proposed by the Civil Auditor that I should be authorized to draw at the rate of Rs.5,000 per month on account; but it was finally determined that the amount to be in the first instance drawn should be limited to the average expenses of Bencoolen, viz. about Rs.3,700, and that any excess incurred beyond that sum should be separately drawn, and accounted for as Durbar charges. The disbursement in question, and the charges now referred to, were for such expenses incurred during the Mission to Acheen and Singapore, and for the period from my quitting Calcutta till my leaving Singapore to return to Bencoolen.

"A regular account of these expenses was kept by my Acting Secretary, Captain Crossley, of the Bengal Establishment, and on my return to Bencoolen, where a similar account had been kept of the Government House Establishment expenses, which had also been kept there by Captain Travers, the second assistant, the two amounts were added together, and the aggregate was found to exceed the average of the Resident's usual expenses by the sum stated. This excess was consequently charged in a separate account, and this being duly certified according to the regulation provided in such cases, forwarded to the Civil Authorities in Bengal, the receipt of it was duly acknowledged, and some further explanation having been subsequently furnished, no further notice was taken of it, and I of course concluded that it had been regularly carried to account.

"At all events, this item may be considered, if not already carried to account, at any rate under audit to Bengal. I request to claim the benefit of that audit, and, in the meantime, it may perhaps be satisfactory to the Honourable Court to observe how much the sum actually drawn by me fell short of the amount which, according to the calculations of the Civil Auditor, I might have been expected to have drawn.

"On the principle adopted by former Residents, I might have drawn the actual expense on honour, without limitation as to the amount, and it was only at my request, and to simplify the accounts, that any change in form was made. It was arranged that the amount regularly drawn and carried to account should be limited to an average of what had been formerly drawn in ordinary times, and that what was incurred on extraordinary occasions should be drawn in a separate account, and according to a prescribed form. The extraordinary case did occur in the Mission to Acheen and Prince of Wales's Island, and in the establishment of Singapore; and that such an extra charge should be incurred in excess of the ordinary charge at Bencoolen will be satisfactorily explained when it is considered that at Bencoolen there was a Government House and paid Establishment and a regular succession of expenses consistent with the nature and duties of that Establishment; and that it became my duty not only to provide for our Establishment and its expense, entirely independent of these, while employed on Foreign Service, on a distant Mission on distinct and political authority, as was the case on the Mission to Acheen and Singapore; and moreover, had not only to provide for the whole of the paid Establishment at Bencoolen during my absence, but to pay and entertain an extra Establishment while in the Straits of Malacca and Singapore, hired only for the time, and consequently at high rates.

"On the second item, viz. 'In 1822-23 charges at Singapore, Rs.17,785.'

"I beg to state that these must have been charges on the Public Account, and can in no way be connected with the amount drawn by me for personal expenses, which, on the occasion of my second visit toSingapore, when I had time to make arrangements to limit the charge, did not exceed the ordinary average of the Bencoolen Resident, and were charged and carried to account accordingly, without any excess.

"On the third item, viz. 'House rent at Singapore,' I trust that a few words will be sufficient.

"I have already stated that during my last visit to Singapore, during which the charge was incurred, I drew no additional sum for personal expenses beyond the ordinary charge of Bencoolen, but I had, of course, to be provided, while I resided at Singapore, with a house and accommodation for myself and Establishment. There was no house belonging to the Government, and I did not intrude on the accommodation of the Resident, who occupied his own quarters. The most reasonable that offered was the upper part of a house occupied by the Master Attendant [Flint], which was engaged at 150 Dollars per month, and for the most part occupied by the writers and servants of the Establishment, and latterly entirely as an office, at which I attended daily when my health admitted—my indisposition during the latter months compelling me to sleep on the Hill, where I occupied a temporary bungalow.

"This charge was as necessarily incurred as every other public charge at Singapore, and I am at a loss to know on what principle it can be charged against me personally—why it is now disputed. That it should be an extraordinary charge accounts for itself, and that it was actually incurred cannot be questioned; and I know not how it was to be avoided, unless I had paid the money out of my own pocket, which could not be expected.

"The sum authorized by the Honourable Court, under the head of Deputation Allowances, I consider to be a compensation or remuneration for extra duty; and, although the largest portion of it was actually expended by defraying my personal expenses, it could not be expected that such a charge as an official house and office to the Chief Authority was to form part of these expenses.

"In explanation of the amount of £592, 5s. 10d. which the Court has called upon me to pay, as the balance due on account of the proceedings of spices per Borneo in 1822, I request to refer to the adjustment made by me previous to my leaving Bencoolen, and then submitted in my Dispatch to the Honourable Court and to express a hope that, under the circumstances, the Court will still be inclined to consider it in the light of a remittance, as it was expressly intended and declared to be, and that, instead of my being subjected to a loss on a commercial speculation, the accounts may be adjusted on the principle of a fair rate of exchange between the money paid into the Bencoolen Treasury in Rupees and the amount Sterling paid by the Honourable Court in England to my agent. In this case it only remains to be decided whether the adjustment made at Bencoolen, at the rate of 2s. 3d. the Rupee, was a fair rate or not, and if not, I shall be ready to pay any difference that may arise by substituting any other rate of exchange that may be determined upon.

"Should any further explanation be required, in addition to my former statements respecting the commission drawn by the first Assistant and Storekeeper, I shall be happy to afford it on being permitted to refer to the Bencoolen Books; but as the same are entirely unconnected with the present call which has been made upon me, and cannot in the remotest degree apply to me personally with any pecuniary reference, it may not be necessary that I should swell this letter with further detail respecting them.

"Having now submitted to the Honourable Court such explanations and observations respecting the several items contained in your Letter, I request to recapitulate them as follows, for the convenience of reference:—

"First.—The amount drawn as arrears of salary from March 1816 to March 1818. . . . For these amounts,[1] calculated with interest and converted into Sterling money by the Auditors, I have requested payment may be received in Calcutta, where the funds are deposited for the purpose.

"However serious the repayment of so large an amount may be, I have no right to complain, as the express condition on which the sums were provisionally drawn was their being subject to the confirmation of the Honourable Court, which has been denied. It will, however, appear that with regard to the first and most important item, viz. the arrears of salary, it could not have constituted a claim but from the circumstances of my removal from Java, and the tenor of my appointment to Bencoolen by the Earl of Minto; and as my appeal to the Honourable Court on that question, viz. my removal form Java, is still before the Honourable Court,

[1] The first three items in the claim.

and it remains to be decided upon how far my unfortunate recall was merited by my conduct, I trust that if it shall appear, on the general review of my administration, that such recall occurred under partial and defective information, which has been since supplied, and that subsequent enquiry has proved that such administration was, upon the whole, sound and creditable to myself and my employers, I may still look to the Honourable Court's liberal consideration of the heavy pecuniary loss to which I was subjected on the occasion, and of which this item forms a part. Had I been allowed to remain until the transfer to the Dutch, and proceeded to Bencoolen direct, I should at any rate not have lost two of the most important years of my life by the necessity of proceeding to England.

"The other item, viz. the loss by discount on paper, being an actual abstraction from the amount of my salary as Lieutenant-Governor, will, I hope, also be considered with reference to the small amount of that salary, and to the loss being occasioned by my sudden recall at a moment no less injurious to my character than pecuniary interests, for had I remained till the transfer, I should have derived the advantage of the notes being all at par and paid off.

"Second.—The amount drawn as commission on exports, Rs.73,791, 15a. 8p., left for the final decision of the Honourable Court under the explanation I have offered.

"Third. — Extraordinary charges at Acheen and Singapore, Rs.49,840. These being actual disbursements, cannot be supposed to have afforded me any pecuniary advantages, and, at all events, should the explanations offered not be sufficient, I claim the benefit of the audit in Bengal on such amounts as may be before that Government.

"Fourth.—The balance on account of a remittance in spices of £592, 5s. 10d. This I have requested may be adjusted on the principle of a remittance as it was intended, at any rate the Court may give.

"The commission drawn by the Assistant to the Resident and Storekeeper can have no reference to myself personally.

"In conclusion, I have to apologize for any accidental error that I may have been led into from the want of any documents to refer to, the whole of my papers and accounts having been destroyed, and my being under the necessity of making these explanations from memory."

While it may be true that the Company was technically justified in debiting Raffles with the various amounts, it certainly seems that in equity the greater part should have been written off, or, if this was impracticable from an accountancy point of view, the Court, had it so wished, could have debited him with the full amount, but, because of his most meritorious services—which, incidentally, had saved the Company far more at Bencoolen than it was now claiming—could have awarded him a gratuity sufficient at least to cover the amounts he was required to repay. It was, in any case, grossly unjust that claims dating back to 1816 should have been allowed to remain unsettled if the Court had been so convinced that the amounts should and must be refunded. By letting the matter hang in suspense for all this time and then charging interest on the amounts outstanding, the Court behaved in a way that was as discreditable to the Company as it was unfair to Raffles.

The last letter from Raffles to his cousin is dated 15th June 1826. It was written from High Wood. Dr Raffles was shortly leaving on a visit to Hamburg.

"I have just received your welcome letter of the 12th," wrote Raffles, "and should send this immediate acknowledgment to Liverpool, if it did not appear that I should best ensure its delivery and meet your arrangements by forwarding it to Highbury Place.

"We are here, thank God, once more out of the trammels and disorders of a London life. We came down last week, and are looking forward to the hope of remaining some time. We have nearly dismantled the house in Grosvenor Street, so that I fear you would find but poor accommodation there: *here* we cannot have you too much with us; and from the nature of the house you can best judge the accommodation we can afford.

"We have the same dread of the measles that you appear to have. Neither of the children have had them; and, as they have had a sad *bout*, and are only just recovering from the hooping-cough, which I caught from them, we cannot be too particular.

"As to my engagements for the next three weeks, I know but of one or two likely to interfere with any arrangement which we can make for being together, as much as possible, while you are in the vicinity of London.

"We are daily waiting a summons from Lady Harcourt to go to St Leonard's, where we have promised to take the children for a week. We are also under the necessity of going into Essex after the Midsummer holidays, to put Charles to school, and spend a few days with Mr Sotheby, the poet, and our friend Mr Hamilton: with these exceptions the coast is clear.

"You do not say the time that Mrs Raffles proposes being in Town: but I hope you will arrange for her coming to us when she does arrive: and that, at all events, we may be able to make a comfortable family circle, previous to your trip to Hamburgh [*sic*].

"Let me have a line from you when you reach Highbury, should you not stop by way of Barnet, and first look in upon us. I generally go into Town once a week, and we must lose no time in meeting.

"I have had a great deal to annoy me since I saw you last; but it is a worldly affair, and I trust will not materially affect our happiness.

"Sophia is quite well, and desires her kindest love."

There was this postscript:

"We suffer a little from the heat; but as we hope to make our hay in the course of next week I don't complain; High Wood is now in its best dress, and will, I am sure, please you.

"My neighbour, Mr Wilberforce, takes possession to-morrow, and will previously spend the day with us."

Wilberforce moved in, but departed for Norfolk a week later and did not settle down in his new house until the middle of August. So he and Raffles were actual neighbours only for one week.

Dr Raffles left High Wood for Hamburg about 25th June. In the early hours of Wednesday, 5th July, Sophia found Raffles, unconscious if not already dead, at the foot of a small spiral staircase connecting the ground and first floors. Travers left in his diary the story of what had happened.

"The poor dear fellow got up and left his room at five o'clock and at six was a corpse, found seated upon the stairs after life had fled. Sir Everard Home who was attached I believe sincerely, came to High Wood, and under his superintendence the body was opened and his report stands a striking proof how little the best medical opinions are to be depended upon. For years had I witnessed the sufferings of my friend and whenever medical aid was called in, whether in India or in Europe, no notice was ever taken of the sufferings of the head but as they were said to denote disease of stomach or liver. Yet, on dissection, it was found that both liver and stomach were quite perfect and sound in every respect, whilst the head gave the clearest proofs of long continued disease. And the opinion was that if death had not occurred, idiocy or madness must have soon appeared, an opinion which reconciled his best friends to his early death, for he was only forty-five years of age."

A few additional details are to be found in the *Gentleman's Magazine* for July 1826.

"... He had passed the preceding day in the bosom of his family, and, excepting a bilious attack under which he had laboured for some days, there was nothing in his appearance to create the least apprehension that the fatal hour was so near. Sir Stamford had retired to rest on the Tuesday evening between ten and eleven o'clock, his usual hour when in the country. On the following morning at five o'clock, it being discovered that he had left his room before the time at which he generally rose, six o'clock, Lady Raffles immediately rose, and found him lying at the bottom of a flight of stairs in a state of complete insensibility. Medical aid was promptly procured, and every means resorted to, to restore animation, but the vital spark had fled. The body was opened, under the direction of Sir Everard Home, the same day, who pronounced his death to have been caused by an apoplectic attack, beyond the controul of all human power. It was likewise apparent that the sufferings of the deceased must, for some time past, have been most intense. . . ."

John Crawfurd mentioned in his *Descriptive Dictionary* that he died from the effect of an abscess on the brain.

He was buried in Hendon parish church, the vicar refusing to allow any memorial tablet to be put up.

For epitaphs let these suffice, from two men who knew him well:

"Although he was not generally known he was certainly a man of first rate genius and Talents, and if he was not able to do all the good he wished, he proved his desire to be beneficial and pointed out a noble path for others to follow. Pity he was lost to his country at so early an Age when so much was expected from him."

This from the pen of Thomas Otho Travers. The second, which has already been quoted in another context, is by 'Abdullah.

"There are many great men besides him, clever, rich and handsome, but in good disposition, amiability and gracefulness, Mr Raffles had not his equal, and were I to die and live again such a man I could never meet again, my love of him is so great."

EPILOGUE

DEATH for once had been merciful to Raffles. But the quality of mercy was not conspicuous at East India House. There the Committee of Accounts was coldly considering how much he should be called upon to repay of those sums drawn by him in the past, to which technically he had not been entitled. Before it had reached a final decision, the news of his death was received, so that the only question then remaining was how far his estate would suffice to meet the amount the Committee of Accounts had in mind. It was assumed, no doubt, that anyone who had held such high positions as had Raffles could not have failed to accumulate vast wealth. William Hull, to whom application for information was made, had some difficulty in dispelling this notion. Writing to Thomas Love Peacock from 16 Kensington Square on 12th February 1827, he first referred to the considerable legal charges due from the estate in connexion with the purchase of 23 Lower Grosvenor Street and High Wood.

"I wish as little difficulty may be found in *paying* as in making out the bills. I declare to you that I expect they will be more than the estimate (£1,700). As to the debts, £6,000 may in the aggregate appear large, but when two houses have been furnished, and most handsomely furnished, carriages had, I speak in the plural, foreign wood [Amboina] made up at great expense into chairs and tables of an unusual size, birds and beasts stuffed and framed, with all the other curiosities and a thousand other items, among them the funeral expenses, all which I really cannot specify and which are left unpaid by his sudden and unexpected death, surprise will probably cease at the sum set down. Once for all let me assure you candidly that no attempts have been made to *vamp up* the account; claims are *bona fide*, and it will be necessary to realize all that can be realized to meet them. An early settlement, therefore, of the Company's claim is of moment, to enable my sister to arrange for getting rid of High Wood, and without which no steps can be taken."

Sophia wrote soon after this to Joseph Dart. The letter is undated, but would have been between 12th and 27th February.

"I am naturally anxious to bring the subject of the demands of the East India Company against Sir Stamford Raffles to a final settlement.

"After defraying the claims brought against the estate, it appears by the Statement of Property laid before you, Sir, that there is little more than £10,000 to meet the demands of the East India Company.

"I therefore beg to offer to transfer to the Company six thousand pounds now in Bengal, together with the India Stock, amounting now to about two thousand four hundred and fifty pounds, and Consols one thousand one hundred and fifty, which will leave a balance of between five and six hundred pounds to make up the ten thousand, and which balance shall be made good on the first realization from the estate.

"I beg to apologize to you for trespassing upon your personal kindness, thro' which I hope the matter may be finally concluded."

The Committee of Correspondence held its final meeting on 27th February. After dealing with each of the principal items and Raffles' remarks thereon in his various letters to the Court, the Committee minuted the following:

"The foregoing letters were referred to your committee and yr. comttee. were about to submit their opinion to the Court when they received intelligence of the death of Sir Thomas Raffles. In consequence of that event the further consideration of the subject was necessarily postponed. Lady Raffles subsequently addressed a letter to the Chairman . . . soliciting that the Company would be pleased to accept the sum of £10,000 in liquidation of their claim, that sum being as nearly as could be calculated all that would remain after the other debts were satisfied. Your committee . . . are induced under all the circumstances of the case to recommend to the Court to accept the sum of £10,000 in satisfaction of all claims by the East India Company on the estate of the late Sir Thomas Raffles."

The Court accepted this recommendation and conveyed its decision to Sophia on 7th March. A bond of mutual release was executed, and so the sorry affair ended.

Sophia seems to have retained for some time both 23 Lower Grosvenor Street and High Wood. Travers recorded a visit to the former in June 1827.

"Finding Lady Raffles in the house where I left her in Lower Grosvenor Street, I wrote to express my wish to see her, and had my interview next day, when I was surprised to find her so wonderfully cheerful and well, poor soul. Within a few months her lot had been sadly changed. I had left her in the enjoyment of great happiness. I found her solitary and after the greatest affliction and distress, the loss of one of the best husbands living, and one who could not fail in attaching to him all with whom he was connected. Poor Lady Raffles had at this time only just lost her sister, and from her accounts the death of the poor Father would be quite a blessing. Just at such a moment an interview was of course not the most pleasant, but still I was most anxious to see the Wife of my late never to be sufficiently regretted Friend. The first hour of our meeting was rather nervous but we soon got over it and we passed a pleasant day together."

In the following January Travers recorded:

"Lady Raffles wrote to me a very kind and affectionate letter early this month informing me of her intention to publish The Life of Sir Stamford, and requested me to afford her any assistance in my power which of course I was most anxious to do, and accordingly I commenced a small sketch of all I knew of my lamented friend from the time of our first becoming acquainted at Pinang till our separation, if I may so call it, in England on our being married. It was a task not easy to perform because in writing for another to cull or Extract for a person one knows not what to dwell upon or what to leave out. Had I been drawing a Sketch of his character from my own personal knowledge it would have been far easier. However I felt a pleasure in contributing as far as I was able to a work in which I felt a very sincere interest. The Memoirs of such a character are well worth recording."

Here followed the sentences quoted at the end of the previous chapter.

Later in the same year Travers visited Sophia at High Wood and spent two or three days helping her with the book. This was published in 1830, and is an invaluable source of information for all biographers of her husband. Farquhar took the opportunity to renew his claim to being the true founder of Singapore. In a letter to the London *Courier* dated 21st April (published on 1st May), he invited attention to a reply to Lady Raffles that he had sent to the *Asiatic Journal*. This was published by the *Asiatic Journal* in its June issue. Farquhar sent a copy to the *Singapore Chronicle*, which published it on 2nd December, though not without critical editorial comment. Farquhar died a major-general in 1839, at the age of sixty-eight.

At some period after the publication of the *Memoir*, Sophia disposed of the lease of 23 Lower Grosvenor Street and settled down to live permanently at High Wood. Until the death of Wilberforce in 1833, she was a frequent and welcome visitor to his house next door, and throughout the rest of her life she was a well-known and greatly respected resident in the districts of Hendon and Mill Hill.

By his early death, Raffles not only escaped a lingering and tragic illness, but was also spared further personal loses that would have grieved him keenly. On 10th June 1827, less than a year after his own death, his devoted friend and confidante, Charlotte, Duchess of Somerset, died. In 1837, the last of his sisters, and his favourite, Mary Anne—"dear Pussy", as he called her—died, followed in 1840 by Ella, the sole surviving child of the tragedy at Bencoolen, at the age of nineteen.

Sophia, her constitution unimpaired by all she had undergone, lived on till 1858, when on 12th December, she died at the age of seventy-two. She was buried in the graveyard at St Paul's, Mill Hill. In 1947 the grave was restored by the Association of British Malaya.

Thomas Raffles, who in 1830 had conferred upon him the Degree of Doctor of Divinity (Union, Schenectady, Connecticut), became, in 1839, chairman of the Congregational Union of England and Wales. He continued in charge of Newington Chapel, Liverpool, until it was destroyed by fire in February 1840. Great George Street Chapel was then built for him and his congregation, and there he continued until his retirement in 1861. From 1842 to 1863 he was chairman of the committee of Lancashire Independent College, Manchester, where a Raffles Scholarship and Memorial Library, presented to mark his fiftieth anniversary at Great George Street, Liverpool, still exist. He died on 18th August 1863.

"Such a funeral", wrote Picton in his *Memorials of Liverpool*, "has rarely been witnessed in the town of Liverpool. The shops along the line of procession were closed, the bells of the churches rang muffled peals; the mayor and magistrates and principal inhabitants joined in the procession, which was lined along the route by 50,000 persons. . . ."

And of his home in Mason Street:

"Many of the most eminent public men, both of England and America, have here, at one time or another, been the doctor's guests. His company was much sought after. His genial flow of conversation, full of anecdote and fun; his inimitable dramatic power in telling a story, set off by his portly presence and the silver tones of his voice; his extensive collection of autographs and relics, many of them unique, which he delighted to exhibit, and to bring out their points to the best advantage, rendered a visit to Mason Street something to be stored up in the mind for future pleasant reminiscence."

His eldest son, Thomas Stamford Raffles, can be briefly mentioned: B.A., Glasgow, 1836; barrister, Inner Temple, 1841; judge, Salford Court of Record, 1859-60; police stipendary magistrate for city of Liverpool, 1860-91; published *Memoirs of Rev. Thos. Raffles, D.D., LL.D.*, 1864; died in Liverpool on 23rd January 1891.

There was no memorial to Raffles in Hendon parish church till 1887, when a brass tablet was placed in the church by members of the Raffles family. The whereabouts of the grave could not by then be traced, and it was not until April 1914 that, during the course of alterations, it was accidentally discovered in a vault beneath the church. Mr J. H. Curle describes in *The Shadow Show* how, having descended into the vault out of curiosity, he came upon the coffin bearing Raffles' name. Shortly afterwards the vault was sealed up once more.

High Wood is now known as Highwood House. Except that its grounds have been sold and built upon, it remains to-day externally much as it must have been in Raffles' time. The spiral staircase, at the foot of which he was found by Sophia, is still to be seen. But nowhere is there anything to indicate that in this house one of England's great servants lived and died.

APPENDIX I

OLIVIA MARIAMNE RAFFLES

ALL biographers of Raffles must have been intrigued by the mystery of the antecedents of his first wife. Extensive researches over a number of years have failed to penetrate the mystery completely, but there has accumulated a certain amount of evidence on which one can at least build a theory; it has strengthened the suspicion that Olivia was born in India, and that there was something about her parentage that caused the omission of the marriage from the records of the Devenish family.

This is to some extent supported by a letter dated 8th July 1813 from John Palmer to Raffles. Palmer had planned to visit Java, but on the way had been shipwrecked off the coast of Borneo, and had been lucky to be picked up by a passing ship. As this vessel was on passage from Java to India, Palmer's trip had had to be abandoned. After referring to this in the letter, he went on:

"I had almost identified myself with your Family on my progress towards Java; a little conceited with a project of reclamation, which meant to restore Mrs R. to a country where first I drew my breath—and of which I had heard she was unjustly (provokingly to me) ashamed."

This passage is not as clear as could be wished, but the words "Family" and "reclamation", coupled with the fact that Palmer himself was born in India, suggest that Olivia was also born there. But why "unjustly ashamed"? Was Olivia not proud of her descent?

A tradition in the Raffles family may throw light on her parentage and subsequent history. It is said that she was the daughter of George (or Godfrey) Devenish, of Castle Dana,[1] Co. Roscommon. Her mother was a Circassian, to whom "she owed her large expressive eyes, her high nose, her colouring and her charm". In her twenty-second year, she, Olivia, was sent out to relatives in India to look for a husband. She sailed in an East Indiaman called the *Rose*, of which the master was Captain Hamilton Dempster of Dunnichen, Co. Forfar. On the long voyage she had an affair with Captain Dempster and, on arrival at Madras, was hastily married to Fancourt on 26th May 1793.

That is the tradition. These are the ascertained facts:

The first three voyages of the *Rose* to Madras and Bengal were made in 1787, 1789 and 1792. On each occasion she was commanded by Captain Dempster. On the third voyage she arrived at Madras outward bound on 25th August 1792, continued to Calcutta, and called at Madras

[1] No castle of this name, or any name like it, can be traced.

again, homeward bound, on 17th February 1793. She left Madras on 4th March. The logs of the three voyages, which are preserved in the India Office Library, reveal no trace of Olivia, or of any woman who might have corresponded to her. Nevertheless, masters of East Indiamen have been known to carry passengers not recorded in the official list.

The suggestion that Olivia's mother was a Circassian, and that Olivia was sent out to relatives in India, reinforces the suspicion that she was born there. In Madras at that date there was a considerable Circassian community; if her father did marry a Circassian, it is more probable that he met her in Madras than in Co. Roscommon. If Irish society frowned on mixed marriages, the exclusion of this one from the records of the Devenish family is explained. John Palmer might have seen no objection to marriage with a Circassian, yet all would not have shared his views.

An elaborate monograph, *The Devenish Families*, by Mr R. J. Devenish and Professor C. H. McLaughlin, was published privately in Chicago in 1948. It is tentatively recorded therein that Olivia may have been the daughter of Christopher Devenish, the son of William Devenish, of Rush Hill, Co. Roscommon. A Christopher Devenish served as an officer in India and was reported to have died at Madras in 1783. This supplied the authors with a link between Olivia and Madras, but there is a difficulty. If Christopher Devenish was the one of that name who entered Trinity College, Dublin, in 1774 at the age of sixteen, he must have been born in 1757-58, a date appropriate in relation to the other children of the same parents. But according to *Bengal Army Officers*, Lieutenant Christopher Devenish obtained his original cadetship in 1780. If, therefore, he was the same Christopher Devenish as he who had entered Trinity College in 1774, he could have been only fourteen years older than Olivia. According to another biography, Christopher Devenish of Co. Roscommon might have been born about 1745. This would have made him old enough to be the father of Olivia, but meant that he did not obtain his first cadetship until the age of thirty-five.

Christopher seems to have been a common name in the Devenish family, and Lieutenant Christopher Devenish may have been neither of those referred to. Among the Leyden letters in the National Library of Scotland is one from Olivia to John Leyden dated 3rd August 1808 (see page 64), in which she wrote: "I feel an affection for you such as I feel for my only and beloved brother." This suggests that the brother was still alive, but not necessarily so. It is not certain that Lieutenant Christopher Devenish did die in 1783; it is only presumed. He might have been not her father but her brother. Who, then, was their father? The Raffles tradition gives him as George or Godfrey Devenish. Both names appear in the Devenish family tree in different generations. There was one George born about 1717-30, the younger brother of Christopher

Devenish of Carrowneclogher and William Devenish of Rush Hill. Little is known about him except that he lived an indolent life and married beneath him—this information being forthcoming from a note made in the 1777 pedigree by his nephew, George Devenish, of Mount Pleasant. Might he not have gone out to India and married a Circassian who bore him two children? Might he not have called his son "Christopher" after his own elder brother? Might he not have called his daughter "Olivia" after her mother (Olivia is not a Devenish name), and "Mariamne", which is a most unusual name, after Mariamne Etherington, who was a witness at the marriage of Raffles and Olivia, and may well have known Olivia's parents in India? All the dates fit reasonably well, and Christopher would have obtained his cadetship at a suitable age.

The vague and scattered evidence does suggest that Olivia was born in India, probably Madras; that her father was George Devenish, younger brother of William Devenish of Rush Hill, Co. Roscommon, and that her mother was a Circassian; that the family in Ireland declined to recognize the wife; and that Olivia was ashamed of her parentage.

But it still remains a theory.

A few lines can be added here concerning the gossip in Penang while Raffles was stationed there. On the face of it, it sprang from the scandalous story that Olivia had been William Ramsay's mistress, and that Raffles had obtained his appointment at Penang as a reward for marrying her. But is it possible that a different story was current in Penang and later became confused with the ill-natured tittle-tattle in London? One fact that might be relevant was that on her fourth voyage from England to India, the *Rose* was commanded not by Captain Dempster but by Captain Alexander Gray, who, in 1805, was one of the members of the new government of Penang. Had there been a scandal about Olivia on board the *Rose*, who would have been more likely to hear about it than the new master? Gray might well have told the story in Penang, thus giving rise to the stigma attaching to Olivia there. His story may have been embroidered, as stories often are; and if there had been gossip affecting Olivia and Raffles in Leadenhall Street, the two stories may have got mixed up in Penang.

This, too, remains a theory.

APPENDIX II

CHAIRMEN AND DEPUTY CHAIRMEN OF THE EAST INDIA COMPANY

	Chairman	*Deputy*
1805	Charles Grant	George Smith
1806	Hon. Wm. Fullarton Elphinstone	Edward Parry
1807	Edward Parry	Charles Grant
1808	Edward Parry	Charles Grant
1809	Charles Grant, M.P.	William Astell, M.P.
1810	William Astell, M.P.	Jacob Bosanquet
1811	Jacob Bosanquet	Sir Hugh Inglis, Bart.
1812	Jacob Bosanquet	Sir Hugh Inglis, Bart.
1813	Robert Thornton	Hon. Wm. Fullarton Elphinstone
1814	Hon. Wm. Fullarton Elphinstone	John Inglis
1815	Charles Grant, M.P.	Thomas Reid
1816	Thomas Reid	John Bebb
1817	John Bebb	James Pattison
1818	James Pattison	Campbell Marjoribanks
1819	Campbell Marjoribanks	George Abercrombie Robinson
1820	Campbell Marjoribanks	George Abercrombie Robinson
1821	George Abercrombie Robinson	Thomas Reid
1822	James Pattison	William Wigram, M.P.
1823	James Pattison	William Wigram, M.P.
1824	William Astell, M.P.	Sir George Abercrombie Robinson, Bart.
1825	Campbell Marjoribanks	Sir George Abercrombie Robinson, Bart.
1826	Sir George Abercrombie Robinson, Bart.	Hon. Hugh Lindsay, M.P.

APPENDIX III

PRESIDENTS OF THE INDIA BOARD OF CONTROL

		Appointed[1]
1784	Rt. Hon. Baron Sydney (afterwards Viscount Sydney)	4th September
1790	Rt. Hon. W. W. Grenville (afterwards Baron Grenville)	6th March
1793	Rt. Hon. Henry Dundas (afterwards Viscount Melville)	24th December
1801	Viscount Lewisham (afterwards Earl of Dartmouth)	19th May
1802	Viscount Castlereagh (afterwards Marquis of Londonderry)	12th July
1806	Lord Minto (afterwards Viscount Melgund and Earl of Minto)	12th February
	Rt. Hon. Thomas Grenville	16th July
	Rt. Hon. George Tierney	1st October
1807	Rt. Hon. Robert Dundas (afterwards Viscount Melville)	4th April
1809	Earl of Harrowby	11th July
	Rt. Hon. Robert Dundas (afterwards Viscount Melville)	7th November
1812	Earl of Buckinghamshire	4th April
1816	Rt. Hon. George Canning	4th July
1821	Rt. Hon. Charles Bathurst	12th January
1822	Rt. Hon. Charles Watkins Williams Wynn	7th February
1828	Robert Dundas, Viscount Melville	7th February

[1] The dates of appointment refer to the dates of the Letters Patent.

APPENDIX IV

DUTCH GOVERNORS-GENERAL OF JAVA

FROM 1610 until the advent of the British in 1811 there were thirty-seven Dutch Governors-General, of which the last eleven were as follows:

Gustaaf Willem Baron van Imhoff	1743–1750
Jacob Mossel	1750–1761
Petrus Albertus van der Parra	1761–1775
Jeremias van Riemsdyk	1775–1777
Reynier de Klerk	1777–1780
Willem Arnold Alting	1780–1796
Pieter Gerardus van Overstraten	1796–1801
Johannes Siberg	1801–1804
Albertus Henricus Wiese	1804–1808
Herman Willem Daendels	1808–1811
Jan Willem Janssens	1811

APPENDIX V
THE RAFFLES FAMILY *1

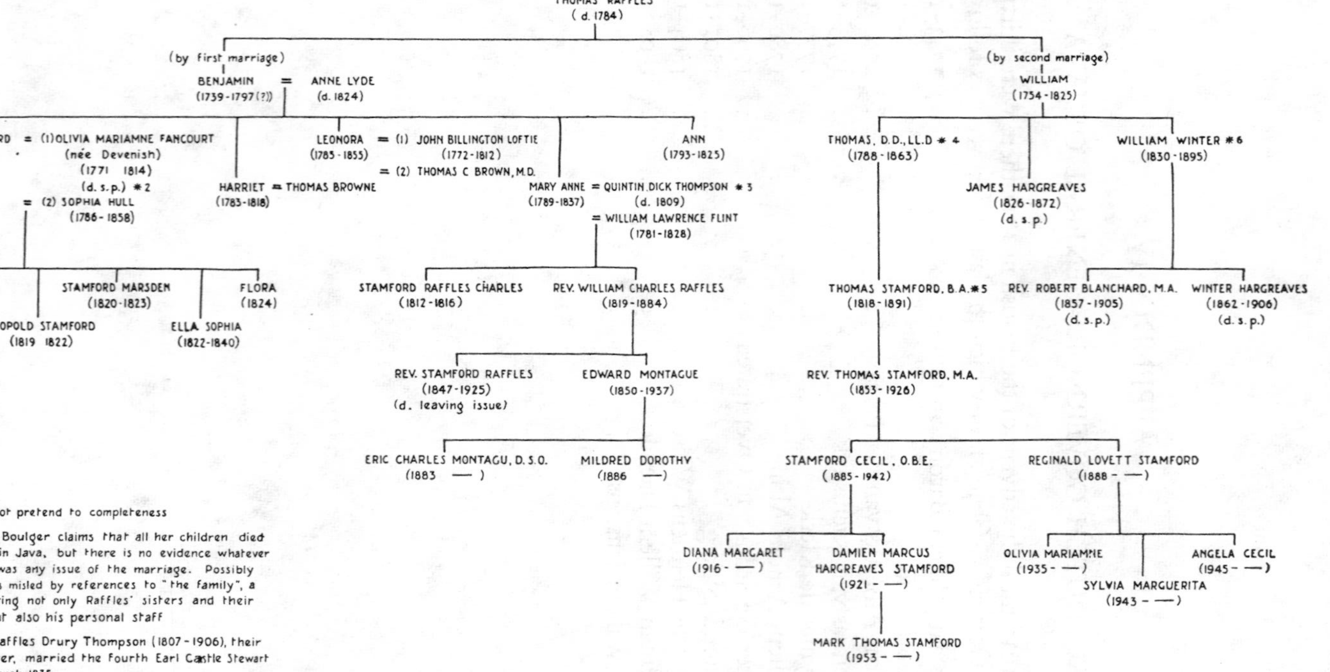

*1 This does not pretend to completeness

*2 Demetrius Boulger claims that all her children died with Olivia in Java, but there is no evidence whatever that there was any issue of the marriage. Possibly Boulger was misled by references to "the family", a term covering not only Raffles' sisters and their children, but also his personal staff

*3 Charlotte Raffles Drury Thompson (1807-1906), their only daughter, married the Fourth Earl Castle Stewart on 24th March 1835

*4 Had also one daughter

*5 Had also three daughters

*6 Had also five daughters

APPENDIX VI

RULERS OF RHIO-JOHORE AND SINGAPORE

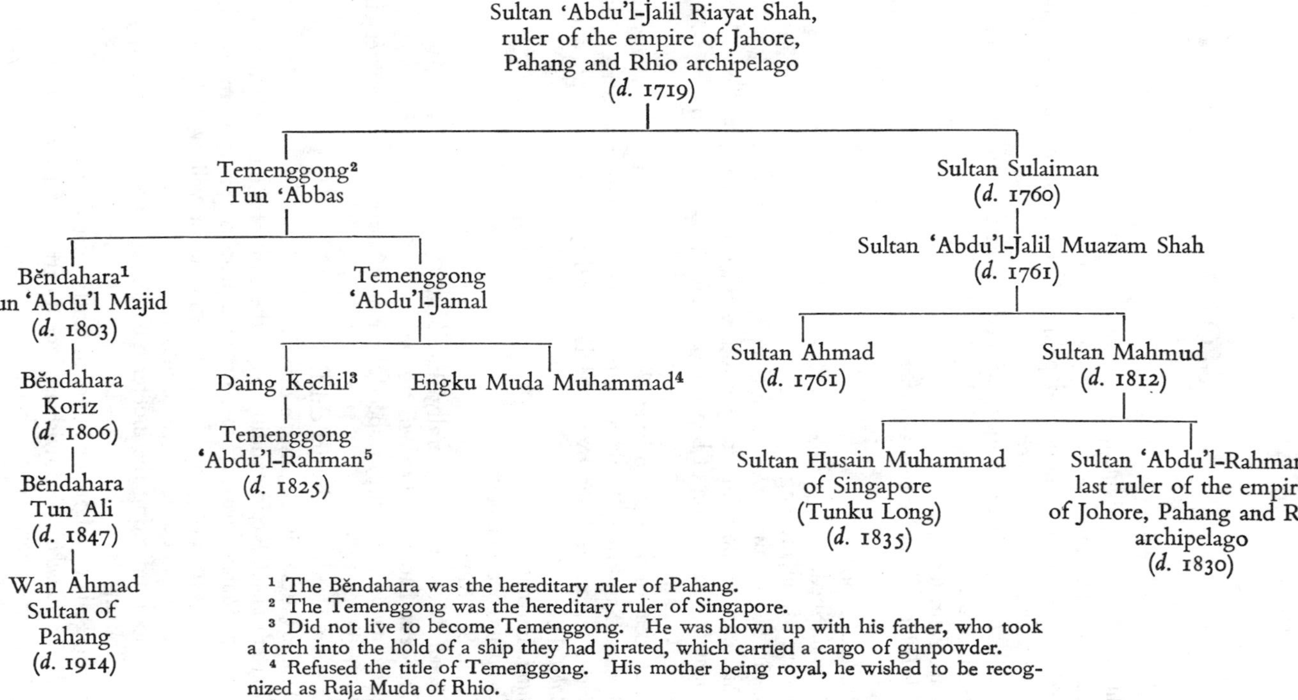

[1] The Bĕndahara was the hereditary ruler of Pahang.
[2] The Temenggong was the hereditary ruler of Singapore.
[3] Did not live to become Temenggong. He was blown up with his father, who took a torch into the hold of a ship they had pirated, which carried a cargo of gunpowder.
[4] Refused the title of Temenggong. His mother being royal, he wished to be recognized as Raja Muda of Rhio.
[5] Installed Temenggong of Singapore in 1806.

GLOSSARY

Adat. Law of custom.
Adipati. See *Radin Adipati.*
Alam. World, universe.
Areca. Genus of pinnate-leaved palms. The nut is chewed with the leaves of the betel pepper (*sireh*).
Arrack. Any spirituous liquor, distilled from rice, molasses, coconuts, etc.
Asam. Sour.
Atap. Palm-leaf thatch.
Bakal. Hereditary heir to an office.
Balam. Dove.
Bandar. Seaport.
Bangsal. Shed.
Banjar. Mountain range.
Banjir. Flood caused by a high tide.
Bĕndahara. Prime minister. Hereditary chief of Pahang.
Benjamin. Corruption of benzoin, aromatic balsamic resin.
Bĕsar. Great.
Betel. Leaf of the betel pepper (*Piper betle*), known to the Malays as *sireh.*
Bhatara (Sanskrit). "Exalted", a title of Hindu gods and Javanese rulers.
Bugis. The name given by the Malays to the dominant people of Celebes.
Bukit. Hill.
Bumi. Earth.
Campong. See *Kampong.*
Cayu. See *Kayu.*
Chandi. Monument, generally Buddhist.
Chĕngkau. Monkey (*Presbytis cristata*).
Dato', datok. Grandsire; respectful term of address to commoner chiefs of any rank.
Demang. Headman, district chief.
Desa. Javanese village; also, a district.
Dragon's blood. Resin exuding from the fruit of the rattan palm.
Dugong (Malay *duyong*). Sea-cow, an aquatic herbivorous mammal.
Durian. Large evergreen tree. Its fruit has a yellow pulp with a pleasant flavour, but a disagreeable odour.
ĕ. Symbol indicating the indeterminate sound between two consonants, as in "bitten".
Engku. Raja of Johore or Rhio, distantly related to royalty.
Gambier (*Gambir*). Yellowish astringent extract of a shrub. It is used for dyeing, also for chewing with betel.
Gamĕlan. Javanese orchestra.
Godown. Warehouse; corruption of *gedong.*
Gunong. Mountain.

H.C.C. Honourable Company's Cruiser. Another designation was H.E.I.C.'s Cruiser.
Hikayat. Story, biography.
Hilir. Lower reaches of river.
Hitam. Black.
Hukum. Sentence, judgment, order.
Indra. See footnote, page 365.
Jauhar. Jewel.
Jayang Sĕkars. See footnote, page 247.
Kabaya (Portuguese). Loose cotton gown
Kampong. Village.
Karang. Reef, ridge of rock.
Kayu. Wood.
Kayubuku. See footnote, page 418.
Kechil. Small, little.
Kĕratun. See text, page 199.
Kiai. Noble, a title for high officials.
Kijang. Barking deer (*Cervulus muntjac*).
Klings. See footnote, page 671.
Kris (*Kĕris*, *Creese*). Dagger, generally with a wavy blade.
Kulen. West.
Lalang. Long, coarse grass.
Landdrost (Dutch). Governor of a province, high bailiff. Cf. *Landraad*, N.I. district court.
Lanuns. See footnote, page 300.
Loji. Factory, trading station.
Lontar. See footnote, page 652.
Mangku-bumi. Prime minister.
Masin. Salty.
Menghiri. Debt slave.
Muda. Young.
Munshi (*Moonshee*). Writer or secretary, especially Asiatic teacher of languages.
Nakhoda. Master of native vessel.
Orang. Man.
Orang laut. Man of the sea.
Orang outang (Malay *hutan*). Man of the woods.
Padris. See pages 562–3.
Panembahan. Madurese chief.
Pangeran. Title of sons of a Javanese ruler.
Panglima. Leader.
Parang. Chopper; sheathless, blade broadest at transverse blunt end.
Penghulu. Territorial chief.
Pĕrang. War.
Pesirehan. Receptacle for betel.
Pikul. 133.3 lb.
Pulau. Island.
Pura. City.

Puchuk (*Pachak*, etc.). Costus root, used as incense by the Chinese.
Puteh. White.
Putěri. Title of ruler's consort when of royal blood.
Radin. Raja, prince. If used alone, it generally means a lesser prince.
Radin Adapati. Eldest son of a ruler; under the Dutch, also prime minister of the Susuhunan of Surakarta (Solo).
Ragus. Title of Javanese noblemen and occasionally added to princely titles.
Rambutan (from *rambut*, hair of the head). Fruit related to the litchi-nut. The name is taken from the coarse-haired rind, which contains an acid pulp pleasant to the taste.
Ratten (from *rotan*, object pared or trimmed). Long, pliable stem of a climbing palm, used for basketwork, cordage, etc.
Ratu. Javanese prince, raja.
Rumah. House.
Ryotwari. See footnote, page 234.
Sagi. Achinese chief.
Saif. Sword.
Sarong. Skirt tucked round the waist and worn by both sexes.
Sayid. Descendant of the Prophet.
Sěri. Illustrious, prefixed to titles.
Sireh. Betel pepper.
Sree. See *Sěri*.
Sticklack (*Stick-lac*). Resinous substance found on certain insects and the twigs on which they live.
Susuhunan. "Object of Adoration", the title by which the Emperor of Surakarta (Solo) was known.
Tanah mati. Dead land (land dead).
Tanjong. Spit of land, cape.
Tělok. Bay.
Temenggong (strictly *Těměnggong*). Title of Malay ministers of defence; formerly also hereditary ruler of Singapore.
Těnok. Tapir.
Tuanku. His Highness (addressing a ruler).
Tunku, Her Highness (addressing a queen or female raja), or His Highness (addressing a male raja).
Tutenague (tutenag). Crude zinc.
Undang-undang. Legal digest.
Wakil. Agent.
Wangi. Fragrant.
Wedono. Senior official not of royal blood.

BIBLIOGRAPHY

ABBREVIATIONS

B.T.L. en V. van Ned. Indië.—Bijdragen tot de Taal-, Land- en Volkenkunde van Nederlandsch-Indië ("Contributions to the Knowledge of the Language, Country and People of the Netherlands Indies").
J.I.A.—Journal of the Indian Archipelago.
J.M.B.R.A.S.—Journal of the Malay Branch of the Royal Asiatic Society.
J.S.B.R.A.S.—Journal of the Straits Branch of the Royal Asiatic Society. (Renamed *J.M.B.R.A.S.* in 1923.)

A. SOURCES QUOTED OR REFERRED TO IN THE TEXT

Published Works

ADDISON, GEORGE AUGUSTUS. *Oringinal familiar correspondence between residents in Indies, including sketches of Java.* Edinburgh, 1846.
ASSEY, CHARLES. *Review of the Administration, Value and State of the Colony of Java with its Dependencies, as it was,—as it is,—and as it may be.* London, 1816.
On the Trade to China and the Indian Archipelago: the Insecurity of the British Interests in that Quarter. London, 1819.
BAMFORD, FRANCIS, and the DUKE OF WELLINGTON. *The Journal of Mrs Arbuthnot,* 1820-1832. London, 1950.
BOSCH, Dr F. D. K. Article in special Raffles number of *Inter-Ocean,* Weltevreden, March 1930.
BOULGER, DEMETRIUS CHARLES. *The Life of Sir Stamford Raffles.* London, 1897.
BOXER, Professor C. R. *The Mandarin at Chinsurah.* Published by the Koninklÿk Vereniging Indsch Instituut (Royal Institute for the Indies). Amsterdam, 1949. See also Section "*B*".
BUCKLEY, C. B. *An Anecdotal History of Old Times in Singapore.* Singapore, 1902.
BURKILL, I. H. *Jack's Letters to Wallich. J.S.B.R.A.S.,* Singapore, 1916.
CAREW, Colonel P. *Facing the Music. Blackwood's Magazine,* October 1949.
COLBURN, HENRY. *Biographical Dictionary of the Living Authors of Great Britain and Ireland* (Supplement). London, 1816.
CRAWFURD, JOHN. Report on Raffles' *History of Java* in the *Edinburgh Review* (Vol. 31), 1819. (The contribution is anonymous, but authorship is attributed to Crawfurd.)
History of the Indian Archipelago. Edinburgh, 1820.
Journal of an Embassy to the Courts of Siam and Cochin China. London, 1829.
Descriptive Dictionary of the Indian Islands and Adjacent Countries. London, 1856.
CURLE, J. H. *The Shadow-Show.* London, 1928.
CURZON OF KEDLESTON, MARQUIS. *British Government in India.* London, 1925.
DEVENISH, R. J., and MCLAUGHLIN, C. H. *Historical and Genealogical Records of the Devenish Families.* Chicago, 1948.

DOEFF, HENDRIK. *Herinneringen uit Japan* ("Reminiscences of Japan"). Haarlem, 1833.

Dropmore Papers (Vol. 1). Published by Historical Manuscripts Commission. London, 1892.

EARL, GEORGE WINDSOR. *Eastern Seas*. London, 1837. See also KOLFF, D. H., Section "*B*".

EGERTON, HUGH EDWARD. *Sir Stamford Raffles*. London, 1900.

ELLIOT, SIR GEORGE. *Memoir of Admiral the Honble. Sir George Elliot*. London, 1863. Reprinted 1891.

FARINGTON, JOSEPH. *Diary of Joseph Farington* (8 vols.). Edited by J. Greig. London, 1922-28.

FARQUHAR, WILLIAM. *The Establishment of Singapore. Asiatic Journal and Monthly Register*. London, May 1830.

Singapore. Singapore Chronicle, 2nd December 1830.

FAULKNER, T. *History and Antiquities of the Parish of Hammersmith*. London, 1820.

FORSTER, JOHN. *The Life of Dickens*. London, 1872-74.

FURNIVALL, J. S. *Netherlands India*. Cambridge, 1948.

HAHN, EMILY. *Raffles of Singapore*. New York, 1946; London, 1948.

HAMILTON, Captain ALEXANDER. *New Account of East India*. Edinburgh, 1727.

HASTINGS, MARQUIS OF. *The Private Journal of the Marquis of Hastings*. Edited by the Marchioness of Bute. London, 1858.

HAUGHTON, H. T. *Landing of Raffles in Singapore by an Eye Witness* (Wa Hakim). *J.S.B.R.A.S.*, Singapore, 1882.

HICKEY, WILLIAM. *The Memoirs of William Hickey*. London, 1919.

HOGENDORP, DIRK VAN. *Bericht van den Tegenwoordigen Toestand der Bataafsche Bezittingen in Oost-Indië* ("Report on the Present State of the Batavian Possessions in the East Indies"). Delft, 1799.

JENSEN, JOHANNES V. *Olivia Mariamne*. Copenhagen, 1915.

KEMP, P. H. VAN DER. *De Singapoorsche Papieroorlog* ("The Singapore Paper War"). *B.T.L. en V. van Ned. Indië* (Vol. 49). The Hague, 1898. For other essays, see Section "*B*".

LEVYSSOHN NORMAN, Dr H. D. *De Britsche Heerschappij over Java en Onderhorigheden* (1811-16) ("The British Rule over Java and its Dependencies (1811-16)"). The Hague, 1857.

LEYDEN, Dr JOHN CASPAR. *Dissertation on the Indo-Persian, Indo-Chinese, and Dekkan Languages*. London, 1807.

A translation of *Sějarah Mělayu* ("Malay Annals"). London, 1821.

Poems and Ballads, with a memoir of the author by Sir Walter Scott. Kelso, 1858.

LOCKHART, JOHN GIBSON. *Life of Sir Walter Scott* (7 vols.). Edinburgh, 1836-38.

LUCAS, E. V. *Life of Charles Lamb*. London, 1905.

MACDONALD, Captain D. *Narrative of Early Life and Services*. Weymouth, 1830.

MARSDEN, WILLIAM. *History of Sumatra*. London, 1811.

Grammar of the Malayan Language. London, 1812.

MILBURN, W. *Oriental Commerce*. London, 1813.

MILLER, H. ERIC. *Extracts from the Letters of Colonel Nahuijs* (Nahuys), a translation. *J.M.B.R.A.S.*, Singapore, 1941.

MINTO, COUNTESS OF. *Life and Letters of Sir Gilbert, First Earl of Minto*. London, 1874.

Lord Minto in India. London, 1880.

MITCHELL, SIR PETER CHALMERS. *Centenary History of the Zoological Society of London*. London, 1929.

NAHUIJS (or NAHUYS), H. G. *Reminiscences of the Public and Private Life 1799–1849) of Major-General H. G. Baron Nahuijs van Burgst*. Arnhem, 1858.

PICTON, J. A. *Memorials of Liverpool*. Liverpool, 1903.

RAFFLES, SOPHIA, LADY. *Memoir of the Life and Public Services of Sir Thomas Stamford Raffles: F.R.S.: &c.* (2 vols.) London, 1830. Abridged edition (also 2 vols.), London, 1835.

RAFFLES, DR THOMAS. *Letters, during a Tour Through Some Parts of France, Savoy, Switzerland, Germany, and the Netherlands, in the Summer of 1817*. Liverpool, 1818.

RAFFLES, SIR THOMAS STAMFORD. Discourse at a meeting of the Batavian Society of Arts and Sciences, 24th April 1813. Printed as an appendix to Lady Raffles' *Memoir*.

Discourse at a meeting of the Batavian Society of Arts and Sciences, 11th September 1815. Printed as an appendix to Lady Raffles' *Memoir*.

On the Malayu Nation, with a translation of its Maritime Institutions. Calcutta, 1816.

History of Java (2 vols.). London, 1817.

Report on Crawfurd's *History of the Indian Archipelago* in the *Quarterly Review*, October 1922.

Statement of the Services of Sir Stamford Raffles. London, 1824. Also included in the first (1830) edition of Lady Raffles' *Memoir*.

Letter to Colonel Addenbrooke concerning the founding of Singapore (see page 519), subsequently published in *J.S.B.R.A.S.*, Singapore, 1878.

Translation of the Maritime Code of the Malays, subsequently published in *J.S.B.R.A.S.*, Singapore, 1879.

See also Unpublished Works, Sections "*A*" and "*B*".

RAFFLES, THOMAS STAMFORD, B.A. *Memoirs of Rev. Thos. Raffles, D.D., LL.D.* London, 1864.

RAYNAL, ABBÉ W. T. *A Philosophical and Political History of the Settlements and Trade of the Europeans in the East and West Indies*. Brussels, 1770; London, 1813.

READ, W. H. *Note on the landing of Raffles in Singapore. J.S.B.R.A.S.*, Singapore, 1883.

ROBINSON, HENRY CRABB. *Diary, Reminiscences and Correspondence*. London, 1869.

SCHOUTE, DR DIRK. *Occidental Therapeutics in the Netherlands East Indies during Three Centuries of Netherlands Settlement*, 1600–1900. Batavia, 1937.

SHELLABEAR, REV. R. G. *Autobiography of Munshi Abdullah*. Singapore, 1918.

SMITH, VINCENT A. *Oxford History of India*. London, 1923.

SOLLEWIJN GELPKE, DR J. F. H. *De Landerijen Onder het Engelsche Tusschenbestuur Verkocht en het Verbod van Heeren Diensten Aldaar* ("The Lands Sold During the English Interregnum and the Prohibition of Feudal Services Thereon"). Cheribon, 1889.

THOMPSON, EDWARD J. *Life of Lord Metcalfe*. London, 1937.

THOMSON, JOHN TURNBULL. *Translations from Hikayat Abdulla*. London, 1874. See also Section "*B*".

THORN, Major WILLIAM. *Memoir of the Conquest of Java*. London, 1815.
Memoir of Sir R. R. Gillespie. London, 1816.

VETCH, R. H. *Life of General Sir Andrew Clarke*. London, 1905.

WAKEHAM, Major ERIC. *The Bravest Soldier—Robert Rollo Gillespie*. Edinburgh, 1937.

WATSON, Lieutenant Thomas. *Journal of a Tour in the Island of Java. Asiatic Journal and Monthly Register* (Vol. 1). London, 1816.

WELLINGTON, DUKE OF. *Supplementary Despatches and Memoranda* (Vol. 1). London, 1858.

WILBERFORCE, R. I. and S. *Life of William Wilberforce*. London, 1838.

WINSTEDT, SIR RICHARD O. *Britain and Malaya*. London, 1934 and 1949. See also Section "*B*".

Unpublished Works

CRAWFORD, Captain J. G. F. *Diary of Captain Crawford*, in the possession of Mr C. R. Wylie of Kirribilli, Adelaide.

FORTESCUE, J. B. Manuscript preserved at Dropmore. See Vol. 1, *Dropmore Papers* (Hist. MSS Comm.), London, 1892.

GILLESPIE/RAFFLES. *Charges preferred by Major General Gillespie against T. S. Raffles, Esq. Lieut. Governor of Java with Mr Raffles's defence*. This title is written by hand on the cover of the book, which bears no date, but was privately printed for Raffles in 1814 (see page 330). It formed part of the collection of the late C. E. Wurtzburg and is now at Cambridge University.

LEYDEN, Dr JOHN. Correspondence with Raffles and Olivia Raffles, together with a valuable collection of papers concerning Leyden, in the possession of the National Library of Scotland, Edinburgh.

PALMER, JOHN. Private letter books, in the possession of the Bodleian Library, Oxford.

RAFFLES, OLIVIA. Letter to John Leyden, 3rd August 1808, in the possession of the National Library of Scotland, Edinburgh.

RAFFLES, SIR THOMAS STAMFORD. *Substance of a Minute recorded by the Honourable Thomas Stamford Raffles, Lieutenant-Governor of Java and its Dependencies, on the 11th February* 1814. Printed (but not published) for *Black, Parry and Co., London,* 1814.
A collection of letters to his mother, uncle and cousin, Thomas Raffles, in the possession of Mrs Stamford Raffles of Guernsey.

ROBARTS, EDWARD. *Narrative of Edward Robarts*, in the possession of the Advocates' Library, Edinburgh.

TRAVERS, Captain THOMAS OTHO. *Diary of Thomas Otho Travers*, in the possession of Mr M. T. L. Travers of Kingston, Co. Dublin.

WALLICH, Dr NATHANIEL. Private letter books, in the possession of the Botanic Gardens, Calcutta.

Periodicals, Official Publications, etc.

Asiatic Journal and Monthly Register, London (1816-45), 1816, 1830.

Bijdragen tot Taal-, Land- en Volkenkunde van Nederlandsch-Indië ("Contributions to the Knowledge of the Language, Country and People of the Netherlands Indies"). Published by the Koninklijk (Royal) Instituut voor de Taal-. Land- en Volkenkunde van Nederlandsch-Indië. Vol. 49, The Hague, 1898.

Blackwood's Magazine, London, October 1949.

Calcutta Journal, 19th March 1819.

Colombian Magazine: or Monthly Miscellany, June 1797.

Courier, London, 1st May 1830.

Edinburgh Review (Vol. 31), 1819.

Gentleman's Magazine, London, July 1826.

Inter-Ocean, Weltevreden, March 1930.

Java Government Gazette, Batavia, 1812-16.

Journal of the Indian Archipelago (Vol. vi), Penang, 1852.

Journal of the Malay Branch of the Royal Asiatic Society, Singapore, 1941.

Journal of the Straits Branch of the Royal Asiatic Society, Singapore, 1878, 1879, 1882, 1883, 1916.

Malayan Miscellanies, Bencoolen, 1820 and 1822.

Prince of Wales's Island Gazette, Penang, 1806-26.

Proceedings of the Agricultural Society Established in Sumatra, Bencoolen, 1821.

Proceedings of the Batavian Society of Arts and Sciences, Batavia, 1814-1816.

Quarterly Review, London, April 1817, October 1822.

Singapore Chronicle, 2nd December 1830.

United Service Journal, London, January 1836.

B. SOURCES NOT QUOTED OR REFERRED TO IN THE TEXT

Published Works

ALMEIDA, W. B. D'. *Life in Java*. London, 1864.

ANDERSON, J. *Political and Commercial Considerations relative to the Malayan Peninsula and the British Settlements in the Straits of Malacca*. Penang, 1824. Reprinted in *J.I.A.*, Penang, 1854.

Mission to the East Coast of Sumatra. London, 1826.

ANG GIM TONG. 130th Anniversary of Singapore. *Nanyang Siang Pau*, Singapore, 6th February 1949.

ANSON, Colonel A. E. H. *About Others and Myself*. London, 1920.

BAKER, A. C. *Anglo-Dutch Relations in the East at the Beginning of the 19th Century*. *J.S.B.R.A.S.*, Singapore, 1913.

BALLARD, G. A. *Rulers of the Indian Ocean*. London, 1927.

BANNER, HUBERT STEWART. *The Clean Wind*. London, 1931.

Sir Stamford Raffles—Brother Mason. *British Malaya*, London, December 1931.

These Men Were Masons. London, 1934.

BARTLEY, W. *Population of Singapore in* 1819. *J.M.B.R.A.S.*, Singapore, 1933.

BATTEN, C. G. *Daendels—Raffles.* London, 1894.

BAUD, J. C. *Palembang in* 1811 *en* 1812. *B.T.L. en V. van Ned. Indië* (Vol. 1), Amsterdam, 1852.

De Bandjermasinsche Afschuwelikheid ("The Banjermasin Abomination"). B.T.L. en V. van Ned. Indië (Vol. 7, 3rd of New Series). Amsterdam, 1860.

BEGBIE, J. *Malayan Peninsula.* Vepery Mission Press, 1834.

BICKMORE, A. S. *Travels in the East Indian Archipelago.* London, 1868.

BLUNDELL, E. A. *Notices of Penang. J.I.A.*, Penang, 1850.

BLYTHE, W. L. *Historical Sketch of Chinese Labour in Malaya. J.M.B.R.A.S.*, Singapore, 1947.

BOXER, Professor C. R. *Jan Compagnie in Japan*, 1600–1850. The Hague, 1950. See also Section "*A*".

BOYS, H. S. *Some Notes on Java.* Allahabad, 1892.

BRADDELL, SIR R. ST. J. *The Law of the Straits Settlements.* Singapore, 1915.

BRADDELL, SIR T. *On the History of Acheen. J.I.A.*, Penang, 1851.

The Commencement of Abdullah's Schooling—translated from the Hikayat Abdullah. J.I.A., Penang, 1852.

Concerning Colonel Farquhar's going to look for a place to establish a Settlement—translated from the Hikayat Abdullah. J.I.A., Penang, 1852.

Notices of Singapore. J.I.A., Penang, 1853.

The Ancient Trade of the Indian Archipelago. J.I.A. (New Series), Penang, 1858.

The Europeans in the Indian Archipelago in the 16th and 17th Centuries. J.I.A. (New Series), Penang, 1858.

BRADSHAW, J. *Sir Thomas Munro.* Oxford, 1894.

BRAYLEY, E. W. *Some account of the Life and Writings and contributions to Science of the late Sir T. Stamford Raffles. Zoological Journal*, London, 1853.

BROOKE, SIR JAMES. *The Private Letters of Sir James Brooke.* Edited by J. C. Templer. London, 1853.

BROOKS, C. J. *English Tombs and Monuments in Bencoolen. J.S.B.R.A.S.*, Singapore, 1918.

BROWN, J. M. *The Dutch East.* London, 1914.

BRYANT, ARTHUR. *The Years of Endurance*—1793–1802. London, 1942.

Years of Victory—1802–1812. London, 1944.

The Age of Elegance—1812–1822. London, 1950.

CAMERON, J. *Our Tropical Possessions in Malayan India.* London, 1865.

CAMPBELL, D. M. *Java.* London, 1915.

CHASEN, F. N. *Delegation to Java: Presentation of Sir Stamford Raffles' Bust to the Royal Batavian Society. J.M.B.R.A.S.*, Singapore, 1930.

Old Singapore. J.M.B.R.A.S., Singapore, 1931.

CHEESEMAN, H. R. *Dr Robert Morrison and Malaya. British Malaya*, London, July 1950.

CLIFFORD, SIR HUGH. *Further India.* London, 1904.

CLODD, H. P. *An Eighteenth Century Pioneer: the Life of Captain Francis Light. British Malaya*, London, January-April, 1930.

Malaya's First British Pioneer. London, 1948.

COLENBRANDER, Professor H. T. *Koloniale Geschiedenis* ("Colonial History"). The Hague, 1925-26.

COLLET, OCTAVE J. A. *L'Ile de Java sous la Domination Française*. Brussels, 1910.

COLLIS, MAURICE. *British Merchant Adventurers*. London, 1942.

Foreign Mud. London, 1947.

COOK, J. A. B. *Sir Stamford Raffles*. London, 1918.

COOLHAAS, W. PH. *Baud on Raffles*. *J.M.B.R.A.S.*, Singapore, 1951.

COTTON, SIR EVAN. *East Indiamen*. Edited by Sir Charles Fawcett. London, 1949.

COTTON, J. J. *List of Inscriptions on Tombs and Monuments in Madras*. Madras, 1905.

COUPLAND, SIR REGINALD. *Wilberforce, a Narrative*. London, 1923.

Raffles. Oxford, 1926.

Raffles of Singapore. London, 1946.

COURT, Major M. H. *Relations of the British Government with Palembang*. London, 1821.

COWAN, C. D. *Early Penang and the Rise of Singapore*, 1805-1832. *J.M.B.R.A.S.*, Singapore, 1950.

Governor Bannerman and the Penang Tin Scheme, 1818-19. *J.M.B.R.A.S.*, Singapore, 1950.

CULLEN, E. G., and ZEHNDER, W. F. *Early History of Penang*. Penang, 1905.

DALRYMPLE, ALEXANDER. *A Plan for Extending the Commerce of this Kingdom and of the East India Company*. London, 1769. See also *Formation of the Establishment on Poolo Peenang*. (Dalrymple was the first hydrographer to the British Admiralty (1795) and spent most of his life in the service of the E.I.C.)

DALTON, CLIVE. *Men of Malaya*. London, 1942.

DAVIDSON, G. F. *Trade and Travel in the Far East*. London, 1846.

DAY, CLIVE. *The Policy and Administration of the Dutch in Java*. New York, 1904.

DENNYS, N. B. *Descriptive Dictionary of British Malaya*. London, 1894.

Description Géographique, Historique et Commerciale de Java et des Autres Iles de L'Archipel Indien. Par MM. Raffles. . . . et John Crawfurd. Translated into French by M. Marchal. Brussels, 1824.

DEVENTER, M. L. VAN. *Het Nederlandsch Gezag over Java en Onderhorigheden sedert* 1811 ("The Dutch Rule over Java and its Dependencies since 1811"). The Hague, 1891.

DODWELL, H. H. *The Private Letter Books of Joseph Collet*. London, 1933.

DU PERRON-DE ROOS, E. *Correspondentie van Dirk van Hogendorp met zijn broeder Gusbert Karel* ("Correspondence of Dirk van Hogendorp with his brother Gusbert Karel"). *B.T.L. en V. van Ned. Indië* (Vol. 102). The Hague, 1943.

ELTON, LORD. *Imperial Commonwealth*. London, 1945.

EMERSON, H. *Malaysia*. New York, 1937.

FINLAYSON, GEORGE. *Mission to Siam and Hue*, with a preface by Sir T. S. Raffles. London, 1826. (Published posthumously; see page 662.)

Formation of the Establishment on Poolo Peenang. Miscellaneous Papers relating to Indo-China (Vol. I). London, 1886. Reprinted from Dalrymple's *Oriental Repertory* (Vol. II).

FOSTER, W. *East India House*. London, 1924.

FURBER, H. *John Company at Work.* Cambridge, 1948.

GARNIER, Rev. KEPPEL. *Early Days in Penang. J.M.B.R.A.S.*, Singapore, 1923.

GEORGE, S. C. *Bright Moon in the Forest.* London, 1946.

GIBSON-HILL, C. A. *Notes on the Cocos-Keeling Islands. J.M.B.R.A.S.*, Singapore, 1947.

GOULD, S. BARING, and BAMPFYLDE, C.A. *Sarawak under its Two White Rajahs.* London, 1909.

HAAN, Dr F. DE. *Priangan* (3 vols.). Batavia, 1910-12.

Oud Batavia ("Old Batavia"). Batavia, 1922.

Personalia der periode van het Engelsche Bestuur over Java, 1811-16. ("Personalia of the period of the English Government of Java, 1811-16"). *B.T.L. en V. van Ned. Indië* (Vol. 92). The Hague, 1935.

HAILEY, LORD. *The Future of Colonial Peoples.* Oxford University Press, 1943.

HAMILTON, W. *The East Indian Gazetteer.* London, 1815.

Handbook of the Netherlands East-Indies. Buitenzorg, 1930.

HAYWARD, A. *Diaries of a Lady of Quality.* London, 1864.

HILL, A. H. *Munshi Abdullah's Account of Malacca Fort. J.M.B.R.A.S.*, Singapore, 1950. See also Section "*A*".

HOUGH, G. G. *The Educational Policy of Sir Stamford Raffles. J.M.B.R.A.S.* Singapore, 1933.

HOWE, S. E. *In Quest of Spices.* London, 1946.

HUBBACK, J. H. and E. C. *Jane Austen's Sailor Brothers.* London, 1906.

HUGHES, J. S. *Kings of the Cocos.* London, 1950.

HUGHES, T. D. *A Portuguese Account of Johore. J.M.B.R.A.S.* Singapore, 1935.

HYMA, A. *The Dutch in the Far East.* Michigan, 1942.

INNES, RODERICK. *The Life of Roderick Innes written by himself.* Stonehaven, 1844.

IRELAND, ALLEYNE. *The Far Eastern Tropics.* London, 1905.

JARDINE, SIR W., Bart. *Memoir of Sir T. S. Raffles.* Naturalists Library, Vol. iv. Edinburgh, 1834.

JARVIS, H. W. *Let the Great Story be Told.* London, 1946.

KAT ANGELINO, Dr A. D. A. DE. *Colonial Policy.* The Hague, 1931.

KAYE, J. W. *The Administration of the East India Company.* London, 1853.

KEMP, P. H. VAN DER. *The following essays in B.T.L. en V. van Ned. Indië:*

Fendall's en Raffles' opvattingen in het algemeen omtrent het Londensch Tractaat van 13 *Augustus* 1814 ("Fendall's and Raffles' opinion in general of the London Treaty of 13 August 1814"). Vol. 47, 1897.

Het afbreken van onze betrekking met Bandjermasin onder Daendels en de herstelling van het Nederlandsche gezag aldaar op den 1 *Januari* 1817 ("The breaking off of our relation with Banjermasin under Daendels and the re-establishment of Dutch authority there on 1 January 1817"). Vol. 49, 1898.

Sumatra's Westkust naar aanleiding van het Londensch Tractaat van 13 *Augustus* 1814. ("Sumatra's west coast in connexion with the London Treaty of 13 August 1814"). Vol. 49, 1898.

Raffles' bezetting van de Lampongs in 1818. ("Raffles' occupation of the Lampongs in 1818"). Vol. 50, 1899.

Palembang en Banka in 1816-1820. Vol. 51, 1900.

KEMP, P. H. VAN DER. *Raffles' Atjeh-Overeenkomst van* 1819. ("Raffles' Achin agreement of 1819"). Vol. 51, 1900.

Raffles' betrekkingen met Nias in 1820-1821. ("Raffles' relations with Nias in 1820-1821"). Vol. 52, 1901.

Also:

Sumatra in 1818. The Hague, 1920.

See also Section "*A*".

KEPPEL, Admiral Hon. SIR HENRY. *A Sailor's Life under Four Sovereigns.* London, 1899.

KINCAID, D. *British Social Life in India,* 1608-1936. London, 1938.

KOLFF, D. H. *Voyages of the Dutch Brig of War Dourga,* 1825-26. Translated by G. W. Earl. London, 1840.

LEITH, SIR GEORGE. *Short account of Prince of Wales Island.* London, 1805.

LIM ENG PHEOW. *Penang in the Past.* Penang, 1925.

LINEHAN, W. *The Kings of 14th Century Singapore. J.M.B.R.A.S.*, Singapore, 1947.

LOGAN, J. R. *Temminck's General view of the Dutch Possessions in the Indian Archipelago. J.I.A.*, Penang, 1847.

Commercial Intercourse with Japan. J.I.A., Penang, 1851.

Notes Illustrative of the Life and Services of Sir Stamford Raffles. J.I.A., Penang, 1855.

Gambling and Opium Smoking in the Straits of Malacca. J.I.A. (New Series), Penang, 1856.

Raffles and the Indian Archipelago. J.I.A. (New Series), Penang, 1856.

LORD, WALTER FREWEN. *The English Conquest of Java. The Nineteenth Century,* London, 1890.

Lost Possessions of England. London, 1896.

LOVAT, LADY. *Life of Sir Frederick Weld.* London, 1914.

LOVE, H. D. *Vestiges of Old Madras,* 1640-1800. London, 1913.

LOW, Captain (afterwards Lieut.-Colonel) J. *Soil and Agriculture of Penang.* Singapore, 1836.

Account of the Origin and Progress of the British Colonies in the Straits of Malacca. J.I.A., Penang, 1849.

LOW, URSULA. *Fifty Years with John Company.* London, 1936.

LUSCOMBE, F. M. *Singapore,* 1819-1930. Singapore, 1930.

MACALISTER, N. *Historical Memoir Relative to Prince of Wales Island.* London, 1803.

MACDONALD, M. *Malacca Buildings. J.M.B.R.A.S.*, Singapore, 1934.

MAGNUS, SIR P. *Edmund Burke.* London, 1939.

MAKEPEACE, W., and others. *One Hundred Years of Singapore.* London, 1921.

Malays in Malaya—by one of them. Singapore, 1928.

MALCOLM, H. *Travels in Hindustan and China.* Edinburgh, 1840.

MARRYAT, F. S. *Borneo and the East India Archipelago.* London, 1848.

MATHESON, C. *The Life of Henry Dundas, First Viscount Melville*—1742-1811. London, 1933.

MAXWELL, W. E. *Founding of Singapore. Notes and Queries,* Singapore, 1886.

MCNAIR, F. *Perak and the Malays.* London, 1878.

McQuoid, Thomas. *Notes of Dutch History in the Archipelago, extracted from the Records at Batavia under the Administration of Sir Stamford Raffles. J.I.A.* (New Series), Penang, 1856.

Meyer, F. V. *Britain's Colonies in World Trade.* London, 1948.

Mills, L. A. *A History of British Malaya, 1824-1867. J.M.B.R.A.S.*, Singapore, 1925.

British Rule in Eastern Asia. London, 1942.

Britain and Ceylon. London, 1945.

Money, J. W. B. *Java, or How to Manage a Colony.* London, 1861.

Moor, J. H. *Notices of Indian Archipelago.* Singapore, 1837.

Morley, J. A. E. *The Arabs and the Eastern Trade. J.M.B.R.A.S.*, Singapore, 1949.

Morrison, Robert. *Notes on Memoirs of the Life and Labours of Robert Morrison, D.D.*, compiled by his widow, with critical notices of his Chinese works, by Samuel Kidd (2 vols.). London, 1839.

Neilson, J. B. *A History of the Raffles Institution.* Published serially in the *Rafflesian*, Singapore, 1927-29.

Newbold, T. J. *British Settlements in Malacca.* London, 1839.

Nicolson, Hon. Harold. *The Congress of Vienna.* London, 1946.

Norman, H. *People and Politics of the Far East.* London, 1900.

O'Brien, H. A. *Old Minute by Sir Stamford Raffles. J.S.B.R.A.S.*, Singapore, 1891.

Oman, Carola. *Nelson.* London, 1947.

Osborn, Captain S. *Quedah: Or Stray Leaves from a Journal in Malayan Waters.* London, 1857.

Journal in Malayan Waters. London, 1860.

Osler, E. *The Life of Admiral Viscount Exmouth.* London, 1835.

Ottow, Samuel Julius. *De Verwarring Raffles* ("The Raffles Entanglement"). Utrecht, 1937.

De Oorsprong van de Conservatieve Richting van het Kolonisatierapport—van der Capellen ("The Cause of the Conservative Trend of the van der Capellen Colonization Report"). Utrecht, 1937.

Parkinson, C. Northcote. *Edward Pellew, Viscount Exmouth.* London, 1934.

Trade in the Eastern Seas, 1793-1813. Cambridge, 1937.

Pasqual, J. C. *Prince of Wales Island: an Historical Memoir of Penang. Pinang Gazette*, 25th May 1922.

Payne, E. A. *South-East from Serampore.* London, 1945.

Petrie, Sir Charles A. *George Canning.* London, 1930 and 1946.

Philips, C. H. *The Secret Committee of the East India Company*—1784-1858. *Bulletin of the School of Oriental Studies*, London, 1940.

Plummer, Samuel. *The Journal of Samuel Plummer.* London, 1821.

Popham, Sir Home. *A Description of Prince of Wales Island, in the Streights of Malacca: with its real and probable advantages and sources to recommend it as a Marine Establishment.* London, 1799.

Prinsep, A. *Voyage from Calcutta to Van Diemen's Land.* London, 1833.

Purcell, Dr V. W. S. *Early Penang.* Penang, 1928.

PURCELL, Dr. V. W. S. *Malaya—Outline of a Colony*. London, 1946.
The Chinese in Malaya. London, 1948.
The Chinese in South-East Asia. London, 1951.
Rambles in Java and the Straits—by a Bengal Civilian. London, 1853.
READ, W. H. M. *Play and Politics by an Old Resident*. London, 1901.
RICHMOND, Admiral SIR HERBERT W. *Statesmen and Sea Power*. Oxford, 1946.
ROBERTS, P. E. *India Under Wellesley*. London, 1929.
RONKEL, Dr PH. S. VAN. *Een Maleische Afscheidbrief van Raffles*. ("Raffles' Malay Letters of Farewell"). *B.T.L. en V. van Ned. Indië*. (Vol. 103). The Hague, 1946.
ROSE, J. HOLLAND. *Man and the Sea*. Cambridge, 1935.
ST JOHN, H. *Indian Archipelago*. London, 1853.
SCOTT, DAVID, Director and Chairman of the East India Company. *Correspondence relating to Indian Affairs*, 1787-1805. Edited by C. H. Phillips. Royal Historical Society, London, 1951.
SCHELTEMA, J. F. *Monumental Java*. London, 1912.
SETH, M. J. *Armenians in India from the Earliest Times to the Present Day*. Calcutta, 1937.
SHELFORD, W. H. *Sir Thomas Stamford Raffles. British Malaya*, July 1926.
A Free Translation of Freemasonry. British Malaya, January 1932.
Singapore Local Laws and Institutions. London, 1824.
Singapore Sixty Years Ago. Singapore, 1883.
SKINNER, A. M. *Outline History of British Connexion with Malaya. J.S.B.R.A.S.*, Singapore, 1882.
A Geography of the Malay Peninsula and Surrounding Countries (Part I). Singapore, 1884.
Memoir of Captain Francis Light. J.S.B.R.A.S., Singapore, 1895.
SMITH, ADAM. *An Inquiry into the Nature and Causes of the Wealth of Nations*. London, 1776.
SMITH, M. PASKE. *Report on Japan by Sir Stamford Raffles*. Kobe, 1929.
SONG ONG SIANG. *One Hundred Years' History of the Chinese in Singapore*. London, 1923.
STEUART, A. F. *A short sketch of the Lives of Francis and William Light, Founders of Penang and Adelaide*. London, 1901.
STEVENS, F. G. *Early History of Prince of Wales's Island. J.M.B.R.A.S.* Singapore, 1929.
STOCKDALE, JOHN JOSEPH. *Sketches, Civil and Military, of the Island of Java*. London, 1811.
STOWELL, W. H. *The Missionary Church*. London, 1840.
Straits Settlements Records, 1800-1867. Singapore, 1928.
Straits Settlements Records. J.M.B.R.A.S., Singapore, 1949.
SWETTENHAM, SIR FRANK A. *British Malaya*. London, 1906. Revised edition, 1929.
TAN SOO CHYE. *A Note on Early Legislation at Penang. J.M.B.R.A.S.*, Singapore, 1950.
TAYLOR, Rear-Admiral A. H. *Admiral the Honourable Sir George Elliot. Mariner's Mirror*. October 1949.

TEMPERLEY, H. *Foreign Policy of Canning*. London, 1925.
THOMSON, J. *Straits of Malacca, Indo China and China*. London, 1875.
THOMSON, JOHN TURNBULL. *Sequel to Glimpses into Life in the Far East*. London, 1865. See also Section "*A*".
TRAPAUD, E. *Short Account of Prince of Wales's Island*. London, 1788.
Treaties and Engagements affecting the Native States of the Malay Peninsula. Singapore, 1889.
TREVELYAN, G. M. *British History in the Nineteenth Century* (1782-1901). London, 1922.
TROTTER, N. Letter concerning the original British treaty with Java in 1811. *J.S.B.R.A.S.*, Singapore, 1887.
TUUK, H. N. VAN DER. *Short Account of the Malay Manuscripts belonging to the Royal Asiatic Society. Miscellaneous Papers relating to Indo-China* (Vol. II). London, 1887.
VERHOEVEN, Dr F. R. J. *De Jonge Jaren van de Harmonie, uit de Geschiedenis eener Bataviasche Sociëteit* ("The Early Years of the Harmonie, from the History of a Batavian Society"). Published in *Koloniale Studiën*, 11th June 1939.
VLEKKE, B. H. M. *Nusantara*. Cambridge, Mass., 1943.
WALKER, W. *Tom Cringle's Jottings*. Bombay, 1865.
WALLACE, ALFRED RUSSEL. *The Malay Archipelago*. London, 1869.
WATHEN, J. *Journal of a Voyage in* 1811 *and* 1812 *to Madras and China*. London, 1814.
WEBSTER, (SIR) CHARLES KINGSLEY. *Foreign Policy of Castlereagh*. London, 1925.
WELSH, Major JAMES. *Military Reminiscences*. London, 1830.
WHEELER, L. R. *The Modern Malay*. London, 1928.
WHITE, R. *Poems and Ballads of Dr John Leyden*. Kelso, 1858.
WILKINSON, R. J. *History of the Peninsular Malays*. Singapore, 1923.
Old Singapore. *J.M.B.R.A.S.*, Singapore, 1935.
Bencoolen. *J.M.B.R.A.S.*, Singapore, 1938.
More on Bencoolen. *J.M.B.R.A.S.*, Singapore, 1941.
WILLIAMSON, J. A. *Great Britain and the Empire*. London, 1944.
WINSTEDT, SIR RICHARD O. *History of Kedah*. *J.S.B.R.A.S.*, Singapore, 1920.
Founder of Old Singapore. *J.S.B.R.A.S.*, Singapore, 1920.
Early History of Singapore, Johore and Malacca. *J.S.B.R.A.S.*, Singapore, 1922.
Malaya. London, 1923.
Gold Ornaments dug up at Fort Canning, Singapore. *J.M.B.R.A.S.*, Singapore, 1928.
A Malay History of Riau and Johore. *J.M.B.R.A.S.*, Singapore, 1932.
A History of Johore, 1365-1895. *J.M.B.R.A.S.*, Singapore, 1932.
'Abdu'l-Jalil Sultan of Johore (1699-1719), *'Abdu'l-Jamal, Temenggong* (ca. 1750) *and Raffles' Founding of Singapore*. *J.M.B.R.A.S.*, Singapore, 1933.
Outline of a Malay History of Riau. *J.M.B.R.A.S.*, Singapore, 1933.
A History of Malaya. *J.M.B.R.A.S.*, Singapore, 1935.
Malaya and its History. London, 1944.
The Malays: A Cultural History. Singapore, 1947. See also Section "*A*".
WINT, GUY. *The British in Asia*. London, 1947.

WORSFOLD, W. B. *Visit to Java and Account of the Founding of Singapore*. London, 1893.
WRIGHT, A. *Twentieth Century Impressions of British Malaya*. London, 1908.
Early English Adventurers in the East. London, 1914.
Singapore and Sir Stamford Raffles. *Quarterly Review*, New York, 1919.
WRIGHT, A., and REID, T. H. *Malay Peninsula*. London, 1913.
WURTZBURG, CHARLES E. *Early References to the Suitability of Singapore*. *J.M.B.R.A.S.*, Singapore, 1925.
The Birthday of Sir Stamford Raffles. *J.M.B.R.A.S.*, Singapore, 1947.
Grave of Lady Raffles. *British Malaya*, London, December 1947.
Raffles and the Palembang Massacre. *J.M.B.R.A.S.*, Singapore, 1949.
The Private Letter Books of John Palmer *J.M.B.R.A.S.*, Singapore, 1949.
Reminiscences of Colonel Nahuys. *J.M.B.R.A.S.*, Singapore, 1950.
Baptist Mission Press at Bencoolen. *J.M.B.R.A.S.*, Singapore, 1950.
Olivia Raffles and Thomas Moore. *J.M.B.R.A.S.*, Singapore, 1951.
Who Planned the Sea Route of the Java Expedition in 1811? *Mariner's Mirror*, April 1951.
YVAN, Dr. *Six Months Among the Malays*. London, 1955.

Unpublished Works

Official and Secret Papers relating to the Sale of Lands and Other Subjects during the British Administration of Java. Printed privately at The Hague, 1883.
RAFFLES/HORSFIELD. A small collection of Letters on zoological subjects, in the possession of the Koloniale Bibliotheek, Koninklijk Instituut voor Taal-, Land- en Volkenkunde, the Hague.
RAFFLES/MCQUOID. A small collection of letters, formerly held by the late Mr C. E. Wurtzburg and now in the possession of Cambridge University.
Collections of letters and other papers in the possession of Mrs Stamford Raffles of Guernsey, Major R. L. S. Raffles of Southwold, Suffolk, Major E. Raffles Flint of Torrington, North Devon, Mr A. Dickson Wright, F.R.C.S., of London, and Mrs M. R. Drake of Aviemore, Inverness-shire.

Periodicals, Official Publications, etc.

Annual Register, 1819. Chap. xiv: *Asia*.
Bijdragen tot de Taal-, Land- en Volkenkunde van Nederlandsch-Indië, Amsterdam and The Hague. Vol. 1, 1852; Vol. 7 (3rd of New Series), 1860; Vol. 47, 1897; Vol. 49, 1898; Vol. 50, 1899; Vol. 51, 1900; Vol. 52, 1901; Vol. 92, 1935; Vol. 103, 1946.
British Malaya, London, July 1926, January-April 1930, December 1931. January 1932, December 1947, July 1950.
Bulletin of the School of Oriental Studies, London, 1940.
East India Papers Respecting Prince of Wales's Island. E.I.C.'s Committee of Correspondence, London, 7th November 1804.
Fortnightly Review, London, 1878. *The Dutch in Java*.
Geographical Magazine, London, June 1874. *The Taking of Singapore*.

Hansard's Parliamentary Debates, 1st February 1819. Debate in the House of Lords.

Investigator, London, 1824 (Vol. VIII). *Memoir of Sir Thomas Stamford Raffles.*

Java Annual Directory and Almanack, Batavia, 1814. (This was the first issued.)

Journal of the Indian Archipelago, Penang. Vol. I, 1847; Vol. III, 1849; Vol. V, 1851; Vol. VI, 1852; Vol. VIII, 1854; Vol. IX, 1855; Vol. X, 1856.

Journal of the Malay Branch of the Royal Asiatic Society, Singapore, 1923, 1925, 1927, 1929, 1930, 1931, 1932, 1933, 1934, 1935, 1938, 1941, 1947, 1949, 1950, 1951.

Journal of the Straits Branch of the Royal Asiatic Society, Singapore, 1882, 1887, 1891, 1895, 1913, 1918, 1920, 1922.

Koloniale Studiën, 11th June 1939.

London Literary Gazette, 10th November 1821. Review of John Leyden's *Malay Annals.*

Malayan Police Magazine, Singapore, April 1932. *Notes on the History and Development of the Straits Settlements Police.*

Mariner's Mirror, London, October 1949, April 1951.

Miscellaneous Papers relating to Indo-China, Vol. I, 1886; Vol. II, 1887.

Nineteenth Century, London, 1890

Notes and Queries, Singapore, 1883, 1886. References to the foundation of Singapore.

Pinang Gazette, 25th May 1922.

Proceedings of the Committee of Assessors, Singapore, 1929.

Proclamations, &c. Printed and Published by the British Government of Java, September 1811 *to September* 1813, Batavia. Vol. I, 1813.

Quarterly Review, New York, 1919.

Rafflesian, Singapore, 1927-29.

Saturday Magazine, London, 1842.

Zoological Journal, London, 1853.

C. MUSEUMS, LIBRARIES, ETC.

(see also Unpublished Works, Sections "*A*" and "*B*")

London

Association of British Malaya.

British Museum. There is some useful material in the Library. Doubtless more could be found.

India Office Library. An immense mass of material, offering wide scope for further research.

Linnean Society. Certain zoological papers.

Malayan Government Agency.

Public Record Office. The Foreign Office material concerning the Anglo-Dutch Treaty of 1824 is preserved here.

Royal Asiatic Society.

Singapore

Raffles Museum. The records formerly in the Colonial Secretariat, Singapore, have been deposited in the Museum. They include the early Penang Consultations and a large number of letters dealing with Singapore from its foundation. Two volumes of records disappeared during the Japanese occupation.

The Hague

Government Archives. The sources used (through the courtesy of the late Professor H. T. Colenbrander) were the Falck Collection and the Colonial and Foreign Affairs Archives, all in the 2nd Department.

Djakarta (Batavia)

Indonesian Government Archives. Further research here might also be productive. During the Japanese occupation, the records became disordered and individual documents are now difficult to trace.

NOTE

Mr Wurtzburg accumulated during his lifetime a large collection of books, manuscripts, newspaper cuttings and other papers, all relating in some way to his projected Life of Raffles. Under the terms of his will, this library has now been dispersed, some volumes going to Cambridge University and the remainder to the University of Malaya, Singapore.

INDEX

Matters relating particularly to Bencoolen, Java, Singapore and Sumatra are grouped under each of those four headings.

R. represents Raffles.

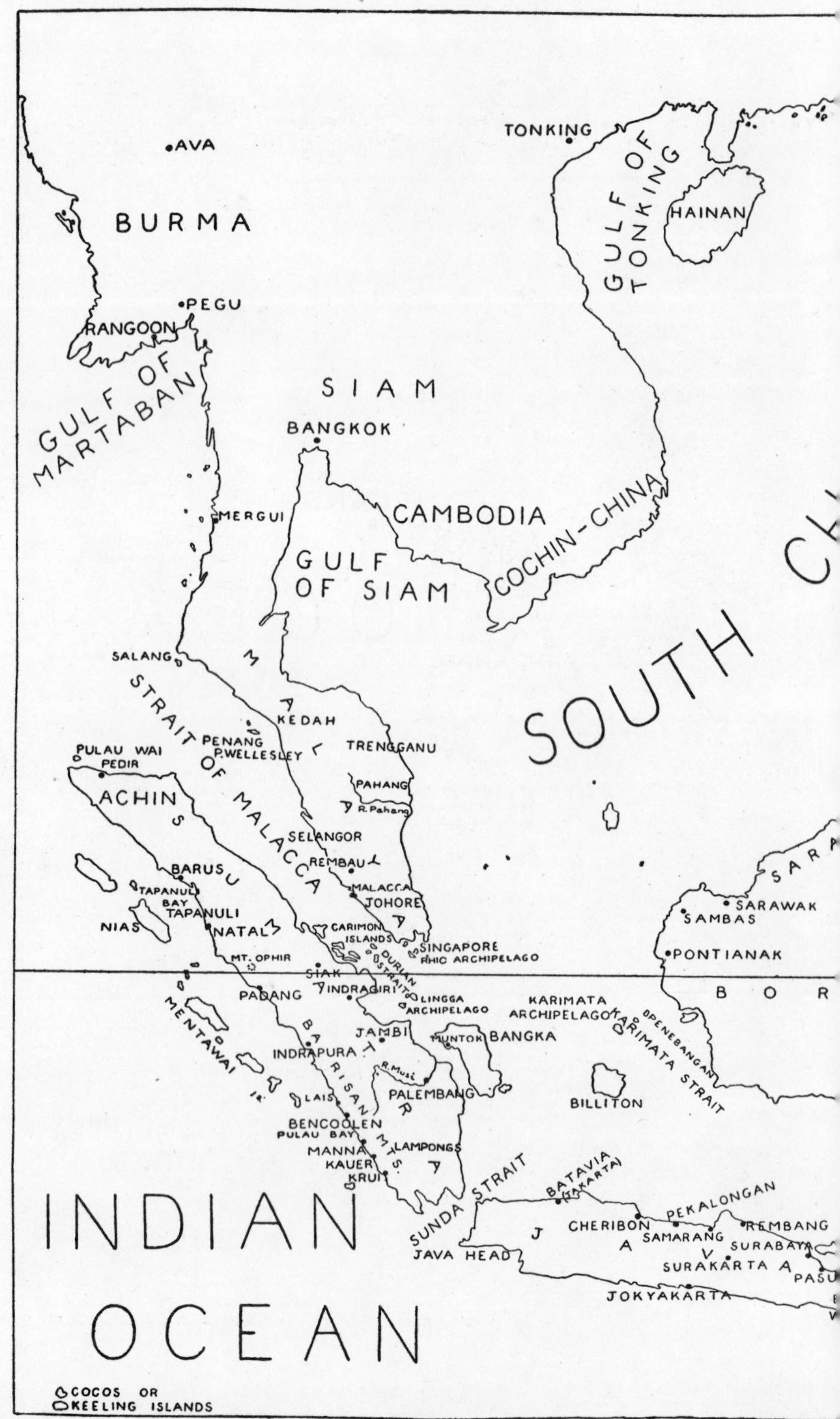

TONKING
AVA
BURMA
GULF OF TONKING
HAINAN
PEGU
RANGOON
GULF OF MARTABAN
SIAM
BANGKOK
MERGUI
CAMBODIA
COCHIN-CHINA
GULF OF SIAM
SOUTH CH
SALANG
MALAYA
STRAIT OF MALACCA
KEDAH
PENANG
P. WELLESLEY
TRENGGANU
PULAU WAI
PEDIR
ACHIN
PAHANG
R. Pahang
SELANGOR
REMBAU
SUMATRA
BARUS
TAPANULI BAY
TAPANULI
MALACCA
JOHORE
NIAS
NATAL
CARIMON ISLANDS
SINGAPORE
RHIO ARCHIPELAGO
DURIAN STRAITS
MT. OPHIR
SIAK
SARAWAK
SAMBAS
PONTIANAK
BOR
INDRAGIRI
PADANG
LINGGA ARCHIPELAGO
KARIMATA ARCHIPELAGO
KARIMATA STRAIT
PENEBANGAN
MENTAWAI IS.
JAMBI
MUNTOK
BANGKA
INDRAPURA
BARISAN MTS.
R. Musi
PALEMBANG
LAIS
BILLITON
BENCOOLEN
PULAU BAY
MANNA
LAMPONGS
KAUER
KRUI
SUNDA STRAIT
BATAVIA (JAKARTA)
PEKALONGAN
INDIAN
OCEAN
CHERIBON
REMBANG
JAVA
SAMARANG
SURABAYA
JAVA HEAD
SURAKARTA
PASU
JOKYAKARTA
COCOS OR KEELING ISLANDS